DESSERTS

Favorite Recipes of Home Economic Teachers

Too good to be forgotten...

2,000 Favorite Recipes

DESSERTS

Favorite Recipes of Home Economic Teachers

Copyright © 2007 by

FRP

P. O. Box 305142
Nashville, Tennessee 37230
1-800-358-0560

ISBN: 978-0-87197-541-6

Cover and chapter opener design by Rikki Odgen Campbell/pixiedesign, llc

Printed in China

Other books in this series:

CASSEROLES

MEATS

SALADS

VEGETABLES

To order this and many other award-winning cookbooks, visit www.cookbookmarketplace.com or call 1-800-269-6839.

Revised slightly from the version published in 1965.

TABLE OF CONTENTS

Choosing a Dessert

The nutritional balance of the entire meal must be the major factor when choosing the proper dessert as well as a pleasant taste treat for rounding out the family meal.

Desserts are excellent means for improving the diet of the poor eater. They also give the homemaker an opportunity for fostering family unity through the preparation of desserts which can become traditional when celebrating special festive occasions.

Remember if the meal is light select a heavy dessert such as pie or cake, but if the meal is heavy you should serve a fruit custard, gelatine, sherbet, or another light dessert. Other considerations before making your recipe selection are time and energy required for preparation, cost, and the necessary equipment.

You will remember, of course, never to serve the same dessert too often. These many delicious recipes afford you an excellent opportunity for giving pleasure to your family and friends by creating desserts which will be real treats and the happy ending to perfect meals.

Preparation Methods for Freezing Desserts

Freezing is so easy that you will want to plan desserts for weeks rather than days ahead. Time is saved by preparing desserts for tomorrow while cooking today. Exceptions, however, are desserts with cream fillings, cream puddings, or some custard pies which are not recommended for freezing.

When freezing desserts the first consideration is *quality* since the quality of the frozen dessert can never be better than the quality of the dessert chosen for freezing. Quality also demands that care be taken to *freeze* and *maintain* desserts at Zero Fahrenheit or below.

The second consideration is space in your freezer. Desserts demand considerable space and should not be crushed by crowding in a small space.

Careful wrapping is the third rule as all frozen desserts must be wrapped in moisture-vapor-proof material to exclude as much air as possible. Contents, number of servings, and the date frozen should be plainly marked on each package.

Freezing Chart

DESSERT	PREPARATION	PACKAGING & APPROXIMATE STORAGE TIME	SERVING
CAKES			
Butter or Sponge	Baking before freezing is recommended. Cool on rack after baking.	Wrap in moisture-vapor-proof material. Freeze in quantities for meal. Store up to 4 months.	Unwrap frosted cakes while defrosting. Allow 30 minutes for angel or sponge, others two hours.
Fruit	Bake and age before freezing.	Wrap as above and store up to 1 year.	
Frostings	Uncooked or butter icings are recommended.		
CANDIES	Prepare according to recipe and cool.	Freeze in container or wrap in foil with waxed paper between layers. Store up to 1 year.	Remove from freezer before serving time and defrost in container.
COOKIES			
Baked	Use desired recipe. Cool before wrapping.	Place in layers with foil or waxed paper between layers and freeze in container or moisture-vapor-proof material. Store up to 6 months.	Thaw at room temperature for about 15 minutes.
Unbaked: Rolled	Cut and stack with wax paper between layers.	Wrap and store as above for 1-2 months.	Bake without thawing.
Dropped	Shape on cookie sheet and then freeze.	Remove from cookie sheet and store in moisture-vapor-proof box or bag for 1-2 months.	Bake without thawing and serve.
FRUITS			
Apples: Baking	Prepare firm, ripe apples; bake according to recipe. Cool quickly.	Wrap in foil or freezer proof paper. Store 8-12 months.	If wrapped in foil may be placed directly in 300 degree oven for heating.
Sauce	Prepare according to recipe. Cool before freezing.	Package in freezer containers.	Defrost in refrigerator before serving.
Other fruits to serve uncooked	Select fully ripened fruit. To prevent light colored fruit from turning brown when exposed to air, ascorbic acid may be added to the sugar or cool syrup before combining with the fruit.	Package in freezer containers. Store up to 1 year.	Defrost rapidly in unopened container 30-60 minutes. Serve icy cold.
ICE CREAM AND SHERBET	Prepare according to recipe. Proper crystal formation is necessary for smoothness.	Store in carton wrapped in moisture-vapor-proof paper. Store up to 2 months.	Do not defrost before serving or refreeze ice cream or sherbet that has melted.
NUTS	Fresh nut meats and in the shell can be frozen but salted nuts do not hold well.	Pack to exclude air in freezer container.	Defrost for serving.
PIES			
Baked: Chiffon	Prepare filling according to recipe and pour into baked or crumb crust. Cool and chill until set.	Press saran wrap down on filling. Wrap pie in moisture-vapor-proof paper. Store up to 1-2 months.	Defrost in refrigerator 4-6 hours before serving.
Unbaked: Fruit Mincemeat Pecan Pumpkin Sweet Potatoes	It is recommended that these pies be frozen before baking. Prepare according to recipe.	Use metal, foil, or glass pie plates. Press saran wrap on filling of one-crust pies. Wrap in moisture-vapor-proof material. Store up to 6 months.	Remove from freezer and cut steam vent in top crust. Bake unthawed in preheated oven. The use of dull aluminum or glass pans with sufficient time for baking will prevent an underbaked bottom crust.
WHIPPED CREAM	Whip by hand or electric mixer until stiff. Add sugar and flavoring. Make rosettes on cookie sheet using pastry tube and rapidly freeze unwrapped.	When frozen remove from cookie sheet and store in moisture-vapor-proof bags or box.	Do NOT defrost before serving as a garnish on pies or other appropriate desserts.

DESSERTS CALORIE CHART

		Number of calories
Apple betty	½ cup	175
Cakes:		
Angelcake	2-inch sector (¹⁄₁₂ of 8-inch round cake)	110
Butter cakes:		
Plain, without icing	1 piece, 3 by 2 by 1½ inches	180
	1 cupcake, 2¾ inches in diameter	130
Plain, with icing	2-inch sector (¹⁄₁₆ of 10-inch round layer cake)	320
	1 cupcake, 2¾ inches in diameter	160
Chocolate, with fudge icing	2-inch sector (¹⁄₁₆ of 1-inch round layer cake)	420
Fruitcake, dark	1 piece, 2 by 2 inches by ½ inch	105
Gingerbread	1 piece, 2 by 2 inches by ½ inch	180
Pound cake	1 slice, 2¾ by 3 inches by ⅝ inch	130
Sponge cake	2-inch sector (¹⁄₁₂ of 8-inch round cake)	115
Candy:		
Caramels	1 ounce (3 medium caramels)	120
Chocolate creams	1 ounce (2 to 3 pieces, 35 to a pound)	110
Chocolate, milk, sweetened	1-ounce bar	145
Chocolate, milk, sweetened, with almonds	1-ounce bar	150
Chocolate mints	1 ounce (1 to 2 mints, 20 to a pound)	110
Fudge, milk chocolate, plain	1 ounce (1 piece, 1 to 1½ inches square)	115
Gumdrops	1 ounce (about 2½ large or 20 small)	95
Hard candy	1 ounce (3 to 4 candy balls, ¾ inch in diameter)	110
Jellybeans	1 ounce (10 beans)	65
Marshmallows	1 ounce (3 to 4 marshmallows, 60 to a pound)	90
Peanut brittle	1 ounce (1½ pieces, 2½ by 1¼ inches by ⅜ inch)	125
Cookies, plain and assorted	1 cooky, 3 inches in diameter	110
Cornstarch pudding	½ cup	140
Custard, baked	½ cup	140
Figbars, small	1 figbar	55
Fruit ice	½ cup	75
Gelatin dessert, plain, ready-to-serve	½ cup	80
Ice cream, plain	1 container (3½ fluid ounces)	130
Ice milk	½ cup (4 fluid ounces)	140
Pies:		
Apple	4-inch sector (⅐ of 9-inch pie)	330
Cherry	4-inch sector (⅐ of 9-inch pie)	340
Custard	4-inch sector (⅐ of 9-inch pie)	265
Lemon meringue	4-inch sector (⅐ of 9-inch pie)	300
Mince	4-inch sector (⅐ of 9-inch pie)	340
Pumpkin	4-inch sector (⅐ of 9-inch pie)	265
Prune whip	½ cup	100
Rennet dessert pudding, ready-to-serve	½ cup	125
Sherbet	½ cup	120

Dessert Cooking Terms and Definitions

A La Mode—*Served with a topping of ice cream.*

Bake—*To cook by dry heat in an oven.*

Batter—*A mixture of liquid, flour, eggs, leavening etc., before cooking such as cake, pancake or waffle batter. A coating for food to be fried.*

Baste—*To spoon juices or liquids over food which is cooking.*

Beat—*To whip with spoon, hand beater or electric mixer in order to combine food or incorporate air as in beating egg whites, and whipping cream.*

Blend—*To mix ingredients until thoroughly combined.*

Coat-the-spoon—*The mixture adheres to the stirring spoon in a thin layer.*

Condensed Milk—*Canned milk which is concentrated and sweetened.*

Confectioners' Sugar—*Sugar that has been ground to the consistency of powder.*

Cream—*To work or beat shortening until light and fluffy. Sugar and/or flour may be creamed into the shortening.*

Cut—*To combine shortening with flour and other dry ingredients by chopping it into the mixture by spatulas, or two knives.*

Dissolve—*To melt or liquify.*

Dough—*Mixture of flour, other dry ingredients and liquid thick enough to knead.*

Evaporated Milk—*Canned milk that is concentrated and unsweetened.*

Fold—*To combine ingredients by blending with a spoon or wire whisk, using an up-and-over motion.*

Freeze—*To chill until solid in freezing compartment of refrigerator or freezer.*

Frost—*To cover with icing.*

Grease—*To rub inside of pan or dish with fat to prevent foods sticking to it.*

Icing—*Frosting for cakes and pastries.*

Meringue—*Egg whites, beaten stiff, combined with sugar.*

Prepared pan—*One that has been rubbed with fat and dusted with flour.*

Shortening—*Fats such as butter, margarine, lard, and vegetable shortening.*

Sift—*To shake dry ingredients through a sieve or sifter.*

Simmer—*To cook in liquid that is just below the boiling point.*

Spatula—*A flexible knife.*

Whip—*To incorporate air into a mixture by beating rapidly by hand or in a mixer.*

Dessert Spice Chart

ALLSPICE   Plum Pudding; fruit cake; fruit compote; baked bananas; all cranberry dishes; spice cake; molasses cookies; tapioca pudding; chocolate pudding; mincemeat.

ANISE   Coffee cake; sweet breads; cookies; fruit compote; stewed apples; all fruit pie fillings; licorice candies.

CARAWAY   Coffee cake; cookies.

CARDOMON   Danish pastry; buns; coffee cake; custards; baked apples; fruit cup; pumpkin pie; cookies; frozen ice cream pudding.

CINNAMON   Buns; coffee cake; spice cake; molasses cookies; butter cookies; custards; tapioca; chocolate pudding; rice pudding; fruit pies; stewed fruit; hot cocoa and chocolate drinks; sprinkle over vanilla ice cream.

CLOVES   Stewed fruits; apple, mince and pumpkin pies; spice cake; rice pudding; chocolate pudding; tapioca.

CUMIN   Fruit pies.

FENNEL   Coffee cake; sugar cookies; apples in any form.

GINGER   Cookies; spice cake; pumpkin pie; Indian pudding; baked, stewed and preserved fruits; apple sauce; custard.

MACE   Gingerbread batter; stewed cherries; doughnuts; cakes; pound cakes; fruit pies.

MINT   Ice cream; custard; fruit compote; frostings.

MUSTARD   Add ½ teaspoon to steamed pudding; molasses cookies.

NUTMEG   Doughnuts; custards; puddings; whipped cream; ice cream; fried bananas; stewed fruits; spice cake; coffee cake; cookies; pumpkin pies.

POPPY   Coffee cake; cookies; pie crusts.

SAFFRON   Cakes.

SESAME   Cookies; coffee cakes; pies.

Abbreviations Used in This Book

Cup	c.	Gallon	gal.
Tablespoon	T.	Large	lge.
Teaspoon	t.	Package	pkg.
Pound	lb.	Square	sq.
Ounce	oz.	Dozen	doz.
Degrees Fahrenheit	°F.	Slice	sl.
Minutes	min.	Pint	pt.
Seconds	sec.	Quart	qt.

In measuring, remember . . .

3 t. = 1 T.
2 T. = ⅛ c.
4 T. = ¼ c.
8 T. = ½ c.
16 T. = 1 c.
5 T. + 1 t. = ⅓ c.
12 T. = ¾ c.
4 oz. = ½ c.
8 oz. = 1 c.
16 oz. = 1 lb.
1 oz. = 2 T. fat or liquid
2 c. fat = 1 lb.
2 c. = 1 pt.

2 c. sugar = 1 lb.
⅝ c. = ½ c. + 2 T.
⅞ c. = ¾ c. + 2 T.
2⅔ c. powdered sugar = 1 lb.
2⅔ c. brown sugar = 1 lb.
4 c. sifted flour = 1 lb.
1 lb. butter = 2 c . or 4 sticks
2 pts = 1 qt.
1 qt. = 4 c.
A Few Grains = Less than ⅛ t.
Pinch is as much as can be taken
between tip of finger and thumb.
Speck = Less than ⅛ t.

Substitutions

1 tablespoon *cornstarch* (for thickening) = 2 tablespoons flour (approximately).

1 cup sifted *all-purpose flour* = 1 cup plus 2 tablespoons sifted cake flour.

1 cup sifted *cake flour* = 1 cup minus 2 tablespoons sifted all-purpose flour.

1 teaspoon *baking powder* = ¼ teaspoon baking soda plus ½ teaspoon cream of tartar.

1 cup *bottled milk* = ½ cup evaporated milk plus ½ cup water.

1 cup *sour milk* = a cup sweet milk into which 1 tablespoon vinegar or lemon juice has been stirred; or 1 cup buttermilk.

1 cup *sweet milk* = 1 cup sour milk or buttermilk plus ½ teaspoon baking soda.

1 cup *cream, sour, heavy* = ⅓ cup butter and ⅔ cup milk in any sour-milk recipe.

1 cup *cream, sour, thin* = 3 tablespoons butter and ¾ cup milk in sour-milk recipe.

1 cup *molasses* = 1 cup honey.

Order Blanks For Additional Books on Page 384

Approximate Measures of Food Materials

ONE POUND OF	MEASURE	ONE POUND OF	MEASURE
Apples, dried	5 c.	Gelatin, granulated	4 c.
Apples, med. size	3	Lard	2 c.
Apricots, dried	3 c.	Lemons	3-5
Apricots, fresh	8-12	Marshmallows	64 or 4 c.
Baking powder	2½ c.	Molasses	1⅓ c.
Bananas, large	2	Nuts, chopped	3¼ c.
Bananas, very small	5	Peaches, dried	3 c.
Butter	2 c.	Peanuts in shell	1¾ c.
Cashew nuts	4 c.	Pears, med. size	3
Cherries	120	Pecan meats	3-4 c.
Chocolate	16 squares	Pecans in shell	2 c.
Cocoa	4½-6 c.	Prunes, dried	2½-3 c.
Coconut, shredded	6-8 c.	Raisins, seedless	2-3 c.
Crackers, graham	40	Sugar, brown	2⅔ c.
Cranberries	4-5 c.	Sugar, domino	90
Dates, chopped, dried	2 c.	Sugar, confectioners'	2⅔ c.
Eggs	8-10	Sugar, granulated	2 c.
Flour, cake, sifted	4½ c.	Tapioca	3 c.
Flour, all-purpose	4 c.	Walnuts, shelled	4-5 c.

ONE OUNCE OF	MEASURE	ONE OUNCE OF	MEASURE
Baking powder	2½ T.	Liquid or fluid	2 T.
Bread crumbs	¼ c.	Oil	2 T.
Butter	2 T.	Salt	1 T.
Chocolate	1 square	Spices	4 T.
Cornstarch	3 T.	Sugar	2 T.
Flour	4 T.	Vanilla	2 T.
Gelatin, granulated	4 T.		

ONE CUP MEASURE

Crackers, graham, coarsely crumbled	9
Crackers, graham, finely crumbled	11
Crackers, salted, coarsely crumbled	7
Wafers, vanilla, coarsely crumbled	22
Wafers, vanilla, finely crumbled	26

Submitted By
Marguerite Holloway
Petersburg High School
Petersburg, Illinois

Cakes

About Cakes

Cake is really the aristocrat of foods. Cakes are a homey food when served warm with no frosting, or elegant when beautifully frosted and decorated.

There are two commonly used methods for making cakes: the Creaming method and the Quick method.

CREAMING METHOD

In the Creaming method, the shortening, sugar, eggs and salt are creamed or blended together until light and smooth, then the dry ingredients and the liquid are added alternately and blended until smooth. Most of the old-time favorite cake recipes are made by this method.

QUICK METHOD

In the Quick method, the shortening, dry ingredients and part of the liquid are mixed for two minutes, then the eggs and remaining liquid are added and mixed for two more minutes. This is a modern method and takes advantage of today's improved products.

The special properties of a top quality vegetable shortening make it possible to bake excellent cakes by either method. We have included both Creaming and Quick method cake recipes in this book.

About Cake Pans

Cake pans may be aluminum, heavy tin, or glass. (Glass usually requires baking at a lower temperature. Follow the manufacturer's direction when using glass baking dishes.) Use the pan size recommended in the recipe. Check the pan size by measuring it across the top.

Use bright, shiny pans. Discolored pans cause uneven browning. Avoid warped pans. They will cause uneven baking.

YOUR CAKES
MAY VARY IN SIZE

A recipe for two 8″ layers will make:
Round, two layers (8″ x 1½″)
Cupcakes:
   1½ dozen large (3″ x 1½″)
   2 dozen medium (2½″ x 1¼″)
   2½ dozen small (1½″ x ¾″)
Loaf cake (9″ x 5″ x 3″)
Oblong cake (13″ x 9½″ x 2″)
Square, two layers (8″ x 8″ x 2″)
SIZE OF PANS: A cake recipe calling for 2 cups flour should be baked in two 8-inch, round pans, 1½ inches deep. A cake recipe calling for 2½ to 3 cups flour should be baked in two 9-inch, round pans, 1½ inches to 2 inches deep, or in two 8-inch, square pans, 2 inches deep.

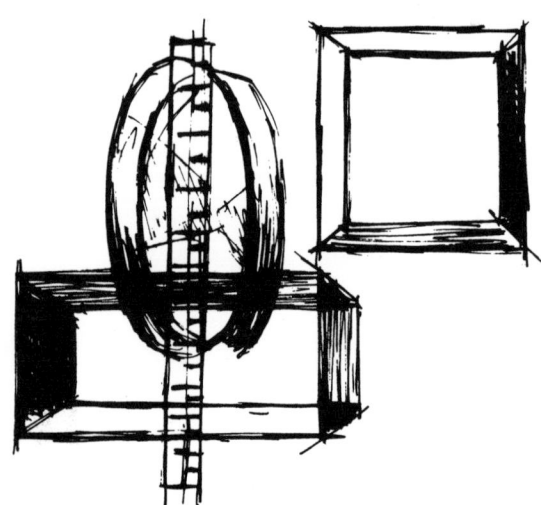

For Successful Cakes

L. WIN PANTRY PRIZES ...

A. Read the recipe carefully before starting to work. Be sure to choose the correct pan size—it makes a difference!

B. Always prepare baking pans before filling them. Here's how: grease the bottom and sides of the pan well, then sprinkle lightly with flour.

C. Have all ingredients at room temperature, and you'll have a lighter, more handsome cake.

D. Cups, spoons and such . . . don't guess, measure correctly, using standard equipment. Simple secrets to remember are:

1. Shortening should hold its shape when turned out of the measuring cup. The same is true of brown sugar.

2. Dry ingredients are lightly spooned into the measuring utensil.

3. A level measurement is obtained by running a spatula or knife across the top of the utensil.

E. Remove large air bubbles from batter before baking, by tapping pan lightly on work surface, or by cutting gently through the batter with a knife.

F. Keep the bowl sides tidy. Have a rubber scraper handy to blend in each delicious drop.

II. FRESH 'N' FOOLPROOF FROM THE OVEN ...

A. When using oven-glass baking pans, always lower the temperature 25 degrees.

B. Place cake pans in the center of the oven, and space them on the rack for good circulation of heat.

C. Although the fragrance is mighty tempting, don't peek! Be sure you wait until the baking time is up before opening the oven.

D. Always test for doneness before removing cake from the oven. It's ready if:

1. A toothpick comes out clean when inserted in the center of the cake . . . or

2. The cake springs back when lightly touched with the finger . . . or

3. The cake begins to pull away from the sides of the pan.

E. Cool cake in the pan five to ten minutes before turning out on wire rack to cool. Then, loosen it around all sides before turning out.

F. Handle it carefully because it's fragile! Turn the cake right side up to cool, unless directed otherwise in the recipe.

III. THE FINISHING TOUCHES ...

A. For a glamorous cake, it is important to cool it thoroughly before frosting.

B. No crumbly cake for you! Be sure to brush away all the crumbs before frosting.

(Continued on Next Page)

C. For a tidy plate, place four strips of waxed paper four inches wide around the edges of the plate. After frosting the cake, pull out the pieces of waxed paper, and you're ready to serve, quick as a wink.

D. You will want to have straight sides after the cake is frosted, so place one layer upside down on the cake plate. After spreading it with filling or frosting, top with the second layer which is right side up.

E. There is no compromise—the frosting must be the proper consistency. If it is too soft, it will eventually slide down the sides, or if it is too stiff, it will tear the cake.

F. Use a small, flexible spatula for frosting the cake. The easy way is to frost the sides of the cake first, using an upward motion, and then the top. To be strictly fancy, use a spoon or spatula and swirl the top into a decorative design.

G. Don't burden the cake with too much frosting; keep it light and fluffy.

H. For serving, cut the cake with a knife that has been dipped in warm water for even, attractive slices.

IV. FANCY FIXINS' . . .

A. For your own special touch, try adding a few frills such as these:
   1. Use plain coconut, or tint coconut and sprinkle over the top and sides of the cake.
   2. Have a variety—frost only half of the cake, and serve the other half plain with fresh fruits or sauces.
   3. Sliced bananas, strawberries or raspberries are favorites.
   4. Accent with melted chocolate, curls or shavings.

B. Festive Holiday Delights—
   1. Use unsalted nuts or blanched almonds, either halves or chopped for special occasion treats.
   2. Candied fruits are ideal during the Holiday Season.

V. GOOD TO THE LAST CRUMB . . .

1. Store cake in a cake keeper, covered container, or invert a large bowl over the cakes.
2. For a good "tote" cake, which will travel easily and safely, frost the cake in the pan, cover with a metal cover that slides on the pan, aluminum foil, or plastic wrap.
3. Cream-filled cakes must be stored in the refrigerator for safety.

Cake Baking helps

IF THIS HAPPENS WITH A TESTED RECIPE	IT MAY BE CAUSED BY THIS	TRY THIS
CAKE CRACKS OR HUMPS	1. Baking at too high temperature	Reduce heat. Have oven thermostat checked for accuracy.
CAKE FALLS	1. Insufficient baking	Test for doneness—cake shrinks away from sides of pan. No imprint left when touched lightly on top.
	2. Using self-rising instead of regular flour without reducing the leavening	Use ingredients specified in tested recipe.
CAKE RUNS OVER EDGE OF PAN	1. Too much batter for pan	Use proper pan size. If smaller pans are used, fill them half full and bake remaining batter as cupcakes.
CAKE BREAKS	1. Improper pan preparation	Brush pan generously with shortening, then dust lightly with flour.
	2. Improper cooling	Let cake cool in pan on rack about 15 minutes, top crust up. Loosen cake from sides of pan. Place rack on cake and invert both. Remove pan and turn cake top side up immediately to finish cooling.

Common Causes of Cake Failure

WHEN CAKE HAS COARSE TEXTURE: Too slow an oven. Butter cake: Insufficient creaming of shortening and sugar or too much leavening. Angel or sponge cake: Underbeaten eggs or insufficient blending of ingredients.

WHEN CRUST IS STICKY: Too much sugar or cake underbaked.

WHEN SPONGE CAKE HAS HEAVY, STICKY LAYER AT BOTTOM: Underbeaten egg yolks or insufficient mixing of egg yolks with other ingredients.

WHEN CAKE HUMPS IN THE MIDDLE OR CRACKS ON TOP: Butter cake: Flour overmeasured or liquid undermeasured, or too hot an oven. Sponge or angel cake: Overbeaten egg whites, too much sugar, or too hot an oven.

WHEN CAKE IS HEAVY: Butter cake: Extreme overbeating, too much shortening or sugar, or too slow an oven. Sponge or angel cake: Ingredients overmixed or oven too hot.

WHEN SPONGE OR ANGEL CAKE IS RUBBERY AND TOUGH: Too hot an oven.

WHEN BUTTER CAKE IS CRUMBLY AND FALLS APART: Too much shortening, too much leavening, or too much flour.

High Altitude Baking

At sea level, atmospheric pressure is 14.7 pounds per square inch; at 5,000 feet altitude, it is 12.28 pounds per square inch; and at 10,000 feet, 10.2 pounds per square inch. The relationship is a reverse one—the higher the elevation, the lower the pressure. Air becomes thinner at higher altitudes and consequently exerts less pressure.

As air pressure drops, water boils at lower temperatures. At sea level, water boils at 212°F. Each 500-foot increase in altitude causes a drop of about 1°F. in the boiling point. At very high altitudes, boiling water is relatively "cool." Since heat, not boiling, cooks foods, more time is required for food to reach the desired internal cooking temperature at higher altitudes.

Problems of altitude cookery are of two classes—boiling and leavening.

At altitudes above 3,500 feet, **increase** the oven temperature 25° over the temperature required at sea level. For example, cakes baked at sea level at 350°F. should be baked at 375°F. at *all* altitudes over 3,500 feet. The faster baking "sets" the cell framework within the flour mixture and helps to prevent falling.

In high altitudes, flour may become excessively dry unless it is stored in airtight containers. More liquid than the recipe calls for may be necessary to bring a batter or dough to the correct consistency.

CAKES

Some sea-level cakes are delicate and defy adjustment to varying altitudes. In which case, choose a new favorite from altitude tested recipes. Some other recipes are so well balanced that little if any adjustment may be necessary up to 5,000 feet. This is especially true of some of the commercial cake mixes. Keep a written record of any adjustments you make.

WITHOUT FAT   Air, incorporated in the beaten eggs, is the leavening agent in cakes without fat. The eggs should be beaten less at high altitudes, so less leavening power is given to the batter. In angel food cakes beat the whites just until they form soft peaks; in sponge cakes beat the egg or eggs (yolks) only until they are slightly thickened.

WITH FAT   The emulsified shortening available on the market today gives good results in altitude baking. Because the emulsifier enables the shortening to tolerate a larger amount of liquid, it is preferable for the "speed-mix" cakes with high sugar ratio.

FLOUR   All purpose flour is preferable in most recipes. Sift before measuring and make the following adjustments:

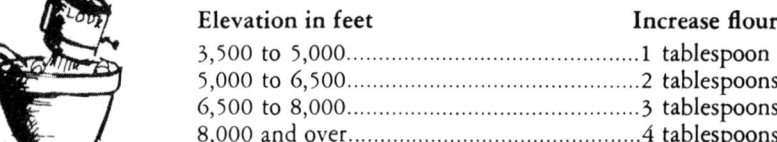

Elevation in feet	Increase flour
3,500 to 5,000	1 tablespoon
5,000 to 6,500	2 tablespoons
6,500 to 8,000	3 tablespoons
8,000 and over	4 tablespoons

EGG   An additional egg may be added to prevent the cake from being too dry and too tender.

LEAVENING   All types of baking powders and baking soda are treated alike in reductions for increased altitudes. When both baking powder and soda are used in a recipe, make the suggested adjustments in both ingredients. Accurate measurement of leavening is of increased importance as the altitude increases. The leavening adjustments begin with 2,000 feet elevation.

Elevation in feet	Decrease leavening
2,000 to 3,500	¼ to ⅓ teaspoon
3,500 to 5,000	⅓ to ½ teaspoon
5,000 to 6,500	½ to ⅔ teaspoon
6,500 to 8,000	⅔ to ¾ teaspoon
8,000 and over	¾ teaspoon

Decrease each teaspoon the lessen amount for the lower altitude within each given range and the larger amount at higher altitudes within the given range.

Cake Cutting Ideas

There is a satisfactory method of cutting each kind of cake. The factors to keep in mind are the size and number of servings and the cutting utensil to be used. The size and number of servings depend upon the size and number of layers in the cake. A knife with a sharp straight-edged, thin blade is most suitable for cutting batter cakes. To make a clean cut, dip the blade into warm water before cutting each portion and keep the blade free from frosting and cake crumbs.

Fruit cake, which also is a batter type cake, may be cut in the same manner. Because of its richness, the size of fruit cake servings generally are smaller than those shown for layer cakes.

The following diagrams illustrate *unusual* methods of cutting cakes of various sizes and shapes. The average number of servings per cake are given.

LAYER CAKES

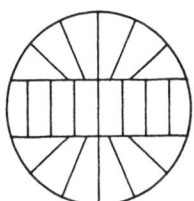

10″—2 layer cake
Yield: 20 servings

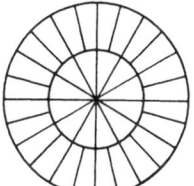

12″—2 layer cake
Yield: 36 servings

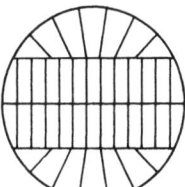

14″—2 layer cake
Yield: 40 servings

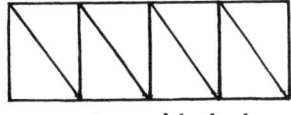

1 pound loaf cake
Yield: 8 servings

18″ x 25″
Yield: 48 servings

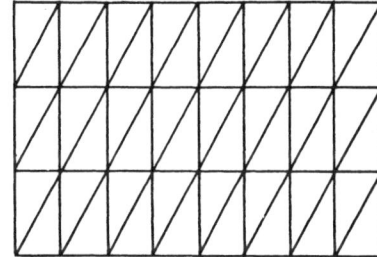

TIER CAKES

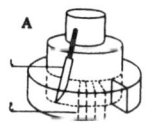

A—Cut vertically through the bottom layer at the edge of the second layer as indicated by the dotted line marked 1; then cut out wedge-shaped pieces as shown by 2.

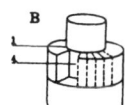

B—When these pieces have been served, follow the same procedure with the middle layer: cut vertically through the second layer at the edge of the top layer as indicated by dotted line 3; then cut out wedge-shaped pieces as shown by 4.

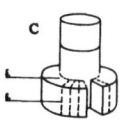

C—When pieces from the second layer have been served, return to the bottom layer and cut along dotted line 5; cut another row of wedge-shaped pieces as shown by 6.

D—The remaining tiers may be cut into the desired size pieces.

Cakes

ANGEL FOOD CAKE

Number of Servings — 15

1½ c. egg white
1½ t. cream of tartar
1 c. granulated sugar
⅛ t. salt
1 t. vanilla
1 c. cake flour
1½ c. confectioners' sugar

Beat eggs until feathery, add cream of tartar, beat until stiff, but not dry. Add granulated sugar little at a time. Add salt and vanilla. Sift cake flour and confectioners' sugar three times. Sift into mixture and fold in. Bake in tube pan 65 minutes at 325°F.

Icing:

2 c. sugar
¾ c. water
¼ t. cream of tartar
2 egg whites

Cook sugar, water, to soft ball—238°F. Beat egg whites and cream of tartar until stiff. Add syrup to egg whites. Beat to spreading consistency.

Mrs. Kathleen K. Horne, Powell Valley H. S.
Big Stone Gap, Virginia

CHOCOLATE ANGEL FOOD CAKE

Number of Servings — 18-24

Set out but do not grease:
Tube pan
Measure and sift together 3 times:
¾ c. cake flour
¼ c. cocoa
½ c. sugar

Measure into large bowl and beat until meringue holds stiff peaks:
1¼ c. egg whites
1½ t. cream of tartar
¼ t. salt
Beat in 2 T. at a time:
1 c. sugar

Fold in flour-sugar mixture and 1½ teaspoons vanilla. Put batter in ungreased pan. Cut through with knife. Bake at 325-350°F. about 1 hour. Invert pan until cake is cool.

Mrs. Florence Wood, Fairmount H. S.
Fairmount, Indiana

COFFEE ANGEL FOOD CAKE

Number of Servings — 16

1½ c. sifted sugar
1 c. sifted cake flour
½ t. salt
1¼ c. egg whites (10-12)
1½ t. cream of tartar
½ t. vanilla
1 T. powdered instant coffee

Add ½ cup of the sugar to flour. Sift together 4 times. Add salt to egg whites and beat with flat wire whisk or rotary egg beater until foamy. Sprinkle cream of tartar over eggs and continue beating to soft-peak stage. Add the remaining cup of sugar by sprinkling ¼ cup at a time over egg whites and blending carefully, about 20 strokes each time. Fold in flavorings. Sift flour-sugar mixture over egg whites about ¼ (one-fourth) at a time and fold in lightly, about 10 strokes each time. Pour into ungreased round 10-inch tube pan. Bake at 350°F. for 35-45 minutes. Remove from oven and invert pan on cooling rack.

Butter Icing for Angel Food Cake

½ c. butter
¼ t. salt
2½ c. sifted confectioners' sugar
3-4 T. milk
1 t. vanilla
2 T. instant coffee

Cream butter, add salt and sugar, a small amount at a time, beating all the while. Add milk as needed, and flavoring. Beat until light and fluffy. Spread and sprinkle generously with slivered or chopped toasted almonds.

Jeannette Peel Morrow, Campbellton H. S.
Graceville, Florida

ANGEL-RUM DESSERT

Cake:
1 package white angel food mix
3 T. cocoa

Sift the dry ingredients with the cocoa and then proceed according to the directions on the package. When cake is baked and cooled cut it in half to make two layers. Put the two layers together and frost the top with the following filling. Sprinkle ¼ cup almonds over top.

Filling:
1 pt. thick whipping cream
¼ c. sugar
3 T. cocoa
¼ c. white rum
¾ c. chopped toasted almonds

Beat whipping cream until stiff. Sift together sugar and cocoa and fold it into the cream. Combine white rum with cream mixture. Add chopped toasted almonds. Place dessert in refrigerator for several hours before serving. This dessert will be good several days after it is prepared.

Mrs. Marie Strand, Junior H. S.
Stillwater, Minnesota

YELLOW ANGEL FOOD

Number of Servings — 20

12 egg yolks
1¾ c. sugar
2 t. baking powder
1 t. vanilla and lemon flavoring
½ c. water

(Continued on Next Page)

⅛ t. salt
2½ c. flour

Add part of water to egg yolks and beat until lemon colored; add baking powder, sugar and rest of water. Now add flour and salt. Beat well. Add flavoring. Bake 1 hour at 350°F. Grease pan slightly.

Mrs. Vic C. Hickson, Seminole County H. S.
Donalsonville, Georgia

APPLE CAKE

Number of Servings — 16

1½ c. cooking oil
2 c. sugar
3 eggs
3 c. flour
1 t. salt
1 t. soda
1 t. vanilla
1 c. pecans (chopped)
3 apples grated (Winesap)

Cream oil and sugar, add eggs one at a time. Add flour sifted three (3) times with salt and soda. Add vanilla, pecans and apples. Bake in three 8″ pans at 350°F. for 30 to 35 minutes.

Filling:
1 c. brown sugar
¼ c. evaporated milk
1 stick margarine

Cook brown sugar, milk, and margarine in top of double boiler for five (5) minutes. Spread on cake.

Kathleen Garrett, Albertville H. S.
Albertville, Alabama

APPLE CHIP CAKE

Number of Servings — 15 to 20

1¼ c. peanut oil
2 c. sugar
3 well beaten eggs
3 c. flour
1 t. salt
1 t. soda
1 c. nut meats
3 c. chopped apples
2 t. vanilla

Combine in large bowl the oil, sugar, and eggs. Sift flour, salt, and soda together and add to first mixture. Add nuts, apples and vanilla. Bake at 325°F. for 45 minutes either in two 9″ layer cake pans or long oblong pan.

½ c. margarine
1 c. brown sugar
¼ c. cream

Heat margarine and brown sugar over low heat, Add cream and let come to a full boil. Remove from heat and cool then pour over the cake. This cake is better 2 or 3 days after baking.

Mrs. Juanita Williams, Graceville H. S.
Graceville, Florida

DELICIOUS APPLE CAKE

Number of Servings — 16

1 t. each cloves, cinnamon, nutmeg, allspice
2½ c. flour

¼ t. salt
1 c. shortening
2 c. sugar
4 eggs
2 c. Delicious apples diced the size of peas
1 t. soda dissolved in ½ c. cold water
1 t. vanilla
1 c. nuts (optional)

Mix flour, salt and spices and sift twice. Cream sugar and shortening. Add eggs which have been well beaten. Beat mixture for 1 minute. Add dry ingredients alternately with apples and water and soda mixture. Add vanilla. Add nuts if desired. Pour into well greased and floured pans. Should make three layers. Bake at 350°F. for 30 minutes or until done.

Sarah Musgrave, Rattan H. S.
Rattan, Oklahoma

FRESH APPLE CAKE

Number of Servings — 20

2 c. sugar
1 c. shortening or butter
4 eggs
2½ c. flour
½ c. water
1 t. cloves, cinnamon, nutmeg
1 t. soda
1 t. vanilla
½ t. salt
1 c. nuts
2 c. fresh apples, chopped fine or grated

Mix like most any cake. Bake in loaf pan at 350°F. for 45 minutes to 1 hour.

Billye Hartman, Princeton H. S.
Princeton, Texas

FRESH APPLE CAKE

Number of Servings — 20 to 24

2 c. sugar
1½ c. cooking oil
2 t. vanilla extract
2 well beaten eggs
Juice of ½ lemon
1 t. salt
3 c. flour
1¼ t. soda
3 c. peeled and chopped fresh apples
1½-2 c. chopped pecans

Combine sugar, oil, vanilla, eggs, lemon juice, and salt in a mixing bowl. Beat well. Mix flour and soda. Add to first mixture and beat well again. Add apples and pecans. Mix well. Bake in a tube pan which has been greased and dusted with flour. Bake 1½ hours at 325°F.

Mrs. Ouida Hiroms, Istrouma Senior H. S.
Baton Rouge, Louisiana

FRESH APPLE CAKE

Number of Servings — 12

1 c. cooking oil
2 c. sugar
2 well beaten eggs
3 c. flour

1 t. soda
½ t. salt
1 t. cinnamon
2 t. vanilla
3 c. chopped fresh apples

Combine cooking oil and sugar. Add well beaten eggs, measure and sift together dry ingredients. Add dry ingredients to first mixture. Add vanilla and chopped apples. Bake in loaf pan (13x9) 55 minutes at 300°F. This cake will keep moist and fresh for days.

Thelma Hughes, Mississippi County H. S.
West Ridge, Arkansas

APPLE CAKE (Knobby)

Number of Servings — 16

3 T. butter
1 c. sugar
1 egg, beaten
½ t. cinnamon
½ t. nutmeg
½ t. salt
1 c. flour
1 t. soda
3 c. chopped apples
½ c. chopped nuts
1 t. vanilla

Cream shortening and sugar, add egg, mix well. Sift dry ingredients together. Add to creamed mixture. Stir in chopped apples and vanilla. Pour in greased 8x8 pan, bake in 350°F. oven about 45 minutes. Serve warm with whipped cream or ice cream.

This recipe submitted by the following teachers:
Mrs. M. J. McMillion,
South Lebanon Township H. S.
Lebanon, Pennsylvania
Barbara Mash, Rylie H. S.
Dallas, Texas
Mrs. Betty J. Hempel, Lyman Memorial H. S.
Lebanon, Connecticut
Mrs. Nanette Banks, Edgerton H. S.
Edgerton, Wisconsin
Mrs. Deanna House, Edgerton H. S.
Edgerton, Wisconsin

GREEN APPLE CAKE

Number of Servings — 15

2 c. sugar
1 c. shortening
4 eggs
3 c. flour
1 t. soda
½ t. salt
1 t. cinnamon
½ t. cloves
⅓ t. nutmeg
1 t. vanilla
4 green apples, finely chopped
¼ c. warm water

Blend sugar and shortening until light and fluffy. Beat in eggs. Sift flour before measuring. Resift with soda, salt, cinnamon, cloves, nutmeg. Add to first mixture. Beat until smooth. Blend in

vanilla. Pour water over apples and mix thoroughly with other mixture. Bake in three 9″ paper lined pans for about 30 minutes (350°F.).

Filling:
2 c. milk
1 c. sugar
2 egg yolks
3 T. flour
1 c. nuts

Combine milk, sugar, egg yolks, and flour. Boil until thick. Add nuts and spread between layers of Green Apple Cake.

Mrs. Dorothy Carter, Cunningham Junior H. S.
Corpus Christi, Texas

RAW APPLE CAKE

½ c. shortening
2 c. sugar
2 well beaten eggs
2 c. flour
½ t. nutmeg
1 t. cinnamon
1 t. soda
1 t. salt
1 c. chopped nuts
1 c. chopped dates
4 c. diced raw apples (preferably of tart variety)

Cream together shortening and sugar. Add eggs and mix well. Sift together flour, nutmeg, cinnamon, soda and salt. Add this to creamed mixture, stirring well. Now stir in nuts, dates and apples. Pour into well greased and floured pan. Makes 1 tube pan or 2 small loaves. Bake 1 hour at 325°F.

Mrs. Betty Hall, Fort Cobb School
Fort Cobb, Oklahoma

APPLE TART CAKE

Number of Servings — 8-10

3 c. sugar
8 T. flour
5 t. baking powder
½ t. salt
4 eggs
2 c. chopped nuts (pecans)
2 c. finely chopped tart apples
2 t. vanilla

Mix the sugar, flour, baking powder, and salt together, set aside. Beat the eggs until they are lemon colored. Add the eggs, nuts, apples, and vanilla to the dry ingredients, mix well. Pour batter in greased loaf pan (9x12). Bake 45 minutes at 350°F. It rises real high and then falls. It makes its own crust and does not need a topping.

Mrs. Kay Pitts, Humble H. S.
Humble, Texas

APPLESAUCE CAKE

Number of Servings — 12

2 c. sifted all-purpose flour
2 T. cocoa
¾ t. salt
1½ t. cinnamon
¼ t. cloves
½ t. nutmeg

(Continued on Next Page)

½ t. allspice
½ t. soda
1½ t. baking powder
1 c. raisins, cut up, or 1 c. snipped dates
¾ c. chopped walnuts, if desired
½ c. soft shortening
1½ c. granulated sugar
2 eggs
1½ c. canned applesauce

Set oven at 350°F. to preheat. Grease, line with wax paper or dust with flour, bottom of 13x9x2 pan. Sift together flour, cocoa, salt, cinnamon, cloves, nutmeg, allspice, soda and baking powder. Add fruit and nuts and toss to coat. In a large mixing bowl, cream shortening and sugar on No. 7 speed 2 minutes, then add eggs, 1 at a time while beating 2 minutes. Add flour mixture alternately with applesauce while beating on No. 2 speed. Scrape bowl as necessary, beat only until blended, about 4 minutes. Bake about 30-35 minutes or until done. Cool. Frost with caramel or coffee frosting.

Mrs. Mary Ellen Burchfield, Minco H. S.
Minco, Oklahoma

APPLESAUCE CAKE

Number of Servings — 12

3½ c. flour
2 c. white sugar
2 t. cinnamon
½ t. salt
1½ t. allspice
1½ t. cloves
2 t. soda
2 c. applesauce
2 whole eggs
1 c. cooking oil
2 c. raisins
1 c. chopped nuts

Soak raisins and nuts in water, while mixing cake. Mix flour, sugar, cinnamon, salt, cloves, allspice and soda. Make a hole in the middle of mixture and add applesauce, eggs, and oil. Mix well for about 5 minutes. Drain raisins and nuts that have been soaking in water. Dredge in flour. Fold into cake mixture. Pour into a greased lined tube pan and bake 45 minutes at 350°F. and 15 minutes at 375°F. When done, cover tightly until cool, preferably over night.

Mrs. John F. Hendrickson, Jr., Pineville H. S.
Pineville, Kentucky

APPLESAUCE CAKE WITH BROWN SUGAR TOPPING

Number of Servings — Full Size Cake

1 c. soft butter
2 c. sugar
4 eggs
2½ c. applesauce
1½ c. chopped nuts
1 box raisins or 2 boxes dates, chopped
4 c. all-purpose flour
3 t. soda
1 t. cinnamon
½ t. cloves

½ t. nutmeg
½ t. salt

Cream butter and sugar. Add eggs and beat until fluffy. Sift dry ingredients. Add raisins and nuts. Mix alternately with applesauce to the butter and sugar mixture. Mix thoroughly and turn into well greased tube pan. Bake 1 hour at 325°F. or until done.

Frosting:
⅔ c. brown sugar
¼ c. melted butter
⅛ t. salt
2 T. milk
1 c. shredded coconut

Mix all ingredients together. Spread over the top of hot cake. Place under broiler for a few minutes until delicately brown.

Mrs. Ruth M. Smith, D. W. Daniel H. S.
Central, South Carolina

APPLESAUCE CAKE (With Lemon Icing)

½ c. shortening
1 c. granulated sugar
1 egg
1 c. unsweetened applesauce
1¾ c. sifted flour
1 t. baking soda
½ t. nutmeg
½ t. allspice
1 t. cinnamon
½ t. salt
1 c. seedless raisins
(More or less spice may be used)

Cream the shortening, add sugar and blend thoroughly. Add the beaten egg and applesauce, mix well. Sift the dry ingredients together into the mixture, add the raisins and mix well. Pour into a greased and floured pan 10x10x2 or line the pan with waxed paper. Bake at 350°F. for one hour or until done. Remove from the oven, set pan on cake rack for about five minutes. Loosen edges of cake from the pan, invert on rack, remove pan and turn cake right side up. When cool, top with lemon icing if desired.

Lemon Icing:
2 T. butter or margarine
Grated rind of ½ lemon
1½ c. confectioners' sugar
1½ T. lemon juice

Cream butter, add grated lemon rind and blend. Gradually add the confectioners' sugar alternating with the lemon juice until icing has a creamy, spreading consistency.

This recipe submitted by the following teachers:
Adrienne Carter, Alleghany District H. S.
Shawsville, Virginia
Mrs. Estelle Rayton, Mt. Baker Jr.-Sr. H. S.
Deming, Washington

BUTTERSCOTCH CHIP APPLESAUCE CAKE
Number of Servings — 12 slices
½ c. shortening (do not use margarine)
1 c. granulated sugar
2 eggs
1¾ c. sifted flour
1 t. soda
¼ t. salt
¼ t. ground cloves
½ t. mace, or allspice
1 t. cinnamon
Thick sweetened canned applesauce*
½ c. raisins
½ c. chopped nuts (optional)
About 1 cup butterscotch chips

*With vegetable shortening, use 1 cup applesauce. With butter, use ¾ cup.

Cream shortening. Add sugar gradually and cream until fluffy. Add eggs one at a time, beating well. Sift together dry ingredients. Add alternately with applesauce in small amounts, beating after each addition until smooth. Stir in raisins, nuts and half of butterscotch chips. Pour batter into 9x5x3 inch loaf pan which has been lined on bottom with foil or paper. Sprinkle remaining butterscotch chips over batter. Bake at 325°F. about 1 hour and 15 minutes, or until done. Cool cake. Cover tightly with plastic wrap or foil and store overnight.

Joan Lichter, Newell-Providence Community H. S. Newell, Iowa

APPLESAUCE SPICE CAKE—Low Cholesterol
Number of Servings — 16
⅓ c. oil
1 c. sugar
1 egg
1 c. sweetened applesauce
1¾ c. flour
1 t. salt
1 t. soda
1 t. cinnamon
1 t. cloves
1 c. raisins
1 c. currants
In a large bowl combine with rotary egg beater or electric mixer the oil, sugar and egg. Beat in the applesauce. Sift together the dry ingredients. Add the flour mixture to the batter gradually, continuing to beat until smooth. Stir in the raisins and currants; transfer to an oiled and floured cake pan (9x13). Bake in a moderate oven 350°F. for 40 minutes.

Mrs. Anita H. Reece, Boonville H. S. Boonville, North Carolina

HOLIDAY APPLESAUCE CAKE
½ c. shortening
1½ c. sugar
3 eggs (beaten)
2 c. cold unsweetened applesauce
½ to 1 c. flour, just enough to hold ingredients together
1 t. baking powder
1 t. salt
2 t. mixed spices
1 t. soda
1 c. seedless raisins (either whole or cut up)
2 or 3 c. pecan meats (chopped)
1 c. coconut
1 pkg. dates (chopped)
Heat oven to 350°F. Grease and flour two layer pans, 9x1½ or an oblong pan, 13x9½x2. Cream shortening and sugar, add beaten eggs. Stir mixture into applesauce. Sift dry ingredients onto waxed paper. Add to first mixture and beat 2 minutes. Stir in raisins, pecans, coconut and dates. Pour into prepared pans. Bake layers 35 to 40 minutes, oblong 45 to 50 minutes or until cake tests done. Cool. Frost with Penuche Icing.

Penuche Icing:
½ c. butter
1 c. brown sugar (packed)
¼ c. milk
1¾ to 2 cups sifted confectioners' sugar
Melt butter in saucepan. Stir in brown sugar. Boil and stir over low heat 2 minutes. Stir in milk. Bring to boil, stirring constantly. Cool to lukewarm 120°F. Gradually stir in confectioners' sugar. Place pan in ice water and stir until thick enough to spread.

Gail C. Oyler, Grove H. S. Grove, Oklahoma

RAISIN-APPLESAUCE CAKE
2½ c. sifted all-purpose flour
1½ t. soda
1 t. salt
1 t. cinnamon
½ t. cloves
½ t. nutmeg
¾ c. shortening
1¼ c. sugar
2 eggs
½ c. light molasses
1 can (17 oz.) thick applesauce
½ c. finely chopped nuts
English Walnut halves
Sift flour with soda, salt, and spices. Cream shortening, add sugar gradually, and beat until fluffy. Add eggs one at a time. Add molasses and beat thoroughly. Stir in applesauce and nuts. Gradually blend in sifted dry ingredients. Pour batter into two wax-paperlined and greased 8" or 9" square baking pans, or three 8" round layer pans. Bake in moderate over (350°F.) for 20 to 25 minutes. Spread cooled layers with Raisin Penuche icing and stack. Frost sides. Rim cake with English walnut halves.

Raisin Penuche Icing:
Combine ⅓ cup butter, ⅓ cup brown sugar, and ⅓ cup light cream. Bring to a full boil over medium heat. Remove from heat. Gradually stir in 3 to 3½ cups sifted powdered sugar until of a velvety, spreading consistency. Add 1 teaspoon vanilla, ¼ cup chopped nuts, and 1 cup coarsely cut raisins. Spread on Raisin-Apple Cake.

Mrs. Eldena Koger, Pickett County H. S. Byrdstown, Tennessee

BANANA CAKE

1⅓ c. sugar
½ c. butter or shortening
2 eggs, separated
½ c. buttermilk
1 t. soda
½ t. baking powder
3 mashed bananas
1 t. vanilla
2⅓ c. all-purpose flour sifted 3 times

Cream sugar and shortening, or butter. Add egg yolks and beat thoroughly. Add milk, soda, baking powder and bananas. Add flour, egg whites (not beaten) and vanilla. Place in three well greased and floured 9" cake pans. Bake at 350°F. for about 25 minutes. Cool in pans 10 minutes. Remove and ice with butter icing, spreading generously between layers as well as the outside.

Butter Icing:
2 c. sugar
1 c. butter
1 c. milk
1 t. vanilla

Place in heavy saucepan and boil until it will form a soft ball in cold water when dropped from a spoon. Add vanilla and beat until thick and creamy.

Effie Lois Greene, Tishomingo H. S.
Padea, Mississippi

BANANA CAKE (Layer)

Number of Servings — 14 to 16

2 c. sifted cake flour
1 t. baking powder
1 t. soda
½ t. salt
½ c. butter
1½ c. sugar
1 whole egg plus 1 yolk
1 c. mashed bananas
½ c. broken nut meats
¾ c. sour milk or buttermilk
1 t. vanilla

Sift flour once, add baking powder, soda and salt. Sift together 3 times. Cream butter, add sugar gradually, creaming together until light and fluffy. Add eggs and beat well. Add bananas and nuts and beat again. Add flour to creamed mixture alternately with milk, beating after each addition until smooth. Add vanilla. Bake in layer pans in 375°F. oven for 25 minutes. Cool.

Jane S. Scates, Rogers H. S.
Florence, Alabama

BANANA LAYER CAKE

2¼ c. sifted all-purpose flour
1¼ c. sugar
2½ t. double-acting baking powder
½ t. soda
½ t. salt
½ c. shortening
1½ c. mashed ripe bananas
2 eggs
1 t. vanilla

Preheat oven to 375°F. Sift into a large mixing bowl: flour, sugar, baking powder, soda, and salt. Add shortening, ½ cup mashed bananas and eggs. Beat 2 minutes at medium speed with electric mixed. Scrape down bowl and beaters. Add remaining 1 cup mashed bananas and vanilla. Beat 1 minute. Bake in two greased 8" round layer pans for 25 minutes.

Speedy Banana Frosting (2 cups):
¼ c. butter or margarine
1 lb. confectioners' sugar
½ c. mashed ripe bananas
½ t. lemon juice

Cream butter until soft and glossy. Add half of the sugar; beat until blended. Add mashed bananas and lemon juice; blend. Add remaining sugar and beat until frosting is light and fluffy.

Mrs. Maggie Beth Watts, Era H. S.
Era, Texas

BANANA NUT CAKE

2 c. sugar
½ c. shortening
2 eggs
3 c. flour
Pinch of salt
1½ t. soda
8 to 10 T. buttermilk
3 bananas, mashed
½ c. chopped nuts

Mix in order given. Add soda to buttermilk. Bake in loaf or tube pan at 350°F. for 1 hour. For holidays, add 1 cup mixed candied fruits.

Mrs. Susan Bailey, Baileysville H. S.
Baileysville, West Virginia

BANANA NUT CAKE

Number of Servings — 16

2½ c. cake flour
1⅔ c. sugar
1¼ t. baking powder
1 t. salt
⅔ c. shortening (oleo)
⅓ c. buttermilk
1 t. soda
1¼ c. mashed bananas (3)
⅓ c. buttermilk
⅓ c. unbeaten egg (2)
½ c. chopped nuts

Sift dry ingredients together. Add soda to buttermilk. Add shortening, buttermilk and mashed bananas. Beat 2 minutes on medium speed. Add buttermilk and eggs. Fold in ½ cup chopped nuts. Bake 350°F. for 30-35 minutes.

Icing:
1 c. white sugar
1 c. brown sugar
1 c. milk
1 c. nuts
1 c. raisins, ground

Boil white sugar, brown sugar, milk together 5 minutes. Add nuts and ground raisins. Beat, spread on cool cake.

Mrs. Mary R. Whipple, Ballard Memorial H. S.
Barlow, Kentucky

BANANA LOAF

Number of Servings — 10 to 12

¾ c. sugar
¼ c. shortening
2 eggs
1 c. mashed bananas
2 c. sifted flour
2 t. baking powder
½ t. salt
¼ t. soda
1 c. chopped walnuts

Heat oven to 350°F. Grease 9x5x3 loaf pan. Mix sugar, shortening and eggs, beat hard until light. Add mashed bananas. Stir in sifted dry ingredients, beating smooth. Add walnuts. Pour into pan. Bake 60 to 70 minutes. Cool on rack.

Les V. Edmonds, Franklin H. S.
Franklin, Louisiana

BANANA SPICE CAKE WITH SEAFOAM FROSTING

2½ c. sifted cake flour
1⅔ c. sugar
1¼ t. baking powder
1¼ t. baking soda
1 t. salt
1½ t. cinnamon
¾ t. nutmeg
½ t. ground cloves
⅔ c. hydrogenated vegetable shortening
⅔ c. buttermilk
1¼ c. mashed ripe bananas (3 medium)
2 eggs, unbeaten

Sift dry ingredients into large mixer bowl. Add shortening, buttermilk, and mashed bananas; mix until all flour is dampened. Beat at low speed for 2 minutes. Add eggs; beat 1 minute. Bake in three 8" or two 9" greased and floured layer-cake pans at 350°F. 30-35 minutes. Spread Sea-Foam frosting between cooled layers, top with banana slices. Frost cake; make swirls.

Sea-Foam Frosting:
2 unbeaten egg whites
1½ c. brown sugar (firmly packed)
5 T. water
1 dash of salt
1 t. vanilla

Combine egg whites, brown sugar, water, and salt in top of double boiler. Beat slightly to mix. Place over rapidly boiling water. Beat with rotary egg beater or electric mixer at high speed until frosting stands in peaks, about 7 minutes. Remove from heat; add vanilla; beat 1-2 minutes, or until thick enough to spread.

Lorene English, Norcross H. S.
Norcross, Georgia

BLITZ TORTE CAKE

Number of Servings — 12

½ c. butter
½ c. sugar
3 egg yolks, slightly beaten
1 c. sifted flour
2 t. baking powder
⅓ c. milk
½ t. vanilla
½ c. chopped pecans

Meringue:
5 egg whites
¾ c. sugar

Cream shortening and sugar, add egg yolk and beat. Sift flour and soda together and add alternately with milk and vanilla. Spread batter in two lightly greased and floured 8" pans, leaving ½" margin around sides. Make meringue by beating egg whites until stiff. Fold in sugar gradually, beating after each addition. Spread meringue over uncooked batter, leaving 1" around edge. Sprinkle nuts over uncooked meringue. Bake at 350°F. for 25-30 minutes.

Filling:
2½ T. flour
⅓ c. sugar
⅛ t. salt
2 egg yolks
1 c. milk

Prepare filling by blending sugar, flour, and salt together. Add egg yolks and milk. Cook until thick, stirring constantly. Let cake and filling cool. Place one layer of cake on plate, meringue side down. Spread filling over this layer. Place other layer on top, meringue side up. (Meringue will be on both the top and bottom of cake.)

Frances Rudd, State Department of Education
Little Rock, Arkansas

BUTTERMILK CAKE

Number of Servings — 16 Slices

1 c. butter
2½ c. sugar
4 eggs
3 c. flour
1 c. buttermilk
½ t. soda
1 T. boiling water

Cream butter and sugar. Add 1 egg at a time. Beat well after each addition. Then add flour and buttermilk alternately. Stir in soda that has been dissolved in boiling water. Bake in loaf pan 1 hour, or until done. Temperature 325°F.

Mrs. B. H. Canter, Oakdale H. S.
Oakdale, Louisiana

BUTTERMILK CAKE

3 c. sugar
1 c. butter
5 eggs (separated)
3 c. plain flour
⅓ t. soda (dissolved in 2 T. warm water)
1 c. buttermilk
1 t. vanilla
½ t. salt

Cream butter and sugar. Add egg yolks, one at a time, beating after each. Add half of the milk to the soda water and then add this to the creamed mixture. Mix thoroughly and add vanilla. Sift flour and salt together and add alternately with the remaining milk to the first mixture. Begin and

(Continued on Next Page)

end with flour. Fold in well beaten egg whites. Pour into a large tube cake pan which has been greased and floured. Bake at 350°F. for approximately one hour. This will be somewhat crusty on the outside and the inside will be somewhat like pound cake.

This recipe submitted by the following teachers:
Mrs. Pauline S. Slate, Greensville County H. S.
Emporia, Virginia
Evelyn H. Duke, Grayson H. S.
Grayson, Louisiana

BUTTERMILK CAKE

2 c. sugar
1 c. shortening
4 eggs (beaten)
½ t. soda
1 c. buttermilk
½ t. vanilla
3 c. flour
½ t. baking powder
½ t. lemon flavoring

Cream sugar and shortening. Add beaten eggs. Add soda to buttermilk. Sift flour and baking powder. Add in small portions to other ingredients. Add vanilla and lemon flavoring. Bake approximately 1 hour and 15 minutes at 350°F. in large greased and floured tube pan.

Mrs. Anne Havel, Gonzales H. S.
Gonzales, Texas

BUTTERMILK CAKE

1 c. hydrogenated shortening
3 c. sugar
1½ t. vanilla flavoring
6 eggs
3 c. flour
¼ t. soda
½ t. salt
1 c. buttermilk

Cream shortening and sugar. Add flavoring. Add eggs, one at a time, beating after each addition. Sift dry ingredients together and add alternately with buttermilk. Pour batter into greased 10" tube cake pan. Bake at 325°F. for 1 hour or until tests done.

Jane H. Robinson, Quitman H. S.
Quitman, Texas

CARROT CAKE

Number of Servings — 20
2 c. flour
2 t. soda
2 t. cinnamon
1 t. salt
2 c. sugar
4 eggs
1¼ c. cooking oil
2 c. finely grated carrots

Sift dry ingredients together. Mix eggs, cooking oil and carrots together and add to dry ingredients. Beat hard. Bake in 2 layer pans at 350°F. for 45 minutes.

Icing:
1-8 oz. pkg. cream cheese

1 stick oleo
1 box powdered sugar
1 c. chopped nuts

Cream cheese and oleo. Add sugar gradually. Blend in nuts.

Lucinda Beuerage, Monterey, H. S.
Monterey, Virginia

CARROT CAKE

1½ c. oil
2 c. sugar
4 eggs
2 c. flour
1½ t. soda
1 t. salt
2 t. cinnamon
2 c. grated carrots

Combine oil ad sugar. Add eggs, beating mixture after each egg. Add gradually flour, soda, salt, cinnamon. Mix well. Fold in carrots. Bake in greased rectangular pan at 325°F.

Icing:
½ stick oleo
1-3 oz. pkg. cream cheese
½ box powdered sugar
½ t. vanilla
Nuts (as desired)

Cream butter and cream cheese. Add powdered sugar gradually, mixing until smooth and creamy. Add vanilla. Add nuts and spread on cake.

Glenda Brodnax, Memorial Junior H. S.
Kingsville, Texas

CARROT CAKE

Number of Servings — 20 to 24
3 c. flour
2 t. soda
½ t. salt
3 t. cinnamon
1½ c. salad oil
2 c. sugar
2 c. grated carrots
1 flat can crushed pineapple
⅛ c. chopped nuts
2 t. vanilla
3 eggs

Sift together flour, soda, cinnamon and salt. Mix together salad oil and sugar. Add half of dry ingredients. Mix well and beat in carrots, pineapple and nuts. Add vanilla and rest of dry ingredients. Add eggs one at a time. Beat until well blended after each addition. Bake in greased 8x12x2 pan at 350°F. until brown and toothpick comes out clean when tested. Ice with Cream Cheese Icing.

Cream Cheese Icing:
1 lge. pkg. cream cheese, 8 oz.
½ stick margarine
1 box powdered sugar
½ t. lemon extract
1 t. vanilla

Melt margarine and blend in with sugar, cheese and extract. Mix well. Ice top of cake.

Mrs. Florence Lenox, Runnels Junior H. S.
Big Spring, Texas

CARROT CAKE

Number of Servings — Approx. 16

Mix together:
2 c. grated carrots
2 c. granulated sugar
½ c. black walnuts
1½ c. salad oil
4 eggs, well beaten
Add to first mixture:
2 c. flour
2 t. soda
½ t. baking powder
½ t. salt
2 t. cinnamon

Bake 1 hour (more or less) at 300°F. Excellent baked as loaf cake, plain or iced. Easy Penuche Icing is very flavorful.

Mrs. Alberta Lanham, Bellevue H. S.
Bellevue, Kentucky

CARROT CAKE

Number of Servings 20 Slices

1 c. sugar
¾ c. salad oil
1½ c. flour
1 t. baking powder
1 t. baking soda
1 t. cinnamon
¼ t. salt
1 c. grated carrots
2 eggs
½ c. chopped nuts

Mix sugar and oil, then add sifted dry ingredients. Now add carrots. Next add eggs, one at a time, beating well. Add nuts last. Blend well. Bake in a medium-sized loaf pan at 375°F. for 55 minutes.

Elaine Rose Rotter, Pettus H. S.
Pettus, Texas

CARROT CAKE

Number of Servings — 20 to 25

1½ c. cooking oil
2 c. sugar
4 eggs
1 T. hot water
1½ c. grated carrots
2½ c. cake or plain flour
2½ t. cinnamon
1½ t. soda
1½ t. salt

Cream oil, sugar, egg yolks and hot water. Add the grated carrot. Sift together the flour, cinnamon, soda, and salt. Add to the first mixture. Beat the egg whites until stiff and add to mixture by folding in. Pour into prepared pans. Will make three 8″ layers or two 9″ layers. Bake at 350°F. for 30 minutes. Ice with cream cheese icing or coconut and pecan frosting.

This recipe submitted by the following teachers:
Mrs. Mildred N. Mallette, Greenville H. S.
Greenville, Alabama
Hilda S. Wright, Hanceville H. S.
Hanceville, Alabama

CARROT CAKE

1¼ c. cooking oil
2 c. sugar
4 eggs
2 c. flour
1 t. cinnamon
2 t. baking powder
⅛ t. soda
¼ t. salt
1 c. chopped nuts

Sift dry ingredients together. Mix all ingredients and add 2 cups cooked carrots, chopped finely, or shredded raw carrots. Bake at 350°F. 35 to 45 minutes. Cool and remove from tube pan. Spread with icing.

Icing:
1 small pkg. (3 oz.) cream cheese
1 box powdered sugar
1 c. pecans, chopped
Milk enough to make spreading consistency.

Mrs. Pat Chambers, Abilene H. S.
Abilene, Texas

CARROT CAKE

Number of Servings — 12

1½ c. Wesson oil
2 c. sugar
4 whole eggs (well beaten)
2 c. flour
2 t. cinnamon
2 t. soda
2 t. baking powder
1 c. broken up pecans
3 c. grated carrots

Mix Wesson oil and sugar and beat well, then add the eggs that have been beaten. Sift flour, cinnamon, soda and baking powder for 2 or 3 times. Then add nuts and mix with the above mixture. Last add the grated carrots small amount at a time. Bake 1 hour in moderate oven 350°F. This may be baked in layers if desired about 30 minutes.

Filling:
1-8 oz. pkg. cream cheese
1 stick oleo
1 box powdered sugar
2 t. vanilla

Beat all ingredients well. Spread on cake.

Sharon Turner, Red Boiling Springs H. S.
Red Boiling Springs, Tennessee

CARROT CAKE (With Buttermilk Icing)

3 c. all-purpose flour
2 t. baking powder
1 t. salt
1½ t. cinnamon
1½ t. nutmeg
2 c. sugar
1¼ c. salad oil
1 t. vanilla
3 eggs, separated
2 c. carrots, shredded (fine)
1 small can crushed pineapple and juice
1 c. chopped nuts

(Continued on Next Page)

Sift together flour, baking powder, salt, cinnamon, nutmeg, and set aside. Cream the sugar and oil together. Add vanilla and egg yolks one at a time and mix thoroughly. Add the dry ingredients to the oil mixture and mix thoroughly. Add carrots, pineapple and nuts. Mix well. Fold in stiffly beaten egg whites. Bake in tube pan at 350°F. for 80 minutes.

Buttermilk Icing:
2 c. white sugar
1 t. soda
1 stick butter or oleo
1 c. buttermilk
2 T. white syrup

Mix all of this together thoroughly. Cook stirring often, until a soft ball forms when dropped in water. Cool and beat.

Faye Stanley, Waterloo H. S.
Waterloo, Alabama

CARROT CAKE (Self-rising Flour)
Number of Servings — 16
2 c. self-rising flour
2 c. sugar
1 t. soda
1 t. salt
1 t. cinnamon
1¼ c. Wesson oil
4 eggs
3 c. finely shredded carrots

Mix first five ingredients, add Wesson oil, eggs, and carrots, beat well. Pour into two 9″ pans or three 8″ pans. Bake at 350°F. for 40 to 45 minutes. Cool.

Icing:
1-8 oz. pkg. cream cheese
1 stick margarine
1 box sifted confectioners' sugar
2 t. vanilla
1 c. chopped nuts
1 c. coconut

Mix first five ingredients. Add pecans and coconut.

Nancy G. Jones, Pink Hill School
Pink Hill, North Carolina

CARROT CAKE (With Coconut)
Number of Servings — 12 to 15
2 c. sugar
1½ c. Wesson oil
4 eggs
2 c. flour
1 t. salt
2 t. soda
2 t. cinnamon
3 c. finely grated carrots, raw
1 c. finely chopped nuts
½ c. coconut

Mix sugar, oil, and eggs. Add flour, salt, soda, and cinnamon. Stir in carrots, nuts, and coconut. Bake in a layer cake pan, at 300°F. for 45 minutes.

Mrs. Harriette Wilson, Western Ky. State College
Bowling Green, Kentucky

CARROT CAKE (With Pineapple)
Number of Servings — 24
3 c. flour
2 c. sugar
2 t. soda
1 t. cinnamon
2 t. vanilla
½ t. salt
2 c. grated carrots
1½ c. vegetable oil
1½ c. nuts
1 small can crushed pineapple (juice and all)
3 eggs
2 T. orange rind or ½ c. coconut (if desired)

Mix all dry ingredients, add carrots, oil, pineapple, and eggs. If desired add orange rind or coconut. Bake in an oiled and floured tube pan for 1 hour at 350°F. or until set. Cool and serve or wrap for freezing. Best after about 3 weeks.

Billie Lue Bosher, Amherst H. S.
Amherst, Texas

CARROT CAKE (With Pineapple)
2 c. flour
2 t. baking powder
1½ t. soda
1 t. salt
2 t. cinnamon
1½ c. cooking oil
2 c. sugar
4 eggs
2 c. grated carrots
1 small can crushed pineapple
¾ c. chopped nuts

Sift all dry ingredients together and set aside. Mix oil, sugar, and eggs, beating after each addition. Add dry ingredients. Mix well. Add carrots, pineapple, and nuts. Grease and flour two 13x9x2½ pans. Bake 30-35 minutes at 325°F. Cool.

Pecan Frosting:
1 c. evaporated milk
1 c. sugar
3 egg yolks
1 t. vanilla
1 c. chopped nuts

Combine milk, sugar, egg yolks, and vanilla. Cook until thickened over medium heat. Add chopped nuts. Beat and spread on layers.

Nadine Flippo, Biggers-Reyno H. S.
Biggers, Arkansas

CARROT CAKE (With Black Walnuts)
Number of Servings — 15-20
2 c. sugar
1½ c. Wesson oil
4 eggs (add one at a time)
3 c. flour
2½ t. baking powder
½ t. salt
1 t. cinnamon
1 t. nutmeg
2 c. grated carrots
1 c. black walnuts (chopped fine)

(Continued on Next Page)

Mix in order given. Bake in greased tube pan 1 hour at 350°F.

Mrs. Glenn C. Peak, Bibb County H. S.
Centreville, Alabama

CHERRY NUT CAKE

½ c. shortening
1½ c. sugar
½ c. chopped nuts
16 maraschino cherries, chopped
2⅛ c. cake flour
3 t. baking powder
¼ t. salt
¼ c. evaporated milk, diluted with 1 t. vanilla, and ¼ c. cherry juice
4 egg whites, stiffly beaten

Cream shortening, add sugar and cream together thoroughly. Mix nuts and cherries together, dredge with ⅛ cup flour. Sift remaining flour, salt, and baking powder together, add to creamed mixture alternately with diluted milk. Blend in nuts and cherries, fold in beaten egg whites. Pour into a greased 8x8 square loaf pan and bake in moderate oven 350°F. about 45 minutes.

Annie Lillian Brewton, Escambia H. S.
Pensacola, Florida

CHERRY NUT CHIFFON CAKE

2¼ c. sifted cake flour
1½ c. sugar
3 t. baking powder
1 t. salt
½ c. cooking oil
5 unbeaten egg yolks
¼ c. maraschino cherry juice
½ c. cold water
1 t. vanilla
1 c. egg whites (7 or 8)
½ t. cream of tartar
½ c. very thinly sliced and finely chopped maraschino cherries
½ c. very finely chopped nuts

Measure and sift together into mixing bowl, cake flour, sugar, baking powder, and salt. Make a well and add in order, cooking oil, unbeaten egg yolks, maraschino cherry juice, cold water, and vanilla. Beat until smooth with spoon or beat with electric mixer on medium speed for 1 minute. Measure into large mixing bowl, egg whites and cream of tartar. Beat until whites form very stiff peaks. Pour egg yolk mixture gradually over beaten egg whites, gently folding with rubber scraper just until blended. Do not stir. Mix together, chopped maraschino cherries and chopped nuts. Sprinkle over top of batter, gently folding in with a few strokes. Pour into ungreased pan immediately. Bake in a tube pan 10x4, 325°F. 65-70 minutes; oblong pan, 13x9½x2, 350°F. 45-50 minutes or until top springs back when lightly touched. Immediately turn pan upside down, until cool. Loosen from sides and tube with spatula. Frost, if desired.

Mrs. Violet Kueker, Unit 5 H. S.
Waterloo, Illinois

CHERRY-NUT CAKE

Number of Servings — 24 or More
1 c. sifted all-purpose flour
1 t. baking powder
1 t. salt
4 c. pecan halves (do not chop)
4 large eggs
1 t. vanilla
1 c. granulated sugar
½ lb. whole candied cherries
1 lb. pitted dates uncut
2 large slices candied pineapple, cut into one-half inch cubes

Save some of the cherries, cubed candied pineapple and pecan halves to decorate the top of the cake. Sift the flour, measure, add the baking powder and salt, and sift again. Beat the eggs, then gradually add the sugar and beat until thick and light colored. Fold in the flour, vanilla, fruits, and pecans. Line the bottom of a well greased tube cake pan, or loaf bread pan, then grease the paper. Pour batter into pan. Cover the top of the pan with a brown paper bag which has been dampened with water. Bake in a slow oven 250°F. for two hours. When done, remove from the pan, remove the paper lining from the cake, and let cool on rack on a folded cloth. This may be served plain, or with whipped cream.

Mrs. Vada Belle Zellner
South San Antonio Senior H. S.
San Antonio, Texas

MAPLE-NUT CHIFFON CAKE

Number of Servings — 15-20
2¼ c. sifted cake flour
¾ c. granulated sugar
3 t. baking powder
1 t. salt
¾ c. brown sugar
½ c. salad oil
5 egg yolks
¾ c. cold water
2 t. maple flavoring
1 c. (8) egg whites
½ t. cream of tartar
1 c. finely chopped walnuts

Sift flour, granulated sugar, baking powder, and salt into mixing bowl; stir in brown sugar. Make a well in dry ingredients. In this order, add: salad oil, egg yolks, water, and flavoring. Beat till satin smooth. Combine egg whites and cream of tartar in large mixing bowl. Beat until they form very stiff peaks (stiffer than for meringue or angel cake). Pour egg-yolk batter in thin stream over entire surface of egg whites, gently cutting and folding—down, across bottom, up the side, and over—just till blended. Fold in nuts. Bake in ungreased 10" tube pan in slow oven (325°F.) 55 minutes; increase heat to 350°F. and bake 10 to 15 minutes more. Invert pan and let cool. Ice with butter frosting if desired.

Carol L. Patrick, Holmes County H. S.
Bonifay, Florida

CHIFFON CAKE

Number of Servings — 20

2¼ c. sifted flour
1½ c. sugar
3 t. baking powder
1 t. salt
¾ c. water
¼ t. almond extract
1 t. vanilla
½ c. salad oil
5 egg yolks, unbeaten
7 egg whites, beaten
½ t. cream of tartar

Start oven at 325°F. Have all utensils and ingredients ready. Sift flour before measuring. Sift flour again with sugar, baking powder and salt into a large bowl. Measure water and mix in extracts. Measure salad oil. Separate eggs and note well, this recipe calls for 5 unbeaten egg yolks and 7 egg whites beaten very stiffly. Now dump everything except egg whites and cream of tartar into the dry ingredients and beat until smooth. About 1 minute. Beat egg whites and cream of tartar very stiff or until whites can be cut with a knife. Pour batter into the beaten whites gradually, folding in gently until thoroughly mixed. Bake in a tube pan 1 hour.

Mrs. Billie A. McCarroll, Slidell H. S.
Slidell, Texas

BURNT SUGAR CHIFFON CAKE

2 c. sifted flour
1½ c. sugar
3 t. baking powder
1 t. salt
½ c. vegetable oil
7 unbeaten egg yolks
½ c. burnt sugar mixture
¼ c. cold water
1 t. vanilla
1 c. egg whites
½ t. cream of tartar

To make burnt sugar mixture—melt 1 cup sugar until medium brown. Slowly stir in ½ cup boiling water.

Sift together into mixing bowl the flour, sugar, baking powder, and salt. Form a well in the dry ingredients and add the vegetable oil, egg yolks, burnt sugar mixture, cold water, and vanilla. Beat with wooden spoon or batter beater until smooth. Beat egg whites and cream of tartar in large bowl until they hold very stiff peaks, and a dry rubber scraper drawn through them leaves a clean path. Do not underbeat. Pour egg yolk mixture in thin stream over egg whites. Fold in gently. Bake in ungreased cake pan 325°F. for 65 to 70 minutes.

Elizabeth McClure, Greencastle H. S.
Greencastle, Indiana

CHOCOLATE CHIFFON CAKE

Number of Servings — 16

2 eggs, separated
1½ c. sugar
1¾ c. cake flour
¾ t. soda
¾ t. salt
⅓ c. Wesson oil
1 c. buttermilk
2 sq. chocolate (melted)

Beat egg whites. Gradually add ½ cup sugar. Beat until stiff and glossy. Sift dry ingredients into bowl. Add oil and half buttermilk. Beat 1 minute at medium speed. Add remaining buttermilk, egg yolks and chocolate. Beat one minute again. Fold in meringue gently. Add vanilla. Pour in pan. Bake at 350°F.

Verlys M. Malme, Erskine H. S.
Erskine, Minnesota

ORANGE CHIFFON CAKE

2¼ c. sifted cake flour
1½ c. sugar
3 t. baking powder
1 t. salt
½ c. cooking (salad) oil
5 egg yolks, unbeaten
¾ c. orange juice
1 c. egg whites (7 or 8 eggs)
½ t. cream of tartar

Sift together in a bowl cake flour, sugar, baking powder, and salt. Make a "well" and add in order cooking oil, unbeaten egg yolks, and orange juice. Beat until smooth. Measure into a large mixing bowl, egg whites and cream of tartar. Beat until whites form very stiff peaks. Pour egg yolk mixture gradually over beaten whites, gently folding with rubber scraper just until blended. Pour into ungreased tube pan (10x4). Bake at 325°F. for 55 minutes then at 350°F. for 10 to 15 minutes, or until top springs back when lightly touched. Invert on funnel. Let hang until cold.

Helene Barnett, Huntley Project H. S.
Worden, Montana

SUNSHINE CAKE (Chiffon Cake)

8 egg whites
¾ t. cream of tartar
¾ t. salt
1 c. sugar
6 egg yolks
½ c. sugar
1 c. flour
2 T. cold water
1 t. lemon extract
1 t. vanilla

Beat egg whites until foamy. Add cream of tartar and salt and mix well. Add sugar gradually, continuing to beat until stiff peaks are formed. Let meringue stand while preparing egg yolk mixture. Beat egg yolks until thick and light colored. Add ½ cup sugar gradually and continue to beat until fluffy. Spoon flour into dry cup. Add flour alternately with water and flavorings, beginning and ending with flour. Fold in meringue. Pour into greased 10" tube pan. Bake at 325° for 60-65 minutes. Invert pan to cool. Frost with fluffy white frosting and decorate with pineapple and cherries.

Bonita Liles, Central Junior H. S.
Helena, Arkansas

CHOCOLATE CAKE

Number of Servings — 24

¼ stick oleo
3 T. cocoa or 2 blocks chocolate
3 eggs
1 c. sugar
¾ c. flour
¼ t. each of soda, baking powder, and salt
1 c. chopped nuts
1 pkg. marshmallows

Put oleo and chocolate on slow heat to melt. Beat eggs well, add sugar. Gradually add flour (salt, soda and baking powder added). Add melted oleo and chocolate. Add chopped nuts. Put in floured pan. Bake in hot oven 375-400°F. for 20 minutes. Cover with marshmallows and return to oven (heat off) and allow to melt. Spread over cake.

Frosting:

½ stick oleo
2 sq. chocolate
2 to 3 c. confectioners' sugar

Melt oleo and chocolate. Add sugar (sifted). If too stiff add a little milk until right consistency to spread. Allow to cool thoroughly before cutting in blocks.

Mrs. Margaret A. Scruggs,
Alabama Institute for Deaf and Blind
Talladega, Alabama

CHOCOLATE CHIP CAKE

Number of Servings — 12

1 t. soda
1 c. hot water
1 c. chopped dates
½ c. shortening
1 c. sugar
2 eggs
1 t. vanilla
1 T. cocoa
½ t. salt
1¾ c. flour
½ c. chopped nuts
1-6 oz. pkg. chocolate bits

Dissolve soda in hot water, pour over dates and cool. Cream shortening and sugar. Add beaten eggs and vanilla. Sift cocoa and salt with flour and add to creamed mixture alternately with date mixture. Spread in oiled pan. Sprinkle nuts and chocolate bits over top and bake 40 minutes at 350°F.

Shirley Asher, Lebanon Junction H. S.
Lebanon Junction, Kentucky

CHOCOLATE ALMOND CAKE

Number of Servings — 18

2 c. sugar
1 c. oleo
1 t. butter flavoring
4 egg yolks (beaten until lemon colored)
2½ c. all-purpose flour sifted with 1 pinch of salt
¾ c. buttermilk
1 pkg. German sweet chocolate
½ c. boiling water
1 t. soda
¼ c. buttermilk
1 t. vanilla
4 egg whites beaten until stiff

Cream oleo and sugar until fluffy, add butter flavoring. Add egg yolks. Add flour and salt alternately with ¾ cup buttermilk. Melt chocolate in boiling water, dissolve soda in ¼ cup buttermilk mix these two until smooth. Fold into creamed mixture. Fold in beaten egg whites. Add vanilla. Pour into three 9″ layer cake pans, greased and floured on bottom. Bake in moderate oven 350°F. 25 to 30 minutes. Cool.

Toasted Almond Filling:

Brown 1 cup blanched almonds (chopped) slowly in 4 tablespoons of butter. Remove from fire, add 6 tablespoons cream, 3 cups confectioners' sugar, pinch of salt, 2 teaspoons vanilla, 2 drops almond extract. Beat until of spreading consistency. Use as filling to stack the 3 cake layers.

Frosting:

In electric mixer blend 1 box confectioners' sugar, 6 tablespoons cream, 1 teaspoon vanilla. Melt 3 tablespoons butter, 4 squares bitter chocolate and 1 pinch salt, add to sugar mixture. Frost cake.

Nancy Jo Murphy, Throckmorton H. S.
Throckmorton, Texas

CHOCOLATE COCONUT CAKE

⅔ c. butter or margarine
1 t. soda
½ t. salt
½ t. baking powder
1½ c. sugar
2⅓ c. sifted cake flour
1 t. vanilla
1 c. buttermilk
1 bar German sweet chocolate (melted and cooled)
2 eggs
1 can angel flake coconut

Cream butter until softened. Sift in dry ingredients. Add vanilla and ¾ cup buttermilk; mix until flour is dampened. Beat 2 minutes at medium speed of electric mixer. Add chocolate, eggs and remaining buttermilk. Beat one minute. Pour into 2 paper-lined 9″ layer pans. Bake at 350°F. about 35 minutes. Cool. Fill and frost layers with 7-minute frosting (tinted pink). Sprinkle cake with coconut. Serve.

Bonnie N. Warner, Wells H. S.
Wells, Texas

RICH CHOCOLATE CAKE

1 c. shortening
2 eggs
2 c. sugar
2½ c. flour
2 t. soda
1c. sour milk (well curdled)
½ c. cocoa
1 c. hot water
Pinch salt
1 t. vanilla

Sift flour, cocoa, salt, and soda together. Cream shortening and sugar. Add eggs (beaten) and beat with the sour milk. Add dry ingredients and flavoring and mix. Add hot water gradually and then beat a few minutes. Bake for 25 minutes at 350°F. or until a toothpick comes out clean. Ice with 7-minute frosting.

Mrs. Thelma Bishop, Greenville H. S.
Greenville, West Virginia

CHOCOLATE CHIP CAKE

Number of Servings — 12 to 16
2 c. all-purpose flour
3 t. baking powder
½ t. salt
½ c. shortening
1⅓ c. sugar
1 t. vanilla extract
1 c. milk
2-1 oz. cakes sweet chocolate, finely shredded
3 egg whites

Sift flour, measure, sift again with baking powder and salt. Cream shortening, add 1 cup of the sugar gradually, creaming until light and fluffy. Add flavoring to milk, add milk and flour mixtures to shortening mixture alternately in small amounts, beating until smooth after each addition. Fold in chocolate. Beat egg whites until stiff but not dry; add remaining ⅓ cup sugar gradually, continue beating until mixture will hold a peak, fold into cake batter. Pour into 2 well greased 8″ layer cake pans. Bake in moderate oven 350°F. 30 minutes or until done. Remove cake from pan, cool on rack. When cool, spread chocolate cream filling between layers and frost top and sides of cake with 7-minute frosting. Sprinkle curled shavings of sweet or milk chocolate over top of cake.

Mrs. L. M. Wallace, Grayson H. S.
Henryetta, Oklahoma

CHOCOLATE COKE CAKE

½ c. shortening
1¼ c. granulated sugar
2 eggs
2 sq. unsweetened chocolate (melted)
1 c. coke (8 oz.)
1¾ c. flour
¾ t. soda
1 t. salt

Cream shortening and sugar. Add eggs (beaten) and melted chocolate. Add coke and dry ingredients alternately. Beat well. Bake at 350°F. 30 to 40 minutes.

Mrs. Alvenia Nimmo, Burns Flat School
Burns Flat, Oklahoma

DABERGE CAKE

½ c. butter
½ c. shortening
2 c. sugar
¼ t. sugar
¼ t. salt
4 eggs
3 c. sifted cake flour
3 t. baking powder
½ c. milk
½ c. water
1 t. vanilla

Cream butter and sugar. Add egg yolks one at a time. Add milk and flour alternately. Fold in beaten egg whites and vanilla. Bake in four 8″ cake pans at 375°F. for 20-25 minutes. Cool. Split each layer. Spread with the following filling.

Filling:
4 sq. unsweetened chocolate
1 qt. milk
½ c. flour
1½ c. sugar
2 eggs, beaten

Melt chocolate. Add milk and bring to a boil. Combine flour and sugar in a bowl and stir in a small amount of hot liquid. Add eggs. Blend into remaining liquid. Cook until very thick. Cool.

Chocolate Frosting:
¼ c. butter
4 sq. unsweetened chocolate
2 c. sifted confectioners' sugar
½ c. boiling water

Melt butter and chocolate on lowest heat position. Blend in sugar and water and beat until smooth. Frost top and sides.

Verna Lea Franklin, Poteet H. S.
Poteet, Texas

DOUBLE CHOCOLATE DELIGHT

2 c. sifted all-purpose flour
1 t. salt
1¾ c. sugar
½ c. shortening
2 unbeaten eggs
½ c. cocoa
1 c. hot coffee
1 t. soda
½ c. boiling water

Sift together flour and salt. Set aside. Add sugar to shortening, creaming well. Blend in unbeaten eggs, beat well. Combine cocoa and hot coffee, stir to dissolve cocoa. Add to creamed mixture. Add the dry ingredients gradually, blend thoroughly. Dissolve soda in water, add to batter, mix well. Turn into pan or pans (see sizes below), well greased and lightly floured on the bottom. Bake in moderate oven 375°F.

Two 8″ or 9″ round pans, 30 to 35 minutes; 13x9x2 pan, 30 to 35 minutes; two 8″ square pans, 25 to 30 minutes; two 9″ square pans, 20 to 25 minutes. Makes 2½ dozen cupcakes, 18 to 22 minutes.

When using self-rising flour, omit salt and decrease soda to ¼ teaspoon.

Charlene Green, Permian H. S.
Odessa, Texas

CHOCOLATE CREOLE CAKE

⅔ c. boiling coffee
1½ sq. chocolate
1¾ c. flour
1½ c. sugar
1 t. baking powder
1 t. soda
1 t. salt
¾ t. cloves
⅜ c. shortening
½ c. sour milk
½ t. vanilla
2 eggs

Pour boiling coffee on chocolate. Let set and cool. Sift together dry ingredients. Cream in shortening and add liquids and eggs. Beat two minutes before one after the addition of eggs. Pour in a 14x9x2 pan and bake 35-40 minutes at 350°F.

Mrs. Andrea Johnson, Climax Public School
Climax, North Dakota

GRANDMA'S CHOCOLATE CAKE

1 c. shortening
2 c. sugar
1 t. salt
1 t. vanilla
2 eggs
2¼ c. unsifted flour
1 c. buttermilk
½ c. cocoa
2 t. soda
1 c. hot water

In large mixing bowl cream shortening, sugar, salt, and vanilla. Add eggs and beat with mixer till mixture is very light and creamy. Add flour and buttermilk and beat 2 more minutes. In small mixing bowl mix cocoa, soda, add hot water. Add to rest of batter. Put into three 8" round pans or one 9x12x2 loaf pan. Bake at 350°F. for about 40 minutes. Frost with Glossy Chocolate Frosting.

Glossy Chocolate Frosting:
2 c. sugar
6 T. cornstarch
2 c. water
4 sq. semi-sweet chocolate
2 T. butter
1 t. vanilla

Mix sugar and cornstarch in 2 quart saucepan. Add water and chocolate. Cook over medium flame until thickened. Add butter and vanilla. Will frost a two or three layer or one large loaf cake.

Joyce Birdwell, Hemet H. S.
Hemet, California

HERSHEY CAKE

2 sticks butter
2 c. sugar
4 eggs
2½ c. cake flour
1 c. buttermilk
8—5¢ Hershey bars
½ t. vanilla
1 c. chopped nuts

Cream butter, add sugar, creaming well. Add eggs one at a time, beating well. Add flour alternately with buttermilk. Add Hershey bars that have been melted. Add nuts and vanilla. Mix well. Bake in greased and floured angel food cake pan for 1 hour at 350°F.

Margaret Williams, Miami H. S.
Miami, Texas

GERMAN CHOCOLATE CAKE

Number of Servings — 18-20
1 pkg. German sweet chocolate
½ c. boiling water
1 c. butter, margarine or shortening
2 c. sugar
4 egg yolks, unbeaten
1 t. vanilla
½ t. salt
1 t. baking soda
2½ c. cake flour
1 c. buttermilk
4 egg whites, stiffly beaten

Melt chocolate in boiling water. Cool. Cream butter and sugar until fluffy. Add egg yolks, one at a time and beat well after each. Add melted chocolate and vanilla. Mix well. Sift together salt, soda and flour. Add alternately with buttermilk to chocolate mixture, beating well. Beat until smooth. Fold in beaten egg whites. Pour into three 8" or 9" cake layer pans, lined on bottoms with paper. Bake in moderate oven 350°F. 30 to 40 minutes. Cool. Fill layers and frost top and sides of layers with coconut-pecan filling.

Coconut-Pecan Frosting:
1 c. evaporated milk
1 c. sugar
3 egg yolks
¼ lb. margarine (1 stick)
1 t. vanilla
1⅓ c. coconut (1 can)
1 c. chopped pecans

Combine milk, sugar, egg yolks, and margarine, add vanilla. Cook over low heat, stirring constantly until thickened (about 12 minutes). Add coconut and chopped pecans. Beat until thick enough to spread.

This recipe submitted by the following teachers:
Mrs. Mary L. Whitley, Caledonia H. S.
Caledonia, Mississippi
Mrs. Peggy Hogan, Fannindel H. S.
Ladonia, Texas
Betty Sue Gregory, Zama H. S.
Zama, Mississippi
Mrs. Emily Daniel, Talbot County H. S.
Woodland, Georgia
Mrs. Wilma B. Carroll, Excelsior H. S.
War, West Virginia
Mrs. Catherine C. Prince, Montour Joint Schools
McKees Rocks, Pennsylvania
Jo Dunn, Arab H. S.
Arab, Alabama
Dudley B. Hambright, Roby H. S.
Roby, Texas
Mrs. Chalice Harden, Wetumpka H. S.
Wetumpka, Alabama

HERSHEY LAYER CAKE

Number of Servings — 20

1—49¢ Hershey bar or
    2—25¢ Hershey bars
2 sticks margarine
2 c. sugar
4 eggs
2¾ c. sifted flour
½ t. salt
½ t. baking soda
1 t. baking powder
1 c. buttermilk
1 c. nuts (chopped)

Melt Hershey bar in top of double boiler over hot water. Cool. Cream margarine with sugar. Beat till smooth. Add eggs one at a time beating well after each. Sift dry ingredients and add to creamed mixture alternately with buttermilk beginning and ending with dry ingredients. Stir in nuts. Bake in 2 greased and floured 9″ square cake pans in 350°F. preheated oven for about 35 to 40 minutes. Frost cake with your favorite frosting.

Sylvia Daude, Mullin H. S.
Mullin, Texas

FABULOUS CHOCOLATE CAKE (Chocolate Nut Cake)

Number of Servings — 24-2 inch squares

½ c. butter
2 c. sugar
4 oz. bitter chocolate
2 eggs
2 c. sifted flour
2 t. baking powder
1½ c. milk
1 c. chopped nuts
2 t. vanilla

Cream butter and sugar. Melt chocolate. Beat eggs and add to creamed mixture, then add melted chocolate. Mix dry ingredients and add alternately with the milk. Add vanilla and nuts. Bake in a loaf pan, 8x12x2 at 350°F. 45 minutes.

Frosting:
¼ lb. butter
3 oz. chocolate
1 lb. powdered sugar
1 unbeaten egg
1 t. lemon
1 t. vanilla
1 c. nuts

Combine melted butter and melted chocolate, then add sugar. Beat egg and add to sugar mixture, then add flavoring and nuts. This icing is not to be cooked. If too dry add a little cream. Blend well and spread.

This recipe submitted by the following teachers:
Carolyn Lutkemeier, Frankfort H. S.
Frankfort, Kentucky
Robbie Nell Petty, Sudan H. S.
Sudan, Texas

HEAVENLY CHOCOLATE CAKE

Number of Servings — 20

1 c. butter or oleo
2½ c. sugar
2 eggs, unbeaten
3 c. flour
¼ t. salt
2 T. cocoa
2 T. vanilla
2 c. buttermilk
2 t. soda

Cream butter, add sugar and cream well. Add eggs, one at a time, and beat well after each. Add milk and dry ingredients alternately. Bake in 4 greased and floured layer pans at 350°F. for 25 minutes or until done.

Filling:
2 c. sugar
2 eggs, well beaten
2 T. flour
1 c. evaporated milk, undiluted
1 c. angel flake coconut
1 c. chopped pecans
1 T. vanilla

Mix flour and sugar. Add eggs that have been added to milk. Cook over low heat until thick. Add coconut, pecans, and vanilla. Let cool before putting on cake. Ice with white frosting or use filling all over cake.

Mrs. Lucille King, Nazareth H. S.
Nazareth, Texas

CHOCOLATE MARBLE CAKE

Number of Servings — 12

⅔ c. butter
2 c. sugar
4 eggs, well beaten
3 c. flour
4 t. baking powder
1 c. milk
1 t. vanilla
1 sq. chocolate

Cream the butter and sugar together, add the well beaten eggs and mix well. Sift flour and baking powder, add alternately with the milk to the first mixture. Put ⅓ of mixture into a bowl and add the melted chocolate. To the white batter, add the vanilla. Drop white batter, then chocolate, by spoonsful into a well-greased tube pan. Bake in a moderate oven 350°F. for 1 hour. Cool 1 hour before removing from pan.

Icing:
1 T. butter
3 c. confectioners' sugar
Cream
1 t. vanilla
1 sq. chocolate

Cream the butter, add the confectioners' sugar and enough cream to make it spread smoothly. Add the vanilla and the melted chocolate.

Janice M. Mountz,
Brandywine Heights Joint Jr.-Sr. H. S.
Topton, Pennsylvania

LAZY DAISY CHOCOLATE CAKE

Number of Servings — 9

½ c. milk
1 T. butter
2 eggs
1 c. sugar
1 c. flour
1 t. baking powder
⅛ t. salt
1 t. vanilla

Put milk and butter in saucepan to heat. Beat eggs, add sugar, beat together vigorously. Stir in dry ingredients that have been sifted together. Add vanilla. Now add hot milk mixture stirring carefully as it is added. Pour into greased 8x10½ pan. Bake 25-30 minutes in a moderate oven 350°F.

Topping:
⅝ c. brown sugar
⅓ c. melted butter
1 T. cream
½ c. coconut

Mix ingredients. Spread on warm cake and return to oven for 5-10 minutes.

Mrs. Reuben Wunderlich, Round Top-Carmine H.S.
Carmine, Texas

LIGHT CHOCOLATE CAKE

Number of Servings — 12 to 20

1 c. brown sugar
1 c. white sugar
½ c. plus 2 T. oleomargarine
2 eggs
⅝ c. water
2 c. sifted all-purpose flour
⅓ c. cocoa
1 t. salt
1 t. baking soda
⅝ c. sour milk
1 t. vanilla extract
2 t. red food coloring

Cream the brown and white sugar with the margarine. Beat in the whole eggs. Add water, stirring constantly. Sift together flour, cocoa, salt, and baking soda. Add alternately with the sour milk to the sugar mixture. Stir in vanilla and red coloring. Bake in two 9" pans (the bottoms of which have been greased, wax papered and greased), in a moderate oven, 350°F. for 30 minutes.

Wanda Reeves, Sanger H. S.
Sanger, Texas

CHOCOLATE MACAROON CAKE

1 egg white (reserve yolk for frosting)
2 t. vanilla
2½ c. sugar
2 c. fine grated coconut
1 T. flour
½ c. cocoa
¾ c. hot coffee
3 eggs (whites and yolks separated)
1 t. soda
½ c. sour cream
½ c. shortening
1 T. salt
2 c. sifted flour

Beat egg white with 1 teaspoon vanilla until soft mounds form. Add ½ cup sugar gradually beating until stiff peaks form. Stir in coconut and 1 tablespoon flour. Dissolve cocoa in hot coffee. Beat 3 egg whites until soft mounds form. Add ½ cup sugar gradually, beating until meringue stands in stiff peaks. Add soda to sour cream. Beat 1¼ cup sugar, shortening, egg yolks, 1½ teaspoon salt, 1 teaspoon vanilla and half of cocoa mixture until light and creamy, about four minutes. Add 2 cups flour, the sour cream and remaining cocoa mixture, blend well. Fold in egg whites. Turn ⅓ of chocolate batter into 10" tube pan, greased on bottom. Place ½ of coconut mixture on top. Cover with ½ of remaining chocolate batter. Top with remaining coconut, then chocolate batter. Bake at 350°F. for 55 to 65 minutes. Cool completely before removing from pan. Frost top and sides. Makes 10" tube cake.

Icing:
2 c. sugar
4 T. cocoa
1 stick butter
¼ c. white karo
½ c. sweet milk
1 t. vanilla

Mix sugar and cocoa. Add remaining ingredients. Let boil only 1 minute. Let cool and beat until spreading consistency. Start timing when it begins to boil. Do not overcook. Add the vanilla.

This recipe submitted by the following teachers:
Mrs. Rena Nell Taylor, Royse City H. S.
Royse City, Texas
Mrs. Frances B. Wilson, Cherokee County H. S.
Centre, Alabama

MAHOGANY CAKE

1½ c. sugar
½ c. butter
4 egg yolks
2 T. cocoa
5 t. hot water
2 t. baking powder
1¾ c. flour, sifted
½ c. milk
1 t. vanilla
4 egg whites

Cream softened butter and sugar. Add egg yolks one at a time, beating well after each addition. Combine the cocoa and hot water. Blend into egg mixture. Sift together the flour and baking powder. Add the dry ingredients alternately with the milk. Add vanilla. Fold in the stiffly beaten egg whites. Bake in three 8" cake pans that have been lined with wax paper and greased. Bake at 350°F. for about 25 minutes.

Mahogany Frosting:
½ c. butter
1 box confectioners' sugar
2 T. cocoa

(Continued on Next Page)

5 t. hot coffee
1 egg yolk

Mix butter and sugar gradually. Put cocoa in hot coffee and mix well. Add to butter and sugar mixture. Add egg yolk. If too thick add cream until right consistency.

Mrs. Marshall King, Gatesville, H. S.
Gatesville, Texas

CHOCOLATE COOKIE SHEET CAKE

Number of Servings — 24
2 c. flour
2 c. sugar
½ t. salt
1 stick oleo, ½ c. shortening or 2 sticks oleo
1 c. water
3 T. cocoa
2 eggs, well beaten
1 t. soda
½ c. buttermilk
1 t. vanilla
1 t. cinnamon (if desired)

Sift flour, measure, resift with sugar and salt. In a saucepan, put oleo, shortening, water, and cocoa. Bring to a boil and pour over flour and sugar mixture. In another bowl put eggs, soda, buttermilk and vanilla. Add to above mixture and mix well. Bake in a greased and floured shallow cake pan (15½x10½x1). Bake for 20 minutes at 350°F. Start icing the last 5 minutes cake is baking.

Chocolate Frosting—Quick 'n Easy:
1 stick oleo
3 T. cocoa
6 T. milk
1 box confectioners' sugar
½ c. pecans (chopped)
1 t. vanilla

Mix oleo, cocoa, and milk in saucepan. Heat over low flame, but do not boil. Remove from heat and add confectioners' sugar, chopped pecans, and vanilla. Mix well. Frost Cookie Sheet Cake as soon as removed from oven. Cut cake in squares to serve. Makes 24 servings or 48 party sized squares.

This recipe submitted by the following teachers:
Mrs. Pat Thompson, Central H. S.
Delhi, Louisiana
Margie Alford, Spearman H. S.
Spearman, Texas
Dorothy B. Morrison, Colorado City Jr. H. S.
Colorado City, Texas
Beadie L. Kilpatrick, Travis Jr. H. S.
Temple, Texas
Mrs. Frances W. McKenzie, Lufkin H. S.
Lufkin, Texas

CHOCOLATE MAYONNAISE CAKE

Number of Servings — 12-16
2 c. flour
1 c. sugar
4 T. cocoa
1 t. baking powder
1 t. soda
1 c. mayonnaise

1 c. cold water
1 t. vanilla

Sift together flour, sugar, cocoa, baking powder, and soda. Add mayonnaise, cold water, and vanilla. Beat 2 minutes. Bake in a shallow loaf (11x7) or layer (two 9″) pans at 350°F. 30 to 35 minutes. Frost if desired.

Alice McChesney, Clarion-Lime Stone H. S.
Strattanville, Pennsylvania

SOUR CREAM CHOCOLATE CAKE

2 Layers
2 eggs
1¼ c. sugar
1 c. thick sour cream
1½ c. cake flour
½ c. cocoa
¼ t. salt
1 t. soda in ½ c. warm water
1 t. vanilla

Sift together cake flour, cocoa, and salt. Beat eggs until light, add sugar, then cream and flour and cocoa mixture. Last stir in the water and soda and vanilla. Pour into well greased and lightly floured pans. Bake at 350°F. 30 to 35 minutes.

Mrs. Cleta Salyers, Malvern Community H. S.
Malvern, Iowa

CHOCOLATE SOUR CREAM CAKE

3 eggs
1½ c. sour cream
1 t. vanilla
1½ c. sifted flour (cake)
1½ c. sugar
1½ t. soda
½ t. salt
6 T. cocoa

(For best results do not use cultured sour cream, use naturally soured cream.)

Beat eggs until mixed. Add sour cream and vanilla and blend. Sift dry ingredients together and add to egg mixture. Blend until smooth. Pour into greased and floured pan (13x9x2). Bake at 350°F. about 25-30 minutes or until cake springs back when touched by a finger.

Corinne Stene, Lake Benton H. S.
Lake Benton, Minnesota

EASY DEVIL'S FOOD CAKE (Sour Cream)
Number of Servings — 1 Cake—2 Layers
1 c. sugar
1 c. sifted flour
4 T. cocoa
1 c. sour cream
1 t. soda
1 t. vanilla
2 eggs

Sift sugar, flour and cocoa together. Dissolve the soda in the sour cream, add to the flour mixture. Add the eggs and vanilla. Mix all at once. Pour into prepared cake pans. Bake in a slow oven at 300°F. for 25 to 30 minutes.

Mrs. Jo Nita Schwarz, Central H. S.
San Angelo, Texas

CHOCOLATE CAKE (Sour Cream)

Number of Servings — 8

2 sq. chocolate
½ c. boiling water
1 c. sugar
¼ c. vegetable shortening
1 egg
½ c. sour cream
1 t. vanilla
¼ t. salt
1 c. flour
½ t. soda

Melt the 2 squares of chocolate in the ½ cup of boiling water over low heat and set aside to cool. Cream the 1 cup of sugar with the ¼ cup of shortening, add the egg, sour cream, vanilla and cooled chocolate. Add the sifted dry ingredients. Pour into a greased loaf pan or cup cake tins and bake at 350°F. until done. Makes a small, moist cake.

Mrs. Lois E. Pritchard, Consolidated School
Susquehanna, Pennsylvania

RICH CHOCOLATE PECAN CAKE

4 sq. unsweetened chocolate
½ c. butter
2 c. sugar
2 eggs
2 c. plain flour
2 t. baking powder
¾ t. salt
1½ c. milk
2 t. vanilla
1 c. chopped pecans

Melt chocolate. Allow to cool. Meanwhile, cream butter and sugar. Add chocolate. Add eggs and mix well. Sift together flour, baking powder, and salt. Add flour mixture and milk alternately, mixing well after each addition. Stir in vanilla and pecans. Bake in a greased and floured tube pan for 1 hour at 325°F.

Frosting:
½ c. butter
2 sq. unsweetened chocolate
1½ c. powdered sugar
Pinch of salt
1 t. vanilla
1 t. lemon juice (optional)
1 c. pecans

Melt butter and chocolate in top of double boiler. Stir in other ingredients and mix well. Frost cake after it has cooled.

Virginia L. Langston,
State Department of Education
Baton Rouge, Louisiana

TIME-SAVER CHOCOLATE CAKE

Number of Servings — 15

2 c. all-purpose flour
2 c. sugar
1 stick margarine
4 T. cocoa
½ c. shortening
1 c. water
2 eggs
½ c. buttermilk
1 t. soda
1 t. cinnamon
1 t. vanilla

Sift together in large mixing bowl, flour and sugar. Bring to boil in saucepan, margarine, cocoa, shortening and water. Pour over flour mixture, beat and add eggs, cinnamon, vanilla, and buttermilk which has soda added. Beat thoroughly. Pour into greased loaf pan (9x13x2) and bake at 375°F. until done to touch. Just before cake is done, bring to boil in saucepan, 1 stick margarine, 4 tablespoons cocoa, and 6 tablespoons milk. Add to this 1 box powdered sugar and stir. Fold in 1 cup pecans and pour over cake as soon as it is removed from oven. May serve hot or cold.

Rachel Brewster, Petrolia H. S.
Petrolia, Texas

QUICK CHOCOLATE CAKE

Number of Servings — 16

1 oz. sq. chocolate
¼ c. margarine
½ c. boiling water
1 c. sugar
1 c. flour minus 1 T.
½ t. soda
¼ t. salt
1 egg
¼ c. buttermilk
1 t. vanilla

Sift flour, soda and salt together. Cut chocolate into small pieces and put in bowl with butter. Add water and stir until chocolate melts. Add remaining ingredients as listed stirring well after each addition. Bake in 350°F. oven for 25 minutes in an 8″ square pan.

Quick Chocolate Icing:
Enough for one 8″ layer
¼ c. margarine
1 oz. sq. chocolate
¼ c. brown or white sugar
2 T. cream
1 T. white corn syrup
1½ c. powdered sugar
1 t. vanilla
¼ c. chopped nuts (optional)

Melt chocolate and butter in pan on low heat. Add brown sugar, cream, and syrup. Bring to boiling point. Add powdered sugar and stir well. Add vanilla and nuts. Spread on cake. If frosting is too cool to spread nicely, return to unit to warm.

Gwendollen Beaty, Red Oak H. S.
Red Oak, Oklahoma

VERY MOIST CHOCOLATE CAKE

2 c. sugar (1 brown and 1 white)
1 scant c. Crisco
1 t. salt
3 eggs
1 t. soda
⅓ c. hot water
1 c. milk
2 c. flour

(Continued on Next Page)

2 t. vanilla
4 sq. semi-sweet chocolate (melted) or
½ pkg. German sweet chocolate

Cream well in mixing bowl sugar, Crisco, and salt. Add eggs one at a time and beat well after each egg. In separate bowl mix soda in hot water. Add milk alternately with flour and vanilla. Add melted chocolate or German sweet chocolate. Combine mixtures. Bake 350°F. for 30 minutes.

Mary Beth Ince, Mason H. S.
Mason, Texas

WACKY CAKE
Number of Servings — 8

1½ c. flour
1 c. sugar
3 T. cocoa
1 t. soda
1 t. vanilla
1 T. vinegar
6 T. cooking oil or melted fat
1 c. water
½ t. salt (if desired)

Grease a 9" square pan with oil. Sift flour, sugar, cocoa, and soda together directly into pan. Make three depressions in mixture; in one put vanilla, in one put vinegar, in other put oil. Pour water over all, mix well with fork. Bake thirty minutes 350°F.

This recipe submitted by the following teachers:
Mrs. Alice L. Brooks, Strawn H. S.
Strawn, Texas
Shirley Andersen, Enterprise H. S.
Enterprise, Oregon
Mrs. Jeanne M. Steffen,
Griswold Community School
Griswold, Iowa
Dorothy Sills, Hearne H. S.
Hearne, Texas
Ilene Wahl, Riverside H. S.
Milan, Washington
Mrs. Patricia Mohns, Lemont Township H. S.
Lemont, Illinois

WACKY DEVIL'S FOOD CAKE
Number of Servings — 6

⅓ c. cocoa
1½ c. flour
1 c. sugar
1 t. soda
1 t. vinegar
1 t. vanilla
1 stick melted margarine
1 c. water

Sift flour, cocoa, sugar, and soda together. Melt margarine. Add melted margarine, vanilla, and vinegar to the water. Pour liquid ingredients into dry ingredients. Stir until well mixed. Pour into ungreased 7x12 pan or 9x9 pan. Bake at 350°F. for about 30 minutes.

Icing:

1 c. sugar
¼ c. cocoa
¼ c. milk
½ stick margarine

Bring entire mixture to boil and boil for 1 minute. Remove from heat and add 1 teaspoon vanilla. Beat until it thickens and then spread over the cake in the pan. Cut in squares to serve.

Mrs. Elizabeth Ann Walrond, Young H. S.
Knoxville, Tennessee

WALDORF-ASTORIA CHOCOLATE CAKE OR $100 CAKE

¼ lb. oleo (½ c.)
2 c. sugar
2 eggs
4 sq. (oz.) bitter melted chocolate
2 c. cake flour
2 t. baking powder
½ t. salt
1½ c. milk
1 c. chopped nuts
1 t. vanilla

Cream together the oleo and sugar. Add eggs and cooled melted chocolate. Add baking powder and salt to sifted cake flour and add this alternately with the milk to the creamed sugar, oleo, and chocolate. Add chopped nuts and vanilla. Grease and flour angle food cake pan or oblong loaf pan and bake one hour at 350°F. (If 2 layer pans are used bake 25-30 minutes.)

Icing:

1½ sq. (oz.) melted chocolate
⅛ lb. or ½ stick oleo
Pinch of salt

Cream the above together. When chocolate is cool, add 1 beaten egg. Then add 1 tablespoon vanilla, 1 tablespoon of lemon juice, and 1½ cups of powdered sugar and 1 cup chopped nuts.

This recipe submitted by the following teachers:
June Wright, Hamshire-Fannett H. S.
Hamshire, Texas
Mary M. Shelton, Waterproof H. S.
Waterproof, Louisiana
Mrs. Theresa H. Smith, Warner Robins H. S.
Warner Robins, Georgia

CHOCOLATE NUT DEVIL'S FOOD CAKE

½ c. shortening
2 c. sugar
4 egg yolks
2 oz. chocolate, melted
2½ c. cake flour
3 t. baking powder
½ t. salt
1 c. milk
1 c. chopped nuts
1 t. vanilla
4 stiffly beaten egg whites

Cream shortening and add sugar. Cream until smooth. Add beaten egg yolks. Beat 30 seconds. Add melted chocolate and beat. Sift together dry ingredients. Add to sugar mixture alternately with milk, nuts and flavoring. Fold in stiffly beaten egg whites. Bake in 3 greased and floured 9" round cake pans 350°F. for 30 minutes.

Mrs. Maxine Bohart, Belt Line Jr. H. S.
Richardson, Texas

DEVIL'S FOOD CAKE

1 lb. brown sugar
¾ c. butter
2 eggs
1 c. sour milk
1 t. vanilla
¾ c. cocoa
1 c. boiling water
1 t. soda
3 c. flour

Combine cocoa, boiling water, soda, and flour, beat thoroughly and set aside to cool. Mix brown sugar, butter, eggs, sour milk, and vanilla. Beat about 2 minutes with electric mixer. Add the cocoa mixture to the sugar mixture and beat another 2 minutes. Bake in two 9" cake pans (well greased) in 375°F. oven for 35 minutes.

Icing:
1 c. sugar
¼ c. cocoa
¼ c. butter
¼ c. milk
1 t. vanilla

Mix sugar and cocoa. Add butter and milk. Place on range unit and stir constantly until the mixture comes to a rolling boil. Continue to boil one minute or to the count of 60. Remove from unit, add vanilla and beat until right consistency to spread.

Mrs. Helen B. Wilmoth, Decatur H. S.
Decatur, Arkansas

CHOCOLATE CUSTARD DEVIL'S FOOD CAKE

3-1 oz. sq. chocolate, melted
½ c. milk
1 beaten egg
⅔ c. sugar
½ c. shortening
1 c. sugar
2 beaten egg yolks
2 c. cake flour
¼ t. salt
1 t. soda
1 c. milk
1 t. vanilla extract

Combine first four ingredients and cook over low heat until thick. Cool. Cream shortening and remaining cup sugar. Add egg yolks and mix well. Add sifted dry ingredients alternately with 1 cup milk. Add vanilla. Stir in chocolate custard mixture. Bake at 350°F. Two 8" pans for 25 to 30 minutes. Rectangular pan for 45 minutes. When cool frost with fudge icing.

Mrs. G. Sue Lacy, Kermit H. S.
Kermit, West Virginia

MOIST DEVIL'S FOOD CAKE

Number of Servings — 10-12
First Mixture:
½ c. cocoa
1 c. sugar
1 c. milk
2 egg yolks, well beaten

Blend cocoa and sugar in top of double boiler.

Add milk and beaten egg yolks. Blend well and cook, stirring until thickened.

Second Mixture:
1 stick oleomargarine
1 c. sugar
2¼ c. flour
1 t. soda
½ t. salt
½ c. buttermilk
2 eggs well beaten
1 t. vanilla

Cream shortening and sugar. Sift flour with soda and salt and add alternately with the milk. Add beaten eggs and vanilla. Blend and combine with first mixture. Bake in two greased and floured 9" layer pans in moderate oven 350°F. about 25 minutes. Allow to cool. Use your favorite frosting.

Mrs. Sara H. Barlow, Whitesburg H. S.
Whitesburg, Tennessee

GRANDMA'S DEVIL'S FOOD CAKE

Sift Together:
2 c. flour
1 c. sugar
¼ c. cocoa
2 t. soda
⅛ t. salt
Add:
1 c. salad dressing
1 c. cold water
1 t. vanilla

Mix well and bake in well greased floured pans at 350°F. for 25 to 30 minutes.

Mary Patrick, Grand Ridge H. S.
Grand Ridge, Florida

MOISTY-RICH DEVIL'S FOOD CAKE

2 c. granulated sugar
½ c. shortening
½ c. cocoa
1 t. vanilla
1 c. boiling water
½ c. sour milk
2 eggs (whole)
2 c. flour (sift before measuring)
¼ t. salt
1¼ t. soda

Cream sugar, shortening, cocoa, and vanilla. (Vanilla flavoring added at this point is held in by the shortening.) Pour the boiling water over the beaters to prevent bowl from cracking. Then just dump in milk and eggs. Then sift in half of the flour mixture until all is wet and then sift in remaining flour mixture. Continue mixing until all ingredients are well mixed. Grease pan on the bottom lightly. Do not flour it. Bake at 350°F. for 30-40 minutes depending on the pan size. This is a MOIST CAKE. Test with a tooth pick until it comes out almost clean. The crumb in this cake is large. Ice with a chocolate fudge icing.

Ann Elizabeth Morris, South Park Jr. H. S.
Corpus Christi, Texas

ONE BOWL DEVIL'S FOOD
Number of Servings — 2 9" Layers
1½ c. sifted cake flour
1¼ c. sugar
½ c. cocoa
1¼ t. soda
¼ t. cream of tartar
1 t. salt
⅔ c. shortening
1 c. sweet milk
1 t. vanilla
2 eggs (unbeaten)

Sift flour, sugar, cocoa, soda, cream of tartar, and salt into a mixing bowl. Add shortening, ⅔ cup of milk, and vanilla. Beat until smooth (150 strokes by hand or 2 minutes with mixer). Scrape sides of bowl often. Add eggs and beat 250 strokes by hand or 2 minutes on low speed on mixer. Add remaining milk and beat 50 strokes. (If using mixer add eggs and remaining milk at same time.) Bake in two 9" pans at 350°F. for 25 minutes or until springs back when touched by fingers. Frost with 1-minute fudge frosting.

Mrs. Jack Walton, Fouke H. S.
Fouke, Arkansas

REAL RED DEVIL'S FOOD CAKE
Sift together:
1¾ c. sifted cake flour
1½ c. sugar
1¼ t. soda
1 t. salt
⅛ c. cocoa
Add:
½ c. soft shortening
⅔ c. milk
Beat 2 minutes. Add:
⅛ c. milk
2 eggs (¼ to ½ c.)
1 t. vanilla

Grease and flour two 8" or 9" layer pans. Pour into pans. Bake until cake tests done, 8" layers 35 to 40 minutes at 350°F. Cool. Finish with "Satiny Beige Frosting."

Mrs. Cleda Morris, Timbo Home Economics Depart.
Timbo, Arkansas

DEVIL'S FOOD CAKE— TUTTI FRUTTI FILLING
Number of Servings — 20
1 c. butter
2 c. sugar
3 eggs
¼ c. hot water
¼ c. cocoa
3 c. cake flour
1 t. soda
1 t. vanilla
1 c. buttermilk

Cream butter and sugar until light and fluffy. Add whole eggs one at a time beating well. Combine cocoa and hot water in one container and in another, soda and buttermilk. Then combine the two. Add flour and soda (sifted together) alternately with liquid. Bake in three 8" layer pans 350°F. Cool and spread with filling.

Filling:
1½ c. sugar
4 T. flour
2 c. milk—cherry juice
2 eggs
1 T. butter
1 t. vanilla
Fruit Mixture:
Small bottle cherries
½ c. pecans
½ c. raisins

Combine ingredients in order given, leaving out fruit mixture. Cook at low temperature. Sprinkle fruit mixture on last.

Lillian Y. Wynn, Sicily Island H. S.
Sicily Island, Louisiana

RED DEVIL'S FOOD CAKE
½ c. shortening
1½ c. sugar
2 eggs
½ c. sour milk (or buttermilk)
½ c. cocoa
1 t. vanilla
1½ c. sifted cake flour
1 t. soda
¼ t. salt
½ c. boiling water

Cream shortening and sugar. Add eggs, beat until light and fluffy. Add sour milk, cocoa, and vanilla. Blend well. Working quickly add remainder dry ingredients. Add the boiling water last, blend until smooth, quickly and pour into prepared pans. Bake 350°F. Loaf cake 1 hour, layers 45 minutes, cupcakes 35 minutes.

Patricia O'Malley, Washington H. S.
East Chicago, Indiana

SNOW PEAK DEVIL'S FOOD CAKE
Number of Servings — 12-15
1½ c. sifted flour
1¼ c. sugar
½ c. cocoa
1¼ t. soda
1 t. salt
⅔ c. vegetable shortening
1 c. buttermilk or thick sour milk
1 t. vanilla
2 eggs unbeaten

Sift flour, sugar, cocoa, soda, and salt, into bowl. Drop in shortening. Add milk, then vanilla and beat 200 strokes (2 minutes) at low speed. Scrape. Add eggs and beat 200 strokes (2 minutes). Bake in two deep 8" greased layer pans in 350°F. oven about 25 to 30 minutes or in 9x13 pan 30 to 40 minutes. Frost with 7-minute white frosting, to which 6 quartered marshmallows have been added after cooking.

Mrs. Elizabeth Stump Rice, Colonial H. S.
Orlando, Florida

CHOCOLATE CAKE (Sour Milk)
Number of Servings — 12
1 c. granulated sugar
½ c. shortening
2 eggs
1½ c. all-purpose flour or 2 c. cake flour

(Continued on Next Page)

1 t. baking soda
1 t. baking powder
½ t. salt
½ c. sour milk
2 sq. baking chocolate
½ c. boiling water
1 t. vanilla

Cream well, sugar and shortening, add 2 well beaten eggs. Sift together flour, baking soda, baking powder, and salt. Add dry ingredients alternately with sour milk. Melt chocolate in boiling water and add to mixture, plus vanilla. Bake 30 minutes at 375°F.

Mrs. Lucille Glover, Cambridge H. S.
Cambridge, Maryland

COCOA CAKE

Number of Servings — 25

1½ c. butter
3 c. sugar
4 eggs
3 c. flour
1 t. baking powder
Pinch of salt
4 T. cocoa
1 c. milk
1 t. vanilla

Cream butter and sugar together. Add eggs one at a time and beat well after each. Mix dry ingredients together and add alternately with milk. Add vanilla. Bake in a greased and floured tube pan at 325°F. for about 1½ hours.

Mrs. Ramona Hext, Newton H. S.
Newton, Texas

COCOA CAKE

1¼ c. sifted all-purpose flour
1½ t. baking powder
½ t. soda
1 t. salt
1⅓ c. sugar
½ c. Baker's cocoa
½ c. vegetable shortening
1 c. milk
1 t. vanilla
3 eggs

Measure into sifter, sifted flour, baking powder, soda, salt, sugar, and cocoa. Stir shortening (room temperature) just to soften. Sift dry ingredients into bowl with shortening. Add ¾ cup milk and vanilla. Mix until all flour is dampened. Then beat 2 minutes with mixer (at low speed) or 300 strokes by hand. Add 3 eggs (unbeaten) and ¼ cup more milk. Beat one minute longer or 150 strokes. Bake in two 8" layer pans, lined on bottom with wax paper, in moderate oven 350°F. about 35 minutes. Frost top and sides with Cocoa Frosting.

Cocoa Frosting:

3½ c. confectioners' sugar
¼ t. salt
⅓ c. Baker's cocoa
⅓ c. butter or margarine
⅓ c. warm milk
½ t. vanilla

Sift confectioners' sugar, salt, and cocoa together. Cream butter or margarine, add part of sugar mixture gradually, mixing well. Add remaining sugar, alternating with the warm milk, beating until smooth. Add vanilla, blend. Makes about 2 cups frosting, sufficient to frost layers, top and sides of Cocoa Cake.

Mrs. Frances C. Reynolds, Calhoun H. S.
Laurel, Mississippi

COCOA CAKE

Number of Servings — 12

2 c. sugar
½ c. shortening
½ t. salt
2 eggs
⅔ c. cocoa
1 t. vanilla flavoring
½ c. buttermilk or sour milk
½ t. soda
2 c. sifted flour
1 c. hot water

Mix sugar, shortening and salt. Add unbeaten eggs one at a time, stir after each addition. Add cocoa and vanilla flavoring and stir. Add soda to buttermilk (this may be done before you begin to mix). Add flour which has been sifted 3 times alternately with buttermilk mixture to the sugar shortening mixture. Add hot water. Pour into two prepared 8" layer pans. Bake at 350°F. for 30 minutes. Ice as desired.

Mrs. Grace Nowlin, Dime Box H. S.
Dime Box, Texas

FUDGE CAKE

2 Layers

½ c. butter or oleo
1½ c. sugar
2 eggs
2 sq. melted chocolate
1 t. vanilla
2 c. sifted cake flour
¼ t. salt
1½ t. baking soda
1 c. buttermilk

Cream butter, adding the sugar gradually, add whole eggs, one at a time and beat well after each addition, add chocolate and vanilla, beat well and scrape the bowl and beaters. Sift the flour, salt, and soda together and add the dry ingredients alternately with the buttermilk. Pour into two wax paper lined pans or grease and flour the bottom of the pans. Bake 350°F. oven for 30 to 35 minutes.

Fudge Cake Frosting:

3 c. powdered sugar (sift if lumpy)
⅓ c. soft butter or oleo
Dash of salt
¼ c. milk
1½ t. vanilla
2 sq. melted chocolate

Melt the chocolate and butter, add milk to the sugar and salt, then pour in the chocolate and butter mixture. Beat well and add the vanilla.

Mrs. Carlton Bierschwale, Junction H. S.
Junction, Texas

CHOCOLATE "QUICK" CAKE
Number of Servings — 6

1½ c. all-purpose flour
3 T. cocoa
1 c. sugar
1 t. soda
½ t. salt
1 t. vinegar
1 t. vanilla
5 T. cooking oil
1 c. water

Sift dry ingredients into greased 8" cake pan. Make 3 depressions in dry ingredients. Pour vinegar into one, vanilla into another, oil into third. Pour water over all. Mix well until smooth. Bake at 350°F. for 35 minutes. When cool, cut into squares. Serve topped with vanilla ice cream, whipped cream, or chocolate fudge sauce.

Rebecca C. Turner, State Dept. of Education
Little Rock, Arkansas

DOUBLE MIX FUDGE CAKE
Large 2 Layer

1 c. sugar
¾ c. cocoa
1 c. milk
1 egg

Combine sugar and cocoa. Add well-beaten egg. Add milk. Cook in double boiler until thick and smooth. Cool.

¾ c. shortening
1 c. sugar
½ c. milk
2 eggs
2 c. cake flour
⅛ t. salt
1 t. baking powder
1 t. baking soda

Cream shortening and sugar. Add well-beaten eggs. Beat thoroughly. Sift flour, measure, and sift with baking soda and salt. Add alternately with milk to creamed shortening and sugar. Add flavoring. Add cooled cocoa mixture. Beat thoroughly. Pour into well-oiled layer cake pans. Bake in moderate oven 375°F. about 20 minutes. Use 7-minute or fudge icing between layers and over top.

Mrs. Variel S. Garner, Moody H. S.
Moody, Texas

FUDGE CAKE
(May Use Date Cream Filling)

¾ c. butter
2¼ c. sugar
1½ t. vanilla
3 eggs
3 sq. chocolate
3 c. sifted cake flour
1½ t. soda
¾ t. salt
1½ c. ice water

Cream butter, sugar and vanilla. Add eggs. Beat until light and fluffy. Add chocolate. Sift together, cake flour, soda, and salt. Add dry ingredients to creamed mixture alternately with

ice water. Bake in three 8" cake pans that have been greased and sprinkled with flour. Pre-heat oven to 350°F. and bake 30 to 35 minutes.

Date Cream Filling:
1 c. milk
½ c. chopped dates
¼ c. sugar
1 t. flour
1 egg (beaten)
½ c. nuts
1 t. vanilla

Heat in the top of a double boiler, milk and chopped dates. Combine sugar and flour. Add beaten egg and blend until smooth. Add mixture slowly to hot milk. Stir while cooking until thick. Cool and then stir in nuts and vanilla. Ice with Fudge Frosting.

Fudge Cake Frosting:
Blend in heavy saucepan:
2 c. sugar
1 c. cream
2 sq. grated chocolate

Boil over light heat for 3 minutes while stirring. Reduce heat and cook until it reaches soft ball stage. Cool and beat until creamy.

This recipe submitted by the following teachers:
Clarice Qualls, Celina H. S.
Celina, Tennessee
Mrs. W. R. Kilby, Bismarck H. S.
Bismarck, Arkansas
Mrs. Ralph Shipman, Paris H. S.
Paris, Texas
Mrs. Maxine M. Miller, Fairview H. S.
Fairview, West Virginia

SAUCEPAN FUDGE CAKE
Number of Servings — 9

¼ c. shortening
2 sq. baking chocolate
½ c. water
1 c. sugar
1 t. vanilla
1 c. flour, sifted
½ t. salt
½ t. soda
½ t. baking powder
1 egg, unbeaten
¼ c. sour milk or buttermilk

Melt shortening and chocolate in two-quart saucepan over low heat, or double boiler. Add water and sugar, stir until well blended. Remove from fire, cool to room temperature, add vanilla. Sift dry ingredients together. Add egg to cooled chocolate mixture, beat thoroughly. Add dry ingredients alternately with milk, stirring well after each addition. Beat vigorously until smooth. Bake in greased, floured, 8x8x2 pan at 350°F. for 30-35 minutes. Serve warm with whipped cream, or cool and frost.

This recipe submitted by the following teachers:
Barbara Myers Shaw, Hemlock H. S.
Hemlock, Michigan
Mrs. Augusta B. Peacock, Cleveland H. S.
Cleveland, Mississippi

NEW FUDGE CAKE (Large Cake)

Number of Servings — 15

2 c. sugar
2 t. baking powder
¼ t. soda
1 t. salt
¼ c. soft shortening
1½ c. milk
1 t. vanilla
4 sq. unsweetened chocolate, melted
1 c. chopped nuts

Grease and flour two 8″ or 9″ layer pans or 13x9 oblong pan. Sift together into bowl, sugar, baking powder, soda, and salt. Add shortening, milk, and vanilla. Beat 2 minutes. Add melted chocolate. Beat 2 more minutes. Stir in chopped nuts. Pour into prepared pans. Batter will be thin in first stage. Bake at 350°F. until cake tests done. Layers 35 to 40 minutes, oblong 40 to 45 minutes, square 35 to 40 minutes. Cool. Ice with a fudge frosting.

Mrs. Ruth W. Williams, Belmont H. S.
Belmont, North Carolina

FUDGE CAKE

1 c. oleomargarine
2 c. sugar
4 eggs, well beaten
2 c. sifted cake flour
⅛ t. salt
1½ t. baking soda
⅔ c. buttermilk
3 sq. bitter chocolate
⅔ c. boiling water
⅔ t. vanilla

Cream oleomargarine and sugar. Add eggs, beat well. Sift flour with salt. Mix soda with buttermilk. Add flour alternately with buttermilk to creamed mixture. Begin and end with flour. Beat well. Stir chocolate into boiling water to melt. Stir until smooth. While hot add to cake batter. Mix well. Add vanilla. Beat well. Bake in a well greased 9x13 pan at 325°F. for 1 hour. Cool cake and frost. When frosting is set, melt 2 squares of bitter chocolate and dribble or spread over top.

Jacquelyn Gentry, Clemiston H. S.
Clemiston, Florida

FUDGE NUT CAKE

Number of Servings — 20

2¼ c. sifted flour
1 t. soda
1 t. baking powder
½ t. salt
½ c. shortening
1½ c. sugar
1 t. black walnut flavoring
2 eggs
1 c. sour milk
⅓ c. hot water
½ c. cocoa
1 c. chopped black walnuts

Preheat oven to 350°F. Grease well and dust with flour, three 8″ or two 9″ layer cake pans. Sift together 2 cups flour, soda, baking powder, and salt, set aside. Cream shortening and sugar. Add flavoring and well-beaten eggs, beat until light and fluffy. Beat in flour mixture alternately with sour milk. Mix cocoa and hot water to form a paste, beat into batter. Mix chopped nuts with ¼ cup flour and mix thoroughly into batter. Pour into prepared pans and bake for 30-35 minutes. Cool. Spread with any chocolate frosting.

Clara Mae Chatham, Smithville H. S.
Smithville, Oklahoma

COCONUT CAKE

½ lb. butter
2 c. sugar
4 eggs
2⅔ c. cake flour
4 t. baking powder
1 c. milk
Pinch salt
1 t. vanilla

Grease and line three 8″ cake pans. Set oven at 375°F. Cream butter and sugar well. Add egg yolks. Sift flour, baking powder, and salt together and add alternately with the milk. Add vanilla. Beat egg whites until stiff and fold into mixture. Bake at 375°F. for 20-25 minutes.

Coconut Filling:
1 egg yolk
1 c. milk or part coconut milk
1 c. sugar
1 T. cornstarch
1 t. vanilla
1 c. coconut, grated

Mix together all ingredients except coconut and cook in a double boiler over low heat until thickened. Cool partly, then add coconut before icing cake.

Mrs. Jo Ann Rockett Bridges, White Castle H. S.
White Castle, Louisiana

FRESH COCONUT CAKE

3 egg whites
1½ c. sugar
¾ c. shortening
½ t. vanilla
3 egg yolks
¼ c. grated coconut
2¼ c. flour (cake flour)
2¼ t. baking powder
½ t. salt
¾ c. coconut milk

Beat egg whites until stiff, but not dry. Beat in ½ cup sugar, 2 tablespoons at a time. Cream shortening and add vanilla. Beat in 1 cup sugar, add egg yolks well-beaten. Beat well. Stir in grated coconut. Sift dry ingredients together and add alternately with coconut milk. Fold in egg whites. Spoon into two 9″ pans lined with wax paper. Bake 25 to 30 minutes at 350°F. Use 7-minute frosting. Sprinkle with coconut. A Japanese fruit cake filling is also delicious to use between layers.

Mrs. Marion H. Osborne, West Wilkes H. S.
Millers Creek, North Carolina

COCONUT CAKE
Number of Servings — 2 Layers
1½ c. sugar
¼ t. salt
½ c. butter (or margarine)
¾ c. water (do not substitute milk)
2½ c. sifted flour (cake)
3 t. baking powder
5 beaten egg whites
1 t. vanilla

Cream butter and sugar. Mix dry ingredients and add alternately with water. Add vanilla and fold in beaten egg whites. Bake at 350°F. until light brown. (Do not over-bake.) Use marshmallow filling, spreading fresh or canned coconut on top and sides.

Marshmallow Filling:
⅞ c. sugar (1 c. less 2 T.)
⅛ t. cream of tartar
3 T. cold water
1 egg white

Cook in double boiler. When water begins to boil start timing or put mixture in top of double boiler, beating with electric mixer during entire cooking. Cook and beat 3 minutes, then add 6 marshmallows. Continue cooking for 4 minutes. Remove from fire and beat until thicker. Spread on top and between layers, putting coconut on top after spreading filling.

Mrs. Alice E. Blackburn, H. E. Supervisor
Montevallo, Alabama

CHRISTMAS DELIGHT CAKE (Coconut)
Number of Servings — 24
⅔ c. shortening
2 c. sugar
3 c. flour
½ t. salt
3 t. baking powder
1 c. warm water
8 egg whites beaten stiff
1 t. orange extract

Cream shortening well, add sugar gradually. Sift flour, measure, add salt, baking powder and sift together. To creamed shortening and sugar add warm water, flour mixture and beaten egg whites alternately. Add flavoring. Divide into 2 layers. Place in cold oven. Bake 15 minutes at 150° then increase every fifteen minutes. Remove when done. It takes about 45 minutes. Cake should not brown.

Filling:
4 c. sugar
2 c. hot water or coconut juice
Pinch salt
4 egg whites beaten stiff
2 large grated coconuts

Boil sugar, water or juice and pinch salt until soft ball stage 236°F. Gradually add hot syrup to stiffly beaten egg whites, beating constantly. Continue beating until frosting is of spreading consistency. Frost cake and spread coconut on top of each layer.

Mrs. Nonie Lee Hardage, Carthage H. S.
Carthage, Mississippi

WHITE BUTTER CAKE WITH FRESH COCONUT ICING
Number of Servings — 10
⅔ c. butter
1¾ c. sugar
3 c. cake flour
3 t. baking powder
½ t. salt
1 c. milk (use part coconut milk)
5 egg whites (beaten)
1 t. vanilla (added to milk)

Cream butter and sugar. Sift flour, baking powder, and salt together 3 times. Add flour mixture alternately with milk mixture. Fold in beaten egg whites (40 times). Bake in 2 layers at 350°F. for 30 minutes.

Fresh White Coconut Icing:
2 c. sugar
2 T. white syrup
½ c. water
2 egg whites
1 t. vanilla (before thick enough to spread)

Beat the egg whites (not too stiff). Cook the sugar, syrup and water until it spins a thread 8" long. Then beat into the beaten egg whites adding a little at a time, until thick enough to stand up. Spread. Grate the meat of a fresh coconut and sprinkle over entire cake.

Mrs. Viola Lee Roy, Eubank H. S.
Eubank, Kentucky

COCONUT CAKE WITH LEMON FILLING
Number of Servings — 14
¾ c. butter (soft)
1½ c. sugar
5 egg whites
3 c. cake flour
4½ t. baking powder
½ t. salt
1 c. milk (warm)
1½ t. vanilla
1 t. lemon extract

Cream butter and sugar. Add slightly beaten egg whites. Sift flour, measure, and sift twice with baking powder and salt. Add flour mixture alternately with milk. Beat with mixer for one minute on low speed. Add vanilla and lemon. Pour batter into two greased and floured 9" round cake pans. Bake at 325°F. for 30 minutes. Cool.

Lemon Filling:
½ c. sugar
1½ T. cornstarch
½ c. boiling water
1 beaten egg yolk
½ T. butter
3 T. lemon juice

Mix sugar and cornstarch. Add boiling water. Cook over low heat stirring constantly for two minutes until thickened. Add beaten egg yolk and cook for one minute. Add butter and lemon juice. Cool. Spread mixture between the two cakes. Ice with 7-minute frosting. Sprinkle coconut on sides and top of cake.

Jeanne A. Simpson, Carrollton H. S.
Carrollton, Kentucky

LAZY DAZY CAKE (Coconut)
Number of Servings — 12

1 c. sifted enriched flour
1 t. baking powder
¼ t. salt
1 T. butter or margarine
½ c. hot milk
2 eggs
1 c. sugar
1 t. vanilla

Sift together flour, baking powder, and salt. Add butter to milk, keep hot. Beat eggs till thick and lemon-colored, about 3 minutes at high speed on mixer. Gradually add sugar, beating constantly at medium speed 4 to 5 minutes. Add sifted dry ingredients to egg mixture alternately with hot milk mixture. Add vanilla. Pour into greased and floured 9x9x2 glass pan. Bake in moderate oven 325°F. about 25 minutes. Cool cake slightly (do not remove from pan), frost top. Brown in broiler. Serve from glass pan. This cake packs nicely for picnics.

Frosting:
1 c. sugar
1 c. coconut
½ c. cream
5 t. melted butter

Mix together and frost warm cake.

Mrs. Dorothy Crabb, Lockett H. S.
Vernon, Texas

CHOC-CHIP DATE CAKE
Number of Servings — 8

1 c. dates, cut up
1 t. soda
1 c. boiling water
1 c. white sugar
1 c. oleo
1¾ c. flour
1 T. cocoa
2 eggs
1 t. vanilla
1 c. Choc-chips (6 oz.)
½ c. pecans, cut up

Mix together in a bowl, dates, soda, and boiling water. Cream sugar and oleo. Combine together and add flour, cocoa, eggs, and vanilla. Blend. Then add Choc-chips and pecans. Bake in 9x12x2 pan for 40 minutes in oven at 350°F. No frosting is needed.

Mrs. Joan R. Dean, Stephens County H. S.
Eastanollee, Georgia

CHOC-CHIP-DATE CAKE
Number of Servings — 12-15

1 c. sugar
1 c. shortening
2 eggs
1 c. chopped dates
1 c. hot water
1¾ c. flour
2 T. cocoa
½ t. salt
1 t. soda
1 t. vanilla
¾ c. chopped nuts
1-6 oz. pkg. chocolate chips

Pour hot water over chopped dates and let cool until lukewarm. Cream sugar, shortening, and eggs. Sift flour, cocoa, salt, and soda together. Add sifted dry ingredients alternately with date mixture to creamed mixture. Add vanilla. May put half of chocolate chips and nuts into mixture and remaining on top, or put nuts and chocolate chips all on top. Put in greased and floured pan (about 9x14). Bake at 350°F. for 35 minutes. Serve plain, sprinkle with powdered sugar, or with whipped cream, topped with a cherry.

This recipe submitted by the following teachers:
Mrs. Patsy Steffensen, Lake Norden Ind. School
Lake Norden, South Dakota
Lucy White, Wethersfield H. S.
Kewanee, Illinois

DATE CAKE
Number of Servings — 8

1 c. boiling water
1 c. chopped dates
1 t. soda
½ c. shortening (butter or Crisco)
1 c. white sugar
1 egg
1½ c. sifted flour
1 t. salt
1 t. vanilla

Cover chopped dates and soda with boiling water and let stand while mixing batter. Cream shortening and sugar. Add egg and blend well. Sift flour and salt together and add to creamed mixture, with dates and soda mixture. Add vanilla. Pour into a greased and floured square baking pan. Bake 45 minutes or until done at 350°F. While still hot spread top with the following:

Topping:
4 T. butter
½ c. brown sugar
2 T. cream or milk
1 c. chopped nuts or coconut

Blend all together and spread over hot cake in pan in which it was baked. Place under broiler until it becomes bubbly and slightly browned.

Mrs. Cleo Waltrip, Hanes Junior-Senior H. S.
Winston-Salem, North Carolina

DATE-NUT CAKE

½ c. butter or shortening
2 c. sugar
2 eggs, well beaten
1 pkg. dates
1 c. walnuts
3 c. all-purpose flour
2 t. soda
2 c. hot water

Pour 1 cup hot water over seeded dates and let stand. Cream butter and sugar. Add well beaten eggs, then pour in dates and chopped nuts. Mix soda in other cup of hot water. Add flour and hot water alternately to first mixture. Bake in moderate oven 350°F. for about 45 minutes or until done.

Mrs. Rosemary Harwood, North Stanly H. S.
New London, North Carolina

DATE CAKE
Number of Servings — 9
PART I:
½ pkg. dates
1 c. hot water
1 t. soda
Mix together, allow to cool, then add:
½ c. walnuts
1½ c. cake flour
1 t. baking powder
PART II:
2 T. soft butter
1 c. sugar
½ t. salt
1 egg
Mix Part I and Part II together. Bake in a 9x9 cake pan, 25 minutes at 350°F.

Frosting:
½ pkg. dates
½ c. walnuts
¾ c. sugar
⅔ c. water
Mix together and cook until syrupy. Spread on cake after it is baked (while still hot).

Mrs. Ruth Reich, Meyersdale Joint H. S.
Meyersdale, Pennsylvania

BLIND DATE CAKE
Number of Servings — 12 to 15
1 c. dates, cut fine
1¼ c. boiling water
1 t. soda
½ c. shortening
1 c. sugar
2 eggs, well beaten
1 t. vanilla
1¼ c. flour
3 T. cocoa (level)
½ t. salt
Topping:
¼ c. sugar
1 c. chocolate chips
½ c. chopped nuts
Stir dates in boiling water. Mash and cool before adding soda. Cream shortening with the 1 cup sugar, eggs, and vanilla. Combine the mixtures. Add flour sifted with cocoa and salt. Sprinkle topping of the ½ c. sugar, chocolate chips, and chopped nuts over cake and **press down with** hand. Bake at 350°F. for 30-35 minutes.

Pauline Brown, Lone Wolf H. S.
Lone Wolf, Oklahoma

DATE-NUT CAKE
Number of Servings — 16
1 c. pitted dates, cut
1 t. soda
1 c. boiling water
1 egg
Pinch of salt
1 c. sugar
1½ c. flour
1 t. vanilla
1 T. butter or oleo
½ c. nuts

Recipe may be doubled.
Put dates in pan. Sprinkle the soda over the dates and pour on the boiling water, Let cool. Mix other ingredients. Add dates. Bake in slow oven 350°F.

For a doubled recipe for icing use:
2 c. brown sugar
6 T. cream
6 T. butter
Cook until it forms a soft ball in water. Do not stir. Let cool, but not entirely cold. Beat and spread on cake.

Mrs. Ann Hoit, Ousley Junior High
Arlington, Texas

DATE NUT CAKE
Number of Servings — 12-15
4 eggs
1 c. sugar
1½ c. flour
2 t. baking powder
½ t. salt
2 t. vanilla
1 qt. nut meats
1 lb. pkg. pitted dates
Beat eggs, add sugar and beat until light and fluffy. Add flour, baking powder, and salt which have been sifted together and beat well. Add vanilla, chopped nuts, and chopped dates. Mix thoroughly. Pack into a well greased loaf pan. Place in a 300°F. oven for 30 minutes, reduce temperature to 250°F. and bake 1 to 1½ hours longer. Allow to cool slightly before removing from pan.

Mrs. Grace L. Thompson, Valdosta H. S.
Valdosta, Georgia

ORANGE DATE CAKE
Number of Servings — 20
1 c. butter
2 c. sugar
4 eggs
1 t. soda
1¼ c. buttermilk
4 c. flour
2 T. grated orange rind
1 c. chopped pecans
1 lb. chopped dates
Cream butter and sugar. Beat in eggs one at a time. Dissolve soda in buttermilk. Add sifted flour in about 3 parts to butter mixture, alternately with milk. Beat batter until smooth. Add orange rind, dates, and nuts which have been dredged in the flour measured for cake. Bake in tube pan 1½ hours at 325°F. When cake is done, pour orange sauce over hot cake and let cool in pan.

Orange Sauce:
2 c. sugar
2 T. orange rind
1 c. orange juice
Stir until sugar is dissolved. Do not beat.

Estelle J. Garrison, Fayette County H. S.
Fayette, Alabama

DATE-NUT MAYONNAISE CAKE

1 c. sugar
3 T. cocoa
½ t. salt
1 t. cinnamon
1 c. mayonnaise
1 c. chopped walnuts
1 c. dates or raisins
1 t. baking soda
1 c. boiling water
2 c. sifted flour

Mix sugar, salt, cocoa, and cinnamon. Add mayonnaise and blend. Mix dates and nuts and pour hot water and soda over them. Add to mayonnaise mix. Add flour and blend in thoroughly. Make at 360°F. for 40 minutes in loaf or 35 minutes in layer pans. Serve with whipped cream icing.

Esther J. Swinden, Reno H. S.
Reno, Nevada

ORANGE DATE CAKE

1 c. shortening
2 c. sugar
1 t. soda
4 eggs
1 c. chopped pecans
2 c. chopped dates
½ t. salt
2 T. orange peeling
1½ c. buttermilk

Set oven at 325°F. Cream shortening and sugar. Add soda to ½ cup buttermilk. Add other ingredients and mix well with the buttermilk added last. Bake in a tube pan for 1½ hours.

Filling:
2 c. sugar
1 c. orange juice

Mix filling while cake is baking. Mix sugar and orange juice. Stir often until cake is done. After cake has baked the 1½ hours remove from oven and punch holes in the top with an ice pick. Pour juice slowly until all is absorbed in cake.

Mrs. Patsy Evans, Bridge City H. S.
Bridge City, Texas

DATE ORANGE CAKE
Number of Servings — 20

1 c. butter
2 c. sugar
4 eggs
1½ c. buttermilk
4 c. sifted flour
1 t. soda
2 c. chopped pecans
2 c. chopped dates
2 T. grated orange peel

Cream butter and sugar. Add eggs one at a time beating after each addition. Sift dry ingredients together, add to first mixture alternately with buttermilk. Add nuts, dates and orange peel last. Bake in a greased and floured tube cake pan for two hours at 300°F.

Glaze for Cake:
1 c. orange juice
2 c. sugar
2 t. grated orange peel

Just before the cake is done, mix glaze and place on a slow burner. Do not boil. As soon as you remove the cake from the oven pour steaming glaze over top and stick top of cake with a toothpick to allow glaze to soak in. This cake will keep several weeks if properly wrapped.

Mrs. Betty Prince, Mt. Ida H. S.
Mount Ida, Arkansas

ORANGE-NUT-DATE CAKE

1 c. butter
2 c. sugar
4 eggs
1⅛ c. buttermilk
1 t. soda
4 c. flour
2 T. grated orange rind
1 lb. dates (chopped)
1 c. broken pecans

Cream butter and sugar. Beat in eggs one at a time. Dissolve soda in buttermilk. Add sifted flour in about three parts to the butter mixture, alternately with the buttermilk. Beat until smooth after each addition. Add orange rind, dates and pecans that have not been floured. Bake in stem pan 1½ hours in moderate oven, about 325°F.

Sauce for Top of Cake:
2 c. sugar
1 c. orange juice
2 T. grated orange

When cake is done, pour the above sauce over the cake. Make holes in top of cake with toothpick to allow juice to soak well into cake. Allow to cool in pan. This cake may be served with or without an icing.

Mrs. Julia B. Willey, Lone Grove H. S.
Lone Grove, Louisiana

DATE AND WALNUT CAKE
Number of Servings — 12

1 t. soda
1 c. chopped dates
1 c. boiling water
1 c. sugar
1 T. butter

(Continued on Next Page)

1 egg, beaten
1⅛ c. flour
½ (or more) c. chopped walnuts

Put soda over dates and pour boiling water over dates and soda, add sugar and butter. When cool add beaten egg, flour and nuts. Bake either in layer or loaf pan, 350°F. oven 30-40 minutes.

Icing:
2 small (or 1 large) pkg. cream cheese
1 pkg. powdered sugar
Cherries and/or nuts

Beat cream cheese, and add powdered sugar gradually. Smooth for easy spreading. Garnish with cherries and/or nuts.

Mrs. Mary Irey, Red Bluff Union H. S.
Red Bluff, California

GOLDEN DATE CAKE

2⅛ c. (2 c. and 2 T.) flour
1½ c. sugar
3 t. baking powder
1 t. salt
½ c. Crisco
1 c. milk
1½ t. vanilla
2 medium eggs
1 c. dates
½ c. chopped pecans

Sift together in mixing bowl flour, sugar, baking powder, and salt. Add Crisco, milk, and vanilla. Beat with spoon for 2 minutes (150 strokes per minute) or beat 2 minutes with electric mixer on medium speed. Add unbeaten eggs and dates cut fine. Beat 2 minutes longer. Fold in nuts. Pour in cake pans lined with wax paper, or greased and dusted with flour. Bake in 350°F. (moderate) oven.

Fresh Orange Icing:
3 c. sifted confectioners' sugar
⅛ c. Crisco
3 T. orange juice
1½ T. coarsely grated orange rind

Blend sugar into Crisco, orange juice, and rind adding small amount at each addition. Spread on cake.

Mrs. W. C. Robertson, Collins H. S.
Collins, Mississippi

EASY-TO-MAKE FRUIT CAKE

Number of Servings — 16
2 cans sweetened condensed milk
2 cans of coconut
2-1 lb. pkg. dates
½ lb. candied cherries
½ lb. candied pineapple (more may be used)
1 lb. shelled walnuts (or 2 c. pecans)
1 lb. pecans
½ t. salt (if desired)

Mix and bake 1 hour at 250 degrees in an angel food cake pan.

This recipe submitted by the following teachers:
Lona W. Capshaw, Hermitage Springs School
Red Boiling Springs, Tennessee
Mrs. Pearl Dawson, Marion County H. S.
Guin, Alabama

DELTA DELIGHT FRUIT CAKE

8 c. pecans
1 lb. candied cherries
1 lb. candied pineapple
2 lb. dates
2 c. sugar
3 c. flour
8 eggs
2 t. baking powder
2 t. salt
3 T. vanilla flavoring
1 T. almond flavoring

Beat eggs together, add sugar and cream well. Add flour, baking powder, salt, vanilla, and almond flavoring. Add dates, cherries, pineapple, and nuts (cut in pieces). Pack into paper lined, greased and floured pans. Bake 1½-2 hours at 250°F. over a pan of water.

Mrs. Sudie M. Bell, Isola H. S.
Isola, Mississippi

FRUIT CAKE IN GRAPEFRUIT SHELLS
(For a Gift)

Number of Servings — 6
Grapefruit Shells:

Select large grapefruit of good shape and color. Cut in half, making zig-zag edges. Remove pulp, being careful to leave all the thick part of the peel and not to break the shell. Cover shells with cold, salted water, bring to a boil, cook 10 minutes. Drain off water. Repeat three or four times to remove bitter flavor from peel. Cool. Make a syrup with equal parts of sugar and water. Cook to medium thick syrup, let fruit stand in syrup for 24 hours, turning several times. Cook to very thick syrup. Remove from syrup and cool. If shells are large, invert each over a small bowl to dry.

Fruit Cake:
1 pkg. instant yellow cake mix
½ c. applesauce
4 eggs unbeaten
1 t. salt
1 t. orange extract
2 c. cut dates (about 1 lb.)
½ lb. candied green pineapple cut in strips
½ lb. whole candied red cherries
⅛ lb. candied fruits and peels
1 lb (4 c) walnut halves, broken
½ c. flour

Empty cake mix into bowl, add applesauce, eggs, salt, and extract. Beat 3 minutes until smooth and creamy. Combine fruits and nuts mixed well with flour. Stir into batter. Fill candied grapefruit shells almost full. Bake in slow oven (275°F.) about 2¼ hours. Cool thoroughly. Wrap cakes tightly in moisture proof cellophane, pliofilm, or aluminum foil. Store in refrigerator or freezer until ready to use. Cakes should be stored for from two to four weeks before using to allow fruits to mellow and flavors to blend. This makes enough to fill six large grapefruit shells.

Genevieve A. Miller, Tyrone Jr. H. S.
St. Petersburg, Florida

EASY FRUIT CAKE

1 lb. chopped pecans
1 lb. chopped dates
1 lb. coconut
12 oz. candied fruits
2 cans sweetened condensed milk

Mix all ingredients together and bake in a greased and floured tube or loaf pan. (Cover with foil half of baking time while it is baking, to prevent too much browning). Bake one hour at 350°F.

Mrs. J. W. Duncan, Purcell H. S.
Purcell, Oklahoma

NEVER FAIL FRUIT CAKE

Number of Servings — 30-50
1 lb. candied cherries
1 lb. candied pineapple
1 lb. pitted dates
1 lb. shelled pecans
4 cans coconut or 2 boxes (7½ oz. size)
3 T. flour
2 cans sweetened condensed milk

Chop fruit and nuts in a large mixing bowl. Add coconut and mix well with hands. Add flour, mix, then add sweetened condensed milk. Mix well. Pack firmly in 10″ lightly greased spring form tube cake pan with bottom lined with greased wax paper. (If desired decorate top with a few pecan and cherry halves.) Bake 1½ hours at 300°F. Remove from oven. Run knife around edge and remove rim of pan. When barely warm, remove tube bottom and wax paper from cake. Keeps indefinitely in refrigerator.

Mrs. Annie Lou Wigley, Buckhorn H. S.
Huntsville, Alabama

HONEY FRUIT CAKE

Number of Servings — 8-10
1 c. liquid honey
⅔ c. strong coffee
5 eggs
1 c. sugar
⅔ c. vegetable cooking oil
3½ c. sifted all-purpose flour
½ t. salt
2 t. double-acting baking powder
1 t. baking soda
1½ t. ground cinnamon
½ t. ground allspice
¼ t. ground cloves
½ c. chopped nuts
½ c. chopped citron
1 c. chopped seedless raisins

Combine coffee and honey, heat and set aside. Beat eggs until thick and lemon-colored. Gradually beat in sugar. Stir in oil. Sift flour, salt, baking powder, baking soda, and spices together. Mix with nuts, citron, and raisins. Gradually stir into the egg mixture alternately with the honey-coffee mixture. Mix well after each addition. Pour into well-greased, lightly floured 8½″ tube pan. Bake at 325°F. 1½ hours, or until done. Cool on a wire rack 15 minutes. Invert pan and finish cooling. Cake will drop out when cool. When cold pack in tightly closed cake box and allow to stand 7-10 days.

Mrs. Mary Alice Smith, Pine Knot H. S.
Pine Knot, Kentucky

HOLIDAY CAKE (Fruit)

1 lb. butter
2 c. sugar
6 eggs
3 c. all-purpose flour
1 t. baking powder
¼ t. salt
1 t. vanilla flavoring
1 t. almond extract
½ lb. candied cherries
½ lb. candied pineapple
1 lb. chopped pecans
1 c. flour

Preheat oven 250°F. Cream butter with sugar. Beat in eggs, 1 at a time, beating after each addition. Mix together 3 cups sifted all-purpose flour, baking powder, and salt. Add gradually to creamed mixture. Add vanilla flavoring and almond extract. Dredge candied cherries, candied pineapple and chopped pecans with 1 cup flour. Add to first mixture. Bake in large tube cake pan about 3 hours.

Mrs. Maxine Edwards Tuten, Hardeeville H. S.
Hardeeville, South Carolina

FRUIT CAKE

1 c. powdered sugar
1 c. flour
½ t. salt
1 t. baking powder
½ lb. candied pineapple
½ lb. candy orange slices
½ lb. candied cherries
1 lb. dates
2 c. pecans
4 eggs
1 t. vanilla

Sift together sugar, flour, salt, baking powder. Combine chopped nuts and fruits. Beat eggs well, add vanilla and pour over first mixture. Blend well. Grease and flour pan. Bake at 325°F. for 35 to 40 minutes.

Mrs. Lorretta Steakley, Cranfills Gap H. S.
Cranfills Gap, Texas

JAPANESE FRUIT CAKE

8 egg whites
2 c. sugar
1 c. butter
4 c. flour
½ c. milk
2 t. baking powder
1 c. raisins
1 c. chopped cherries
1 c. pecans
1 t. spice
1 t. cinnamon
1 t. cloves (ground)

Cream butter, sugar, add flour (sifted with baking powder) and milk gradually. Then fold in egg whites stiffly beaten. Bake 3 layers at 350°F. for 25 minutes. To the remaining batter add raisins, chopped cherries, pecans, spice, cinnamon and cloves. Bake these 2 layers at 350°F. for 30 minutes. Frost cake with following filling.

(Continued on Next Page)

Filling:
2 c. sugar
1 c. boiling water
3 T. cornstarch
1 can pineapple (No. 2 crushed)
Juice and grated rinds of 2 lemons
2 c. fresh coconut

Cook for 5 minutes in double boiler. Cool and spread on layers. Sprinkle with coconut.

Mrs. Sara M. Gantt, Wagener H. S.
Wagener, South Carolina

JAPANESE FRUIT CAKE

Number of Servings — 16
1 c. butter
2 c. sugar
4 eggs
1 t. vanilla
3 c. flour
3 t. baking powder
½ t. salt
1 t. cloves
1 t. cinnamon
1 t. allspice
½ lb. chopped raisins
¾ c. chopped or slivered almonds
Filling:
Juice and rind of 3 lemons
1 coconut, grated fine (2 cans)
2 c. sugar
1 c. boiling water
1 t. cornstarch

Cream together butter, sugar, eggs and vanilla Sift together flour, baking powder, and salt, add flour mixture alternately with milk into egg mixture. Separate batter into 3 parts. To 1 part add spices, raisins, and nuts. Bake in 3 layers. Mix lemon juice, coconut, sugar, water and cornstarch, bring to a boil, cook until it falls in lumps from a spoon. Put layers together with filling, placing spiced layer in the center. Ice cake with 7-minute frosting and cover with grated coconut or slivered almonds.

Charlotte R. Turner, Hendersonville H. S.
Hendersonville, North Carolina

LAYER FRUIT CAKE

Mix together and set aside:
½ lb. fruits
1 lb. pecans
1 lb. English walnuts
1 lb. cherries
Put in large container and sift:
1 c. flour
1 t. allspice
1 t. nutmeg
1 t. cinnamon
1 t. cloves

Then sift 1 cup flour with 3 teaspoons baking powder and mix again.

6 eggs (beat slightly)
2 c. sugar
½ lb. butter
1 c. milk (melt butter in milk over low heat)

Cream sugar and slightly beaten eggs, pouring

milk and melted butter over and mix well. Add to mixture of fruit. Grease pans and dust with flour. Bake 25 minutes at 350°F.

Filling:
6 peeled oranges, ground
1 c. crushed pineapple
3 c. sugar

Cook until thick and pour over layer fruit cake.

Mrs. Anona Moore, Alvin H. S.
Alvin, Texas

LAST MINUTE FRUIT CAKE

2 c. sugar
1 c. butter or margarine
3 eggs well beaten
1 c. buttermilk
1 t. soda
1 c. blackberry jam
1 c. chopped pecans
1 c. chopped raisins
1 c. grated coconut
3 c. flour

Cream butter and sugar, add eggs and mix well, add buttermilk to which the soda has been added. Add blackberry jam, nuts, raisins, and coconut, mixing thoroughly. stir in flour. Bake in three 9" layer pans (greased and lined) at 350°F. for 25-30 minutes. Cool and spread with frosting.

Frosting:
2 c. sugar
4 T. flour
1 c. butter or margarine
1½ c. sweet milk

Cook until thick, then beat until creamy.

Mrs. Homer Jolly, Wortham H. S.
Wortham, Texas

ORANGE FRUIT CAKE

1 c. soft margarine
2 c. granulated sugar
6 eggs
3½ c. self-rising flour
1 c. plain milk
1 T. vanilla flavoring
1 T. lemon flavoring
1 lb. pitted dates, chopped
1 lb. pecans, chopped

Using ½ cup of the flour, dredge the nuts and dates. Cream together sugar, margarine, and eggs, adding one at a time. Add remaining flour alternating with milk, add flavoring and beat, add nuts and dates. Pour into 10" tube pan (line bottom with greased wax paper). Bake at 325°F. one hour or until done. Remove from oven, pour orange syrup over cake immediately. Let cool in pan 30 minutes, turn out, let stand upsidedown overnight, turn.

Orange Syrup:
2 c. fresh orange juice
1 box confectioners' sugar
Mix together.

Doris Joe Campbell, Great Falls H. S.
Great Falls, South Carolina

ORANGE FRUIT CAKE
4 lb. Cake
½ lb. candied pineapple
½ lb. candied cherries
½ lb. blanched almonds
¼ lb. citron
1 c. shortening
1½ c. sugar
1 c. orange juice
6 egg yolks
½ lb. coconut
2 T. rosewater
3 c. cake or pastry flour
1 c. raisins

Shred pineapple, cherries and almonds. Shave citron into thin slices, cover with ½ cup orange juice, let stand overnight. Cream shortening and add sugar. Add well beaten egg yolks and the coconut soaked ½ hour in the rosewater. Then beat in ½ cup orange juice and 3 cups flour. Add the mixed fruits and raisins, chopped and dredged with flour. Bake in a well greased tube pan at 300°F. for 3 hours.

Margaret Phalen McKenzie, Rainelle H. S.
Rainelle, West Virginia

PORK FRUIT CAKE
Number of Servings — 18
1 lb. fresh ground pork
1 c. boiling water
2 c. sugar
1½ c. sorghum
1 pkg. mincemeat
1 c. raisins
1 c. nuts
2 apples diced
½ t. cinnamon
½ t. nutmeg
½ t. allspice
1 t. soda
Flour to stiffen

Mix ingredients in order listed. Pack in tube or loaf pan. Place in oven. Turn oven on low heat. Bake on low for 2 hours. Increase heat to 250°F. and bake for 1 hour. Increase heat to 300°F. and cook 1 hour. Test with straw. This cake keeps extra well.

Mrs. Wilford Taylor, Hoxie Consolidated School
Hoxie, Arkansas

SOUTHERN FRUIT CAKE
1 lb. (4½ c.) flour
1 t. baking powder
1 t. allspice
2 t. apple pie spice
1 lb. (2 c.) butter
1 lb. (2¼ c.) sugar
½ c. honey
2 T. lemon juice
1 doz. eggs
1 T. almond extract
1½ c. strawberry preserves
1 c. fig preserves
2 lb. red cherries
2 lb. green pineapple
2 lb. yellow pineapple
2 lb. dates
½ lb. figs
½ lb. orange peel
1 large coconut, grated
½ lb. black walnuts
¾ lb. English walnuts
1 qt. pecans
½ box white raisins
½ lb. almonds
1 box seeded raisins
½ c. bourbon

Sift flour, baking powder, and spices together. Cream butter until smooth. Add sugar gradually and cream until fluffy. Add lemon juice and honey to well beaten eggs, beating thoroughly. Add to creamed mixture. Add flour mixture to first mixture a small amount at a time, mixing completely. Stir in almond extract, strawberry preserves, and fig preserves. Cut the fruit and nuts into small pieces, dredge with flour, and add to cake batter. Add bourbon as needed to thin batter. Grease and line with brown paper 2 large loaf pans, 3 small loaf pans, and 1 dozen paper cups in muffin rings or 1 large tube pan and 2 loaf pans. Bake in 250°F. oven until done. Blanch almonds for decorating tops of fruitcake. Also save part of the pineapple and cherries for decoration.

Mrs. Suanne Lett Black, Sidney Lanier H. S.
Montgomery, Alabama

TUTTI-FRUTTI CAKE
Number of Servings — 20
1-1 lb. pkg. pitted dates, chopped (3 c.)
4 oz. red candied pineapple
4 oz. green candied pineapple
4 oz. red candied cherries
4 oz. green candied cherries
3 c. nuts (pecans or Brazil nuts)
1 c. sifted enriched flour
1 c. sugar
1 t. baking powder
¼ t. salt
4 well beaten eggs
1 t. vanilla or rum extract

Cut fruit in chunks. Combine with whole cherries and nuts. Sift together dry ingredients, add to fruits and nuts, coating well. Stir in eggs and add vanilla. Line two 8½x4½x2½ loaf pans with heavy paper (greased). Pour in batter. Bake in slow oven 325°F. 1 hour. Cool. Trim top with gumdrop rose.

Gumdrop Rose:
Between sugared sheets of wax paper, roll 3 or 4 big pink gumdrops into flat ovals. Cut each in half crosswise. Fold corner of 1 piece at an angle and wind to make rose center, place atop cake. Tuck and press other half-ovals around center to make petals. Roll out green jelly string for stem, green gumdrops for leaves, cut out, arrange.
This recipe submitted by the following teachers:
Martha Mae Tate, Stigler Sr. H. S.
Stigler, Oklahoma

Mrs. Yvonne T. Napp, Choctaw County H. S.
Butler, Alabama

YULE CAKE

1½ c. whole Brazil nuts
1½ c. walnut halves
1 pkg. (7¼ oz.) pitted dates
⅔ c. candied orange peel (2-3 oz. cans)
⅔ c. red maraschino cherries (drained)
½ c. green maraschino cherries (drained)
½ c. seedless raisins
¾ c. sifted all-purpose flour
¾ c. sugar
½ t. baking powder
½ t. salt
3 eggs
1 t. vanilla

Grease bottom and sides of loaf pan 10x5x3 or star shaped 1½ quart pan or two 1 lb. coffee cans. Line bottom with brown paper. Place Brazil nuts, walnuts, dates, orange peel, red and green cherries and raisins in large bowl. Measure flour, sugar, baking powder, and salt into sifter; sift over nuts and fruits. Mix well. Beat eggs until light in small bowl, add vanilla, blend into nut mixture, batter very stiff. Spoon mixture into pan, spread evenly. Bake loaf, 300°F. 1¾ hours. Star pan or coffee cans 2½ hours at 300°F. Cool cake in pan 10 minutes, loosen edges and turn. Can be stored in refrigerator 2 or 3 months.

Maxine Fowler, Mount Hope H. S.
Mount Hope, Alabama

WHITE FRUIT CAKE (Layer)

Number of Servings — 12
1 c. butter
2 c. sugar
1 t. vanilla
3¼ c. all-purpose flour
3 t. baking powder
¾ t. salt
1 c. milk
8 egg whites or 1 c.

Cream butter well, add sugar gradually, beating until light and fluffy. Add vanilla, then sifted dry ingredients alternately with milk, beating until smooth. Beat egg whites until stiff but not dry. Fold in egg whites. Pour batter into layer cake pans, 1″ deep, lined on the bottom with paper, then greased. Bake in moderate oven, 375°F. for about 15 minutes, then turn out on racks to cool. Spread frosting between layers.

Filling:
½ lb. butter
8 well beaten egg yolks
½ lb. sugar
½ lb. English walnuts
½ lb. almonds
½ lb. citron
1 large coconut, grated
1 t. vanilla

Melt butter, add beaten eggs, add sugar and cook in a double boiler, stirring often. When thickened, add chopped walnuts, coconut, blanched chopped almonds and chopped citron. Add vanilla. When cool, spread between layers and on top if desired. A white icing may be used on outside.

Mrs. Josephine P. Clark, Fairview H. S.
Fairview, Tennessee

WHITE FRUIT CAKE

Number of Servings — 20
¾ c. butter
1½ c. sugar
3 c. cake flour (reserve 1 c. for dredging)
3 t. baking powder
4 egg whites or 3 whole eggs
1 c. sweet milk
1 t. flavoring (vanilla or lemon)
1 c. coconut
1 c. white raisins
1 c. drained maraschino cherries
1 c. chopped nuts

Cream butter and sugar until very fluffy and smooth, adding sugar gradually. Sift flour before measuring. Sift flour with baking powder. Put flavoring in milk. Mix coconut, raisins, cherries, and nuts with 1 cup of the flour. Add flour and milk alternately to the butter and sugar mixture, beginning and ending with flour. Fold in the fruit. Beat the egg whites until stiff and fold in last. If whole eggs are used, the yolks should be added to the creamed butter and sugar mixture. Oil and dust a loaf pan with flour. Cook 1 hour at 325°F. Serve plain or with ice cream.

Mrs. Edna Earle Beck, Anson H. S.
Anson, Texas

WHITE FRUIT CAKE

1 c. butter
2 c. sugar
12 egg whites or 6 whole eggs
1 t. vanilla
3 c. flour
1 t. baking powder
¾ lb. crystallized cherries
¾ lb. pineapple
½ lb. citron, if desired
1 lb. pecans
¼ lb. white raisins

Cream butter, add sugar and mix. Add eggs and beat thoroughly. Add vanilla. Sift dry ingredients together and mix with fruits. Add this mixture to creamed mixture. Pour into large greased tube pan lined with heavy brown paper and bake in a slow oven 250°F. for 2 hours or until done when tested.

Mary R. Copley, Bluestone H. S.
Shipwith, Virginia

LIGHT FRUIT CAKE

Number of Servings — 12 lbs.
2 lb. white raisins
1 lb. preserved citron
2 lb. preserved pineapple
2 lb. glace cherries
½ lb. crystallized orange peel
½ lb. crystallized lemon peel
3 lb. broken nuts (pecans and walnuts)
6 c. all-purpose flour
1 lb. butter
2 c. granulated sugar
10 eggs
½ t. salt
4 t. baking powder
½ c. pineapple or orange juice
3 T. vanilla flavoring

(Continued on Next Page)

Cut fruits and nuts coarsely, and mix thoroughly with 2 cups flour. Cream butter until fluffy, gradually add sugar while continuing to cream. Add eggs one at a time, beating vigorously after each addition. Sift remaining four cups of flour with salt and baking powder, and add to the mixture alternately in thirds with the fruit juice and vanilla. Fold in floured fruits and nuts. Bake in three loaf pans or one large funnel and 1 loaf pan at 250°F. Store for one month in a cool place.

Mrs. Ben Elkin, East Duplin H. S.
Wallace, North Carolina

WHITE FRUIT CAKE

8 egg whites, stiffly beaten
1 c. margarine
2 c. sugar
4 c. flour
1 c. milk
2 t. baking powder
¼ t. salt
2 t. vanilla
2 t. orange flavoring
2 t. lemon flavoring
2 c. candied cherries
½ lb. candied pineapple
2 c. white raisins
1 c. pecans
1 c. almonds
1 c. coconut

Heat oven to 325°F. Line with heavy brown wrapping paper a tube pan. Cream sugar and margarine. Sift flour, measure, use 1 cup for dredging fruits and nuts. Sift remainder with baking powder, and salt. Add alternately with milk to sugar and butter mixture. Add flavorings, fruits, coconut and nuts. Mix thoroughly. Fold in stiffly beaten egg whites. Pour into pan and bake at 325°F. from 2 to 2½ hours or until toothpick stuck in center of cake comes out clean. Cool. Wrap in wax paper or foil and store in air tight container in a cool place.

Laura C. Jackson, McCreary County H. S.
Whitley City, Kentucky

WHITE COCONUT FRUIT CAKE

3 c. sugar
1 lb. butter
1 doz. eggs
4½ c. flour
2 lb. white raisins
2 coconuts, grated
¼ lb. orange peel
1 lb. citron
¼ lb. lemon peel
1½ lb. pecans
½ lb cherries, half red, half green
¼ lb. pineapple
1 t. nutmeg
1 glass brandy or wine

Grease pans and line bottoms with heavy brown paper. (Will fill a 10″ tube pan and 2 small loaf pans.) Make a batter of sugar, butter, and eggs. Dredge fruit in flour. Add other ingredients. Bake in pan with another pan turned over the top. Bake at 275°F. for 2½ to 3 hours.

Mrs. Rose Lynn, Auburndale H. S.
Auburndale, Florida

WHITE FRUIT CAKE WITH CUSTARD SUPREME

Number of Servings — 16-20

1½ c. butter or Crisco
2 c. sugar
2 c. sifted cake flour
1 T. baking powder
1 c. milk plus 1 t. vanilla
2 c. sifted cake flour
2 c. nut meats, chopped fine (hickory nuts or pecans)
1 lb. white seedless raisins
8 oz. candied cherries
8 oz. candied pineapple
8 oz. angel flake coconut
1½ c. egg whites, room temperature

Cream Crisco and sugar very smooth. Sift flour, measure, add baking powder and sift again. Add alternately with milk, beating well after each addition. Sift other cups of flour. Add raisins and nuts to it and mix until each nut and raisin is well covered with flour. Add gradually to above mixture beating each time until no flour is seen. Add cherries, pineapple and coconut, blending evenly. Beat egg whites until they stand in peaks and fold into mixture. Bake in stem or angel food cake pan which has been lined with Reynolds Wrap or with brown paper, which has been greased and floured. Bake at 325°F. for 1 hour. Reduce heat and continue baking for 2 hours at 275°F. or until done when tested. Cool in pan, remove, wrap well and store in air-tight place. Age if desired.

Polly's Custard Supreme:

1 gal. milk
1 c. sugar
½ c. flour
1 additional c. milk
10-12 egg yolks (from White Fruit Cake)
10-12 bananas
½ gal. vanilla ice cream

Scald the 1 gallon of milk. Beat egg yolks until smooth, add the flour and sugar which has been blended together. Blend in the 1 cup of milk. Very slowly add the egg mixture to the scalded milk. Cook in large heavy cooker over low heat or cook over water until mixture coats a metal spoon. Chill. Add 2 teaspoons of vanilla. In large glasses put cut-up bananas, pour in custard and top with generous dip of ice cream.

Mrs. Pauline G. Adkins, Sandy Hook H. S.
Sandy Hook, Kentucky

WHITE FRUIT CAKE

Number of Servings — 20

2 c. sugar
1 lb. butter or oleomargarine
8 eggs
1-2 oz. bottle lemon extract
4 c. flour
2 t. baking powder
1 lb. pecans
1 lb. candied cherries
1 lb. candied pineapple

(Continued on Next Page)

Mix sugar and butter together. Add eggs one at a time mixing after each addition, add lemon extract, 2 cups of the flour with baking powder sifted in flour. Cut fruit and dredge with 2 cups of the flour. Add dredged fruit and nuts to batter. Bake in ungreased tube pan 2½ to 3 hours at 275°F. Put pan of water under cake while baking on lower rack. Keeps cake moist while baking.

Mrs. Murel McKnight, Olton H. S.
Olton, Texas

FRUIT COCKTAIL CAKE
Number of Servings — 9-12

1 c. flour
1 c. sugar
1 t. baking soda
Pinch salt
1 egg
1 No. 303 can fruit cocktail, drained
1 t. vanilla

Mix flour, sugar, soda, salt, and egg in mixing bowl. Add 1 cup drained fruit cocktail. Pour into ungreased 9″ square pan. Mix brown sugar and nuts together and sprinkle over top. Bake at 350°F. for 45 minutes. Serve with whipped cream or ice cream.

Topping:
1 c. brown sugar
½ c. chopped nuts

This recipe submitted by the following teachers:
Mrs. Madra Fischer, Mendota H. S.
Mendota, Illinois
Mrs. Sally Bicker, Knoch H. S.
Saxonburg, Pennsylvania
Mrs. Less Feichtinger, Minnetonka H. S.
Excelsior, Minnesota

FRUIT COCKTAIL CAKE
Number of Servings — 12 to 15

1¾ c. sugar
2 c. flour
2 t. soda
1 No. 2 can fruit cocktail
¼ c. brown sugar
½ c. coconut

Mix sugar, flour, soda, and fruit cocktail. Pour into 8x14x1½ greased and floured loaf pan. Sprinkle brown sugar and coconut over top. Bake at 325°F. until done. Cake will spring back when touched.

Icing:
1 c. sugar
1 stick margarine
1 c. evaporated milk
½ c. chopped pecans
½ c. coconut
1 t. vanilla

Mix and cook until slightly thick the sugar, margarine and evaporated milk. Remove from burner. Add pecans, coconut, and vanilla. Spread on cake while still warm. Serve directly from pan.

Mrs. Lynn Mathews, Centerville H. S.
Centerville, Texas

FRUIT COCKTAIL CAKE
Number of Servings — 15

2 eggs
1½ c. sugar
2 c. flour (plain)
2 t. soda
¼ t. salt
1 No. 2 can fruit cocktail (juice and fruit)
1 t. vanilla

Beat eggs. Add sugar and beat about 5 minutes. Add sifted dry ingredients to egg and sugar mixture. Add fruit cocktail and mix. Bake in 2 wax paper lined pans in moderate oven 350°F. 30 minutes.

Icing:
1 small can evaporated milk
⅔ c. sugar
1 stick oleo
½ t. vanilla
½ c. coconut
¼ c. nuts (if desired)

Mix milk, sugar and oleo. Cook in saucepan until thick. Add vanilla, nuts and coconut.

Mrs. Ivadine G. Blevins, Ider H. S.
Ider, Alabama

FRUIT COCKTAIL CAKE
Number of Servings — 12

2 c. flour
1½ c. sugar
2 t. soda
¼ t. salt
1 No. 303 can fruit cocktail
2 eggs
¼ c. brown sugar
½ c. nuts

Sift together flour, sugar, salt, and soda. Add fruit cocktail, and eggs. Mix well. Pour into two 8″ cake pans or one loaf pan. Sprinkle with nuts and brown sugar. Bake at 350°F. for 25 minutes. Spread with German Chocolate Cake icing.

Marie H. Welch
Oak Grove, Louisiana

FRUIT COCKTAIL CAKE AND ICING
Number of Servings — 18

2 c. sifted all-purpose flour
1½ c. sugar
1 No. 303 can fruit cocktail
2 t. soda
1 t. vanilla

Mix all ingredients together and pour into an ungreased 9x13 loaf pan. Sprinkle the top with 1 cup brown sugar and ½ cup chopped pecans. Bake at 425°F. about 30 minutes.

Icing:
½ c. oleo
½ c. sugar
⅔ c. evaporated milk
1 can angle flake coconut
1 t. vanilla

In a saucepan bring the oleo, sugar, evaporated milk, and coconut to a boil and let it boil 5 minutes, stirring constantly. Remove from heat, add vanilla, and pour on hot cake.

Mrs. Mary Jane Wilson, Woodland Jr. H. S.
Fayetteville, Arkansas

GUMDROP CAKE

Number of Servings — 24

½ c. butter
1 c. sugar
2 eggs, beaten
2¼ c. sifted flour
¼ t. salt
2 t. baking powder
1 t. vanilla
¼ c. milk
¾ c. raisins
1 lb. gumdrops (black ones removed) chopped fine

Cream butter, while adding sugar and beaten eggs. Sift flour, salt, and baking powder together over chopped candy and raisins. Dredge well. Add vanilla to milk and add flour mixture and milk alternately to first mixture. Bake in a large greased loaf tin in a slow oven 275 to 300°F. 1½ hours.

Ardery Peery, Keota H. S.
Keota, Oklahoma

GUMDROP CAKE

1 can sweetened condensed milk
½ lb. shredded coconut
1 lb. dates (chopped)
10 lge. red gumdrops (chopped)
10 lge. green gumdrops (chopped)
2 c. pecans, cut
1 slice each of green, red, and white candied pineapple, cut

Mix thoroughly with hands and pack tightly in bread pan lined with greased brown paper. Bake about 1 hour at 275°F. Keeps for a year if wrapped in foil and stored in refrigerator.

Myrtle B. Sellie, Ellis Jr. H. S.
Austin, Minnesota

ORANGE CANDY SLICE CAKE

2 sticks butter
2 c. sugar
4 eggs
1½ c. buttermilk
1 t. soda
¼ t. salt
4 c. flour
1 lb. dates, chopped
1 lb. orange jelly candy slice (halved)
2 c. mixed nuts, chopped

Cream the butter and sugar. Add eggs one at a time, beating well. Add 1 cup buttermilk. Beat well. Add soda to the other half cup buttermilk. Add to mixture. Combine dry ingredients, add orange slices (halved). Add dates and nuts, blend. Line tube pan with well greased brown paper. Bake slowly 2½ hours at 275°F.

To Ice:

1 small can frozen orange concentrate (thawed). Add ½ cup light brown sugar. Let stand while cake bakes. Pour on cake while hot. Let cake cool in pan before removing.

Mrs. Dorothy A. Foster, Mathews H. S.
Mathews, Virginia

BLACKBERRY JAM CAKE (Layer)

2 c. sifted all-purpose flour
1 t. baking powder
⅛ t. salt
1 t. each cinnamon, allspice, cloves, nutmeg, ginger
½ c. shortening
1 c. sugar
3 eggs
2 c. jam (blackberry)
½ c. milk
1 c. raisins

Sift all dry ingredients together. Cream shortening and sugar. Add eggs one at a time, beating well. Add milk and flour mixture alternately. Fold in jam and floured raisins. Bake in greased and floured 8″ or 9″ layer pans 25-30 minutes at 350°F.

Joyce M. Asbury, Fleming County H. S.
Flemingsburg, Kentucky

JAM CAKE (Layer)

¾ c. shortening
1 c. sugar
3 eggs
1 c. strawberry or blackberry jam
2 c. sifted all-purpose flour
1 t. soda
1 t. salt
1 t. nutmeg
3 t. cinnamon
1 c. buttermilk or sour milk

Combine shortening, sugar, and eggs. Add jam and mix well. Stir in sifted dry ingredients alternately with milk. Pour into greased and lightly floured 9x13 oblong pan or two 9″ layers, or muffin tins. Bake in moderate oven 350°F. for 30 to 40 minutes or until done. Cool. Frost with a cooked fluffy white frosting. Spread thin layer of jam between layers and on top before spreading with frosting.

Dorothy Petty, Calhoun H. S.
Port Lavaca, Texas

BLACKBERRY CAKE (Layer)

Number of Servings — 20

1 c. shortening
2 c. sugar
2 eggs
3½ c. flour
1 t. cinnamon
½ t. cloves
2 t. soda
2 c. blackberries (juice and berries)
Nuts and raisins if desired

Blend shortening and sugar and add well beaten eggs. Blend cinnamon, cloves, and flour. Put the soda in the blackberries and add to the mixture, alternately with the flour mixture. Add nuts and raisins if desired. Bake in two 9″ layer pans, in a 325°F. oven for 45 minutes or until done. Frost with favorite frosting.

Mrs. Jane Thurman, Henry County H. S.
New Castle, Kentucky

JAM CAKE

1½ c. sugar
2½ c. flour
1 c. buttermilk
4 eggs
1 t. soda
¾ c. margarine or butter
1 c. blackberry jam
1 t. cinnamon
1 t. cloves
1 t. nutmeg

Cream sugar and shortening. Add beaten eggs. Sift together the flour, cinnamon, cloves, and nutmeg. Add soda to milk. Add flour and milk alternately to creamed mixture. Add jam. Bake in 2 layers 25 to 30 minutes in 350°F. oven.

Filling:
3 c. sugar
1 c. water
1 c. coconut
1 c. chopped nuts
Juice from 2 oranges
1 T. grated orange rind
1 c. raisins
12 marshmallows

Cook sugar and water together until mixture spins a thread. Add remaining ingredients. Cook mixture until it begins to thicken. Spread on bottom and top layers.

Mrs. Doris Beville, Walker Jr. H. S.
Bradenton, Florida

JAM CAKE (Layer)

Number of Servings — 20

1½ c. butter
2 c. sugar
6 eggs
1 c. buttermilk
3 c. flour
1 t. soda
4 t. spices (cloves and cinnamon)
1 c. raisins (ground)
1 c. pecans (ground)
1 c. coconut (ground)
1 c. blackberry jam

Cream butter and sugar and add well beaten eggs. Add milk and dry ingredients alternately. Add remaining ingredients and mix thoroughly. Bake in very thin layers, preferably in an iron skillet at 300°F.

Filling:
3 c. sugar
1 t. soda
1 c. buttermilk
1 c. butter
1 c. pecans (chopped)
2 t. vanilla
½ c. raisins (ground)
½ c. blackberry jam (ground)
½ c. coconut (ground)

Mix all ingredients and cook until thick. Stir to keep from burning. Put plenty of filling between each layer and decorate as desired.

Macie H. Drake, J. B. Pennington H. S.
Blountsville, Alabama

JAM CAKE (Caramel Filling)

Number of Servings — 16-20

1 c. butter or margarine
2 c. sugar
4 eggs
3½ c. flour
1 T. each cloves, cinnamon, allspice, and cocoa
1 c. buttermilk
1 t. soda
1 T. vanilla
1 c. jam (strawberry is best)
½ c. wine (blackberry)

Cream shortening and sugar, add eggs one at a time. Sift spices with flour and add alternately with milk that has soda dissolved in it. Add vanilla, jam, and wine. Bake in moderate oven, 350°F. in three 9½ or 10″ pans. When cool frost with caramel or favorite filling.

Caramel Filling:
1 c. sugar browned with large cut of butter
3 c. sugar
1 c. milk
½ lb. butter

Cook the 3 cups sugar, milk, and butter together until slightly thickened. Then add caramel while both are boiling. Cook until it forms a soft ball in cold water.

Mrs. Sue C. Batchelor, Palmetto H. S.
Reform, Alabama

BLACKBERRY CAKE (Layer)

2 c. sugar
1 c. butter
6 eggs, separated
2 t. allspice
2 t. cinnamon
2 t. cloves
2 t. nutmeg
½ c. sour cream or buttermilk
2 t. soda
1½ c. blackberry jam
3 c. flour

Cream butter, add sugar gradually, cream together until light and fluffy. Add unbeaten egg yolks one at a time beating thoroughly after each addition. Add allspice, cinnamon, cloves, and nutmeg. mix thoroughly. Add sour cream or buttermilk into which soda has been dissolved. Mix thoroughly. Add blackberry jam and flour. Mix thoroughly. Then fold in the well beaten whites of eggs. Pour into four 8″ or 9. layer pans. Bake at 350°F. for 30-35 minutes. Ice cake with 7-minute icing. A lemon frosting may be used. Blackberry jelly or nuts may be placed between layers of cake. Black walnuts and Blackberry jelly are especially good when using 7-minute icing.

Helen Doris Stephens, Rabun County H. S.
Clayton, Georgia

JAM CAKE (Layer)

2 c. sugar
1 c. butter or margarine
5 eggs, separated
1½ c. jam
1 c. buttermilk

(Continued on Next Page)

3 c. flour, sifted
1 t. soda
1 t. baking powder
1 t. allspice
1 t. cinnamon
1 t. nutmeg
1 T. cocoa
1 c. nuts
¼ c. citron
1 c. raisins

Cream butter, add sugar and cream until light and fluffy. Add egg yolks and beat well. Sift together dry ingredients then take out some to dredge nuts and raisins. Add jam to creamed mixture and beat thoroughly. Add buttermilk and flour mixture alternately. Add fruit and nut mixture. Fold in stiffly beaten egg whites last. Turn batter into three 9" layer pans that have been greased and lined with wax paper. Bake for 35 minutes at 325°F. Cover with caramel icing.

Wilma C. House, London H. S.
London, Kentucky

JAM CAKE (Loaf)

1 c. butter
2 whole eggs
1 t. soda
1 t. each cinnamon, cloves, nutmeg
1 t. vanilla
2 c. sugar
1 c. buttermilk
4 c. flour
2 c. blackberry jam
1 c. nuts

Cream butter and sugar. Add eggs and beat until fluffy. Add soda to milk and add to mixture alternately with flour. Add spices to flour before sifting. Use small amount of flour to coat nuts. Add jam, nuts and vanilla. Bake in mold 1 hour at 325°F. Use caramel frosting if desired.

Mrs. Elizabeth Spillman, Madison H. S.
Richmond, Kentucky

BLACKBERRY JAM LOAF CAKE

1¼ c. flour, sifted
¾ c. sugar
½ t. baking soda
¼ t. salt
½ c. butter or shortening
2 eggs
1 c. blackberry jam with seeds
¼ c. buttermilk
½ c. chopped pecans
½ c. seedless raisins
Optional: 1 t. allspice, 1 t. nutmeg, 1 t. cinnamon
  (add with other dry ingredients)

Place flour, sugar, baking soda, salt, butter, eggs, and jam in mixing bowl. Mix until well blended. Add buttermilk, blend in thoroughly. Add pecans and raisins, stir in with a spoon. Pour into a lightly greased and floured loaf pan. Bake in 350°F. oven 1 hour and 20 minutes or until done when tested with toothpick. Cool five minutes before removing from pan.

Sula Mae Majure, Tchula H. S.
Tchula, Mississippi

JAM CAKE

Number of Servings — 20

1 c. sugar
½ c. butter
3 eggs
3 T. sour milk
1 t. soda
1 c. jam or jelly
1 t. each nutmeg, cloves, allspice
2 t. cinnamon
2 c. flour

Cream butter and sugar then add other ingredients and mix well. Bake in either a loaf or two layers. Use caramel filling. Delicious served with applesauce.

Mrs. Mark Strawn, Lyerly Jr. H. S.
Lyerly, Georgia

JAM CAKE (Loaf)

1 c. shortening or 2 sticks oleo
1 c. sugar
1 c. jam
5 eggs
½ c. buttermilk
1 t. soda
2½ c. flour
½ t. salt
1 t. cinnamon
1 t. nutmeg
1 t. allspice
1 c. raisins
1 c. fruit cake mix or crystallized cherries
1 c. pecans

Beat egg whites stiff. Save 1 cup flour to dredge fruit. Add soda to buttermilk. Cream shortening and sugar and add jam. Add beaten egg yolks and add 1½ cups flour and spices alternately with buttermilk and soda. Fold in egg whites and add floured fruit. Bake in 325°F. oven for 30 minutes. Reduce heat to 225°F. and bake 2 hours or until done.

Willie B. Matthews, Stevenson H. S.
Stevenson, Alabama

JAM CAKE (Layer)

Number of Servings — 4 Layers

2 c. sugar
1 c. butter
4 eggs
1 t. cloves
1 t. cinnamon
1 t. nutmeg
1 t. allspice
3 c. flour
1 t. soda
1 c. buttermilk
1 c. strawberry preserves
1 c. chopped nuts

Cream sugar and butter together. Add beaten eggs. Beat well. Sift spices with flour, add soda. Add flour mixture and milk alternately. Add preserves and nuts. Bake in prepared pans (4) for 30 minutes in 350°F. oven. Make cream filling with nuts.

Imogene Shofner, Crawford H. S.
Crawford, Texas

LEMON CHEESE CAKE
Number of Servings — 20
¾ c. butter
2 c. sugar
1 c. milk
3½ c. flour
3½ t. baking powder
1 t. lemon extract
6 egg whites
Cream butter, add sugar gradually. Sift together flour and baking powder three times and add to butter alternately with milk and flavoring. Fold in beaten egg whites. Bake in layers at 375°F. for 35 minutes.

Filling:
6 egg yolks
1 c. sugar
1 c. butter
Juice and rind of 3 lemons
Mix all ingredients and cook in double boiler until thick.

Mrs. Maude Pruitt, Dadeville H. S.
Dadeville, Alabama

EASY LEMON CAKE
Number of Servings — 15
2 c. sugar
1 c. butter or 1¼ sticks whipped oleo
¼ t. salt
3 c. sifted cake flour
3 t. baking powder
4 eggs
1 c. milk
Cream butter and sugar, add 1 egg at a time and beat one minute. Add sifted dry ingredients alternately with milk. Bake at 350°F. Three layers. Grate 2 lemons (juice and rind). Add 1 cup sugar and stir until sugar is dissolved. When cake is baked, spoon on this mixture while cake is hot. use 7-minute frosting to stack cake.

Mrs. Eunice S. Tate, Malvern Sr. H. S.
Malvern, Arkansas

LEMON EXTRACT CAKE
1 lb. butter (not margarine)
2½ c. sugar
6 eggs
3 oz. lemon extract
3½ c. sifted flour (all-purpose)
1½ t. baking powder
½ t. salt
½ lb. candied cherries, chopped
2 slices candied pineapple, chopped
¾ c. golden raisins
4 c. pecans, chopped
½ c. flour
Cream together butter and sugar. Add eggs. Blend until well mixed then add lemon extract. Mix well. Add the 3½ c. flour, baking powder, and salt which have been sifted together. Blend all together. Fold in the fruits, nuts, and ½ cup flour which have been mixed together (preferably the night before). Bake in 2 greased and floured loaf pans in a 300°F. oven for 1½ to 2 hours.

Mrs. Mary Jo King
Mize, Mississippi

LEMON GOLD CAKE
2 Layer Cake
2½ c. cake flour
2½ t. baking powder
½ t. salt
½ c. shortening or butter
1 T. grated lemon rind
1¾ c. sugar
6 egg yolks, unbeaten
1 c. plus 3 T. milk
Preheat oven to 350°F. Grease and flour two 9″ round layer pans. Combine flour, baking powder, and salt. Sift together 3 times. Cream shortening and lemon rind together. Add sugar gradually, creaming until fluffy. Beat in egg yolks one at a time. Add flour alternately with milk. Beat after each addition until smooth. Bake in two layers at 350°F. for 30 to 35 minutes. Frost with any lemon flavored frosting or a 7-minute white frosting.

Mrs. Peggy S. Jackson, Fairforest H. S.
Fairforest, South Carolina

LEMON PECAN CAKE
Number of Servings — 30
1 lb. oleo
1 lb. brown sugar
6 whole eggs
4 c. flour
2 t. baking powder
1 lb. pecans
1 lb. candied cherries
1 lb. candied pineapple
2 oz. lemon extract (pure)
Cream oleo and brown sugar together. Add remaining ingredients in the order listed and mix thoroughly. Bake in a large angel food cake pan at 275°F. over a pan of water for 2 hours or until done when tested with a toothpick.

Dolphia Dawson Dies, Hamlin Jr. H. S.
Corpus Christi, Texas

LEMON PINEAPPLE CAKE
2 c. sugar
1 c. shortening or oil
8 egg whites
3 c. flour
2 t. baking powder
1 c. milk
1 t. vanilla
Cream shortening and sugar. Sift flour and baking powder. Add flour and milk alternately. Add well beaten egg whites and vanilla. Pour in 8″ cake pans and bake at 350°F.
Filling:
8 egg yolks
1 c. sugar
Juice of 2 lemons
1 tall can crushed pineapple
1 T. oleo
2 T. flour
Grated rind of 1 lemon
(Lemon flavoring may be substituted for rind)
Mix, cook over low heat until thick enough to spread.

Mrs. R. S. Clark, Troup H. S.
La Grange, Georgia

LEMON LOAF CAKE

Number of Servings — 10-12

1 c. butter
1¾ c. sugar
5 eggs
2 c. sifted cake flour
1 T. lemon extract

Cream butter and sugar thoroughly. Add eggs one at a time and blend thoroughly after each addition. Add flour gradually and then extract. Bake in a 10" tube cake pan for approximately 1 hour at 325°F.

Willie Hawkins, Lovelady H. S.
Lovelady, Texas

BLACK WALNUT CAKE

½ c. shortening
1 c. sugar
1 t. vanilla
2 c. sifted cake flour
2 t. baking powder
½ t. salt
⅔ c. milk
4 egg whites
⅓ c. sugar
1 c. minced black walnut meats
Chopped nuts

Cream shortening well, add 1 cup sugar, beating until light and fluffy. Add vanilla. Then sift in dry ingredients alternately with milk, beating until smooth. Beat egg whites until foamy, add ⅓ cup sugar gradually, continuing to beat until stiff but not dry. Fold into batter. Add 1 cup minced nuts. Pour into two square 8" pans. Bake 375°F. for about 25 minutes. Spread frosting between layers and on top and sides of cake. Sprinkle with chopped nuts. (English walnuts may be substituted.)

Mrs. Mildred Frazier, Sullivan County School
Sonestown, Pennsylvania

HICKORY NUT CAKE

Number of Servings — 10

1½ c. sugar
½ c. shortening
1 c. milk
2 c. sifted flour
2 t. baking powder
½ t. nutmeg
¼ t. salt
1 c. nut meats (chopped fine)
3 egg whites

Mix sugar, fat, and milk. Add sifted flour and other ingredients (alternate dry with milk). Add nut meats. Fold in beaten egg whites. Bake in moderate oven in two layer cake pans.

Creamy Nut Filling and Frosting:
2½ T. flour
½ c. milk
½ c. butter
½ c. sugar
Pinch of salt
½ t. vanilla
½ c. chopped nut meats
1 c. powdered sugar

Blend flour and milk. Cook over low heat to a very thick paste (about 10 minutes) stirring constantly. Cool to lukewarm. Meanwhile, cream butter with sugar, add pinch of salt. Beat with egg beater until fluffy. Fold in vanilla and chopped nut meats. Use about ⅓ of this for the filling between the layers. To the remainder blend in powdered sugar (a small amount at a time). Spread on top and sides of cake.

Fern Todd, Bloomington H. S.
Bloomington, Wisconsin

HICKORY NUT CAKE

3 c. flour (sifted)
½ t. salt
2 c. sugar
1 t. vanilla
3 t. baking powder
⅔ c. butter
1 c. milk
5 egg whites (beaten stiff)
1½ c. hickory nuts

To flour, add baking powder and salt and sift together three times. Cream butter thoroughly. Add sugar gradually and cream together until light and fluffy. Add flour mixture, alternately with milk, a small amount at a time. Beat after each addition until smooth. Add vanilla, fold in eggs and nut kernels. Bake in 3 layers at 350°F.

Fay Harper, Bell County H. S.
Pineville, Kentucky

TOASTED BUTTER PECAN CAKE AND FROSTING

Number of Servings — 16-18

1⅓ c. pecans (chopped)
1¼ c. butter
3 c. sifted enriched flour
2 t. baking powder
½ t. salt
2 c. sugar
4 unbeaten eggs
1 c. milk
2 t. vanilla extract

Toast pecans in ¼ cup butter for 20-25 minutes at 350°F. Sift flour, baking powder, and salt. Cream 1 cup butter, gradually add sugar, creaming well. Blend in eggs, beating after each addition. Add dry ingredients, alternately with milk. Add vanilla and pecans. Bake at 350°F. for 20-30 minutes. Makes 3 layers.

Frosting:
¼ c. butter
1 lb. powdered sugar
1 t. vanilla
4-6 T. cream
⅔ c. pecans

Cream butter, powdered sugar and vanilla. Add cream. Add pecans. Will frost a 3 layer cake.

This recipe submitted by the following teachers:
Mrs. Mazie M. Rogers,
Seminary Attendance Center
Seminary, Mississippi
Mrs. Ione G. Straud, El Paso H. S.
El Paso, Texas

NUT CAKE (Pecans)
Number of Servings — 12

½ lb. butter (1 c.)
1 lb. sugar (2 c.)
6 eggs
½ lb. candied cherries
½ lb. candied pineapple
1 box seeded white raisins
1 qt. pecans
1 lb. flour (4 c.)
1 t. baking powder
Pinch of salt
¾ c. sweet milk
1 t. vanilla

Cream butter and add sugar and eggs. Flour fruits and nuts, add remainder of flour, baking powder and salt (sifted together). Add milk and vanilla. Pour in a large tube cake pan greased and lined with wax paper. Bake at 275°F. about 2 hours.

Mrs. Rodney A. Russell, John de la Howe School
McCormick, South Carolina

PECAN CAKE
Number of Servings — 4 x 9 Loaf Pan

½ lb. butter
2 c. white sugar
6 eggs
1 t. nutmeg
1 t. baking powder
¼ t. soda
1 c. liquid
4 c. flour
2 lb. pecans
1 lb. golden raisins

Cream butter and sugar. Add eggs one at a time. Mix in liquid, spices, and ½ of flour alternately. Mix remaining flour with pecans and raisins and add to cake batter. Line pan with wax paper. Bake at 250°F. for 3 hours.

Roberta Sims, Shepherdsville H. S.
Shepherdsville, Kentucky

HARVEST PECAN CAKE

2 c. butter or margarine
4½ c. sifted flour
¼ t. salt
1 t. baking powder
6 eggs
1 lb. brown sugar
½ c. milk
1 t. vanilla
3 T. instant coffee dissolved in 3 T. hot water
4 c. chopped pecans

Set out butter to soften. Sift together flour, salt, baking powder. Grease bottom of 10″ tube pan. Separate eggs, beat yolks well, beat egg whites until stiff. In large mixing bowl, cream together butter and brown sugar. Add beaten egg yolks, mixing well. Combine milk, vanilla, dissolved coffee. Add alternately with dry ingredients. Fold in pecans and egg whites. Bake at 325°F. 1½ hours. Let cool in pan on cake rack. Remove from pan. Serve plain, with a dessert sauce, or whipped cream.

Bettye Antwine, Midway H. S.
Henrietta, Texas

FRANKLIN PECAN CAKE
Number of Servings — 16

½ lb. butter
2 c. sugar
6 eggs
4 c. flour
1 t. baking powder
¼ t. salt
½ lb. candied cherries
½ lb. candied pineapple
1 lb. pecans
2 t. vanilla

Cream butter and sugar. Add beaten eggs. Add 3 cups of the flour, which has been sifted with the baking powder and salt. Mix remaining flour with cherries, pineapple and the broken pecans. Stir this mixture into the batter. Add vanilla. Pour into a greased tube pan. Bake at 250°F. for 3 hours. Allow cake to cool in pan.

This recipe submitted by the following teachers:
Dudley Magee, Mt. Hermon H. S.
Mt. Hermon, Louisiana
Mrs. Ethel McCardle, Hazlehurst H. S.
Hazlehurst, Mississippi

TEXAS PECAN CAKE

2 c. butter
2 c. sugar
6 well beaten eggs
1 T. lemon extract
4 c. sifted flour
1½ t. baking powder
2 c. white raisins
4 c. whole pecans

Cream butter and sugar, add the well beaten eggs and lemon extract and blend. Sift dry ingredients together and combine with raisins and pecans. Add to creamed mixture and blend thoroughly. Pour in a well greased and floured tube pan. Bake 2 hours at 275°F.

This recipe submitted by the following teachers:
Rita Dickinson, Melrose H. S.
Melrose, New Mexico
Mrs. Dorothy Chapman, Irwin County H. S.
Ocilla, Georgia

TEXAS PECAN CAKE
Number of Servings — 12 to 15

1 lb. butter
1 lb. brown sugar
1 lb. pecans
½ lb. glace′ cherries
½ lb. glace′ pineapple
4 c. flour
6 egg yolks
6 egg whites (beaten)
1 t. baking powder
1½ oz. pure lemon extract

Cream butter, then butter and sugar, add egg yolks one at a time alternately with 2 cups flour and baking powder. Beat well after each addition. Use other 2 cups flour to dredge fruits and nuts. Add lemon extract. Fold in egg whites, fruits and

(Continued on Next Page)

nuts. Let stand over night in refrigerator. Next morning put into large angel food pan or 2 loaf pans. Bake slowly 3 hours or over 225°F. Cool. Wrap well in wax paper or foil and store in air tight container. If cake seems dry to your taste use the following sauce poured over cake while warm.

1 c. orange juice
2 c. sugar
2 t. orange peel

Edna Ruth Strickland, Heavener School
Heavener, Oklahoma

OATMEAL CAKE AND TOPPING
Number of Servings — 8
1½ c. boiling water
1 c. quick-cooking oats
½ c. salad oil or ½ c. oleo or shortening
1½ c. flour
1 t. cinnamon
1 t. soda
½ t. salt
1 c. brown sugar
1 c. white sugar
2 eggs

Pour boiling water over oats. Let stand while preparing the following: Sift together flour, cinnamon, soda, and salt, add to sugar, eggs, and oil, then add oatmeal. Mix well, bake at 350°F. for 30 or 40 minutes or until done.

Topping:
1 stick butter or margarine
1 c. brown sugar
½ c. evaporated milk or plain milk
½ c. chopped nuts (pecans)
1 t. vanilla
1 can coconut

Dissolve thoroughly the sugar and milk, add butter and cook. Stir almost constantly, until mixture boils and becomes thick. Take from heat, add vanilla, nuts, and coconut. Pour on cake while hot.

This recipe submitted by the following teachers:
Julia Ann Shumaker, Francis Hammond H. S.
Alexandria, Virginia
Beverly J. Byrne, Fowler H. S.
Fowler, Colorado
Mrs. Anne McCord, Kilgore H. S.
Kilgore, Texas
Mrs. Sue Kennon, Bartow Senior H. S.
Bartow, Florida
Joy T. Limbaugh, Childersburg H. S.
Childersburg, Alabama

OATMEAL CAKE AND TOPPING
Number of Servings — 12
1 c. 3-minute oatmeal
1½ c. boiling water
½ c. butter, shortening or cooking oil
1 c. firmly packed brown sugar
1 c. white sugar
2 eggs
1⅛ c. flour
1 t. cinnamon
1 t. soda

½ t. salt
(½ t. nutmeg may be added if desired)
1 t. vanilla

Pour boiling water over oatmeal and set aside. Cream shortening and sugars until fluffy. Add eggs one at a time beating well. Add oatmeal-water mixture, Sift dry ingredients together and add beating well. Bake in well greased and floured loaf or tube pan at 350°F. 30 to 35 minutes.

Topping for Oatmeal Cake:
(Many variations may be used)
1 stick oleo or butter
½ c. brown sugar
½ c. milk, or cream, or evaporated milk
1 c. coconut
½ c. chopped nuts

Melt oleo, add sugar and milk, bring to boil. Cook slightly. Add nuts and coconut. Pour on top of hot cake and place in broiler until topping is bubbly.

This recipe submitted by the following teachers:
Mrs. Maurice Silk, Cooper H. S.
Abilene, Texas
Mrs. Gary Hilker, Holbrook H. S.
Holbrook, Nebraska
Mrs. Wilma L. Greenway, Flat H. S.
Flat, Texas
Lois Hieronymus, Clinton H. S.
Clinton, Illinois
Mrs. Kate S. Berry, Latta H. S.
Latta, South Carolina
Mrs. Hazel M. Brown, McAdoo H. S.
McAdoo, Texas

OATMEAL CHOCOLATE CAKE
1 c. oatmeal
1½ c. boiling water
½ c. shortening
1½ c. sugar
2 eggs
1 c. sifted flour
½ c. cocoa
1 t. soda
1 t. vanilla
½ t. salt

Mix oatmeal with boiling water, let stand until cool. Cream shortening with sugar and eggs. Add oatmeal mixture with flour, cocoa, soda, salt, and vanilla. Beat until smooth. Bake in 8x12 pans at 350°F. for 35 minutes.

Lillian R. Congdon, Winter Haven H. S.
Winter Haven, Florida

OATMEAL CAKE WITH TOPPING
Number of Servings — 20
Place in mixing bowl:
1¼ c. boiling water
1 c. quick-cooking oats
1 stick oleo
Cover and let stand 20 minutes.
Add:
1 c. white sugar
1 c. brown sugar

(Continued on Next Page)

2 eggs
1½ c. sifted flour
1 t. soda
1 t. cinnamon
1 t. salt

Mix well and bake in oblong pan. 350°F. oven, 35 minutes.

Topping:
2 T. oleo
¼ c. evaporated milk
½ c. sugar
½ c. coconut
½ t. vanilla
½ c. chopped nuts

Spread on cake while it is still hot. (If desired, return to oven for 2 minutes, or place under broiler until bubbly.)

This recipe submitted by the following teachers:
Keren Payne, Canton H. S.
Canton, Oklahoma
Sister M. Josella, O.S.F., Bishop Luers H. S.
Fort Wayne, Indiana
Pauline Arnold, Albin H. S.
Albin, Wyoming
Grace Montgomery, Twisp H. S.
Twisp, Washington
Mrs. J. E. Proctor, Dilley H. S.
Dilley, Texas
Jean Cline, Rowan County H. S.
Morehead, Kentucky

ORANGE CAKE

Number of Servings — 20

1 c. sugar
½ c. butter or oleo
1 egg
1 c. buttermilk
1 t. soda
½ t. salt
2 c. flour
Rind of 1 orange, ground
1 c. raisins
½ c. nut meats, chopped
Juice of 1 orange plus 2 t. sugar

Cream sugar and butter. Add beaten egg and buttermilk. Mix a small amount of dry ingredients with orange rind, raisins and nut meats. Add dry ingredients and then the fruit and nut mixture. Bake in a 11x7 greased cake pan at 350°F. for 35 to 40 minutes. Five minutes after cake comes from the oven, spoon orange juice over cake. Frost cake.

Frosting for Orange Cake:
1 T. butter
1½ T. brown sugar
Sprinkle of salt
Cook a few minutes, then add:
2 T. cream
¾ c. powdered sugar
Until right consistency to spread on cake.

Mrs. Irma B. Morley, Senior High
Allegan, Michigan

OATMEAL CAKE AND TOPPING

Number of Servings — 10

1 c. quick oatmeal soaked in 1¼ c. boiling water for 20 minutes
1 c. granulated sugar
1 c. brown sugar
1 c. shortening
2 eggs, beaten
1⅓ c. flour (1½ c. may be used)
1 t. vanilla
1 t. soda
1 t. baking powder
1 t. cinnamon
½ t. salt

Mix sugar and add to the shortening. Cream. Add eggs beating after addition. Add oatmeal to the creamed mixture. Sift dry ingredients, flour, soda, baking powder, cinnamon, and salt. Stir to mingle the ingredients. Add vanilla. Bake in a baking pan greased lightly and floured. Bake about 35 minutes in a 350°F. oven. Add topping.

Topping:
1 c. brown sugar
4 T. butter or margarine
1 c. coconut
⅓ c. cream or milk
½ c. nuts, chopped

Cream sugar with margarine. Add coconut. Moisten with the cream. Spread nuts on top of the cake after it is done. Put under broiler and broil until the topping bubbles up and spreads over the top of the cake.

This recipe submitted by the following teachers:
Mrs. Zelota M. Yates, Needham Broughton H. S.
Raleigh, North Carolina
Ruby Akers, McDowell H. S.
McDowell, Kentucky
Donnalie Stratton, Johns Creek School
Pikeville, Kentucky
Mrs. W. R. Meade, Jr., Paintsville H. S.
Paintsville, Kentucky
Mrs. Irene Allen, Wall H. S.
Wall, Texas
Mrs. Estelle B. Nickell, Morgan County H. S.
West Liberty, Kentucky

GLAZED ORANGE CAKE

Number of Servings — 14-16

1 c. butter
2 c. sugar
½ t. vanilla
2 T. grated orange rind
5 eggs
3 c. cake flour
1 T. baking powder
¼ t. salt
¾ c. milk

Grease and flour 10″ tube pan. Cream butter and sugar until light. Add vanilla, orange rind and eggs, one at a time, beating after each. Sift flour, baking powder and salt. Add alternately with milk, beginning and ending with flour. Beat well after each addition. Spoon into greased tube

(Continued on Next Page)

pan and bake at 350°F. for about 1 hour. Cool cake for 2 minutes after removing from oven and pour glaze over cake in pan.

Glaze:
¼ c. butter
⅔ c. sugar
⅓ c. orange juice

Heat ingredients for glaze until the sugar is dissolved. Allow cake to thoroughly cool in the pan.

Mrs. Louise H. Little, Edison H. S.
Edison, New Jersey

FRESH ORANGE CAKE

2½ c. sifted cake flour
2¼ t. baking powder
¼ t. salt
½ c. butter or margarine
½ t. vanilla
⅓ c. fresh ground orange, pulp and peel
1½ c. sugar
2 eggs, slightly beaten
⅔ c. milk

Grease and flour two 8" cake pans. Sift together dry ingredients. Work butter until creamy. Stir in vanilla and orange. Add sugar gradually, then beat until fluffy. Add eggs, one at a time, beating after each. Add stifted dry ingredients by thirds, alternately with milk. Beat only enough to blend thoroughly. Pour into pans and bake at 350°F. 35 to 40 minutes. Frost with a clear orange filling or spread a clear orange filling between layers, and ice with a 7-minute frosting.

Elaine Simnacher, Silverton H. S.
Silverton, Texas

ORANGE CAKE

Number of Servings — 15

½ c. butter
1 c. sugar
2 eggs, well beaten
¾ t. soda
¾ t. baking powder
2 c. flour
½ c. milk
1 c. ground raisins
Nuts if desired
Rind of 1 orange

Cream butter and sugar. Add eggs well beaten. Sift dry ingredients together and add alternately with milk. If raisins and nuts are used add ¼ cup of your flour to them and add at this time. Stir in grated orange peel. Bake in an angel food cake pan at 300°F. usually about 45 minutes. While still hot and in pan pour over it the juice of 1 orange and 1 cup of sugar well mixed.

Nana E. James, Southeastern H. S.
Hammond, Louisiana

ORANGE BISHOP CAKE

Number of Servings — 15

5 eggs
2 sticks butter
2 c. flour
2 c. sugar
1 T. orange juice
1 t. vanilla

Cream 2 sticks of butter well. Add sugar slowly creaming well. Add eggs one at a time beating well after each addition. Add orange juice. Sift flour three times. Stir in with mixer at low speed. Pour into a greased 10" tube pan. Cook for 1 hour and 15 minutes at 350°F. While cake is still in pan pour over the mixture of sugar and orange juice.

Filling:
½ c. sugar
¾ c. orange juice

Mrs. Mary George Elliott, Walnut H. S.
Walnut, Mississippi

ORANGE CAKE

Number of Servings — 12

1 c. shortening
2 c. sugar
4 eggs
1 T. grated orange rind
1 c. buttermilk
1 t. soda
3 c. flour

Cream shortening and sugar. Add eggs one at a time, beating after each addition. Add orange rind. Mix soda in milk and add alternately with flour. Bake in loaf or tube pan at 350°F. until well done.

Topping:
1½ c. sugar
1 c. orange juice
1 T. grated orange rind

Mix ingredients and dribble over cake while the cake is hot. Pierce the surface of the cake with a fork while dribbling the topping so it will soak into the cake.

Mrs. Frances Hicks, Utopia H. S.
Utopia, Texas

FRENCH ORANGE CAKE

Number of Servings — 24

½ lb. dates
½ c. hot water
1 t. soda
½ c. shortening
1 c. sugar
1 egg
2 c. flour
1 t. baking powder
¼ t. salt
1 c. milk
1 grated orange rind
1 c. chopped pecans

Chop dates. Mix soda and water and pour over dates. Cream shortening and sugar, add egg and beat well. Add date mixture. Add sifted dry ingredients alternately with milk. Beat well. Add grated orange rind and pecans. Bake at 350°F. for about 45 minutes in greased 9x13x2 loaf pan.

Topping:

Mix 1 cup sugar and juice of an orange and pour over cake while hot. Put back in oven for 10-15 minutes, until glazed.

Mrs. Aleta B. Nelson, Tidehaven H. S.
Blessing, Texas

IRENE'S FAMOUS ORANGE CAKE
Number of Servings — 12
1 T. grated orange rind
2¼ c. flour
3 lge. eggs
1½ c. sugar
¾ c. orange juice (4 or 5 oranges)
¼ c. water
¾ c. shortening
½ t. salt
3½ t. baking powder

Combine flour, eggs, sugar, ½ cup orange juice, grated orange rind shortening, salt, and baking powder. Beat 2 minutes on medium speed. Add remaining ¼ cup of orange juice and water. Beat 1 minute longer. Bake in two 9" cake pans 35 to 40 minutes at 350°F. Cool and frost with orange butter icing.

Icing:
1 stick butter or margarine
1 T. white Karo
1 box confectioners' sugar
1 T. grated orange rind
3 T. orange juice

Mix ingredients together.

Virginia Boxley, Berryville School
Berryville, Arkansas

HEAVENLY PINEAPPLE CAKE
Number of Servings — 12
1 c. butter
2 c. sugar
4 eggs
3 c. flour
1½ t. baking powder
1 t. salt
1¼ c. milk

Separate eggs and beat yolks and whites separately. Cream butter and sugar, add beaten egg yolks. Mix salt, flour, and baking powder and sift together. Add flour mixture and milk alternately to butter mixture. Fold in stiffly beaten egg whites. Divide mixture and place in three prepared cake pans. Bake 30 to 40 minutes in a hot oven 400°F.

Pineapple Filling:
1 lge. can crushed pineapple
1 c. sugar
2 T. flour
2 T. butter

Drain pineapple. Add the sugar, flour, and butter to the pineapple juice. Cook until thick, then add pineapple pulp and spread on hot cake

Mrs. Rachel M. Pearce, Castleberry H. S.
Fort Worth, Texas

PINEAPPLE TREAT
Number of Servings — 8
¾ c. butter
¾ c. sugar
4 egg yolks
2 c. cake flour
1½ t. baking powder
1 t. vanilla
1 c. milk

Preheat oven to 350°F. Cream butter with sugar. Add egg yolks. Beat 1 minute. Add cake flour, baking powder, vanilla, and milk. Beat 2 minutes. Spread batter in a greased floured pan (15½x10½x1) and bake at 350°F. 15 minutes.

Topping:
1 No. 2 can crushed pineapple, drained
4 egg whites, beaten stiff
5 T. sugar
1 can shredded coconut

Drain pineapple. Prepare meringue from egg whites and sugar. Quickly take cake from pan and spread with pineapple, top with meringue, sprinkle with coconut. Return to 375°F. oven until meringue is browned.

Mrs. Ruth Sloan, Ridgeville H. S.
North Ridgeville, Ohio

PINEAPPLE-NUT CAKE
Number of Servings — 16
1 c. sugar
1 stick margarine
2 eggs, separated
2 t. baking powder
24 graham crackers, crushed
1 c. milk
1 t. vanilla
1 c. chopped nuts

Cream sugar and margarine, add egg yolks. Mix baking powder with graham crackers. Mix vanilla with milk. Alternately add the milk mixture and the dry mixture to the sugar mixture. Add nuts. Fold in whipped egg whites. Bake in a moderate 350°F. oven for 30 minutes. Use oblong cake pan or two 9" square cake pans.

Topping:
½ No. 2 can crushed pineapple
1 c. sugar

Mix crushed pineapple and sugar and cook until thick. Pour over baked cake. Cut in squares and serve with whipped cream.

Rosemarie Barber, Tuskegee Public School
Tuskegee, Alabama

IRISH POTATO CAKE
Number of Servings — 12-14
½ c. butter
2 c. sugar
1 c. warmed mashed potatoes
1 t. vanilla
1 t. cocoa
2 c. flour
2 t. baking powder
¼ t. salt
1 t. soda
½ c. sweet milk

(Continued on Next Page)

1 c. nuts, chopped fine
3 egg whites, beaten light
Beat egg whites light. Cream sugar and butter. Add vanilla, cocoa and potatoes. Add sifted dry ingredients alternately with milk. Fold in nuts and egg whites. Bake in 2 prepared layer pans for 35 minutes at 350°F.

Filling:
1 c. sweet cream,
1 c. sugar
3 beaten egg yolks
1 lump butter
1 c. chopped nuts
1 box angel flake coconut
Cook sweet cream, sugar, and beaten egg yolks until thick. Add butter and stir until it melts. Stir in chopped nuts and coconut. Cake can be frozen after it has the filling on it. Delicious!

Mrs. Patsy Cooper, Goree H. S.
Goree, Texas

IRISH POTATO CAKE
Number of Servings — 24
2 c. sugar
¾ c. butter (or Crisco)
4 eggs (separated)
2 c. flour
2 t. baking powder
1 t. cinnamon
1 t. nutmeg
¼ t. salt
1 c. cocoa
½ c. sweet milk
1 c. mashed Irish potatoes
1 c. chopped black walnuts
1 c. raisins
1 t. vanilla
Cream the sugar and butter well, add egg yolks and beat well. Sift together the flour, baking powder, cinnamon, nutmeg, cocoa, and salt. Flour raisins in small portion of the flour mixture. To the creamed mixture add the mashed potatoes. Alternate the flour mixture and milk, beating after each addition. Add vanilla. Add raisins and nuts. Last fold in stiffly beaten egg whites. Bake in greased stem cake pan in a 325°F. oven for one hour or until done, frost with your favorite chocolate frosting, either cooked or uncooked.

Mrs. Betty H. Foust, Bledsoe County H. S.
Pikeville, Tennessee

POTATO CAKE
Number of Servings — 20
2 c. sugar
1 c. butter
4 egg yolks, beaten separate
1 c. chopped walnuts
1 c. chopped raisins
1 t. cinnamon
1 t. ginger
1 t. baking powder
3 c. flour
1 c. sour cream
½ t. soda
2 sq. chocolate
1 c. hot mashed potatoes

4 beaten egg whites
1 t. vanilla
Cream the sugar, butter, and eggs together. Then drop in and mix the walnuts and chopped raisins together. Next sift the cinnamon, ginger, baking powder together with the flour. Then mix the soda and sour cream together. Alternate the flour and milk and add to the mixture. When this has all been added, then add the melted chocolate. Add the hot mashed potatoes and mix thoroughly. Last add the flour, beaten egg whites, and vanilla. Bake in three 8″ layer cake pans for 45-50 minutes at 350°F.

Betty Clyburn, Man H. S.
Man, West Virginia

POTATO CAKE
Number of Servings — 20
2 c. sugar
¾ c. butter
1 c. unseasoned mashed potatoes
1 c. flour
1 t. each of salt, cloves, allspice, nutmeg, and cinnamon
2 t. baking powder
½ c. cocoa
4 egg yolks
1 c. raisins
2 c. chopped nuts
1 c. coconut
½ t. soda mixed in 1 c. buttermilk
4 egg whites stiffly beaten
Cream sugar, butter and mashed potatoes. Sift flour, cocoa, baking powder, salt, all the spices, and cocoa together, reserving 1 cup for dredging the fruit and nuts. Add the egg yolks and beat thoroughly. Mix alternately the flour and buttermilk beginning and ending with the flour mixture. Add raisins, nuts and coconut and mix thoroughly. Fold in stiffly beaten egg whites. Pour into well greased and floured 9x13x2 pan. Bake in a 350°F. oven for one hour.

Frosting:
½ pkg. dates, cut in pieces
2 T. flour
1½ c. milk
2¼ c. sugar
1 c. pecans, chopped
1 c. coconut
Combine the sugar, flour, chopped dates, and milk in saucepan and cook until thick, about eight to ten minutes. Cool, add nuts and coconut and spread on cake.

Mrs. Dorothy E. Perryman, Alpine H. S.
Alpine, Texas

YAM LOAF CAKE
Number of Servings — 12
⅔ c. butter or shortening
2 c. sugar
1 c. yams, mashed well
4 eggs, beaten separately
2 c. sifted cake flour
2 t. cocoa (heaping)
2 t. pumpkin pie spice

(Continued on Next Page)

64

1 T. baking powder
½ t. soda
½ t. salt
1 c. chopped pecans
½ lb. seedless raisins
1 t. vanilla

Sift 1½ cups flour with other dry ingredients three times. Dust raisins and nuts with other ½ cup flour. Cream butter and sugar, add potatoes, then egg yolks. Add flour mixture and milk alternately. Stir in nuts and raisins, fold in beaten egg whites. Bake in loaf. Use icing if desired.

Gussie Mae Beard, Pelican H. S.
Pelican, Louisiana

OLD FASHIONED POUND CAKE

Number of Servings — 40
1 lb. butter
3½ c. sugar
4 c. sifted flour
1 t. baking powder
12 eggs
1 t. vanilla flavoring
1 t. almond flavoring

Cream butter thoroughly, gradually add sugar and cream until light and fluffy. Mix baking powder with flour. Add 3 tablespoons flour mixture and beat well. Add 2 eggs and beat well. Add flour and eggs alternately until all have been added. Add flavoring and bake in two 10″ tube cake pans for 1 hour at 325°F.

Rebecca L. Yarbrough, St. Clair County H. S.
Odenville, Alabama

GRANNY'S POUND CAKE

1 lb. butter (not oleo)
3 c. sugar
3 c. sifted flour
10 whole eggs

Be sure butter is room temperature. Thoroughly cream butter and sugar. Add eggs alternately with flour. Bake in a well greased and floured tube pan approximately 1½ hours at 325°F. Makes a very large cake.

Verlee Heard, Dillingham Junior H. S.
Sherman, Texas

POUND CAKE

Number of Servings — 15-18
3 c. sugar
1 c. butter
½ c. Crisco
5 eggs, beaten
3 c. flour and ½ t. baking powder
1 c. sweet milk
1 t. vanilla
1 t. lemon

Cream butter, sugar, and Crisco until sugar dissolves. Add beaten eggs. Sift together flour, baking powder. Add flour and milk alternately to above mixture. Add flavorings. Place in cold stove and turn oven to 325°F. for 1½ hours.

Mrs. Mary Frances C. Boyd, Stovall H. S.
Stovall, North Carolina

POUND CAKE

Number of Servings — 25
3 c. sugar
1⅛ c. shortening or butter
9 eggs
3 c. flour
½ t. salt
1 t. vanilla

Cream sugar and shortening until light and creamy. Add eggs, one at a time, beating constantly. Add flour and salt and mix well. Add vanilla. Bake in a greased tube pan at 300°F. for 1 to 1¼ hours.

Marilyn Cannon, Berry H. S.
Berry, Alabama

POUND CAKE

1 lb. margarine or butter
8 eggs
2¾ c. sugar
3½ c. flour, sifted
8 T. evaporated milk or coffee cream
1 t. vanilla

Separate eggs and hold out ⅔ cup sugar to beat with egg whites. Cream margarine and 2 cups sugar. Add egg yolks one at a time and beat well after each addition. Alternately, add flour and milk. Beat egg whites with sugar until stiff. Fold into batter and beat vigorously. Add vanilla. Bake for 1½ hours at 350°F. in tube pan lined with wax paper.

This recipe submitted by the following teachers:
Mrs. Wilda Jean Davis, Lumpkin County H. S.
Dahlonega, Georgia
Tommie Cooke, West Bainbridge H. S.
Bainbridge, Georgia

POUND CAKE

1 c. butter
½ c. Crisco
5 lge. eggs
3 c. sugar
3 c. cake flour
1 t. baking powder
1 c. milk
1 t. vanilla
1 t. lemon flavoring

Cream shortening. Add eggs one at a time. Add sugar gradually. Combine baking powder with flour and add alternately with milk. Add flavorings. Bake at 350°F. for 1 hour.

Thelma Dilday, B. F. Grady School
Albertson, North Carolina

POUND CAKE

1 c. butter
1¾ c. sugar
5 eggs
2 c. flour

Cream butter and sugar. Add eggs one at a time, beating well. Add flour last. Bake at 350°F.

Virginia Dale Rawls, Pearl River Junior H. S.
Pearl River, Louisiana

POUND CAKE (Very Rich and Moist)
Number of Servings — 16
½ lb. butter
2 c. sugar
6 eggs
2 c. flour
1 t. vanilla

Cream butter well, gradually add sugar, beat after each addition. Add eggs, one at a time, beating well after each addition. Add vanilla. (This first step may be done with an electric mixer.) Sift flour, measure and add by folding in a little at a time by hand. Grease and flour 10″ tube cake pan. Pour in batter and bake at 350°F. about 45 minutes. Cool before removing from pan. No icing is needed.

This recipe submitted by the following teachers:
Mary W. DeMyer, Fulton H. S.
Fulton, Kentucky
Mrs. Helen Windham, Greenwood H. S.
Greenwood, Florida

POUND CAKE
Number of Servings — 16
2 c. sugar
2 sticks oleo
6 eggs
2 c. sifted all-purpose flour
1 t. vanilla
1 t. lemon extract

Cream together thoroughly sugar and oleo. Add eggs, one at a time. Add flour, vanilla, and lemon extract and mix thoroughly. Bake at 325°F. in a tube pan for 1 hour.

Jane Laetsch, Sands H. S.
Ackerly, Texas

POUND CAKE WITH CRISP CRUST
Number of Servings — 15 to 18
1½ c. shortening
1¾ c. sugar
5 eggs
2 t. flavoring (1 vanilla and 1 lemon)
2 c. flour

Cream shortening and sugar well. Add eggs, one at a time. Beat well. Add flavoring and flour last. Do not over beat while adding flour but mix it well. Pour into lightly greased, lined 9″ tube pan and bake at 325°F. for 1 hour and 5 or 10 minutes. (Makes small cake.)

Mrs. Nell Wilson, Clarke County H. S.
Grove Hill, Alabama

CRISCO POUND CAKE
Number of Servings — 20
3 c. sugar
1 lb. Crisco
10 eggs
3 c. cake flour
¼ c. evaporated milk

Cream sugar and Crisco. Add eggs, one at a time, beating after each egg. Add flour and milk alternately. Bake in a tube pan 10″ for 2 hours at 300°F.

Mrs. Dorothy McGoogan, St. Pauls H. S.
St. Pauls, North Carolina

POUND CAKE (Using Confectioners' Sugar)
Number of Servings — 15
3 sticks butter or margarine
1 box confectioners' sugar
6 whole eggs
3 c. cake flour
1 t. almond or lemon extract
1 t. vanilla

Cream butter, add sugar and mix thoroughly in electric mixer. Add eggs one at a time, beating well after each egg. Add flour, 1 cup at a time and blend well. Add flavorings. Bake in a greased stem pan 1 hour and 25 minutes at 325°F. Start the cake in a cold oven.

This recipe submitted by the following teachers:
Mrs. Sue Bevill, Winnfield H. S.
Winnfield, Louisiana
Mrs. Nancy York, St. Andrew's H. S.
Charleston, South Carolina
Mrs. Frances S. Clark, North Side H. S.
Jackson, Tennessee

POUND CAKE (Using Confectioners' Sugar)
3 c. flour
1 t. baking powder
¼ t. salt
1 lb. confectioners' sugar
1 c. margarine or butter
4 eggs
1 c. milk
1 t. vanilla flavoring
1 t. lemon flavoring

Sift flour, baking powder and salt together. Mix sugar, butter and eggs and beat until light and fluffy. Add flour and milk alternately to the sugar, butter and egg mixture. Bake at 325°F. for 1½ hours.

Mrs. Hal Puett, North Cobb H. S.
Acworth, Georgia

POUND CAKE (Using Confectioners' Sugar)
1 lb. butter
1 lb. confectioners' sugar
1 t. vanilla flavoring
½ t. almond flavoring
½ t. lemon flavoring
6 eggs
4 c. flour

Cream butter and sugar. Add flavorings. Add eggs, one at a time, and beat well. Add flour and beat well. Bake in greased and floured tube pan for 1 hour at 325°F.

Mrs. Nina Lotito, Pocahontas H. S.
Pocahontas, Virginia

POUND CAKE (Using Confectioners' Sugar)
1 lb. butter or margarine
1 lb. confectioners' sugar
1 lb. cake flour
1 t. salt
6 eggs

(Continued on Next Page)

1 T. lemon juice
1 t. vanilla
1 t. almond flavoring

Cream butter or margarine until fluffy. Add sugar gradually and blend well. Add 1 egg at a time, blend well. Add flour and flavoring. Bake in ungreased tube pan at 325°F. for 1 hour and 15 minutes.

Elizabeth Miller,
Itawamba Agricultural H. S. and Jr. College
Fulton, Mississippi

POUND CAKE

2 c. sugar
1 c. vegetable shortening
2½ c. cake flour
½ c. self-rising flour
1 c. sweet milk
1 T. vanilla flavoring
1 t. lemon flavoring
6 eggs

Cream sugar and shortening. Mix in flour and milk alternately. Add flavorings. Add eggs one at a time beating after each addition. Place batter in deep tube pan. Bake 1 hour at 325°F. then bake 20 minutes more at 350°F. Place pan of water in oven during baking.

Betty C. Stephens, Cowpens H. S.
Cowpens, South Carolina

FAVORITE POUND CAKE

Number of Servings — 25

1 lb. butter or margarine
3 c. plain flour
1 c. self-rising flour
8 eggs
2 c. sugar
1 t. vanilla

Cream butter in large bowl of mixer gradually add flour (sifted twice together) until thoroughly blended with butter. In small bowl beat eggs and add sugar, blend. Add small bowl mixture to large bowl mixture and beat at medium speed 5 minutes. Add vanilla. Bake in greased tube pan 1½ hours at 275°F. Cool in pan.

Anne G. Rollins, J. C. Lynch H. S.
Coward, South Carolina

WHITE POUND CAKE

Number of Servings — 10-12

3¾ c. sifted flour
1½ t. baking powder
1¾ c. butter
2 c. sugar
1¼ c. egg whites (10-12 whites)
½ t. vanilla
¼ t. almond extract

Measure and sift flour and baking powder three times. Cream butter and sugar. Add egg whites ¼ cup at a time beating two minutes after each addition. Add flavoring and beat at medium speed one minute. Turn into two loaf pans greased and lined with wax paper and bake at 275°F. for 40 minutes. Increase heat to 325°F. and bake another 40 minutes.

Loura D. Selph, Cotton Valley H. S.
Cotton Valley, Louisiana

FAVORITE POUND CAKE

Number of Servings — 16

1 stick margarine
½ c. Crisco
2 c. sugar
6 eggs
2 c. flour minus 2 T.
1 t. vanilla flavoring

Cream margarine and Crisco. Gradually add sugar beating continually as added. Add one egg at a time beating after each addition until all 6 have been added. Sift and measure 2 cups flour, remove 2 tablespoons flour (use all-purpose flour). Fold flour into first mixture, then add vanilla flavoring. Grease tube cake pan, sprinkle lightly with flour. Bake in tube cake pan at 325°F. for 30 minutes, then lower to 300°F. and bake 30 minutes longer or until done.

Mabel Heath, Jacksonville Sr. High
Jacksonville, Texas

APRICOT BRANDY POUND CAKE

Number of Servings — 20-24

3 c. sugar
2 sticks margarine
6 eggs
½ t. rum flavoring
1 t. orange flavoring
¼ t. almond flavoring
½ t. lemon flavoring
1 t. vanilla flavoring
1 t. butter flavoring
3 c. flour
¼ t. soda
½ t. salt
1 c. sour cream (commercial)
¼ c. apricot brandy or ½ c.

Cream margarine and sugar. Add eggs, one at a time. Beat well. Add flavorings. Add dry ingredients (Flour, sifted with salt and soda), alternating with sour cream and brandy. Bake in greased tube pan at 300-325°F. for 1 hour and 10 minutes.

This recipe submitted by the following teachers:
Mrs. Madeline H. Cleere, Lawrence County H. S.
Moulton, Alabama
Lorene Featherstone, North Side H. S.
Jackson, Tennessee

BROWN SUGAR POUND CAKE

2 sticks butter
½ c. shortening
1 box dark brown sugar
5 eggs
1 c. milk
3 c. cake flour
½ t. salt
1 t. baking powder
1 t. vanilla

Cream butter, shortening, and sugar. Add eggs and beat well. Add flour, sifted with salt and baking powder, alternately with milk. Add vanilla. Bake at 275°F. for 30 minutes, 300°F. for 15

(Continued on Next Page)

minutes and at 325°F. for 45 minutes. Ice with caramel icing.

Caramel Icing:
1 box light brown sugar
1 small can evaporated milk (5¼ oz.)
⅛ stick butter
Bring sugar, milk, butter to hard boil, and thicken to spreading consistency with powdered sugar.

Mrs. Frances W. Register, Atkinson H. S.
Atkinson, North Carolina

BROWN SUGAR POUND CAKE

½ lb. butter
½ c. shortening (Crisco)
1 box and 1 c. brown sugar
5 eggs
1 c. sweet milk
3½ c. flour
½ t. baking powder
1¼ t. vanilla

Cream butter and shortening (Crisco) until fluffy. Add sugar, one cup at a time, and cream thoroughly. Add eggs, one at a time, and beat thoroughly after each addition. Sift flour. Measure. Sift flour and baking powder together. Add alternately, into creamed mixture, dry ingredients and milk. When thoroughly mixed, add vanilla. Pour into a well greased and floured tube pan. (Pan may be lined with wax paper.) Bake at 325°F. for 1½ hours.

Annie Laura Sayers, George Washington H. S.
Danville, Virginia

BUTTERMILK POUND CAKE

3 c. sifted all-purpose flour
¼ t. soda
1 c. butter or margarine
2¾ c. sugar
4 eggs
1 T. grated lemon rind or 1 t. vanilla or both
1 c. buttermilk

Sift flour and soda together. Cream butter or margarine and sugar until well blended. Add eggs, one at a time, beating well on high speed of the mixer after each addition until light and fluffy. Using low speed of mixer, mix in lemon rind or add vanilla to buttermilk and add dry ingredients alternately with milk to creamed mixture. (Add flour in 3 portions and milk in 2.) Mix only until all flour is moistened. Pour into greased 10″ tube pan and bake at 350°F. for one hour and 10 minutes.

Vera H. Martin, Glen Oaks H. S.
Baton Rouge, Louisiana

BUTTERMILK POUND CAKE

Number of Servings — 12

1 c. (½ lb.) butter
3 c. granulated sugar
5 medium eggs
1 t. vanilla or almond flavor if desired
3 c. all-purpose flour
1 c. thick buttermilk
⅔ t. baking soda

Cream butter, add sugar gradually. Cream well.

Add eggs one at a time beating well after each addition. Add flavor if desired. If butter is of good flavor, omit vanilla. Add sifted flour alternately with buttermilk to which soda is added (⅛ teaspoon to each ½ cup). Batter should be smooth. Bake in 10″ tube pan (greased only on bottom) 1 hour and 15 minutes at 350°F. Cool 10 minutes. Remove from pan.

Mrs. Helen P. Sims, Spearsville H. S.
Spearsville, Louisiana

BUTTERMILK POUND CAKE

1 c. butter
2 c. sugar
4 eggs
1 t. lemon flavoring
1 c. buttermilk
½ t. soda
3 c. flour
⅛ t. salt

Cream butter, add sugar gradually and cream well. Add eggs one at a time, beating well after each addition. Add flavoring and mix well. Add flour, salt, and soda alternately with buttermilk. Bake at 300° F. for 1 hour.

Helen Willard, Anahuac H. S.
Anahuac, Texas

CHOCOLATE POUND CAKE

Number of Servings — 20-25

1 c. butter or oleo
½ c. shortening
3 c. sugar
5 eggs
3 c. flour
½ t. baking powder
½ t. salt
4 T. cocoa (may be heaping if desired)
1 c. milk
1 t. vanilla

Cream together butter and shortening. Add sugar. Add eggs one at a time, beating after each. Add vanilla. Sift all dry ingredients together. Add dry ingredients and milk alternately to creamed mixture. Bake in 10″ tube pan at 325°F. for 80 minutes.

This recipe submitted by the following teachers:
Nola P Allen, Russellville Sr. H. S.
Russellville, Alabama
Betty Coe, District Supervisor
Montevallo, Alabama
Mrs. Annie G. Childress, Mangham H. S.
Mangham, Louisiana
Mary Hanna Markham, Lumberton H. S.
Lumberton, North Carolina

CHOCOLATE POUND CAKE

2 sticks butter or margarine and ½ c. shortening (1½ c. Crisco, or butter, or margarine may be used)
3 c. sugar
5 eggs
3 c. cake flour
½ t. baking powder
½ c. cocoa

(Continued on Next Page)

¼ t. salt
1¼ c. milk
1 T. vanilla

Cream butter and shortening, add sugar. Add eggs one at a time, beating after each addition. Sift flour, baking powder, cocoa, and salt. Add dry ingredients alternately with milk. Add vanilla before last flour. Bake in greased and floured tube pan 1 hour and 15 minutes at 325°F.

This recipe submitted by the following teachers:
Mrs. Imogene D. Crawford, East Henderson H. S.
Flat Rock, North Carolina
June Brooks, Stephens County H. S.
Eastanollee, Georgia
Mrs. Barbara McDaniel, Ajax H. S.
Marthaville, Louisiana
Johnnie T. Broome, Blackshear H. S.
Blackshear, Georgia

GERMAN CHOCOLATE POUND CAKE

2 c. sugar
1 c. shortening
4 eggs
2 t. vanilla
2 t. butter flavor
1 c. buttermilk
3 c. sifted all-purpose flour
½ t. soda
1 t. salt
1 pkg. German sweet chocolate

Cream sugar and shortening. Add eggs, flavors and buttermilk. Sift together flour, soda and salt and add. Mix well. Add softened sweet chocolate and blend together well. Cook in 9″ stem pan that has been well greased and dusted with flour, or in 2 loaf pans prepared in the same manner. Bake about 1½ hours at 300°F. Remove cake from pan while still hot and place under a tight fitting cake cover and leave covered until cold.

This recipe submitted by the following teachers:
Mrs. Dianna M. Watson, LaVernia H. S.
LaVernia, Texas
Marjorie Chaney, Zachary H. S.
Zachary, Louisiana
Pat Coley, Magdalina H. S.
Magdalina, New Mexico

BUTTERMILK POUND CAKE

Number of Servings — 20

1 c. soft butter or oleo
3 c. sugar
5 eggs (at room temperature)
1 c. buttermilk
4 c. sifted flour, all-purpose
¼ t. soda
1 T. water
2 t. vanilla

Use mixer to make. Beat butter until fluffy. Add sugar gradually, beating constantly. Then beat some more. Add eggs, one at a time, beat well after each addition. Dissolve soda in water, add to ½ cup of buttermilk. Add 1 cup of flour alternately with milk-soda mixture and beat well. Add remaining flour and milk alternately, blending

well. Add vanilla. Pour into 10″ tube cake pan and stick spatula every ½″ vertically in batter. Bake 1 hour and 30 minutes at 325°F. Grease only bottom of pan. Cool in pan on rack.

Sarah Miller, Moorhead H. S.
Moorhead, Mississippi

OLD FASHIONED POUND CAKE

1 c. butter or oleo
1¾ c. sugar (white)
1 t. vanilla flavoring
4 lge. eggs
2 c. all-purpose plain flour

Cream butter, sugar and flavoring until fluffy. Add 1 egg at a time and beat, continue beating at high speed for 10 minutes. Fold in flour (do not beat). Pour into greased and floured tube cake pan. Bake in a 350°F. oven for 1 hour.

Elizabeth Cofield Harrington, Colonial H. S.
Orlando, Florida

PECAN POUND CAKE

1 c. shortening
1½ c. sugar
2 T. milk
5 eggs
2 c. flour
½ t. mace*
1 t. salt
¾ c. pecans (toasted)
2 t. lemon juice
1 t. grated lemon rind
*May substitute ¼ t. cinnamon and ¼ t. cloves for mace.

Cream together shortening and sugar, add milk. Mix well. Add eggs one at a time, beating after each. Sift together flour, mace, and salt, add to creamed mixture. Add pecans, lemon juice and rind. Pour into greased 9″ tube pan and bake at 325°F. 1 hour and 15 minutes. Cool 5 minutes. Remove cake from pan and cool on wire rack.

Laura H. Wilkins, Pickens County H. S.
Reform, Alabama

RUM POUND CAKE

Number of Servings — 16-20

1 lb. margarine (at room temperature)
1 box (1 lb.) sifted confectioners' sugar
1 measure of cake flour (using box of confectioners' sugar as a measure)
6 eggs
1 t. rum flavoring
½ t. nutmeg

Beat margarine with electric beater until frothy. Add confectioners' sugar ¼ cup at a time beating constantly. Add cake flour, sifted four times before measuring, to sugar-margarine mixture ¼ cup at a time beating after each addition. Add eggs one at a time beating after each addition. Add rum flavoring and nutmeg. Beat. Pour into large greased and floured tube cake pan, bake for 90 minutes at 350°F. Remove from oven, cool 5 minutes. Remove from pan.

Mrs. Evelyn Roberts, Alba Golden H. S.
Alba, Texas

ORANGE-DATE POUND CAKE

1 c. butter or 2 sticks margarine
2 c. sugar
4 eggs
1⅛ c. buttermilk
1 t. soda
4 c. flour
2 t. grated orange rind
1 lb. chopped dates
1 c. broken pecans

Cream butter and sugar. Add eggs one at a time, beat after each addition until smooth. Dissolve soda in buttermilk, add sifted flour and milk alternately in 3 parts. Beat until smooth after each addition. Add orange rinds, dates, and nuts. Mix well. Bake in greased stem pan (angel food cake pan). Cover pan with foil. Bake 30 minutes at 325°F. Remove foil and bake 1 hour at same temperature. When done pour sauce over cake and allow to cool in the pan.

Sauce:
2 c. sugar
1 c. orange juice
2 t. orange rind

Mix until sugar dissolves. Do not heat.

Mrs. Milton Holmes, Danville H. S.
Danville, Alabama

SOUR CREAM POUND CAKE

2 sticks butter, soft (or oleo)
3 c. sugar
6 eggs
1 c. sour cream or 1-8 oz. carton
¼ t. soda
3 c. sifted flour
1 t. vanilla or lemon extract or ½ t. almond
   flavoring if desired

Sift flour and measure. Resift twice with soda. Set aside. Cream butter and add sugar slowly, beating constantly to cream well. Add eggs one at a time, beating well after each addition. Stir in dairy sour cream. Add flour mixture ½ cup at a time, beating well and constantly. Stir in lemon extract and turn batter into well greased and floured 10" tube pan. Use salt-free shortening or fat for greasing pan. Bake in moderate oven 325°F. about 1½ hours or until cake is done. Place pan on rack to cool 5 minutes. Loosen cake around edge of pan and edge of tube with dull side of knife. Press toward pan rather than toward cake. This protects crust. Turn cake onto rack to cool completely. Serve plain. When freezing this cake either whole or cut, wrap in several thicknesses of clear plastic or aluminum foil.

This recipe submitted by the following teachers:
Mrs. Vivian R. Harrison, Millington Central H. S.
Millington, Tennessee
Mrs. Minnie Van W. Stuart, Livingston H. S.
Livingston, Alabama
Jean Bugg, Highland Home H. S.
Highland Home, Alabama
Mrs. Ethel F. Johnson, New Brocton H. S.
New Brocton, Alabama
Mrs. Rebecca McGaughy, Montevallo H. S.
Montevallo, Alabama

PRUNE CAKE

Number of Servings — 15

1 c. cooking oil
1½ c. sugar
3 eggs
2 c. flour
1 t. soda
1 t. salt
1 t. cinnamon
1 t. nutmeg
1 t. allspice
1 c. buttermilk
1 t. vanilla
1 c. cooked chopped prunes
1 c. nuts

Blend sugar and oil, add eggs, add dry ingredients alternately with milk, add vanilla, nuts, and prunes, pour into greased pans, bake at 300°F. for 1 hour. When brown remove from oven and while hot cover with icing.

Icing:
1 c. sugar
1 c. buttermilk
1 t. soda
1 T. white corn syrup
¼ c. butter
½ t. vanilla

Boil until forms a soft ball in water, pour on hot cake without beating.

Gail Frances Gardner, Haines City H. S.
Haines City, Florida

PRUNE CAKE

2 c. flour
1 t. salt
1 t. soda
1 t. cloves
1 t. cinnamon
1 t. nutmeg
1 c. shortening
1½ c. sugar
3 eggs
2 c. flour
1 c. buttermilk
1 t. vanilla
1 c. cooked prunes
1 c. nuts

Sift together flour, salt, soda, and spices. Cream shortening and sugar. Add eggs one at a time and beat. Add flour and milk alternately. Add vanilla, prunes, and nuts. Bake in layers at 350°F.

Filling:
2 c. brown sugar
1 c. cream or top milk
½ lb. dates
½ c. pecans
2 T. butter

Boil sugar and milk until soft ball. Add dates and butter, cook one minute. Add pecans. Beat until stiff enough to spread on cake.

This recipe submitted by the following teachers:
Mrs. Frank G. Haltom, Prescott H. S.
Prescott, Arkansas
Mrs. Dorothy McAlister, Northside School
Vernon, Texas

PRUNE CAKE
Number of Servings — 16 to 20

1½ c. sugar
1 c. salad oil
3 eggs
3 c. sifted flour
1 t. cinnamon
1 t. nutmeg
1 t. allspice
¼ t. salt
1 c. buttermilk
1 t. soda
1 t. vanilla
1 T. lemon juice
1 c. chopped prunes
1 c. chopped nuts

Mix sugar and salad oil. Add eggs one at a time and beat. Sift together flour, spices, and salt. Add alternately with buttermilk and soda. Beat in vanilla, lemon juice, prunes, and nuts. Bake in oblong cake pan 1 hour at 325°F.

Topping:
1 c. sugar
½ c. buttermilk
½ t. soda
½ t. salt
1 T. white corn syrup
¼ c. butter

Boil 5 minutes and pour over warm cake while still in pan.

Ruth Lee, Teague H. S.
Teague, Texas

PRUNE CAKE

1 c. cooking oil
2 c. white sugar
3 eggs (1 egg, 2 whites, save 2 yolks for icing)
1 c. buttermilk
1 t. soda
2 c. flour
1 t. baking powder
½ t. salt
1 c. cooked cut prunes
¼ c. prune juice
1 t. vanilla
½ t. each: cloves, allspice nutmeg, cinnamon

To oil add sugar. Beat in eggs, one at a time (1 whole egg, 2 whites). Add soda to buttermilk. Sift all other dry ingredients. Add flour mixture alternately with milk mixture to oil and sugar mixture. Fold in prunes, prune juice and vanilla. Bake in three well greased layer pans or a large sheet pan in moderate oven until done (about 30 minutes).

Frosting:
¼ lb. butter
Grated rind and juice of 1 lemon
2 egg yolks
1 lb. confectioners' sugar

Cook butter, juice and grated lemon rind, and egg yolks in top of double boiler until thick. Put in mixer and add confectioners' sugar. Beat until smooth.

Mrs. G. K. Waters, Thomas Dale H. S.
Chester, Virginia

OLD FASHIONED PRUNE CAKE
Number of Servings — 12

½ c. butter or vegetable shortening
1 c. sugar
2 eggs
1 c. prune pulp
2 c. flour
½ t. salt
½ t. allspice
½ t. cinnamon
½ t. ginger
1 t. soda dissolved in 2 T. hot water
1 c. nut meats, optional

Cream butter and sugar. Beat in eggs. Add prune pulp and beat. Sift spices and flour twice and add to creamed mixture. Add soda and hot water mixture. Beat together. Add nut meats if desired. Bake in one layer, approximately 9x13 pan, or in layer cake pans. Bake at 350°F. for 40-45 minutes. Frost with orange or lemon butter cream frosting or serve with whipped cream.

Orange Frosting for Prune Cake:
1¾ c. sifted confectioners' sugar
¼ c. melted butter or margarine
¼ c. orange juice
1 T. cream
¼ t. grated orange peel
1⅛ c. sugar

Combine sugar with butter, orange juice, cream, and orange peel. Beat until smooth. Add remaining 1⅓ cup sugar. Beat until spreading consistency is reached. Spread on sheet cake or frost two 9" layers.

Helen Harbour, Pomona H. S.
Pomona, California

PRUNE SPICE CAKE
Number of Servings — 12-15

2 c. sifted flour
¾ t. salt
1 t. soda
1 t. baking powder
2-3 t. cinnamon
2 t. nutmeg
1½ t. allspice
½ c. shortening
1½ c. granulated sugar
3 eggs (unbeaten)
1 c. sour milk or buttermilk
1 c. finely cut, well drained prunes

Sift together the first seven (7) dry ingredients. Cream shortening and sugar for 2 minutes. Add eggs and beat about 2 minutes longer. Add flour mixture and sour milk alternately to the creamed mixture. Beat only until blended. Add prunes and stir until blended. Grease bottom of two 9" pans or use a round 13x9x2 mold. Bake layers 35 minutes, round molds about 45-50 minutes. Serve plain, or with orange, cream cheese or sea foam frosting.

Virginia Lee Puffinburger, Greenbelt Jr. H. S.
Greenbelt, Maryland

PRUNE WHIP CAKE

2 c. sifted cake flour
1⅛ c. sugar
2 t. baking powder
¼ t. baking soda
½ t. salt
½ t. nutmeg
½ t. cinnamon
½ t. allspice
½ c. shortening
1 c. prune juice
1 t. vanilla
2 eggs

Sift dry ingredients together. Add shortening and ¾ cup prune juice. Beat 2 minutes with electric mixer. Add remaining prune juice, vanilla, and eggs, beat 2 minutes longer. Bake in greased and floured 13x9x2 pan in moderate oven 350°F. 25 to 30 minutes. Cool and frost with Prune Whip Frosting.

Prune Whip Frosting:

2 egg whites
1 c. brown sugar
½ c. granulated sugar
⅛ c. prune juice
¼ t. salt
Vanilla

Place egg whites, brown sugar, granulated sugar, prune juice, and salt in top of double boiler. Beat 1 minute with electric mixer to blend. Beat constantly until frosting forms stiff peaks (about 7 minutes). Remove from boiling water, add vanilla, and beat to spreading consistency.

Mrs. Leland Mulder, Holmen H. S.
Holmen, Wisconsin

PRUNE SPICE CAKE

Number of Servings — 15

1½ c. dried prunes
2 c. flour
1½ c. sugar
1¼ t. soda
1 t. cinnamon
1 t. nutmeg
¼ t. cloves
½ c. salad oil
3 eggs
1 t. salt

Cover prunes with water and simmer 20 minutes (do not sweeten). Drain, reserving ⅔ cup liquid (add water it necessary). Chop prunes. Sift together dry ingredients, add reserved prune liquid and salad oil. Mix to blend. Beat vigorously 2 minutes. Add eggs, beat 1 minute longer. Stir in prunes. Pour into greased and floured 13x9x2 baking dish. Sprinkle with crumb top. Bake at 350°F. 35 minutes. Serve warm or cold with whipped cream.

Crumb Top:

½ c. sugar
2 T. flour
2 T. butter
½ c. broken nuts

Cut in sugar, flour, and butter. Add nuts.

Mrs. Mary Sue Worley, Gate City H. S.
Gate City, Virginia

EASY PRUNE CAKE

1 c. oil
3 eggs
2 c. sugar
2 c. self-rising flour
1 T. cake spice or the following: 1 t. nutmeg, 1 t. cinnamon, 1 t. allspice
1 jar junior baby food prunes
½ c. chopped nuts

Mix sugar and oil, then add eggs. Sift flour and spices together and add to mixture. Add prunes. Mix well. Drop in nuts, and mix. Pour into greased, floured tube pan. Bake at 300°F. for 1 hour.

Mrs. Bobbie G. Ross, North Mecklenburg H. S.
Huntersville, North Carolina

PRUNELLA CAKE

Cream together:
½ c. butter
1 c. sugar
2 eggs
⅔ c. cooked prunes (seeded)
Stir in:
⅔ c. buttermilk
Add sifted dry ingredients:
1⅓ c. flour
½ t. salt
2 t. soda
1 t. cinnamon
1 t. allspice
1 t. nutmeg

Mix well. Bake in 300°F. oven 30 to 40 minutes.

Icing:

Cook until thick:
2 eggs
1 c. sugar
1 c. seeded cooked prunes
½ c. sour milk
Add:
1 t. vanilla

Jolene Corcoran, Lefors H. S.
Lefors, Texas

PRUNELLA CAKE

Number of Servings — 16

1 c. Crisco or butter
2 c. sugar
3 eggs
1 c. stewed prunes
1 c. sour milk
2½ c. flour
1 t. soda
1 t. baking powder
½ t. salt
½ t. each nutmeg, allspice

Blend Crisco with sugar, eggs, chopped prunes. Stir in milk and sifted dry ingredients alternately. Pour into greased pans and bake moderately 350°F.

Icing:

2 c. sugar
2 T. flour
½ c. milk
½ c. prune juice

(Continued on Next Page)

Blend sugar and flour. Stir in milk and prune juice. Boil until thick.

Mrs. Corrie Parker, Linville H. S.
Linville, Louisiana

RED VELVET CAKE (Waldorf)

½ c. shortening
1½ c. sugar
2 eggs
2 oz. red food coloring
2 T. cocoa
2¼ c. plain flour
1 scant t. salt
1 t. vanilla
1 t. soda
1 c. buttermilk
1 T. vinegar
1 t. butter flavoring (if desired)

Cream shortening, sugar, and eggs. Make a paste with coloring and cocoa and add to mixture. Add salt and flour with buttermilk and vanilla. Alternately add soda and vinegar and don't beat hard, just blend. Bake 30 minutes at 350°F. Bake in two 8" pans greased and floured. Layers may be split to make 4.

Frosting:

3 T. flour
1 c. butter, oleo or shortening
1 t. vanilla
1 c. milk
1 c. granulated sugar

Cook flour and milk on low heat until thick. Cool. Cream sugar and butter and vanilla until fluffy. Add to flour milk mixture. Beat until mixture is like whipped cream. Spread on layers. Sprinkle with coconut or nuts if desired. (Keep cake cool.)

This recipe submitted by the following teachers:
Mrs. David L. Keathley, Waco H. S.
Waco, Texas
Elsie Snellgrove, Corner H. S.
Warrior, Alabama
Maggie Johnson, Varnado H. S.
Varnado, Louisiana
Harriet J. Harless, Logan Sr. H. S.
Logan, West Virginia
Ann S. Belair, Jennings H. S.
Jennings, Louisiana
Mrs. Dorothy Sue T. Hill, Oberlin H. S.
Oberlin, Louisiana
Mrs. Velma Strickland, Mynick H. S.
Laurel, Mississippi
Nan Lindsey, Wade Hampton H. S.
Greenville, South Carolina
Katie Whorton, Cabot H. S.
Cabot, Arkansas
Ann N. Thompson, Athens H. S.
Athens, Alabama
Mrs. Jim Neeley, Bearden H. S.
Bearden, Arkansas

RED EARTH CAKE

½ c. Crisco
1½ c. sugar
2 whole eggs
4 T. cocoa
1 t. red cake coloring
3 T. hot coffee
1⅞ c. flour
1 t. salt
1 t. soda
1 c. sour milk with soda dissolved in it
1 t. vanilla

Cream Crisco, add sugar gradually. Cream until fluffy. Beat in eggs. Mix cocoa, coloring, and hot coffee until it forms a smooth paste. Add to creamed mixture. Sift flour, measure and sift three times with salt added. Add flour alternately with milk. Add vanilla. Bake 40 minutes at 350°F.

Icing:

1 stick butter or oleo
1 box powdered sugar (sifted)
4 T. cocoa
4 T. coffee
1 t. red cake coloring
1 t. vanilla

Cream butter or oleo. Add sifted sugar and make a soft paste of cocoa, coloring, and coffee. Add sugar. Add enough coffee to make a consistency to spread. Put between and on top and sides of Red Earth Cake when cool.

Mrs. Dalpha Baley, Splendora H. S.
Splendora, Texas

SPECIAL SPICE CAKE
Number of Servings — 12

2 c. sifted all-purpose flour
1 c. sugar
1 t. baking powder
½ t. salt
¾ t. baking soda
2 t. cinnamon
2 t. nutmeg
½ t. cloves
¾ c. brown sugar
½ c. soft shortening
1½ t. vanilla
⅔ c. evaporated milk
⅓ c. water
1 T. vinegar
3 eggs

Sift into a 3-quart bowl, flour, sugar, baking powder, salt, baking soda, cinnamon, nutmeg, and cloves. Add brown sugar, shortening, and vanilla. Add a mixture of milk, water, vinegar. Beat hard 2 minutes with electric mixer at medium speed, or by hand. Add 3 eggs and beat hard 2 minutes more. Bake in a greased and floured 9x12 cake pan at 350°F. for 35-40 minutes. Bake near center of oven. When cool, frost with Creamy Caramel Frosting.

Mrs. Beverly Russell Parker, Dunbar H. S.
Okmulgee, Oklahoma

DELICIOUS SPICE CAKE
Number of Servings — 16
1 c. brown sugar
½ c. lard or butter
1 whole egg and egg yolk
¼ t. salt
½ t. soda
½ t. cloves
½ t. cinnamon
1¼ c. cake flour
½ c. sour milk
Meringue:
1 egg white
½ c. brown sugar
¼ c. nut meats

Cream sugar with shortening, add eggs and beat. Sift together all dry ingredients and add alternately with the sour milk. Spread batter in greased 8" baking pan and cover with the meringue. Beat the egg white stiff, add the brown sugar and nut meats. Place in a moderate oven and bake 35 minutes.

Catherine R. Mordan, Millville Area H. S.
Millville, Pennsylvania

SOUR CREAM CHOCOLATE SPICE CAKE
Number of Servings — 12-18
2 c. sour cream
4 eggs
2 c. sugar
2½ c. flour
4 t. cocoa
2 t. soda
1 t. cloves
1 t. salt
1½ t. cinnamon
¾ t. mace
1 c. raisins
½ c. nut meats

Whip sour cream and eggs, add sugar and blend, all remaining ingredients except nuts and raisins, stir well for 1 minute with electric mixer, then add nuts and raisins. Bake in a medium oven 300°F. for 1 hour. Will make 2 layers 8x8 or 1 large loaf cake.

Icing:
1 c. brown sugar
4 T. melted butter
4 t. flour
1 c. chopped nuts
Mix all ingredients together. Spread on cake top and bake 10 minutes at 300°F.

Mrs. J. Caroline Kenyon, Holyoke H. S.
Holyoke, Colorado

CHERRY SPICE CAKE
Number of Servings — 18-24
2 c. sugar
½ c. butter
2 eggs
1 c. grated fresh apple
3 c. sifted flour
2 t. soda
1 t. allspice
1 c. chopped cherries (maraschino)
1 c. chopped nuts

Cream butter and sugar well, add eggs and beat. Add apple and beat well, add flour, sifted with soda and allspice. Stir in cherries and nuts. (Reserve cherry juice for filling). Bake in a 9" tube pan, with bottom lined with wax paper. Do not grease sides of pan. Bake approximately 1½ hours at 300°F. Let cake cool thoroughly then cover with filling.

Filling:
1½ c. sugar
2½ c. milk (add cherry juice, then milk to make 2½ c.)
¼ stick butter or margarine
Combine all 3 ingredients in a heavy 2-quart saucepan and cook until thick, approximately 8-10 minutes, at a rolling boil. Remove from heat, cool, then beat until creamy. Apply to cake.

Janell Samford, C. O. Wilson Jr. H. S.
Nederland, Texas

1880 CHOCOLATE SPICE CAKE
Number of Servings — 8-10
1 c. sugar
½ c. butter
1 egg
1½ c. flour
½ t. salt
1 T. cocoa (heaping)
1 t. cinnamon
1 t. cloves
1 t. nutmeg
1 c. buttermilk
1 t. soda
1 t. vanilla

Cream sugar, butter, and egg together. Sift dry ingredients together. Dissolve soda in sour milk and add alternately with dry ingredients to creamed mixture. Beat 3 minutes at No. 3 speed. Pour in greased and floured 12x8x2 pan. Bake at 350°F. for 25 to 30 minutes. Spread on hot cake the following icing.

Boiling Icing:
5 T. melted butter
7 T. brown sugar
5 T. cream
½ c. coconut
Mix all ingredients and spread on cake. Place in oven and broil until icing bubbles all over and is light brown. Careful not to burn.

Mrs. Alice Dyer, Bixby Jr. H. S.
Bixby, Oklahoma

CIDER SPICE CAKE
Sift together:
3 c. flour
1½ t. soda
1 t. cinnamon
1 t. nutmeg
¼ t. ground cloves
¾ t. salt
Cream:
¾ c. shortening
1½ c. brown sugar
Add:
3 eggs
1 c. apple cider (add 1 T. of lemon juice if the cider is sweet)

(Continued on Next Page)

Add the flour and spices to the creamed mixture. Blend well. Pour into a greased and floured cake pan. (8x11 loaf pan or three 8″ layer pans.) Bake at 350°F. for 30 to 35 minutes.

Cider Icing:

¼ c. melted butter
2 T. flour
¼ c. apple cider
3 c. confectioners' sugar
½ c. chopped black walnuts

Blend together melted butter and flour. Add apple cider. Cook over low heat until thick, about 1 minute. Remove from heat. Add confectioners' sugar and chopped black walnuts.

Rose Tiller, Blue River H. S.
Blue River, Wisconsin

YAM SPICE CAKE
Number of Servings — 20

1¾ c. sugar
1 c. mashed cooked yams
¾ c. soft shortening
1 t. cinnamon
½ t. nutmeg
⅛ t. salt
3 unbeaten eggs
1 t. baking soda
1 c. buttermilk
2 c. sifted all-purpose flour
1 c. pecans, chopped
2 T. flour

Combine sugar, yams, shortening, spices, and salt. Cream well. Add eggs, beating until blended. Combine baking soda and milk. Add alternately with flour to creamed mixture, beginning and ending with flour. Coat pecans with 2 tablespoons flour, stir into batter. Turn into greased and floured 13x9 pan. Bake in moderate oven 350°F. for 50 to 60 minutes. Cool and frost with Yam Topping.

Yam Topping:

1 c. evaporated milk
1 c. sugar
3 egg yolks
¼ lb. margarine
1 t. vanilla
1¼ c. angel flake coconut
½ c. mashed yams
1 c. chopped pecans

Combine milk, sugar, egg yolks, margarine, and vanilla in a saucepan. Cook and stir over medium heat until mixture thickens, about 12 minutes. Add coconut, mashed yams, and chopped pecans. Beat until cool and thick enough to spread.

Mrs. Bobbie McFatter, Merryville H. S.
Merryville, Louisiana

BUTTER SPONGE CAKE

11 beaten egg yolks
2 c. sugar
1 c. milk, scalded
1 t. vanilla extract
2¼ c. cake flour
2 t. baking powder
½ c. melted butter

Beat egg yolks with sugar until light-colored and fluffy, add slightly cooled milk and vanilla. Add sifted dry ingredients. Fold in butter. Bake in 2 wax paper lined 8″ square pans in moderate oven 350°F. 30 to 40 minutes. Frost if desired. This cake may be used for strawberry shortcake.

Mrs. Sarah Smith, West Mifflin South H. S.
Dravosburg, Pennsylvania

CHOCOLATE SPONGE CAKE
Number of Servings — 16

6 eggs
1 c. sugar
1 c. cake flour
¼ c. melted butter, cooled
4 oz. melted chocolate, cooled
4 T. brandy or rum

Beat eggs, add sugar gradually, beat until mixture holds shape. This can't be overbeaten. Sift and measure cake flour. Fold flour into mixture. Mix together the butter, chocolate, and liquor. Fold into batter. Bake in a spring form pan, which has been greased and floured, at 325°F. for 50 minutes. Turn out of pan immediately.

Mrs. Lucille Murray, Havre H. S.
Havre, Montana

DATE SPONGE CAKE
Number of Servings — 21

2 c. pitted dates
2 c. sugar
6 egg yolks
1 c. flour
2 t. baking powder
1 t. vanilla
2 c. chopped pecans
6 egg whites beaten stiff

Pour boiling water over dates, pour off when skins will slip off. Cream sugar with dates while still warm, add well beaten egg yolks. Sift baking powder with flour. Prepare nuts with 2 tablespoons flour. Add rest of flour to date mixture. Add vanilla, add pecans. Whip egg whites until stiff, fold into mixture. Turn into a pan (10x14) which has been greased and flour dusted over it. Bake in moderate oven 350°F. 40 minutes or until the cake shrinks from sides of pan.

Mrs. Louise J. McDonald, Bernice H. S.
Bernice, Louisiana

GOLDEN SPONGE LOAF
Number of Servings — 15

1¾ c. sifted cake flour
1 t. baking powder
½ t. salt
10 egg yolks (at room temperature)
½ c. hot water
1 t. lemon extract
1 c. sugar

Sift flour once, measure, add baking powder and salt, and sift together. Beat egg yolks with rotary egg beater until thickened slightly, add hot water gradually, beating until mixture is very thick and light (about 10 minutes). Electric mixer 5 minutes. Add flavoring to egg yolks. Then add sugar gradually, beating constantly. Fold in flour, a

(Continued on Next Page)

fourth at a time, folding just until blended. Turn into ungreased round 10" tube pan and bake in moderate oven 375°F. 40 minutes or until done. Remove from oven, invert pan and let stay 1 hour, or until cake is cool.

Barbara A. Ferster, Middleburg Joint H. S.
Middleburg, Pennsylvania

HOT MILK SPONGE CAKE

Number of Servings — 10

3 eggs
1½ c. sugar
1½ t. vanilla
1½ c. cake flour
1½ t. baking powder
⅛ t. salt
¾ c. milk
3 T. butter (scant)

Combine eggs, sugar and vanilla in large bowl of an electric mixer. Beat until very light and foamy. Beat while preparing dry ingredients. Heat milk just to the boiling point. Fold in dry ingredients. Melt butter in milk. Stir hot milk and butter into eggs and sugar. Pour into buttered pan (8" or 10" or size for cake the thickness you need). Bake at 350°F. for 30 to 40 minutes. Serve topped with favorite sauces or fruits.

Mrs. Paulene Bierman, Osceola Area Schools
Osceola, Wisconsin

SUNSHINE SPONGE CAKE

Number of Servings — 8-12

6 eggs
¼ t. salt
1½ c. sugar
½ c. water
1 c. flour
¾ t. cream of tartar
1 t. flavoring

Cook together sugar and water until it spins a thread. Separate eggs, beat whites and salt until stiff, do not overbeat. Slowly pour hot sugar syrup over whites beating constantly. Set aside to cool slightly. Beat yolks until thick, add flavoring. Fold yolks into whites gently. Then fold in sifted flour and cream of tartar. Pour into 10" Turk's-head pan and bake at 325°F. 50-55 minutes. Cool inverted before removing from pan. Ice with 7-minute boiled frosting and freshly grated coconut.

Margaret C. Montgomery, Williamstown H. S.
Williamstown, New Jersey

AUNT MONIE'S CAKE

Number of Servings — 12

1¾ c. sugar
½ lb. butter
5 eggs
2 c. sifted flour
3 T. lemon juice

Cream sugar and butter thoroughly. Add eggs, one at a time, beating well. Add flour and lemon juice, beat until well blended. Bake in greased stem pan 45 minutes in 375°F. oven.

Barbara E. Vines. Rupert H. S.
Rupert, West Virginia

BLACKBERRY CAKE

Number of Servings — 12

1 c. brown sugar
½ c. shortening
1 egg
1 c. crushed blackberries
½ c. sour milk
2 c. flour
1 t. soda
¼ t. salt
½ t. cinnamon
½ t. cloves
1 t. baking powder

Sift flour, soda, salt, cinnamon, cloves, and baking powder together. Cream sugar and shortening. Add egg and beat well. Add crushed blackberries. Alternate sour milk and the dry ingredients. Pour into a greased loaf pan. Bake at 350°F. 35 minutes.

Topping:
½ c. brown sugar
1 c. chopped walnuts or salted cocktail peanuts
2 T. water
4 T. flour
4 T. melted butter

Ora Goodrich, Coudersport Area H. S.
Coudersport, Pennsylvania

GRANDMOTHER'S BOILED RAISIN CAKE

Number of Servings — 12

1 c. raisins
1½ c. water
1 egg, slightly beaten
2 c. flour
1 c. sugar
1 t. soda
1 t. cinnamon
1 t. nutmeg
1 t. cloves
3 t. boiling water
½ t. vanilla
½ c. melted shortening

Boil raisins slowly in the water until there is 1 cup of water left and the raisins are plump. Allow mixture to cool. Add the sugar and egg. Add flour which has been mixed and sifted with the soda, spices which have been wet with 3 teaspoons of boiling water and last, the melted shortening. Bake in 325°F. oven 40 to 50 minutes.

Mrs. Effie G. Hoyle, Warwick H. S.
Newport News, Virginia

BUTTERSCOTCH CAKE

⅔ c. butterscotch morsels
¼ c. water
2¼ c. cake flour
1 t. baking soda
½ t. baking powder
½ t. salt
1¼ c. sugar
½ c. shortening
3 unbeaten eggs
1 c. buttermilk

Melt butterscotch morsels in the water in saucepan. Cool. Sift flour with salt, soda, and baking

(Continued on Next Page)

powder. Set aside. Cream sugar and shortening, add eggs and beat well. Add melted butterscotch and mix well. Add dry ingredients alternately with the buttermilk. Bake in two 9" round layer pans at 350°F. for 25 minutes. Cool and frost with your favorite frosting.

Mrs. Ivy C. Stacy, Wilber H. S.
Wilber, Nebraska

CARAMEL CAKE

Number of Servings — 18-20

2 c. brown sugar
½ c. shortening
2 eggs
½ c. milk
½ c. coffee
1 t. vanilla
2¾ c. flour
3 t. baking powder
½ c. coconut

Cream brown sugar and shortening. Add eggs and blend. Add milk, coffee, and vanilla, blending after each addition. Add flour, baking powder (no need to sift, add as is), and coconut. Bake 45 minutes at 350°F. Use oblong cake pan.

Icing:
1 c. brown sugar
¼ lb. butter or oleo
½ c. coconut
Cream or milk to moisten

If more icing desired, increase amount. Put icing on cake and place under broiler. It takes a very short time and will brown easily. Place upper rack in oven so cake will be about 3-4" from top unit.

Lois S. Gass, Mahanoy Joint H. S.
Herndon, Pennsylvania

MOMO'S CARAMEL CAKE

1 c. butter
2 c. sugar
4 egg yolks, slightly beaten
3 c. cake flour
1 t. salt
3 t. baking powder
1 c. milk
1 t. vanilla
4 egg whites, beaten until stiff but not dry

Cream butter. Add sugar, cream together thoroughly. Add slightly beaten egg yolks. Sift together dry ingredients, add alternately with milk. Add vanilla. Fold in beaten egg whites. Pour batter into three greased and floured layer cake pans. Bake at 350°F. 35-45 minutes.

Filling and Frosting:
2½ c. sugar
2 c. cream
2 c. coarsely ground pecans
4 T. sugar for caramelized syrup

Mix 2½ cups sugar and milk together in a saucepan. Cook to soft ball stage. In a skillet, caramelize 4 tablespoons sugar. Add to first mixture, cool then stir until thickened. Remove from heat and add ground pecans. Spread between

layers and on top and sides of cake.
Note: To caramelize sugar place in heavy skillet over medium heat until it is a rich golden brown, stirring constantly.

Mrs. Odessa N. Smith,
State Department of Education
Baton Rouge, Louisiana

CINNAMON CARROT CAKE

2 c. sifted cake flour
2 t. soda
1 t. salt
2 c. sugar
2 t. cinnamon
1¼ c. oil
3 c. grated raw carrots
4 eggs

Sift flour, soda, salt, sugar and cinnamon, add oil and stir. Add eggs all at once, stir well, add carrots, mix well. Bake in 2 layer pans at 350°F. about 35 minutes.

Icing:
1 8 oz. pkg. cream cheese
1 lb. confectioners' sugar
1 c. chopped pecans
½ stick oleo
2 t. vanilla

Mix well and spread on cake.

Ann C. Daniels, Escambia H. S.
Pensacola, Florida

THE CONFECTIONER CAKE

1 box confectioners' sugar
1 lb. butter, sweet or salt or oleo
3 c. cake flour
6 whole eggs
1 t. flavoring (your choice)

Have butter at room temperature. Blend sugar and butter together until smooth. Add eggs one at a time. Blend small portions of the cake flour with each egg. Beat well after each mixture. Continue adding eggs and flour together until all are blended well. Place in a round tube pan for 1¼ to 1½ hours. at 275°F.

This recipe submitted by the following teachers:
Mrs. Swanie Smoot, Scott H. S.
Madison, West Virginia
Mrs. Virginia Bond, Scott H. S.
Madison, West Virginia

CRANBERRY CAKE WITH
HOT BUTTER SAUCE
Number of Servings — 9

2 T. butter
1 c. sugar
1 t. vanilla
2 c. sifted cake flour
3 t. baking powder
½ t. salt
1 c. milk
2 c. whole, raw cranberries

Thoroughly cream butter and sugar. Beat in vanilla. Sift flour, baking powder, and salt. Add dry ingredients to creamed mixture alternately

(Continued on Next Page)

with milk. Fold in cranberries. Pour into greased floured 8" or 9" square pan. Bake in hot oven 400°F. about 35 minutes or until done. While hot cut into squares and top with Hot Butter Sauce.

Hot Butter Sauce:
½ c. butter
½ c. coffee cream
1 c. sugar

Melt butter in saucepan, blend in sugar. Stir in cream. Simmer 3 to 4 minutes, stirring occasionally. Serve immediately over warm Cranberry Cake.

Mary C. Shaw, Kress H. S.
Kress, Texas

CRANBERRY CAKE
Number of Servings — 12
1 c. sugar
3 T. butter
2 c. all-purpose flour
2 t. baking powder
¼ t. salt
2 c. raw cranberries
1 c. milk

Cream sugar and butter. Sift dry ingredients and add alternately with milk to creamed mixture. Add cranberries. Bake in two greased bread tins at 350°F. until done (about 40 minutes).

Butter Sauce:
½ c. butter
1 c. sugar
½ c. cream
1 t. vanilla

Bring butter, sugar, and cream to boil slowly. Add vanilla. Serve hot on cake.

Mrs. Myrtle Halvorson, Simmons Jr. H. S.
Aberdeen, South Dakota

CRUNCH CAKE
Number of Servings — 20
2 c. sugar
2 c. cake flour (sifted)
1 c. Crisco
6 eggs
1 t. vanilla
1 t. lemon

Mix sugar, flour, Crisco, and eggs in a mixing bowl until it is creamy and smooth. In a mixer, beat about 8-10 minutes or by hand mix about 12 minutes. Add vanilla and lemon flavoring. Mix well, about one minute. Pour into a slightly greased angel food cake pan. Bake at 350°F. for 1 hour. If cake is not brown then, bake about 10 minutes longer, until it is firm and brown. *Note:* In warm weather be sure the Crisco and eggs are cold.

Mrs. R. D. Dyson, Cairo H. S.
Cairo, Georgia

CRUMBLE CAKE
Number of Servings — 16
2 c. brown sugar, packed
2 c. flour, sifted
½ c. butter
1 egg, beaten

1 t. vanilla
1 t. soda
1 c. sour milk
½ c. raisins
½ c. walnuts

Mix sugar, flour, and butter. Reserve one cup of mixture. Add beaten egg and vanilla to flour mixture. Add soda to sour milk and gradually add to mixture. Add raisins and nuts. Put in shallow (9x12) greased pan and sprinkle with reserve crumbs for frosting. Bake 35 to 40 minutes in 375°F. oven.

Mrs. Annette R. Helgelien, Faulkton H. S.
Faulkton, South Dakota

CUERO CAKE
1 c. butter
2½ c. sugar
5 eggs (separated)
1 orange rind (grated)
2 sq. melted chocolate
½ c. orange juice
1 t. vanilla
1 c. buttermilk
3 c. cake flour
1 t. soda

Cream butter and add sugar. Mix well. Add beaten egg yolks and mix well. Add melted chocolate and grated orange rind, orange juice and vanilla. Alternately add the flour and buttermilk adding the soda to the last portion of the milk before putting into batter. Mix well. Fold in stiffly beaten egg whites. Pour into three 9" cake pans that have been greased and wax paper placed in the bottom. Bake 350°F. about 30 minutes or until loosened around edges.

Filling:
1 small can crushed pineapple (cup)
2 eggs
1 c. sugar
3 T. flour
1 T. butter
1 T. lemon juice
1 c. coconut

Mix the first four ingredients well in top of double boiler. Cook the mixture until thickened. Take from heat and add butter, lemon juice, coconut and mix well. Set aside to cool. Spread between layers of cake. Ice the top and sides of the cake with your favorite 7-minute icing.

Mrs. Joalice Poehler, Reagan County H. S.
Big Lake, Texas

EGGLESS BUTTERLESS CAKE
Number of Servings — 10-20
1 lb. seeded raisins
1½ c. sugar
2 c. water or coffee
½ t. salt
2 T. shortening
4 c. flour
1 t. soda
1 t. baking powder
1 t. cinnamon
1 t. nutmeg
½ t. cloves (ground)

(Continued on Next Page)

Boil raisins, sugar, coffee, salt, and shortening together for 5 minutes. Cool and then add dry ingredients which have been sifted together 3 times. Bake in two loaf pans or one tube pan at 275°F. for 90 to 105 minutes.

Mrs. Barbara-Jane Houle, Bennington H. S.
Bennington, Vermont

FALL DELIGHT
Number of Servings — 12

1 c. chopped dates
1 c. chopped apples
1 t. soda
1 c. boiling water
½ c. shortening
1 c. sugar
1 egg
1 t. vanilla
1½ c. sifted flour
1 t. salt
1 c. chopped nuts
4 T. melted butter
½ c. brown sugar
2 T. milk

Mix dates, apples, soda, and boiling water together. Let stand until cool. Cream shortening and sugar, add beaten egg. Sift flour and salt together, add alternately with fruit mixture. Add vanilla and nuts. Bake at 350°F. for 35 minutes. Spread the mixture of melted butter, brown sugar, and milk, over baked cake and broil until it bubbles. Serve with whipped cream.

Mrs. Pauline Kirby, Marcellus H. S.
Marcellus, Michigan

FIG PRESERVE CAKE
Number of Servings — 2 Loaves

2½ c. sugar
¾ c. butter
4 eggs
1 c. buttermilk
1 t. soda
2 c. fig preserves
3 c. flour
1 t. nutmeg
1 t. cloves
1 t. cinnamon
1 t. vanilla
1 c. nuts

Cream sugar and butter, add well beaten eggs. Mix soda with buttermilk and add to first mixture, gradually add flour, nutmeg, cloves, and cinnamon. Add fig preserves, vanilla, and nuts. Bake in loaf pan 1 hour at 300°F. Frost with icing below if desired.

Icing:
1 c. brown sugar
1 can evaporated milk
1 T. butter
1 T. vanilla

Boil sugar and milk until soft ball stage. Add butter and vanilla. Beat well and spread.

Marilyn Lively, Irvin H. S.
El Paso, Texas

FIG CAKE
Number of Servings — 15

2 c. flour
1 t. salt
1 t. soda
1½ c. sugar
1 c. cooking oil or oleo
3 eggs
1 c. buttermilk
1 c. fig preserves
1 c. chopped nuts
1 T. vanilla

Sift together flour, salt, soda, sugar. Add oil and beat well. Add eggs. Then add buttermilk gradually. Add figs, nuts and vanilla. Pour into greased loaf pan. Bake at 325°F. for 45 minutes. While hot, pour this sauce over cake in pan.

Sauce:
1 c. sugar
1 stick oleo
1 T. corn syrup
1 T. vanilla
½ c. buttermilk
¼ t. soda

Mix ingredients and boil for 3 minutes.

Mrs. Jo Marler, Forest H. S.
Forest, Mississippi

FLUFFY WHITE CAKE
Number of Servings — 8

½ c. soft shortening (half butter)
1½ c. sugar
2½ c. sifted cake flour
2½ t. baking powder
1 t. salt
1 c. milk
1½ t. flavoring
4 egg whites (½) c., stiffly beaten

Grease generously and flour two 8" or 9" layer pans or 13x9 oblong pan. Cream together until fluffy the shortening, butter and sugar. Sift together the flour, baking powder and salt. Mix in alternately with milk and flavoring. Fold in egg whites stiffly beaten. Pour into prepared pans. Bake in moderate oven 350°F. for 30 to 35 minutes for layers and 35 to 45 minutes for oblong. Cool. (Cooked white icing with coconut sprinkled over it. May use any 7-minute icing.)

Helen E. Pyle, Christian County H. S.
Hopkinsville, Kentucky

HILL-BILLY CAKE

Boil together for one minute:
1 c. sugar
1 c. cold water
½ c. nuts
½ t. salt
½ t. cloves
½ t. allspice
½ c. butter
1 c. seeded raisins
1 t. cinnamon
Add:
2 c. flour, sifted with 1 t. soda
Bake ½ hour at 350°F. in 9x12 pan.

(Continued on Next Page)

Icing:
⅔ c. melted butter
1½ c. brown sugar
6 T. cream
1 c. coconut

Blend all ingredients and spread on top of warm cake. Put under slow broiler for a few minutes until brown and bubbly.

Betty J. Hardman, Valley Head H. S.
Valley Head, Alabama

HEATH BAR CAKE
Number of Servings — 10-12
2 c. brown sugar
2 c. sifted flour
½ c. butter
1 egg, beaten
1 c. milk
1 t. soda
1 t. salt
1 t. vanilla

Stir sugar into flour and mix well, with pastry blender cut in butter until mixture is like cornmeal. Measure out 1 cup of mixture and set aside. To rest of mixture, add egg, milk, soda, salt, and vanilla, beat well. Pour into greased and floured 9x13x2 pan, spread with topping and bake in 350°F. oven for 35 minutes.

Topping:
Put 6 Heath bars in freezer, when hard, break bars with hammer (leave wrappers on while crushing). Remove crushed Heath bars from wrappers and blend broken candy with ½ cup broken pecans and the 1 cup of reserved crumb mixture.

Mrs. Rex Todd Withers, Home Economics and
Family Life Education Service
Lansing, Michigan

HUSBAND'S CAKE
Number of Servings — 20
¾ c. butter
1½ c. sugar
1 c. canned tomato soup
¾ c. water
1 t. soda
3 c. flour
¾ t. salt
3 t. baking powder
1½ t. cinnamon
1 t. cloves
1½ c. raisins
1½ c. nuts

Cream butter and sugar, combine tomato soup with water and soda. Add soup mixture alternately with sifted dry ingredients, stir in raisins and nuts. Bake at 350°F. about 1 hour.

Icing:
2 pkg. cream cheese
1 egg yolk
3 c. confectioners' sugar
⅛ t. salt
1 t. vanilla

Cream cheese, add egg yolk, stir in salt and 1 cup sugar, add vanilla. Stir in remaining sugar 1 cup at a time.

Mrs. Virginia Bonds, Shady Spring H. S.
Beaver, West Virginia

JOHN'S FAVORITE CAKE
(A Mile High Altitude Recipe)
2 c. sugar
1 c. butter
4 eggs
1 c. mashed potatoes
2 c. flour
½ t. each cinnamon, cloves, allspice, nutmeg, and vanilla
½ c. cocoa
2 t. baking powder
1 c. milk
1 c. nuts (pecans)

Cream butter and sugar, add eggs, one at a time.
1 small bottle cherries (cut in fourths)

Add potatoes. Sift flour, cocoa, spices, and baking powder sifted alternately with milk. Have cherries cut and drained on a towel, add nuts and cherries to mixture. Bake in tube pan in 350°F. oven. Ice with mocha icing if desired.

Mrs. Laurel Alexander Webb, Marfa H S.
Marfa, Texas

JUNE MOON CAKE
½ lb. butter
2 c. sugar
5 eggs
3 c. flour
1 t. baking powder
¾ c. water
1 t. vanilla

Cream butter and sugar, add one egg at a time, then 7 tablespoons flour. Add all water and remaining flour to which baking powder has been added. Add vanilla. Bake in two rectangular pans at 350°F.

Filling:
2 c. apricots, drained
1 lge. can crushed pineapple and juice
1 c. sugar
1 can flaked coconut

Combine and cook together for 15 minutes. Put on top and between the two layers, then cover with another can of coconut.

Mrs. Carolyn Hubbard, Bibb County H. S.
Centreville, Alabama

MARTHA WASHINGTON CAKE
Number of Servings — 20
1 c. shortening
2 c. sugar
4 egg yolks
1 t. vanilla
3 c. flour
¼ t. salt
3 t. baking powder
1 c. milk
4 stiffly beaten egg whites

Cream the shortening and sugar. Add egg yolks and vanilla. Beat well. Add sifted dry ingredients alternately with milk. Fold in egg whites. Bake in three wax paper lined 8" round layer cake pans. Bake at 350°F. for 30 minutes. Ice with fudge frosting.

Eileen Miller, Deuel County H. S.
Chappell, Nebraska

LANE CAKE

1 c. butter
2 c. sugar
3 c. sifted flour
1 c. milk
⅛ t. salt
1 t. vanilla
7 egg whites (beaten stiff)

Cream butter, add sugar gradually and cream until fluffy. Add sifted dry ingredients alternately with milk. Add vanilla. Fold in beaten egg whites. Pour into layer pans and bake at 350°F. (about 25 minutes).

Filling:
7 egg yolks (beaten well)
1 c. sugar
½ c. butter or oleo
1 c. chopped nuts
1 c. coconut (more may be used)
1 box seedless raisins
1 t. vanilla
½ c. wine (if desired)

Cook egg yolks, sugar and butter until thick (over low heat or double boiler). Stir constantly. Add raisins, nuts, coconut, vanilla and wine. Spread thick between layers, on top and sides.

Mildred Mason, Cherokee H. S.
Cherokee, Alabama

MARSHMALLOW CHOCOLATE CAKE

¼ lb. pkg. marshmallows
2 sq. chocolate, grated
½ c. hot water
1½ c. sifted pastry flour
1 t. vanilla
1 t. soda
1 t. salt
2 eggs, beaten
1 c. sugar
1 c. sour cream

Melt marshmallows and chocolate over water, add hot water, beating to smooth paste, cool. Sift pastry flour, measure 1½ cups and resift twice with soda and salt. Beat eggs, add sugar, whip until creamy. Add sour cream, stir until smooth, fold flour mixture gradually into egg mixture. Carefully fold in chocolate-marshmallow paste and vanilla, turn batter into 2 layer cake pans and bake 30-35 minutes at 375°F. Frost with chocolate fudge icing.

Mary Jane Bertrand, Blackfoot H. S.
Blackfoot, Idaho

MATRIMONIAL CAKE

12-2 Inch Squares
1½ c. flour
1 t. soda
1 c. butter
1½ c. quick cooking oatmeal
½ t. salt
½ c. brown sugar

Sift flour, measure. Place all ingredients in mixing bowl together. Blend shortening into ingredients. Place about half the quantity in a greased 8″ pan. Pat down firmly. Add date filling. Sprinkle the other half of mixture on top. Pat lightly. Bake in moderate oven 350°F. until light brown (about 20 minutes). When cold cut in squares.

Date Filling:
½ lb. dates (pitted)
½ c. water
1 T. vanilla
½ c. brown sugar
1 T. butter

Place all ingredients in boiler, cook until soft. Add vanilla and butter.

Mrs. J. Kenneth Smallwood, Bowdon H. S.
Bowdon, Georgia

MILKY WAY CAKE

Number of Servings — 10
8 Milky Way bars
2 sticks oleo
2 c. sugar
4 eggs
2½ c. flour
½ t. soda
1¼ c. buttermilk
1 c. chopped pecans

Melt Milky Way bars and 1 stick oleo, set aside. Cream sugar and 1 stick oleo. Add eggs. Add alternately flour, soda with buttermilk. Add melted candy and oleo mixture. Add pecans. Bake in tube pan at 325°F. for 1 hour and 10 minutes or until done.

Milky Way Cake Icing:
2½ c. sugar
1 c. evaporated milk
6 oz. semi-sweet chocolate chips
1 c. marshmallow cream
1 stick oleo

Cook to soft ball stage. Add chocolate chips, marshmallow cream, and oleo. Stir until all are melted.

Gayle Scott, Olton H. S.
Olton, Texas

MINCEMEAT CAKE

Number of Servings — 10
2 c. sifted cake flour
3 t. baking powder
½ t. cinnamon
½ t. cloves
½ c. cooking oil
½ c. milk
¾ c. moist mincemeat
2 eggs
1 c. sugar

Sift together the flour, baking powder, salt, cinnamon, and cloves. Add the oil, milk, and mincemeat, beat until it forms a smooth batter. In a separate bowl beat the eggs until thick and foamy. Gradually add the sugar and continue beating until very well blended. Fold this egg and sugar mixture thoroughly into the batter. Pour into a wax paper lined 9″ square pan. Bake in a moderate oven 350°F. 45 to 50 minutes.

Vivian Watson, Licking Valley H. S.
Newark, Ohio

NO SHORTENING CAKE
Number of Servings — 8
2 eggs
No. 2 can crushed pineapple
1½ c. sugar
¼ t. salt
2 t. soda
2½ c. plain flour (sifted)
Mix all ingredients together. Bake 30 minutes at 350°F.
Icing:
1½ c. sugar
1 c. Pet milk
2 sticks oleo
1 can angel flake coconut
½ c. chopped nuts
Heat and let boil 4 minutes. Add coconut and chopped nuts.

Sue Harrison, Keiser H. S.
Keiser, Arkansas

NUTMEG FEATHER CAKE WITH BROILED ICING
Number of Servings — 12
2¼ c. sifted cake flour
1 c. sugar
1 t. baking powder
¾ t. soda
1 t. salt
2 t. nutmeg
¾ c. brown sugar (packed)
½ c. soft shortening
1 c. buttermilk
3 eggs (½ to ⅔ c.)
6 t. soft butter
¾ c. brown sugar (packed)
4 T. rich cream
1 c. shredded coconut
Sift together in bowl flour, sugar, baking powder, soda, salt, and nutmeg. Add brown sugar, shortening, and buttermilk to dry ingredients and beat two minutes. Add eggs and beat two minutes. Pour mixture into a 13x9 oblong pan which has been greased and floured lightly. Bake 45-50 minutes at 350°F. Mix together butter, brown sugar, cream, and coconut for "Broiled Icing" about ten minutes before cake is done. Spread on top of warm cake. Place about 3" under broiler (low heat) until mixture bubbles and browns evenly over entire surface.

Mrs. Mary Jo Kinser, Calhoun H. S.
Calhoun, Tennessee

O SO GOOD CAKE
2-9 Inch Layers
¾ c. butter
2 c. sugar
2 c. buttermilk
3 t. soda
1 t. cinnamon
1 t. nutmeg
1 t. allspice
1 t. cloves
4 c. sifted flour
1 pt. seeded raisins in 1 c. water. Simmer while mixing other ingredients

Cream butter and sugar. Add milk. Sift all dry ingredients together and add to mixture. When it is well mixed reserve 1 cup of the dough for filling. Drain raisins and add to mixture. Save juice for filling. Pour into two 9" cake pans that have been well greased and floured. Bake in moderate oven until done.
O So Good Cake Filling:
1 c. raisin juice
2 c. sugar
1 c. cake dough
1 c. nuts
Put raisin juice, sugar, and cake dough into a saucepan and cook until it is caramelized. Add nuts and cook a few minutes more. Remove from heat and beat until thick enough to spread on cake.

Mrs. Annie May Jones, Hobbs School
Rotan, Texas

PENNSYLVANIA DUTCH PLUM CAKE
Number of Servings — 10-12
¼ c. shortening
¾ c. sugar
2 eggs
1 c. sifted flour
¼ c. milk
1 t. baking powder
½ t. vanilla
¼ t. salt
2 lb. blue plums
½ c. chopped nuts
½ t. cinnamon
¼ c. sugar
2 T. butter
Cream the shortening and sugar until blended, add the unbeaten eggs and stir until mixed. Add the milk, flour, baking powder, and salt. The vanilla may be added with the milk. Beat until the dough is well blended. Spread the dough evenly on a well-greased baking dish that is about 12x8. Cut the plums and remove the seeds. Lay the cut side of the plums up in even rows on the dough. Let the fruit overlap slightly. Mix ½ cup chopped nuts, cinnamon, with ¼ cup sugar and strew the mixture over the fruit. Spread the 2 tablespoons of butter over all the mixture. Bake at 350°F. for about 45 minutes. Serve with ice cream.

Mrs. George Simpson, Sterling H. S.
Sterling, Kansas

PLUM SAUCE CAKE
Number of Servings — 12
1 c. white sugar
½ c. butter
1 c. plum sauce
1 t. soda
1 c. seeded raisins
1 t. cinnamon
½ t. each cloves and nutmeg
1¾ c. flour
Cream sugar and butter. Add plum sauce (or any sauce) with the soda stirred into the mixture. Add raisins, cinnamon, cloves, nutmeg, and flour.

Ann Coughlin, Gary Public School
Gary, South Dakota

PIG AND WHISTLE CAKE

½ c. butter
½ c. milk
2 eggs
1 c. sugar
1½ c. flour
½ t. salt
1 t. baking powder
1 t. vanilla

Combine butter and milk, heat until hot and butter melts. Beat eggs until light yellow, add sugar. Beat until light and fluffy. Add hot milk and mix thoroughly. Add flour, baking powder, salt and vanilla. Blend well. Batter will be thin. Pour into greased 8x11x2 or 9x9x2 pan. Bake for 30 minutes at 350°F.

Topping:
1 c. brown sugar
3 T. cream
¼ c. butter
½ c. chopped walnuts

Mix, spread on hot cake and broil until brown.

Mrs. J. A. Myron, Chester H. S.
Chester, Montana

PINK AZALEA CAKE

2-9 Inch Layers

Grease generously and flour two 9″ layer pans for thick layers or three pans for thinner ones. Cream together until fluffy:
1 c. soft shortening (½ butter for flavor)
2 c. sugar
Sift together:
3 c. sifted cake flour
4 t. baking powder
1 t. salt
Stir in alternately with:
1¼ c. thin milk (½ water)
2 t. flavoring
Fold in:
6 egg whites (¾ c.) stiffly beaten

Tint batter for one layer a delicate pink. Bake at 350°F. for 30-35 minutes until cake tests done. Cool. Prepare favorite fluffy white frosting. Divide in half and into one portion fold cut-up maraschino cherries or strawberries and nuts. Put together with this filling. Tint remaining frosting pink and frost top and sides of cake.

Janet R. Stark, Blooming Prairie H. S.
Blooming Prairie, Minnesota

PLANTATION CAKE

1 t. vanilla
2 c. all-purpose flour
½ t. salt
6 eggs
1 c. Crisco
2 c. sugar

Combine Crisco, sugar, and vanilla, cream together until smooth. Add the eggs, one at a time, beating after each addition. Add sifted flour and salt. Bake in a tube or loaf pan in a slow oven 300-350°F. for one hour.

Mrs. Bernice Bagwell, Connally H. S.
Waco, Texas

PINTO FIESTA CAKE

1 c. sugar
¼ c. butter
1 egg, beaten
2 c. cooked pinto beans, mashed
1 c. flour
1 t. soda
½ t. salt
1 t. cinnamon
½ t. cloves
½ t. allspice
2 c. diced raw apples
1 c. raisins
½ c. chopped nuts
Vanilla

Cream sugar and butter, add beaten egg. Add mashed beans. Sift all dry ingredients together and add to sugar mixture. Add apples, raisins, chopped nuts, and vanilla. Pour into well greased 10″ tube pan and bake in 375°F. oven for 45 minutes. Glaze and decorate with maraschino cherry halves and walnut halves.

Mrs. Lola P. Smith, Aztec Public School
Aztec, New Mexico

POPCORN CAKE

1 c. sugar
1 c. white corn syrup
½ c. water
2 T. butter or margarine
Food coloring
18 c. popped corn
1 c. colored gumdrops

Combine sugar, syrup, water and butter in a saucepan. Switch to high until boiling, switch to low and cook until mixture reaches 240°F. Allow to cool slightly, then add food coloring. Combine popped corn and gumdrops and pour syrup over them. Mix well. Press mixture into a well greased 10″ tube pan. Unmold immediately. To serve, slice with a sharp knife. May be wrapped and frozen if desired.

Marilyn Benjamin, Niantic-Harristown H. S.
Niantic, Illinois

POPPY SEED CAKE

Number of Servings — 16-20

1 c. milk
½ c. poppy seed
½ c. shortening
1½ c. sugar
1 t. vanilla
2 c. flour
2 t. baking powder
4 egg whites

Scald milk and pour over poppy seed. Let stand for two hours or overnight, in refrigerator. Cream shortening and sugar until light and fluffy and add vanilla. Sift flour and baking powder together. Add flour mixture and poppy seed mixture alternately to creamed mixture, beginning and ending with flour mixture. Beat egg whites until stiff and fold into batter. Pour batter into 3 greased and floured 9″ cake pans and bake at 350°F. approximately 30 minutes, or until lightly browned.

(Continued on Next Page)

Filling:
4 egg yolks
¾ c. sugar
2 T. flour
1½ c. milk
1 c. coarsely chopped pecans

Beat egg yolks, add sugar, flour, and milk. Cook in heavy pan over low heat, stirring constantly, until thick. Add nuts, reserving a few to decorate top. When custard is cool enough to spread, fill and frost cake, add extra nuts on top.

This recipe submitted by the following teachers:
Mrs. Betty Thompson, Star H. S.
Star, Texas

Nancy Smith, Falfurrias H. S.
Falfurrias, Texas

POPPY SEED CAKE

2¼ c. sifted cake flour
4 t. baking powder
1 t. salt
1½ c. sugar
½ c. poppy seed
½ c. shortening
1 c. skim milk
1 t. vanilla
4 egg whites (½ c.)

Sift dry ingredients including sugar into a mixing bowl. Stir in poppy seed. Add shortening and ⅔ cup milk to dry ingredients. Beat for 2 minutes. Add unbeaten whites and remaining ⅓ cup milk, beat for 2 minutes more. (Thin batter.) Bake in two layers at 350°F. for 30-35 minutes.

Filling:
½ c. sugar
4 T. sifted flour
½ c. scalded milk
Juice of 1 lemon and rind
1 egg yolk
Dash of salt
1 T. butter

Combine sugar and flour in saucepan, mix well. Add cooled, scalded milk, lemon juice, and slightly beaten egg yolk. Cook over medium heat until thick, stirring constantly. Remove from heat, add butter and lemon rind. Cool. Spread between cooled layers of Poppy Seed Cake.

Aunt Mayme's Frosting (7-minute)
1½ c. white sugar
½ t. cream of tartar
5 T. cold water
1½ t. light syrup
2 egg whites
½ c. ground raisins

Combine all ingredients except ground raisins in top of double boiler. Cook over boiling water while beating with rotary or electric beater at high speed. Continue until frosting stands in soft peaks. Remove from heat, stir in ground raisins. Frost top and sides of cake with lemon filling between layers. This recipe makes enough to use as layer filling too.

Mrs. Ramona Scharf, Bangor H. S.
Bangor, Michigan

QUEEN ELIZABETH'S CAKE
Number of Servings — 18
1 c. boiling water
1 c. dates
1 t. soda
1 c. sugar
¼ c. butter
1 egg (beaten)
1½ c. flour
1 t. salt
1 t. baking powder

Sprinkle the soda over the dates and pour the boiling water over it. Let stand to cool while mixing the following: Cream the sugar and butter. Add the beaten egg, flour, salt and baking powder to the creamed mixture and mix well. Add to date mixture and pour into a 9x12 greased pan. Bake at 375°F. for 35 minutes.

Icing:
5 T. brown sugar
5 T. cream
2 T. butter
½ to 1 c. chopped nuts

Mix brown sugar, cream, and butter in a saucepan. Boil for 3 minutes and spread on the cake while still warm. Sprinkle with chopped nuts.

Katie Lou Krause, Van Vleck H. S.
Van Vleck, Texas

SHEATH CAKE
2 c. flour
2 c. sugar
1 stick butter or oleo
3 to 4 T. of cocoa
1 c. water
½ c. shortening
½ c. buttermilk
1 t. soda
2 eggs
1 t. vanilla

Pre-heat oven to 400°F. Mix sugar and flour together in a mixing bowl. Heat butter, cocoa, water and shortening in a saucepan until it reaches the boiling point. Pour hot mixture over the dry ingredients and add buttermilk with soda, egg and vanilla. Mix well. Pour batter into pan 11x15x1. Bake for 20 minutes.

Icing:
1 stick oleo
3 T. cocoa
6 T. milk
1 box powdered sugar
1 t. vanilla
½ c. chopped nuts

Put oleo, cocoa and milk in pan and heat until it begins to boil. Remove from stove and add sifted powdered sugar. Blend well and add vanilla and nuts. Pour over hot cake. Add coconut if desired.

This recipe submitted by the following teachers:
Mrs. Wanda Fae Gray, Longview Sr. H. S.
Longview, Texas
Arlene Riddle, Commerce H. S.
Commerce, Texas
Mrs. Naomi Austin, Gainesville Sr. H. S.
Gainesville, Texas

SPRING CAKE
Number of Servings — 30
4 c. flour
4 t. baking powder
¼ t. salt
2½ c. sugar
1 c. butter
1⅛ c. milk
1 t. vanilla or almond extract
6 egg whites

Sift flour, then measure. Add baking powder and salt. Sift three times. Cream butter, then gradually add the sifted sugar. Begin adding the flour and milk alternately starting with flour and ending with flour. Add the flavoring and fold in the beaten egg whites. Grease and flour five 8x12 pans. Bake in very thin layers at 350°F. Let cool.

Filling for Spring Cake:
Whip 1 pint of heavy cream. Take out ⅓ of it for the top frosting. Dividing the remainder of it in five portions. Keep cream as cold as possible. Mix ½ cup strawberry preserves with one portion of cream. Add red food coloring to make a pretty strawberry red. Spread on one layer of the cake. Put on another layer of cake. Spread with a mixture of cream and pineapple topping and enough yellow coloring for a pretty light yellow. The other fillings are made in the same manner. Use apricot topping or preserves with a good bit more yellow coloring. Pineapple and green coloring was used for one filling. Grape may be used. Spread cream over the top of the whole cake, sprinkle with chopped nuts. A 7-minute icing may be used for the top and sides. Chill for several hours before slicing.

Mrs. C. B. Carter, Kirbyville H. S.
Kirbyville, Texas

SWEET POTATO CAKE
Number of Servings — 14-16
⅜ c. oleo or butter
2 c. sugar
1 t. soda
2 c. flour
2 T. cocoa
1 t. allspice
1 t. cinnamon
1 t. cloves
1 t. nutmeg
½ t. salt
4 egg yolks, beaten
1 c. mashed, cooked sweet potatoes
1½ c. raisins
2 c. chopped nuts
1 c. buttermilk
4 egg whites, beaten stiff
1 t. vanilla

Cream together oleo and sugar. Sift together dry ingredients. Add to oleo and sugar. Add beaten egg yolks and potatoes. Combine raisins and nuts, add to the sweet potato mixture. Add buttermilk. Fold in beaten egg whites and vanilla. Bake in an angle food cake pan at 325°F. for 1 hour. Reduce temperature to 300°F. and bake 45 more minutes.

Mrs. Shirley Boddie, Calvin H. S.
Calvin, Louisiana

STRUMPET CAKE
Number of Servings — 16 or more
3 sticks oleomargarine (room temperature)
6 eggs (room temperature)
1 box confectioners' sugar
2½ c. flour
1 t. pure vanilla (2 t. imitation)
1 t. lemon extract

Cream oleomargarine and slowly add confectioners' sugar. Sift and measure flour and sift again. Alternate flour and 2 eggs at a time. Add vanilla and lemon. Cover top of cake pan with foil and bake at 325°F. for about 30 minutes. Remove foil and bake 45 minutes more. If you do not intend to ice, sprinkle greased tube pan sides and bottom with flour to make sides crusty.

Mrs. Willie Fay Spurlock, M. C. Napier H. S.
Hazard, Kentucky

TEN DOLLAR CAKE
1 c. butter
2½ c. sugar
3 c. flour
¼ t. salt
1 t. soda
5 t. strong coffee
1 c. buttermilk
3 t. cocoa
1 t. vanilla
1 t. lemon extract
5 egg whites, beaten (fold into cake)

Cream butter and sugar together until fluffy, add egg yolks one at a time and beat well. Sift together flour, soda, cocoa, and salt, add buttermilk and flour alternately, add coffee and extract, mix well. Fold in egg whites. Bake in three 9" pans 350°F. for 30-35 minutes.

Icing:
¼ c. butter
1 box powdered sugar
3 t. strong coffee
1 t. vanilla
1 t. lemon
1 egg yolk
5 T. cream
1 box coconut

Melt butter, add sugar and coffee and mix well. Add egg yolk and beat, add extracts, cream and beat at high speed until creamy, then add coconut.

Sandra Crawford, Savoy H. S.
Savoy, Texas

TOASTED BUTTER PECAN CAKE
2 c. pecans, chopped
1¼ c. butter
3 c. flour
2 t. double acting baking powder
½ t. salt
2 c. sugar
4 unbeaten eggs
1 c. milk
2 t. vanilla

Toast pecans in ¼ cup butter in 350°F. oven 20-25 minutes, stir frequently. Sift flour with baking powder and salt, cream 1 cup butter, gradually add sugar, creaming well. Blend in eggs, beat well

(Continued on Next Page)

after each, add dry ingredients alternately with milk. Blend well after each addition, stir in vanilla and 1¼ cups pecans. Turn into two 9″ or three 8″ round layer pans (greased and floured). Bake at 350°F. for 25-30 minutes. Cool, spread frosting between layers and top.

Butter pecan frosting:
¼ c. butter
1 lb. sifted powdered sugar
1 t. vanilla
4-6 T. evaporated milk
Cream butter, add sifted powdered sugar, vanilla and evaporated milk until frosting is spreading consistency. Stir in remaining pecans.

Mrs. Perry Laconte, Elbert County H. S.
Elberton, Georgia

RUM CAKE
Number of Servings — 14
1 c. shortening
2 c. sugar
4 eggs
3 c. cake flour
1 t. soda
¼ to ½ t. salt
1 c. buttermilk
1½ t. rum flavoring
½ t. vanilla flavoring
Cream shortening, add sugar to shortening gradually and cream well. Add eggs and blend well. Sift dry ingredients together. Add dry ingredients and buttermilk alternately, beginning and ending with the dry ingredients. Beat well after each addition. Add flavorings. Bake in a slightly greased and floured tube pan at 375°F. for 15 minutes, then decrease temperature to 350°F. for 30 minutes. Let the cake remain in the pan for 5 minutes after removing from the oven.

Rum Sauce:
1 c. sugar
2 T. brown sugar
½ c. water
1½ t. rum flavoring
Combine all ingredients in a saucepan. Heat the mixture until it boils, then remove from the heat immediately. Dip the sauce over the entire surface of the cake. Place the cake in a covered box to allow the sauce to penetrate into the cake.

Emma Jewel Goodwin, Bertram H. S.
Bertram, Texas

TIPSY CAKE
Number of Servings — 10
1 c. flour
1 t. baking powder
¼ t. salt
3 eggs
1 c. sugar
3 T. hot water
1 t. lemon extract
Sift flour, baking powder, and salt together. Separate eggs. Beat whites stiff and gradually beat in one-half sugar. Add water and extract to egg yolks, beat until light and gradually beat in remaining sugar. Sift in flour, mix gently, add

whites. Fold for a very light cake and beat together for a finer grained cake.

Custard:
1 qt. milk
4 to 6 eggs
1 c. sugar
Vanilla
Scald milk and pour eggs beaten with sugar in double boiler. If 6 eggs are used no flour is needed but if 4 eggs are used, add 1 tablespoon flour to sugar. Return to double boiler and cook custard until somewhat thickened. Flavor with vanilla. While cakes are hot pour ⅔ cup wine (scuppernong or sherry) over them. Blanch ¼ lb. almonds and stick about in cakes. Place cold cakes in large bowl and pour over the cakes the cold custard. Let stand several hours and serve with whipped cream, seasoned with wine or brandy.

Mrs. Mary Katherine Rymell, Boyd H. S.
Boyd, Texas

VANILLA WAFER CAKE
Number of Servings — 18
2 sticks margarine
2 c. sugar
6 whole eggs
1-12 oz. box vanilla wafers
½ c. milk
1-7 oz. pkg. flaked coconut
1 c. chopped pecans
Cream margarine and sugar. Add eggs, one at a time, and beat after each. Crush the vanilla wafers and add alternately with the milk. Add coconut and chopped pecans. Bake in greased and floured tube pan at 325°F. for 1 hour and 15 minutes.

This recipe submitted by the following teachers:
Faye L. Greenway, Dublin H. S.
Dublin, Texas
Frances J. Holbrook, South Habersham H. S.
Cornelia, Georgia
Mrs. Doveta Hunt, Pecos H. S.
Pecos, Texas
Mrs. J. Y. Smith, Greenwood H. S.
Greenwood, Mississippi

WESTERN CAKE
Number of Servings — 20
3 sticks butter or margarine (at room temperature)
1-1 lb. box powdered sugar
6 eggs at room temperature
Grated rind of 1 lemon
1 T. lemon juice
Sift sugar box full of all-purpose flour
Cream butter and powdered sugar until fluffy. Add one egg at a time. Cream after each addition, never stop beater (scrape from sides of bowl often). Sift flour into creamy mixture in four steps, beating all the time. Add grated rind of lemon and 1 tablespoon lemon juice. Bake in ungreased stem pan at 325°F., 1 hour and 30 minutes. This cake will keep in freezer.

Sevola Fulgham, Safford H. S.
Safford, Arizona

WATERMELON RIND PRESERVE CAKE (May Use Pear Preserves)

3 c. flour
1 t. soda
½ t. allspice
½ t. cloves
1 t. cinnamon or ½ cinnamon and nutmeg if desired
Few grains of salt
1 c. watermelon rind preserves and juice
1 c. pecans
¾ c. butter
2½ c. sugar
4 eggs
1-2 t. vanilla
1 c. buttermilk

Mix and sift flour, soda, allspice, cloves, cinnamon, and salt. Chop watermelon rind preserves and cover with juice, chop pecans. Cream butter and sugar. Beat eggs into the creamed mixture 1 at a time. Add vanilla. Mix buttermilk with the juice from the preserves. Mix pecans and watermelon preserves. Dredge with a little of the flour. Add flour alternately with the milk mixture. Bake in three greased pans at 350°F.

Frosting:
2 c. sugar
½ c. milk
½ c. cream
⅛ c. well packed brown sugar

Boil sugar with milk and cream. After it begins to boil add brown sugar. Cook to just below soft ball, cool, beat and spread.

Myrtle Jennings, Brownsville H. S.
Brownsville, Texas

WHITE DELIGHT CAKE

½ c. Crisco
1¼ c. sugar
4-5 egg whites
2 c. cake flour (sift twice before measuring)
3 t. double-acting baking powder
1 t. salt
1 c. milk
1 t. vanilla

Blend thoroughly together Crisco and sugar. Combine flour, baking powder, and salt and add alternately with milk and vanilla mixture. Beat well. Beat egg whites until very firm. Add to mixture by folding gently in. Spread in one 13x9x2½ cake tin lined with plain paper or rubbed with Crisco and floured. Bake at 350°F. 35 to 40 minutes. *Test*: If done, cake will spring back when touched lightly with finger. Cool over cake rack 10 to 20 minutes. Loosen sides of cake from pan with spatula, then place cake rack over cake and invert together. Turn cake bottom side down to finish cooling before frosting. When cake is cool cut through center and add Jello. Strawberry or some light shade, lime, orange, etc. Place cake together just as you would do with a two layer cake. Top with Jello and Dream Whip. You may add a little Dream Whip with the center filling also. Add a few cut cherries.

Sister Mary Louise, S.S.J., Notre Dame H. S.
Clarksburg, West Virginia

WHIPPED CREAM CAKE

1 c. cream
1 c. sugar
1 t. vanilla
2 t. baking powder
2 eggs
1½ c. cake flour
¼ t. salt
Shredded coconut

Whip cream until slightly thickened but not until it holds a peak. Fold in sugar, then eggs beaten to a froth, add vanilla. Sift cake flour, baking powder, and salt. Fold into the egg mixture, do not beat. Bake in two 8" layer cake pans at 375°F. Frost with 7-minute frosting, sprinkle generously with shredded coconut.

Mrs. Cornelia C. Peterson, North Stanly H. S.
New London, North Carolina

WHITE MOUNTAIN CAKE

2 c. sugar
1 c. shortening (country butter)
1¼ c. sweet milk
6 egg whites
3 c. flour
1 t. salt
1 t. vanilla
3 t. baking powder

Cream shortening and sugar well. Add salt. Add milk and flour alternately. Reserve 1 cup of flour to mix with baking powder, to be added to cake last. Add vanilla. Fold in well beaten egg whites. This will make 3 layers. Bake at 350°F. for 30 minutes.

Maurita Taylor, Estelline H. S.
Estelline, Texas

APPLE TOPSY-TURVY CAKE

Number of Servings — 6-8

3 T. butter
⅔ c. apricot preserves
3-4 med. apples, pared, cored
¼ c. seedless raisins
1¾ c. sifted flour
1 c. granulated sugar
2½ t. baking powder
¼ t. salt
1 t. cinnamon
¼ t. cloves
¼ t. nutmeg
⅓ c. soft shortening
¾ c. milk
1 egg

Combine butter or margarine and preserves in small pan and bring to boil. Pour into a 9x9x2 pan. Cut apples into ¼" rings, chop end slices. Place 1 ring in center of pan, cut remaining rings in half and arrange around center ring. Press raisins in centers of rings. Sift flour, sugar, baking powder, salt, cinnamon, cloves and nutmeg. Add shortening and milk. Beat 2 minutes. Fold in chipped end slices. Spoon batter over rings in pan. Bake in moderate oven 350°F. 45-50 minutes. Invert cake on plate. Leave pan over cake for 5 minutes so topping will run down over cake. Serve warm.

Helen Janis Hale, Somerset H. S.
Somerset, Kentucky

APRICOT UPSIDE-DOWN CAKE

Number of Servings — 8-10

1½ c. cooked, sweetened dried apricots
2 T. water
⅓ c. brown sugar, firmly packed
3 T. butter or margarine
½ t. cinnamon

Turn oven to 375°F. Combine sugar, butter, cinnamon, and water in skillet about 9x2, place in oven until butter is melted, remove from oven, evenly distribute sugar mixture in bottom of skillet, and place apricots uniformly over syrup.

1¾ c. sifted cake flour
2½ t. baking powder
½ t. salt
½ c. shortening
1 c. sugar
⅔ c. milk
1 t. vanilla

Sift flour, salt, and baking powder and cream with shortening, gradually add sugar and vanilla, beat until fluffy. Beat eggs and add to sugar and shortening.

Mrs. Earl Spriestersbach, Cyril H. S.
Cyril, Oklahoma

CHOCOLATE UPSIDE DOWN CAKE

Number of Servings — 8

1 c. cake flour
1 t. baking powder
¼ t. salt
⅔ c. sugar
¼ c. softened butter
½ c. milk
1 egg, well beaten
½ t. vanilla
1 sq. unsweetened chocolate
3 T. butter
½ c. sugar
2 c. sliced drained peaches

Sift flour, measure, add baking powder, salt, and ⅔ cup sugar, and sift together again. Add ¼ cup butter. Combine egg, milk and vanilla. Add to flour mixture, stirring until all flour is dampened. Add chocolate and blend. Beat vigorously 1 minute. Melt 3 Tablespoons butter in a 8x8 cake pan. Add ½ c. sugar and cook until well mixed. Arrange peaches on this. Turn batter on contents of pan. Bake in a moderate oven 50 minutes or until done. Serve upside down with whipped cream.

Mrs. Rush Valentine, Starkville H. S.
Starkville, Mississippi

CHOCOLATE FUDGE UPSIDE DOWN CAKE

Number of Servings — 10

¾ c. sugar
1 T. butter
½ c. milk
1 c. flour
½ t. salt
1 t. baking powder
1½ T. cocoa
½ c. chopped nuts
½ c. granulated sugar
½ c. brown sugar
¼ c. cocoa
1¼ c. boiling water

Cream together the ¾ cup sugar and tablespoon butter and add ½ cup milk and stir. Sift together flour, salt, baking powder and 1½ tablespoon cocoa and add to mixture. Stir well and put in a 9″ buttered round pan. Sprinkle with chopped nuts. Then mix together ½ cup granulated sugar, ½ cup brown sugar, ¼ cup cocoa and spread over top of dough in pan. Pour the boiling water over the top of it all and bake in 350°F. oven for 30 or 40 minutes. Let cool in pan. Cut in wedge-shape serving pieces. Turn up-side-down to serve and top with whipped cream or vanilla ice cream.

Sandra King, Lyeffion H. S.
Evergreen, Alabama

PEACH UPSIDE-DOWN CAKE

Number of Servings — 6-8

4 T. butter
½ c. brown sugar

Make a syrup of the butter and brown sugar, adding the sugar to the melted butter, using an iron skillet. Arrange six sliced peaches, smoothly, over the syrup in the skillet.

¾ c. sugar
1 egg
4 T. butter
1¼ t. baking powder
½ t. salt
1¼ c. sifted flour
½ c. milk
1 t. vanilla

Pour batter over the peaches and bake 40 minutes at 400°F. When done turn out on a flat dish upside down, peaches and syrup on top. Serve hot, as is, or with whipped cream or a scoop of ice cream.

Mrs. Margaret I. Lott, New Oxford H. S.
New Oxford, Pennsylvania

PINEAPPLE UPSIDE DOWN CAKE

Number of Servings — 8 or 9

½ c. butter
1 c. brown sugar
1 No. 2 can sliced pineapple
2 T. lge. whole pecans
1 c. sifted cake flour
1 t. baking powder
⅛ t. salt
3 eggs (separated)
1 c. granulated sugar
5 T. pineapple juice

Melt butter in large baking pan. Spread brown sugar evenly in pan and arrange pineapple slices on sugar filling in spaces with pecans. Sift flour, baking powder and salt together. Beat egg yolks until light, adding sugar gradually, add pineapple juice, and sifted flour. Fold in stiffly beaten egg whites. Pour batter over pineapple. Bake in moderate oven 375°F. 30 to 35 minutes. Turn upside down on cake plate. Serve with whipped cream if desired.

Mrs. Carolyn Ibert, Hammond H. S.
Hammond, Louisiana

PINEAPPLE UPSIDE-DOWN CAKE

2 T. butter
½ c. brown sugar
4 pineapple slices, drained
6 maraschino cherries
⅓ c. shortening
1¼ c. sifted flour
½ c. sugar
2 t. baking powder
½ t. salt
½ c. minus 1 T. pineapple syrup
½ t. grated lemon peel
1 egg

Melt butter in 8x8x2 pan. Stir in brown sugar. Halve pineapple slices, place in mixture, center with 3 cherry pieces. Sift dry ingredients together over softened shortening. Add remaining ingredients. Beat 2 minutes. Pour over pineapple. Bake at 375°F. for 45 minutes. Let stand 5 minutes, turn upside down.

Mrs. Kathryn Janicek, Buckholts H. S.
Buckholts, Texas

PINEAPPLE UPSIDE DOWN CAKE

Number of Servings — 6
¼ c. butter
½ c. sugar
½ c. pineapple syrup
1¼ c. flour
2½ t. baking powder
½ t. salt
1 egg (separated)
½ t. vanilla

Cream butter with sugar, add beaten egg yolk. Add pineapple syrup alternately with sifted mixture of flour, baking powder, and salt. Fold in stiffly beaten egg white, add vanilla.

Filling:
3 T. butter (melted)
¾ c. brown sugar
½ c. sliced pineapple

Melt butter in frying pan, add brown sugar. When melted spread on sliced pineapple. Pour cake batter over this and bake in moderate oven 375°F. Turn up-side-down to put fruit on top.

Mrs. Margia S. Roberts, Rowan County H. S.
Morehead, Kentucky

PINEAPPLE UPSIDE DOWN CAKE

Number of Servings — 6 to 8
¼ c. butter or oleomargarine
⅔ c. brown sugar
6 to 8 pineapple slices
Maraschino cherries
2 egg yolks
¾ c. sugar
¼ c. boiling pineapple juice
¾ c. cake flour
⅛ t. salt
½ t. baking powder
½ t. vanilla
2 stiffly beaten egg whites

Melt butter in an 8x12 pan while oven is heating. Add brown sugar. Arrange pineapple and cherries over this and return to oven to heat while you make the cake batter. Beat egg yolks, add sugar gradually. Add hot juice, then dry ingredients and extract. Fold in stiffly beaten egg whites. Bake ½ hour at 325°F. A longer baking time is required if a Pyrex pan is used. Invert cake on plate to serve.

Phyllis J. Taylor, George Washington H. S.
Alexandria, Virginia

BUTTER CAKE

Number of Servings — 18
1 c. butter
2 c. sugar
5 eggs
2 c. flour (all-purpose)
1 t. flavoring

Cream butter and sugar. Then add eggs one at a time, beating after each egg. Then add flavoring and flour using the mixer until cake is ready for the pan. Bake in a well greased and floured tube cake pan for 45 minutes at 375°F.

Mrs. Ina C. Hooper, Elizabeth H. S.
Elizabeth, Louisiana

PLAIN CAKE

Number of Servings — 12
2 c. sifted cake flour
2½ t. baking powder
½ t. salt
½ c. shortening
1 c. sugar
2 eggs
⅔ c. milk
1 t. vanilla extract

Sift together flour, baking powder, and salt. Cream shortening. Add sugar gradually and cream together until light and fluffy. Add eggs, one at a time, and beat well after each addition. Add sifted dry ingredients alternately with milk, a small amount at a time, beating after each addition until smooth. Add vanilla. Pour into two greased 8" layer pans and bake in a 375°F. oven for 25 to 30 minutes.

Wanda Clark, Porter H. S.
Maryville, Tennessee

FOUNDATION CAKE

30 Cupcakes or 3 Layers
¾ c. butter
2 c. sugar
4 eggs
3 c. plain flour
3 t. baking powder
1 t. salt
1 c. sweet milk
1 t. vanilla

Cream butter until soft. Add sugar gradually while beating. Add eggs one at a time, beating well after each. Sift flour, baking powder and salt together three times. Add vanilla to milk. Alternately add dry ingredients and milk to the butter, sugar and egg mixture, beating well after each addition. Place in three 9" cake pans which have been lined with wax paper and greased. Bake at 375°F. for 25 minutes.

Doris Gunter, Pelion H. S.
Pelion, South Carolina

PLAIN CAKE
Number of Servings — 25
3 c. sugar
½ c. Crisco
1 stick oleomargarine
5 lge. eggs
3 c. flour (plain)
1 c. milk (sweet)
1 t. butternut flavoring or 1 t. vanilla, 1 t. lemon

Cream sugar, Crisco and oleo together until creamy. Add one egg at a time and beat, fold in flour and milk alternately. Add flavoring. Bake at 350°F.

Martha R. Rankin, Calhoun Falls H. S.
Calhoun Falls, South Carolina

PLAIN CAKE WITH BROILED TOPPING
Number of Servings — 10
½ c. shortening
2 c. flour
1½ c. sugar
3 t. baking powder
1 t. salt
1 c. milk
1½ t. vanilla
2 eggs

Soften shortening in mixing bowl. Sift in dry ingredients. Add milk, beat until smooth. Vanilla should be in milk. Add eggs, beat 2 minutes or until smooth. Pour into well greased and floured rectangular 9x18 pan. Bake in 375°F. oven for 50 minutes or until done.

Topping:
¼ c. butter, melted
¾ c. brown sugar
1 c. coconut, shredded

Mix topping ingredients, sprinkle over surface of cake. Place under broiler, broil until mixture bubbles.

Mrs. Jilma G. Vidaurri, Cunningham Jr. H. S.
Corpus Christi, Texas

1-2-3-4 CAKE
Number of Servings — 20
1 c. butter or margarine
2 c. sugar
3 c. sifted flour
4 eggs
2 t. baking powder
1 c. sweet milk
1 t. vanilla

Cream together butter and 1 cup sugar. Add well beaten egg yolks. Sift together flour and baking powder and add alternately with the milk to the butter-sugar mixture beating well after each addition. Add vanilla. Beat egg whites until stiff but not dry. Add remaining cup sugar to egg whites and fold into the cake batter. Line stemmed cake pan or three layer cake pans with two thicknesses of brown paper. Grease pan and papers. Bake at 350°F. for about 25 to 30 minutes for layers or one hour for loaf cake. Serve plain or frosted. Keeps moist for several days.

Mrs. Ella Furr Long, Terry H. S.
Terry, Mississippi

1-2-3-4 CAKE
Number of Servings — 16
1 c. shortening
2 c. sugar
4 eggs
3 c. flour
3 t. baking powder
1 t. salt
1 c. milk
2 t. vanilla

Cream together shortening and sugar in a bowl. Add eggs to shortening and sugar one at a time and beat. Sift together flour, baking powder, and salt. Alternate milk with flour. Add vanilla and stir. Grease and flour three 8" cake pans or two 9" cake pans. Bake 350°F. for 35 to 40 minutes.

Maude M. Henderson, Gunston Jr. H. S.
Arlington, Virginia

1-2-3-4 CAKE
3-9 Inch Layers
3 c. sifted cake flour
3 t. baking powder
¼ t. salt
1 c. shortening
2 c. sugar
1 t. vanilla
¼ t. lemon
4 eggs, separated
1 c. milk

Sift flour, baking powder and salt together. Cream shortening with sugar until fluffy. Add beaten egg yolks and beat thoroughly. Add sifted dry ingredients and milk alternately in small amounts, beating well after each addition. Beat egg whites until stiff but not dry and fold into batter. Pour into greased pans and bake in moderate oven 375°F. about 30 minutes. Makes three 9" layers. 350°F. 1 hour.

Mary Helen Candee, Williamsburg Jr. H. S.
Arlington, Virginia

BROILER CAKE
Number of Servings — 20
3 eggs
1½ c. sugar
1½ c. flour
1½ t. baking powder
6 T. butter
⅔ c. milk
1 t. vanilla
Few grains of salt

Beat eggs, add sugar. Sift dry ingredients, add to eggs and sugar. Melt butter, add milk and bring to boil. Add to above mixture. Add vanilla. Bake 30 minutes in loaf pan 13x9x2 325°F.

Topping:
10 T. butter (melted)
18 T. brown sugar
8 T. cream
1 c. chopped pecans
1 c. shredded coconut or pineapple

Beat together butter, sugar, and cream. Add nuts and coconut or pineapple. Pour over cake and place in broiler until brown.

Mrs. May Campbell, Orangefield H. S.
Orangefield, Texas

rostings, Fillings, Sauces & Toppings

Frosting the Cake

These steps make frosting a cake easy:

1. COOL CAKE AND FROSTING

Frost the cake as soon as it is thoroughly cool. Frosting protects the cake—keeps it fresh and moist. To prevent the cake from becoming soggy, both frosting and filling should be cool. For best results, apply frostings in a cool room.

2. PROVIDE A CONVENIENT PLACE FOR APPLYING THE FROSTING

Set the cake plate on rim of large mixing bowl—with plate extending beyond rim of bowl, so that the cake can be turned around easily while frosting and decorating.

3. GET THE CAKE READY FOR FROSTING

Brush loose crumbs away with hand and trim ragged edge with scissors. This keeps crumbs out of frosting. If desired, strips of waxed paper may be placed under the edges of the cake to catch frosting that might be spilled on the cake plate. When the cake has been frosted, carefully pull out the strips.

4. SINGLE-LAYER CAKES

Place one-layer and sheet cakes *right side* up on the cake plate. Frost sides and top. (Frostings go on top sides of cake more smoothly than on the bottom sides.)

5. TWO-LAYER CAKES

Place one layer, *upside down,* on cake plate. Spread with frosting or filling. Let stand until set. Then place second layer, *right side up,* on top of filling. If layers tend to slip, thrust a wire cake tester through both layers to anchor them until filling sets. This can be removed before frosting the top or left until frosting is set, then removed. The mark may be covered with decorations.

6. THREE-LAYER CAKES

Proceed as for a two-layer cake, then spread top of second layer with filling or frosting. Let stand until set. Place third layer, *right side up,* on top of filling.

7. ANGEL FOOD AND OTHER CAKES BAKED IN TUBE PANS

Turn upside down on cake plate. These cakes may be cut into layers and put together with fillings. Use a thin sharp knife and sawing motion for cutting. Use toothpicks in sides of cake as markers for cutting even slices. If desired, the hole in center of cake can be covered with a piece of waxed cardboard and frosting spread over it. If hole is not covered, spread inside with frosting.

8. FROSTING THE OUTSIDE OF THE CAKE

Frost sides of cake, holding spatula in vertical position. Pull up toward top. Let the frosting reach the bottom of the cake all around. Pile remaining frosting on top and spread—smoothly if the cake is to be decorated—in swirls and ridges if it is to have no other decoration.

To make the cake look taller, pull spatula around the top to form a ridge at edge of cake.

To obtain a smooth surface on cakes that are to be decorated, first frost with a thin layer of frosting to set crumbs. Fill in spaces at base and between layers. Let stand until set. Then frost with a thick layer of frosting. If necessary, smooth surface with spatula dipped into hot water.

TOOLS TO MAKE CAKE DECORATING EASY

You will find these tools in stores which sell home furnishings:

> A flexible spatula about 8 inches long
> A cake decorator set
> Wooden toothpicks
> Waxed paper
> Scissors
> Sharp knife

EXTRA HELPS TO MAKE CAKE DECORATING MORE FUN

You will find these in grocery and dime stores:

> Maraschino cherries
> Food coloring sets
> Gold and silver dragees (these are little candy balls covered with edible silver and gold coating)
> Red cinnamon candies
> Colored gumdrops
> Cake candy pellets (these are tiny, bright-colored balls of candy. They are usually sold in small jars)
> Paper lace doilies
> Paper patterns for outlining designs on cake
> Bright colored jellies and jams
> Chocolate
> Nuts
> Coconut
> Peppermint stick candy
> Raisins

SEE CANDY SECTION FOR HIGH ALTITUDE ADJUSTMENTS.

How to Use a Cake Decorator

Inexpensive cake decorator sets may be purchased at department and dime stores. Many of these give excellent results and if thoroughly washed and dried after each using, they last for years.

A cake decorator consists of a plastic-lined bag or a metal gun and various tips or tubes which fit into the bag or gun. The frosting is forced through the tips much the same way that toothpaste is forced from the tube. Just as different size and shape toothpaste tubes give different shaped ribbons of toothpaste, the different size decorator tips form different size and shaped frosting ribbons.

When the toothpaste tube is squeezed gently, only a small amount of toothpaste comes out on the brush and if the pressure is released and the tube lifted, a little point will form on the bit of toothpaste. In the same manner, if frosting is squeezed from the decorator, then the pressure released and the tip lifted, a little leaf or flower petal is formed.

Directions for using the decorator come with the sets. You can gain skill in using the set by practicing on a piece of waxed paper or the bottom of an enameled pan or cake pan. (The frosting can be scraped back in the decorator and used over and over until you have mastered the design you desire.)

Test the consistency of the frosting by placing a little in the decorator with the tube or tip to be used. It should be thin enough to force easily but should be thick enough to hold its shape. Variations in weather and temperature may cause variations in consistency. If frosting should be too thin, beat in a little *Powdered (Confectioners') Sugar*. If too thick, add a few drops of water.

Most decorator sets have 4 tips or tubes—plain, rosette, leaf and shell or star tips.

THE PLAIN TIP

The plain tip has a small round opening, much like that in the end of a mechanical pencil. This tip is used for fine writing and lines.

To use, first trace the letters or design on the frosted cake with a toothpick. Place the plain tip in the decorator and fill decorator two-thirds full of frosting. Hold tip barely touching the cake. Squeeze bag, or force gun, so that frosting flows with steady even pressure. Follow the toothpick tracing. Once you have started a line or word, continue until it is finished. Stopping leaves a ragged line.

Many simple designs may be made with this tip. For flower stems, make curved lines. For flowers, make dots by forcing a bit of the frosting on the cake, releasing the pressure, then lifting the tip.

Use the plain tip to pipe lines diagonally across the cake to form diamonds. Place a flower dot on the crossed line.

For a beautiful web effect, pipe circles one inch apart on cake, extending from center to edge of cake. While frosting is still soft, draw a toothpick through the lines, starting first in the center, then from the edge to the center.

For a marbled effect, pipe lines of contrasting color straight across the cake, making them about three-fourths inches apart. Before the lines harden, draw a toothpick through them, first from the bottom to the top, then from top to bottom.

For borders, use piped lines of loops and curves around the cake.

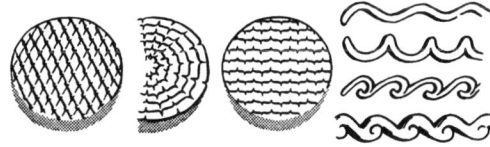

THE ROSETTE TIP

This tip has a much larger opening than the plain tip. The opening consists of several slots or notches cut into the metal. Frosting forced through this tube forms a ridged, rope-like ribbon. It is used to write large letters or greetings or it may be used to make borders.

To make flower rosettes, hold tube upright, about one-fourth inch from the cake, press out frosting, release pressure, then lift tip away. Other flower shapes may be made by holding the tip at different angles.

THE LEAF TIP

 The leaf tip has a narrow opening, formed by long, narrow notches. Frosting forced through this tip forms a wide, flat ribbon with lines or veins. Use it for leaves, borders, and decorating sides of cake.

For leaves, hold tip at an angle, press (increasing pressure widens leaf), release pressure, then lift tip. This tip may also be used to make flower petals.

SHELL OR STAR TIP

 These tips have smaller openings than rosette tips. They may be used for borders and decorations in much the same way as rosette tip.

FLOWER NAILS

Roses and other large flower shapes may look flat if piped directly on the cake. To avoid this flat look, you can do as the baker does—make the flower on a flower nail, let stand over night, then place on the cake.

 A flower nail has a sharp point, much like a common nail. The heads are of various sizes, depending on the size flower to be made. Flower nails, as well as cake decorators with a great variety of tips, may be purchased from bakery supply houses. A flower nail helps you do a

better job shaping petals because you can rotate the nail while piping.

To use a flower nail, first pipe a little mound of frosting in center of the greased nail head. Stick nail in cardboard box. Let stand until set. Then, with leaf tip, pipe petals around the frosting mound, turning the nail in your hand as you pipe the petals. Let stand until set. For best results, each row of petals should be allowed to set before another row is added. Stick the nail with the finished flower into the cardboard box and let stand several hours before placing on cake.

If you have no flower nail, get a dozen or so 6 or 8 penny common nails from a hardware store. Cut pieces of cardboard the size you wish your flowers to be. Thrust the nails through the cardboard so that the underneath side of the nail head touches the cardboard. Brush tops of nails and cardboard with melted paraffin. Let dry before using.

LAYING OUT THE DECORATIONS

Before applying decorations, it is usually easier to trace the design on the frosted cake with a toothpick. Rulers, compass, tape measure, and paper patterns are helpful in spacing the designs evenly.

For an easy way to space the designs on sides of a round cake, first use a tape measure to measure around the pan in which the cake was baked. Then determine the number and width of designs. For instance, a cake which measured 28 inches could have 7 designs that are 4 inches wide ($7 \times 4 = 28$) or it could have 8 designs $3\frac{1}{2}$ inches wide ($8 \times 3\frac{1}{2} = 28$).

Use a compass or paper pattern as a pattern for marking where the designs begin and end.

GIVE YOUR CAKES A LIFT...

White, chocolate, spice or sponge — they're all delicious, but most can stand a little help to make them glamorous. You need not be an artist to decorate cakes that give pleasure to your family and friends. Here are suggestions for decorating your cakes for special occasions with special consideration for the days when you have little time. (You can follow these ideas without doing any overtime in the kitchen.) A suggestion to follow is to design your pattern on paper, then transfer to cardboard and cut out. Trace the letters or design on the frosted cake with a toothpick. Take your time and have fun.

New Year's Eve Cake

Christmas Cake

Heart Cake

Jack-O-Lantern Cake

Wedding or Anniversary Cake

Shamrock Cake

Patriotic Cake

Mother's Day Cake

Easter Egg Cake

ALMOND CREAM FILLING

Number of Servings — 12

¼ c. flour
¼ c. sugar
¼ c. cold milk
1 c. hot milk
½ c. butter or margarine
½ c. confectioners' sugar
2 t. vanilla
½ c. slivered almonds
1 T. butter

Combine flour, sugar, and cold milk. Add to hot milk in saucepan and cook, stirring constantly until thick (5 minutes). Remove from heat, and cool until lukewarm. Cream butter, confectioners' sugar and vanilla and add to cooled cooked mixture. Add almonds that have been browned in 1 tablespoon butter. Chill until firm enough to spread on cake or chiffon roll.

Irene H. Nelson, Alabama School for Deaf
Talladega, Alabama

BANANA CAKE ICING

1½ c. sugar
1 T. flour
½ c. sweet milk
Butter
3 bananas

Mix sugar, flour, and milk. Place over medium heat, and let boil 2 minutes. Take off heat, add butter size of an egg. Beat until thick enough to spread. (If you double the recipe, which is preferred, boil 3 minutes.) Cover bottom of layer cake with slices of bananas, use ½ icing recipe over these. Repeat for top layer. Cover sides of cake last, using no bananas. To be used on a two-layer yellow butter cake.

Mrs. Anita K. Smith, Bowie H. S.
El Paso, Texas

LADY BALTIMORE FROSTING AND FILLING

2 egg whites, unbeaten
1½ c. sugar
5 T water
1½ t. light corn syrup
½ t. vanilla
¾ t. rose water
6 figs, chopped
½ c. raisins, chopped
½ c. nut meats, chopped
Candied cherries

Combine egg whites, sugar, water, rose water, and corn syrup in top of double boiler, beating with mixer until thoroughly mixed. Place over rapidly boiling water, beat constantly with mixer, and cook 7 minutes, or until frosting will stand in peaks. Remove from boiling water, add flavoring and beat until thick enough to spread. For filling, scald figs and raisins and chop. Add enough frosting to chopped fruit and nuts to make a filling that will spread easily. Spread between layers. Spread remaining frosting on top and sides of cake. While frosting is soft, sprinkle top of cake with chopped cherries and additional chopped figs, raisins, and nuts. Makes enough for tops and sides of two 9″ layers.

Mrs. Virginia C. Alexander, Jumpertown School
Booneville, Mississippi

CARAMEL FROSTING

4 Layer Cake

½ c. milk
½ c. butter
2 T. corn syrup
3 c. sugar
¼ t. soda
¼ c. boiling water, to make ¼ c. caramelized sugar
1 t. vanilla
Pecan halves on top, if preferred

Melt ¼ cup (of the 3 cups) sugar in a heavy skillet or saucepan. Add boiling water and let the lumps dissolve. Add this syrup to all remaining ingredients except vanilla. Cook in a large saucepan (because it will boil high), until there is a heavy trace on the spoon, or forms a soft ball when dropped in cold water. When done, remove from heat. Cool, before beating. Add vanilla. If it gets too hard before you spread, add a few drops of boiling water. Enough to use on 4 layers.

Mrs. Edwin F. Cook, Union County H. S.
Blairsville, Georgia

CARAMEL FROSTING

½ c. butter or margarine
1 c. brown sugar, packed
¼ c. milk
2 c. confectioners' sugar (more if needed)

Melt butter in saucepan, add brown sugar. Boil over low heat 2 minutes, stirring all the time. Add milk. Keep stirring until mixture boils. Remove from heat. Cool. Add sifted sugar. Beat well after each addition. Add pecans if desired. May be pressed on sides of cake.

This recipe submitted by the following teachers:

Mrs. Bobbie Sharpe, Irving College School
McMinnville, Tennessee

Mrs. D. J. Dear, Stringer H. S.
Bay Springs, Mississippi

CARAMEL ICING

½ c. sugar
2 c. sugar
¾ c. milk
1 stick butter
1 egg
1 t. vanilla

Place ½ cup sugar in iron skillet over low heat. Mix in saucepan remaining 2 cups sugar, milk, butter, slightly beaten egg. Stir this mixture over low heat until butter melts. Increase heat and cook until it boils rapidly. When the sugar in the skillet is light brown, pour it into the other boiling mixture stirring fast and constantly. Cook until soft ball stage is reached. Add vanilla. Beat until spreading consistency then spread on cake.

Mrs. Tommy Long, Allen County H. S.
Scottsville, Kentucky

CARAMEL FILLING

3 c. sugar
1 c. sweet milk
1 T. butter or margarine
1 t. vanilla flavoring

Melt slowly 1 cup sugar in a saucepan. Mix 2 cups sugar and sweet milk in another saucepan. Boil second mixture until first cup of sugar is melted (about 10-15 minutes). Stir constantly. Mix all together. Cook slowly until it forms a soft ball. Remove from heat, add butter, let cool 5 minutes. Add vanilla. Beat until smooth. Covers a 3 layer cake.

Mrs. Selma H. Turner, Scotland Neck H. S.
Scotland Neck, North Carolina

CARAMEL ICING

2 c. light brown sugar
2 T. flour
6 T. cream or milk
4 T. butter
2 t. vanilla or ½ t. maple flavoring
½ c. pecans

Mix sugar, flour, cream and butter. Boil for 2 minutes. Take off and beat. Add flavoring. Spread on cake and sprinkle pecans on top. This freezes well.

Mrs. Sue P. Jones, Marriott H. S.
St. Stephens Church, Virginia

CREAMY CHOCOLATE FILLING

For One Cake
2⅓ c. sifted confectioners' sugar
1 egg
¼ c. granulated sugar
2 T. water
½ c. Crisco (do not melt)
2 sq. chocolate (melted)
1 t. vanilla

Combine confectioners' sugar and egg. Combine granulated sugar and water and boil one minute. Add slowly to first mixture and blend well. Add Crisco, melted chocolate, and vanilla. Beat until creamy. (Spreads easly. Does not dry out.)

Mrs. Opal Pockrus, Collinsville H. S.
Collinsville, Texas

NEVER-FAIL CREAMY CARAMEL ICING

For 2 Layer Cake
2½ c. sugar
1 slightly beaten egg
1 stick of butter or margarine
¾ c. milk
1 t. vanilla

Melt ½ cup of sugar in an iron skillet slowly, until brown and runny. Mix egg, butter, remaining sugar, and milk in a saucepan and cook over low flame until butter melts. Turn the heat to medium and add the browned sugar. Cook until it reaches the soft ball stage or until mixture leaves sides of pan (about 10 minutes). Remove from heat. Cool slightly. Add vanilla. Beat until right consistency to spread. If too thick add a little cream.

Erin T. Mayes, Mason Hall H. S.
Kenton, Tennessee

BAKED MAGIC FROSTING

1-8 Inch Cake
¾ c. coconut
½ c. chopped nuts
¾ c. light brown sugar
½ t. salt
⅓ c. margarine
2 T. milk

Combine all ingredients in saucepan. Heat on medium unit until sugar melts. Spread lightly over top of warm cake. Place in a 400°F. oven for about 10 minutes to brown lightly. Tops two 8″ layer cakes, or one 8″ square cake, or an oblong 7x11 cake.

Barbara Price Russell, Rule H. S.
Knoxville, Tennessee

CHOCOLATE FUDGE FROSTING

2 c. sugar
½ c. cocoa
½ c. margarine or butter
¼ c. milk
1 t. vanilla

Mix all ingredients except vanilla. Bring to full rolling boil and boil 1 minute, or until mixture forms soft ball in cold water. Add vanilla and beat until creamy.

Hilda Harman, Smithville H. S.
Smithville, Mississippi

CHOCOLATE FROSTING

2-9 Inch Layers
4 sq. unsweetened chocolate
3 egg yolks, well beaten
¾ c. milk
2¼ c. sugar
1½ T. butter
Dash of salt
2 t. vanilla

Melt chocolate over low heat. Beat egg yolks until light and thick. Add milk, sugar, and butter. Cook over low heat stirring constantly. Boil 1 minute. Remove from heat. Stir in melted chocolate, salt, and vanilla. Beat until of desired consistency.

Mrs. Eleanor J. Lewis, Union Point School
Union Point, Georgia

NEVER-FAIL CHOCOLATE FROSTING

3 Layer Cake
3 c. sugar
½ c. cocoa
¼ lb. butter
¾ c. sweet milk
1 t. vanilla
½ c. broken walnut or pecan meats

Mix cocoa and sugar. Add milk and stir until dissolved. When mixture comes to a boil, cover pot and boil HARD for one minute. Remove from stove, add vanilla and butter. Beat until right consistency to spread. Add nuts.

Mrs. Norma M. Womble, Broadway H. S.
Broadway, North Carolina

INSTANT FUDGE FROSTING (Uncooked)

1 lb. unsifted powdered sugar
½ c. dry cocoa
¼ t. salt
1 t. vanilla
7 T. boiling water
6 T. (¾ stick) soft butter or margarine

Mix powdered sugar, cocoa, and salt thoroughly so no lumps of cocoa can be seen. Add vanilla and boiling water, stir smooth. Add soft (not melted) butter or margarine and stir or beat until smooth, just stiff enough to spread. (The frosting may seem too thin at first, but it thickens as it cools. If it should get too thick while spreading, stir in a few drops of hot water.) Makes enough to cover two 8″ or 9″ layers generously.

Mrs. Maurice E. Eskridge, Tryon H. S.
Bessemer City, North Carolina

CHOCOLATE ICING

2 c. sugar
½ c. water
1 stick oleo
1 T. white corn syrup
2 egg whites (beaten stiff)
3 sq. melted chocolate
1 t. vanilla

Beat egg whites. Cook sugar, syrup, water, and oleo until it forms a soft ball when dropped in water. Pour slowly over beaten egg whites, and add chocolate and vanilla. Beat until thick enough to spread.

Mattie Mary Green, McLain H. S.
McLain, Mississippi

CHOCOLATE FUDGE FILLING OR FROSTING

3 c. sugar
4 T. cocoa
3 T. white corn syrup
1 c. milk
½ stick butter or oleo
1 t. vanilla

Mix in a saucepan the first four ingredients in the order listed. Cook without stirring until the soft ball stage is reached (when tested in cold water). Remove from heat. Add butter and vanilla. Beat until creamy and thick. Spread on cake.

Ruth Stovall, State Department of Education
Montgomery, Alabama

MINUTE BOIL FROSTING (Chocolate)

1½ c. sugar
2 oz. chocolate
2 T. butter
1 T corn syrup
¼ c. milk (approximately)

Boil until mixture forms soft ball in water. Cool slightly. Beat, spread on cake. If mixture becomes too thick add a little cream.

Monna Smith Miller, Lake City H. S.
Lake City, Tennessee

CREAMY CHOCOLATE FROSTING

2 Cups

2½ c. sifted confectioners' sugar
1 egg, unbeaten
2 T. water
¼ c. granulated sugar
¼ t. salt
½ c. shortening
1 t. vanilla extract
2 sq. (2 oz.) unsweetened chocolate, melted

Combine confectioners' sugar and egg in mixing bowl. Combine water, granulated sugar, and salt in saucepan. Stir over medium heat until sugar is dissolved. Boil for 1 minute. Add slowly to the egg mixture, beating constantly. Add shortening, vanilla, and chocolate and beat until creamy. Spread on cake.

Variations: To make basic Creamy Frosting, omit chocolate. Omit chocolate, add 2 tablespoons instant powdered coffee. Omit chocolate, add 2 tablespoons instant powdered coffee and 2 tablespoons cocoa.

Helen E. Snyder, Hughesville H. S.
Hughesville, Pennsylvania

JOAN'S FUDGE ICING

1-3 Layer Cake

4 c. white sugar
1 c. hydrogenated shortening
1 c. cream or milk (or mixture)
½ c. corn syrup (light)
1 t. salt
2 oz. chocolate (slivered)
2 t. vanilla flavoring

Combine all ingredients except vanilla in saucepan. Cook over low heat until chocolate and shortening melt, stirring continuously. Bring to rolling boil, 220°F. and hold one minute. Begin beating and beat until 120°F. Add vanilla. Beat to spreading consistency.

Nellie B. Westbrook, Bessemer H. S.
Greensboro, North Carolina

QUICK COCOA FROSTING

2-8 Inch Layers

½ c. margarine
2 c. sugar
3 T. cocoa
½ c. milk

Cream margarine, sugar, and cocoa in a saucepan. Add milk and bring mixture to a boil. Boil one minute. Remove from heat and beat until icing begins to thicken. Ice cake immediately.

Mrs. Billy Bass, Mooreville H. S.
Mooreville, Mississippi

FRESH COCONUT BUTTER ICING

Covers 3 Layer Cake

2 c. sugar
1 c. milk
⅛ t. salt
1 T. butter
1 average size coconut (grated) or 2 c.
1 t. vanilla

(Continued on Next Page)

Grate medium size coconut. Combine sugar, milk, and salt in saucepan. Bring to boil and cook 7 minutes. Remove from heat, add butter, vanilla, and ¾ of the coconut. Mix well. Spread on the cake while the cake and icing are warm. Sprinkle some of the remaining coconut on top of the icing of each layer. The icing will go into the warm cake.

Ellaine B. Scott, Dekalb H. S.
Dekalb, Mississippi

COCONUT FILLING

2 Layers
2 c. sugar
⅔ c. water or coconut juice
1 pkg. frozen coconut or 2 c. fresh coconut
2 egg whites
1 t. vanilla flavoring

Combine sugar, water or coconut juice in saucepan. Cook until syrupy. Add coconut and cook one minute. Remove from heat and fold in stiffly beaten egg whites and vanilla. Ice plain cake.

Mrs. Jack Hollingsworth,
Pelahatchie Attendance Center
Morton, Mississippi

COCONUT CAKE FILLING

1 Medium Size Cake
2 eggs, beaten
1 c. milk
1 c. sugar
1 c. grated coconut
2 T. flour
1 t. vanilla extract
1 t. lemon extract

Beat eggs in a heavy saucepan. Add milk, sugar, grated coconut, and flour. Cook and stir until thick. Remove from heat. Cool. Add vanilla and lemon extract. Use as filling on a plain layer cake.

Kathleen P. Burton, Star Valley H. S.
Afton, Wyoming

COCONUT PECAN FILLING AND FROSTING

1 c. evaporated milk
1 c. sugar
3 egg yolks
¼ lb. butter or margarine
1 t. vanilla
1⅓ c. flaked coconut (approximate)
1 c. chopped pecans

Combine milk, sugar, egg yolks, butter, and vanilla in a saucepan. Cook over medium heat, stirring constantly, until mixture thickens, about 12 minutes. Remove from heat. Add coconut and pecans. Beat until cool and of spreading consistency. Makes enough to cover tops of three 8″ or 9″ layers, or about 2⅔ cups frosting and filling.

This recipe submitted by the following teachers:
Mrs. Uvonne Jones Van Hecke,
Walnut Grove H. S.
Walnut Grove, Minnesota
Mrs. Wilma Elliston, Blue H. S.
Blue, Oklahoma

PETER PAUL CAKE FILLING (Coconut)

3 Chocolate Layers
1½ c. sugar
1½ c. milk
18 marshmallows
1 lb. ground coconut (not flaked)
1 t. vanilla

Mix sugar, milk, and marshmallows together in top part of double boiler. Heat until marshmallows are melted. Add coconut and cook for approximately 2 minutes, add flavoring. Use this for filling and icing 3 chocolate or devils food cake layers.

Edna Phillips Pritchard, Randleman H. S.
Randleman, North Carolina

COLONADE ICING

4½ c. granulated sugar
1 c. water
6 T. white syrup
6 egg whites
⅓ c. confectioners' sugar

Mix granulated sugar, water and syrup and cook to soft ball stage. Beat egg whites until stiff but not dry. Slowly add hot sugar-syrup mixture to egg whites, beating constantly until icing is like cream. Add confectioners' sugar. Leftover frosting may be refrigerated then heated over warm water to luke warm and used as needed.

Mrs. Gladys Herring, Collins Jr. H. S.
Corsicana, Texas

COLORVISION CAKE ICING

2 Layer Cake
3 T. gelatin dessert granules (Jello)
¼ c. egg whites
1 c. sugar
⅛ t. cream of tartar
¼ c. water

Combine all ingredients. Place over boiling water and beat with electric mixer on high speed until icing holds peaks. Remove from heat and beat about 1 minute longer.

Mrs. Estella Crowell, Whitmore Lake H. S.
Whitmore Lake, Michigan

EGG ICING

1 lb. butter or margarine
2 c. sugar
8 egg yolks
2 c. chopped pecans
1 can or box coconut
1 c. chopped dates
1 c. raisins, if desired

As butter melts add 1 cup sugar, mix well. Beat egg yolks, gradually add remaining 1 cup sugar, beating yolks well after each addition. As melted butter mixture boils, slowly add beaten egg yolk mixture. Cook until thick, stirring constantly. Remove from range, add remainder of ingredients. Cool. Use any three layer white cake. This is a very rich frosting and is best served during the Christmas holiday season.

Mrs. Jo Ann Gray, Waxahachie H. S.
Waxahachie, Texas

BUTTER CREAM FROSTING

2 Layer Cake

1 egg white
1 c. granulated sugar
1 c. warm milk
½ c. shortening
½ c. oleo or butter
1 t. vanilla

Beat egg white until very stiff. Add sugar slowly. Add milk slowly. Put aside. Beat remaining ingredients well. Add egg mixture slowly, beating after each addition, until well mixed. Will resemble whipped cream when done.

Mrs. Ruth Dolsen, Walled Lake Sr. H. S.
Walled Lake, Michigan

FRUIT-NUT FILLING

1 Medium Cake

⅔ c. ground apricots
¾ c. sugar
1 c. water
⅛ c. chopped nuts
1 T. lemon juice
1 t. grated lemon rind

Combine apricots, sugar, and water in saucepan. Simmer for 15 minutes, stirring 2 or 3 times. Cool fruit mixture, add nuts, lemon juice, and rind, stirring. Spread between sliced cake layers.

Mrs. Jo Anne Davis, Ceres Union H. S.
Ceres, California

LEMON CHEESE FILLING

1 c. sugar
2 T. flour
2 lemon rinds (grated)
¼ c. lemon juice
1 egg
1 T. butter

Mix sugar and flour. Add other ingredients in order as given. Cook in double boiler over moderate heat until mixture thickens. This recipe is sufficient for one 2-layer cake. If desired the layers may be split and double the recipe would be needed.

Lois Bray, Oak Grove Jr. H. S.
Tampa, Florida

LEMON ICING

Number of Servings — 8-12

1 orange (grated rind and juice)
1 lemon (grated rind and juice)
2 eggs (well beaten)
1 c. sugar
½ pt. whipping cream (whipped)

Cook orange rind and juice, lemon rind and juice, eggs, and sugar in top of double boiler until thick. Cool. Add whipping cream (whipped). Spread between layers of an angel food or sponge cake you have sliced. Spread on sides and top. Let stand in refrigerator 24 hours before serving. An excellent frosting-dessert to make ahead of time.

Phyllis Barton, Lee H. S.
Springfield, Virginia

HEAVENLY LEMON FILLING
(For Meringues)

Number of Servings — 25

8 egg yolks
1 c. granulated sugar
6 T. lemon juice
2 T. grated lemon rind
¼ t. salt
1 pt. heavy cream
1 pt. heavy cream (for garnishing)

Place egg yolks in double boiler. Beat slightly. Stir in sugar, lemon juice, rind, and salt. Cook over boiling water until very thick (about 10 minutes). Cool. Whip 1 pint cream, fold into lemon mixture. Cover, and chill in refrigerator. Whip 1 pint heavy cream. Using ½ of it, place spoonful in a large meringue shell, top with spoonful of filling, garnish with whipped cream. Serve on dessert plates with fork.

Mrs. Charlene Broome Strickland,
Madison County H. S.
Danielsville, Georgia

HONEY ORANGE FILLING

1 T. flour
2 T. cornstarch
2 egg yolks
½ c. honey
1 t. salt
¼ c. orange juice
2 T. water
1 T. lemon juice
1 t. butter
1 grated orange rind

Mix flour, cornstarch, honey, salt, and egg yolk in top of double boiler. Slowly add orange juice, water, and lemon juice, then add butter and orange rind. Cook over boiling water stirring until mixture thickens. Cool and spread between layers of cake.

Georgia N. Watson, Blossom H. S.
Blossom, Texas

STRAWBERRY FLUFF TOPPING

2 egg whites (unbeaten)
1 c. sugar
Dash of salt
⅔ c. sliced strawberries or 1 pkg. frozen
 strawberries

Combine all ingredients in top of double boiler. Cook as for 7-minute frosting. Makes enough for tops and sides of three 9″ layers.

Fay Taylor, Ingleside H. S.
Ingleside, Texas

STRAWBERRY ICING

3 Layers

2 T. butter
¾ c. strawberries
1 box confectioners' sugar

Cream the butter, add half the sugar and beat until blended. Add the strawberries and the remaining sugar. Spread on the cake.

Mrs. Eva Rae Clark, Elise H. S.
Robbins, North Carolina

WHITE FROSTING (Perfect)

1⅓ c. sugar
½ c. water
1 T. Karo
1 egg white
6 marshmallows cut up or 60 miniatures
½ t. vanilla (I also like ½ t. almond)

Cook sugar, water, and Karo until it forms a firm, soft ball in cold water (not ice water). Beat egg white stiff, add marshmallows and hot syrup. Continue beating until it holds its shape. Spread on cake.

Mrs. Effie Ray, West Blocton H. S.
West Blocton, Alabama

MAGIC FROSTING (White)

1 c. sugar
¼ t. salt
¼ t. cream of tartar
5 T. cold water
2 egg whites
1 t. vanilla

Mix in saucepan sugar, salt, cream of tartar, and water. Stir. Bring to full rolling boil over moderate heat. Place two egg whites in the small mixer bowl. Do not beat until syrup is cooked. Pour syrup slowly over the egg whites while beating at high speed until all the syrup has been added. Reduce speed to medium. Add vanilla and beat until the mixture is of a spreading consistency. Makes enough to ice two layers.

Carolyn Sellers, Wallace H. S.
Wallace, South Carolina

WHITE MARSHMALLOW FROSTING (Non-Fail)

2 Layer Cake

1½ c. sugar
½ c. water
6 lge. marshmallows (chopped)
2 egg whites (beaten stiff)
¼ t. baking powder
2 t. lemon juice

Boil sugar and water to 238°F. Add chopped marshmallows, but do not stir. Pour hot syrup over beaten egg whites, then add baking powder and lemon juice. Continue beating until it forms a peak. Spread between 2 layers and on top and sides of cake. Sprinkle with coconut or chopped pecans if desired.

Mrs. Joyce Nance, Nixon H. S.
Nixon, Texas

REA'S ICING DELIGHT (White)

Frosts Two 9 Inch Layers

1 lb. confectioners' sugar
1 T. powdered milk
Pinch of salt
1 c. vegetable shortening
¼ c. water

Thoroughly mix confectioners' sugar, milk, and salt. Cream shortening and dry ingredients. Gradually add water and beat at high speed until fluffy.

Mrs. Rose Marie Staley, Francis Scott Key H. S.
Union Bridge, Maryland

CAKE FROSTING (White)

2 Layer Cake

3 egg whites
½ c. sugar
½ c. white syrup

Beat egg whites until stiff. Add sugar and white syrup, beat until stiff or consistency of whipped cream. If desired, coloring, fruit or nuts may be added.

Mrs. George Brodie, III, Shawnee H. S.
Joiner, Arkansas

BOILED ICING (White)

Cover for 3 Layers

3 c. sugar
¼ t. cream of tartar or 1 T. light corn syrup
1 c. boiling water
3 egg whites
¾ t. vanilla

Combine sugar, cream of tartar, and boiling water in saucepan and cook until mixture spins a long thread 242°F. Beat egg whites until they hold a stiff peak, then pour on hot syrup in a fine stream, beating constantly. Add flavoring and beat until cool and stiff enough to spread. (This is a good icing to add fruit to when cool, if you want a fruit icing.)

Margaret Hefner Peden, Hoke County H. S.
Raeford, North Carolina

COLONNADE ICING (White)

2-3 Dozen Cupcakes or 1 Large Cake

4½ c. sugar
1 c. water
6 T. white corn syrup
6 egg whites, beaten stiff
⅛ c. confectioners' sugar

Mix sugar, water, and syrup in a saucepan. Cook to soft ball stage, 238°F, on your candy thermometer. Slowly add to stiffly beaten (but not dry) egg whites. Beat thoroughly until the icing is like cream. Add confectioners' sugar. This is a soft-on-the-inside, crusty-on-the-outside icing. Leftovers may be refrigerated, then heated over lukewarm to warm water and use as needed.

Mrs. Elizabeth Ann Weaver,
South Terrebonne H. S.
Houma, Louisiana

ORANGE CREAM CHEESE FROSTING

1⅞ Cups of Frosting

3 T. butter
1-3 oz. pkg. cream cheese (room temperature)
Dash of salt
¼ c. concentrated orange juice (thawed)
4½ c. sifted confectioners' sugar

Cream butter, add cheese, salt, and orange juice. Cream together until light and fluffy. Gradually add sugar, until of right consistency to spread, blending well after each addition. Enough to cover tops and sides of two 8" layers.

Mrs. Sue Buxton, Cowden H. S.
Cowden, Illinois

FROSTING (For Pastry Tube)

½ c. Crisco shortening
1 box powdered sugar
¼ c. hot water
½-1 t. vanilla or other flavoring

Mix on slow speed with electric mixer. Do not beat.

Mrs. Mildred Mahan, Sheridan Rural Agri. School
Sheridan, Michigan

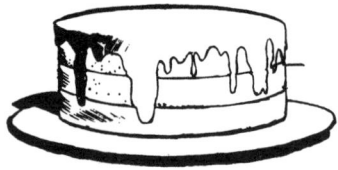

SOUR CREAM NUT FILLING

3 Layer Cake

3 egg yolks
1 c. sour cream
½ c. white sugar
1 c. chopped walnuts

Beat egg yolks until thick. Add sour cream, mix well. Add sugar, mix thoroughly. Add chopped walnuts. Let boil until thick, stirring so that it will not scorch. Use as filling for layer cake. Very good with plain white cake.

Mrs. Anna Delvo, Hankinson Public School
Hankinson, North Dakota

SOUR CREAM FROSTING

Number of Servings — 1 Cake

1 c. sour cream
1 c. white sugar
1 c. walnuts (cut but not fine)
3 egg yolks
1 T. cornstarch

Beat egg yolks, add cream, sugar, cornstarch, and nuts. Cook in a double boiler, stirring constantly until thick. Cool. Spread over cake.

Mrs. Gladys Severance, Huron H. S.
Huron, South Dakota

BUTTERSCOTCH SAUCE

Number of Servings — 12

1½ c. sugar
1 c. light syrup
¼ t. salt
½ c. butter
2 c. heavy cream
1 t. vanilla

Boil sugar, syrup, salt, butter, and 1 cup of the cream until it forms a stiff ball in water. Add the other cup of cream and boil until it reaches the soft ball stage. May be stored in the refrigerator and heated before used.

Mrs. Gary R. Johnson, Jefferson Senior H. S.
Alexandria, Minnesota

CARAMEL TOPPING

Number of Servings — 4 to 6

1 can sweetened condensed milk
½ c. chopped walnuts

Take the label off from the can. Do not open the can. Put the whole (unopened) can into cool water (water should cover the can at all times). Boil can for about 3 hours. Cool can then open it, the milk will be caramelized. Add nuts, and chill in refrigerator until used. This recipe is good as a cake frosting or topping, or candy, or ice cream topping.

Mrs. K. R. Wightman, Lakeview H. S.
Lakeview, Michigan

HOT CHOCOLATE SAUCE

Number of Servings — 3 Cups

2-4 sq. unsweetened chocolate
½ c. butter
½ t. salt
3 c. sugar
1 lge. can evaporated milk

Melt chocolate, butter, and salt together in double boiler. Add the sugar, ½ cup at a time, stirring after each addition. Add the evaporated milk, a little at a time and continue stirring until well mixed. Serve hot over ice cream. Extra sauce may be stored in the refrigerator.

This recipe submitted by the following teachers:
Mrs. Joan Marotzke, Oslo Public School
Oslo, Minnesota
Bernice E. Kirkeby, Willow Lake H. S.
Willow Lake, South Dakota

REGAL CHOCOLATE SAUCE

Number of Servings — 3 Cups

½ c. corn syrup
1 c. sugar
1 c. water
3 sq. chocolate
1 t. vanilla
1 c. evaporated milk

Combine syrup, sugar, and water. Cook to soft ball stage 235°F. Remove from heat. Add chocolate squares. Stir until chocolate melts. Add vanilla. Very slowly add evaporated milk. Mix thoroughly. Cool. Heat over hot water for hot fudge sauce.

Mrs. Jean R. Engelmann, Waconia H. S.
Waconia, Minnesota

CHOCOLATE SYRUP

Number of Servings — 1 pt.

½ c. cocoa
1 c. water
2 c. sugar
⅛ t. salt
¼ t. vanilla

Mix cocoa and water in a saucepan, stir to dissolve cocoa, heat to blend the cocoa and water. Add sugar, stirring to dissolve sugar. Boil for 3 minutes. Add salt and vanilla. Pour into clean sterilized pint jar. Store covered in refrigerator. Will keep for several months. May be used for milk drinks or toppings for ice cream.

Mrs. Grace Kurtz, Estelline H. S.
Estelline, South Dakota

CHOCOLATE-HONEY SAUCE
Number of Servings — 6
4 T. butter
1 T. cornstarch
3 T. cocoa
½ c. honey
½ c. water
6 Marshmallows
¼ t. salt
1 t. vanilla extract
Melt butter, add cornstarch and cocoa. Blend well. Add honey and water. Cook over low heat until thick. Add marshmallows and salt. Cook just long enough to melt marshmallows. Add vanilla. Excellent sauce for ice cream.

Mrs. Patricia Moore, Ionia H. S.
Ionia, Michigan

CHOCOLATE FUDGE SAUCE
Number of Servings — 8 to 10
1 sq. chocolate
1 T. butter
⅓ c. boiling water
1 c. sugar
½ t. vanilla
2 T. light corn syrup
⅛ t. salt
Melt chocolate slowly. Add butter and blend thoroughly (additional butter makes a richer sauce). Add water slowly and bring to a boil. Add sugar, salt, and corn syrup and bring to a boil. Let boil 1 minute. Remove from heat and add vanilla. Serve hot. (Delicious over vanilla ice cream.)

Nancy S. Cobb, Villa Rica H. S.
Villa Rica, Georgia

CREAMY FUDGE SAUCE
Number of Servings — One and 2/3 Cups
3 sq. unsweetened chocolate
½ c. light cream
¾ c. sugar
3 T. butter
Dash of salt
¾ t. vanilla
Add chocolate to cream in saucepan. Cook over low heat stirring constantly until chocolate is melted and mixture is smooth and blended. Add sugar, butter, and salt and continue cooking, stirring constantly, 3 to 5 minutes longer, or until slightly thickened. Remove from heat and add vanilla. Serve warm on ice cream, pudding or cake.

Mrs. Ned R. Mitchell, Charleston H. S.
Charleston, South Carolina

MOCHA SAUCE
1 c. confectioners' sugar
⅓ c. butter
2 t. cocoa
2 T. strong coffee
Add cocoa to sugar. Cream butter and add sugar to the butter gradually while beating until the mixture is fluffy. Add coffee gradually while beating to keep sauce from separating. Serve with a dessert soufflé such as mocha soufflé.

Barbara Gioria, Bellows Falls H. S.
Bellows Falls, Vermont

CITRUS SAUCE
Number of Servings — 8
2 T. flour
½ c. sugar
Few grains of salt
½ lemon, juice and grated rind
1 orange, juice and grated rind
1 T. butter
½ pt. whipping cream
Combine dry ingredients, add juice and grated rind and butter. Cook over medium heat until thick. Chill. Whip the cream and fold in the chilled mixture. Serve on angel food, chiffon, or plain cake.

Mrs. Enid Hedrick, Bolsa Grande H .S.
Garden Grove, California

JIFFY LEMON SAUCE
Number of Servings — 4 to 6
½ c. sugar
2 T. cornstarch
⅛ t. salt
1 c. water
1 t. lemon rind
4 T. lemon juice
2 T. butter or margarine
Mix sugar, cornstarch with ¼ cup water, add remaining water. Bring to a boil and remove from heat. Add remaining ingredients. Cool slightly. Serve over warm cake.

Rosemary C. Patout, Jeanerette H. S.
Jeanerette, Louisiana

LEMON SAUCE
Number of Servings — 8
2 T. flour
Enough water to make a paste
2 eggs
¾ c. sugar
Juice and rind of 1 lemon
½ pt. whipping cream
Combine water and flour in the top of double boiler. Add sugar, eggs, lemon juice, and rind. Cook until thick stirring constantly. Remove from heat and cool. Fold in the whipped cream. Cut angel food cake (or any type sponge cake) into servings and top with sauce.

Mrs. Ruby Walker, Kate Griffin Jr. High
Meridian, Mississippi

LEMON SAUCE
Number of Servings — 1 Cup
4 T. (½ stick) butter
1 c. sugar
1 egg
¼ c. water
¼ t. ground cardamon
1 t. grated lemon rind
3 T. lemon juice
Cream butter (or margarine) and sugar until fluffy in top of double boiler. Beat in egg, stir in water. Cook over boiling water, stirring constantly, about 5 minutes, or until thick. Remove from heat, stir in remaining ingredients. Serve warm over cakes.

Sandra Rountree, Manteo H. S.
Manteo, North Carolina

LEMON SAUCE
(For Chiffon or Angel Food Cakes)
Number of Servings — 6

1 c. sugar
5 T. cake flour
1 egg (beaten slightly)
¼ c. lemon juice
⅔ c. cold water
2 t. butter
1 t. grated lemon rind
½ pt. whipped cream

Combine sugar, cake flour, egg, and lemon juice in top of double boiler. Add water and butter. Mix thoroughly. Place mixture over boiling water and cook until thick (about 10 minutes). Chill. Fold in grated lemon rind and whipped cream just before using.

Maxine Barber, Albambra H. S.
Martinez, California

MINT SAUCE

1½ c. sugar
¾ c. white Karo
1 c. water
4-6 drops green food coloring
4-6 drops oil of spearmint

Combine sugar, Karo and water. Boil hard for 5 minutes, then turn to low heat and cook until it starts to string. When cool add coloring and spearmint oil. Served over vanilla ice cream.

Stephanie T. Mulford, Salem H. S.
Salem, New Jersey

ORANGE SAUCE
Number of Servings — 12 to 18

6 oz. can frozen orange juice, thawed
¼ c. sugar
2 T. cornstarch

Put orange juice into small saucepan. Mix sugar and cornstarch. Add to cold orange juice. Cook over medium heat until it becomes thick. Remove from flame and allow to cool, slightly, before serving.

Irina Nikitin, Ramseur H. S.
Ramseur, North Carolina

SPICY CHESTNUT FRUIT SAUCE
Number of Servings — 3 Cups

1 T. melted butter
5½ oz. can water chestnuts
1 No. 2 can pineapple juice
1-6 oz. can tangerine juice concentrate, undiluted
2 sticks cinnamon
1 T. butter
½ c. sugar
¼ c. cornstarch
¼ t. ground ginger
⅛ t. salt
2 T. lemon juice
2 t. grated lemon rind

Slice the water chestnuts. Add to the melted butter. Stir until butter is absorbed and chestnuts are lightly browned. Remove from heat. In a large saucepan add enough water to the pineapple juice to make 3 cups, add tangerine juice and cinnamon sticks. Bring to a boil, reduce heat and simmer for 5 minutes. Mix the sugar, cornstarch, ginger, and salt in a bowl. Blend thoroughly. Pour a little of the hot juices into the cornstarch mixture. Stir until smooth. Return cornstarch mixture to fruit juices and cook, stirring until clear and thickened. Remove from heat. Add the lemon juice, lemon rind, and butter. Cool to room temperature. Remove cinnamon sticks. Chill. Before serving add sautéed water chestnuts. Keeps well in refrigerator for a week. Use over fruit combinations: apples, watermelon and honeydew mellon balls, strawberries, and green or white grapes.

Mrs. Louise E. Frame, Coraopolis, Jr. H. S.
Coraopolis, Pennsylvania

STRAWBERRY TOPPING
Number of Servings — 12

1 box frozen strawberries (10 oz.)
½ or ¾ c. sugar
1 egg white

Put frozen berries and sugar in large mixing bowl and beat until well blended, and berries are practically dissolved. Beat in egg white 15 minutes at high speed. Mixture will expand and thicken. Serve on slices of cake.

Roxie Ledbetter, Livingston, Academy
Livingston, Tennessee

MOCK WHIPPED CREAM
Number of Servings — 4 to 6

1 egg white
⅓ c. sugar
Juice of 1 lemon
1 lge. ripe banana

Beat egg white until foamy, gradually add sugar and lemon juice. Continue beating until stiff. Slice banana and add to egg white mixture, beat until stiff and well-blended and mixture stands in peaks. Serve on hot gingerbread.

Nancy J. DeLaurent, Tri-City H. S.
Buffalo, Illinois

FOR ADDITIONAL FROSTINGS AND FILLING RECIPES
REFER TO CAKE SECTION

Candies & Confections

The Secrets of Candy Success

FOLLOW THE RECIPE FAITHFULLY

Don't try to substitute ingredients or double the recipes. These formulas have been perfected for home use in a kitchen similar to your own, and call for quantities easily handled with average household utensils.

CHOOSE THE RIGHT COOKING PAN

It should be large enough to let the candy boil freely without running over—heavy enough to eliminate burning—and have a tightly fitted cover to put on during the first few moments of cooking.

BE SENSIBLE ABOUT HEAT

Candies made with milk should be cooked over medium heat to avoid scorching. Candies made with water may be boiled faster.

PREVENT SUGARY RESULTS

Sugary candy is often caused by sugar crystals finding their way into the candy as it cooks or cools. This applies to both types of candies— the crystalline, such as fudge, divinity, panocha and fondant; and the non-crystalline, such as taffy, chewy caramel and crunchy brittle.

AVOID LETTING CRYSTALS FORM

Here is how you can prevent sugar crystals from forming around the sides of the candy pan.
• If recipe calls for butter or margarine, use it to grease sides of saucepan before adding other ingredients.
• Heat the milk or water used in the candy before adding the sugar and it will dissolve faster. Stir the sugar in thoroughly before placing the mixture over the heat.
• Cover the cooking pan during the first part of the cooking or until the mixture boils up well. The steam will melt the sugar crystals down from the sides of the pan. Then uncover the saucepan to permit evaporation.

AVOID INTRODUCING CRYSTALS

To prevent sugar crystals from finding their way into the candy, don't re-use your stirring spoon once the mixture has started to cook. Take a clean spoon each time to dip out samples for the cold water tests.

AVOID CRYSTALS IN COOLING

During the cooling period, be sure that the candy is not moved or jarred, as any agitation will cause the sugar to crystallize and this will result in sugary candy.

AVOID CRYSTALS IN POURING

In non-crystalline candies, such as taffies, caramels or brittles, the syrup is poured from cooking pan to cooling pan. As you pour, hold the saucepan within an inch or so of the cooling pan and never scrape out the last of the syrup.

WATCH CANDY CAREFULLY

Keep a close eye on the candy during last few moments of cooking, as the temperature rises with great speed once it reaches 220°F.

TEST CAREFULLY FOR DONENESS

A candy thermometer is a good investment as it takes the guesswork out of testing. To get an accurate reading, hold thermometer in center of mixture, with bulb above bottom of pan. Without a thermometer, follow the cold-water test (page 6). Be sure to remove candy from heat as you test, for even a few moments extra cooking may be too much.

BE PATIENT ABOUT COOLING

Don't beat the candy before it has cooled. The ideal temperature is 110°F.—or when the saucepan feels lukewarm to palm of the hand.

"STIR-BEAT"

No need to beat furiously. A steady, casual beating will produce just as creamy a candy. We call the motion "stir-beat"—using a wooden spoon to stir the candy around in a wide motion while lifting it up and over as in beating. Cooked and cooled correctly, fudge types need only about 8 minutes of stir-beating.

WHEN IT RAINS

If there is excess moisture in the air, it is advisable to cook candies to a slightly firmer stage— a degree or so above what is given in the recipe.

Candies and Frostings

HIGH ALTITUDE ADJUSTMENTS

Just as water boils at a temperature below 212° F. at the higher altitudes, all other liquids also boil at lower temperatures. Boiling causes loss of moisture through evaporation. The lower the boiling point, the sooner evaporation begins. At high altitudes, when sugar mixtures are cooked at the temperatures suggested in sea-level recipes, the faster loss of water causes the mixture to become too concentrated. Depending on the type of sugar mixture being prepared, the results may be "sugary" (where sugar re-crystallizes out), or "hard."

To adjust sugar recipes for altitude, reduce the finish temperature. If you use a candy thermometer, test first the temperature at which water boils. While there will be minor changes from day to day, due to weather conditions, the range is usually slight. At 5,000 feet altitude, water boils at approximately 202° F., ten degrees less than at sea level. Thus, correct the finish temperature for the candy or frosting by subtracting the 10°. **Example:** If a sea-level recipe for creamy fudge gives a finish temperature for syrup at 238° F., at 5,000 feet the thermometer reading would be 228° F.

The tests in cold water are reliable when a thermometer is not available.

TEMPERATURE TESTS FOR CANDY MAKING AT VARIOUS ALTITUDES

PRODUCT	TEST IN COLD WATER*	DEGREES F. ON CANDY THERMOMETER			
		SEA LEVEL	2000 FEET	5000 FEET	7500 FEET
FUDGE, PANOCHA, FONDANT	SOFT BALL (can be picked up but flattens)	234°-240°F.	230°-236°F.	224°-230°F.	219°-225°F.
CARAMELS	FIRM BALL (holds shape unless pressed)	242°-248°F.	238°-244°F.	232°-238°F.	227°-233°F.
DIVINITY, TAFFY AND CARAMEL CORN	HARD BALL (holds shape though pliable)	250°-268°F.	246°-264°F.	240°-258°F.	235°-253°F.
BUTTERSCOTCH, ENGLISH TOFFEE	SOFT CRACK (separates into hard threads but not brittle)	270°-290°F.	266°-286°F.	260°-280°F.	255°-275°F.
BRITTLES	HARD CRACK (separates into hard and brittle threads)	300°-310°F.	296°-306°F.	290°-300°F.	285°-295°F.

*Drop about ½ teaspoon of boiling syrup into one cup cold water, and test firmness of mass with fingers.

ALMOND BUTTER CRUNCH

1 c. butter
1⅛ c. sugar
1 T. light corn syrup
3 T. water
1 c. coarsely chopped blanched almonds, toasted
4-4½ oz. bars milk chocolate, melted
1 c. finely chopped blanched almonds, toasted

Melt butter in large saucepan. Add sugar, corn syrup, and water. Cook, stirring occasionally, to hard-crack stage 300°F.° Quickly stir in coarsely chopped nuts. Spread in ungreased 13x9½x2 pan. Cool thoroughly. Turn out on wax paper, spread top with half the chocolate, sprinkle with half of finely chopped nuts. Cover with wax paper, invert and spread again with the chocolate. Sprinkle the top with the remaining nuts. If necessary, chill to firm chocolate. Break in pieces. °Watch carefully after the temperature reaches 290°F.

This recipe submitted by the following teachers:
Margaret E. Gilliland, Columbia Jr.–Sr. H. S.
Columbia, Pennsylvania
Joyce Bradford, Lincolnwood H. S.
Raymond, Illinois

APPLETTS

1 c. applesauce
1 pkg. apple gelatin
1 c. sugar
½ c. nuts
Powdered sugar

Heat applesauce to boiling, add gelatin and sugar and stir until dissolved. Add nuts. Pour in buttered pan. When set hard, cut and dip pieces in powdered sugar.

Mrs. Louisa M. Krebs, Rapid City Sr. H. S.
Rapid City, South Dakota

APRICOT CONFECTION

Number or Servings — 100

2 lb. dried apricots
3 cans coconut
1 can Eagle Brand milk

Put uncooked apricot through food chopper. Add coconut and Eagle Brand milk. Chill in refrigerator over night. Form into balls walnut size. Roll in powdered sugar. Store in refrigerator in covered container. Will keep indefinitely.

Mrs. Florence Thompson, Lamar Jr. H. S.
Austin, Texas

BON BONS

¼ c. fresh lemon juice
¼ c. fresh orange juice
1 T. grated lemon or orange rind
3 c. vanilla wafers crushed fine
2 T. cocoa
1 c. confectioners' sugar
1 c. nuts chopped fine

Mix together in a medium sized bowl. Blend well, roll into balls and roll in granulated sugar.

Mrs. Wilda Jean Davis, Lumpkin County H. S.
Dahlonega, Georgia

ARIZONA CREAMS

Number of Servings — 1½ Pounds

3 c. granulated sugar
1 lge. can evaporated milk
1 T. butter
1 c. chopped nuts

Caramelize (not too brown) 1 cup sugar. Add and dissolve evaporated milk. Add remaining 2 cups sugar. Cook to soft ball stage 236°F. Remove from heat, add butter. Place pan in cold water, beat. Add chopped nuts. Beat until stiff and holds its shape. Put in buttered square cake pan 8x8 or on platter. Cut when cool.

Gloria R. McHenry, East Jr. H. S.
Mesa, Arizona

AUNT BILL'S CANDY

Number of Servings — 4 Pounds

6 c. sugar
2 c. cream or evaporated milk
1 T. white corn syrup
½ c. butter
¼ t. soda
1 t. vanilla
2 c. pecans, chopped

Caramelize 2 cups sugar, by melting it in heavy skillet. Combine 4 cups sugar and cream or milk and corn syrup in large saucepan, bring to boil while sugar is caramelizing. Pour caramelized sugar slowly into boiling mixture, stirring constantly. Cook to 245°F., stirring frequently. Remove from fire and immediately add soda, stirring vigorously as it foams up. Add butter and stir only until melted. Cool 20 minutes. Add vanilla and beat until thick and creamy. Add pecans. Pour in buttered pan (9x13). Cool. Cut in squares. Keeps indefinitely in tight containers.

Mrs. Ardyce Gilbert, Scotland H. S.
Scotland, South Dakota

BUTTERMILK FUDGE

Number of Servings — 1 Pound

1 c. buttermilk
1 t. soda
2 c. sugar
3 T. white syrup
1 t. vanilla
1 c. nuts

Add soda to buttermilk and let stand for at least 5 minutes. To this add sugar and syrup and cook until it reaches the soft ball stage or 238°F. Remove from the heat and cool until lukewarm. Add vanilla and nuts and beat until it begins to thicken, loses its glossy appearance and holds its shape. Pour into a buttered pan or dish. Cut into square when firm and cool.

Agnes Sublette, Fulton County H. S.
Hickman, Kentucky

BUTTERMILK CANDY

1 c. buttermilk
1 t. soda
2 c. sugar
2 t. corn syrup

(Continued on Next Page)

2 T. butter
1 t. vanilla
1 c. chopped nuts

Add soda to buttermilk in a 4 quart saucepan. Stir well and let stand one minute. Add sugar, corn syrup, and butter. Cook to the soft ball stage 236-238°F. Add vanilla and nuts. Beat until begins to thicken. Drop by teaspoon onto buttered cookie sheet. To vary: Double the recipe and to half the finished product add ½ cup coconut instead of nuts.

Juno B. Mulder, French H. S.
Beaumont, Texas

BROWN CANDY
Number of Servings — 4 Dozen Squares

3 lb. white sugar (6 c.)
1 pt. cream (2 c.)
¼ lb. butter
1 t. vanilla
¼ t. soda
2 lb. pecan meats

Caramelize 2 cups of sugar. Boil slowly 4 cups of sugar with cream. Pour caramelized sugar very slowly into sugar and cream mixture, stirring constantly. Turn heat on low, cook until mixture forms a firm ball in cold water. Remove from heat. Add butter, vanilla, and soda. Cool 10 minutes. Beat 6 minutes, add pecans and turn out on greased cookie sheet, cool slightly and cut into squares.

Mrs. Jackie F. Taplin, John McDonogh Sr. H. S.
New Orleans, Louisiana

CARAMEL CANDY
Number of Servings — 24-30

2 c. sugar
½ can Pet milk (lge.)
2 egg yolks (well beaten)
½ c. brown sugar
2 t. vanilla
2 T. butter
½ c. chopped nuts (if desired)

Mix together white sugar, milk, and egg yolks. Bring to a boil. Add brown sugar and cook to soft ball stage stirring frequently. Add vanilla and butter, chopped nuts if desired. Beat until cool. Spoon on wax paper into individual pieces. Can also be used for cake frosting.

Mrs. Patsy Simmons Morris, Carlowville H. S.
Minter, Alabama

CARAMELS (Chocolate)
Number of Servings — 108 Caramels

2 c. sugar
1 c. brown sugar
½ c. butter
1 c. corn syrup
1 c. cream
⅛ t. salt
1 t. vanilla
3 sq. unsweetened chocolate

To chocolate add sugar, butter, salt, syrup, and cream. Cover, boil 5 minutes. Uncover, boil

slowly, stirring constantly to firm ball stage 240°F. Remove from heat, add flavoring. Pour into a buttered pan (6x10). Cool (best to let set over night). Cut into ¾″ squares. Wrap in wax paper.

Mrs. Layne Storment, Kahlotus H. S.
Kahlotus, Washington

DELICIOUS CARAMELS
Number of Servings — 25

4 c. white sugar
2 c. white syrup
1 pt. cream
1 qt. whole milk
2 c. pecans
Dash of salt

Combine cream and milk in a large bowl. In large cooking utensil put sugar, syrup, salt, and 1 pint of milk-cream mixture. Cook and stir constantly until it reaches soft ball stage. Add 1 pint milk-cream mixture. Cook to firm ball stage. Add remaining milk-cream mixture. Cook to hard ball stage. Add nuts. Stir. Set in cool place 1-2 hours. Cut into squares. Wrap in wax paper.

Carol M. Oberle, Silver Lake H. S.
Silver Lake, Kansas

PATIENCE CANDY (Caramels)
Number of Servings — 4 Pounds

4 c. sugar
1 c. milk
1 t. salt
2 c. nuts
2 T. butter

Place 1 cup sugar in a heavy saucepan or skillet to caramelize. Place three cups of sugar and milk in a saucepan and cook over low heat. When sugar is completely melted (or caramelized), add to mixture in saucepan slowly, stirring constantly. Continue cooking until the soft ball stage is reached. (Forms a softball when a few drops are dropped into cold water.) Remove from fire and add salt, nuts, and butter. Beat until creamy. Pour into well greased pan to cool and cut into squares.

Mary Ella Porter, Como Independent School
Como, Texas

COCKTAIL MIX
Number of Servings — 100

1 lb. box Wheat Chex
1 regular box Cheerios
1 lb. margarine or butter
1 lb. mixed nuts or pecans (raw)
1 medium size box pretzel sticks
1 T. celery salt
1 T. onion salt
1 T. garlic salt

Place the ingredients in a large roaster or pot and cook (roast) in the oven for 2 hours at 250°F. Stir the mixture well every half hour. Serve cold as nuts are served. This mixture may be stored and kept indefinitely.

Mrs. Geraldine M. Beveridge, Beaufort H. S.
Beaufort, North Carolina

CHOCOLATE COATED COCONUT BALLS
(Bon-Bons, Mounds, Dreams)

2 boxes confectioners' sugar
1 can sweetened condensed milk
1 stick butter or margarine
1 can flaked coconut
1 pinch of salt
1-4 c. chopped pecans (more or less or none)
2 pkg. chocolate chips, semi-sweet chocolate or German sweet chocolate
⅓ cake paraffin
1 stick or 1 block paraffin (¼ lb.)

Melt butter slowly and add milk. Stir in sugar and salt. Add coconut and pecans. Chill until it can be easily handled. Roll into balls. Insert a toothpick and place in refrigerator or freezer until firm. (Toothpicks may be omitted and balls handled on long fork when dipping in chocolate.) Melt chocolate and paraffin together in top of double boiler. Remove from heat and dip each candy ball in chocolate. Remove candy from chocolate quickly and place on wax paper. Use another toothpick to push ball from inserted toothpick. If hole remains where toothpick was inserted, smooth with spoon and a small amount of coating. Take a small number of balls from refrigerator at a time to prevent them from getting soft.

This recipe submitted by the following teachers:

> *Mrs. Theora A. Webber, McKinney H. S.*
> *McKinney, Texas*
> *Faye Hobson, Bibb Graves H. S.*
> *Millerville, Alabama*
> *Mrs. Howard Pierce, Trimble H. S.*
> *Trimble, Tennessee*
> *Mary E. Roddam, Curry H. S.*
> *Jasper, Alabama*
> *Ann Derrick, Amarillo H. S.*
> *Amarillo, Texas*
> *Mrs. Sharon Wheeler, Hot Springs County H. S.*
> *Thermopolis, Wyoming*
> *Mrs. Trudy Fulmer, Springfield H. S.*
> *Springfield, South Carolina*
> *Dolores Moore, Glennville H. S.*
> *Glennville, Georgia*
> *Mrs. Lera Harrison Manley, Beatrice H. S.*
> *Beatrice, Alabama*
> *Peggy Mullens, Northside Jr. H. S.*
> *Corpus Christi, Texas*
> *Mrs. Ruth Irwin, Shawnee H. S.*
> *Wolf Lake, Illinois*

CHOCOLATE COVERED CHERRIES AND NUTS

1 box powdered sugar
4 T. butter
Pinch of salt
1 t. vanilla
4 T. sweetened condensed milk
⅛ c. nuts
1 bottle cherries
1 box block chocolate
¼ cake paraffin

Cream butter and sugar together adding milk in small amounts. Add salt and vanilla. Drain bottle of cherries. Roll cherries in cream mixture to cover each cherry well. Add ½ cup nuts to what is left of mixture and roll in oblong rolls. Melt chocolate and paraffin over boiling water. Dip cherries and nut rolls one at a time in melted chocolate. Lay on wax paper to cool.

> *Mrs. Frances E. Poole, Mary Persons, H. S.*
> *Forsyth, Georgia*

CHOCOLATE PEANUT BUTTER CRESCENTS
(With Dates)

1 c. powdered sugar
1 c. peanut butter
Vanilla
1 T. butter
½ c. nuts, ground
½ c. dates

Melt the above ingredients over a very low heat. Shape into balls or shape of dates.

½ c. chocolate chips
1 T. butter
¼ c. parawax

Melt in double boiler. Dip balls in melted mixture.

> *Audrey Walker, Walsh County Agricultural H. S.*
> *Park River, North Dakota*

CHOCOLATE CHEWS
Number of Servings — 4 Dozen

1½ c. sugar
1 c. white Karo
1 small can evaporated milk
3 oz. sq. chocolate
1 c. pecans
½ c. butter or margarine
2 t. vanilla

Melt butter and chocolate. Add Karo and milk, and sugar. Cook slowly in heavy utensil until temperature 245°F. is reached. Remove from heat. Add nuts and vanilla. Pour into large buttered platter. When cool enough to handle, take by handfuls and make into rolls about the size of a ladys ring finger, and any length. Place the rolls on a cool flat surface like a porcelain table top. Cut in lengths of 1". Wrap each piece in a square of cellophane, and twist ends. At Christmas time a large candy dish filled with "Chocolate Chews" wrapped in red and green cellophane adds to decorations.

> *Willie B. Barry, Martin H. S.*
> *Laredo, Texas*

MARTHA WASHINGTON CANDY
(Chocolate)
Number of Servings — 75

2 boxes confectioners' sugar (sifted)
1 stick oleo or butter
1 can sweetened condensed milk
1 t. vanilla
4 c. pecans (chopped)
1 pkg. (½ lb.) bitter or semi-sweet chocolate sq.
1 block paraffin

(Continued on Next Page)

Cream the first five ingredients. Add nuts. Roll into balls the size of a walnut. (Use powdered sugar to dip hands into as you roll balls.) Melt the chocolate and paraffin over low heat. Dip balls into this mixture, one piece at a time, holding each with a toothpick. Drop on wax paper. (This candy is moist inside and has a hard coating of chocolate. It stays fresh for several weeks.)

This recipe submitted by the following teachers:

Mrs. Marion Adair Cloud, Cuthbert H. S.
Cuthbert, Georgia

Barbara Jean Hemeter, New Augusta H. S.
New Augusta, Mississippi

Kirby Breland, Pascagoula H. S.
Pascagoula, Mississippi

Mrs. Rowena McCarty, Beaumont H. S.
Beaumont, Mississippi

CREAM CANDY

2 c. white sugar
½ c. white Karo
1 pt. whipping cream
½ t. vanilla
½ c. walnuts

Combine ½ of the cream, the syrup, sugar and cook until light brown and creamy. Add remaining cream a little at a time and keep boiling. Cook until the candy forms a firm ball in water. Remove from heat and beat. Add nuts and vanilla. Pour into buttered pan.

Mrs. Luolo Walch, Coeur d'Alene Jr. H. S.
Coeur d'Alene, Idaho

DATE ROLL (Or Loaf)

3 c. sugar
1 c. milk
6 candied or maraschino cherries, chopped (may be omitted)
1 pkg. pitted dates (chopped)
1 T. butter
1 c. pecans

Mix sugar and milk, bring to the boiling point, and add cherries and dates. Boil slowly until a small amount of the mixture forms a soft ball 234-240°F. when tried in cold water. Remove from heat. Add butter, set in a pan of cold water. When cool, beat until thick. Add nuts. Pour into dampened cloth and shape into desired roll. Chill and slice when cold.

This recipe submitted by the following teachers:

Mrs. Jean S. Brown, Pleasant Home H. S.
Andalusia, Alabama

Jessie Musgrove, Ragley H. S.
Ragley, Louisiana

DATE NUT ROLL

Number of Servings — 1½ Pounds

2 c. sugar
1 c. milk
1 T. butter
1 c. chopped dates
1 t. vanilla
½ c. finely chopped nuts
1½ c. coarsely chopped nuts

Combine sugar, milk, and butter in heavy 2 quart saucepan. Blend thoroughly. Place over low heat. Stir until sugar is dissolved and mixture is boiling moderately. Cover. Cook 3 minutes. Remove cover. Remove crystals from sides of pan with damp cloth. Cook to soft ball stage 234°F., stirring occasionally. Add dates, mix well. Again cook to soft ball stage. Remove from heat. Add vanilla. Cool, without stirring, to lukewarm 110°F. Beat until very thick, add finely chopped nuts. Knead until smooth. Divide into 3 equal parts, shape each into a roll. Coat each with ½ cup of the coarsely chopped nuts. Chill and cut into ½" slices.

Leasle H. Maze, Eva H. S.
Eva, Alabama

DATE ROLL

Number of Servings — 2-6 Inch Rolls

2 c. sugar
1 c. milk
¼ c. butter
1 c. dates
1 c. chopped nuts
1 c. shredded coconut

Combine the sugar, milk, and butter in a heavy saucepan. Cook until the syrup forms a soft ball, test. Add the dates and continue cooking and stirring until candy becomes very thick. The bubbles will pop with a hissing sound and the mixture will follow the spoon. Remove from the heat. Add nuts and coconut. Stir until the mixture has a consistency of a soft cooky dough. Turn out on a cloth dipped in cold water and form into two long rolls about 1½" in diameter. Cool and cut in slices. This type of candy will freeze well and will keep wrapped in wax paper several weeks in the refrigerator

Mrs. Norma H. Dubbe, Sturgis H. S.
Sturgis, South Dakota

PECAN DIVINITY ROLLS

Number of Servings — 5-6 Rolls

Ingredients for Inside:
2½ c. sugar
⅔ c. light corn syrup
½ c. water
2 egg whites
½ t. vanilla
Ingredients for Caramel Covering:
1 c. sugar
½ c. brown sugar
½ c. light corn syrup
½ c. cream
1 c. milk
¼ c. butter
(1½ c. coffee cream may be substituted for cream and milk)

Cook sugar, syrup and water until the syrup is hard when dropped in water (hard crack stage). Pour slowly over two egg whites that have been beaten until stiff. Add vanilla. Continue beating until very stiff and cool enough to handle. Form into rolls. Cook caramel ingredients until they

(Continued on Next Page)

form a firm ball. Cool slightly. While still quite warm dip rolls of divinity into caramel and roll in nuts. Divinity rolls should be very cold. (This recipe will take about a quart of coarsely chopped nuts.)

Mrs. Myrtle M. Joy,
Meredosia-Chambersburg H. S.
Meredosia, Illinois

DIVINITY
Number of Servings — 30

2 c. granulated sugar
½ c. light corn syrup
¼ t. salt (if desired)
½ c. water
2 egg whites
1 t. vanilla extract (almond or lemon extract may be used)
¾ c. candied cherries or 1 c. chopped nuts (or both) may be added if desired

Dissolve sugar, syrup, and salt over low heat, stirring (or use hot water). Cook, without stirring to 248°F., or to firm ball stage (or light crack stage 265°F.). Wash down with a damp cloth any crystals that may form on the sides of the pan during cooking. Remove from heat and pour gradually over the stiffly beaten egg whites. Add extract and continue beating until mixture will hold its shape when dropped from a spoon. Add nuts or fruit if used. Drop by spoonfuls on wax paper.

This recipe submitted by the following teachers:
Muriel Liles, Sterling H. S.
Sterling, Oklahoma
Mrs. Julia M. Jones, Estill Public Schools
Estill, South Carolina

DIVINITY FUDGE
Number of Servings — 50

3 c. granulated sugar
1 c. Karo (red label)
½ c. water
¼ t. salt
1 t. vanilla
2 egg whites
1 c. chopped nuts (pecans or english walnuts)

Combine Karo, water, salt, and sugar in a 3 quart saucepan, boil to 265°F. (hard ball stage). Beat egg whites stiff in large mixer bowl, and gradually beat in the boiling syrup. Beat until it begins to stiffen, add vanilla and nuts. Beat again and pour into a pan slightly oiled with cooking oil or butter. (It can be dropped by teaspoon onto wax paper if preferred.) If poured into pan, cut into squares when cool.

Mrs. Mary W. Hall, Mabelvale H. S.
Mabelvale, Arkansas

DIVINITY
Number of Servings — 36

2½ c. sugar
¼ c. white corn syrup
½ c. water
2 egg whites, beaten stiff
1 t. vanilla

Mix sugar, syrup, and water together. Cook over moderate heat until mixture forms a soft ball in cold water. Pour hot syrup mixture slowly into beaten egg whites, beating constantly. Beat until mixture begins to hold its shape. Add vanilla. Mix thoroughly. Spoon lightly into soft mounds on wax paper. Let set and serve.

Mary Louise Sexton, Warsaw H. S.
Warsaw, Ohio

EASTER EGGS

4 c. sugar
1 c. Karo syrup (white)
1 c. cold water
4 egg whites beaten
1 pkg. coconut
1 t. vanilla
1 lb. melted chocolate

Cook sugar, water, and syrup until it forms a hard ball (not brittle) when dropped in cold water. Pour hot syrup into beaten egg whites and beat until you can shape the mixture. Add vanilla and coconut and blend well. Shape. Drop into melted chocolate to coat, then decorate after cool.

Mrs. Fern Garland, Forbes Road H. S.
Harrisonville, Pennsylvania

EASTER EGG (Fruit and Nut)
Number of Servings — 2 Pounds

2 c. white sugar
½ c. white Karo syrup
½ c. warm water
1 small jar candied cherries
1 c. chopped nuts
¾ c. coconut
2 egg whites

Boil sugar, syrup, and water until you hear it crack in cold water when tested. Add, slowly to stiffly beaten egg whites, and beat until mixture begins to thicken. Add fruit and nuts. Cool slightly and form into shape using confectioners' sugar to keep from sticking to the hands. When cold spread with melted semi-sweet chocolate.

Dorothy Kitko, Union City Area H. S.
Union City, Pennsylvania

CHOCOLATE FUDGE
Number of Servings — 25-30

2 c. sugar
1 small can milk
80 small or 10 lge. marshmallows
1 stick margarine
¾ t. vanilla
1 small pkg. chocolate chips
Pinch of salt
1 small can nuts

Cook sugar, milk, marshmallows, vanilla, salt, and margarine in heavy saucepan 6 minutes. Put chocolate chips in large bowl and pour hot mixture over them. Beat until well blended and creamy. Drop by teaspoon on wax paper and press one nut on each piece.

Mrs. Mavis Toms, Saline H. S.
Saline, Louisiana

CHOCOLATE FUDGE

Number of Servings — 1¼ Pounds

2 c. granulated sugar
1 c. milk
½ t. salt
2 sq. unsweetened chocolate
2 T. white corn syrup
2 T. butter or margarine
½ t. vanilla extract
½ c. broken nut meats

Combine sugar, milk, salt, chocolate, and corn syrup in a saucepan over low heat, stirring constantly until sugar is dissolved. Cook gently, stirring from the bottom occasionally, to 238°F. or until soft ball forms in cold water. Remove from heat, drop in the butter, but do not stir. Set aside to cool, without stirring to 110°F. or lukewarm. Add vanilla and beat until mixture loses gloss and a small amount will hold its shape. Fold in nut meats and turn into a buttered pan about 9x5x3. Cool and cut into squares.

Mrs. Adelaide Wolf, Harbor Creek H. S.
Harbor Creek, Pennsylvania

CARAMEL CHOCOLATE FUDGE

Number of Servings — 30-35 Squares

2 c. light brown sugar (firmly packed)
2 T. chocolate
⅛ t. salt
½ c. white Karo
½ c. evaporated milk
½ c. whole milk (room temperature)
1 t. vanilla
2 c. chopped pecans
2 T. butter

Blend sugar, chocolate, and salt. Add Karo and milk. Place on medium heat, stirring until boiling begins. Lower heat slightly and cook until mixture reaches the firm soft ball stage. Careful occasional stirring may be done while mixture is cooking for more accurate testing. Remove from heat and cool (about 10 minutes). Add butter, vanilla, butter, and pecans. Beat until gloss disappears completely. Pour into buttered square pan. Cut in squares.

Mrs. Florine M. Suire, Henry H. S.
Erath, Louisiana

CONDENSED MILK FUDGE

Number of Servings — 6-8

1 can condensed milk
1 c. sugar
¼ c. milk
1 t. vanilla
1 c. nuts (pecans)

Combine condensed milk, sugar, and milk, mix well and cook over medium heat. Stir constantly, using a wooden spoon. When mixture turns away from the sides of the saucepan remove from heat. Add vanilla and nuts, beat until mixture thickens and changes color. Spread in buttered dish. Cool and cut in squares.

Mrs. Cherrie Y. Manuel, Mamou H. S.
Mamou, Louisiana

CHOCOLATE FUDGE

Number of Servings — 5 Pounds

2 sticks margarine
4 c. sugar
1 can (lge.) evaporated milk
2 pkg. (small) chocolate chips
1 lge. jar marshmallow creme
1 c. nuts

Mix chocolate chips and marshmallow in bowl. Mix butter, sugar, and milk and boil 9 minutes. Pour over chips and mallow mixture. Beat until glossy. Cut in squares. Wrap each piece in wax paper. Store in refrigerator.

Alice Neel Eidson, Sans Souci Jr. H. S.
Greenville, South Carolina

MARY BALL FUDGE

3 pkg. chocolate bits
1 tall can evaporated milk
1 jar marshmallow creme
1 stick oleo
5 c. sugar

Combine sugar, milk, and oleo, bring to boil and boil for 7 minutes. Remove from heat and add chocolate bits and marshmallow creme. Beat until creamy, add nuts if desired, and pour into buttered pan.

Evelyn D. Wester, Crossville H. S.
Crossville, Alabama

MILLION-DOLLAR FUDGE

Number of Servings — 5 Pounds

4½ c. white sugar
1 lge. can evaporated milk
2 sticks butter or oleo
18 oz. chocolate chips
1½ t. vanilla
2 c. broken nuts

Bring sugar and milk to a boil and boil constantly (while stirring) for 10 minutes. Have butter or oleo and chocolate chips in another large pan. Add boiling sugar and milk mixture to chips and oleo and beat quickly. Beat—beat—beat. Add vanilla and nuts. Pour into large oblong pan (8x12). Let cool.

June Elizabeth Rector, Abingdon H. S.
Abingdon, Virginia

MILLION DOLLAR FUDGE

1 lge. can evaporated milk
4½ c. sugar
3 bags chocolate chips
2 jars marshmallow creme
1 c. nuts (more or less)

Stir and cook evaporated milk and sugar for 6 minutes. After it boils take off heat. Stir in chocolate chips, marshmallow creme and nuts. Set marshmallow creme in hot water to soften while sugar and milk are cooking. Grease pans and line with wax paper, pour fudge in pans and let stand 8 hours. Turn out, take off wax paper and cut. This recipe yields 5 pounds of candy. If properly stored, will keep moist for a long time.

Martha M. Tate, Stigler Sr. H. S.
Stigler, Oklahoma

NEVER-FAIL FUDGE

Number of Servings — 5 Pounds
1 (14½ oz.) can evaporated milk
5 c. sugar
2 sticks butter or margarine
1 pkg. chocolate chips (semi-sweetened)
4 sq. unsweetened chocolate
1 lb. pkg. marshmallows
2 c. chopped nuts

Melt butter in large saucepan. Add sugar and milk. Bring to a boil and boil 6 minutes, stirring constantly. Remove from flame. Add marshmallows, chocolate chips, chocolate squares (chipped up), and nuts. Stir until the chocolate and marshmallows are melted. Beat rapidly for 1 minute. Pour into large well buttered cake pan (17½x12). Cool and cut into squares.

Emaline Davis, Coal Hill H. S.
Coal Hill, Arkansas

PEANUT BUTTER FUDGE

1 lb. light brown sugar
1 T. butter
3 T. granulated sugar
½ c. milk
1 t. cornstarch
1 t. vanilla
1-8 oz. jar smooth peanut butter

Dissolve brown sugar, butter, and granulated sugar with milk. Cook until it forms a soft ball in cold water (234-240°F. on candy thermometer). Add cornstarch dissolved in a little cold water. Stir in. Take immediately from the stove and beat well. Add vanilla and peanut butter.

Mrs. Elizabeth Burleigh Totman,
Waterville Sr. H. S.
Waterville, Maine

PINEAPPLE FUDGE

Number of Servings 1-2/3 Pounds
1 c. evaporated milk
3 c. granulated sugar
2 T. butter or oleo
1 c. crushed pineapple, well drained
2 t. lemon juice

Combine milk, sugar, and butter. Heat slowly to boiling point. Add crushed pineapple and cook over medium heat to soft ball stage 235°F., stirring constantly to prevent burning, allow about 25 minutes. Cool. Add lemon juice. Beat until crystalline. Turn into buttered pan. Mark in squares. Decorate with pecan halves, if desired.

Louise Bollinger, Newman H. S.
Sweetwater, Texas

SOUR CREAM FUDGE

2 c. sugar
2 T. white corn syrup
2 T. butter
¾ to 1 c. sour cream depending upon its
   consistency
1 t. vanilla
½ c. black walnuts

Mix sugar, corn syrup, butter and sour cream together thoroughly. (Note: If commercial sour cream is used thin with milk until it is the consistency of thick whipping cream.) Cook over medium or low heat until it reaches the soft ball stage. Cool, add vanilla. Cool to room temperature. Beat until thick and pour all at once onto buttered platter. Do not spread. Top will be glossy and uneven. Cut into ¾" squares when firm.

Mrs. James L. Patton, Bryan Station Sr. H. S.
Lexington, Kentucky

SOUR CREAM FUDGE (Chocolate)

Number of Servings — 9x9 Pan
3 c. sugar
1 c. sour cream
⅛ t. soda
4 T. dark corn syrup
6 T. cocoa
⅛ t. salt
1 t. vanilla
1 c. nuts

Combine all ingredients, except vanilla and nuts in a saucepan. Cook with a minimum of stirring until mixture reaches the soft ball stage. (Dissolve sugar crystals on side of pan by placing cover on mixture during first few minutes of cooking.) Set mixture to cool. When bottom of pan feels cool to the touch, add vanilla, and begin beating. When mixture begins to lose gloss, add chopped nuts and continue to beat until mixture begins to set. Pour into buttered pan. Cut into squares. Freezes well.

Mrs. Audrey Krengel, Hawley Public H. S.
Hawley, Minnesota

MERINGUE FUDGE DROPS

Number of Servings — 24
Beat until stiff but not dry:
4 egg whites
¼ t. cream of tartar
¼ t. salt
Add a little at a time:
1 c. sugar
¼ t. almond extract

Continue beating until stiff and satiny. Drop by teaspoon into mounds 2" in diameter on cookie sheet covered with brown paper. With spoon, press contours to form a cup Bake at 250°F. for 50 minutes. Let cool on paper. Remove gently. (Yield approximately 2 dozen.)

Filling:
Combine and melt over hot (not boiling water):
1 pkg. or 1 c. semi-sweet chocolate morsels
½ c. butter or margarine
Combine and beat well:
4 egg yolks
2 T. corn syrup or sugar

Add to chocolate mixture. Cook stirring for 5 minutes. Remove from heat. Beat until mixture is of spreading consistency. Fill meringue with chocolate mixture. Sprinkle with 2 tablespoons of ground nutmeats.

Ruth G. Seitz, North Hills H. S.
Pittsburgh, Pennsylvania

HOLIDAY DELIGHT

3 c. sugar
1 c. light corn syrup
1½ c. light cream
1½ t. vanilla
½ lb. Brazil nuts cut in half
½ lb. pecan halves
½ lb. black walnuts broken coarsely
½ lb. candied red cherries cut in halves
½ lb. green candied pineapple cut in cubes
   or wedges

Combine sugar, corn syrup, and cream and cook to soft ball stage over medium flame (or heat). Remove from flame and begin beating immediately. It will begin to thicken and change color. Add vanilla and continue beating. Have ready the above fruits and nuts. Add slowly to mixture. The mixture will be thick and sticky. Pack into a wax paper lined loaf pan, pressing down firmly with a wet spoon. Place in refrigerator to chill. Slice after 24 hours. Will keep soft for several months.

Mrs. Sue H. Calhoun, Downsville H. S.
Downsville, Louisiana

MARSHMALLOWS (Homemade)

Number of Servings — 3 Dozen

1 pkg. unflavored gelatin
⅛ c. cold water
½ c. sugar
⅔ c. white corn syrup
⅛ t. salt
1 t. vanilla

Combine gelatin and water in top of double boiler. Stand five minutes to soften. Place over boiling water and heat until gelatin dissolves. Add sugar and stir over hot water until completely dissolved. In large mixer bowl, combine corn syrup, vanilla, and salt. Add hot gelatin-sugar mixture Beat at high speed until light and fluffy (about 15 minutes). Lightly grease a 9" square cake pan. Pour in mixture. Let stand in cool place until set, about 1½ hours. Cut into 1" squares. Roll in powdered sugar.

Bertha Keller Benthien,
Clermont Northeastern H. S.
Owensville, Ohio

AFTER DINNER MINTS

Number of Servings — 150

1 box powdered sugar
1 egg white (unbeaten)
1 T. cream
1 t. vanilla
1 heaping t. soft butter or white shortening
3 drops of oil flavoring of your choice (oil of
   peppermint, cinnamon, etc.)
Food coloring to make pastel color

Combine egg white, cream, vanilla, oil flavoring, and coloring. Stir well. Add the box of sugar all at once, mix thoroughly, add butter, or (white shortening for white mints) and more sugar, if necessary, to make the mixture the right consistency to roll into a firm small ball. Arrange the balls on wax paper and press each ball with tines of a fork dipped in powdered sugar or cornstarch. When mixing in the sugar a bit more cream may need to be added. Cream also makes the white mints look a creamy white. Let stand overnight to form a crust, then pack in tins with wax paper between each layer. May be frozen and kept several months.

Shirley Andersen, Dalton H. S.
Dalton, Nebraska

PULLED MINT CANDY

Number of Servings — 100-110 Small Mints

2 c. white sugar
1 stick butter or margarine
½ c. water
Few drops oil of peppermint or wintergreen
Food coloring (4 drops)

Combine first three ingredients together in a heavy saucepan. Shake the pan or stir lightly with a wooden spoon until sugar has dissolved enough to start cooking. Do not stir again. Place a candy thermometer in pan and cook rather rapidly until thermometer registers 260°F. or to a "soft crack stage" (if you do not have a thermometer). Pour at once on a cold, buttered, marble slab. Pour flavoring and color on top of candy while it cools for a minute or so. Butter hands and begin pulling while still quite hot. When it hardens sufficiently, twist and cut with kitchen shears at once. (Do not make on a rainy day.) Store in airtight container.

This recipe submitted by the following teachers:
Mrs. Katy Jo Powers, Haysi H. S.
Haysi, Virginia
Cynthia S. Picha, Wheaton H. S.
Wheaton, Maryland
Georgia H. Putney, Cumberland H. S.
Cumberland, Virginia

SOUR CREAM SUGARED NUTS

½ c. cultured sour cream
1⅓ c. sugar
1½ t. vanilla
13 oz. walnuts

Mix cream and sugar. Heat to 223°F. stirring constantly. Add vanilla and walnuts. Stir rapidly until mixture has coated nuts and sugared. Spread on tray and separate nuts. Cool thoroughly. Store in an air tight container. (Will keep 3 to 4 months.)

Mrs. Mary Esther Rowe, Swartz Creek H. S.
Swartz Creek, Michigan

ORANGE CANDY

Number of Servings — 20 to 30 Pieces

2 c. sugar
½ c. white Karo syrup
½ c. evaporated milk
2 T. margarine
Grated rind of 1 lge. orange
1 c. chopped nuts

Combine all ingredients except the nuts and cook until it forms a soft ball in cold water. Stir to

(Continued on Next Page)

mix the ingredients at the beginning, and then only enough to prevent sticking. Let cool and beat until creamy, add the nuts just before the candy is ready to dip or pour. Either dip by teaspoonfuls on wax paper or pour into a buttered container and cut into squares.

Mrs. H. M. Thomas, Breckenridge H. S.
Breckenridge, Texas

ORANGE PEEL (With Coconut)
Number of Servings — 1 Pound
2 lge. oranges
Cold water
2 c. sugar
2-3 c. flaked coconut

Wash oranges. Remove peel in quarters. Scrape off excess white inner skin. Cut peel in strips. Place in saucepan and cover with water. Bring to boil, then drain off water. Repeat 2 more times. Measure peel and combine in saucepan with an equal amount of sugar. Cover with water. Bring to boil and cook until syrup is almost absorbed. Remove from heat and drain on racks for 1 minute. Roll quickly in coconut.

Marianne Woolsey, Monmouth H. S.
Decatur, Indiana

MEXICAN ORANGE CANDY
Number of Servings — 36 Pieces
1 c. granulated sugar
1½ c. whole milk
2 c. granulated sugar
Pinch of salt
¼ c. butter
Grated rind of 2 oranges
1 c. pecan meats, broken

Melt the first cup of sugar in a large kettle (4 to 6 quart capacity) while the milk is scalding in a double boiler. When the sugar is melted and a light golden color, add the hot milk all at once. This will boil up quickly so stir it vigorously. Add the 2 cups of sugar and stir until dissolved. Continue cooking to 246°F. (a little dropped into cold water forms a firm ball). Remove from heat, add the salt, butter, grated orange rind and the nuts. Beat until creamy and cool enough to hold its shape when dropped from a teaspoon. Drop by the teaspoonful onto buttered plates. Top each with a pecan half if desired.

Hazel Bussey, William Adams H. S.
Alice, Texas

ORANGE SNOW BALLS
Number of Servings — 3½ Dozen
2¾ c. vanilla wafer crumbs
¼ c. melted margarine
1 c. powdered sugar
1 c. chopped nuts
¼ c. frozen orange juice, undiluted

Mix and shape into small balls with hands. Dip balls in butter icing.
2 T. soft margarine
2 c. powdered sugar

Enough milk to spread. Roll in fine coconut. Store in air-tight container. These will freeze nicely and are better after setting a few days.

Mrs. Willie Mae Cornwell, Midway H. S.
Waco, Texas

PRISSY NUTS (Pecans)
Number of Servings — 1½ Cups
2 t. instant coffee
¼ c. sugar
¼ t. cinnamon
2 T. water
Dash of salt
1½ c. pecan halves

Combine ingredients in saucepan, bring to a boil over medium flame. Boil for 3 minutes stirring constantly. Spread on wax paper. Use 2 forks and separate pecan halves as they cool.

Mrs. Myrna Parsons, Burleson H. S.
Burleson, Texas

SUGARED NUTS
Number of Servings — 24-30
2 c. sugar
½ c. water
5 T. white Karo
8 marshmallows
1 t. vanilla
1 qt. nuts

Mix sugar, water, Karo, cook to little more than soft ball stage, 240°F. Add marshmallows, stir until dissolved. Add vanilla and nuts. Stir until it begins to sugar. Pour out on wax paper and separate with fork.

Joan Wilf, Walnut Ridge H. S.
Walnut Ridge, Arkansas

PEANUT BRITTLE
Number of Servings — 20-25
1½ c. sugar
½ c. white Karo
1 t. soda or 1½ t.
¼ t. salt
¼ c. water
2 c. shelled raw peanuts

Combine sugar, Karo, and water, bring to a boil. Stir in peanuts gradually so as not to lose the boil. Keep at a rolling boil until peanuts pop and turn brown. Remove from heat, add soda stirring well, add salt. Pour on a well greased platter. Allow room for candy to spread. When cold break in clumps.

This recipe submitted by the following teachers:
Mrs. Billye Tingle, Forrest County Agri. H. S.
Brooklyn, Mississippi
Mrs. Ruth D. Jordan, Benjamin Russell H. S.
Alexander City, Alabama

PEANUT BRITTLE
2 c. sugar
½ c. water
1 c. light Karo syrup
2 c. raw peanuts
Dash of salt
1 heaping t. soda
1 t. vanilla

Combine sugar, water and Karo syrup in a heavy, large saucepan and boil to the hard-ball stage. Check either by the cold water method or use a candy thermometer. Remove from heat. Add raw

(Continued on Next Page)

peanuts and salt. Mixture will be quite thick. Return to fire and boil to golden brown and the nuts smell done. Take from the fire. Add baking soda and vanilla. Pour out on a buttered pan. When thoroughly cooled crack into pieces and serve.

Mrs. Shirley Newcombe, Reed City Public Schools
Reed City, Michigan

PEANUT BRITTLE
Number of Servings — 15-20
2 c. sugar
3 c. peanuts, raw
¾ c. white Karo
¼ c. water
Dash of salt
3 t. baking soda

Combine sugar, peanuts, Karo, water, and salt. Cook on medium heat, stirrin continuously until peanuts are very brown, to hard crack stage. Remove from heat, add soda and stir. Pour on well buttered baking sheet and spread as thin as possible.

Mrs. Iris B. Christopher, Glencoe H. S.
Glencoe, Alabama

PEANUT CLUSTERS
Number of Servings — 1½ Dozen
⅔ c. condensed milk
1½ c. spanish peanuts salted
1-6 oz. pkg. chocolate chips
1 t. vanilla

Melt chocolate chips over double boiler, remove from heat. Add condensed milk, vanilla, and peanuts. Mix and drop by teaspoonfuls onto a buttered cookie sheet or on wax paper.

Mary Lou Meyer, Aviston Community H. S.
Aviston, Illinois

PENUCHE
2 c. brown sugar
¾ c. sweet milk
1 t. vanilla flavoring
1 c. chopped nut meats
2 T. butter

Boil sugar and sweet milk slowly until it forms a soft ball when tested in cold water. Stir constantly to prevent curdling. Remove from heat and add vanilla, chopped nut meats, and butter. Beat until creamy and pour into a greased pan. Cut into squares when firm.

Sarah Judith Pitts, Century H. S.
Century, Florida

POPCORN BALLS
Number of Servings — 12 Medium Size Balls
3 qt. popcorn
1 c. sugar
⅓ c. white syrup
⅓ c. water
¼ c. butter
¾ t. salt
¾ t. vanilla

Mix sugar, corn syrup, water, butter, and salt in saucepan and cook, stirring until the sugar is dissolved. Continue cooking without stirring until syrup forms a brittle ball in cold water. Add vanilla and stir only enough to mix it through the hot syrup. Place the popped corn in a bowl large enough for mixing. Pour the cooked syrup slowly over the popped corn and mix well. Wet the hands slightly and shape corn into balls, using only enough pressure to make the balls stick together.

Bonnie O'Connell, Tracy H. S.
Tracy, Minnesota

CONFETTI POPCORN
2 c. sugar
2 T. butter
½ c. water

Cook ingredients together until mixture spins a fine thread. Remove from stove and add food coloring (pink) and flavoring if desired. Pour over corn and stir until each kernel is coated. Serve as a snack or light dessert.

Mrs. Eva Malerich, Colfax H. S.
Colfax, Washington

POTATO PINWHEELS
Number of Servings — 2 Dozen
1 medium sized potato
2½-3½ c. powdered sugar
Chunk style peanut butter

Boil until done, one medium potato, either peeled or unpeeled. While still hot, mash thoroughly. Begin adding powdered sugar, small amounts at a time until the potato and powdered sugar mixture is at a rolled dough stage. Roll out to ¼" thickness. Spread evenly with chunk style peanut butter and roll up. Chill 5 to 6 hours or overnight. Slice into ¼" or ½" pieces. Serve cold.

This recipe submitted by the following teachers:
Ardis Boyd, Lead Public School
Lead, South Dakota
Mrs. Ruth H. Green, Leakesville H. S.
Leakesville, Mississippi

MASHED POTATO CANDY
Number of Servings — 32 Pieces
¾ c. cold mashed potatoes
4 c. confectioners' sugar
4 c. shredded coconut
1½ t. vanilla
½ t. salt
8 sq. baking chocolate

Mix potatoes and confectioners' sugar. Stir in coconut, vanilla and salt, blend well. Press into large pan so that candy will be about ½" thick. Melt chocolate over hot water (do not allow water to boil). Pour chocolate on top of candy. Cool. Cut in squares.

Mary Nicholella, Peters Twp. Jr.-Sr. H. S.
Canonsburg, Pennsylvania

CREAMY PRALINES
Number of Servings — 20 Pieces
1 c. brown sugar
1 c. evaporated milk or 1 c. thin cream
⅛ t. salt

(Continued on Next Page)

2 t. vanilla
1 c. white (granulated) sugar
⅛ t. soda
½ stick butter
2 c. slightly toasted pecans

Mix all ingredients except vanilla. Cook over low heat until it reaches the soft ball stage on candy thermometer (or forms soft ball in cold water). Stir occasionally to prevent sticking. Add vanilla. Cool. Beat until thick. Drop by spoonfuls on wax paper. Leave on paper until firm and cool.

Hilda Harmon, Crowley H. S.
Crowley, Louisiana

PRALINES (Creamy)

1 box light brown sugar
1 small can evaporated milk
2 T. Karo
2 T. water
½ stick butter
1 t. vanilla
1½ c. pecan halves

Boil together sugar, milk, water, and Karo until soft ball is formed when tested in cold water. Remove from heat. Add butter, cool. Add vanilla. Beat until creamy. Add pecans and drop by spoonfuls on wax paper or greased marble.

Ruth Stovall, State Department of Education
Montgomery, Alabama

CREAMY PRALINES

1 c. brown sugar
1 c. granulated sugar
2 c. pecans (½ lb.)
½ c. evaporated milk

Mix all ingredients thoroughly. Cook over medium heat to soft ball stage, stirring constantly. Cool slightly. Beat until mixture starts to thicken. Drop candy rapidly from a spoon onto greased wax paper to form patties. If candy becomes to stiff to make smooth patties, stir in a little hot water.

Mrs. Barbara Hinegardner, Bel Air Jr. H. S.
Bel Air, Maryland

CREAMY PRALINES

Number of Servings — 6 Dozen

2 c. sugar
1 c. brown sugar
½ c. milk
½ c. condensed milk
¼ c. butter
¼ t. salt
3 c. broken pecans

Combine sugars and milks with butter and salt in a heavy saucepan. Bring slowly to a full rolling boil over medium heat. Add the nuts and continue boiling until candy reaches the soft ball stage, 234°F. on the candy thermometer. Remove from heat and stir only enough to give a creamy look. Spoon out on wax paper or a buttered baking sheet.

Mrs. Agnes La Fleur, Lawtell H. S.
Lawtell, Louisiana

CHOCOLATE COVERED PRALINES

Number of Servings — 16

1 t. cornstarch
½ c. evaporated milk
½ c. honey
¾ c. maple syrup
2 T. butter
¼ t. salt

Make a paste with the starch and 1 teaspoon milk. Add the remaining ingredients and stir again. Put on direct heat and heat to 250°F., stirring all the time as this candy will stick to the pan and scorch easily. Butter a cookie sheet and dust with confectioners' sugar. Place the pecans in groups of 3 or 4 on the dusted sheet about 3″ apart. Use 3 pecans if large, 4 or 5 if small. Drop the candy on top of the pecans after the candy has cooled slightly. Coat each piece with chocolate melted at about 100°F. and cooled to 82°F., after the candy has cooled to room temperature.

La Rue B. Fleming, Senior H. S.
Bogalusa, Louisiana

EASY PRALINES

1 pkg. butterscotch pudding
1 c. granulated sugar
1 c. brown sugar
½ c. evaporated milk
1 T. butter or margarine
½ c. pecans (more if desired)

Combine all ingredients except the pecans and cook at a low temperature until the sugar is dissolved. Then boil until the soft ball stage is reached. Add pecans. Stir until it just begins to harden. This candy hardens very quickly once it has started to thicken in the pan. Quickly drop by spoonfuls into 2″ patties on wax paper. Let stand until firm.

This recipe submitted by the following teachers:
Nancy Newman, Joliet Township H. S. & Jr. Col.
Joliet, Illinois

Mrs. Sarah Henry, Redwater H. S.
Redwater, Texas

PRALINES

Number of Servings — 16

1 c. white sugar
1 c. brown sugar
2 c. nuts
2 T. Karo
½ c. cream (may use undiluted evaporated milk)
Dash of salt
¼ stick oleo
¼ t. cream of tartar (dash)

Add sugars, syrup, cream, cream of tartar, and salt. Boil to soft ball stage. Remove from fire and beat 2 minutes. Cool 15 minutes. Beat again 10 times, add pecans and drop on wax paper. If it gets too hard, add a little hot water.

Mrs. Sallie Hilley
Abilene, Texas

ORANGE PRALINES

3 c. sugar
1 c. top cream
2 T. corn syrup
1 orange peel
2 c. pecans

Cook the first three ingredients together until a soft ball is formed when tested in cold water. Remove from heat and add peel from 1 orange chopped fine. Let cool. Add pecans. Drop on wax paper.

Mrs. Martha Thompson, Nocona H. S.
Nocona, Texas

PECAN PRALINES

Number of Servings — 24 Pieces

2 c. brown sugar
½ c. evaporated milk
½ T. butter
16 marshmallows
1 lb. shelled pecans (about 2 c.)

Place the brown sugar, milk, and butter in a saucepan and cook to the soft ball stage. Add the warm softened marshmallows and stir until dissolved. Add pecans. Drop on wax paper. Will be firm when cool.

Mrs. Laquita B. Neill, J. Z. George H. S.
North Carrollton, Mississippi

SEAFOAM NUT KISSES

Number of Servings — 2 Dozen

1 egg white
¼ c. instant dry milk
1 T. water
¾ c. brown sugar
⅛ t. salt
1 T. flour
1 c. nuts (cut up)

With electric mixer at high speed, beat egg white, dry milk and water in small mixer bowl until stiff. Beat brown sugar in, a tablespoon at a time, to make thick, glossy meringue-like mixture. Scrape sides of bowl often. Fold in a mixture of the salt, flour, and nuts. Drop teaspoonfuls of mixture onto greased and floured cookie sheet. Bake in 325°F. oven about 15 minutes, or until light brown. Take from sheet, cool on wire rack.

Mrs. Ann Rushing, Jefferson H. S.
Fayette, Mississippi

CANDY STRAWBERRIES

Number of Servings — 64

2 boxes strawberry Jello
¾ c. Eagle Brand milk
1 c. fine shredded coconut
1 c. finely chopped pecans

Mix all the ingredients and form into strawberries. Dip the pointed end in red sugar and the stem end in green sugar. Place on wax paper in refrigerator for several hours. Green toothpicks and green hulls may be attached if desired. (Note: granulated sugar may be colored by placing in a jar, adding food coloring and shaking.)

Ettie Belle Robinson, Dawson H. S.
Dawson, Texas

SNOWBALLS

Number of Servings — 24-30

1 c. chopped dates
1 c. finely chopped walnuts
1 c. peanut butter
1½ c. confectioners' sugar
2-4 T. light cream
1½ cans (2 c.) flaked coconut

Blend together dates, walnuts, and peanut butter. Shape into small balls about 1″ in diameter. Make a thin icing with the confectioners' sugar and cream. Roll balls in icing and then in flaked coconut. Let stand until the icing is set. May be served after chilling or placed in covered refrigerator dishes and stored in the refrigerator.

Mrs. Retha George, Biloxi H. S.
Biloxi, Mississippi

CHOCOLATE ALMOND TOFFEE

1 c. brown sugar, packed
1 c. white sugar
⅓ c. syrup, white
½ c. water
⅛ t. salt
¼ c. butter
1-6 oz. pkg. semi-sweet chocolate, melted
½ c. toasted almonds, chopped

Combine sugars, syrup, water, and salt in heavy saucepan. Blend thoroughly. Place over medium heat. Stir until sugar is dissolved and mixture is boiling moderately. Cook to firm ball stage 245°F. Add butter and continue cooking to hard crack stage 290°F. Pour into lightly oiled 9x9 pan. Cool until hard and brittle. Spread with half the melted chocolate and top with half the chopped almonds. Loosen and do the same to other side and break into various sized pieces.

Darlene M. Johnson, Senior H. S.
New Richmond, Wisconsin

BUTTER CRUNCH

Number of Servings — 1 Pound

1 c. margarine
1 c. sugar
2 T. water
1 T. light corn syrup
¾ c. nut meats, chopped fine
4 sq. (4 oz.) semi-sweet chocolate

Melt the margarine in a 2-quart saucepan over low heat. Remove from heat, add the sugar. With a wooden spoon, stir the mixture until it is well blended. Return to low heat, stir rapidly until thoroughly mixed and begins to bubble. Add water and corn syrup, mix well. Keep heat low, stirring frequently, cook until candy thermometer registers 290°F. (brittle stage, 15 to 20 minutes). Remove from heat at once. Sprinkle nuts over surface and quickly mix in. Pour out on lightly greased cookie sheet. With spatula, spread ¼″ thick. Cool to room temperature. Partially melt 2 squares chocolate over boiling water. Remove from water, stir until melted. Spread evenly over crunch. Set aside until firm, then turn over, melt rest of chocolate and spread other side. When firm, break in pieces. Store in tightly covered container in cool place.

Mrs. Wanda Brian, Brock H. S.
Weatherford, Texas

BUTTER TOFFEE

Number of Servings — 2 Dozen

1 c. sugar
½ t. salt
¼ c. water
½ c. butter
1½ c. chopped walnuts
1 lge. pkg. chocolate bits

Combine sugar, salt, water, and butter. Cook to light crack stage 285°F. on candy thermometer. Add ½ cup chopped walnuts. Pour onto well greased cookie sheet. Cool. Melt chocolate bits over hot water. Spread half chocolate on the top of toffee and sprinkle with ½ cup chopped walnuts. Cool. Turn the toffee and repeat the spreading of chocolate and nuts on the other side. Cool. Break into pieces.

Pauline Baskett, Blue Rapids H. S.
Blue Rapids, Kansas

ENGLISH TOFFEE

1 c. chopped almonds
1 c. butter
1 c. brown sugar
4-10¢ chocolate bars (Hershey)

Sprinkle ½ cup nuts in greased 9x12 pan. Melt butter in saucepan. Add sugar and mix well. Boil for 12 minutes stirring constantly. Add remaining ½ cup of nuts. Pour hot mixture over nuts in pan. Place bars on top. When melted, spread to cover.

Elizabeth M. Sandness, Aitkin Public School
Aitkin, Minnesota

MUNCHY CRUNCHIES

Number of Servings — 60

1-6 oz. pkg. semi-sweet chocolate bits
1-6 oz. pkg. butterscotch morsels
2-3 oz cans chow mein noodles
1 c. peanuts

Spread candy evenly in 11" or 12" skillet. Set control at 200°F. Cover, cook 5 minutes. Stir to combine softened candy, mixture may not be smooth. Add noodles and nuts, stir until coated with candy mixture. Remove from heat. Drop by teaspoonfuls onto wax paper.

Mrs. Dorothy T. Rousseau, Baker H. S.
Baker, Louisana

PECAN TOFFEE

Number of Servings — 8

½ c. granulated sugar
¼ lb. butter
1-5¢ Hershey bar
1½ c. chopped pecans

Place in a heavy skillet, sugar and butter. Cook, stirring constantly, until lightly browned. Pour at once onto flat buttered pan that is covered with pecans, placed closely together. Break Hershey bar over top and spread around when melted. Sprinkle with chopped pecans. Yields about 7x9 sheet of candy.

Mrs. Laverne Littrel, Wapello Community School
Wapello, Iowa

TWO-TONE TRUFFLES

1½ c. chopped nuts
1½ c. powdered sugar
1 egg white
1 T. rum extract
1½ c. chocolate bits
¾ c. condensed milk
1 T. butter

Combine nuts, sugar, egg white, and rum. Mix and spread in buttered, wax paper lined pan. Melt chocolate bits, stir in milk and butter. Cook until thick (approximately 5 minutes). Pour over nut mixture. Cut into squares when firm. Wrap individually in Saran Wrap if stored.

Dana Ray Owens, Schleicher County School
Eldorado, Texas

WITCHES' HATS

Number of Servings — 8

1 oz. (1 sq.) unsweetened chocolate
16 lge. fresh marshmallows
3 T. corn syrup
3 c. puffed wheat cereal

Melt together chocolate, marshmallows, and corn syrup over low heat. Stir to blend. While chocolate mixture is melting, place puffed wheat in shallow pan. Heat in moderate oven 350°F. 10 minutes. Place in greased bowl. Pour chocolate mixture over puffed wheat. Stir to coat kernels evenly. With greased hands, form mixture into 8 cone shapes. Roll in chocolate. Place each cone-shaped witches' hat in 3½" circle for brim.

Phyllis T. Smith, Bryan Station Jr. H. S.
Lexington, Kentucky

Cookies, Squares & Bars

Cookie Capers

I. CLUES FOR "BUTTON POPPIN'" SUCCESS...

A. Be sure to read the recipe carefully before beginning to work.

B. Cookie sheet conversation...

1. Choose a shiny cookie sheet which is 2 inches smaller around all sides than the oven; this allows for good circulation of heat.

2. Here's a trick—for extra cookie sheets, cut pieces of aluminum foil the same size as the cookie sheet. Drop dough onto foil and slip onto the cookie sheet as soon as it comes from the oven. A real timesaver!

3. Without a cookie sheet? Simply turn a baking pan over and use the bottom, and your problem is solved!

4. If the cookie sheet is to be greased, always grease it lightly. You can avoid brown spots if you will only grease the spots where dough is to be dropped.

C. Have all ingredients at room temperature for more glamorous, perfect cookies.

D. A pinch of this, a dash of that ... no guessing game this! Measure correctly and accurately, using standard equipment. Simple secrets to remember are:

1. Shortening should hold its shape when turned out of the measuring cup. The same applies to brown sugar.

2. Dry ingredients are lightly spooned into the measuring utensil.

3. A level measurement is obtained by running a spatula or knife across the top of the utensil.

E. A tidy bowl is important. Use a rubber scraper often, so the ingredients are well blended. Do leave a few drops for "bowl lickin'" fun though ...

II. THE HEAT'S ON...

A. So watch those cookies! A good rule is to check them when the minimum baking time is up.

B. When using oven-glass baking pans, always lower the temperature 25 degrees.

C. Cookies should be baked near the center of the oven if a single cookie sheet is used. If two cookie sheets are placed in the oven at the same time, they should be spaced far enough apart to allow for proper circulation of heat.

D. Timely tip ... use a handy clock or timer to check the baking time, but don't trust your memory!

E. Done or undone, that is the question ...

1. Bars or squares are done when the sides shrink from the pan, or the top springs back when lightly touched with the finger. Soft cookies will also spring back when touched.

2. Crisp cookies are done when they are fairly firm, and lightly browned around the edges.

F. Unless otherwise directed, remove cookies from cookie sheet right after taking from oven, and place on wire rack to cool. Never overlap, pile, stack, or store warm cookies.

G. Use a wide spatula to take cookies from cookie sheet ... pretty cookies must have a good figure, you know!

III. IN THE COOKIE JAR...

A. Storage conditions must be just right to "lock in" the homemade flavor and aroma.

   1. Soft cookies, bars and squares should be stored in a tightly covered container or right in the baking pan, covered with aluminum foil. If cookies begin to dry, add a piece of bread, apple, or orange to supply the needed moisture.

   2. Crisp cookies should be stored in a container with a loose fitting cover. If cookies soften and become limp and tired, freshen them in a 300 oven (slow) for about five minutes before serving.

B. Be wise... soft and crisp cookies should *never* be stored together.

IV. A TRAVELIN' THEY WILL GO...

A. For a delightful gift on birthdays, holidays, or other special occasions, send a box of cookies. Choose cookies that are heavenly, but hardy, so they can stand the trip. Soft cookies generally are the best travelers.

B. Use a strong cardboard box or metal container. Line with waxed paper or aluminum foil, and put a cushion of crumpled waxed paper, plastic wrap, or cellophane straw on the bottom.

C. Wrap cookies in pairs, back to back, with waxed paper between. A moisture-vapor proof material, such as plastic wrap, safely holds the fine flavor while the cookies bounce along the miles.

D. Pack snugly in rows, with heavy cookies at the bottom. Tuck popcorn, puffed cereal, or crushed waxed paper into the holes to prevent jiggling.

E. Cover each layer with a cushion of waxed paper or paper towels, and don't forget to put an especially fat layer on the top!

F. Tape box shut, print address on box (if paper becomes torn en route, the address will not be destroyed with it) and wrap in heavy brown paper. Tie securely.

G. Print name and address plainly on front of package, and label "Fragile, Handle with Care."

AMBROSIA DROP COOKIES

Number of Servings — 2½ to 3 Dozen Cookies

½ c. butter or margarine
½ c. sugar
1 egg
1¼ c. sifted all-purpose flour
½ t. baking powder
½ t. salt
1 T. grated orange rind
1 c. coarsely chopped pecans
1 c. grated coconut
Whole pecans

Cream butter, add sugar gradually and cream together until light and fluffy. Add egg and beat well. Mix in dry ingredients which have been sifted together, and then stir in orange rind, chopped nuts and coconut. Drop by teaspoonfuls onto oiled cookie sheet, press a whole pecan into the center of each cookie, and bake in 375°F. oven for 12 to 14 minutes, until lightly browned.

Allene Elliott, Gulfport H. S.
Gulfport, Mississippi

SPICED APPLESAUCE DROPS

Number of Servings — 3 Dozen

½ c. shortening
1 c. sugar
1 egg, unbeaten
2 c. sifted all-purpose flour
1 t. baking powder
¼ t. cloves
½ t. baking soda
½ t. salt
½ t. cinnamon
1 c. thin unsweetened applesauce°
1 c. chopped dates
1 c. chopped nuts

Cream shortening, gradually beat in sugar. Add egg, beat until light and fluffy. Sift dry ingredients together. Use ½ cup to mix with dates and nuts. Add dry ingredients alternately with applesauce to egg mixture. Stir in floured fruit and nut mixture. Drop from teaspoon on greased baking sheet. Bake in moderate oven 350°F. until tops spring back under finger tip pressure, about 15 minutes.

°Use apple butter instead of applesauce, if desired.

Thyra Krauss, Concordia Junior-Senior H. S.
Concordia, Kansas

BROWN SUGAR COOKIES

Number of Servings — 4 Dozen

1 c. butter or oleo
1 lb. brown sugar
2 eggs
4 c. sifted flour
½ t. salt
1 t. baking powder
1 c. nut meats

Cream butter, add brown sugar, beaten egg, sifted dry ingredients. Mix well, drop by teaspoons on cookie sheet. Bake at 350°F. for 7 minutes.

Mrs. Opal Alexander, Sundown H. S.
Sundown, Texas

BACHELOR BUTTON COOKIES

Number of Servings — 5 to 6 Dozen

2 c. sifted flour
¾ t. salt
1 t. soda
¾ c. shortening
1 c. firmly packed brown sugar
1 egg
1 t. vanilla
½ c. chopped nuts or ½ c. coconut or ½ c. chopped candied or maraschino cherries or ½ c. chocolate chips or ½ c. raisins

Measure and sift together flour, salt, and soda. Measure and put in a bowl shortening and brown sugar. Beat with a mixer until soft and then add egg, beating until light and fluffy. Add vanilla and nuts or fruit. Stir with rubber spatula to blend. Stir in flour. Drop from a teaspoon onto greased cookie sheet or shape into crescents with floured fingertips. Bake in moderate oven at 375°F. about 12 minutes.

Mrs. Joyce Mauldin Redstone, Weir H. S.
Weir, Mississippi

BUTTEROONS

Number of Servings — 3 Dozen

½ c. butter
½ c. sugar
1 egg
2 t. grated lemon rind
2 t. grated orange rind
¼ t. salt
1 c. all-purpose flour
1 small can crushed pineapple, drained
1 c. fine, flaked coconut

Cream butter, add sugar, egg, lemon and orange rind, and salt, cream thoroughly. Blend in flour and drained pineapple. Drop by ½ teaspoon on coconut and roll until cookie mixture is coated with coconut. Place on ungreased baking sheet 1″ apart. Bake at 325°F. until light golden brown.

Ruth Dantzler, Columbia H. S.
Columbia, South Carolina

CHOCOLATE CHIP SAND TARTS

Number of Servings — 6 Dozen

1 c. butter
⅛ t. salt
1 t. vanilla
½ t. almond extract
1¼ c. sugar
1 egg
2 c. sifted flour
1-6 oz. pkg. (1 c.) semi-sweet chocolate morsels

Preheat oven to 350°F. Combine and blend well butter, salt, vanilla, and almond extract. Beat sugar in gradually. Beat in egg. Stir in sifted flour. Add chocolate morsels. Drop by teaspoon on ungreased cookie sheet. Bake at 350°F. 15 minutes.

Mrs. Linda Gage, Pflugerville H. S.
Pflugerville, Texas

CHOCOLATE CHIP COOKIES
Number of Servings — 60
2 small pkg. chocolate chips
4 T. sugar
1 can condensed milk
1 stick butter
1 c. flour
1 t. vanilla
1 c. chopped nuts

Melt chocolate chips and sugar in double boiler. Add condensed milk and butter and stir until butter is melted. Pour mixture over flour in bowl. Stir and add vanilla and nuts. Let set awhile. Drop by teaspoon on greased cookie sheet and bake exactly 8 minutes at 350°F.

Lucillie H. Stewart, Farmerville H. S.
Farmerville, Louisiana

CHOCOLATE CHIP BROWN SUGAR COOKIES
Number of Servings — 36
¼ lb. butter or oleomargarine
1 c. brown sugar
2 eggs
⅛ c. milk
2 c. flour
2 t. baking powder
1 t. salt
1 c. chocolate chips
1 c. walnuts or pecans

Combine butter and sugar. Add eggs, one at a time, unbeaten. Mix thoroughly. Add dry ingredients alternately with milk. Add chocolate chips and nuts. Drop on ungreased baking sheet. Bake at 400°F. for 15 minutes.

Ruth Bailey, Jonesboro H. S.
Jonesboro, Tennessee

CHOCOLATE DROP COOKIES (Iced)
Number of Servings — 3 Dozen
½ c. butter or shortening
1 c. brown sugar
1 egg, slightly beaten
1½ c. flour
½ c. cocoa
¼ t. soda
¼ t. baking powder
¼ t. salt
½ c. sour milk
1 c. nut meats
Combine ingredients in order listed. Drop from teaspoon on greased and floured pan and bake at 400°F.
Icing:
1 egg, slightly beaten
1¾ c. powdered sugar
¼ c. cocoa
1 t. vanilla
1 T. cream
Mix powdered sugar with cocoa, add to egg, add cream slowly, then add vanilla.

Mrs. Ruby W. Harkey, San Saba H. S.
San Saba, Texas

CHOCOLATE NUT WAFERS
Number of Servings — 5 Dozen
½ c. soft shortening
1 c. sugar
1 egg
1 t. vanilla
2 sq. chocolate
¾ c. flour
¾ t. salt
¾ c. nuts (finely chopped)

Cream the shortening and sugar. Add the egg, vanilla, and melted chocolate. Mix well. Add the sifted dry ingredients and finely chopped nuts. Drop by teaspoons 2" apart on a lightly greased cookie sheet. Use the bottom of a glass with a slightly dampened cloth over it to press the dough into flat rounds. Bake 10 to 12 minutes at 325°F.

Helen Chase, Canby Public Schools
Canby, Minnesota

CHOCOLATE COOKIES
Number of Servings — 4 Dozen
2 c. sugar
½ c. cocoa
½ c. canned milk
1 stick oleo
¼ t. salt
3 c. quick cooking oats
1 c. coconut
½ c. chopped nuts
1 t. vanilla

Mix first five ingredients and cook to rolling boil. Then add the remaining ingredients. Mix well and drop by teaspoonfuls on wax paper.

Mrs. Jean Pearson, San Felipe H. S.
Del Rio, Texas

COFFEE COOKIE
Number of Servings — 5 Dozen
1½ c. brown sugar
1 c. shortening (half & half)
3 eggs
1 t. soda
4 T. hot coffee
2½ c. flour
1 t. cinnamon
½ t. cloves
½ t. allspice
½ t. salt
1 c. chopped nuts
1 c. seedless raisins

Cream sugar and shortening, add eggs one at a time beating well. Dissolve soda in strong, hot coffee (one tablespoon of instant coffee to four tablespoons of hot water.) Add soda and coffee to first mixture. Beat well. Sift, measure and mix dry ingredients together. Add to other mixture gradually. Add nuts and raisins. Drop by teaspoon on greased baking sheet 2" apart. Bake at 375°F. for about 10 minutes. To add flavor, frost with a mocha icing when cooled.

Elizabeth C. Norman, Madison H. S.
Madison, Minnesota

COCONUT MACAROONS
Number of Servings — 2½ Dozen

2 c. finely grated coconut
¾ c. sweetened condensed milk
Dash of Salt
1 t. vanilla
¼ t. almond extract

Combine all ingredients and mix well. Drop by teaspoonfuls, 1″ apart, on greased baking sheets. Bake at 325°F. about 15 minutes, or until golden brown. Remove from baking sheet at once.

Peggy Sue Rozell, Bagdad H. S.
Bagdad, Arizona

FOUR-IN-ONE-COOKIES
Number of Servings — 5½ Dozen

1 c. shortening, soft
1 c. brown sugar
1 c. granulated sugar
2 eggs
1¼ c. sifted flour
1 t. soda
½ t. salt
½ t. vanilla
3 c. rolled oats (uncooked quick or old fashioned)
1 c. pecans
1-6 oz. pkg. chocolate chips

Heat oven to moderate 350°F. Place shortening, sugars, and eggs in mixing bowl, beat thoroughly. Sift together flour, soda and salt, add to shortening mixture. Mix thoroughly. Stir in vanilla and oats. Add pecans and chocolate chips. Drop from teaspoon onto greased cookie sheets 2″ apart. Bake in preheated oven 350°F. 12 to 15 minutes. Cool about 2 minutes, then remove from cookie sheets. For variety: Omit pecans and chocolate chips and add 1 cup raisins, 1 cup peanuts.

Mrs. Dorothy Cross, Whitney H. S.
Whitney, Texas

FROSTED DEVIL'S-FOOD DROP COOKIES
Number of Servings — 4½ Dozen

½ c. butter or margarine
1 c. brown sugar
1 egg
1 t. vanilla
2-1 oz. sq. unsweetened chocolate, melted and cooled
2 c. sifted all-purpose flour
½ t. soda
¼ t. salt
¾ c. dairy sour cream
½ c. chopped walnuts

Cream butter and sugar until fluffy, beat in egg and vanilla. Stir in chocolate. Sift together dry ingredients, add to chocolate mixture alternately with sour cream. Mix well. Stir in nuts. Drop from teaspoon, 2″ apart, on greased cookie sheet. Bake at 350°F. 10 minutes or until done. Remove from cookie sheet, cool and frost.

Mocha Frosting:
¼ c. soft butter or margarine
2 T. cocoa (regular type, dry)
2 t. instant coffee
Dash of salt
3 c. confectioners' sugar
3 T. milk
1½ t. vanilla

Cream butter, cocoa, instant coffee, and salt, slowly cream 1 cup confectioners' sugar. Add remaining 2 cups confectioners' sugar, milk, and vanilla. Beat smooth.

Mrs. Mary Louise Sawyer, Smyer H. S.
Smyer, Texas

DATE COOKIES
Number of Servings — 3 Dozen

1 c. chopped dates
¾ t. soda
2 T. butter
1 egg
1 c. sugar
1 t. vanilla
1½ c. flour
Pinch of salt

Put soda in measuring cup and fill cup with boiling water. Add butter and pour over dates. Combine beaten egg, sugar, flour, and vanilla. Drop by teaspoon on cookie sheet. Bake at 400°F. 8-10 minutes.

Madge Arlene Humphrey, Weston H. S.
Cazonovia, Wisconsin

FRUIT CAKE COOKIES
Number of Servings — 15 or 20

2 sticks margarine
1 c. brown sugar
4 eggs
½ t. nutmeg
3 c. flour
1 t. soda
½ t. salt
3 T. buttermilk
½ c. wine (optional)
1 lb. candied cherries
1 lb. white raisins
1½ lb. pecan halves

Cream margarine and sugar. Add eggs one at a time. Add dry ingredients, buttermilk, and (wine or whiskey, if desired). Add chopped fruit.

Mrs. Reba Jean Fite Cook
Clarksdale-Coahoma H. S.
Clarksdale, Mississippi

FRUIT CAKE DROP COOKIES
Number of Servings — 7 Dozen

½ c. butter
1 c. brown sugar
4 eggs
3 c. flour (cake flour)
1 t. soda
½ t. nutmeg
3 T. sour milk
1 t. vanilla
1 lb. white raisins
1 lb. glazed pineapple
¼ lb. red glazed cherries

(Continued on Next Page)

¼ lb. green glazed cherries
1½ lb. chopped pecans
½ c. flour to dredge nuts and fruit

Cream butter and sugar, add eggs one at a time and beat after addition. Sift flour and measure, add soda and nutmeg to above mixture alternately with the milk. Add vanilla and mix well. Chop pecans, and cut fruit in small pieces, mix, add the ½ cup flour and dredge. Add to batter and mix well. Drop by teaspoon on greased baking sheet. Bake at 350°F. for about 15 minutes.

Mrs. Mabel Flanagan, Bogue Chitto H. S.
Bogue Chitto, Mississippi

FRUIT CAKE COOKIES
Number of Servings — 9 Dozen

1 c. brown sugar
½ c. butter or margarine
4 whole eggs
1 scant t. soda
3 T. milk

Mix soda and milk and add to above mixture.

1½ lb. shelled pecans
1 lb. pineapple (candied)
1 c. white raisins
½ lb. cherries (candied)
3 c. sifted flour
1 t. cinnamon
1 t. allspice
1 t. nutmeg
1 c. whiskey

Drop by teaspoon on lightly greased cookie sheet and bake in 300°F. oven for 15 to 20 minutes.

Martha Carden, East Junior H. S.
Tullahoma, Tennessee

FRUIT CAKE COOKIES
Number of Servings — 50

½ c. butter
1 c. brown sugar
4 eggs
3 T. sweet milk
3 c. sifted flour
2 t. soda
1 t. cloves
1 t. cinnamon
¾ lb. raisins
1 t. nutmeg
½ lb. broken pecans
1 lb. pecan halves
½ lb. candied cherries
½ lb. candied pineapple
¼ c. fruit juice (grape, pineapple, orange)

Cream the butter and sugar, add the eggs and beat well, add the sweet milk and mix. Sift the flour, soda, and spices together and add to the butter and sugar mixture, stir in the fruit and nuts, add fruit juice last. Drop by teaspoons on greased cookie sheet. Bake in 325°F. oven until cookies are firm but not very brown. These cookies may be kept for several weeks in a covered container.

Mrs. Marie Lovil, McLeod H. S.
McLeod, Texas

FRUIT CAKE COOKIES
Number of Servings — 4 Dozen

½ c. shortening
1 c. brown sugar
1 egg
¼ c. buttermilk
1¾ c. sifted flour
½ t. soda
½ t. salt
½ c. chopped nuts
1 c. chopped dates
1 c. quartered cherries

Mix thoroughly shortening, sugar, and egg. Stir in buttermilk. Sift together flour, soda, and salt. Stir in. Mix in nuts, cherries and dates. Chill. Drop with a teaspoon about 2" apart onto a lightly greased baking sheet. Top each one with a pecan half or a cherry. Bake in a 400°F. oven for 8 to 10 minutes.

Mrs. Margaret Hollingsworth, Montevallo H. S.
Montevallo, Alabama

CHRISTMAS FRUIT COOKIES
Number of Servings — 150-160

½ lb. candied mixed fruit
¼ lb. candied cherries
2 lb. dates
½ lb. blanched almonds
½ lb. shelled pecans
2½ c. sifted all-purpose flour
1 t. baking soda
1 t. salt
1 t. cinnamon
1 c. butter
1½ c. sugar
2 eggs

Pit dates, cut all fruit into small chunks, chop almonds coarsely and toast until golden, chop pecans. Sift flour, baking soda, salt and cinnamon together. Cream butter and sugar until mixture is smooth. Beat in eggs thoroughly, then stir in sifted dry ingredients and all the fruits and nuts. Drop cookie batter from teaspoon on ungreased cookie sheets and bake 10 minutes at 400°F. Do not overbake. Cool slightly before removing from cookie sheet.

Mrs. Margaret Treber, Walt Whitman H. S.
Bethesda, Maryland

LIZZIES (Christmas Cookies)
Number of Cookies — 34 Dozen

2 lb. candied cherries
2 lb. candied pineapple
1 lb. dark raisins
1 lb. white raisins
6 c. pecans
1 stick butter
1½ c. dark brown sugar
4 eggs
1 c. pineapple juice
3 T. sweet milk
1 t. cinnamon
1 t. allspice
1 t. nutmeg
1 t. cloves
3 t. soda
5-6 c. flour (plus 1 c. flour to dredge)

(Continued on Next Page)

Cut fruit into small pieces. Break pecan halves. Add all raisins. Dredge this in 1 cup flour. Cream butter and sugar. Add eggs one at a time. Add the pineapple juice, milk, and dry ingredients. Add fruit and nuts. Work well with hands so fruit is well mixed. Drop from teaspoon onto greased sheet. Cook at 275°F. for 12 minutes.

Nelda L. Roark, LaSalle H. S.
Olla, Louisiana

FRUIT COCKTAIL COOKIES
Number of Servings — 75 Cookies
1 c. shortening, vegetable or oleo
1 c. brown sugar
½ c. granulated sugar
3 eggs (well beaten)
1 No. 2 can fruit cocktail including juice
1 c. chopped walnut meats
1 t. vanilla
4 c. pre-sifted flour, all-purpose
1 t. each soda, baking powder, cinnamon & cloves
1 t. salt
Cream shortening and sugar, add well beaten eggs, fruit cocktail, nut meats, and vanilla. Sift dry ingredients together and add. Mix thoroughly. Drop by teaspoonfuls on greased cookie sheets and bake at 375°F., 12 to 15 minutes or until a light brown.

Carol Jean Worrell, Beth-Center H. S.
Fredericktown, Pennsylvania

FUDGE BALLS
2 small pkg. chocolate chips
1 can sweetened condensed milk
1 c. flour
1 c. chopped nuts
2 T. butter
2 t. vanilla
Melt over hot water chocolate chips and sweetened condensed milk. Remove from heat and add flour, chopped nuts, butter and vanilla. Let set for approximately 10 minutes. Drop by teaspoon on greased cookie sheet. Bake at 300°F. for 5 minutes.

Mrs. Mildred Spanihel, Louise H. S.
Louise, Texas

GUM DROP COOKIES
Number of Servings — 6 Dozen
1 c. shortening
2 c. brown sugar
2 eggs
½ c. water
3½ c. flour
1 t. soda
1 t. salt
3 c. cut up gum drops
Mix all ingredients together. Chill for 1 hour. Drop by teaspoon on a greased cookie sheet. Bake for 10 minutes at 400°F.

Mrs. Grace Womack Buford, Plainview-Rover H. S.
Plainview, Arkansas

(Gum) ORANGE CANDY COOKIES
Number of Servings — 6 Dozen
1½ c. brown sugar
½ c. shortening
2 eggs

2 c. sifted flour
1 t. soda
½ t. baking powder
½ t. salt
1 lb. orange slice candy, diced and mixed with
   ½ c. flour
½ c. flaked coconut
½ c. chopped nuts
½ c. rolled oats
Cream sugar and shortening until light and fluffy. Beat in eggs. Sift flour, soda, baking powder and salt and blend into creamed mixture. Fold in candy, coconut, nuts, and rolled oats, mixing well. Roll into balls, about 1" in diameter. Place on greased baking sheet and press down with the tines of a dinner fork. Bake at 325°F. for about 12 minutes or until lightly browned.

Virginia Snyder, Grant Public School
Grant, Michigan

HERMITS
Number of Servings — 36
½ c. shortening or margarine
1½ c. brown sugar
3 eggs, well beaten
2½ c. cake flour, sifted
¾ T. baking soda
½ T. cinnamon
½ T. nutmeg
½ T. salt
1 c. raisins
1 c. chopped walnuts
Work shortening with a spoon until fluffy and creamy. Add sugar while continuing to work with a spoon until light. Then add eggs. Sift 2 cups flour with soda, spices and salt. Add to mixture. Dredge raisins and nuts in ½ cup flour. Add to mixture. Drop by teaspoon on a greased or oiled cookie sheet about 2" apart. Bake at 375°F. for 15 minutes.

Mrs. Virginia Lewis Sullivan, St. Charles H. S.
St. Charles, Virginia

MARSHMALLOW COOKIES
Number of Servings — 6 Dozen
½ c. shortening
1 c. sugar
1 egg
1 t. vanilla
½ c. cocoa
1¾ c. sifted flour
½ t. soda
½ t. salt
½ c. milk
½ c. nuts
36 marshmallows cut in half
Combine shortening, sugar, egg, vanilla, cocoa, flour, soda, salt, and milk. Mix until smooth. Drop cookies on an ungreased cookie sheet. Bake at 375°F. for 8 minutes. When done, top each cookie with a half marshmallow (out side down) and return to oven 1 minute. Cool and frost cookies with favorite chocolate frosting. Decorate each cookie with a half nut placed on top, or chop nuts and sprinkle on top.

Mardeen Christiansen, Eddyville H. S.
Eddyville, Oregon

MAPLE NUT DROPS

3 c. & 2 T. sifted flour
1 t. baking powder
1 t. baking soda
1 t. salt
1 c. butter
3 eggs
1 c. maple flavored syrup
¼ t. maple flavoring
1 c. cut up dates
1 c. chopped nuts

Sift together the flour, baking powder, baking soda and salt. Set aside. Cream butter, add eggs, maple flavored syrup and maple flavoring. Blend in the dry ingredients gradually. Add ¼ cup boiling water. Mix well. Stir in dates and nuts. Chill at least 1 hour. Drop by teaspoons on greased cookie sheets. Bake at 350°F. 13-16 minutes. Cool and frost tops with maple icing.

Maple Icing:
¼ c. butter
2 T. cream
1 t. vanilla
1 T. maple flavored syrup
2 c. sifted confectioners' sugar

Melt butter. Add cream, vanilla, and maple flavored syrup. Blend in confectioners' sugar. Beat until smooth.

Barbara Widmyer, Conneaut Lake Area H. S.
Conneaut Lake, Pennsylvania

MERINGUE MINT COOKIES

Number of Servings — 24
2 egg whites
Pinch of salt
½ t. cream of tartar
¾ c. sugar
1 pkg. mint chocolate chips
Few drops green food coloring

Mix egg whites, salt, and cream of tartar until stiff. Add sugar, chips, and food coloring. Drop on cookie sheet covered with wax paper. Preheat oven to 375°F. for 15 minutes. Turn oven off and put cookies in. Leave in over night.

Phyllis Christmann, Sheyenne H. S.
Sheyenne, North Dakota

MINCEMENT COOKIES

Number of Servings — 4 Dozen
1 c. soft shortening
1½ c. sugar
3 eggs, well beaten
1 pkg. mincemeat
3¼ c. all-purpose flour
1 t. soda
½ t. salt

Cream shortening and sugar. Add eggs and beat until mixture is smooth. Break mincemeat into small pieces and mix in well. Sift together flour, soda, and salt. Add to batter, mix well. Drop by teaspoon about 2″ apart on a lightly greased baking sheet. Bake at 400°F. 10 to 12 minutes or until lightly browned.

Grace M. Shepard, Palmetto H. S.
Williamston, South Carolina

GRAMMY YOUNG'S MOLASSES COOKIES

Number of Servings — 30 Cookies
½ c. white sugar
⅓ c. shortening
½ c. molasses
1 egg
1 t. soda
1 t. cinnamon
½ t. ginger
1 t. salt
2 c. flour or flour to roll
2 T. water
1 T. vinegar

Cream shortening, sugar, until creamy. Add molasses and unbeaten egg. Blend well. Sift dry ingredients and add to creamed mixture alternately with vinegar and water. Drop by teaspoon on ungreased cookie sheet or add sufficient flour to roll, and roll thin and cut. Bake at 375°F. for approximately 10 minutes or until brown.

Martha R. Phillips, Kennett H. S.
Conway, New Hampshire

MONKEY FACE COOKIES

Number of Servings — 3 Dozen

1 egg
1 c. sugar
¼ c. sour milk
2 T. shortening, melted
2 c. sifted flour
1 t. soda
½ t. salt
1 t. vanilla
Raisins

Mix egg, sugar, shortening, and sour milk. Sift together flour, soda, and salt. Add gradually to first mixture. Add vanilla. Drop by teaspoon on a greased cookie sheet. Put 3 raisins on each cookie for eyes and nose. Bake at 350°F. for 8 to 10 minutes.

Louise Temple, Exeter H. S.
Exeter, New Hampshire

BANANA-OATMEAL COOKIES

Number of Servings — 3 Dozen
2 c. flour
1 t. cinnamon
¼ t. nutmeg
½ t. salt
1 t. baking powder
¼ t. soda
1 c. sugar
1 c. shortening
1 c. mashed bananas
2 eggs
2 c. rolled oats

Sift together first 7 ingredients. Add shortening, mashed bananas, eggs. Beat until smooth (about 2 minutes). Fold in rolled oats. Drop from spoon onto greased cookie sheet. Bake in 375°F. oven for about 15 minutes.

Mrs. Nelma Ruggles, Portland Public Schools
Portland, Michigan

OATMEAL DROP COOKIES
Number of Servings — 5 Dozen

1 c. shortening
2 c. brown sugar (free from lumps)
2 eggs
2 c. rolled oats (preferably slow cook variety)
1½ c. flour
2 t. baking powder
½ t. salt
1 t. vanilla
1 T. vinegar
½ c. raisins
½ c. nut meats

Cream shortening 2 minutes at high speed in large bowl. Add brown sugar to shortening and cream 3 minutes. Add eggs, 1 at a time, beating 1 minute at high speed after each. Add rolled oats, mix a few seconds. Sift together flour, baking powder, and salt and add beating at high speed, after mixing with spatula. Stir in remaining ingredients and drop by teaspoonfuls on an ungreased cookie sheet. Bake at 375°F. for 10 to 12 minutes. Remove from sheet while hot. Store in jar or tins, will remain crisp for days.

Mrs. Albert T. Butler, Eau Gallie Jr. H. S.
Eau Gallie, Florida

CHOCOLATE CHIP OATMEAL COOKIES
Number of Servings — 5 Dozen

1½ c. sifted flour
1 t. soda
1 t. salt
1 c. shortening
¾ c. white sugar
¾ c. brown sugar
2 eggs unbeaten
1 t. hot water
½ to 1 c. chopped nuts (if desired)
1 pkg. chocolate chips
2 c. oatmeal
1 t. vanilla

Sift flour, measure, add soda and salt and sift. Cream fat until fluffy. Add sugars, cream well. Beat in eggs, add hot water, add sifted ingredients. Add nuts, chocolate chips and oatmeal. Mix well. Add vanilla. Drop by spoonfuls on greased cookie sheet. Bake at 350°F. 10-12 minutes.

This recipe submitted by the following teachers:
Cecelia Butler, Clayton Junior H. S.
Clayton, New Mexico
Mrs. Mildred G. Grundy
South Middleton Twp. H. S.
Boiling Springs, Pennsylvania
Mrs. Betty Kyle, Troy H. S.
Troy, Texas

HATTIE CARAWAY'S OAT COOKIES
Number of Servings — 60

2 c. flour
2 t. soda
½ t. salt
1 t. cinnamon
½ t. nutmeg
1 c. sugar
1 c. bacon drippings
5 T. sweet milk
2 eggs
½ box raisins
1 c. chopped nuts
2 c. uncooked rolled oats

Sift all the dry ingredients into a large bowl of mixer. Add bacon drippings, milk, and eggs and mix well at slow speed, about 2 minutes. Remove bowl from mixer, add raisins and nuts. Mix with spoon or rubber spatula. Add oats last and mix. Drop from teaspoon on greased cookie sheet. Bake about 20 minutes at 325°F.

Paralee Coleman, Wellington H. S.
Wellington, Texas

RANGER COOKIES
Number of Servings — 10 Dozen

1 c. shortening
1 c. brown sugar
1 c. white sugar
2 eggs
2 c. flour
1 t. baking powder
2 t. soda
½ t. salt
2 c. crushed corn flakes
2 c. oatmeal
1 c. pecans (if desired)
1 c. coconut

Cream shortening and sugar until smooth. Add eggs and beat until smooth. Sift flour, soda, baking powder and salt together and add to the creamed mixture. Then add corn flakes, oatmeal, pecans, and coconut. Mix until all is combined together. Drop by teaspoons on ungreased cookie sheet and bake 15 to 20 minutes in a 400°F. oven.

This recipe submitted by the following teachers:
Mrs. Nancy King, Hallsville H. S.
Hallsville, Texas
Mrs. Carolyn Dyer McKinney H. S.
McKinney, Texas

SPEEDY OATMEAL COOKIES
Number of Servings — 3 Dozen

Stir until smooth:
1 c. brown sugar
½ c. oleo or shortening
1 egg
½ t. soda
½ t. baking powder
¼ t. salt
1 t. vanilla
Add:
1 c. flour
1 c. oatmeal
½ c. nut meats

Stir until smooth. Drop by teaspoon on ungreased baking sheet. Bake in 350°F. oven, 12 to 15 minutes.

Mrs. Myrtle Wood, Rogers H. S.
Rogers, Texas

ORANGE COOKIES

1 lb. margarine
1 c. brown sugar
1 c. white sugar
1 t. soda
5 c. flour
2 eggs
½ t. vanilla
3 T. orange juice and rind
1 pkg. chocolate miniature bits

Cream margarine and sugars. Sift together soda and flour. Add eggs to the sugar and butter mixture. Beat well. Combine the creamed and dry ingredients and blend in vanilla, orange juice and rind, and chocolate bits. With a teaspoon place on lightly greased cookie tin. Bake at 350°F. for 8 to 10 minutes.

Jane Roberts, Quincy H. S.
Quincy, Michigan

ORANGE DELIGHT COOKIES
Number of Servings — 4 Dozen

1½ c. sugar
¾ c. shortening
2 eggs
1½ T. grated orange rind
3 c. all-purpose flour
½ t. soda
2 t. baking powder
1 t. salt
⅓ c. sour milk
½ t. vanilla
¾ c. chopped nuts (optional)

Mix sugar, shortening, eggs until creamy. Add orange rind, sifted dry ingredients, sour milk, and vanilla. Add nuts, if desired. Drop by teaspoon on greased cookie sheet. Bake 12-15 minutes at 375°F.

Topping:
2 t. grated orange rind
1 c. sugar
⅓ c. orange juice

Mix ingredients for topping before mixing cookies. Let stand. When cookies are removed from oven. spoon on topping while cookies are hot. Cool and serve.

Mrs. Corinne Clark, Riverdale H. S.
Riverdale, North Dakota

PEANUT BUTTER COOKIES
Number of Servings — 4½ Dozen

½ c. peanut butter
¼ c. shortening
½ c. brown sugar
½ c. granulated sugar
1 egg, well beaten
1 c. sifted flour
1 t. soda

Cream peanut butter and shortening together. Add sugar gradually, continuing until mixture is light and fluffy. Add beaten egg. Sift flour and soda together, add, mix well. Drop mixture by teaspoon on cookie sheet. Press down with tines of a fork. Bake 10-15 minutes at 350°F.

Lucy T. Babb, Hillcrest H. S.
Fountain Inn, South Carolina

PAT COOKIES

1 c. shortening
1 c. brown sugar
1 c. white sugar
2 eggs
2 c. flour
½ t. baking powder
1 t. soda
¼ t. salt
2 c. quick oats, uncooked
1 c. Wheaties
1 c. shredded coconut

Cream the shortening and sugars. Beat in eggs. Sift flour, baking powder, soda, and salt, then add to above mixture. Add oats, Wheaties, and shredded coconut. Drop rounded teaspoonfuls of cookie batter on greased cookie sheet. Flatten with bottom of glass which has been floured. Bake in moderate oven 375°F. for 10 minutes. Makes 7 to 8 dozen cookies about 2″ in diameter.

Mrs. Effie Gish, Castleberry H. S.
Fort Worth, Texas

PECAN DELIGHTS
Number of Servings — 7 Dozen

1 c. shortening
2 c. brown sugar, packed
1 t. vanilla
2 eggs
2½ c. sifted flour
1 t. salt
2 t. baking powder
1 c. chopped pecans

Cream shortening, sugar, and vanilla. Add eggs to creamed mixture and beat well. Sift together dry ingredients and add. Add pecans and mix well. Drop by teaspoon on a cookie sheet. Bake at 350°F. about 10 minutes.

Betty Horn, Seagraves H. S.
Seagraves, Texas

PECAN DROPS
Number of Servings — 4 Dozen

1 c. pecans
½ c. butter or margarine
½ c. plus 2 T. shortening
1 c. confectioners' sugar
2½ c. sifted cake flour
2 t. vanilla extract

Start your oven at 325°F., or slow, and chop pecans rather coarsely. Cream butter or margarine and shortening together until smooth. Then beat in the confectioners' sugar gradually. Stir in the flour thoroughly and add vanilla extract and pecans. Mix well and drop by teaspoon on an ungreased baking sheet. Bake 15 to 20 minutes or until a delicate light brown.

Fay Foster, Brownsboro H. S.
Brownsboro, Texas

PERSIMMON COOKIES
Number of Servings — 6 Dozen

1 c. sugar
½ c. shortening
1 egg

(Continued on Next Page)

2 c. flour
1 t. baking powder
½ t. soda
½ t. cinnamon
¼ t. cloves
½ t. salt
1 c. persimmon pulp
½ c. raisins
½ c. chopped nuts

Cream shortening and sugar. Add egg and mix well. Sift dry ingredients and add alternately with persimmon pulp. Add the raisins and nuts. Blend thoroughly: and drop on greased cookie sheet 1½″ to 2″ apart. Bake at 350° for 12 to 15 minutes.

Mrs. Adeline B. Wiser, Calaveras H. S.
San Andreas, California

PINEAPPLE COCONUT COOKIES

Number of Servings — 4 Dozen

1 c. shortening
1 c. white sugar
1 c. brown sugar
1 c. crushed pineapple
2 eggs, well beaten
4 c. flour
2 t. soda
½ t. salt
2 t. vanilla
1 c. nuts (optional)
1 c. shredded coconut

Cream shortening with white and brown sugar, add crushed pineapple. Add beaten eggs. Sift flour with soda, salt. Add flour and vanilla. Mix well. Add nuts and coconut. Drop by teaspoon on greased cookie sheet. Bake 10-12 minutes in 350°F. oven. Do not overbake. Do not mix or cream shortening and sugar with electric mixer. Mix by hand.

Win McMullin, Dawson County H. S.
Glendive, Montana

PINEAPPLE COOKIES

Number of Servings — 5 Dozen Cookies

1 c. soft shortening
1½ c. sugar
1 egg
9 oz. can crushed pineapple with juice (1 c.)
3½ c. sifted flour
1 t. soda
½ t. salt
¼ t. nutmeg
½ c. chopped nuts

Mix thoroughly shortening, sugar, and egg. Stir in pineapple. Sift together dry ingredients and add to mixture. Mix in nuts. Chill at least 1 hour. Drop rounded teaspoonfuls about 2″ apart on lightly greased baking sheet. Bake at 400°F. 8 to 10 minutes, or until, when touched lightly with finger, no imprint remains.

Mrs. Sandra G. Gay, Plains H. S.
Plains, Georgia

PUMPKIN NUT COOKIES

Number of Servings — 2 Dozen

¼ c. shortening
½ c. sugar
1 egg, beaten
½ c. canned pumpkin
1 c. sifted flour
2 T. baking powder
½ t. salt
1¼ t. cinnamon
¼ t. nutmeg
⅛ t. ginger
½ c. raisins
½ c. nuts, chopped

Cream shortening. Add sugar gradually. Cream until light and fluffy. Add egg and pumpkin. Mix well. Sift flour, baking powder, salt and spices together. Stir in dry ingredients. Mix until blended. Add raisins and nuts. Drop by teaspoonfuls on greased cookie sheet. Bake in a moderate oven 350°F. for about 15 minutes.

Nona L. Dutson, Marsh Valley H. S.
Arimo, Idaho

RAISIN DROP COOKIES

Number of Servings — 3 Dozen Large — 100 Small

2 c. raisins
1 c. water
4 c. sifted flour
1 t. baking powder
1 t. baking soda
1 t. salt
½ t. cinnamon
½ t. nutmeg
1 c. shortening
1¾ c. sugar
2 eggs, slightly beaten
1 t. vanilla
½ c. chopped nuts

Bring raisins and water to a boil. Boil until the raisins are plump, about 3 minutes. Cool. Sift flour, baking powder, soda, salt, and spices together. Cream shortening and suger together until light and fluffy. Add eggs and vanilla and mix well. Stir in the raisins and any remaining water. Gradually add the flour mixture, blending thoroughly after each addition. Stir in nuts. Drop by tablespoon about 1″ apart on ungreased baking sheets. Bake at 375°F. 12-15 minutes.

This recipe submitted by the following teachers:
Katherine Brooks, Pleasanton Rural H. S.
Pleasanton, Kansas

Mrs. Dora Clark Fleming, Centerville H. S.
Sand Coulee, Montana

ROCKS (Della's)

Number of Servings — 9 Dozen 2″ Cookies

1 c. soft butter
1½ c. sugar
3 c. flour
1 t. cinnamon
1 t. allspice
½ t. soda
3 eggs

(Continued on Next Page)

1½ c. chopped raisins
2 c. chopped black walnuts

Cream butter and sugar. Sift flour, cinnamon, allspice, and soda. Add dry ingredients to creamed mixture, alternately with the eggs, beating after each addition. Add raisins and nuts with the last part of the dry mixture. Drop by teaspoonfuls about 2″ apart, on lightly greased cookie sheet. Bake at 400°F. for 8 to 10 minutes.

Mrs. Armalea Hopperstad
Independence Community College
Independence, Kansas

SOUR CREAM COOKIES
Number of Servings — 3 Dozen

1½ c. sugar
¾ c. shortening
2 eggs, slightly beaten
1 c. commercial sour cream
½ t. soda
3½ c. flour
2 t. baking powder
½ t. salt
½ t. vanilla

Cream the sugar and shortening together. Add eggs. Add soda to sour cream, then add this to egg mixture. Combine the flour, baking powder and salt together and sift. Add gradually to the egg mixture. Add vanilla. Drop from teaspoons on greased cookie sheets. Bake at 375°F. for 15 minutes or until slightly browned.

Barbara J. Snyder, Selinsgrove Area Sr. H. S.
Selinsgrove, Pennsylvania

SOFT SOUR CREAM DATE-NUT COOKIES
Number of Servings — About 5 Dozen Cookies

2 c. brown sugar, packed
1 c. butter
2 eggs
1 c. sour cream
1 t. vanilla
1 t. baking soda
½ t. salt
1 t. cloves
½ t. cinnamon
3 c. all-purpose flour
1½ c. dates (measured after pitting and chopping)
1 c. nut meats, chopped

Cream butter and sugar together. Add unbeaten eggs. Mix well. Add the sour cream and vanilla. Mix and sift all the dry ingredients together. Add them to the butter mixture. Then add the chopped nuts and dates. Drop by spoonfuls onto greased cookie sheet. Bake at about 350-375°F. These cookies remain soft after baking. The batter may be kept in the refrigerator a week.

Agnes Van Oosten, Park County H. S.
Livingston, Montana

STUFFED DATE DROPS
Number of Servings — 6 Dozen

1 lb. dates
70 to 80 walnut or pecan
¼ c. shortening
¾ c. light brown sugar

1 egg
1¼ c. sifted flour
½ t. baking powder
½ t. soda
¼ t. salt
½ c. cultured cream

Stuff each date with a nut half, set aside. Cream the shortening and gradually add the brown sugar. Add the egg and thoroughly mix. Combine the flour, baking powder, soda and salt. Add the dry mixture to the fat, sugar and egg mixture alternately with the sour cream. Stir in the dates, drop on a greased cookie sheet (one date per cookie). Bake at 400°F. for 8 to 10 minutes. Cool and top with a frosting made by slightly browning ½ cup butter, 3 cups confectioners' sugar, ¾ teaspoon vanilla. Slowly add enough water until icing is of thin spreading consistency. It may be divided and colored.

Mrs. Naomi Blatt, Fairfield Union H. S.
Lancaster, Ohio

SAND TARTS (Rolled)
Number of Servings — 60 Cookies

½ c. butter
1 c. sugar
2 egg yolks
1 T. milk
½ t. vanilla
1½ c. flour
1 t. baking powder
½ t. salt
Split blanched almonds
Sugar-cinnamon mixture

Cream butter well, add sugar and blend, add slightly beaten egg gradually, stirring thoroughly after each addition. Add milk and vanilla and beat until light. Sift together flour, baking powder, and salt, add to first mixture and blend well. Chill for several hours. Roll dough very thin and cut with 3″ star cookie cutter. Place on greased baking sheets and put a split blanched almond on each cookie. Brush with unbeaten egg whites. Sprinkle with sugar and cinnamon mixture. Bake in preheated, 375°F. oven for 10 minutes. Remove from sheet at once to a cooling rack.

Frankie E. Dreyfus, Edison Jr. H. S.
Milwaukee, Wisconsin

SUGAR COOKIES (Rolled)
Number of Servings — 2 Dozen Large

1 c. butter
1 c. sugar
2 eggs
1 T. milk
1 t. vanilla
3 c. flour, sifted
3 t. baking powder

Cream butter and add sugar gradually. Add eggs, milk and vanilla and cream well. Then add flour and baking powder sifted together. Chill for 10 minutes. Roll and cut into desired shape. May be frosted or decorated with colored sugar or left just plain.

Mrs. Fern Bowen, Mount Gilead H. S.
Mount Gilead, Ohio

SUGAR COOKIES (Rolled)
Number of Servings — 3 Dozen

1 c. shortening
2 c. sugar
4 eggs
2 T. cream
4 c. flour
⅛ t. salt
4 t. baking powder
1 t. vanilla

Cream together shortening and sugar. Add eggs one at a time beating well after each. Add cream then flour sifted with baking powder and salt. Mix well and add vanilla. Chill mixture 20 minutes. Roll very thin. Cut and bake at 400°F. until brown.

Carrie Eas. Hinton, Stone H. S.
Wiggins, Mississippi

CLARKSVILLE CRESCENTS
Number of Servings — 2 Dozen

2 c. sifted flour
1 cake compressed yeast
½ c. (1 stick) margarine
2 egg yolks
½ c. sour cream
Confectioners' sugar
Melted margarine

Put sifted flour into a large mixing bowl. Crumble in compressed yeast. Cut in margarine with pastry blender until mixture is crumbly. Add egg yolks and sour cream. Mix well. Form into a ball. On lightly floured board, knead until smooth (5 to 10 minutes). Divide dough into 3 equal parts. Wrap in wax paper. Chill in refrigerator at least 1 hour. On a board sprinkled with confectioners' sugar, roll each part of the dough into an 8" circle and cut into 8 pie-shaped wedges. Fill wide end of each wedge with 1 tablespoon of Pecan Filling. Roll up from wide end to point. Place on greased baking sheets, curving ends to form crescent shape. Bake in moderate oven 375°F. about 25 minutes, or until golden brown. Dust with confectioners' sugar.

Pecan Filling:
1 c. finely chopped pecans
½ c. sugar
1 t. vanilla
2 egg whites, stiffly beaten
Combine pecans, sugar, and vanilla. Fold in stiffly beaten egg whites.

Mrs. L. H. Scott, Clarksville H. S.
Clarksville, Texas

CREAM WAFERS
Number of Servings — 5 Dozen Double Cookies

1 c. soft butter
⅓ c. whipping cream
2 c. sifted flour

Mix well the butter, cream and flour. Chill the mixture in the refrigerator. Roll one-third of the dough at a time, keeping the remainder refrigerated. Roll out dough ⅛ inch thick on floured board. Cut 1½" circles. Transfer rounds to wax paper heavily covered with granulated sugar. Turn each round so that both sides are coated. Place on ungreased baking sheet and prick with a fork. Bake at 375°F. 7-9 minutes. Cool. Put 2 cookies together with the filling.

Filling:
¼ c. soft butter
¾ c. confectioners' sugar
1 egg yolk
1 t. vanilla

Blend ingredients in the order listed. Tint filling if desired.

Valerie Barnum, Jonesboro-Hodge H. S.
Jonesboro, Louisiana

DATE CRESCENT COOKIES
Number of Servings — 2 Dozen

1½ c. sifted cake flour
½ t. salt
2 T. powdered sugar
⅓ c. butter or margarine
2 to 3 T. cold water
1 c. fresh dates, pitted and chopped
½ c. chopped walnuts
⅓ c. sugar
½ t. grated orange rind
2 T. orange juice
Powdered sugar

Sift together flour, salt and the 2 tablespoons powdered sugar. Cut in butter or margarine until mixture resembles coarse meal. Sprinkle with water and toss lightly with fork until dough is moist enough to hold together. Form into a ball. Roll thin on floured board. Cut into 3" squares. Combine dates, walnuts, sugar, orange rind, and juice, mixing well. Put a spoonful of the date mixture on each square and bring edges together to form a triangle. Seal with tines of fork and curve slightly when placed on greased baking sheet. Bake in 375°F. oven for about 20 minutes. Roll in powdered sugar while still warm.

Mrs. Dorothy Morris, Ooltewah H. S.
Ooltewah, Tennessee

EASY FILLED DATE COOKIES
Number of Servings — 5 to 6 Dozen

1 c. soft shortening
2 c. brown sugar (packed)
2 eggs
½ c. water or buttermilk
1 t. vanilla
3½ c. sifted flour
½ t. salt
1 t. soda
⅛ t. cinnamon

(Continued on Next Page)

Mix thoroughly shortening, brown sugar, and eggs. Stir in water and vanilla. Sift together and stir in dry ingredients. Drop by teaspoons on greased baking sheet. Place ½ teaspoon Date Filling on dough, cover with another ½ teaspoon dough. Bake at 400°F. until lightly browned (10 to 12 minutes).

Date Filling:
2 c. dates, finely cut up
¾ c. sugar
¾ c. water
½ c. nuts

Cook all together until thick. Add nuts. Cool.

This recipe submitted by the following teachers:

Nancy Withrow Sensabaugh, Rockbridge H. S.
Fairfield, Virginia

Alice M. Eckerle, Hart H. S.
Hart, Michigan

DATE PINWHEEL COOKIES

Number of Servings — 5 Dozen

¾ c. pitted dates
6 T. granulated sugar
6 T. water
2 t. lemon juice
¼ c. nut meats, chopped
2 c. sifted all-purpose flour
¼ t. soda
¼ t. salt
⅔ c. butter or oleo
1¼ c. brown sugar
1½ t. grated orange rind
1 egg
1 T. vinegar

Combine in saucepan, sugar, water, and dates. Cook until thick, about five minutes. Remove from heat and add nuts and lemon juice. Cool. Sift together flour, soda and salt. Cream butter and brown sugar. Add orange rind. Beat in egg and vinegar. Blend in dry ingredients. Chill dough several hours or over night. Roll dough out into 10x15 rectangle. Spread with date mixture and roll up as for jelly roll. Chill one hour. Slice ¼" thick. Place on greased cookie sheet and bake in 375°F. oven 12-15 minutes. Cool on cake rack.

Mrs. Mildred J. Wehman, Columbus H. S.
Columbus, Texas

DATE SWIRLS

½ c. butter
½ c. brown sugar
½ c. white sugar
1 egg
2 c. flour
½ t. soda
¼ t. salt

Combine ingredients. Beat well. Roll dough about ¼" thick. Spread dough with date and nut mixture. Roll up like a jelly roll. Wrap in wax paper. Leave in refrigerator overnight. Slice and bake in moderate oven.

Filling:
½ lb. dates
1 t. lemon juice
⅓ c. water
¼ c. sugar
½ c. chopped nuts

Cook together 5 minutes, dates, lemon juice, water, and sugar. Remove from heat. Add nuts. Let cool.

Mrs. Estelle Beard Craney, Ellisville H. S.
Ellisville, Mississippi

FILLED DATE COOKIES

Number of Servings — 2 to 3 Dozen

2 c. brown sugar
1 t. cinnamon
1 t. soda
3 eggs
1 c. melted fat (use part butter)
1 pinch of salt
Flour, all-purpose

Add cinnamon, soda, salt to sugar. Add unbeaten eggs one at a time, to sugar mixture, beating well after each addition. Add melted fat. Add flour (several cups) to make dough of consistency to roll out. Cut. Place cookie on lightly greased sheet. Place 1 teaspoon filling on each and top with remaining cookies. Press edges together. Bake at 350°F. for 10 minutes.

Filling:
1 lb. dates, pitted and chopped or ground
1 c. brown sugar
1 c. water
½ c. nut meats (if desired)

Combine dates, brown sugar, and water. Cook until thick. Add nut meats at end of cooking period. Cool.

Mrs. Doris Kruger, Peotone H. S.
Peotone, Illinois

PECAN TASSIES

Number of Servings — 4 Dozen

6 oz. pkg. cream cheese
1 c. butter
2 c. sifted all-purpose flour

Cream softened cheese and butter together. Blend in flour. Chill dough at least 1 hour. Cream 2 tablespoons butter and brown sugar together. Add salt, vanilla and 2 eggs, beat well. To form cookies, make 48 balls of chilled dough, spread in small (greased) muffin tins. Sprinkle each cookie with a few chopped pecans, place 1 teaspoon of filling on each, then sprinkle with a few more pecans. Bake at 350°F. 12-15 minutes. Remove from tins immediately.

Filling:
2 T. butter
1½ c. brown sugar
1 T. vanilla
Dash of salt
2 eggs
1⅓ c. broken pecans

Patricia C. Harker, West Greene H. S.
Rogersville, Pennsylvania

ROSKY COOKIES
Number of Servings — 3 to 5 Dozen
4 c. flour
1 lb. butter or margarine
2 egg yolks
1 c. sour cream
Mix together flour and butter, add egg yolk and sour cream. Blend and chill.
Filling:
1 lb. ground walnuts
1-1½ c. pineapple preserves
Small amount of cream

Make filling by mixing walnuts, preserves, and enough cream to moisten mixture. Roll dough to ¼-⅛″ thickness, and cut in 3″ squares. Place a teaspoonful of filling in each square of dough and roll dough cornerwise forming crescents. Bake for 15 to 20 minutes at 350°F. Roll in powdered sugar while still hot.

Mary Ficke, Delta H. S.
Delta, Colorado

STRAWBERRY-COOKIE DESSERT
Number of Servings — 12-15
1 c. butter
1 c. sugar
1 egg
½ t. almond extract
2½ c. sifted flour

Cream butter and sugar. Add egg, flavoring, and flour. Roll thin and cut with large, fluted edge cookie cutter. Place on cookie sheet (ungreased) and bake at 375°F. about 12 minutes. Handle carefully for they are fragile. When cool, place one cookie on a salad plate and add a large spoon of ice cream (not too hard). Cover with strawberries. Then place another cookie on top of berries, more ice cream and berries and juice on top of this.

Florence B. Fisackerly, Inverness H. S.
Inverness, Mississippi

WHOOPEE PIES
Number of Servings — 24
½ c. melted fat
1 c. sugar
3 sq. melted chocolate
2 eggs
½ c. milk
2⅓ c. flour
1 t. baking powder
1 t. soda
¼ t. salt

Mix sugar and shortening, add melted chocolate, eggs. Add alternately milk and flour sifted with soda, baking powder, and salt. Drop by teaspoon on oiled baking sheet. Bake at 350°F. for 10 minutes. Cool thoroughly. This recipe freezes well. The filling is much like ice cream when served frozen.
Filling:
4 T. flour (heaping)
1 c. milk
½ c. butter
1 c. vegetable shortening

Cook flour and milk until thick. Cool. Cream together butter and shortening. Add the cooled flour-milk mixture, which will look much like library paste, to the creamed shortening and sugar. Beat thoroughly with mixer until it is creamy. Spread between two of the chocolate cookies.

Mrs. Mary Kathryn Lands
Amanda-Clearcreek School
Amanda, Ohio

AUNT JAKE'S REFRIGERATOR COOKIES
Number of Servings — 8 Dozen
1 lb. soft margarine or butter
1½ c. white sugar
1 box dark brown sugar
3 t. cinnamon
3 eggs
7 c. flour (not sifted)
1 t. soda
Juice of 1 lemon
½ c. chopped nuts
½ c. powdered sugar

Cream butter and sugars together. Add cinnamon, eggs, flour and soda, lemon juice and nuts. Mix thoroughly with wooden spoon. Take a piece of dough about the size of your fist. Make roll about the size of a half dollar, roll this in powdered sugar. Store in wax paper in refrigerator until thoroughly chilled or until time to bake. Bake at 400°F. 10 minutes on ungreased cookie sheet.

Barbara Hawkins, Midland H. S.
Midland, Louisiana

ICE BOX COOKIES
Number of Servings — 4 to 5 Dozen
2 c. brown sugar
1½ c. shortening
3 eggs
1 t. cinnamon
½ c. nuts
1 t. soda
1 t. cream of tartar
¼ t. salt
Flavoring
5 c. flour

Cream sugar, shortening, and eggs. Add soda, salt, cream of tartar, cinnamon, flavoring, and nuts. Add flour last, working in a little at a time. Roll in two rolls and chill, or let stand in ice box over night. Slice and bake at 425°F. for about 10 minutes. Dough could be divided and different nuts or fruits added to each.

Ethel Spradling, Bixby Sr. H. S.
Bixby, Oklahoma

BACHELOR BUTTONS
Number of Servings — 6 Dozen Cookies
¾ c. butter or margarine
1 c. light brown sugar, firmly packed
1 egg
2 c. sifted flour
1 t. soda
¼ t. ginger
¼ t. cinnamon
¼ t. salt
1 c. chopped nuts
1 t. vanilla

(Continued on Next Page)

Cream butter, add brown sugar gradually, beating well, add egg. Sift and add dry ingredients. Fold in chopped nuts and vanilla. Chill several hours or overnight in refrigerator. Shape dough in tiny balls. Roll in granulated sugar and place 2" apart on greased baking sheet. Bake in moderate oven 375° F. 10-12 minutes.

Mrs. James Risinger, Cooper H. S.
Cooper, Texas

BISCOCHOS
Number of Servings — 34 Cookies
1 c. shortening
3 T. sugar
2 eggs, beaten
2 c. flour
2 t. baking powder
½ t. salt
¼ t. anise
¼ t. crushed stick cinnamon
Cinnamon and sugar mixture

Cream sugar into the shortening. Add beaten eggs and mix. Measure and sift flour twice. Add baking powder and salt to flour. Add gradually to first mixture. If desired, add anise and stick cinnamon. Shape in roll about 1" in diameter. Chill. Slice. Bake on ungreased sheet at 400°F. about 10 minutes or until lightly browned. Roll in cinnamon and sugar mixture while hot.

Mrs. Leda F. Callahan, Ysleta H. S.
El Paso, Texas

BLACK-AND-WHITE PIN WHEELS
Number of Servings — 4 Dozen
1½ c. sifted all-purpose flour
½ t. baking powder
⅛ t. salt
½ c. shortening
½ c. sugar
1 egg yolk
3 T. milk
½ t. vanilla
½ pkg. semi-sweet chocolate morsels

Sift together flour, baking powder, and salt and set aside. Blend together shortening and sugar. Beat in egg yolk. Add milk and vanilla. Add flour mixture. Divide dough into two parts. Leave one half plain. To other half, add semi-sweet chocolate morsels, melted. Chill dough for a few minutes. Roll out black and white parts separately, each between two sheets of wax paper. Place black on white, dough sides touching. Remove top sheet of paper and press doughs together lightly. Roll by hand, as for jelly roll, peeling off dough from bottom piece of paper. Shape into uniform roll. Chill and cut into ⅛" slices. Bake on ungreased cookie sheet at 400°F. 5 to 8 minutes.

Mary W. Nettleton, Teague H. S.
Teague, Texas

BUTTERSCOTCH ICE BOX COOKIES
Number of Servings — 3 Dozen
1 c. butter
2 c. brown sugar
Pinch of salt

2 eggs, beaten
2 t. vanilla
4 c. flour (plain)
1 t. soda
1 c. nuts, broken
Cream butter, sugar, and salt. Add eggs and vanilla. Beat. Sift flour and soda, add to butter, add more flour if needed, also nuts. Make into a roll. Wrap in wax paper. Chill overnight in refrigerator. Slice very thin. Bake in 400°F. oven about 10 minutes.

Mrs. Ora Avant, Tabor City H. S.
Tabor City, North Carolina

CHOCOLATE MELTAWAYS
Number of Servings — 6 Dozen
2 c. sifted cake flour
⅛ t. salt
¾ c. butter
1 c. sugar
½ t. vanilla
1 egg
2 T. milk
2 sq. (2 oz.) unsweetened chocolate
⅓ c. finely chopped walnuts
5 t. sweet cocoa beverage mix

Sift flour and salt together. Cream butter, sugar, and vanilla. Beat egg until thick and ivory colored. Beat into creamed mixture with melted chocolate and milk. Gradually stir in flour. Turn out on wax paper and with spoon or spatula shape into a rectangle. Cover tightly and place in freezer until firm. Cut into 4 portions. Remove one portion just before baking. Shape into 18 balls. Roll balls in nuts mixed with cocoa mix on wax paper (balls will not be covered with nuts). Place on ungreased cookie sheet about an inch apart. Bake in 375°F. oven about 10 minutes. Cool on wire racks.

Janet Linse, Rice Lake H. S.
Rice Lake, Wisconsin

CHOCOLATE PINWHEEL COOKIES
Number of Servings — 4 Dozen Cookies
2 c. sifted flour
1 t. baking powder
½ t. salt
½ c. shortening
⅔ c. sugar
1 unbeaten egg
1 T. milk
1 t. vanilla
1 sq. unsweetened chocolate, melted

Sift flour once, measure, add baking powder and salt and sift again. Cream shortening, add sugar gradually and cream together until light and fluffy. Add the egg and mix well. Add the flour mixture, one or two tablespoons at a time to shortening, mixing well after each addition. Then add milk, then vanilla. Divide the dough into two equal parts. Add the melted chocolate to one part. Roll each part very thin, place white layer on top of chocolate layer and roll as jelly roll. Place in refrigerator overnight. Slice ¼" thick. Bake 15 minutes at 350°F.

Margie E. Mayfield, Mandeville, H. S.
Mandeville, Louisiana

CINNAMON REFRIGERATOR COOKIES
Number of Servings — 25
1 c. shortening (oleo or butter)
1 c. brown sugar
1 c. white sugar
2 eggs
3½ c. all-purpose flour
1 t. baking soda
1 T. cinnamon
1 c. chopped nuts
Cream shortening and sugar until light and fluffy. Add eggs and mix well. Sift flour with dry ingredients and add to the above. Add the chopped nuts. The dough should be very stiff. Flour the hands, form dough into small rolls, wrap in wax paper and chill. Slice thinly and bake in preheated oven at 350°F. for 15 minutes or until brown. These may be kept in the freezer up to 6 months.

Willie M. Trotter, Batesburg Leesville H. S.
Batesburg, South Carolinia

DATE COOKIES
Number of Servings — 11 to 12 Dozen
1 c. shortening
2 c. brown sugar
2 eggs
1 c. nuts, ground
1 c. dates, ground
3½ c. cake flour
1 t. salt
1 t. soda
Cream shortening and sifted sugar thoroughly, add eggs 1 at a time and beat well after each addition. Add nuts and dates. Sift dry ingredients together, add to creamed mixture and mix well. Shape into 2″ rolls, wrap in wax paper and store in refrigerator until firm. Slice thin and bake 8 minutes at 400°F.

Gladyce H. Davis, Poteau H. S.
Poteau, Oklahoma

PECAN CRUNCHES
Number of Servings — 6 Dozen
2 c. melted butter (or oleo)
1 c. brown sugar
1 c. sugar
3 beaten eggs
½ t. almond flavoring or vanilla
4¼ c. sifted flour
1 t. baking powder
½ t. salt
1 t. cinnamon
1 c. chopped pecans
Combine butter, sugars, beaten eggs and flavoring and beat with electric mixer at medium speed for 3 minutes. Combine sifted flour, baking powder, salt and cinnamon, and sift. Add dry ingredients to first mixture. Add pecans and mix at slow speed, only enough to mix thoroughly. Shape in long rolls, size of desired cookie. Chill several hours. Slice thin, bake on ungreased tin at 400°F. for 10 minutes. Dough may be kept for several weeks in refrigerator.

Mrs. Albertin P. McKellar, Rowland H. S.
Rowland, North Carolina

OATMEAL CRISPIES
Number of Servings — 5 Dozen
1 c. shortening
1 c. brown sugar
1 c. granulated sugar
2 eggs, well beaten
1 t. vanilla extract
1½ c. flour
1 t. salt
1 t. soda
3 c. quick cooking oatmeal
½-1 c. chopped nuts
6 oz. chocolate bits (optional)
Thoroughly cream shortening and sugars, add eggs and vanilla, beat well. Add sifted dry ingredients. Add oatmeal, nut meats, and chocolate chips, mix well. Shape in rolls, wrap in wax paper and chill thoroughly or overnight. Slice ¼″ thick, bake on ungreased cookie sheet at 350°F. for 10-12 minutes. Let cool 1 minute. Loosen. Let cool longer before removing from sheet. May be frozen. May be garnished with cherries or nuts before baking.

This recipe submitted by the following teachers:
Mrs. Tina O. Cooper, Jourdanton H. S.
Jourdanton, Texas
Helen B. Loftin, Denton H. S.
Denton, North Carolina
Thrath C. Curry, Carrollton H. S.
Carrollton, Alabama
Maudell C. Cooper, Monticello Attendance Center
Monticello, Mississippi
Hazel C. Johnson, Lake City H. S.
Lake City, Tennessee
Mrs. Ann Click McGaughy, Calera H. S.
Calera, Alabama

PECAN REFRIGERATOR COOKIES
Number of Servings — 12 Dozen
1 c. butter or margarine
2 c. brown sugar (packed)
2 eggs
3½ c. flour
1 t. soda
½ t. salt
1 t. cream of tartar
1 c. pecans (chopped)
Cream butter and sugar. Add beaten eggs and mix well. Sift flour and measure. Add flour, soda, salt and cream of tartar to butter mixture. Mix well. Add nuts and stir until well mixed. Divide mixture into four parts and roll each part in wax paper. Rolls will be about 1½″ in diameter. Chill in refrigerator at least 4 hours. (May be frozen.) Slice into ¼″ slices, place on ungreased cookie sheet and bake 8 minutes at 375°F. Remove from cookie sheet immediately.

Jane Pate Rawson, Little Cypress H. S.
Orange, Texas

BUTTER BON BONS
Number of Servings — 3 Dozen
1 c. butter or margarine, soft
½ c. sifted confectioners' sugar
1 t. vanilla
2 c. sifted all-purpose flour
½ t. salt
½ c. flaked or shredded coconut
1 c. oats (quick or old fashioned kind)
½ c. semi-sweet chocolate pieces

Heat oven to slow 325°F. Beat together butter, sugar, and vanilla until creamy. Sift together flour and salt, blend well into butter mixture. Stir in coconut and rolled oats. Shape dough into balls (1 tablespoon each). Bake on ungreased cookie sheets in preheated oven about 25 minutes. Cool. Melt semi-sweet chocolate pieces over hot (not boiling) water. Swirl chocolate on cookies, sprinkle with coconut.

Mrs. Marilynn Trosper, Bryan Station Jr. H. S.
Lexington, Kentucky

CHRISTMAS BALLS
1 c. light brown sugar
1 c. butter
3 eggs, well beaten
3 c. flour
1 t. soda
1 t. cinnamon
1 t. cloves
½ t. nutmeg
½ lb. raisins
6 slices pineapple (crystallized)
2 c. cherries (crystallized)
7 c. nuts

Cream butter and sugar. Add eggs. Sift flour, soda and chopped spices together. Add to the first mixture. Add nuts and fruits. Roll in hand into balls and bake at 300°F. for 15 minutes.

Mrs. Carolyn Garland, Seneca H. S.
Seneca, South Carolina

CHRISTMAS CHERRIES
Number of Servings — 3 Dozen
½ c. shortening
¼ c. granulated sugar
1 egg, separated
½ t. vanilla extract
1 T. grated orange rind
6 candied cherries
1½ T. grated lemon rind
1 T. lemon juice
1 c. sifted pastry flour
½ c. walnut meats (chopped)

Cream shortening. Add sugar, and cream well. Add beaten egg yolk, vanilla, orange rind, lemon rind and lemon juice. Mix well. Add flour. Mix well, and chill. Roll in small balls ½" in diameter. Roll in egg whites slightly beaten, then in walnut meats. Place on a greased baking sheet and press in a small piece (about ⅛ of a cherry) on each. Bake in a moderate oven 350°F. for 20 minutes.

Mrs. Carley Basco Wright, Readhimer H. S.
Chestnut, Louisiana

COCONUT BALLS
Number of Servings — 8 Dozen Cookies
½ c. cornstarch
1½ c. confectioners' sugar
3 c. sifted flour
2 c. soft butter (or margarine)
1½ t. vanilla
3 c. grated coconut (fresh, frozen or packaged)

Sift cornstarch, sugar, and flour together. Blend in butter and vanilla. Chill. Shape into small balls, ½" diameter. Roll in coconut. Place 1" apart on ungreased baking sheet. Bake in slow oven 300°F. 20 to 25 minutes, or until coconut is golden brown.

Mrs. Rachael K. Cozart, Olympia H. S.
Columbia, South Carolina

COCONUT BALLS
Number of Servings — 4 Dozen

1 c. butter or oleo, softened
¼ c. sifted confectioners' sugar
2 t. vanilla
1 T. water
2 c. sifted enriched flour
1 c. chopped pecans
18 oz. (3 c.) shredded coconut, cut fine
Assorted food colorings

Thoroughly cream butter, sugar, vanilla. Stir in water. Add flour and mix well. Stir in nuts. Roll in 1" balls. Bake on ungreased cookie sheet 300°F. 20 minutes, or until delicately browned. Cool thoroughly before removing from pan. Dip in frosting and roll in tinted coconut (pink, yellow, green). To tint coconut: Place coconut in jar, add few drops coloring, cover, shake until color uniform.

Frosting:
4 c. sifted confectioners' sugar
½ c. milk
Gradually add milk to sugar, blending until smooth.

Mrs. Rosabelle G. Mitchell, Chataignier H. S.
Chataignier, Louisiana

COCONUT SUPRISE POMPONS
Number of Servings — 4 Dozen
1 c. butter
½ c. sugar
2 t. vanilla
2 c. sifted flour
¼ t. salt
2 c. pecan halves
Chopped shredded coconut

Cream butter, sugar, and vanilla. Add flour and salt to creamed mixture, blending well. Shape dough around each half pecan to form 1" ball. Roll in coconut. Place on cookie sheet. Bake at 300°F. for 35 minutes. Cool. Variation: Use whole blanched almond, date, or candied cherry for "surprise" center.

Thelma S. Land, Hickory H. S.
Hickory, Mississippi

GINGER SNAPS
Number of Servings — 3 Dozen

¾ c. shortening
1 c. sugar
4 T. molasses
1 egg
2 c. flour
2 t. soda
1 t. cinnamon
1 t. ginger
1 t. cloves

Thoroughly cream shortening and sugar, add the molasses, and well beaten egg. Add sifted dry ingredients and beat until smooth. Roll into small balls (size of a walnut) dip or roll in granulated sugar and place 2″ apart on greased baking sheet. Bake in moderate oven, store in air-tight container. Longer kept, the better the cookie.
This recipe submitted by the following teachers:
Mrs. H. L. Burleson, West Hyde H. S.
Swan Quarter, North Carolina
Mrs. Foy M. Griffin, Indian Land School
Fort Mill, South Carolina

GUMDROP COOKIES
Number of Servings — 3 to 6 Dozen

1 c. shortening
1 c. brown sugar
1 c. granulated sugar
2 eggs
1 t. vanilla
2 c. sifted flour
1 t. baking powder
½ t. soda
¼ to ½ t. salt
2 c. quick cooking oats
1 c. coconut
1 c. of same flavor gumdrops or different flavors as preferred, cut in small pieces

Thoroughly cream shortening and sugars. Add eggs and beat well. Sift dry ingredients, and add to creamed mixture. Blend. Add oats, coconut, and gumdrops, and mix with spoon until well blended. Roll dough into small balls. Place on greased cookie sheet. Press each ball with a fork. Bake in moderate oven 350-375°F. for about 10 minutes. These improve in flavor if stored for a few days.
This recipe submitted by the following teachers:
Beulah Whitt Dowell, Cuba H. S.
Mayfield, Kentucky
Thelma B. Caballero, Benavides H. S.
Benavides, Texas
Mrs. Elizabeth W. Knape, Douglas Sr. H. S.
Douglas, Arizona

HONEY SUNDIES
Number of Servings — 30

1 c. shortening
2 c. sifted flour
¼ c. honey
½ t. vanilla or almond extract
½ t. salt
2 c. pecans

Cream shortening. Add other ingredients. Roll in small balls. Bake for 30 minutes in a 300°F. oven. Roll in powdered sugar while hot, and again when cold.
Jane Carroll, Avalon H. S.
Avalon, Texas

JELLY JEWEL COOKIES
Number of Servings — 2 Dozen

½ c. butter
¼ c. brown sugar
1 egg, separated
1 c. flour
½ c. finely chopped pecans
1 small jar currant or raspberry jelly

Cream butter and sugar together until fluffy, add well beaten egg yolk, stir in flour. Chill dough. Pinch off small pieces and roll into small balls, dip into slightly beaten egg whites, then into finely chopped pecans. Place on cookie sheet, bake in 360°F. oven for 5 minutes. Remove, make depression in center of each ball, return to oven for 10 minutes. Cool on wire or cake cooler. When cold, drop a small amount of currant or red raspberry jelly in center of each. Makes 2 dozen cookies 1½″ in diameter.
Mrs. Martha Brown Long, McCamey H. S.
McCamey, Texas

LACY ENGLISH JUMBOS
Number of Servings — 5 Dozen

1-6 oz. pkg. semi-sweet chocolate bits
¾ c. shortening
¾ c. sugar
⅛ t. salt
¼ t. ginger
½ c. light corn syrup
1½ c. sifted flour

Combine chocolate bits, shortening, sugar, salt, and ginger. Melt over hot (not boiling) water. Remove from water. Stir in corn syrup and sifted flour. Drop by teaspoonfuls 3″ apart on well greased cookie sheet. Bake at 350°F. for 10 minutes. Cool slightly, approximately 1 minute. Remove from cookie sheet and roll at once, top side out, over handle of wooden spoon, or use finger to form a cane. Press to seal edges. If cookies should stick to the sheet return to oven for a minute. Then proceed as directed.
Juanita Roberts, Cherry Creek H. S.
Englewood, Colorado

NUTTY FINGERS
Number of Servings — 48 Cookies

1 stick oleo
5 T. powdered sugar
1 t. vanilla
1 c. plain flour
1 c. nuts, cut finely

Cream oleo and add powdered sugar and vanilla. Work in flour gradually. Add nuts. Make into rolled cookies about the size of little finger. Bake at 375°F. for 8-10 minutes or until lightly brown. When cool, roll in powdered sugar twice.
Earle H. Vallentine, Edisto H. S.
Cordova, South Carolina

NUT GEMS
Number of Servings — 2½ Dozen

2 c. sifted flour
1 c. butter or oleo
4 T. powdered sugar
1 c. chopped nuts
2 T. water
2 t. rum flavoring or vanilla extract
Confectioners' sugar

Cream butter or oleo, add sugar gradually, cream until smooth. Blend in flour. Stir in nuts, water, flavor. Mix well. Shape into small 1" balls, bake on ungreased baking sheet in oven 350°F., 20 minutes or until golden brown. While still warm, roll into confectioners' sugar.

Hazel C. Johnson, Lake City H. S.
Lake City, Tennessee

NUT LOGS
Number of Servings — 7½ Dozen

2¼ c. sifted flour
2 t. baking powder
½ t. salt
½ c. butter, melted
⅔ c. (½ 15 oz. can) sweetened condensed milk
½ c. dark brown sugar, firmly packed
1 egg
1 t. vanilla extract
¾ c. finely chopped nut meats
Confectioners' sugar

Sift together flour, baking powder and salt into a large bowl. Add butter, sweetened condensed milk, brown sugar and egg, mix until well blended. Stir in vanilla and nut meats. Use about 1 teaspoon dough to form logs. Place on well greased baking sheet. Bake in moderate oven 375°F. about 10 minutes or until lightly browned. Remove from baking sheet immediately. Roll in confectioners' sugar.

Della Louise Carter, Holbrook H. S.
Holbrook, Arizona

PARTY COOKIES
Number of Servings — 6 Dozen

1 c. butter or margarine
1 c. sugar
2 egg yolks
1 t. vanilla
2 c. flour
¼ t. salt
2 egg whites
2 c. finely chopped pecans

Cream butter, sugar, egg yolks and vanilla. Mix flour and salt and stir into creamed mixture. Chill dough. Roll 1 teaspoon dough into balls. Dip in slightly beaten egg whites and roll in nuts (may be rolled in coconut). Place on baking sheet and press finger into center of each. Bake in 350°F. oven for 10 to 12 minutes. Fill cooled cookies with tinted confectioners' sugar icing. Variation: Add 2 squares (2 ounces) melted unsweetened chocolate to dough and fill centers with chocolate icing.

Mrs. L. A. Boyd, Vernon H. S.
Vernon, Texas

PEANUT BLOSSOMS
Number of Servings — 3 Dozen

⅓ c. peanut butter
½ c. sugar
½ c. butter
½ c. brown sugar
1 egg
1 t. vanilla
½ t. salt
1 t. soda
1¾ c. flour
2 pkg. chocolate kisses

Cream first four ingredients. Add egg and vanilla. Sift flour, soda, and salt. Combine with other mixture. Shape into balls and dip in white sugar. Bake at 375°F. for 8 minutes. Press in candy kisses. Return to bake 2-5 minutes.

Mrs. Betty Viens, Turtle Lake H. S.
Turtle Lake, Wisconsin

PEANUT BUTTER COOKIES
Number of Servings — 15

¾ c. fat
¾ c. brown sugar
¾ c. white sugar
1 c. peanut butter
2 eggs (beaten)
2½ c. flour with 1 t. soda, ½ t. salt

Cream fat, add ingredients in order given, blending well after each. Roll into 1" balls and place on ungreased cookie sheet. Flatten with a fork crisscross and bake at 350°F. for 10 minutes. Cool on rack before storing in tightly covered can.

Deanna Patin, Fifth Ward H. S.
Marksville, Louisiana

PEANUT COOKIES
Number of Servings — 4 Dozen

1 c. shortening
2 c. brown sugar
2 eggs
1 t. vanilla
1 c. cornflakes, crushed
2 c. oatmeal
2 c. flour
½ t. salt
1 t. baking powder
½ t. soda
1 c. peanuts (coarsely chopped)

Cream shortening, sugar and eggs until light. Add vanilla, cornflakes, oatmeal. Add flour sifted with salt, baking powder, and soda. Stir in peanuts. Mold with hands into small balls, place on greased baking sheet. Press each with tines of a fork. Bake in a moderate oven 350°F. 12 to 15 minutes.

Mrs. Gladys Paschal, Senior H. S.
Rogers, Arkansas

PECAN STICKS
Number of Servings — 75 Cookies

1 c. butter
⅜ c. sugar
1 t. water
1 t. vanilla or almond extract
2¼ c. flour
½ c. chopped nuts

(Continued on Next Page)

Cream butter. Add sugar and cream well. Add water and vanilla. Gradually add flour until mixed into a stiff dough. Blend in chopped nuts. Chill until dough becomes firm. Roll dough in palm of hand into shape of small cocoons. Place on ungreased cookie sheet. Bake 8 to 10 minutes at 350°F. until lightly browned.

Mrs. Elizabeth L. Blanchard, S. Terrebonne H. S.
Houma, Louisiana

PECAN ROLLS

⅞ c. butter
4 T. Confectioners' sugar
2 c. sifted flour
2 t. vanilla
1 t. water
1 c. pecans (finely chopped)

Cream butter with sugar. Add flour, vanilla, water and pecans. Pinch off small pieces of dough. Make into small rolls. Bake 30 minutes at 275°F. Roll in confectioners' sugar.

Mrs. Jack Searcy, Lewisville H. S.
Lewisville, Arkansas

PRESS COOKIES
Number of Servings — 12 Dozen

1 lb. butter (or 1 c. margarine and 1 c. shortening)
1½ c. sugar
1 egg plus 1 yolk
1 t. vanilla
5 c. flour

Cream butter and sugar. Add slightly beaten egg and yolk. Add vanilla. Beat in flour. Let chill. Shape with cookie gun or press. Bake on ungreased cookie sheet at 375°F. until light golden brown. Remove from cookie sheet while hot.

Mrs. Helen L. Scott, Haynesville H. S.
Haynesville, Louisiana

RANGER COOKIES
Number of Servings — 60 to 72

1 c. granulated sugar
1 c. brown sugar
1 c. shortening
1 t. vanilla
1 t. salt
2 eggs
1 t. soda
½ t. baking powder
2 c. quick oatmeal
2 c. cereal, such as Rice Krispies
1 c. coconut
1 c. chopped nuts

Cream shortening and sugars. Add vanilla, salt, and eggs. Sift dry ingredients together and add to creamed mixture. Add oatmeal, cereal, coconut, and nuts. Mix well and form into balls. Bake 12 minutes at 350°F. These cookies will be soft, but will harden later when cool.

Mrs. Betty Adams, Windthorst H. S.
Windthorst, Texas

SAND COOKIES
Number of Servings — 5 Dozen

1 c. butter (2 sticks)
4 T. powdered sugar
3 c. flour
1 c. pecans

Cream butter (or margarine) and powdered sugar. Gradually add flour and pecans and continue to mix. (Use hands to mix.) When dough holds together, shape into small rolls about 1½" long. Place on an ungreased cookie sheet and bake at 325°F. until golden brown. (20 minutes.) While cookies are still hot, roll in powdered sugar. Let cool. Serve.

Mrs. Mary B. Hodson, Lockport H. S.
Lockport, Louisiana

SANDIES
Number of Servings — 3 Dozen

1 c. butter or margarine
¼ c. confectioners' sugar
2 t. vanilla
1 T. water
2 c. enriched flour
1 c. chopped pecans
⅛ box confectioners' sugar

Cream butter or margarine and ¼ cup confectioners' sugar, add vanilla and water. Add flour, mix well and add chopped nuts. Form small rolls, 1½" long. Bake on ungreased cookie sheet in slow oven 300°F. for 20 minutes or until delicately browned. While hot, roll in confectioners' sugar.

Mrs. Saralu C. Jenkins, Clarkston H. S.
Clarkston, Georgia

SAND DABS
Number of Servings — 2 Dozen

½ c. butter
3 T. confectioners' sugar
½ t. vanilla
1 c. sifted flour
1 c. chopped pecans

Cream butter, add sugar, vanilla and blend. Add flour, mixing thoroughly. Add pecans. Roll a tablespoon full into a ball, crescent or finger shape. Place on slightly oiled baking sheet. Bake at 350°F., 20 minutes. Roll in confectioners' sugar while warm.

Mrs. Hobert Keller, Rabun County H. S.
Clayton, Georgia

SAND DABS (Party)
Number of Servings — 100

1 c. butter
3 c. flour
6 T. sugar
1 T. vanilla
1 c. chopped nuts
Small amount tart jelly
100 whole halves pecans
½ c. powdered sugar

Cream butter and sugar, add flour gradually. Then chopped nuts and vanilla. This makes a firm

(Continued on Next Page)

dough. Pinch off small amounts and roll into balls. Push thumb into balls to make a deep dent. Fill with tart jelly. Cover with ½ pecan. Bake 30 minutes, 300°F. When cool roll in powdered sugar.

Sara A. Ardrey, Rock Hill H. S.
Rock Hill, South Carolina

SAND TARTS

Number of Servings — 6 Dozen

1 c. butter
5 T. powdered sugar
2 c. flour
2 t. vanilla
1½ c. chopped nuts

Cream butter and sugar. Work flour, vanilla, and nuts into creamed mixture. Form into small balls or crescents. Bake on ungreased sheet in oven 350°F. for 30 minutes or until very lightly browned. Roll tarts in powdered sugar while still warm.

This recipe submitted by the following teachers:
Jean Morris, Central H. S.
Florence, Alabama
Mrs. Martha Thomas, Franklin-Simpson H. S.
Franklin, Kentucky

SCOTCH SHORTBREAD

Number of Servings — 2½ Dozen

1 c. soft butter
½ c. brown sugar
2½ c. sifted flour

Mix the butter and sugar thoroughly. Stir in the flour. Mix thoroughly with hands. Chill dough. Shape into 1″ balls, and place on ungreased cookie sheet. Press criss-cross design on top with floured fork. Bake in a 300°F. oven for 20 to 25 minutes. (The shape does not change and the tops do not brown.)

Geraldine Thompson, Sonoma Valley H. S.
Sonoma, California

THUMBPRINTS COOKIES

Number of Servings — 2 Dozen

½ c. soft shortening
¼ c. brown sugar
1 egg yolk
½ t. vanilla
1 c. sifted flour
¼ t. salt
¾ c. finely chopped nuts

Mix thoroughly shortening, brown sugar, egg yolk, and vanilla. Sift together flour and salt and add to first mixture. Roll into 1″ balls. Dip in slightly beaten egg whites. Roll in finely chopped nuts. Place 1″ apart on ungreased baking sheet and press thumb into center of each. Bake at 375°F. until set. Cool. Place in thumbprints jelly or tinted confectioners' sugar. Time 10 to 12 minutes.

Jimmie McGuire, Davis H. S.
Davis, Oklahoma

SNICKERDOODLES

Number of Servings — 5 Dozen

1 c. soft shortening
1½ c. sugar
2 eggs
2¾ c. sifted flour
2 t. cream of tartar
1 t. soda
¼ t. salt

Heat oven to 400°F. Mix shortening, sugar, and eggs thoroughly. Sift together flour, cream of tartar, soda, salt, and stir into above mixture. Form dough into balls about the size of walnuts. Roll in mixture of sugar and cinnamon. Place about 2″ apart on ungreased baking sheet. Bake 8 to 10 minutes at 400°F.

Topping:
2 T. sugar
2 t. cinnamon

This recipe submitted by the following teachers:
Mrs. Ted Trotter, Independence H. S.
Independence, Louisiana
Mrs. Myrtle Teer, Hutto H. S.
Hutto, Texas
Mrs. Laura Montgomery, Wellman H. S.
Wellman, Texas
Mrs. Ruth C. Currier, Stanton Union H. S.
Stanton, Michigan

WALNUT BOURBON BALLS

2½ c. finely crushed vanilla wafers
1 c. powdered sugar
2 T. cocoa
1 c. finely chopped nuts
1 c. coconut (if desired)
3 T. corn syrup
¼ c. bourbon (or wine)
Powdered sugar

Mix first 4 ingredients well. Add corn syrup and bourbon. Mix well. Roll into 1″ balls. Roll in powdered sugar.

Mrs. Jewell T. Johnson, Albany H. S.
Albany, Georgia

GOLDEN APPLE BARS

⅔ c. shortening
2 c. brown sugar
2 eggs, beaten
¼ t. salt
1 t. vanilla
2 c. sifted flour
2 t. baking powder
1½ c. chopped raw apple
½ c. chopped nut meats

Cream the shortening and sugar, add eggs, vanilla and salt and beat well. Sift dry ingredients and add. Stir in apples and nut meats. Bake in 12x8 greased pan, 350°F. 35-40 minutes. Cut in bars when cool or very good served warm with whipped cream or ice cream.

Mrs. Irene Robotham, Bellaire Public School
Bellaire, Michigan

APRICOT BARS

Number of Servings — 12 to 15

⅔ c. dried apricots
½ c. soft butter
¼ c. granulated sugar
1⅓ c. sifted flour
½ t. baking powder
¼ t. salt
2 eggs
1 c. brown sugar
½ t. vanilla
½ c. chopped nuts
Confectioners' sugar

Rinse apricots, cover with water and boil 10 minutes. Drain, cool and chop apricots. Set aside. Heat oven to 350°F. Grease an 8x8x2 pan. Mix butter, granulated sugar and 1 cup flour until crumbly. Pack into pan and bake for 25 minutes. Sift ⅓ cup flour, baking powder, and salt. Beat eggs and add brown sugar. Beat until well mixed. Add flour mixture, vanilla, nuts, and apricots to egg-sugar mixture. Spread over baked layer. Bake 30 minutes. Cool in pan. Cut into squares and roll in confectioners' sugar.

This recipe submitted by the following teachers:
Mrs. Gloria Love, Cumberland Valley H. S.
Mechanicsburg, Pennsylvania
Mrs. Louise S. Ventura, Arnold H. S.
Arnold, Pennsylvania

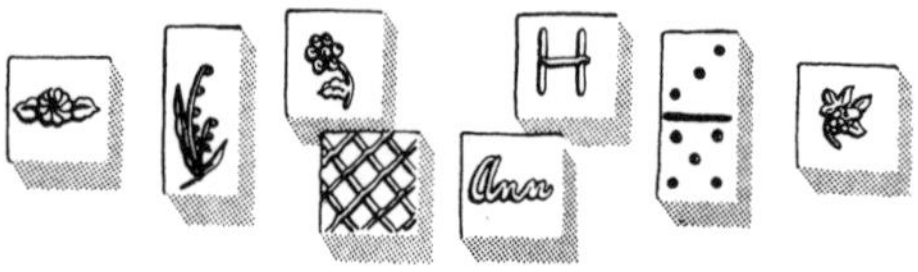

CRUNCHY APPLESAUCE SQUARES

Number of Servings — 9

½ c. butter
¾ c. dark brown sugar
¾ c. flour
1 c. quick oats
½ t. salt

Cream together butter and brown sugar. Add flour, quick oats, and salt. Cut together until crumbly. Press ½ mixture in a 8x8x1½ greased pan. Bake 20 minutes at 350°F.

Filling:
¼ c. dark brown sugar
1½ c. canned applesauce
2 T. flour
½ t. grated lemon rind
1 T. lemon juice
½ c. chopped walnuts
½ t. nutmeg

Pour applesauce in saucepan. Boil rapidly for 5 minutes, stirring constantly. Combine flour with brown sugar. Add to hot applesauce. Cook about 5 minutes or until thickened. Remove from heat, add lemon rind and juice. Cool. Spread evenly over baked mixture. Add nuts and nutmeg to remaining ½ cup crumbs, mix well. Sprinkle over applesauce mixture. Bake 40 minutes at 375°F. Cut when cool. Serve with whipped cream if desired.

Mrs. A. J. Foret, Bayou Chicot H. S.
Ville Platte, Louisiana

BROWNIES

Number of Servings — 20

⅔ c. sifted flour
¼ t. salt
½ t. baking powder
⅓ c. butter or shortening
2 sq. unsweetened chocolate
2 eggs
1 c. sugar
½ c. broken walnuts
1 t. vanilla

Sift flour wth baking powder and salt. Melt butter and chocolate over hot water. Beat eggs well, add sugar gradually, beating well. Beat in chocolate mixture. Mix in flour, then nuts and vanilla. Bake in greased 8x8x2 pan at 350°F. about 25 minutes. Cool in pan. Cut in squares.

This recipe submitted by the following teachers:
Mrs. Mary Ann Calhoun, Meriwether H. S.
Woodbury, Georgia
Mrs. Marion Biscup, North Junior H. S.
Grants Pass, Oregon

BROWNIES (Brown Sugar)

Number of Servings — 35

6 T. butter
2 sq. chocolate, melted
2 eggs
2 c. brown sugar
1 c. all-purpose flour
¼ t. salt
½ t. vanilla
1 c. pecans

Melt butter and chocolate in top of double boiler over low heat. Beat eggs slightly and add remaining ingredients. Spread evenly in buttered 9x13 pan and bake about 30 minutes at 275°F. Mark in squares and take out of pan when slightly cooled.

Mrs. Irene J. Hodges, McKee Laboratory School
Cullowhee, North Carolina

BROWNIES (Self Rising Flour)

Number of Servings — 10

½ c. butter or margarine
1-1 oz. sq. unsweetened chocolate
1 c. sugar
¾ c. chopped pecans
⅔ c. self-rising flour
1 t. vanilla
2 eggs

Melt chocolate and butter in saucepan. Remove from heat. Add all ingredients except eggs. Stir to mix, add eggs and beat well. Pour into greased and floured 9" round pan. Bake at 350°F. about 30 minutes. Cut in squares.

Mrs. Lucille Morse, Caldwell Co., H. S.
Princeton, Kentucky

DELUXE FUDGY BROWNIES (Fayes)

Number of Servings — 2 Dozen

4 sq. unsweetened chocolate and ½ c. butter or margarine or 1½ sticks butter, 3½ oz. bakery chocolate, ½ t. salt (if desired)
4 eggs
2 c. sugar
1 c. sifted flour
1 t. vanilla
1 c. coarsely chopped nuts

Melt chocolate and butter together over hot water. Cool slightly. Beat eggs until foamy, gradually add sugar, beating thoroughly after each addition. Add chocolate mixture and blend. Stir in flour. Then add vanilla and nuts. Spread in greased 9x9x2 pan. Bake at 325°F. 40-50 minutes. Cool in pan, then cut into squares or bars. Will have crunchy top and bottom crust with a center almost like chocolate cream. Delicious served straight from the freezer.

This recipe submitted by the following teachers:

Mrs. Jessie Sue Smith, Fairview H. S.
Cullman, Alabama
Mrs. Nina Diefenbach, Silver Creek Sr. H. S.
Sellersburg, Indiana

FUDGE SQUARES

Number of Servings — 25 Squares

1 c. butter (2 sticks) or 1 c. oleomargarine
2 c. sugar
4 eggs
1 t. vanilla
4 sq. chocolate
1 c. flour
2 c. chopped nuts

Mix and bake for 30 minutes in a moderate oven, about 350°F. When they are cool, they can be iced with chocolate icing.

Chocolate Icing:
2 c. sugar
½ c. white Karo syrup
¾ c. cream
1 sq. melted unsweetened chocolate
1 t. vanilla
3 T. butter

Cook all together until soft ball stage or 234°F. Remove from fire and add vanilla and butter. Beat and spread on top and sides.

Mrs. Annie R. Gonzales, Prescott Junior H. S.
Baton Rouge, Louisiana

BROWNIES (Iced)

Number of Servings — 36

2 c. sugar
½ c. cocoa
1 c. Crisco
Pinch of salt
4 eggs
½ c. evaporated milk
1 c. flour
½ t. vanilla
1 c. nuts

Cream first four ingredients together. Add remaining ingredients. Mix Well. Bake in a greased and floured pan at 350°F. for 20 or 30 minutes.

Icing:
1 pkg. powdered sugar
Pinch of salt
3 T. cocoa
¾ stick margarine, melted

Add enough evaporated milk to mixture to bring to spreading consistency. Spread over the hot brownies. Cut into squares.

Doris S. Hartman, Slocum H. S.
Slocum, Texas

BLACK AND WHITE BROWNIES

Number of Servings — 8

2 eggs
1 c. sugar
⅓ c. butter (melted)
⅔ c. flour
¾ t. baking powder
¼ t. salt
⅔ c. or 1½ oz. coconut
½ t. almond extract
2 sq. chocolate, melted

Beat eggs and sugar. Blend in butter. Sift together dry ingredients. Stir into first mixture. Mix coconut and almond into ⅓ of batter. Blend chocolate in remaining batter. Pour chocolate batter into greased 8x8x2 pan. Spread coconut batter on top. Bake at 350°F. 25-30 minutes. Cool, cut into squares.

Helen Mullikin, Wade Hampton H. S.
Hampton, South Carolina

CANADIAN BROWNIES

Number of Servings — 3 to 4 Dozen

Part I:
½ c. flour
1 T. confectioners' sugar
½ c. butter

Part II:
2 eggs beaten
½ t. baking powder
1¼ c. brown sugar
1 c. coconut
4 T. flour
1 c. nuts

Cream together butter, flour, and sugar (Part I). Bake in oven 425°F. until brown. While first mixture is baking mix second mixture. When first mixture has browned, pour part II over top and bake at 400°F. about 20 minutes. Cut in squares.

Mrs. Ruth N. Powell, Franklinville H. S.
Franklinville, North Carolina

CHOCOLATE CHIP BLONDE BROWNIES

Number of Servings — 12 to 16 Squares

⅓ c. shortening or butter, melted (if shortening, add 1 T. hot water)
1 c. brown sugar
1 egg
1 t. vanilla
1 c. sifted flour
½ t. baking powder
⅛ t. soda
½ t. salt
½ c. chopped nuts (optional)
½ pkg. chocolate chips

(Continued on Next Page)

Add brown sugar to melted shortening or butter. Cool. Add egg and vanilla to mixture and blend well. Add sifted dry ingredients gradually. Stir in chopped nuts. Pour mixture into greased 9x9x2 pan. Sprinkle chocolate chips on top. Bake in 350°F. oven 20-25 minutes. Cut in squares. (Recipe may be doubled and baked in 8x12 pan.)

This recipe submitted by the following teachers:

Mrs. Imogene Spring, Seymour H. S.
Seymour, Texas

Emma Lou Garst, Natural Bridge H. S.
Natural Bridge Station, Virginia

BLONDE BROWNIES
Number of Brownies — 1½ to 2 Dozen
¼ c. butter
1 c. light brown sugar (packed)
1 egg
¾ c. sifted flour
1 t. baking powder
½ t. salt
½ t. vanilla
½ c. coarsely chopped walnuts

Melt butter over low heat. Remove from heat and stir in brown sugar until well-blended. Cool. Stir in egg. Sift together and stir in flour, baking powder, and salt. Then stir in vanilla and walnuts. Spread in well greased 8″ square pan. Bake at 350°F. about 25 minutes. Do not overbake! Cut into bars or squares while still warm.

Mrs. Dixie Dunn Ruby, Charles Town Sr. H. S.
Charles Town, West Virginia

LIGHT BROWNIES (Chocolate Chip)
Number of Servings — 16
¾ stick butter
1 c. brown sugar
1 egg
1 t. vanilla
1 c. flour
½ c. nuts
½ c. chocolate tidbits

Melt butter, add sugar and egg and beat well. Add vanilla, flour and nuts. Pour into greased and floured 8″ square pan. Sprinkle chocolate tidbits on top. Bake at 350°F. 25 to 30 minutes. Cut in squares.

Emily B. Person, John Graham H. S.
Warrenton, North Carolina

FUDGE FROSTED BROWNIES
½ c. butter
1 c. sugar
2 eggs
2-1 oz. sq. unsweetened chocolate
1 t. vanilla
½ c. flour
½ c. chopped walnuts

Cream butter and sugar, add eggs beating well. Blend in melted chocolate and vanilla. Add flour, then nuts. Pour in greased 8x8x2 pan. Bake at 325°F. for 35 minutes. Cool. Spread with Fudge Frosting. Cut in squares while frosting is warm.

Fudge Frosting:
1 c. sifted confectioners' sugar

1 T. cocoa
2 T. cream
1 T. butter

Combine ingredients in order listed. Cook until mixture boils around sides of saucepan. Remove from heat and beat until of spreading consistency. Spread.

Mrs. Requa K. Spears, Mullins School
Pikeville, Kentucky

BROWN SUGAR BROWNIES
(Quantity Recipe)
Number of Servings — 100
2 lb. butter
1 gal. brown sugar
1 pt. eggs
½ gal. flour (all-purpose)
¼ c. vanilla
½ gal. coconut
3 T. baking powder

Cream butter and sugar, add eggs. Beat well. Sift flour and baking powder. Blend into mixture. Add vanilla and coconut. Pour into 3 (17½x11) pans. Bake at 325°F. about 40 minutes. Note: The brownies will not look done and will fall thereby giving a chewy texture.

Inez Galloway, Columbia H. S.
Lake City, Florida

GLORIFIED BROWNIES
Number of Servings — 12 to 15
1 c. sugar
½ c. butter
2 eggs
3 T. cocoa (or 2 sq. chocolate)
¾ c. flour
Pinch of salt
1 t. vanilla
1 c. nuts
12-15 marshmallows

Mix in order given. Spread in pan and bake 20 minutes at 400°F. When done, cut marshmallows fine over top of brownies while still hot and cover with the confectioners' sugar or other favorite fudge icing. Decorate with nuts.

Letha A. Chastain, Pamplico H. S.
Pamplico, South Carolina

FUDGE SQUARES
Number of Servings — 2 Dozen
¾ c. sifted flour
½ t. baking powder
⅛ t. salt
3 T. cocoa
⅓ c. shortening
1 c. sugar
2 eggs, well beaten
½ c. chopped nut meats
1 t. vanilla

Sift flour with baking powder, salt, and cocoa. Melt shortening. Beat sugar into eggs. Add shortening and blend. Add sifted ingredients, nuts, and vanilla. Mix well. Bake in greased and floured (10x15) pan at 350°F. about 30 minutes. Cool. Cut into squares.

Mrs. Joyce H. Jeter, Haskell Jr. H. S.
Haskell, Texas

MARSHMALLOW FUDGE BROWNIES AND ICING

Number of Servings — 8 to 12

½ c. shortening
¾ c. sugar
2 eggs beaten
¾ c. sifted flour
¼ t. baking powder
2 T. cocoa
¼ t. salt
1 t. vanilla
½ c. chopped nuts
18 marshmallows, halved

Cream shortening and sugar, add eggs. Beat well. Sift dry ingredients, add to creamed mixture. Mix well. Add vanilla and nuts. Bake in 12x8 pan 20 minutes at 350°F. Take from oven and put marshmallow halves on top. Return to oven for 3 minutes. Spread until top is covered with marshmallows. Let cool. Frost with following.

Icing:
½ c. brown sugar
¼ c. water
1 sq. unsweetened chocolate
3 T. butter
1 t. vanilla
1½ c. powdered sugar

Combine and boil for 3 minutes brown sugar, water, and chocolate. Add butter and vanilla and let cool. Then stir in powdered sugar. Spread on brownies. Cut in squares.

Mrs. Maxine King, Unity H. S.
Mendon, Illinois

MINT STICK BROWNIES

Number of Servings — 4 Dozen Small Cookies

2 sq. chocolate
½ c. butter
2 eggs, well beaten
1 c. sugar
¼ t. peppermint flavoring
½ c. sifted flour
⅛ t. salt
½ c. chopped nuts

Melt chocolate and butter together over hot water. Cool. Add beaten eggs, sugar, flavoring, flour, salt, and nuts. Pour batter into well greased 9" square pan. Bake at 350°F. for 20-25 minutes. Cool. Frost brownies with this double layer of frosting.

Mint Frosting:
2 T. soft butter
1 c. sifted powdered sugar
1 T. cream
½ t. peppermint flavoring
Few drops green food coloring (if desired)

Mix together until creamy and spread on cooled brownies. Refrigerate while you make glaze topping.

Glaze Topping:
1 sq. baking chocolate
1 T. butter

Combine butter and chocolate and melt over hot water. Blend well. Dribble this glaze over green icing. Carefully tilt pan back and forth to cover surface or very carefully spread over top. Refrigerate to set chocolate glaze. Cut into finger-like sticks. Attractive party cookies can be made by cutting diagonally across the pan and then cutting diagonally the other way to make small brownies.

This recipe submitted by the following teachers:
Mrs. Charles Barber, Monroe H. S.
Monroe, South Dakota
Josephine Grissette, Robert E. Lee H. S.
Montgomery, Alabama
Ruth Elizabeth Cook, University H. S.
Morgantown, West Virginia

MOCHA SAUCEPAN BROWNIES

Number of Servings — 8

1 stick margarine
1½ sq. chocolate
1 c. sugar
1 t. vanilla
⅔ c. sifted flour
1 t. baking powder
2 T. instant coffee
¼ t. salt
2 eggs, well beaten
½ c. chopped pecans

Melt margarine and chocolate in a saucepan over low heat. Cool. Blend in sugar and vanilla. Sift dry ingredients together and blend with sugar mixture. Add eggs and beat well. Add chopped pecans. Spread in an 8x8x2 pan, greased on the bottom, lined with greased wax paper. Bake at 350°F. for 30 minutes. Cool 5 minutes. Remove wax paper. Frost or cut in squares and serve plain or with ice cream.

Mrs. Pauline Wattner, Seagoville H. S.
Seagoville, Texas

PEANUT BUTTER BROWNIES

¼ c. butter
½ c. peanut butter
1 c. sugar
¼ c. firmly packed brown sugar
2 eggs
1 c. sifted flour
1 t. baking powder
¼ t. salt
1 pkg. semi-sweet chocolate bits
½ t. vanilla

Beat butter and peanut butter together until light. Gradually add sugar and brown sugar, creaming well. Add eggs, one at a time, beating well after each addition. Add flour, baking powder and salt, mixing well. Add chocolate bits and vanilla. Spread mixture in well greased, 9" pan. Bake at 350°F. for 30-35 minutes. Cool and cut into squares.

Clara Deiter, Dodge City Junior H. S.
Dodge City, Kansas

CARAMEL NUT COOKIES

Number of Servings — 30

1 c. brown sugar
1 c. melted butter or oleo

(Continued on Next Page)

1 egg
2 c. flour
1 beaten egg
1 c. brown sugar
1 c. chopped nuts

Mix together 1 cup brown sugar, 1 cup melted butter, 1 egg and 2 cups flour. Spread with hands in greased pan, 8x8. Then spread over top 1 beaten egg and ½ cup brown sugar. Over this, sprinkle 1 cup of chopped nuts, then another ½ cup of brown sugar. Bake at 325°F. about 25 minutes. Cut into squares while hot. Candied fruit may also be used on top.

Elberta Martin, Irma Marsh Junior H. S.
Fort Worth, Texas

CARAMEL SQUARES
Number of Servings — 2 Dozen
1 stick oleo
1 lb. brown sugar
2 eggs
2 c. flour
1 t. baking powder
1 c. pecans
1 t. vanilla

Cream margarine, add sugar and eggs. Add dry ingredients, vanilla and nuts in order. Bake in greased pan 9x13, 35 to 40 minutes. Start in oven 400°F. and reduce to 325°F. after 15 minutes. Test with toothpick.

Mona Faye Fordham, Sikes H. S.
Sikes, Louisiana

CARROT COOKIES
Number of Servings — 36
¾ c. shortening
¾ c. sugar
1 T. finely grated orange rind
1 egg
1 c. carrots (cooked and mashed)
2 c. flour
2 t. baking powder
½ t. salt

Cream shortening, sugar, and orange rind. Beat in egg. Add carrots. Beat mixture well. Sift dry ingredients. Add about ⅓ of sifted dry ingredients at a time and beat well after each addition. Pour mixture into shallow baking pan (or sheet with closed end). Bake 350°F. for 20-25 minutes. Cool. Glaze with 2 cups sifted confectioners' sugar and ⅓ cup orange juice. Cut in squares or bars.

Minta McAninch, Raton H. S.
Raton, New Mexico

CHERRY SLICES
Number of Servings — 12
Base:
1 c. flour
½ c. butter
1 T. brown sugar

Mix all above ingredients and pack in shallow pan. Pack up sides. Bake 5 minutes at 400°F.
1 c. brown sugar
¾ c. chopped nuts
½ c. coconut
1 bottle maraschino cherries cut in small pieces

2 eggs
3 T. flour
1 t. baking powder

Mix above ingredients and pour over base, and bake for 25 or 30 minutes at 350°F. Cool. Coat top with powdered sugar icing. Make icing with cherry juice instead of milk. Leave for several days before slicing. This keeps a long time.

Mary Kate Stover, Benjamin H. S.
Benjamin, Texas

CHESS NOELS
Number of Servings — 3½ Dozen
¾ c. butter or margarine
1½ c. sifted flour
3 T. granulated sugar
2¼ c. (1 lb.) dark brown sugar
3 egg yolks, beaten
1 c. chopped pecans
½ t. vanilla
3 egg whites, stiffly beaten
1 c. confectioners' sugar

Cream butter, add flour and granulated sugar gradually. Mix well. Press evenly into 13x9x2 pan. Bake at 350°F. for 15 minutes. Mix brown sugar and egg yolks, add pecans and vanilla. Fold in stiffly beaten egg whites. Spread evenly over baked layer. Bake an additional 25 minutes. Dust with confectioners' sugar and cool. Cut into 40 squares.

Mrs. Cornelia M. Merwin
Lower Dauphin Joint School
Hummelstown, Pennsylvania

COCONUT BARS (Dream Squares or Tea Bars)
Number of Servings — 20 Bars
Bottom Layer:
½ c. butter
½ c. brown sugar
1 c. flour

Mix with a pastry blender to crumbly consistency. Press in bottom of baking pan. Bake 10 minutes at 350-375°F.
Top Layer:
2 eggs
1 c. brown sugar
1 t. vanilla
2 T. flour
½ t. salt
1 t. baking powder
1½ c. shredded coconut
1 c. chopped nuts

Mix eggs, brown sugar, and vanilla. Then mix flour, salt, and baking powder. Sift over coconut and chopped nuts. Add to egg mixture and spread over warm bottom layer. Bake 20 minutes at 375°F. Cool and cut into bars.

This recipe submitted by the following teachers:
Mrs. Earl Austin, Avery H. S.
Avery, Texas
Mrs. Madie Oliver, Centerville School
Groveton, Texas
Mrs. Genevieve Mason, Georgetown Public Schools
Georgetown, Texas

COCONUT-NUT SQUARES
Number of Servings — 20 Cookies

Mix and press into 8x13 pan. Bake 10 minutes at 350-375°F.
½ c. shortening
1 c. flour
½ c. brown sugar

Mix and pour over first mixture after it has baked 10 minutes the following:
1 c. brown sugar
1 t. vanilla
½ t. salt
2-3 T. flour
2 eggs
1 c. nuts
1½ c. coconut

Replace in oven and bake 20 minutes longer at same heat as above. Cut in squares while still warm. (Sprinkle with confectioners' sugar if desired.)

This recipe submitted by the following teachers:
Mrs. Lula Patrick, Monticello H. S.
Monticello, Kentucky
Mrs. Doris Roberts, Custer H. S.
Custer City, Oklahoma

PENUCHE COCONUT BARS
Number of Servings — 3 Dozen 1½" Squares
½ c. butter or Crisco
½ c. brown sugar
1 c. sifted enriched flour
⅛ t. salt
2 T. milk
2 eggs

Blend Crisco and brown sugar. Add flour and the salt. Stir in milk. Pat evenly in lightly greased 9x2 pan. Bake at 325°F. for about 20 minutes, until light brown.

1 c. brown sugar
1 t. vanilla
2 T. enriched flour
½ t. double-acting baking powder
1⅛ c. (1-3½ oz. can) flaked coconut
1 c. chopped pecans

Beat eggs, add brown sugar and vanilla and beat until thick and lemon-colored. Add remaining ingredients and mix well. Spread over baked crust, bake at 325°F. for 20 minutes, until golden brown. Cool and cut into 36 squares.

Ollie Noffsinger, Poca H. S.
Poca, West Virginia

CONGO SQUARES
Number of Servings — 48
¾ c. shortening or oleo
2¼ c. (1 lb.) brown sugar
3 eggs
2¾ c. flour
2½ t. baking powder
½ t. salt
1 c. broken nut meats
1-6 oz. pkg. semi-sweet chocolate morsels

Melt the shortening in a large saucepan. Add brown sugar and mix well. Cool slightly. Add eggs one at a time, beating well after each addi-

tion. Sift together the flour, baking powder and salt. Add the flour mixture to mixture in saucepan. Mix well. Add broken nut meats and chocolate morsels. Pour into 2 greased pans (7½x11x1½). Bake 325°F. to 350°F. for 25-30 minutes. When almost cool, cut into squares.

This recipe submitted by the following teachers:
Mary Ella Ingram, Wagram H. S.
Wagram, North Carolina
Marolyn Howell, Morgan Co. H. S.
Madison, Georgia

CONGO BARS
Number of Servings — 16
¾ c. melted butter
1 lb. brown sugar
2 eggs
2½ c. flour
2½ t. baking powder
1 t. salt
1 t. vanilla
¼ c. milk
12 oz. pkg. chocolate chips

Combine butter and sugar. Beat eggs and add sugar-butter mixture, add flour, baking powder, salt, mix together milk and vanilla. Add to mixture, add chocolate chips. Bake in greased 9x9 pan at 350°F. 30-40 minutes. Cut into squares when cool.

Violett Cheek, Henderson Settlement
Frakes, Kentucky

CRANBERRY JELLY DELIGHTS
Number of Servings — 3 Dozen
1-1 lb. can jellied cranberry sauce
2 pk. orange flavored or red gelatin (flavored)
1 c. granulated sugar
⅔ c. chopped nuts

Beat cranberry sauce until smooth and heat. Dissolve gelatin in hot cranberry sauce. Add sugar and stir over low heat until dissolved. Add nuts. Pour into a greased 9x5x3 loaf pan. Refrigerate until firm. Cut innto 1" squares, roll in granulated sugar. After 24 hours, sugar again.

Mrs. James Potter, Tomah H. S.
Tomah, Wisconsin

DATE BETTY BARS
Number of Servings — 36 Bars
1½ c. sifted all-purpose flour
1 t. baking soda
1 t. salt
½ c. chopped nuts
2½ c. quick rolled oats
½ c. brown sugar
1 c. shortening, melted (heat over water)

Grease 12x8x2 baking dish. Combine first six ingredients. Add melted shortening and mix well. Press half of dough very firmly into dish. Spread with filling below, cover with remainder of dough, pat down well. Bake at 350°F. for 25-30 minutes. Cool in pan. Cut in squares.

Filling:
2-7¼ oz. pkg. pitted dates
½ c. granulated sugar

(Continued on Next Page)

¾ c. light corn syrup
¼ c. orange juice
1 T. grated orange rind
¼ t. salt
Simmer all ingredients, stirring until thick. Cool.

Frances Woolfolk, Palo Verde H. S.
Blythe, California

DREAM BARS

Number of Servings — 24 2" Bars

½ c. shortening
½ c. brown sugar
1 c. flour
½ t. salt

Cream sugar and shortening. Add flour and blend. Spread in 8x12 pan and bake at 350°F. for 15 minutes.

1 c. brown sugar
1 t. vanilla
2 eggs, beaten
2 T. flour
½ t. baking powder
1½ c. shredded coconut
½ c. pecans

Add sugar and vanilla to well beaten eggs. Add flour and baking powder and blend well. Mix in coconut and pecans. Spread on first layer and bake 20 minutes at 300-325°F.

This recipe submitted by the following teachers:
Sister Adrienne Marie, Bishop Forest H. S.
Schulenburg, Texas
Kathryn Brewer, Hermosa Junior H. S.
Farmington, New Mexico
Lynda Rudd, Archer City H. S.
Archer City, Texas

FRUIT CAKE NUGGETS

Number of Servings — 12

6 oz. shelled whole Brazil nuts (1 c.)
½ lb. pitted dates
1 c. English walnut halves
½ lb. red and green candied cherries, mixed
1 slice candied red pineapple, diced
1 slice candied green pineapple, diced
Grease an 8" or 9" square pan. Line with greased brown paper. Cut dates into halves. Distribute nuts and fruits evenly in pan. Press down gently.

¾ c. flour
¼ t. baking powder
¼ t. salt
¾ c. sugar
1 T. butter, melted
2 eggs
1 T. honey
½ c. mashed banana

Sift dry ingredients together. Stir in butter, eggs, banana, and honey. Blend well and pour over fruits and nuts. Cover pan tightly with foil. Bake at 275°F. for 1 hour and 45 minutes. Remove foil after baking one hour. Cool in pan and cut into small squares.

Helen M. Godwin, Northwest H. S.
Greensboro, North Carolina

SOFT GINGER COOKIES

1 c. sugar
⅓ c. shortening
1 egg
½ c. molasses
2 t. soda in 4 T. hot water
1 t. cinnamon
1 t. ginger
1 t. salt
3¼ c. flour
Cream sugar and shortening. Add egg and molasses. Mix well. Sift dry ingredients together and add alternately with soda and hot water. Spread on greased cookie sheet. Bake 15-20 minutes in 350°F. oven. Cool. Frost with a powdered sugar icing. Cut in squares or bars.

Mrs. Kenny Handel, Freeman H. S.
Freeman, South Dakota

GUM DROP COOKIES (Iced)

Number of Servings — 2 Dozen

1 c. gumdrops, cut in small pieces
4 eggs, beaten together
1 T. cold water
2 c. brown sugar
2 c. flour (scant)
1 t. cinnamon
½ t. salt
½ c. pecans
Cut gumdrops, and chop nuts and set aside. Beat eggs, add cold water. Add brown sugar and beat well. Sift dry ingredients together, and beat into sugar and egg mixture. Add gum drops and nuts last, and mix well. Spread in a sheet pan, which has been lined with wax paper. Bake 30 minutes at 322°F. Turn out of pan and remove wax paper while still hot. Cool and spread with orange-butter icing.

Icing:
3 T. orange juice
2-3 T. butter
Enough powdered sugar to thicken
1 t. orange rind

Mrs. J. T. Barnett, Tulia H. S.
Tulia, Texas

ORANGE GUM DROP COOKIES
(With Shortening)

Number of Servings — 3 Dozen

1 c. shortening (1 stick margarine, ½ c. Crisco)
2 c. brown sugar
4 whole eggs
2 c. flour
½ t. baking powder
½ t. salt
1 lb. orange slice candy (cut up)
1 c. pecans (cut up)
Cream shortening, add sugar, mix. Add eggs. Sift together dry ingredients. Combine dry ingredients and add to creamed mixture. Stir in candy and nuts. Bake in lined pan (no shortening) for 45 minutes at 300°F. Take out of oven, cut and roll in powdered sugar. Put in cake box and put top on so they will sweat.

Mrs. Patsy Sawyer, Powell Valley H. S.
Speedwell, Tennessee

ORANGE SLICE COOKIES
(With Shortening)
Number of Servings — 2 Dozen
1 lb. brown sugar
⅔ c. melted butter
2¾ c. flour
3 eggs
2½ t. baking powder
½ t. salt
1½ t. flavoring (vanilla)
1 c. pecans
1 lb. orange slices (candy)

Cut orange slices and nuts in small pieces. Pour melted butter over brown sugar and cream. Add eggs one at a time. Beat after each addition. Sift flour, salt, baking powder together. Add dry ingredients a little at a time. Add vanilla, pecans and orange slices. Bake in 350°F. oven for 35 to 40 minutes. Remove from pan, cool and cut in squares.

Frances Stewart, Frisco H. S.
Frisco, Texas

ORANGE SLICE BARS
(Without Shortening)
Number of Servings — 4 Dozen
1 lb. candy orange slices
2 c. sifted flour
½ t. salt
1 lb. dark brown sugar
3 eggs, slightly beaten
1 c. chopped nuts
1 t. vanilla

Cut orange slices into small pieces. Add flour and salt to orange slices and stir to coat cut edges of candy with flour. Add remaining ingredients and mix well. Spread in 2 greased 9x9x2 pans. Bake at 350°F. for 45 minutes. Cool in pans then cut into bars. Roll in fine granulated sugar if desired. These may be frozen.

Doris Vavra, Muenster Public School
Muenster, Texas

ORANGE SLICE BARS
(Without Shortening)
Number of Servings — 24
1 lb. candy orange slices
2 c. sifted flour
½ t. salt
1 lb. light brown sugar
4 eggs, slightly beaten
1 c. chopped nuts
1 t. vanilla

Cut orange slices with scissors dipped in water, and add to flour and salt in mixing bowl. Toss lightly to coat. Add remaining ingredients and mix well. Spread in greased 13x9x2 pan. Bake at 350°F. for 40-45 minutes. Cut in bars or squares and roll in granulated sugar.

This recipe submitted by the following teachers:
Mrs. June Nesbitt, Springfield H. S.
Springfield, Illinois
Sue Dorman, Earle H. S.
Earle, Arkansas

HALF WAY BARS
Number of Servings — 48
1 c. shortening
½ c. brown sugar
½ c. white sugar
2 egg yolks
1 T. cold water
½ t. soda
2 c. flour
1-6 oz. pkg. chocolate bits
2 egg whites
1 c. brown sugar

Mix first seven ingredients and pat in 13x8 pan. Sprinkle with chocolate bits and push into mixture. Beat egg whites until stiff and add 1 cup brown sugar. Spread over top of mixture. Do not touch sides of pan. Bake at 325°F. until golden brown, about 35 minutes.

Jonda Hallfrisch, Baraga H. S.
Marquette, Michigan

LEMON COCONUT BARS
Number of Servings — 2½ Dozen 3″ x 1″ Bars
½ c. soft shortening (half butter)
½ c. brown sugar (packed)
1 c. sifted flour

Mix shortening and sugar thoroughly. Stir in flour. Press and flatten mixture with hand to cover bottom of ungreased oblong pan, 13x9½x2. Bake 10 minutes at 350°F.

Topping:
1 pkg. lemon fluff frosting mix
1 c. moist shredded coconut (4 oz. can)
1 c. chopped almonds or other nuts

Prepare frosting mix as directed on package. Fold in coconut and almonds. Spread on first layer. Return to oven and bake 25 minutes more until topping is golden brown. Cool slightly. Cut into bars.

Mable Henderson, Tahlequah Senior H. S.
Tahlequah, Oklahoma

LEMON SQUARES
Number of Servings — 36 Squares
Mix in order listed:
¼ c. confectioners' sugar
⅛ t. salt
1 c. flour
½ c. butter or margarine
Bake in an 8″ square cake pan for 15 minutes at 350°F. Remove from oven and spread with the following mixture:
Mix in order listed:
1 c. granulated sugar
½ t. baking powder
⅛ t. salt
2 eggs slightly beaten
2 T. lemon juice and rind
Return to oven and bake 20 minutes longer at 350°F. When the cookie mixture is cold spread with the following glaze:
2 T. lemon juice
¾ c. confectioners' sugar
1 T. butter
These cookies freeze well.

Ruth McRae Carlson
Washington, D. C.

LEMON SQUARES
Number of Servings — 24

1½ c. flour
½ c. brown sugar
1 stick margarine

Mix flour, sugar, and margarine. Pour into 9x13 pan. Bake 10 minutes at 275°F.

Filling:

2 eggs (beaten well)
1 c. brown sugar
1¼ c. coconut
½ c. chopped pecans (optional)
2 T. flour
½ t. baking powder
¼ t. salt
½ t. vanilla

Pour filling over baked pastry. Return to oven and bake an additional 20 minutes at 350°F. Remove from oven and glaze with following while hot.

Glaze:

1 T. melted butter
2 T. lemon juice
1 c. powdered sugar

This recipe submitted by the following teachers:
Clotile Pease, Kasson-Mantorville School
Kasson, Minnesota
Mrs. Josephine B. Lumpkin, Fairfield Jr. H. S.
Richmond, Virginia

DELTA BARS (Meringue Top)
Number of Servings — 48

½ c. butter
1 c. sugar
2 egg yolks
1 c. sifted flour
½ t. baking powder
¼ t. salt
1 t. vanilla

Cream butter and sugar until fluffy. Add egg yolks and beat well. Gradually add sifted flour, baking powder and salt. Add flavoring. Press dough into a 8½x13½x1½ pan. Spread top with meringue made of egg whites, brown sugar and nuts. Bake at 325°F. for 30-35 minutes. Cool in pan and cut in squares.

Topping:

2 egg whites, stiffly beaten
½ c. brown sugar
1 c. chopped pecans

Bessie Boyd, Huntsville Senior H. S.
Huntsville, Texas

MERINGUE TOP COOKIES
Number of Servings — 18

½ c. margarine
½ c. granulated sugar
½ c. light brown sugar
2 egg yolks
1 T. water
1 t. vanilla
2 c. sifted flour
1 t. baking powder
½ t. salt

¼ t. soda
1-6 oz. pkg. chocolate bits

Cream margarine and sugars, add egg yolks, water, and vanilla. Beat. Add dry ingredients which have been sifted together. Mix. (Dough is very stiff.) Spread and press dough into the bottom of a greased 10x12 cake pan. Sprinkle chocolate bits on top and lightly press into the dough, saving a few bits for the top of meringue.

Meringue:

1 c. brown sugar
2 egg whites

Beat the egg whites until stiff. Fold in the brown sugar. Spread lightly over top of dough and chocolate bits. Sprinkle remaining chocolate bits over top of meringue. Bake 30 minutes at 350°F. Cool 5 minutes. Cut into squares. Cool 30 minutes before removing squares from pan.

Mrs. Ruth Peirce, Hutchinson Senior H. S.
Hutchinson, Kansas

PECAN DELIGHTS
Number of Servings — 30

½ c. margarine
1 c. granulated sugar
2 eggs
½ t. salt
1½ c. pastry or cake flour
1 t. baking powder
½ t. vanilla extract

Cream margarine and sugar until light and fluffy. Add beaten eggs and sifted dry ingredients. Add vanilla and mix ingredients well. Spread the batter onto a baking sheet, spreading as thinly as possible.

Frosting:

1 c. brown sugar
1 c. pecans, chopped
1 egg white, stiffly beaten

Remove lumps from brown sugar. Fold sugar into egg white. Spread onto the cookie batter. Sprinkle with nuts. Bake in a moderate oven 325°F. for 30 minutes. Cut in squares.

Mary Free
Assistant State Supv.—Home Economics Education
Carrollton, Georgia

PECAN SQUARES
Number of Servings — 16 Squares

2 eggs
1 c. brown sugar
½ c. all-purpose flour
¼ t. baking powder
¼ t. salt
1 t. vanilla
1 c. pecans, chopped

Beat eggs until thick. Add sugar and beat thoroughly. Stir in flour which has been sifted with baking powder and salt. Add vanilla and chopped nuts and stir until well mixed. Bake in an 8" square pan which is lined with paper and greased in oven at 350°F. for 25-30 minutes.

Mrs. Margaret Q. Snelgrove, Baron DeKalb School
Westville, South Carolina

PETITS FOURS
Number of Servings — 25
¼ c. butter
¼ c. shortening
1 c. sugar
½ t. vanilla extract
¼ t. almond extract
2 c. cake flour
¼ t. salt
3 t. baking powder
¾ c. milk
¾ c. egg white, beaten
¼ c. sugar

Cream shortening and 1 cup sugar, add extracts, sifted dry ingredients alternately with milk. Beat until smooth. Beat egg whites to stiff froth. Add remaining ¼ cup sugar. Beat until mixture forms peaks. Fold into batter. Bake in wax paper lined 9x12 pan in moderate oven 350°F. for 40 minutes. Cut in squares, ovals, and triangles. Use confectioners' frosting.

Charlsie Biggs, McAdory H. S.
McCalla, Alabama

PRALINE COOKIES
Number of Servings — 3 Dozen
2 eggs
2 c. brown sugar (1 pkg.)
1 c. (2 sticks) melted butter
1½ c. all-purpose flour
1 t. vanilla
1 c. pecans

Beat eggs well. Add sugar and blend. Add melted butter. Blend. Add flour gradually. Add vanilla and pecans last. Blend. Pour into 8x11 baking tin and bake at 350°F. for 35-40 minutes. Cut in squares.

Mrs. Lola Weaver, Gaston Independent
Joinerville, Texas

RAISIN MUMBLES
Number of Servings — 6 Dozen
2½ c. raisins
½ c. sugar
2 T. cornstarch
¾ c. water
3 T. lemon juice

Cook raisins, sugar, cornstarch, water, and lemon juice together stirring constantly over low heat until thick. Cool.

Crumb Mixture:
¾ c. soft butter
1 c. brown sugar
1¾ c. sifted flour
½ t. salt
½ t. soda
1½ c. rolled oats

Cream butter and brown sugar. Add dry ingredients, then oats. Press half of mixture into 13x9 pan. Spread with the cool filling. Pat on remaining crumbs. Smooth with back of spoon. Bake at 400°F. for 20 to 30 minutes. Cool before cutting otherwise the cookies fall into pieces.

Patricia Roppel, Ketchikan H. S.
Ketchikan, Alaska

PRINCESS SLICES
Number of Servings — 10
2 c. flour, sifted
2 c. sugar
1 t. salt
1 c. butter
1 egg, beaten
1 c. chopped nuts
1 t. vanilla
½ t. maple flavoring
2 c. grated coconut
Fig jam

Mix the flour, sugar, and salt. Cut in butter and add egg. Add nuts, vanilla, maple flavoring and coconut. Divide mixture in half. Spread half on bottom of square pan. Cover with fig jam. Then spread other half of mixture. Bake in moderate oven, 350°F. Cut in squares.

Mrs. John A. Flynt, New Hebron H. S.
New Hebron, Mississippi

RAISIN SQUARES (Quantity Recipe)
Number of Servings — 50
2½ c. dough fat
4 c. brown sugar
2 t. vanilla
6 c. flour
4 t. soda
1½ t. salt
7 c. rolled wheat (oatmeal, uncooked)

Cream the sugar and fat. Add vanilla. Sift soda, flour, and salt together. Add rolled wheat to flour mixture. Mix flour with sugar and fat. (This makes a crumbly mixture and not a dough.) Sprinkle half of mixture in the bottom of greased large pan. Cover with the filling, spread the other half of the mixture on top. Bake 400°F. for 10 minutes, 350°F. for 20 minutes. Cut in 2½" squares. Serve as cookie or with whipped cream.

Filling:
1 qt. raisins
1 lemon
2 t. cinnamon
2 c. sugar
½ c. flour
2 c. water

Mix sugar, flour, cinnamon, raisins, water, and fruit juice. Simmer until thick, stirring to prevent burning.

Mrs. Mary Geer, Hartman H. S.
Hartman, Arkansas

RASPBERRY JAM COOKIES
Number of Servings — 16 Cookies
½ c. butter or 1 stick margarine
¼ c. sugar
2 eggs, separated
1½ c. flour
½ t. salt

Cream margarine or butter with sugar. Add egg yolks. Add flour in which salt has been sifted. Spread in greased square (8x8x2) pan. Spread with layer of raspberry jam.

Topping:
2 egg whites

(Continued on Next Page)

½ c. sugar
1 t. vanilla
¼ c. nuts

In separate bowl, beat egg whites until stiff. Add sugar and vanilla. Spread on top of jam with nuts sprinkled over the top. Bake 30 minutes at 350°F. Cut in squares when cool.

Mrs. Ruth Aurin Jennings, Eufaula H. S.
Eufaula, Alabama

SCOTCH BARS
Number of Servings — 2½ Dozen
⅓ c. shortening
1 c. brown sugar
1 t. vanilla
1 egg
1 c. flour, sifted
½ t. baking powder
⅛ t. baking soda
½ t. salt
½ c. chopped nuts
1 pkg. chocolate bits

Cream fat, sugar, and vanilla. Blend in egg. Add sifted dry ingredients gradually with nuts in last addition. Spread or press into greased cake pan. Sprinkle with chocolate bits. Bake at 350°F. for 20-25 minutes. Cool and cut into bars.

Frances Sellers, Roosevelt-Wilson H. S.
Clarksburg, West Virginia

SUGAR GEMS
Number of Servings — 15 to 20
¾ c. butter
3 T. sugar
1½ c. all-purpose flour
3 egg yolks (beaten)
2¼ c. light brown sugar
1 c. chopped pecans
¾ c. shredded coconut
3 egg whites (beaten)

Cream butter, add sugar, beat well, then blend thoroughly with flour. Put mixture in 12x12 pan (or 12x15 pan), patting smoothly into pan, which has been oiled. Bake at 375°F. for 15 minutes. Cool. Add brown sugar to the beaten egg yolks and blend well. Add chopped nuts and coconut. Fold in beaten egg whites, pour over baked mixture, return to oven for 30 minutes. Dust with powdered sugar. Cut into 1½" squares.

Evelyn Wilson, Waurika H. S.
Waurika, Oklahoma

THREE LAYER COOKIES
First Layer:
1 c. flour
½ c. butter
Pack together into 8x9 pan. Bake at 350°F. until light brown. Cool.
Second Layer:
2 beaten eggs
1½ c. brown sugar
½ c. coconut
1 c. pecans, chopped
1 t. vanilla
2 T. flour

¼ t. baking powder
½ t. salt
Combine the above ingredients. Spread second layer on the first layer and bake at 350°F. for 25 minutes. Cool and add the following topping:
1 c. powdered sugar
2 T. butter
3 T. orange juice
½ c. chopped walnuts

Gladys Anderson, Mandan Senior H. S.
Mandan, North Dakota

TOFFEE BARS
½ c. soft shortening
½ c. brown sugar
1 c. sifted flour
Mix thoroughly and press in ungreased pan (13x9). Bake about 10 minutes at 350°F.
2 eggs
1 c. brown sugar
1 t. vanilla
2 T. flour
1 t. baking powder
½ t. salt
1 c. moist coconut and/or 1 c. almonds or nuts
Beat eggs well and stir in brown sugar and vanilla. Mix in flour, baking powder, and salt. Stir in coconut and nuts. Spread on first mixture. Return to oven and bake 25 minutes until topping is golden. Cool slightly and cut into bars.

Mrs. Betty Romans, Forsan H. S.
Forsan, Texas

TOFFEE BUTTER COOKIES
Number of Servings — 70 to 80 Cookies
1 c. butter
1 c. sugar (brown)
1 egg
1 t. vanilla
2 c. flour
8-5¢ plain milk chocolate bars or ½ lb. sweet chocolate (melted)
¼ c. chopped nuts
Cream butter and sugar. Beat well, add egg. Beat until light and fluffy, add vanilla. Add flour and blend thoroughly. Spread on 11x17 jelly roll pan. Bake at 350°F. for 15 or 20 minutes. Place 8 bars on top of hot cake or spread melted chocolate. Spread and sprinkle with chopped nuts.
This recipe submitted by the following teachers:
Mrs. R. O. Traugott, Riverview H. S.
Sarasota, Florida
Carol Steele, Powers-Spalding H. S.
Powers, Michigan
Ruth Haislip, Ridgefield Park H. S.
Ridgefield Park, New Jersey
Dorothy L. O'Malley, No. Arlington H. S.
No. Arlington, New Jersey
Inez Waechter, Anna-Jonesboro Comm. H. S.
Anna, Illinois

TOFFEE TREAT DESSERT
Number of Servings — 12
2 c. sifted all-purpose flour
¼ t. salt
2 c. light brown sugar

(Continued on Next Page)

⅓ c. butter or margarine
1 egg, slightly beaten
1½ t. vanilla
1 c. milk
1 t. soda
6 small toffee candy bars (such as Heath bars) chilled
½ c. pecans, chopped
1 qt. vanilla ice cream

Combine flour, salt, and brown sugar, cut in butter or margarine to fine crumbs. Remove 1 cup of the crumbs. Combine egg, vanilla, milk, and soda. Stir into crumb mixture. Pour into greased 8x12 or 9x13 pan. Shave chilled candy bars with knife, or crush. (There will be 1 cup.) Sprinkle batter with reserved cup of crumbs, then nuts and lastly toffee candy bar crumbs. Bake at 350°F., 25-30 minutes. Cut in squares and top with vanilla ice cream.

Mrs. Hallie Christensen, Truman H. S.
Truman, Minnesota

BON BONS
Number of Servings — 2 to 3 Dozen

2 lb. powdered sugar
¼ lb. butter
¼ t. almond or vanilla
Dash of salt
1 lge. pkg. angel coconut
1 can Eagle Brand sweetened milk
Cherries or nuts (optional)

Combine powdered sugar, butter, vanilla, salt, coconut, and sweetened milk. Roll into a ball formation with cherry or nut inside.

Topping:
1 lge. pkg. chocolate chips
⅔ bar paraffin wax

Melt chocolate chips and paraffin over hot water. Dip balls into chocolate-paraffin mixture. Refrigerate 2 hours.

Erna Ziegler, Amboy H. S.
Amboy, Minnesota

CHOCOLATE NO BAKE COOKIES
Number of Servings — 4 Dozen

2 c. granulated sugar
½ c. margarine
2 sq. unsweetened chocolate or 5 T. cocoa
3 c. oatmeal
1 c. coconut
½ t. vanilla

Bring to a boil the sugar, margarine, and chocolate. Pour liquid mixture over dry ingredients, mix and drop from spoon, on buttered cookie sheet. Chill, preferably overnight.

This recipe submitted by the following teachers:
Mrs. Joyce Rapes, Sebewaing H. S.
Sebewaing, Michigan
Mrs. Pat Thompson, Fabens H. S.
Fabens, Texas

FUDGE COOKIES
Number of Servings — 20

2 c. sugar
½ c. cocoa

½ c. milk
1 stick oleo
½ c. crunchy peanut butter
3 c. quick-cook oats

Combine in large saucepan the sugar, cocoa, milk, and oleo. Bring to a boil and boil 1 minute. Stir in the peanut butter and oats. Put out in patties on wax paper.

Maude Haynes, Lawhon School
Tupelo, Mississippi

CHOCOLATE FUDGE COOKIES (Boiled)
Number of Servings — 24 to 30

2 c. sugar
½ c. milk
1 stick butter or oleo
3-4 T. cocoa
½ c. peanut butter
2½-3 c. quick-cooking oatmeal
1-2 t. vanilla
½-1 c. chopped nuts

Boil sugar, milk, oleo, and cocoa for 1 to 1½ minutes (start timing after the mixture reaches a full rolling boil). Remove from heat, add peanut butter, oatmeal, vanilla, and nuts. Beat until blended, then drop on wax paper (by teaspoonfuls). Coconut, or dates may be added if desired.

This recipe submitted by the following teachers:
Mrs. Jacqueline T. Thurmon, Castor H. S.
Castor, Louisiana

Mrs. Patricia Reed, Guilford School
Guilford College, North Carolina

Faye Quinley, Corsicana H. S.
Corsicana, Texas

Janice Bell, McKenzie H. S.
McKenzie, Tennessee

Mrs. Cledith Murphrey, Floyd H. S.
Floyd, New Mexico

Janet Hopf, Hamilton Jr. H. S.
Pittsburgh, Pennsylvania

Lillian Thompson, Kansas H. S.
Kansas, Oklahoma

FUDGE COOKIES
Number of Servings — 3 Dozen

2 c. sugar
½ c. milk
½ c. cocoa
½ c. butter or margarine
1 t. vanilla
3 c. minute cooking oatmeal
1 c. chopped pecans
1 c. confectioners' sugar

Bring the sugar, milk, cocoa, butter, and vanilla to a rolling boil in a heavy saucepan and boil for 1 minute. Pour hot mixture over the oatmeal and chopped nuts and stir until well mixed. Drop from teaspoonfuls into sifted powdered sugar and roll while still hot. Place on wax paper until cookies harden.

Mrs. Willie Jean B. Johnson,
Randolph-Henry H. S.
Charlotte Court House, Virginia

MINNIE PEARL

Number of Servings — 6

½ lb. butter
1 lb. confectioners' sugar
2 c. graham crackers
2 c. almonds (roasted and ground)
2 c. coconut
4 t. almond extract
4 t. vanilla
Pink coloring

Cream butter, add sugar and mix well. Add crackers, almonds, coconut, almond extract, vanilla, and coloring to the butter mixture. Mix well. Spread into a greased baking pan and place in the refrigerator. When firm, cut into squares and serve with ice cream.

Mrs. Reba Wilson, Brainerd H. S.
Chattanooga, Tennessee

NO-BAKE PEANUT BUTTER COOKIES

Number of Servings — 20

1 c. white corn syrup
1 c. granulated sugar
1 (12 oz.) jar peanut butter
4½ c. corn flakes
1 can flaked coconut

Combine sugar and corn syrup. Bring to boil. Remove from heat and stir in peanut butter. Pour this mixture over the corn flakes and coconut. Mix well. Drop by teaspoon on wax paper.

Mrs. Ava Bush, Latexo Independent School
Latexo, Texas

PEANUT BUTTER COOKIES

Number of Servings — 60

1¼ c. corn syrup, light or dark
1¼ c. sugar, granulated or brown
1-12 oz. jar of crunchy peanut butter
1 t. vanilla
5 c. Special K cereal
Butter to oil fingers

Heat syrup and sugar until sugar dissolves. Remove from burner. Add the peanut butter stirring well. Then add vanilla. Pour over Special K that has been measured into a large bowl. Stir well to mix evenly. Oil fingers in butter to prevent sticking. Roll into small balls. Place on wax paper.

Mallie Venn Steger, Montgomery H. S.
Montgomery, Texas

SKILLET COOKIES

Number of Servings — 58 Balls

¼ c. butter
1 c. sugar
2 eggs
1 lb. dates (ground or chopped)
1 t. vanilla
½-1 c. chopped nuts
3 c. cereal, such as Rice Krispies

Cook the butter, sugar, eggs, and dates in an iron skillet or heavy saucepan about 20 minutes or long enough to cook the eggs. Add vanilla, nuts, and cereal. Stir until all ingredients are well mixed. Form into balls about the size of a walnut, then roll the balls in coconut or ground pecans.

This recipe submitted by the following teachers:
Mrs. Viola Johnson, Karnes City H. S.
Karnes City, Texas
Mrs. Lillian Sandlin, Pawhuska H. S.
Pawhuska, Oklahoma

SKILLET COOKIES

1 stick of butter (melted)
1 egg (well beaten)
1 c. sugar
1 c. dates (cut fine)
2-2¾ c. cereal, such as Rice Crispies
¾-1 c. pecans
1 t. vanilla
1 box coconut (small)

Melt butter, add beaten egg, sugar, and dates that have been cut fine. Cook in skillet at 300°F. for 6 minutes, stirring constantly. Remove from stove. Add cereal, nuts and vanilla. Form into balls, and roll in coconut.

This recipe submitted by the following teachers:
Mrs. A. D. Wilder, Contentnea H. S.
Kinston, North Carolina
Mrs. Melba Love, Borden H. S.
Gail, Texas

SKILLET COOKIES (Angel Cookies)

Number of Servings — 5 Dozen

2 eggs, beaten
¾ c. sugar (granulated)
1 stick oleo
1 pkg. dates, chopped
⅛ t. salt (if desired)
1 t. vanilla
2 c. cereal, such as Rice Krispies
1 c. nuts

Coconut, nuts or powdered sugar to roll in

Beat eggs, add sugar and beat well. Melt oleo in saucepan or skillet, pour in egg mixture, and chopped dates. Stir and cook until mixture thickens and turns dark brown (3-5 minutes after mixture boils). Add vanilla. Remove from heat, add Rice Krispies and nuts. Cool slightly. Make into small balls, or into long rolls like refrigerator cookies. Roll in coconut, nuts, or powdered sugar. Put in the refrigerator to harden. These keep indefinitely in the long rolls, and can be sliced as needed.

This recipe submitted by the following teachers:
Mrs. Mary Ray White, Troup H. S.
Troup, Texas
Martha Wilson, Concord H. S.
Concord, Arkansas
Mrs. Annetta Bailey, Agua Dulce H. S.
Agua Dulce, Texas
Gayle Dunn, Henryetta H. S.
Henryetta, Oklahoma

Dessert Breads

APRICOT NUT BREAD
Number of Servings — 15-18 Slices
2¼ c. biscuit mix
1 c. uncooked rolled oats
¾ c. granulated sugar
¼ t. salt
1 t. double acting baking powder
¾ c. snipped dried apricots
1 c. broken walnuts
1 egg
1¼ c. milk

Set oven at 350°F. Grease generously a 9x5x3 loaf pan, flour pan. Combine in a large bowl, biscuit mix, rolled oats, granualed sugar, salt, baking powder, then stir in nuts and apricots. Beat egg well and add milk, add milk and egg mixture to dry mixture, beat hard for 30 seconds. Turn batter into prepared pan and bake for 1 hour or until it comes from sides. Cool 10 minutes, then turn from pan, cool on rack (mellows overnight).

Carole A. Petersen, Cando H. S.
Cando, North Dakota

BANANA BREAD
Number of Servings — 10
½ c. cooking oil (such as Mazola)
1 c. sugar
3 bananas (crushed)
3 eggs (well beaten)
2 T. buttermilk
2 c. flour
1 t. soda
⅛ t. salt
1 c. chopped nuts

Preheat oven 350°F. Sift together dry ingredients. Cream shortening and sugar. Add eggs and bananas, blend well. Add buttermilk and flour alternately. Blend well. Add chopped nuts. Bake 1 hour in medium loaf pan that has been oiled.

Myrtle Brookshire, Johnson Co. H. S.
Mountain City, Tennessee

BANANA CHERRY NUT BREAD
Number of Servings — 12
1 stick margarine
1 c. sugar
3 eggs
2 c. flour
3-4 mashed ripe bananas
1 c. raisins
⅓ c. maraschino cherries
1 t. salt
½ t. soda
½ c. pecans
1 t. vanilla

Cream butter or margarine until fluffy, add sugar and beat well, add eggs, 1 at a time, beating after each addition. Add bananas, beating well, dredge raisins and nuts in 1 cup flour. Add salt and soda to the other cup of flour, add this to butter mixture, then add raisins, nuts, cherries and other flour to mixture. Pour into loaf pan lined with wax paper. Bake at 325°F. until straw emerges clean.

Joye Weaver, Leonard H. S.
Leonard, Texas

BANANA NUT BREAD
Number of Servings — 15-20
2 c. sifted flour
1 t. soda
¼-½ t. salt
½ c. butter or margarine (1 stick)
1 c. sugar
2 eggs
1 t. vanilla
3 large or 4 small mashed bananas
1 c. ground or chopped nuts (may be omitted)

Measure and sift together flour, soda, and salt, cream margarine, add sugar. Cream butter and sugar together, add eggs and vanilla and stir until thoroughly mixed, stir in mashed bananas. Fold in dry ingredients and nuts, place in a well-greased 9x5x3 loaf pan or 8" square cake pan. Bake at 325°F.-350°F. for 55-60 minutes.

This recipe submitted by the following teachers:
Lucy Jo Walker, Tascosa H. S.
Amarillo, Texas
Mrs. Mary Jo Lyle, Putnam Co. H. S.
Eatonton, Georgia
Mrs. Nancy Burke, Ritzville H. S.
Ritzville, Washington

BANANA NUT LOAF
Number of Servings — 20
3 c. sugar
1 c. shortening
4 eggs
2 t. vanilla
1½ c. buttermilk
2 t. soda
4 c. sifted flour
3 mashed bananas
1 c. chopped nuts

Cream sugar and shortening, add eggs one at a time, mix well, add vanilla, combine soda and buttermilk, add flour and buttermilk alternately, beginning and ending with flour, add bananas and nuts. Bake in a well greased and floured tube pan or two 8" loaf pans at 300°F. for 2 hours.

Mrs. Carl K. Park, Dayton H. S.
Dayton, Texas

BISHOP'S BREAD
Number of Servings — 15
1 c. sugar
3 eggs
4 T. baking powder
1½ t. salt
1 c. chopped dates
1 c. maraschino cherries
2 c. nuts
1½ c. flour
¼ c. cherry juice
1 pkg. chocolate bits

Mix as for any loaf cake, using the cherry juice instead of milk. If the mixture seems to be too soft, add more flour, add chopped dates, cherries, nuts and chocolate bits last. Bake in a loaf or tube cake pan in a medium oven.

Mrs. Mildred Drinkard, West Lauderdale H. S.
Collinsville, Mississippi

"DOWN EAST" CRANBERRY RING
Number of Servings — 12

3 T. butter or margarine
2 c. fresh cranberries
1 c. granulated sugar
3 c. sifted cake flour
3 t. double acting baking powder
½ t. salt
½ c. shortening
1 c. granulated sugar
2 eggs
1 t. vanilla extract
1 c. milk

Grease sides of 3-quart ring mold, place butter in it and put in oven to melt butter. Wash cranberries, mix with 1 cup sugar, sift together flour, baking powder and salt. In large bowl, cream shortening with sugar, eggs, and vanilla, until very light and fluffy. Blend in alternately (just until mixed) flour mixture and milk. Remove ring mold from oven, sprinkle cranberries over butter, arrange evenly in mold. Pour batter over cranberries. Bake 45-50 minutes or until done. Invert cake in mold onto large round plate, let stand 1 minute, then lift off mold. Serve cake warm with hard sauce sprinkled with nutmeg.

Maurine Sullivan Frederick, Copperas Cove H. S.
Copperas Cove, Texas

DATE NUT BREAD
Number of Servings — 12

1 pkg. dates (2 c.)
1 c. boiling water
1 egg
1 c. sugar
1¾ c. flour
1 t. soda
⅛ t. salt
1 t. vanilla
1 c. nuts

Cut up dates, pour 1 cup boiling water over and soak. Beat egg and sugar until creamy, add dry ingredients, nuts and dates. Bake in loaf pan 55 minutes in 350°F. oven.

Madge M. Shaw, Borger H. S.
Borger, Texas

DESSERT BREAD
Number of Servings — 18

4 eggs
1 box light brown sugar
1 c. plain flour
1 c. self-rising flour
2 t. vanilla
1 c. nuts

Beat eggs, add sugar and cook in double boiler for 15 minutes. Let cool. Add flour, vanilla, and nuts. Pour in well greased pan. Bake in 275°F. for approximately 45 minutes. Cut in squares and remove from pan. Leave out nuts and may be used in a low fat diet.

Alice W. Keler, Cerro Gordo H. S.
Cerro Gordo, North Carolina

FRUIT BREAD
Number of Servings — 40

1 c. butter
2 c. sugar (white)
4 eggs
3½ c. flour
1 t. soda
1 c. buttermilk
6¼ oz. dates
1 c. chopped nuts
1 c. coconut
2 T. grated orange peel
½ t. salt

Cream butter and sugar, add eggs, beat well, dissolve soda in buttermilk. Add alternately with sifted flour to egg mixture. Fold in fruit and nut mixture. Bake in 2 loaf pans (paper lined) size, angel bar about 4x12 at 350°F. for 1 hour. Remove from pan, pour syrup over cake, punching holes to allow syrup to go into cake.
Syrup: Prepared by mixing 2 cups powdered sugar, 1 cup orange juice and 2 tablespoons orange juice, heat to boiling.

Mrs. Mary S. Dean, Rowlesburg H. S.
Rowlesburg, West Virginia

GINGERBREAD
Number of Servings — 10

½ c. butter and lard mixed
½ c. sugar
1 egg, beaten
1 c. molasses
2½ c. flour
1½ t. soda
1 t. cinnamon
1 t. ginger
½ t. cloves
½ t. salt
1 c. hot water

Cream together butter and lard mixed with sugar. Add egg beaten and molasses. Sift together flour, soda, cinnamon, ginger, cloves, salt, and add to first mixture. Add hot water and beat until smooth. The batter is soft, but it makes a fine cake. Bake in greased shallow pan 35 minutes at 325°F. to 350°F.

Mrs. Margaret R. Huckabee, Istrouma Jr. H. S.
Baton Rouge, Louisiana

SOUTHERN SPICY GINGERBREAD
Number of Servings — 16

2 eggs
¾ c. brown sugar
¾ c. cane syrup or molasses
¾ c. melted shortening
2½ c. flour
2 t. soda
2 t. ginger
1½ t. cinnamon
½ t. powdered cloves
½ t. allspice
½ t. baking powder
1 c. boiling water

Add beaten egg to the sugar, syrup, and melted shortening, add the dry ingredients which have

(Continued on Next Page)

been mixed and sifted, add the hot water last.
Bake in small individual pans or in 2 8x8x2 pans
at 350°F. 30-40 minutes or until done. May be
topped with whipped cream.

Mrs. Beulah K. Sanders, Goldonna H. S.
Natchitoches, Louisiana

GINGERBREAD
Number of Servings — 20
1 c. shortening
1½ c. brown sugar
2 eggs
1 c. molasses
3½ c. flour
1 T. ginger
2 t. cinnamon
2 t. nutmeg
1 c. hot water
1 t. soda

Cream shortening, add sugar and cream again.
Add eggs and beat well. Stir in the molasses, add
dry ingredients alternately with hot water in
which soda has been dissolved. Bake at 350°F.
in a 9x12 pan. Remove from pan, cool, cut in
squares, serve with whipped cream.

Odessa Smith, Foreman H. S.
Foreman, Arkansas

GINGERBREAD
Number of Servings — 20
½ c. butter
½ c. sugar
2 eggs, well beaten
½ c. country syrup
1 t. soda, dissolved in syrup
1½ c. flour
1 t. ginger and cinnamon
¼ t. cloves, allspice, and salt
½ c. water

Cream butter and sugar. Add eggs, syrup, and
soda, then sift dry ingredients together. Bake at
325-350°F.

Mrs. Ann S. Keith, Carbon Hill H. S.
Carbon Hill, Alabama

ORANGE NUT BREAD
Number of Servings — 1 Loaf
1 orange
1 c. raisins
1 egg, beaten
2 T. melted butter
2 c. flour
½ c. sugar
1 t. baking powder
½ t. soda
¼ t. salt
½ c. chopped nuts

Put juice of orange into cup, filling remainder of
cup with hot water if necessary. Grind orange
rind with raisins. Pour juice over ground mixture,
add egg and butter. Sift flour, sugar, baking
powder, soda, and salt, add to first mixture until
blended, add nuts. Pour into greased pan 8x5x3½.
Bake at 350°F. for 1 hour.

Sandra M. Cuchna, La Farge H. S.
La Farge, Wisconsin

CHRISTMAS ORANGE BREAD
Number of Servings — 40
½ c. shortening
¾ c. granulated sugar
3 eggs
½ c. mashed bananas
½ c. orange juice
2½ c. sifted flour
4 t. baking powder
¾ t. salt
1½ c. mixed candied fruit
¼ c. raisins
¾ c. chopped nuts

Cream shortening, add sugar and beat until light
and fluffy, add eggs, 1 at a time, beating well
after each addition. Combine banana and orange
juice, add to creamed mixture alternately with
sifted dry ingredients mixed with fruits and nuts.
Pack into greased and wax paper loaf pan
9x5x3. Bake at 350°F. 1 hour or until done. Cool
about 20 minutes before turning out on rack.

Mrs. Mozelle B. Batchelor, Coopers H. S.
Nashville, North Carolina

CANDIED ORANGE PEEL BREAD
Peel of 6 medium oranges
3 c. sugar
½ c. water
⅞ c. butter
2 eggs
4 c. flour
3 t. baking powder
1 t. salt
1 c. milk

Cut into thin strips with kitchen shears the peel
of 6 medium oranges, cook until tender, drain.
Add 2 cups sugar and ½ cup water and cook
until syrup is almost gone, cool. Cream butter,
add 1 cup sugar and cream well, add well-beaten
eggs, mix well. Combine flour, baking powder,
and salt, add flour mixture alternating with milk
to creamed mixture. Stir cooled orange peel into
mixture, pour into 2 small wax paper lined loaf
pans, let stand for 20 minutes. Bake for 1 hour at
350°F.

Kathy Katri, Linden H. S.
Linden, California

FROSTED PINEAPPLE SQUARES
Number of Servings — 3 Dozen
½ c. sugar
3 T. cornstarch
¼ t. salt
1 egg yolk, lightly beaten
1 can (1 lb., 14 oz.) pineapple chunks, undrained
⅔ c. milk
1 t. sugar
1 pkg. active dry yeast
¼ c. very warm water
4 egg yolks, lightly beaten
4 c. sifted flour
1 c. margarine

Mix ½ cup sugar, cornstarch, and salt in saucepan.
Stir in egg yolk and pineapple chunks, cook over

(Continued on Next Page)

medium heat, stirring constantly, until thick and smooth, about 7 minutes. Cool to lukewarm while preparing dough. Scald milk, add 1 teaspoon sugar, cool to lukewarm. Dissolve yeast in very warm water, add to milk mixture. Stir in beaten egg yolks. Measure flour into large bowl, cut margarine into flour, using pastry blender or 2 knives, until mixture resembles coarse meal. Stir in yeast and milk mixture, blend thoroughly. Dough will be soft and moist. Divide dough in half. Roll ½ out on floured board to fit bottom of a jelly roll pan and overlap edges, about 16x10. Spread with cooled pineapple filling. Roll remaining dough large enough to cover filling, seal edges. Snip top of dough with scissors to let steam escape, cover, let rise in warm place, free from draft, until doubled in bulk, about 1 hour. Bake at 375°F. 35-40 minutes. Frost with confectioners' sugar icing. Serve warm.

Mrs. Lucille Bradbury, San Angelo Central H. S.
San Angelo, Texas

PUMPKIN DESSERT BREAD
Number of Servings — 12-18

3 c. all-purpose flour
1 t. soda
1 t. salt
3 t. cinnamon
2 c. sugar
2 c. pumpkin
4 eggs, beaten
1¼ c. Mazola oil or melted shortening
½ c. nut meats

Place all the dry ingredients in a large mixing bowl, with spoon, make a deep well in center. In this well, add all the other ingredients, stir carefully, just enough to dampen all the dry ingredients. Pour into loaf pans, makes 2. Bake at 350°F. for 1 hour. Delicious served with spiced tea.

Mrs. Joseph Didot, Hartford Center H. S.
Geneva, Indiana

COFFEE CAKE
Number of Servings — 12-15

3 c. flour (all-purpose)
2 c. sugar
¾ c. shortening
½ t. nutmeg, cinnamon, cloves
2 c. buttermilk
2 t. soda
1 c. raisins (boiled, drained)
¼ c. chopped pecans

Mix flour, sugar, shortening, and spices until like coarse meal. Set aside ⅓ cup for topping. Add buttermilk and soda to first mixture. Add raisins. Add nuts to topping. Grease 9x12 pan, add raisin mixture, add nut topping. Bake at 350°F. for 45 minutes. Serve hot with butter, or cold with whipped cream to which has been added apple-butter.

Hope Atkinson McCuskey, Titusville H. S.
Titusville, Florida

COFFEECAKE

⅜ c. butter
2¼ c. flour
¾ t. soda
1½ c. brown sugar
¾ c. sour milk
1 egg

Cream butter and sugar and add flour (save ½ cup of this crumb mixture for topping). Dissolve soda in sour milk and add with egg to first mixture. Pour in square shallow pan 8x8, put crumbs on top. Bake at 350°F. for approximately 40 minutes.

Mrs. Virginia Frost, Bohemia Manor H. S.
Chesapeake City, Maryland

COFFEE CAKE
Number of Servings — 16

1 stick oleo
1 c. sugar
2 eggs
1 t. vanilla
1 c. sour cream
2 c. sifted flour
1 t. soda
½ t. salt
1 t. baking powder
Sugar Mixture:
¼ c. white sugar
1 t. cinnamon
¼ c. brown sugar
½ c. black walnuts

Cream together the oleo, sugar, eggs, vanilla and sour cream. Add flour, soda, salt, and baking powder. Pour one-half batter into greased angel food cake pan. Sprinkle half sugar mixture over batter. Add remaining batter and sugar mixture on top. Bake at 350°F. for 40 to 50 minutes. Let cool in pan.

Glenda Wiggins, Greenville H. S.
Greenville, Alabama

BLUEBERRY CAKE
Number of Servings — 8-10

1 c. brown sugar
½ c. shortening
2 eggs
¼ c. milk
1½ c. flour
2 t. baking powder
¼ t. nutmeg
½ t. cinnamon
2 c. wild huckleberries or cultivated blueberries
   (sprinkled with flour)

Wash and drain berries, cream together sugar and shortening, separate eggs, beat whites and set aside. Beat yolks and add milk, stir yolks and milk into creamed mixture. Sift dry ingredients together and add to the batter. Fold in beaten egg whites. Last, gently fold in the blueberries which have been sprinkled with flour. Place in a flat pan 13x9x2 and sprinkle with granulated sugar. Bake at 375°F. for 35 minutes. May be served as is, warm or cold, or with ice cream or whipped cream topping.

Mrs. Marcia Miller, Petoskey H. S.
Petoskey, Michigan

BLUEBERRY COFFEE CAKE

Number of Servings — 9

¾ c. sugar
¼ c. shortening
1 egg
1 t. vanilla
¾ c. milk
1¾ c. flour
3 T. baking powder
½ t. salt
1½ c. blueberries (drained)

Cream sugar, shortening, egg and vanilla. Add milk and blend well. Add all dry ingredients. Spread half of batter in greased 9" square pan. Spread blueberries and add 2 tablespoons sugar. Cover with remaining batter. Sprinkle with 4 tablespoons sugar and ½ teaspoon cinnamon. Bake at 375°F. for 35 minutes. Serve warm if desired.

Judy Daniels, Bay H. S.
Panama City, Florida

QUICK CHOCOLATE COFFEECAKE

Number of Servings — 8

1 c. sugar
2 T. butter, soft
1 egg
1 c. chocolate milk (may use plain)
½ t. soda
2 t. baking powder
2 c. all-purpose flour
Pinch of salt
Topping:
2 T. butter
¼ c. sugar
½ t. cinnamon

Mix sugar, butter and egg together until smooth, add milk alternately with sifted dry ingredients. Pour into 8" square buttered pan, melt butter and pour over top of cake. Mix sugar and cinnamon and sprinkle over cake. Bake at 350°F. 25-35 minutes or until toothpick comes out clean.

Mrs. Janet Latham, Buhl H. S.
Buhl, Idaho

CRANBERRY COFFEECAKE

Number of Servings — 4-9 Squares

2 c. all-purpose flour
3 t. double acting baking powder
¾ t. salt
½ t. sugar
5 T. butter
1 egg, beaten
½ c. milk
2½ c. fresh cranberries, halved
Topping:
¼ c. flour
½ c. sugar
3 T. butter

Sift dry ingredients together, cut in butter with pastry blender until crumbly. Mix beaten egg and milk, add to flour mixture. Stir slowly to mix, then beat until well blended. Spread evenly on 8x8x2 buttered baking dish, sprinkle halved cranberries evenly over top. Mix topping, sprinkle over cranberries. Bake at 375°F. 30-35 minutes.

Mrs. David Farris, Clark County H. S.
Winchester, Kentucky

COWBOY COFFEECAKE

Number of Servings — 10

2½ c. sifted flour
½ t. salt
2 c. brown sugar
⅔ c. shortening
2 t. baking powder
½ t. soda
½ t. nutmeg
½ t. cinnamon
1 c. sour milk
2 eggs, well beaten
Chopped nuts (optional)
Cinnamon (optional)

Combine flour, salt, sugar, and shortening, mix until crumbly. Reserve ½ cup to sprinkle over batter. To remaining crumbs, add baking powder, soda, and spices, mix thoroughly, add milk and eggs, mix well. Pour into 2 wax paper lined 8x8x2 baking pans and sprinkle with reserved crumbs. Chopped nuts and cinnamon may be sprinkled over crumbs. Bake at 375°F. 25-30 minutes. For variations: Add 1 cup raisins, chopped dates or chopped apples to the batter.

Jessie Thomas, Elida H. S.
Elida, New Mexico

PINEAPPLE COFFEECAKE

Number of Servings — 10

1½ c. sifted flour
⅓ c. sugar
2 t. baking powder
¾ t. salt
1 egg, beaten
¼ c. melted shortening
1 c. pineapple juice
Pineapple topping:
½ c. sugar
1 t. cinnamon
1 T. butter or margarine
⅓ c. crushed pineapple, drained

Sift together flour, sugar, baking powder, and salt, combine egg, shortening, and pineapple juice. Mix liquid and dry ingredients, beat until smooth. Spread in 8" or 9" greased pan, sprinkle with pineapple topping mixture. Bake at 350°F. for 35 minutes or until cake shrinks from side of pan. Cool slightly before serving, about 10 minutes.

Mrs. Glen Ruder, North Adams Public School
North Adams, Michigan

PRUNE AND APRICOT COFFEECAKE

Number of Servings — 8-10

¾ c. dried prunes
¾ c. dried apricots
2 c. sifted all-purpose flour
2 t. double acting baking powder
½ t. salt
⅔ c. light brown sugar, firmly packed
1 T. flour
6 T. butter or margarine, melted
1 T. cinnamon
¾ c. shortening
¾ c. granulated sugar
2 eggs
⅓ c. chopped pecans or walnuts

(Continued on Next Page)

¾ c. milk
1 t. vanilla

Lightly grease and flour a 9" tube pan. Let prunes and apricots stand in hot water, to cover, 5 minutes, drain fruit, chop finely, set aside. Into a medium bowl, sift flour with baking powder and salt, set aside. In a small bowl, combine brown sugar with 1 tablespoon flour and the cinnamon, mixing well. In large bowl of electric mixer, at medium speed, beat shortening with granulated sugar until light and fluffy, beat in eggs, 1 at a time, beating well after each addition. At low speed beat in flour mixture (in 3 additions) alternately with milk and vanilla (in 2 additions), beating just until combined. With rubber scraper, gently fold in prunes and apricots. Turn ⅓ of batter into prepared pan, spreading evenly. Sprinkle with ⅓ of brown-sugar mixture, then with 2 tablespoons melted butter. Repeat layering twice. Sprinkle top with chopped nuts. If desired, refrigerate, covered, about 3 hours. About 1½ hours before serving, let coffee cake stand at room temperature 15 minutes. Also, preheat oven to 350°F. Bake 55 minutes, or until cake tester inserted in center comes out clean. Let cool in pan on wire rack about 25 minutes. Gently remove from pan. Serve warm.

Elizabeth L. Stokes, Sulligent H. S.
Sulligent, Alabama

SOUR CREAM COFFEECAKE

Number of Servings — 8

1 stick butter or margarine
1 c. sugar
2 eggs
¼ t. salt
1 t. vanilla
2 c. cake flour
1 t. baking powder
1 t. soda
1 c. sour cream

Cream butter, and sugar, add eggs, mix well, add salt and vanilla. Sift flour, measure, add baking powder and soda, sift again, add alternately with the sour cream. Pour half of batter into greased 9x13 pan, add ½ of the topping, add remaining batter, and sprinkle batter with a little of the topping. Bake 35-40 minutes at 350°F.

Topping:
¼ c. flour
¼ t. cinnamon
¼ c. brown sugar
2 T. butter or margarine
½ c. chopped nuts

Mix together until crumbly.

Lura Hallford, Stilwell H. S.
Stilwell, Oklahoma

STREUSEL COFFEECAKE

Number of Servings — 9

Cake ingredients:
¾ c. sugar
¼ c. soft shortening
1 egg
½ c. milk
1½ c. sifted flour
2 t. baking powder
½ t. salt

Streusel mix:
½ c. brown sugar
2 T. flour
2 t. cinnamon
2 T. melted butter
½ c. chopped nuts

Mix together thoroughly sugar, shortening and egg, stir in milk. Sift together and stir in flour, baking powder and salt. Spread half the batter in a greased and floured 9" pan. Sprinkle with half the streusel mix, add the remaining batter and sprinkle remaining streusel over the top. Bake 25-35 minutes at 375° until cake tests done. Cut in 3" pieces, serve warm.

This recipe submitted by the following teachers:

Mrs. Mary Kaphingst, Hillsborough H. S.
Tampa, Florida
Joan Robson, Utica H. S.
Utica, Ohio

DELICIOUS CHERRY MUFFINS

Number of Servings — 8 Muffins

½ c. shortening
½ c. brown sugar
¼ c. white sugar
2 eggs
1 4-oz. bottle cherries
Pecans, coarsely chopped
1 c. flour
½ t. baking powder
¼ t. salt
1 t. vanilla
1 T. cherry juice

Cream shortening and sugars, add egg yolks, sift dry ingredients together, add to cream mixture. Add vanilla and cherry juice, then add stiffly beaten egg whites. Grease muffin tins, put a few pecans in bottom of muffin tins. Drop a little dough on top of pecans, add a cherry and then more dough. Bake at 350°F. about 25 minutes.

Lucille Cook, Wilmer-Hutchins H. S.
Hutchins, Texas

CHERRY CUP CAKES OR MUFFINS

Number of Servings — 3 Dozen

4 T. butter or oleomargarine
⅛ c. white sugar
½ c. brown sugar
2 well beaten egg yolks
1 c. pastry flour
¼ t. baking powder
2 T. maraschino cherry juice
2 well beaten egg whites
1 bottle maraschino cherries
Pecans, ground fine
Powdered sugar

Cream together margarine and white and brown sugar. Add well beaten egg yolks. Sift together pastry flour and baking powder. Add to the creamed mixture. Stir in cherry juice. Fold in well beaten egg whites. Butter tiny muffin tins. Sprinkle with finely ground pecans. Put 1 teaspoon batter in each prepared muffin tin, then a cherry, cover

(Continued on Next Page)

the cherry with a second teaspoon of batter. Sprinkle top with ground pecan meats, and bake in a 400°F. preheated oven for 10 minutes. Roll muffins in powdered sugar while warm, let cool. Store muffins in tin box or can tightly covered, store for several days before using. May be frozen successfully.

This recipe submitted by the following teachers:
Mrs. Emogene Parker, Connally H. S.
Waco, Texas
Myrtle Curry, Waco H. S.
Waco, Texas

COFFEECAKE MUFFINS
Number of Servings — 1 Dozen
½ c. brown sugar
½ c. chopped walnuts or pecans
2 T. flour
2 t. cinnamon
2 T. melted butter
1½ c. sifted enriched flour
½ c. granulated sugar
2 t. baking powder
½ t. salt
¼ c. shortening
1 beaten egg
½ c. milk

Combine brown sugar, nuts, flour, cinnamon, and butter, set aside. Sift dry ingredients into bowl, cut in shortening until mixture resembles coarse crumbs. Combine egg and milk, add all at once to flour mixture. Stir just until moistened. Grease muffin pans or line with paper bake cups. Spoon in small amount of batter, top with layer of nut mixture. Repeat layers, filling pans ⅔ full. Bake in moderate oven 375°F. 20 minutes or until done.

Mrs. Douglas W. Sikes, Trent H. S.
Trent, Texas

CHOCOLATE CUP CAKES
Number of Servings — 20
1 c. sugar
1 egg
½ c. cocoa
½ c. margarine
1½ c. flour
½ c. buttermilk
1 t. vanilla
1 t. soda dissolved in ½ c. hot water

Put all ingredients together in order given. Do not mix until everything is in the bowl. Mix or beat vigorously, pour into greased cupcake tins or 9x13 cake pan. Bake at 400°F. (hot oven) 18-20 minutes. Frost with chocolate or favorite frosting.

Mrs. Loren Davis, Lake Preston H. S.
Lake Preston, South Dakota

CHOCOLATE SURPRISE CUP CAKES
Number of Servings — 18
¾ c. sugar
1½ c. sifted flour
1 t. baking powder
⅓ t. soda
½ t. salt
½ c. cocoa
⅔ c. buttermilk
1 egg
3 T. butter
1 t. vanilla

Sift together dry ingredients, add milk, egg, butter and flavoring, beat well. Bake in well-greased muffin tins (about 20 minutes), cool. Cut off the tops and remove some of the center. Fill center with filling. Replace tops, spread with icing.

Filling:
½ pt. cream (whipped)
1 t. sugar
½ t. vanilla
Icing:
1 stick melted butter
1 lb. box confectioners' sugar
½ c. cocoa
¼ c. milk

Sift sugar and cocoa together, add butter and milk, mix well. Spread on cup cakes. Top with cherry or nuts.

Mrs. D. T. Hamilton, Michie H. S.
Michie, Tennessee

LITTLE DATE CUP CAKES
Number of Servings — 18
1 c. dates, finely cut
1 c. boiling water
2 T. butter
1¾ c. cake flour
1 t. soda
1 c. sugar
1 egg, beaten
1 c. nut meats, chopped
1 t. vanilla

Combine cut dates, boiling water and butter, let stand until cool. Sift together 3 times flour and soda, add to cooled date mixture: sugar, beaten egg, nut meats and vanilla. Stir until mixed, add sifted dry ingredients, mix. Bake in greased muffin pans at 375°F. 25 minutes. Dust tops with confectioners' sugar.

Mrs. Audra Taylor, Jacksonville H. S.
Jacksonville, Illinois

MOCHA CAKES
Number of Servings — 18
1 c. shortening
1½ c. sugar
3 eggs
2 oz. baking chocolate
1 c. milk
1 t. soda
2 c. sifted flour
1 t. salt
Icing:
2 c. powdered sugar
3 T. cocoa

(Continued on Next Page)

2 T. butter
2 T. cold coffee
1 t. vanilla
Few drops milk

Heat chocolate and milk until chocolate has dissolved, cool, add soda. Cream shortening and sugar, add eggs 1 at a time. Sift flour and salt, add liquid and dry ingredients alternately. Place batter in greased muffin tins. Bake at 350°F. for 15-20 minutes, ice.

Mrs. Florence Bankston, Hammond H. S.
Hammond, Louisiana

ORANGE MUFFINS
Number of Servings — 16-24

½ c. butter
1 c. sugar
2 eggs
¼ t. salt
1 c. sour milk
1 t. soda
1 c. pecans, chopped fine
1 orange rind, grated
1 c. seeded raisins
2 c. flour

Mix together using the cake creaming method. Pour into greased floured muffin pans, bake at 350°F. for 20-30 minutes. When done, remove from pans, dip in the following hot mixture: juice of 1 orange and ½ cup sugar, heated until sugar has dissolved.

Flora Fry, Coleman H. S.
Coleman, Texas

PEANUT BUTTER CUP CAKES
Number of Servings — 2 Dozen

½ c. peanut butter
¼ c. shortening or butter
1 t. vanilla
1½ c. brown sugar
2 eggs
2 c. sifted all-purpose flour
2 t. baking powder
½ t. salt
¾ c. milk

Cream together peanut butter, shortening, and vanilla. Gradually add brown sugar, beating until light and fluffy. Add eggs, 1 at a time, beating well after each. Sift together dry ingredients, add alternately with milk. Place paper bake cups in muffin pans, fill ½ full. Bake in moderate oven 375°F. 20 minutes or until done. Frost with peanut butter, sift confectioners' sugar atop each.

Dony R. Baker, Lakeview School
Lakeview, Texas

PINEAPPLE CUP CAKES
Number of Servings — 24

½ c. shortening
1 c. sugar
2 eggs, unbeaten
2 c. flour, sifted
½ t. salt
2 t. baking powder
1 t. vanilla
1 8 oz. can crushed pineapple (minus 3
   T. juice)

Cream the shortening, add sugar, cream well. Add unbeaten eggs, beat well, sift flour, salt, and baking powder. Sift together 3 times, and blend into the sugar mixture, add the vanilla and crushed pineapple. Put into paper-lined muffin tins and bake at 375°F. 20 minutes or until lightly brown.

Pineapple glaze:
3 T. pineapple juice
3 c. sifted confectioners' sugar

Add the confectioners' sugar to the pineapple juice, blend until smooth and satiny. Spread over the cup cakes while they are still warm.

Mary Ann Worthy, Mexia H. S.
Mexia, Texas

PUMPKIN CUP CAKES
Number of Servings — 24

½ c. shortening
1½ c. sugar
2 eggs, beaten
2¼ c. all-purpose flour
2½ t. baking powder
½ t. soda
1 t. salt
2 t. cinnamon
½ t. ginger
½ t. nutmeg
1 c. pumpkin, cooked
¾ c. milk
½ c. chopped nuts

Cream shortening, add sugar, blend in beaten eggs. Sift flour, baking powder, soda, salt and spices together. Combine pumpkin and milk. Add dry ingredients alternately with pumpkin mixture. Stir in chopped nuts, pour batter into 24 wax paper cups. Bake in muffin tins to help hold shape. Bake 25 minutes at 350°F., cool. Cover with buttercream icing, flavored with grated orange rind.

Mrs. Arthur Ray, Lewis County H. S.
Hohenwald, Tennessee

PRUNE CUP CAKES
Number of Servings — 21

½ c. butter or margarine
1 c. sugar
1 t. vanilla extract
2 eggs
1 c. pitted prunes
1½ c. sifted flour
1½ t. baking powder
½ t. salt
1 t. cinnamon
¼ t. cloves
½ c. milk
½ c. chopped nuts

Cream butter, gradually add sugar, and cream until light. Add vanilla and eggs, 1 at a time, beating well after each. Fold in prunes, add sifted dry ingredients alternately with milk, beating well, add nuts. Half fill greased 2½" muffin pans, bake in 375°F. oven 20 minutes.

Mrs. Nina T. Smith, Picayune H. S.
Picayune, Mississippi

RAISIN CUP CAKES
Number of Servings — 12

1 c. raisins
½ c. liquid
½ c. butter
¾ c. sugar
1 egg
1½ c. flour
1 t. soda
½ t. salt
1 t. vanilla

Cook raisins in water for 20 minutes, ½ cup liquid should remain, cool. Cream butter, add sugar, mix well, add egg, mix thoroughly. Sift together dry ingredients, add flour mixture alternately with raisin water to creamed mixture, add raisins and vanilla. Spoon into greased cup cake tins, bake at 350°F. for 20-25 minutes.

Margaret Konesky, Starbuck H. S.
Starbuck, Minnesota

SOUR CREAM CUP CAKES
Number of Servings — 30

1¾ c. sugar
2 c. sour cream
4 eggs
2 t. vanilla
3 c. sifted all-purpose flour
3 t. baking powder
1½ t. baking soda
2 t. cinnamon
½ t. salt

Combine sugar, cream, eggs and vanilla and beat well, sift and measure flour. Sift dry ingredients together and add to first mixture, stir until batter is smooth. Bake in greased muffin pans at 375°F. for 20 minutes.

Ruth Henschen, Pana Sr. H. S.
Pana, Illinois

SPICED APPLE CUP CAKES
Number of Servings — 8

¼ c. shortening
⅜ c. sugar
1 egg
¾ c. all-purpose flour
1½ t. baking powder
¼ t. salt and cinnamon
⅛ t. nutmeg
¼ c. milk
½ c. chopped apple (fine)
¼ c. chopped nuts
¼ t. vanilla

Topping:
⅛ c. brown sugar
⅛ c. nuts, finely chopped
¼ t. cinnamon

Cream shortening and sugar, add egg and beat well (2 minutes). Add dry ingredients with the milk, fold in the apples, nuts and vanilla. Fill paper-lined cup cake pans ½ full. Sprinkle topping on top of cup cakes before baking. Bake at 350°F. about 25 minutes.

Mrs. Marie G. Reid, Rochester Area Jr.-Sr. H. S.
Rochester, Pennsylvania

DOUGHNUTS
Number of Servings — 2 Dozen

2 eggs
1 c. granulated sugar
4 T. melted butter
1 c. milk
3 t. baking powder
¾ t. salt
3 c. sifted flour
1 t. vanilla
1 c. sifted flour

Slightly beat eggs in a mixing bowl, add sugar and mix thoroughly. Melt butter, measure, and add to mixture, beat, add milk, mix. Sift flour, measure, sift dry ingredients together, add to mixture, add vanilla, mix well, add last amount of flour. Roll out dough and cut ½" thick. Fry in hot deep fat until golden brown.

Mary Ricketts, Yorkville H. S.
Yorkville, Illinois

ORANGE DROP DOUGHNUTS
Number of Servings — 36

1⅔ c. sifted flour
⅓ c. sugar
½ t. salt
2 t. baking powder
½ t. nutmeg
1 egg, lightly beaten
½ c. milk
2 T. melted shortening
2 t. grated orange rind
Frying fat

Sift together flour, sugar, salt, baking powder, and nutmeg, combine egg and milk, blend thoroughly. Gradually add to dry mixtures, stirring constantly, add shortening and orange rind, beat until smooth and well blended. Drop dough from teaspoons which have been dipped in hot fat to prevent dough sticking to spoons. Use 1 teaspoon to push dough from other teaspoon into hot fat, fry and drain as directed. Dip in honey glaze and roll in coconut.

Honey glaze with coconut:
½ c. honey
4 t. boiling water
1 c. sifted powdered sugar
1 c. shredded coconut

Heat honey in a heavy saucepan, add water and sugar, mix thoroughly. Dip doughnuts in warm glaze, drain, roll in coconut.

Helen Mack Northern Bedford County H. S.
New Enterprise, Pennsylvania

FROSTY PUMPKIN DOUGHNUTS

Number of Servings — 2 Dozen

3 c. flour
½ t. nutmeg
¾ t. soda
2 T. shortening
¾ c. brown sugar, firmly packed
4 egg yolks, or 2 eggs and 1 yolk
1 c. canned or cooked pumpkin
¼ c. thick sour milk
¾ t. cinnamon
1¼ t. salt
⅛ t. cream of tartar

Sift dry ingredients together. Cream shortening and brown sugar. Add egg yolks, mix well, add pumpkin, then milk and mix thoroughly. Sift spices, add to dry ingredients, add sifted dry ingredients to pumpkin mixture, mix until smooth. With as little handling as possible, roll dough on floured board to ⅜" thickness. Let dough stand 20 minutes, cut with 2½" cutter. Fry in deep hot fat 375°F. until brown, turning when first crack appears. Drain on absorbent paper, when cool, shake in a bag with granulated or confectioners' sugar.

Creasia G. Stone, Red Rock H. S.
Red Rock, Oklahoma

RAISED DOUGHNUTS

Number of Servings — 50

4 pkg. dry yeast
1 c. warm water
2 c. milk
½ c. sugar
2 t. salt
¾ c. Crisco
8 c. flour
Glaze:
⅔ c. boiling water
1 pkg. powdered sugar

Add dry yeast to warm water and let stand, scald milk and add to sugar, salt and Crisco. Blend together and cool to lukewarm, add yeast mixture and stir well. Add flour and mix. Place in greased bowl, cover and let raise in warm place 30 minutes. Punch down and turn out on a lightly floured board, roll ½" thick and cut with a doughnut cutter, let raise 5 to 30 minutes. Fry in deep fat until golden. Make glaze by mixing boiling water and powdered sugar, beat well.

Mrs. Patricia Barker, Mancos H. S.
Mancos, Colorado

SPUD NUTS

Number of Servings — 60

1 cake yeast
½ c. warm water
1 t. salt
½ c. sugar
⅔ c. shortening
2 c. scalded milk
1 c. mashed potatoes
2 beaten eggs
6-7 c. flour

Put yeast into water, add salt, sugar, and shortening to scalded milk and cool. Add mashed potatoes, eggs, yeast, and flour. Roll dough out and cut ½" spud nuts. Let dough rise for 1 hour and then fry in fat at 350°F.. Glaze with 2 cups powdered sugar and 1 teaspoon vanilla and a little warm water.

Mrs. Peter Alberda, Manhattan H. S.
Manhattan, Montana

HELEN'S YEAST DOUGHNUTS

Number of Servings — 2 Dozen

1 pkg. or cake of yeast
½ c. lukewarm water
⅔ c. shortening
½ c. sugar
1 t. salt
½-¾ c. mashed potatoes
1 c. scalded milk
2 eggs, well beaten
Enough flour to make a stiff dough
1 c. powdered sugar
½ c. milk

Dissolve yeast in water. Add shortening, sugar, salt to milk. Cool. Add yeast, mix thoroughly and add eggs. Stir in enough flour to make stiff. Knead well on floured board. Let rise slightly in greased bowl. Roll out, cut, and let rise 1 hour. Fry in hot fat and glaze while hot with thin powdered sugar and milk glaze.

Mrs. Mary Dworaczyk, Falls City H. S.
Falls City, Texas

BUTTERMILK PANCAKES

Number of Servings — 5-6

¾ c. powdered buttermilk
2 c. sifted flour
2 t. salt
1½ t. soda
2 eggs, unbeaten
2 c. water
¼ c. butter

Sift dry ingredients together twice, add unbeaten eggs, water and melted butter. Stir lightly to moisten dry ingredients. Mixture will be thick and lumpy. Drop by spoonfuls onto lightly greased griddle, spreading batter with spoon. Turn cakes as soon as browned.

Mrs. Vlasta Blaesi, Holcomb H. S.
Holcomb, Kansas

FEATHERWEIGHT PANCAKES

Number of Servings — 16

3 stiffly beaten egg whites
3 beaten egg yolks
¼ t. salt
¼ c. all-purpose flour
¾ c. cottage cheese

Beat the egg whites, use same beater and beat the yolks. Stir in the salt, flour, and cottage cheese with yolks, fold in the whites. Drop by small spoonfuls onto hot, lightly greased griddle, cook until golden brown on both sides. Serve at once with butter and hot maple syrup.

Janet Schmidecamp, Chadwick, H. S.
Chadwick, Illinois

SUGAR PLUM STRAWBERRY HOT CAKES

Number of Servings — 6-8

2 c. packaged layer or pound cake mix
  (white cake mix)
1 egg
½ c. water
⅓ c. flour
⅓ c. chopped nuts

Add egg and water to cake mix, beat until smooth, stir in flour and nuts. Preheat grill with control set at 3¼ until the light goes out. Drop by tablespoons onto the lightly greased surface. Cook about 5 minutes per side. Makes about 12 to 16 cakes. Serve hot with sweetened strawberries, spooned over the cakes shortcake style, and whipped cream.

Marlene Caszatt, Whitehall H. S.
Whitehall, Michigan

BANANA-SPICE LINCOLN LOG

Number of Servings — 8

¾ c. sifted cake flour
1 t. baking powder
¼ t. salt
¼ t. ground cloves
¼ t. ground nutmeg
½ t. ground cinnamon
½ t. ground ginger
4 eggs
¾ c. granulated sugar

Start heating oven to 400°F. Line a lightly greased 15x10x1 jelly roll pan with wax paper, grease paper. Sift together flour, baking powder, salt and spices. Beat eggs in 2-quart bowl until foamy. Gradually add sugar and beat until thick and tripled in volume. Quickly fold in flour mixture, pour batter into pan. Spread evenly. Bake 13 minutes or until light browned. Turn out on towel dusted with confectioners' sugar, remove paper quickly and roll cake and towel together, cool, unroll. Trim all edges of cake. Spread with banana frosting, roll up. Place on platter, open side down. Frost with remaining frosting. Decorate each slice with maraschino cherry.

Margaret Hustead, Bement H. S.
Bement, Illinois

CHOCOLATE CREAM ROLL

One Roll

¾ c. sifted cake flour
¼ c. cocoa
1 t. baking powder
¼ t. salt
3 lge. eggs, separated
1 c. sugar
5 T. water
1 t. vanilla

Set oven at 325°F. Rub a 9x13½ shallow pan with shortening, line it with heavy wax paper and grease and flour the wax paper. Sift together well, the flour, cocoa, baking powder, and salt. Beat the egg yolks until light, gradually add ¾ cup of the sugar, beating thoroughly, until thick and creamy. Beat in the water and vanilla. Beat the egg whites until frothy, gradually beat in the remaining sugar and beat until the whites are stiff. Gradually fold whites into the egg yolk mixture. Gradually fold in dry ingredients. Pour into the prepared pan and bake about 20 minutes. Quickly invert the cake onto a towel which is dusted with powdered sugar. Cut off the crisp edges and remove the paper. Roll in towel and cool well before filling.

Cream Filling for Chocolate Cream Roll:

2 T. flour
½ c. milk
¼ c. butter
¼ c. shortening
Few grains of salt
½ c. granulated sugar
½ t. vanilla

Mix flour and milk until smooth. Cook slowly until thick, over low heat. Stir constantly. Remove from heat and let cool completely. Add butter and shortening, blend at low speed. Add the salt. Beat until smooth and fluffy at high speed. Blend in sugar at high speed. Add the vanilla. Beat one minute more at high speed. Spread on cooled roll, reroll and chill before serving.

Bernadette M. Vavreck,
Curwensville Joint Jr.-Sr. H. S.
Curwensville, Pennsylvania

CHOCOLATE ROLL AND ICING

Number of Servings — 6

½ c. confectioners' sugar
¼ c. sifted flour
2 T. cocoa
6 eggs, separated
Filling:

1 pt. whipped cream with 1 t. vanilla added

Sift dry ingredients together 5 times. Beat egg yolks until lemon color. Fold in dry ingredients, mix well. Beat egg whites until stiff, fold into mixture. Bake at 450°F. for 8 minutes. Turn out on wax paper, when cool roll, when cold unroll and fill with 1 pint of sweetened whipped cream with vanilla added. Roll again and ice.

Icing:
Butter, size of an egg (melted)

(Continued on Next Page)

2 T. hot strong coffee
4 T. cocoa
Confectioners' sugar to make amount needed
Mix ingredients, flavor and spread.

Marjorie Mitchell, Greer H. S.
Greer, South Carolina

CINNAMON APPLE ROLL
Number of Servings — 8-10
1½ c. water
1½ c. sugar (white)
5 drops cinnamon oil
8-10 drops red food coloring
2 c. sifted all-purpose flour
3 t. baking powder
1 t. salt
2 T. sugar
⅓ c. shortening
⅔-¾ c. milk
3 c. finely chopped apples (Jonathon apples
   are excellent)
1-2 T. butter
½ c. chopped nuts

Place first 4 ingredients in saucepan, stir, bring to boil; turn to simmer, keep warm. Sift flour, baking powder, salt and sugar into bowl. Cut in shortening with pastry blender, stir in enough of the milk for soft dough. Turn on floured pastry cloth, round up dough, knead, roll into 6x12 oblong. Spread apples over dough, dot with butter. Carefully roll in long roll, seal edges. Put syrup in ungreased baking dish 9x12. Cut roll in 1″ or 1½″ slices with sharp knife. Place slices cut side down in hot syrup, sprinkle with nuts. Bake in oven 400°F. for 20-25 minutes. Serve warm with milk, ice cream, whipped cream or plain..

Carol Packer, Spencerville H. S.
Spencerville, Ohio

FRUIT ROLL
Number of Servings — 8
2 c. sifted plain flour
2 T. sugar
3 t. baking powder
1 t. salt
6 T. shortening
⅔-¾ c. milk
3 c. finely cut up fruit
1 T. butter
½ t. cinnamon
Syrup:
1½ c. sugar
2 c. liquid (either juice left from fruit or water)
1 stick oleo

Sift dry ingredients together, cut shortening into mixture until fine, stir in milk to make soft dough. Knead lightly, roll ⅛″ thick into an oblong sheet, spread with 3 cups fruit (fresh raw apples, peaches, blackberries or canned fruit may be used if liquid is drained off well). Dot with 1 tablespoon butter and cinnamon. Roll into oblong roll as a jelly roll, place in greased 13x9 pan and lightly brown at 450°F. (about 15 minutes), then reduce heat to 350°F. and pour boiling syrup over roll and cook approximately 30 minutes longer.

Mrs. Marie R. Duggan, Kite H. S.
Kite, Georgia

OLD FASHIONED JELLY ROLL
Number of Servings — 8
¾ c. sifted flour
¾ t. baking powder
¼ t. salt
4 eggs (room temperature)
¾ c. sugar
1 t. vanilla
1 c. tart red jelly

Sift flour once, measure and set aside. Combine baking powder, salt, and eggs, adding sugar, beating until mixture becomes thick and light colored. Fold in the flour and vanilla. Turn into 15x10 pan which has been lined with greased brown paper. Bake at 400°F. 13 minutes. Turn cake out on a towel dusted with powdered sugar. Remove paper and cut off crisp edges of cake. Roll cake and towel together. Cool ten minutes. unroll. Spread cake with jelly. Roll again.

Mrs. Fern Ruck, Rangely H. S.
Rangely, Colorado

STRAWBERRY ROLL
Number of Servings — 10
5 egg whites
3 egg yolks
½ c. flour (plain)
¾ c. powdered sugar
½ t. cream of tartar
½ t. vanilla
½ pt. whipping cream, whipped and sweetened
1 pt. fresh or frozen strawberries

Beat egg whites until frothy, add cream of tartar. Beat until stiff. Add sugar gradually. Add beaten egg yolks, flour and vanilla. Pour into a greased jelly roll pan. Bake at 325°F. for 20 minutes, turn out on towel sprinkled with powdered sugar. Roll towel up in roll and let cool. When cool, unroll and sprinkle sliced strawberries, over cake, then spread with whipped cream. Roll up and frost with favorite butter frosting flavored with strawberries.

Mrs. Audrey Bowers, James F. Byrnes H. S.
Duncan, South Carolina

YAM ROLL
Number of Servings — 10
⅔ c. eggs (3 large)
1 c. sugar
5 T. water
1 t. vanilla
1 c. flour
1 t. baking powder
¼ t. salt

Start heating oven to 375°F. Grease and flour 15x10⅞ jelly roll pan. Beat until thick, eggs, gradually beat in sugar. Beat in all at one time, water, vanilla, flour, baking powder and salt. Beat until smooth, pour in prepared pan. Bake until it tests done (12-15 minutes). Sprinkle powdered sugar on towel, turn cake onto cloth. Fold hem of towel over long edge, then roll cake gently, rolling towel in it. Cool on wire rack, seam side down. If cake is warm filling will melt.

(Continued on Next Page)

Filling:
¼ c. light brown sugar
2 eggs
⅛ t. salt
1 c. yams (mashed)
¼ t. allspice
1 T. butter
½ c. chopped nuts
½ t. vanilla
1 c. whipping cream

Cook in saucepan, stirring constantly until thick, sugar, eggs, salt and mashed yams. When cooked turn fire off and add allspice, butter, chopped nuts, vanilla. Set aside to cool. After cool, add ½ c. whipped cream.

Topping:
½ cup whipped cream to which 2 tablespoons of sugar has been added, also 1 teaspoon vanilla. Yam roll may be served with or without topping.

Vivian J. Ryland, Lafargue H. S.
Effie, Louisiana

SHORTCAKE

Number of Servings — 6-8

2 c. sifted flour
¼ c. sugar
4 t. baking powder
½ t. salt
Few grains nutmeg
½ c. butter
1 egg, well beaten
⅓ c. milk

Grease 8″ pan lightly. Sift dry ingredients together. Work butter into dry mixture. Mix in beaten egg, then milk. Dump dough in pan and pat to fit pan. Bake 12 minutes at 450°F. Cool on rack. Split and spread with sweetened fruit.

Mrs. Chelsea A. Merritt, Tollesboro H. S.
Tollesboro, Kentucky

STRAWBERRY SHORTCAKE

Number of Servings — 6-8

2 c. sifted flour
4 t. baking powder
1 t. salt
4 T. shortening
⅔ c. milk
1 qt. crushed sweetened strawberries
1 c. whipping cream

Sift flour, baking powder, and salt together in large bowl. Cut shortening into flour mixture with 2 knives or a pastry blender until mixture looks like rice grains. Add milk to flour mixture. Stir quickly with a fork just enough to make a soft dough. Put dough on lightly floured board and knead 6 to 8 times. Roll dough ½″ thick. Cut with 4″ cutter. Place cakes on baking sheet. Bake at 450°F. for 12 to 15 minutes. When slightly cooled, split in half. Place 1 layer on serving plate, cut side up and spread with crushed sweetened strawberries. Top with other half, cut side down, spoon more crushed sweetened strawberries on top. Top with cream which has been whipped or vanilla ice cream and decorate with whole strawberries that have been washed and drained.

Mrs. Walter Holden, Albany H. S.
Albany, Louisiana

STRAWBERRY SHORTCAKE

Number of Servings — 20

½ c. shortening
1½ c. sugar
3 c. flour
4 egg whites
3 t. baking powder
Few grains salt
1 c. sweet milk
Meringue:
1 c. sugar
4 egg whites

Mix ingredients for cake as you would for a butter cake. Spread batter in a greased porcelain baking pan about ½″ thick. Beat egg whites for meringue, add sugar gradually. When stiff, spread smoothly over top of cake batter, baking all at once. Bake at 350°F. about 30 minutes or until brown on top and bottom. This crisp meringue keeps cake from getting soggy. Cut in squares and serve with sweetened berries or other fruits.

Myrtle Frieze Campbell, Rockmart H. S.
Rockmart, Georgia

GRANDMA BYRD'S STRAWBERRY SHORTCAKE

Number of Servings — 6

1½ qt. fresh strawberries, sliced
2 c. sugar
2 c. self rising flour
⅔ c. shortening
⅔ c. milk
1 stick butter, melted

Blend together sliced fresh strawberries and sugar. Set aside to form juice while making shortcake. Sift flour, cut in shortening until particles are the size of rice. Add milk all at once and mix lightly and quickly with a fork, knead lightly. Pat into 2 thin rounds about 8″ across. Bake on cookie sheet at 450°F. until golden brown. To serve, split layers apart, put hot rounds on serving dish, and drizzle with melted butter. Spoon sweetened fresh strawberries and juice generously between each layer and on top. Serve warm with cream or plain.

Mildred Rivers, Wilson Jr. H. S.
Charlotte, North Carolina

Party Beverages

ALMOND PUNCH

Number of Servings — 60

4 pkg. cherry Jello
3 c. sugar
4 c. hot water
6 pkg. strawberry Koolade
1 small bottle almond extract
2 tall cans pineapple juice
2 cans frozen lemonade, plus water
12 7-ups

Dissolve Jello and sugar in hot water. Mix all ingredients except 7-ups. Just before serving add 7-ups.

Mrs. R. E. Cassibry, Simsboro H. S.
Simsboro, Louisiana

ALOHA PUNCH

Number of Servings — 24

2-6 oz. cans frozen orange juice
1½ c. water
1 c. fresh pineapple cubes
½ c. sugar
2 qt. gingerale

Combine all ingredients except gingerale and chill. Just before serving add gingerale. Garnish with ice ring with maraschino cherries frozen in.

Nancy Anderson, Dexter H. S.
Dexter, Michigan

APRICOT PARTY BEVERAGE

Number of Servings — 8

1 can apricot nectar
1 qt. bottle gingerale

Empty one can apricot nectar into an ice cube tray and freeze overnight. At serving time, put two or three apricot cubes into a tumbler and fill with gingerale.

Patricia Parks, Basic H. S.
Henderson, Nevada

BANANA CRUSH

Number of Servings — 60, (6 ounce)

4 c. sugar
6 c. water
1-46 oz. can pineapple juice
2-12 oz. cans frozen orange juice concentrate, (thawed)
1-12 oz. can frozen lemonade concentrate, (thawed)
6 bananas
7-28 oz. bottles lemon-lime carbonated beverages, or equal amounts of lemon juice and gingerale may be used

Dissolve sugar in water. Add juices and mashed bananas. Put through food mill. Stir well into juices.

Mrs. Bert Johnson, Bruce H. S.
Bruce, Mississippi

BRIDE'S PUNCH

Number of Servings — 24

1 can (12 oz.) quick frozen concentrated orange juice
1 can (6 oz.) quick frozen concentrated lemonade

6 c. cold water
2½ c. chilled ginger ale
Frozen fruit ring

Mix concentrated orange juice, concentrated lemonade and water. Chill. To serve, pour orange juice mixture into punch bowl. Add gingerale and mix. Float frozen fruit ring.

Frozen Fruit Ring:
Strawberries (sliced if desired)
Pineapple cubes
Orange sections
Mint leaves
Water

Arrange fruit and mint in a 1½ quart ring mold. Carefully add water and chill until solidly frozen. Unmold and float in the punch.

Joyce Thornton, Rosebud H. S.
Rosebud, Texas

BIRTHDAY PARTY PUNCH

Number of Servings — 25 Small

12 bottles of strawberry soda pop
1 lge. can pineapple juice

Have all ingredients cold. Mix just before serving. (Children love this easy, red punch.)

Mrs. Marie W. Davis, John Rundle H. S.
Grenada, Mississippi

CHAMPAGNE (Mock)

Number of Servings — 10-12

1 qt. apple juice
2 lge. bottles gingerale
Few drops of red food coloring to make a light pink
Freeze ice cubes of red or green cherries with mint leaves in each cherry

Mix apple juice and gingerale just a few minutes before serving. Put ice cubes in glasses. Add beverage. Serve with a meal or as an appetizer with wafers or cheese straws.

Mrs. Sallie P. Satterly, Hitchins H. S.
Hitchins, Kentucky

CRANBERRY PUNCH

Number of Servings — 100 (4 oz. Servings)

1 lb. cranberries
1 qt. water
2 c. sugar
1 lemon (juiced) save rind
3 gal. water
3 (6 oz. frozen) cans pineapple juice
2 (6 oz. frozen) cans orange juice
1 (6 oz. frozen) can grapefruit juice
2 (6 oz. frozen) cans lemonade
3 qt. gingerale

Cook cranberries and lemon rind in 1 quart water until skins pop. Remove lemon rind. Strain through food mill or sieve and add sugar and lemon juice. Cool. Add the frozen juices and water. At serving time add chilled gingerale. An excellent party punch or appetizer.

Mrs. Lois Riggs, Walnut Grove H. S.
Arcadia, Indiana

CRANBERRY FRUIT PUNCH
Number of Servings — 24
3 pt. cranberry juict cocktail
3 c. orange juice
¾ c. lemon juice
1½ c. pineapple juice
1½ c. sugar
3 c. water

Combine the cranberry cocktail, orange, lemon, and pineapple juices. Mix well with sugar and water. Pour over ice. Note: Interesting molds may be frozen from some of the punch, or from other liquids for decorations in the punch bowl.

Beatrice Campbell,
Leland Con. Deon Attendance Center
Leland, Mississippi

HOT SPICED CRANBERRY PUNCH
Number of Servings — 35
Tie in cheese cloth bag:
2 t. nutmeg
2 t. cinnamon
2 t. allspice
1½ c. tea leaves
Steep these in 20 cups water for 20 minutes. Remove bag and add:
6 c. sugar
4 c. orange juice
2 c. lemon juice
1 gal. cranberry juice cocktail
12 c. hot water

Serve piping hot, and all will want your recipe.

Ann Derrick, Amarillo H. S.
Amarillo, Texas

PUNCH DELIGHT (Citric Acid)
Number of Servings — 100
¼ lb. citric acid
2 qt. cold water
4 lb. sugar
2 qt. hot water
2 lge. cans pineapple juice
2 cans frozen orange juice (add water as directed on can)
2 bottles apple juice

Dissolve citric acid in cold water. Dissolve sugar in hot water. Cool. Mix together and add remaining ingredients. Makes 3 gallons.

Joan Lynch, Cuero H. S.
Cuero, Texas

CHRISTMAS PUNCH
Number of Servings — 75
2-5¢ pkg. lime aid mix, such as Kool-aid
2 c. sugar
2 qt. water
46 oz. pineapple juice
2 qt. gingerale

Combine aid, sugar, water, and pineapple juice. Just before serving add the gingerale. Pour the entire mixture over ice cubes. A sprig of mint or bits of maraschino cherries may be added.

Lola G. Weatherman, Blue Ridge School
Ararat, Virginia

PUNCH (Citric Acid)
Number of Servings — 3 Gallons
2 oz. citric
Add:
¼ c. hot water (to melt citric acid)
1 lge. can orange juice
1 lge. can pineapple juice
7½ c. sugar
2 gal. water

Rose A. Campbell, Carolina H. S.
Greenville, South Carolina

PUNCH FOR 150
Number of Servings — 150
12 c. sugar
3 pt. water
6 pkg. lime Jello
12 c. hot water
3 cans frozen orange juice
3 cans frozen lemon juice
3 qt. pineapple juice
1 medium size bottle almond extract

Boil sugar and 3 pints water together for a few minutes, long enough to mix thoroughly. Dissolve Jello in 12 cups hot water, add to first solution. When ready to serve add orange juice, lemon juice, pineapple juice, and almond extract.

Mrs. Billie Sommermeyer, Haltom H. S.
Fort Worth, Texas

CURRANT FIZZ
Number of Servings — 50
7 (13 oz.) glasses currant jelly
6 pt. boiling water
15 c. orange juice (4 doz.)
4 c. lemon juice (2 dozen)
12 pt. gingerale

Beat jelly until frothy. Add boiling water. Continue beating until jelly is dissolved. Add fruit juices and stir well. Chill. Just before serving add gingerale.

Leona Jenson, Amphitheater H. S.
Tucson, Arizona

DELICIOUS PUNCH
Number of Servings — 12
Cook 3 minutes:
½ c. water
½ c. sugar
Add:
½ c. grape juice
½ c. orange juice
1 bottle Canada Dry

Mrs. Jewell P. Simmons, Leflore County H. S.
Itta Bena Mississippi

FROSTED CIDER CUP
½ pt. lemon sherbet
3 c. sweet cider

Drop a generous spoonful of lemon sherbet into each of 8 fancy small juice glasses. Pour chilled sweet cider over. Serve at once.

Dianne J. MacPherson, Garden Spot H. S.
New Holland, Pennsylvania

EVERGREEN PUNCH
Number of Servings — 50
2 pkg. lime Kool-aid
2 c. sugar
2 qt. water
1-46 oz. pineapple juice
1 qt. gingerale

Dissolve sugar in water. Mix in lime Kool-aid, pineapple juice, with sugar and water mixture. Add gingerale just before serving and pour over ice cubes. Serves 50 punch cup servings.

Mrs. Euzelia M. Vollbracht,
Burns At Fallston H. S.
Fallston, North Carolina

FROSTED COCKTAIL
Number of Servings — 6
½ c. sugar
⅔ c. water
⅔ c. unsweetened pineapple juice
⅔ c. lemon juice, fresh, frozen, or canned
2 T. bottled or fresh lime juice
2 unbeaten egg whites
4 c. finely crushed ice

Cook sugar and water 5 minutes, chill. Shake all ingredients in shaker or jar until light and frothy. Serve immediately in small chilled cocktail glasses.

Mrs. Goldia Mae Hanberry, White Springs H. S.
White Springs, Florida

FROSTY SHERBET PUNCH
Number of Servings — 2½ Gallons
3 cans (46 oz. each) orange-grapefruit juice
3 cans (12 fl. oz. each) apricot nectar
3 qt. gingerale
3 qt. pineapple sherbet

Have juice and gingerale thoroughly chilled. Empty 1 can of each juice, and 1 quart of ginger-ale in punch bowl. Add a quart of sherbet. Spoon the liquid over sherbet until partly melted. Serve. When supply runs low repeat the process adding another unit of each ingredient. This requires no ice and is easily handled.

Mrs. Virginia Faith Brown, Prosper H. S.
Prosper, Texas

FRUIT JUICE PUNCH
Number of Servings — 25
1 lge. can (12 oz.) frozen orange juice
1 small can (6 oz.) frozen grape juice
1 small can (6 oz.) frozen lemonade
3 c. sugar
1½ c. water
1 qt. gingerale

Make syrup with water and sugar. Boil 5 minutes. Cool. Dilute frozen juices according to directions on can. Add orange juice, lemonade and grape juice to syrup. When ready to serve, add gingerale.

Mrs. Betty Parrett, Ramona H. S.
Ramona, Oklahoma

GOLDEN PUNCH
Number of Servings — 40 Punch Cups
2-6 oz. cans frozen orange juice concentrate
1½ c. white Karo
2 qt. gingerale
1 pt. sherbet (orange or pineapple)
3 trays ice cubes or cracked ice

Empty the juice and Karo in a punch bowl. Add the sherbet and ice. Pour the gingerale over the mixture. Allow most of the ice to melt. Thin slices of orange may be floated.

Mrs. Maxine Gibson, Bradford County H. S.
Starke, Florida

GRADUATION PUNCH
Number of Servings — 50
2 c. boiling water
4 T. black tea (or 4 tea bags)
Pour water over tea, cover and steep 10 minutes and strain.
Juice and rind of 3 lemons
2 c. sugar
4 c. cold water
1½ t. each of vanilla and almond extracts
2 cans (46 oz. cans) chilled unsweetened pineapple juice
2 qt. gingerale (chilled)
1 pkg. frozen fresh pineapple chunks

Mix lemon rind, sugar, and water and heat to boiling. Remove rinds. Add lemon juice, strained tea and extracts. Cool. At serving time, pour mixture over ice blocks in punch bowl. Add pineapple juice and gingerale. Float pineapple chunks.

Mrs. Jo Ann Braddy, Danville H. S.
Danville, Arkansas

HOT MULLED GRAPE JUICE
Number of Servings — 8
2 qt. grape juice
¼ c. sugar
1-2 cinnamon sticks
4 whole cloves
4 whole allspice

Tie the spices in a small bag and drop into a large saucepan. Pour in the grape juice and sugar, bring the mixture to a boil. Let stand for 10 minutes. Remove the spice bag.

Mrs. Mildred L. Phillips, Santa Cruz H. S.
Santa Cruz, New Mexico

HOLIDAY PUNCH
Number of Servings — 40
2 qt. pineapple juice
2 qt. tea
2 c. sugar
6 lemons
1 can frozen lime concentrate or 2 pkg. lemon-lime aid, such as Miracle Aid
Few drops green food coloring

Steep 2 tea bags in 2 quarts boiling water. Pour pineapple juice into large mixing bowl. Squeeze juice from lemons. Add lemon juice to pineapple juice. Add lime concentrate (or) lemon-lime aid mix after mixing according to directions on can or package. Add sugar and enough food color to give a bright green color. Serve over ice.

Georgia Crawley, Theodore H. S.
Theodore, Alabama

HAWAIIAN PUNCH
Number of Servings — 12 to 15

1-6 oz. can frozen orange juice
1 c. water
5¾ c. pineapple juice
2 small cans Hawaiian punch base
1 box frozen strawberries
1 tray ice

Combine orange juice, water, pineapple juice, and punch base. Crush the strawberries and add to the liquid mixture. Chill thoroughly. Before serving add the ice.

Mrs. Opal A. Salyers, Coeburn H. S.
Coeburn, Virginia

HOLIDAY FRUIT PUNCH
Number of Servings — 60 to 80

2 lge. cans orange juice
2 lge. cans grapefruit juice
2 lge. cans pineapple juice
Juice of 2 doz. lemons
5 c. sugar
5 c. warm water

Juice 24 lemons. Add sugar to warm water. Stir until sugar is dissolved, then add all juices to the sugar syrup. Chill before serving.

Mrs. Carolon Craft, Dexter H. S.
Tylertown, Mississippi

HOT SPICED AFTERNOON TEA
Number of Servings — 30 Punch Cups

4 qt. boiling water
1 t. whole cloves
1 stick cinnamon
15 tea bags or 5 T. tea
1¼ c. sugar
1 c. orange juice
¾ c. lemon juice

Add spices to water and bring to full boil. Remove from heat and add tea bags or tea. Steep for 4 minutes. Strain. Add sugar and stir until dissolved. Pour in fruit juices. Keep spiced tea hot or reheat over low heat, but do not boil.

Velma P. Ellis, Opp H. S.
Opp, Alabama

LIME PUNCH
Number of Servings — 36

1 oz. pkg. lime-lemon Kool-aid
4 c. sugar
Strained juice of 6 lemons
1 lge. can pineapple juice
2 qt. boiling water
2 T. tea
2½ qt. cold water

Mix Kool-aid according to directions on package. Steep tea in boiling water 3 minutes. Strain and sugar hot tea. Stir until dissolved. Add cold water to weaken tea. Add fruit juices. Just before serving add ice cubes or crushed ice to chill. 1 quart lime sherbet may be added. Sliced fruits and cherries may also be added.

Margie Ann Rowzee, Flora H. S.
Flora, Mississippi

LIME PUNCH
Number of Servings — 50 to 60

5 pkg. lime Jello
1 No. 2 can crushed pineapple
1 No. 2 can grapefruit juice
2 qt. pineapple juice (or 3 No. 2 cans)
Juice of 2½ doz. lemons
5 c. sugar
5½ qt. water
6-8 qt. gingerale

Mix juices. Add sugar and water. This punch can be placed in freezer in cartons several days before ready to use. It will freeze only to mushy ice. When ready to serve, add 6 to 8 quarts gingerale.

Faye Pearson, Hayneville School
Hayneville, Alabama

LIME PARFAIT

Three scoops lime sherbet. Place in parfait glass. Fill with beverage such as "Sprite". Top with red or green cherry and mint leaf.

Nelle Avery Erwin, Transylvania Jr. H. S.
Transylvania, Louisiana

MILK PUNCH
Number of Servings — 20

6 oz. can frozen pineapple juice
6 oz. can frozen orange juice
3 c. iced water
3 c. milk
Dash of salt
¼ c. sugar
1 qt. lime or orange sherbet
Pineapple chunks and red or green cherries may be added for a garnish

Place the thawed fruit juices in a large mixing bowl. Add the sugar and salt. Stir to blend. Gradually add the milk and ice cold water, blending to make a smooth mixture. Chill. When ready to serve spoon in softened sherbet and whip with a rotory beater at high speed until punch is foamy and all sherbet mixed in. Place pineapple chunks and cherries (if desired) into punch bowl. Add milk punch and serve.

Sondra Hallerman, Milan H. S.
Milan, Ohio

FRUIT SYRUP FOR "MINT JULEP"
Number of Servings — 12

2 c. water
2½ c. sugar
Juice of 6 lemons
Juice of 2 oranges
Grated rind of 1 orange
A lge. handful of mint leaves or 3 T. dried mint

Boil sugar and water 10 minutes and pour into a quart jar holding the fruit juices, rind and mint. Allow to stand in refrigerator at least 24 hours. Use 3 or 4 tablespoons in a glass of ice water for a refreshing drink. This may be kept as long as 2 weeks or it may be frozen for future use.

Mrs. Allen Mayhew, Greensburg Rural H. S.
Greensburg, Kansas

ORANGE MINT PUNCH
Number of Servings — 12 to 15

2 c. sugar
2½ c. water
Juice from 6 lemons
Juice from 3 oranges
Grated rind of 2 oranges
1 qt. gingerale
2 handsful mint leaves

Boil sugar and water for 1 minute. Put mint leaves, juice and grated rind in half gallon jar that can be sealed. Pour boiling syrup in jar over leaves and juice. Seal and let cool. Strain. Add 1 quart gingerale and enough water to make 1 gallon. Serve over crushed ice, with sprig of mint.
Mrs. Thelma Cravy, Jacksonville Senior H. S.
Jacksonville, Texas

MOCHA PUNCH
Number of Servings — 50

2 c. water
1¾ c. granulated sugar
2 oz. instant coffee
4 qt. milk
½ gal. vanilla ice cream
Vanilla or rum flavoring to taste

Boil the water and the sugar until the sugar is dissolved. Turn off the heat and add the instant coffee. Let the mixture steep with a lid on until cool. In a large container place cold milk. Add the cooled mixture and pour over vanilla ice cream. Flavor with vanilla or rum flavoring to taste.
Mrs. Julian Green, Buchholz Junior H. S.
Gainesville, Florida

MOCHA PUNCH
Number of Servings — 25

1 qt. cold coffee
1 qt. chocolate ice cream
1 qt. vanilla ice cream
¼ t. almond extract
1 c. whipping cream
½ c. sugar
¼ t. salt
½ t. grated nutmeg

Pour cold coffee in punch bowl. Add ice cream broken into walnut-size pieces. Add almond extract. Whip cream with sugar and salt. Fold into the coffee-ice cream mixture. Sprinkle nutmeg on top. Serve at once.
Ula Broun, Waco H. S.
Waco, Texas

PARTY PUNCH (Rose Color)
Number of Servings — 30

1 can (46 oz.) Hawaiian Punch
1 can (6 oz.) frozen lemonade diluted
2 bottles (26 oz.) gingerale

Combine Hawaiian Punch and lemonade, add gingerale just before serving and serve over ice.
Mrs. Sue Dowler, Haltom H. S.
Fort Worth, Texas

ORANGE NOG
Number of Servings — 4

½ c. sugar
1½ c. cold orange juice
1 c. chilled evaporated milk
1 c. ice water
½ c. crushed ice
1 pt. orange sherbet

Dissolve sugar in orange juice. Pour milk into a fruit jar and dilute with ice water. Add crushed ice. Add orange juice slowly to milk. Shake vigorously and serve in glasses over sherbet.
Jean F. Goodman, Robert E. Lee Jr. H. S.
Danville, Virginia

ORANGE SHERBET PARTY PUNCH
Number of Servings — 40

2 pkg. strawberry Jello
2 c. boiling water
2 c. cold water
1½ c. sugar
1 can pineapple juice
1 can orange juice
1 c. lemon juice
1 bottle gingerale
2 qt. orange sherbet

Dissolve gelatin in boiling water. Add sugar and stir until dissolved. Add cold water. Combine juices and add to Jello mixture. Chill. Spoon sherbet into punch. Add gingerale just before serving.
Mrs. Helen S. Underwood, Shepherdsville H. S.
Shepherdsville, Kentucky

PARTY PUNCH
Number of Servings — 100

Make a syrup of:
6 c. sugar
4 c. water
While hot add:
4 pkg. lemon Jello (regular size)
Cool. Add:
1-6 oz. frozen lemon juice
1-6 oz. frozen orange juice
2 lge. cans pineapple juice
1 gal. water
1½ oz. almond extract

Hint: To freeze some of the punch in trays prevents weakening from addition of ice.
Geraldine Eddleman, Weatherford Senior H. S.
Weatherford, Texas

PARTY PUNCH
Number of Servings — 25

2 boxes Jello
4 c. boiling water
1½ c. sugar
2 c. cold water
1-8 oz. bottle of lemon concentrate
1 lge. can (46 oz.) pineapple juice
1 qt. gingerale

Dissolve Jello in boiling water. Then stir in sugar until dissolved, allow to cool slightly and add cold water, lemon concentrate, and pineapple juice. Pour into punch bowl, add crushed ice and

(Continued on Next Page)

gingerale. For green punch use lime Jello, orange from orange Jello, red from cherry or strawberry. Do not let stand in the refrigerator as the Jello will begin to thicken, however it will thin again when you add the gingerale and ice just before serving. (This is a most economical and delicious punch and easy to make.)

Mrs. Obera B. Pruitt, Belton H. S.
Belton, South Carolina

PARTY PUNCH
Number of Servings — 25

2-6 oz. cans frozen orange juice
1-6 oz. can frozen lemonade
1-6 oz. can frozen pineapple juice
1 c. sugar
4 qt. water
2 qt. gingerale
1 qt. club soda

Dissolve sugar into water. Add frozen juices. Mix well. About 30 minutes before serving, add gingerale and club soda. Makes a tasty, sparkling beverage. Can add food coloring to accommodate color scheme.

Sarah A. McCreight, Oak Hill H. S.
Morganton, North Carolina

RACY RED PUNCH
Number of Servings — 2½ Quarts

1-46 oz. pineapple-grapefruit drink
¼ c. red hot cinnamon candies
⅓ c. sugar
1 qt. gingerale

Heat 1 cup of the juice, add cinnamon candies and sugar. Stir until dissolved. Combine with the rest of the juice and chill mixture thoroughly. Add the gingerale just before serving for sparkle.

Mrs. Sue T. Glovier, Old Fort H. S.
Old Fort, North Carolina

RASPBERRY SHERBET PUNCH
Number of Servings — 40 to 50

1½ gal. raspberry sherbet
5 qt. gingerale
5 qt. orange juice
1 pt. lemon juice

Mix gingerale, orange and lemon juice to taste. Mix in part of sherbet and put the rest in the punch bowl.

Mable Gray, Savanna Community H. S.
Savanna, Illinois

CREAM SHERBET PUNCH
Number of Servings — 36

1 qt. orange sherbet
1 qt. vanilla ice cream
2 tall cans pineapple juice
1 qt. gingerale

In a bowl combine pineapple juice, sherbet and ice cream. Beat with electric mixer until well blended. Pour into punch bowl. Gently stir in gingerale. Serve immediately.

Mrs. Martha S. O'Neil, Montgomery Area School
Montgomery, Pennsylvania

RHUBARB PUNCH FLOAT

Rhubarb, fresh (cut up)
Sugar
Ice milk
Carbonated beverage

Cover rhubarb with water and cook until done, then put into strainer or colander to drain off the juice. Add 1 cup sugar for each quart of juice, boil until sugar is dissolved, then cool and store until needed. Red food coloring may be added if pinker color is desired. Pour this juice into tall goblets, half full and add a scoop of ice milk. To this, add carbonated beverage, stick in a straw and enjoy.

Mrs. Florence Wiest, Wishek H. S.
Wishek, North Dakota

RUBY RED FRUIT PUNCH
Number of Servings — 20—4 Ounce Servings

32 oz. can pineapple-grapefruit juice
32 oz. tap water
2 c. sugar
1-5¢ pkg. cherry or strawberry powdered drink mix
1 lemon
1 orange
1 lime

Cut 3 nice slices from each of the fruits, place these in bottom of punch bowl. Mix the other ingredients and chill. When ready to serve, place a few pieces of ice in the punch.

Mrs. Roxy Ann Pike, Hillcrest Jr. High
Fayetteville, Arkansas

SMOKEY PUNCH
Number of Servings — 25 to 30

1 gal. lime sherbet
3 bottles gingerale
1 lb. dry ice

In a large punch bowl pour the sherbet, add the gingerale as needed. To this mixture add a few pieces dry ice for a smokey delight. Serve immediately.

Mrs. Joan Johnson Killgore, Gallup H. S.
Gallup, New Mexico

SPRING-TIME PUNCH
Number of Servings — 35

2 lge. cans pineapple juice
1-6 oz. can concentrated lemon juice, 3 cans water
15-20 unhulled strawberries
1 pt. pineapple sherbet
1 pt. gingerale or 7-Up
12 mint leaves

Pour pineapple juice into a large container, add the lemon juice and water, mix. Fill a 1 quart ring mold with some of the juice, freeze to a mush, insert strawberries, return to freezer. To serve: Place chilled juice in punch bowl, loosen frozen ring and float on juice. In center of ring spoon the sherbet, pour gingerale around it, sprinkle on mint leaves. Many combinations of punch may be made by this recipe. Care must be used in mixing colors, however.

Margaret Lopp, Chandler H. S.
Chandler, Arizona

RUSSIAN TEA
Number of Servings — 50
2 gal. water
2 lb. sugar
3 sticks cinnamon
2 t. whole cloves
¾ c. loose tea
6 lemons
5 oranges

Boil water, add sugar and spice bag (cloves and cinnamon) and boil 10 minutes. Remove from heat and add tea bag and steep for 5 minutes. Remove tea bag, add lemon and orange juices. Serve hot.

Mrs. Frank C. Adams, Cradock H. S.
Portsmouth, Virginia

SLUSH
Number of Servings — 12
2 bananas, mashed
1 c. sugar
1 can crushed pineapple
1 can concentrated orange juice
Grated rind of 1 orange
Grated rind of 1 lemon
3 T. lemon juice
1 pt. gingerale

Combine above ingredients and freeze. Chop finely when frozen. Refreeze. Serve in small cups.

Mrs. Barbara Deane, Sheridan Community H. S.
Hoxie, Kansas

SPICED PUNCH
Number of Servings — 20
4 c. water
3 c. sugar
2 t. whole cloves
4″ stick of cinnamon
2 qt. orange juice
4 c. lemon juice
4 c. grapefruit juice
4 c. pineapple juice

Simmer sugar, water and spices 10 minutes. Strain and cool. Add fruit juice. Serve.

Mrs. T. W. Colby, Abilene Christian H. S.
Abilene, Texas

SPICED TEA
Number of Servings — 20
1 gal. water
3 c. sugar
3 t. whole cloves
3 sticks cinnamon
9 t. tea
Juice of 4 oranges (1½ c.)
Juice of 3 lemons

Boil water with cinnamon and cloves and sugar for 5 minutes. Add tea, turn heat off and let set 2 or 3 minutes. Strain and add juices.

Mrs. Betty Coles, Bowling Green H. S.
Bowling Green, Kentucky

WASSAIL (Christmas)
Number of Servings — 18 to 20
Juice of 6 oranges
Juice of 3 lemons
3 c. strong tea
1 qt. sweet cider
½ t. cloves (in tea strainer)
2 sticks cinnamon
1 t. ginger

Make syrup of 3 cups sugar and 3 cups water. Add spices and let stand several hours or over night. Add rest of ingredients. (Remove spices before serving.) Add red cake coloring for Christmas beverage.

Kathleen Gee, Medicine Lodge H. S.
Medicine Lodge, Kansas

WASSAIL BOWL
Number of Servings — 36 or 18 Cups
2 c. water
2 c. sugar
2 cinnamon sticks
1 t. ginger
1 t. allspice
10 whole cloves
1 qt. sweet cider or apple juice
1 qt. orange juice
½ c. lemon juice
2 qt. gingerale

Simmer water, sugar, and bag of spices about 10 minutes. Stir until sugar is dissolved, then cover. Cool and add the cider and fruit juices. Add gingerale just before serving. (Small red apples may be floated on the bowl of punch.)

Martha Sue Hawkins, Murphy H. S.
Murphy, North Carolina

WEDDING PUNCH
Number of Servings — 25
Boil to make syrup:
2½ c. water
3 c. sugar
Add:
2¼ c. pineapple juice
5 c. orange juice
2 c. lemon juice
3 c. ice water
1 qt. gingerale
1 pt. strawberries (may be omitted)

Eleanor Tedford, Wiggins H. S.
Wiggins, Colorado

WEDDING PUNCH
Number of Servings — 35
2 qt. cider
1 (46 oz.) can pineapple juice
1 orange sliced thin
1 lemon sliced thin
3 sprigs crushed mint
2 qt. gingerale
1 can frozen limeade

Frozen juice may be used instead of sliced orange and lemon.

Madge Landis Capel, Woden H. S.
Woden, Texas

Pies, Pastries, Tarts & Turnovers

Start With the Crust...

Tender, flaky crusts are a cinch to make. Use your favorite pie crust mix, or follow these hints.

1. Sift flour and salt together. Cut in shortening with pastry blender, until size of small peas. Sprinkle water over mixture, while tossing quickly with fork, until particles stick together. Form into smooth ball.

2. For ease in rolling out pastry, wrap dough in waxed paper and allow to chill in refrigerator. Lightly roll pastry into circle 1-inch larger than pie plate. Lift loosely into pie plate. Pat out air. Fold edges under and crimp.

3. Prick entire crust thoroughly before baking. This prevents bubbles and excess shrinkage. Bake in hot oven at 450°F. for about 12 minutes or until golden brown. Cool and fill.

ONE-CRUST 9-INCH PIE SHELL

1 cup sifted all-purpose flour
½ teaspoon salt
⅓ cup shortening
3 tablespoons cold water

About Pastry...

Pies are, by all odds, the favorite American dessert. And anyone who can make a tender, flaky pie crust really has something to boast about.

Pie crust can be used as the base for a main dish—such as meat pie or turnovers, or for a dessert pie. The right proportion of shortening and flour is important in making good tender pastry. Use at least $\frac{1}{3}$ cup of shortening for each cup of sifted flour. Measure ingredients, don't guess, when you want a good pie.

Pastry Making Equipment

A bread board or table top can be used for rolling pastry. A pastry canvas and a stockinette cover for the rolling pin make the dough easier to roll without sticking.

Pie plates are made of glass or ceramic over wear, heavy tin, or aluminum. They are commonly available in 8, 9 or 10-inch sizes, diameter measured across the top. They are usually $1\frac{1}{4}$ inches deep. Check pan side by measuring across the top inside edge.

Pastry for one single 8″ crust will make
Six or seven 4″ tart shells
Topping for deep dish pie
Four to six 4″ turnovers

Pastry for one double 8″ crust will make
Eight or nine 4″ tart shells
Two single 8″ crusts
Latticed pie
Ten or twelve 4″ turnovers

Pastry Tips

IF THIS HAPPENS WITH A TESTED RECIPE	IT MAY BE CAUSED BY THIS	TRY THIS
DRY DOUGH HARD TO WORK WITH	1. Incomplete mixing	Don't worry about over mixing. Final mixing or shaping of dough may be done with hands.
	2. Not enough water	Use level measures of water.
TOUGH PASTRY	1. Not enough shortening or too much flour	Use at least $\frac{1}{3}$ cup shortening for each cup of *sifted* all-purpose flour. Use very little flour on board for rolling.
SHRINKING OR BUCKLING OF PASTRY	1. Pastry stretched during fitting into pie pan	Use large enough recipe to fit pie pan without stretching. Don't stretch dough when fitting to pie plate.
	2. Pastry shell not adequately pricked on sides and bottom before baking	Prick pastry generously over bottom and sides of pie plate.

APPLE PIE

Number of Servings — 6

2 c. all purpose flour
1 t. salt
2/3 c. shortening
1/3 c. whole milk

Sift flour, measure, add salt, and sift into medium-sized mixing bowl. Add shortening, and cut into flour mixture with pastry blender or table fork until mixture is size of peas. Remove 1/4 cup of mixture, and add to 1/3 cup of milk. Add this mixture to remainder of flour mixture, blend well, and roll out between 2 sheets of wax paper, 1" larger than edge of pie plate.

Filling:
4-5 medium, tart cooking apples
1 c. granulated sugar
2 T. all purpose flour
1/2 t. cinnamon
1 T. butter

Peel, core and slice apples very thin. Mix sugar with flour and cinnamon. Sprinkle 3 tablespoons of this mixture over bottom of raw pie crust. Pour in apples and dot with butter. Add top crust which has been punched with holes to permit escape of steam. Flute edges and seal together. Glaze top crust with undiluted evaporated milk. Place in 425°F. pre-heated oven and bake for 10 minutes, lower oven temperature to 375°F. and cook 50 minutes. If crust becomes too brown, you may cover with tent made of aluminum foil.

Leatrice L. Davis, Long Jr. H. S.
Houston, Texas

APPLE PIE

Number of Servings — 6

4 medium apples
1/2 c. orange juice
1/2 c. sugar
1/4 lb. butter
1 T. cornstarch

Peel, core and slice apples very thin. Place apples, orange juice, 1/2 cup sugar and butter in saucepan. Cook until apples are clear. Mix 1/2 cup sugar and 1 tablespoon cornstarch and add to mixture. Cook until slightly thick. Pour into uncooked pastry shell. Strip and bake at 350°F. until golden.

Mrs. C. F. Hammen, West End H. S.
Nashville, Tennessee

ALL-AMERICAN APPLE PIE

Number of Servings — 6

1 c. sugar
2 T. flour
1/2 t. cinnamon
1/4 t. nutmeg
1/4 t. salt
1 t. lemon juice
5 c. thinly sliced apples
2 T. butter or margarine
Pastry for 2 crust (9") pie

Combine sugar, flour, spices, salt, and lemon juice. Add apples, toss to mix. Roll out pastry, line pie pan. Trim off overhang. Roll pastry for top, cut vents near center. Add half the apples, pack well. Dot with butter. Add remaining apples. Moisten rim with water. Adjust top crust. Leave about 1/2" pastry beyond edge, fold it under lower pastry. Seal rim by pressing together, flute it. Brush with milk. Bake at 400°F. 50-60 minutes or until apples test done with fork.

Pastry:
2 1/4 c. flour
Take out 1/3 c. of flour
4 T. water
1 t. salt
3/4 c. shortening

Cut the shortening into remaining flour until pieces are the size of small peas. Mix 4 tablespoons of water with the 1/3 cup of flour to form a paste, add to shortening-flour mixture. Mix and shape into ball. Divide dough into 2 parts. Bake as directed for apple pie. If baked as a single crust, use 425°F.

Maggie Q. Gardner, Franklin County H. S.
Rocky Mount, Virginia

APPLE PIE

Number of Servings — 6

1 c. sugar
2 t. cinnamon
6 c. sliced apples
4 T. butter
Pastry for double crust pie (9")

Mix sugar and cinnamon together and mix lightly through sliced apples. Heap up in pastry-lined pan and dot with butter. Cover with top crust which has slits cut in it. Seal and flute. Bake at 375°F. until crust is nicely browned and apples are tender, approximately 50-60 minutes. Serve warm or cold. May be topped with cheese or ioe cream.

Mrs. Jolene Hartman, Lancaster H. S.
Lancaster, Texas

GREATEST APPLE PIE

Number of Servings — 6-8

6-7 tart apples
3/4-1 c. sugar
2 T. enriched flour
1/2-1 t. cinnamon
Dash Nutmeg
Dash salt
1 recipe of pastry
Butter

Pare apples and slice thin (1/4"). For nice fat pie, you'll need 6 cups sliced apples. Combine sugar, flour, spices and salt, mix with apples. Line 9" pie plate with pastry, fill with apple mixture and dot with butter. Adjust top crust, fluting edges, sprinkle top with sugar for sparkle. Gently fold strip of foil or pie tape around rim of crust, covering fluted edge (this keeps juice in pie, guards against boil over in oven and overbrowning). Bake at 400°F. 55-60 minutes or until apples are done. Serve warm.

Norma Jean Wallace, Marion Sr. H. S.
Marion, Virginia

EASY APPLE PIE

Number of Servings — 6-8

Tart Apples, peeled, sliced thin
⅔ c. sugar
Nutmeg
3 T. water
Butter

Peel and slice tart apples thin, having pan or pie plate heaping full. Sprinkle sugar and a little nutmeg over apples. Dot with butter and add water.

Crust:
1 c. sifted flour
½ c. butter
½ c. brown sugar

Mix together with fingers sifted flour, butter, and brown sugar. Sprinkle on top of apples. Bake at 300°F.-350°F. until brown.

Mrs. Marjorie West, Northeast Voc. H. S.
Lauderdale, Mississippi

APPLE CRISP

Number of Servings — 6

1 c. sifted flour
⅓ c. sugar
1 t. baking powder
¾ t. salt
1 egg, unbeaten
⅓ c. shortening, soft
4-5 c. apples, sliced, peeled

Place the apples in bottom of an 8x8 pan. Sprinkle with sugar and cinnamon as for pie. Sift flour, sugar, salt, baking powder into a small mixing bowl. Add the unbeaten egg and the shortening. Mix together with a fork until crumbly and pat out or sprinkle over the fruit. Bake 35-40 minutes at 350°F. Cut in squares and serve with cream, topping, or ice cream. Variations: use rhubarb, fresh berries or 1 can of prepared cherry or apple pie filling instead of apples.

Dorothy Davey, Junior H. S.
Iron Mountain, Michigan

MRS. PINKIE'S APPLE PIE

Number of Servings — 6

5 small tart apples
¾ c. sugar
½ t. cornstarch
½ t. cinnamon
¼ t. salt
3 drops yellow food coloring
3 T. butter
1 recipe for double pastry shell

Peel, core, and slice apples. Mix sugar, cornstarch, cinnamon and salt together. Arrange sliced apples and sugar mixture in alternate layers in unbaked pastry shell. Drop food coloring on top of layers. Dot with butter. Cover with top crust. Seal top and bottom crust together around edge. Make 6 to 8 ½" slits in top crust. Bake at 425°F. for 45 minutes or until nicely browned.

Mrs. Jerry Cook, Live Oak H. S.
Watson, Louisiana

OPEN APPLE PIE

Number of Servings — One 9 Inch Pie

7 medium-size tart apples, washed, pared, cored and sliced
2 T. flour
⅛ t. nutmeg
¾ c. firmly packed brown sugar
1 T. lemon juice
¼ c. heavy cream
¼ c. granulated sugar
3 T. butter

Prepare ½ standard pastry recipe. Press dough lightly into a ball, wrap, and chill in refrigerator 10-15 minutes. Roll out on a lightly floured pastry cloth or board. Fold overhand under and crimp the edges. Prepare apples and arrange them in the pastry shell in layers. Mix flour, nutmeg, and brown sugar and sprinkle on each layer of apples. Add lemon juice and heavy cream. Top with the granulated sugar and dot with butter. Cover with a small circle of aluminum foil, cut just to cover the apples. Bake at 450°F. for 10 minutes. Then reduce the heat to 400°F. and continue baking for 45 minutes to 1 hour, or until the apples are tender and the filling has bubbled up around them.

Mrs. Verna Wright, Russellville Senior H. S.
Russellville, Arkansas

CHEESE-APPLE PIE

Number of Servings — 8

4 c. sliced tart apples
1 c. sugar
2 T. flour
⅛ t. salt
1 t. cinnamon
¼ t. nutmeg
2 T. butter

Pare apples and slice thin. Add sugar mixed with flour, salt, and spices. Fill 9" pie pan lined with cheese pastry. Dot with butter. Adjust top crust. Bake at 450°F. 10 minutes, then at 350°F. about 40 minutes.

Cheese pastry:
2 c. flour
½ t. salt
½ c. grated sharp cheese
⅔ c. cold butter
4-5 T. ice water

Sift together flour and salt. Stir in cheese. Cut in butter. Add ice water slowly, mixing lightly with folk. Roll out slightly thinner than plain pastry.

Mrs. Margaret W. Lyles, Cleveland H. S.
Madison, South Carolina

DEEP DISH APPLE CRUMB PIE

Number of Servings — 10

6 c. peeled, sliced apples
3 T. lemon juice
1 t. lemon rind (grated)
½ c. sugar
½ c. flour
⅓ c. sugar
½ t. cinnamon
½ t. ginger
¼ t. mace
⅓ c. butter

(Continued on Next Page)

Arrange apples in baking dish. Sprinkle over this the sugar, lemon juice and rind. Sift together the flour, cinnamon, mace, ginger and ⅛ cup sugar, cut in the butter. Spread mixture over apples. Bake at 300°F. for about an hour.

Addie Kellum, Chico H. S.
Chico, Texas

DUTCH APPLE PIE

Number of Servings — 6

8 Jonathan apples
⅓ c. sugar
1 t. cinnamon
1 T. flour
Dash salt

Peel and slice 8 apples, spread them in a 9" pastry shell. Spread mixture of sugar, cinnamon, flour, and salt over the apples.

Topping:
½ c. butter
½ c. flour
½ c. brown sugar

Top with butter, flour and brown sugar which has been mixed together. Bake at 400°F. for 10 minutes, then finish baking at 350°F. for 20-30 minutes.

Mrs. Joe M. Maxson, Bald Knob H. S.
Bald Knob, Arkansas

DUTCH APPLE PIE

Number of Servings — 6

4 tart apples
1 c. sugar
1 T. cinnamon
¾ c. flour
⅓ c. butter

In an unbaked pastry shell, slice the 4 peeled and cored apples. Sift ½ cup sugar and cinnamon over apples. Sift remaining ½ cup sugar and flour together in a small bowl and cut in butter. Sprinkle these crumbs over top of pie. Bake for 15 minutes in a 450°F. oven, then reduce heat to 350°F. and bake until apples are tender.

Homoiselle House, Hempstead H. S.
Hempstead, Texas

SOUR CREAM APPLE PIE

Number of Servings — 6-8

8" or 9" unbaked pastry shell
6 apples
¾ c. sugar
⅓ c. flour
1 t. cinnamon
¼ t. nutmeg
¼ c. butter
½ c. sour cream

Mix sugar, flour, cinnamon, nutmeg and butter until crumbly. Arrange apples in bottom of unbaked pastry shell. Sprinkle the crumbly mixture over the apples. Spoon the sour cream over the top. Bake 30 minutes at 400°F., then reduce heat to 350°F. and bake 25 minutes.

Mrs. Lee Edd Wommack, Crane H. S.
Crane, Texas

PAPER-BAG APPLE PIE

Number of Servings — 6

1 unbaked 9" pastry shell
3-4 lg. baking apples
½ c. sugar (for filling)
2 T. flour (for filling)
½ t. nutmeg
2 T. lemon juice
½ c. sugar (for topping)
½ c. flour (for topping)
½ c. butter or margarine

Make an unbaked 9" pastry shell. Pare, core, and quarter apples, then halve each quarter crosswise to make chunks (7 cups). Place in large bowl. Make filling by combining ½ cup sugar, 2 tablespoons flour, and nutmeg. Sprinkle over apples, toss to coat well. Spoon into shell. Drizzle with lemon. Combine ½ cup sugar, and ½ cup flour for topping, cut in butter. Sprinkle over apples to cover top. Slide pie into a heavy brown paper bag to cover pie loosely, fold open end over twice and fasten with paper clips. Place on large cookie sheet. Bake in hot oven 425°F. 1 hour. Split bag open. Remove pie.

Evelyn Hardman, Wallowa H. S.
Wallowa, Oregon

SCOTCH APPLE PIE

Number of Servings — 6-8

5 apples
¾ c. brown sugar

Slice apples in the bottom of a greased baking dish. Cover with brown sugar.

Crust:
¾ c. brown sugar (packed)
½ c. butter
1 c. flour
Dash of salt
½ c. nuts

Cream butter, add sugar, flour, and salt. Mix thoroughly. Add nuts. Spread mixture over the apples and sugar. Bake 1 hour at 350°F. Serve with whipped cream or ice cream.

Lela A. Tomlinson, State Department of Education
Baton Rouge, Louisiana

APPLE CRISP

Number of Servings — 6-8

4 c. sliced, pared, cored baking apples (approximately 4 medium)
⅔-¾ c. brown sugar (packed)
½ c. sifted flour
½ c. rolled oats
¾ t. cinnamon
¾ t. nutmeg
⅓ c. soft butter

Place in greased 8" square pan 4 cups apples. Blend until crumbly the brown sugar, sifted flour, rolled oats, cinnamon, nutmeg and soft butter. Spread over apples. Bake at 375°F. for 30-35 minutes until apples are tender and topping is golden brown. Serve warm with cream, whipped ice cream, or hard sauce.

Mildred A. Graham, LaRue Co. H. S.
Hodgenville, Kentucky

SOUTHERN APPLE PIE

Pastry:
1 c. flour
⅓ c. shortening
Blend flour and shortening with enough water to make it stick together. Roll and shape into pie pan.

Pie:
6 apples (sliced)
6 T. flour
½ c. sugar
1 t. cinnamon
½ c. brown sugar
½ c. butter
1 scant c. flour
Place apples in pie shell. Mix flour, sugar, and cinnamon. Sprinkle over apples. Make a crumb mixture of other ingredients. Sprinkle over apples. Bake 20 minutes at 450°F. and bake 30-40 minutes at 350°F. Serve with ice cream or whip cream. Top with cherry.

Mrs. Estelle B. Cravey, Ellisville H. S.
Ellisville, Mississippi

SOUTHERN APPLE CREAM PIE

Number of Servings — 6
1 whole egg
2 egg yolks
1¼ c. sugar
4 T. flour
¼ t. salt
1 c. canned apples
¼ c. milk
2 T. butter
1 t. vanilla
1 baked 9" pie shell
2 egg whites, beaten stiff
4 T. sugar
¼ t. baking powder
Beat until light and fluffy whole egg and egg yolks. Add sugar, flour and salt. Add apples, milk, and butter. Cook over low heat until thick. Remove from heat. Add vanilla. Pour into baked 9" pie shell. Let cool. Top with meringue made by using 2 egg whites, beaten stiff, to which has been added 4 tablespoons sugar and ¼ teaspoon baking powder. Brown in slow oven.

Hilda Harman, Smithville H. S.
Smithville, Mississippi

APPLE CRUNCH

Number of Servings — 8
8-12 apples
½ c. sugar
1 c. brown sugar
1 c. flour
½ lb. butter
1 c. nuts (pecans)
Peel and slice apples, place in glass baking dish, cover with sugar. Mix brown sugar, flour with butter to a paste, drop over apples. Bake 350°F. for 30 minutes, take out and sprinkle nuts over top. Bake another 30 minutes. Serve with whipped or ice cream.

Margaret M. Golden, Millport H. S.
Millport, Alabama

SPICY APPLE PIE

Number of Servings — 6
3 c. tart apples, sliced
¼ c. lemon juice
2 c. sugar
¼ t. cloves
¼ t. cinnamon
¼ t. nutmeg
½ c. butter or margarine
Pastry for double crust
Heap apple slices on unbaked pie crust in deep pan. Add lemon juice, mix spices with sugar and cover apples. Add melted butter. Add upper crust with holes to let steam escape. Seal edges. Bake at 400°F. for 45 minutes. Serve with sliced cheese.

Maria Adams, Spring Garden School
Chatham, Virginia

CHEESE CRUMBLE APPLE PIE

Number of Servings — 6-8
2½ c. (1 can) sliced apples
1 c. brown sugar
2 T. flour
1 t. cinnamon
½ t. nutmeg
1 T. lemon juice
⅔ c. flour
⅓ c. butter
⅔ c. grated American cheese
Combine apples, ½ cup sugar, 2 tablespoons flour, cinnamon, nutmeg, and lemon juice. Place in deep-dish pie pan. Mix remaining ½ cup sugar, and ⅔ cup flour, cut in butter with 2 knives or pastry blender. Add cheese, toss lightly. Sprinkle mixture over apples. Bake in hot oven 400°F. 45-50 minutes. Serve with wedge of cheese on top.

Doreen Nielsen, Murray H. S.
Murray, Utah

APRICOT APPLE PIE

2 c. water
2 c. sugar
1 lemon, sliced
1 lg. bay leaf
1 T. apricot (preserves or jam)
⅛ t. cloves
⅛ t. nutmeg
4 c. peeled, cored and crosswise sliced apples
3 T. brown sugar
3 T. softened butter
⅛ t. nutmeg
1 bay leaf
1 egg yolk, beaten
Put all ingredients except apples in a sauce pan and boil gently for 20 minutes, then strain. Poach the apples in the syrup for 12 minutes, drain and cool. Set the apples in a pastry-lined pan, spread over them brown sugar, softened butter, nutmeg, and bay leaf. Cover with thinly rolled pastry. Decorate the edges with a fork and pierce holes in the shape of an apple and leaf in center of pie. Gild top with beaten egg yolk and bake at 400°F. for 10 minutes, then at 325°F. for 20 minutes more.

Mrs. Mary U. Christopher, Deshler H. S.
Tuscumbia, Alabama

APRICOT COBBLER
Number of Servings — 24
Topping: (make first)
2 sticks (½ lb.) butter
2 c. sugar
¼ t. salt
2 t. vanilla
2 beaten eggs
2 c. flour

Let butter soften and cream well. Add sugar and cream well. Add the next four ingredients and mix. Save to spoon on top of apricot mixture.

Apricot mixture:
3 lg. cans apricot halves
½ of the apricot juice
1½ c. sugar
2 T. butter
Juice of 2 lemons

Mix the apricot halves, apricot juice, sugar, and butter. Place in a pan and bring to a boil. Add lemon juice. Pour apricot mixture into fairly flat baking dish or pan. Spoon the topping mixture over the top. Bake about 1 hour at 350°F.

Mrs. Mildred Sanders, Tornillo H. S.
Tornillo, Texas

APRICOT-CARAMEL COBBLER
Number of Servings — 6
1 can (1 lb., 14 oz.) unpeeled apricot halves
2 t. quick-cooking tapioca
⅛ c. light-brown sugar, firmly packed
1 T. butter
1 T. lemon juice
Preheat oven to 425°F. In medium saucepan, combine apricots with remaining fruit ingredients. Stirring constantly, bring to boil. Boil until mixture thickens and becomes translucent (about 5 minutes). Keep hot.

Topping:
1½ c. sifted all-purpose flour
½ c. granulated sugar
2 t. baking powder
2 T. butter
½ c. milk
¼ c. light-brown sugar, firmly packed
Into medium bowl, sift together flour, sugar, and baking powder. Blend butter until mixture resembles course cornmeal. Make well in center of dry ingredients. Add milk all at once, stirring until dry ingredients are dampened. Pour hot fruit into 2-quart baking dish. Drop topping, by 6 heaping spoonfuls, on to hot fruit. Bake 15 minutes. In small saucepan, combine brown sugar with 2 tablespoons water. Boil 1 minute. Spoon over cobbler. Bake 5 minutes more. Serve warm.

Mrs. Elsie Kitchens, Santa Rosa H. S.
Santa Rosa, New Mexico

APRICOT CREAM PIE
Number of Servings — 6-8
1 pkg. dried apricots
1 c. water
1 c. sugar
Cream filling:
⅛ c. cornstarch

⅔ c. sugar
¼ t. salt
2 c. milk, scalded
3 slightly beaten egg yolks
2 T. margarine
½ t. vanilla
1 baked 9″ pastry shell
1 c. heavy cream, whipped
Cook apricots in water until tender. Mash. Add sugar and cool. This should be the consistency of preserves. Mix cornstarch, sugar, and salt. Gradually add milk. Cook on low heat, stirring constantly until mixture thickens and boils. Cook 2 minutes, remove from heat. Add small amount to egg yolks. Stir into remaining hot mixture. Cook 1 minute, stirring constantly. Add margarine, vanilla, cool slightly. Pour half of mixture into baked 9″ pie shell. Spread apricots on cream filling, add remaining cream filling and top with whipped cream.

Mary Ann Lea, Vilonia H. S.
Vilonia, Arkansas

BANANA CREAM PIE
Number of Servings — 6
⅔ c. sugar
3 T. cornstarch
¼ t. salt
3 egg yolks
1 c. evaporated milk
1 c. water
1 t. vanilla
1½ c. sliced, ripe bananas

Mix thoroughly in a saucepan the sugar, cornstarch, salt, and egg yolks. Combine milk and water and stir in gradually until smooth. Cook and stir over low heat until thickened, about 10 minutes. Remove saucepan from heat and stir in vanilla. Cover and cool thoroughly. Put in the bottom of a cold 9″ baked pastry shell the sliced bananas. Cover bananas with cooled custard. Spread with meringue. Bake as directed. Cool thoroughly. Cut with wet knife.

Norma S. Hagy, Martin H. S.
Laredo, Texas

ROYAL HAWIIAN BANANA
Number of Servings — 6-8
4 c. sliced, ripe and firm bananas
    (5 to 6 medium)
½ c. pineapple juice
½ c. granulated sugar
1 t. cinnamon
2 T. butter
1 9″ double pie crust
Slice bananas. Cover with pineapple juice. Toss gently until slices are coated. Let set 30 minutes. Drain. Place bananas in uncooked shell. Mix sugar and cinnamon. Sift over top of bananas. Dot with butter. Put on top crust, seal edges. Vent top with 2 or 3 slashes near center. Bake at 400°F. until crust is golden brown. About 30 minutes. Serve hot or cold.

Vada C. Turnham
Arlington, Texas

BERRY COBBLER

Number of Servings — 10-12

1⅔ c. flour, unsifted
2 t. baking powder
¾ c. sugar
¾ t. salt
1 cube butter, melted
1⅓ c. milk
6 c. berries
1 c. sugar
1 c. water
3 T. butter

Sift flour, sugar, baking powder, and salt together in bowl. Add milk and melted butter and stir until smooth. Spread batter over bottom of buttered 9x13x2 baking dish. Sprinkle berries over batter. Combine water, sugar, and remaining butter in saucepan and bring to a boil. Pour over berries. Bake 400°F. 45 minutes or until nicely browned. Serve warm with vanilla ice cream.

Mrs. Mary Westfall, Colusa H. S.
Colusa, California

BLUEBERRY CRUMBLE

Number of Servings — 4

3 c. fresh blueberries
⅓ c. sugar
Juice of 1 lemon

Topping:

¼ c. butter
⅓ c. sugar
⅔ c. flour

Put washed fresh blueberries in small shallow baking dish. Sprinkle with ⅓ cup sugar and juice of lemon. Blend butter, sugar, and flour. Sprinkle over berries. Bake in moderate oven 350°F. 30 minutes until brown. Serve warm. Serve with a topping of ice cream if desired.

Mary Ellen Rudd, Eaton Rapids H. S.
Eaton Rapids, Michigan

BLUEBERRY PIE

Number of Servings — 6-8

3 c. frozen or canned blueberries
⅔ c. sugar
4 level T. cornstarch
2 T. butter
Dash salt
2½ T. wine vinegar

Drain juice from canned or thawed berries. Let juice come to a quick boil in a heavy saucepan. Add the sugar, cornstarch, butter, salt and vinegar. Cook until slightly thickened. Remove from heat, add berries and cool. Pour into a pre-heated 9″ pastry shell, very crisp. The filling should have a sweet-sour flavor.

Topping:

1½ c. sour cream
2 T. sugar
½ t. vanilla

Combine ingredients and spread evenly over berries. Bake in a 250°F. oven for 10 minutes. Allow to cool and place in refrigerator for at least 2 hours before serving.

Mrs. Margaret Detert, Woodsboro H. S.
Woodsboro, Texas

BLUEBERRY PIE

Number of Servings — 8

2½ c. fresh blueberries
1 c. sugar
¼ c. enriched flour
Dash of salt
1 T. lemon juice, fresh, frozen, or canned
2 T. butter or margarine
1 unbaked pastry shell

Combine blueberries, sugar, flour, salt, and lemon juice. Fill an 8″ pastry lined pie pan. Dot with butter and adjust top crust. Bake in hot oven 400°F. 40-50 minutes.

Dixie T. Giannini, Caldwell Co. H. S.
Princeton, Kentucky

BLUEBERRY BANANA PIE

Number of Servings — 6

1 can blueberries
2½ T. cornstarch
½ c. sugar
2 T. butter
2 T. lemon juice (fresh)
2 bananas
1 c. heavy cream

Drain blueberries. Mix cornstarch and sugar, add to juice. Cook until thick, stirring constantly. Remove from heat. Add butter and lemon juice. Add berries. Cool. Line baked pie crust with rounds of bananas. Pour cooled mixture over crust. Refrigerate until thoroughly chilled. Top with whipped cream.

Mrs. Wilma Adams, Lockney H. S.
Lockney, Texas

FROSTED CRISSCROSS CRANBERRY PIE

Number of Servings — 9 Inch Pie

Filling:

2 c. cranberries
3 eggs
1½ c. sugar
2 T. melted butter

Put cranberries through a food chopper. Beat eggs, combine with sugar and butter. Fold this mixture into the cranberries. Fill pastry-lined 9″ pie plate. Arrange crisscross strips of pastry over the top. Brush with milk. Bake at 400°F. for 15 minutes. Reduce to 350°F. for 30 minutes more.

Pie crust:

3 c. flour
½ t. baking powder
½ t. salt
1¼ c. vegetable shortening
1 egg
1 T. vinegar
3-5 T. water (use your judgment)

Sift dry ingredients together. Add one-half of the shortening. Cut in until the mixture resembles cornmeal. Add the remaining shortening and cut in until the mixture looks like the size of peas. Beat the egg and vinegar. Add it to the flour mixture. Use fork and mix lightly. Sprinkle on the water until the mixture is a workable consistency. When mixture gathers in a ball, it should be ready for rolling (use fork to mix ingredients). Makes 4 single or 2 double crusts.

Janice Leno, Lemmon Public Schools
Lemmon, South Dakota

STRAWBERRY PIE
Number of Servings — 6

1 c. sugar
3 T. cornstarch
3 eggs
1½ c. frozen or fresh strawberries
8 T. melted butter
1 unbaked pastry shell

Combine sugar and flour. Separate eggs and beat yolks slightly. Add egg yolks to dry ingredients and add strawberries. Melt butter and pour into mixture. Mix well. Pour into unbaked pastry shell and bake at 375°F. for 40 to 50 minutes. Top with meringue and bake at 325°F. for 12 to 15 minutes.

Mrs. Allene B. Dunn, Valley H. S.
Fairfax, Alabama

STRAWBERRY PIE
Number of Servings — 6

1 c. sugar
3 T. cornstarch
½ t. salt
1 c. water
2 t. lemon juice
Few drops red food coloring
3 c. sliced strawberries
1 baked 9″ pastry shell

Mix sugar, cornstarch, and salt. Add water, lemon juice, and red coloring. Cook, stirring all the time, until clear and thick. Cool a few minutes. Arrange berries in the pie shell. Pour the cooked mixture over the berries. Refrigerate. Substitute well drained frozen strawberries if you wish.

May Lohmann, Miami H. S.
Miami, Oklahoma

STRAWBERRY PIE
Number of Servings — 5

1 pkg. (10 ozs.) frozen strawberries
1 c. sugar minus 1 T.
1 T. lemon juice
Pinch of salt
2 egg whites
½ c. whipping cream
1 t. vanilla

Place defrosted strawberries, sugar, egg whites, lemon juice, and salt in a large bowl of the mixer. Beat at medium speed for 15 minutes or until stiff. Whip the cream. Add the vanilla and fold into the strawberry mixture. Pour lightly into 1 baked pastry shell or vanilla wafer crust. Freeze over night or several hours. Serve with whipped cream and garnish with a strawberry if desired.

Mary Reeves, Fayette Co. H. S.
Somerville, Tennessee

STRAWBERRY CREAM PIE
Number of Servings — 5

1 qt. fresh strawberries
1⅛ c. water
1 c. sugar
3 T. cornstarch
1 c. heavy cream

1 T. confectioners' sugar
⅛ t. nutmeg
1 baked 9″ pastry shell

Make glaze for top of pie first by putting 1 cup of water, 1 cup sugar, and 1 cup berries in a saucepan. Bring to boil and cook 15 minutes. Mix cornstarch with remaining water and add to mixture. Cook until thick and clear. Put mixture through seive and allow to cool. Beat cream until it stands in peaks. Add confectioners' sugar and nutmeg. Put ¾ of the cream in bottom of pastry shell. Slice remaining berries on top and pour glaze over berries and cream. Rest of cream may be used for garnish. Chill 3 hours before serving.

Mrs. Carol A. Brann, Western Area Jr.-Sr. H. S.
Mifflinburg, Pennsylvania

STRAWBERRY DIVINITY PIE
Number of Servings — 8

2 c. sliced strawberries
½ c. butter or margarine
2 eggs
1½ c. sugar
Pinch salt
1 9″ pastry shell

Roll pastry thin and place in 9″ pastry pan. Place sliced strawberries in bottom. Beat together sugar and butter. Add well beaten eggs and pinch of salt. Spread over berries. Bake in hot oven 425°F. for 10 minutes. Reduce heat to 325°F. and bake 25-30 minutes. Serve hot.

Grace G. Mount, Beauregard School
Opelika, Alabama

FRESH STRAWBERRY PIE (One-Crust)
Number of Servings — 6-8

1 qt. fresh strawberries
2 T. cornstarch
¼ t. salt
1 c. sugar
½ c. boiling water
Red coloring (optional)
1 baked pastry shell
Whipped cream

Wash, hull, and sort berries, saving the perfect berries for placing in the shell. Mash or crush enough berries to make 1 cup. Mix sugar, salt, cornstarch, crushed berries, and boiling water. Cook, stirring constantly, directly over flame until thickened. Add coloring and cool thoroughly. Just before serving, place reserved berries in the cooled, baked pastry shell, pour cooled sauce over the berries in the shell. Garnish with whipped cream.

Elizabeth S. Thornton, Sparkman H. S.
Toney, Alabama

STRAWBERRY CHEESE PIE
Number of Servings — 6-8

1 pkg. cream cheese
3 T. cream
1 qt. strawberries
¾ c. sugar
2 T. cornstarch (heaping)
Pineapple juice
1 baked pie shell (cooled)

(Continued on Next Page)

Blend cheese and cream and spread on cool pie shell. Chill. Wash and hull berries. Slice half of the largest berries. Mash other half and put through sieve to make puree. Add cornstarch to this and mix to paste. Add pineapple juice to make 1½ cups liquid. Add sugar and cook until thick and transparent, stir constantly. Cool. Pour ½ into pie shell and arrange sliced berries on it. Pour on rest and chill. Serve with whipped cream.

Helen Reed, Bassick H. S.
Bridgeport, Connecticut

NUTTY STRAWBERRY PIE

Number of Servings — 6-8

Pastry:
1 c. flour
⅓ c. fat
½ t. salt
2 T. water
½ c. almonds

Measure flour into bowl, mix salt through it. With pastry blender, cut in fat until particles are the size of giant peas. Add almonds. Sprinkle with water and press firmly into a ball. Let stand 5 minutes. Flatten with hand, roll, place in pan and let stand 10 minutes. Bake until golden 375°F.

Filling:
1 (15 oz.) can condensed milk
1 egg yolk
⅓ c. lemon juice
1 t. vanilla
¼ t. almond extract
½ c. whipping cream

Combine condensed milk, egg yolk, lemon juice, vanilla and almond extract. Stir until mixture thickens. Fold in whipped cream and spoon into baked shell.

Glaze*:
½ pt. strawberries
¼ c. sugar
1 T. cornstarch
Juice from ½ lemon

Crush ¼ pint strawberries in saucepan, blend in flour, lemon juice, and sugar. Cook over low heat, stirring constantly until mixture thickens and is clear. Add ¼ pint sliced, fresh strawberries. Spread over filling.

*A cherry glaze of 2 cups drained tart cherries, ⅔ cup cherry juice, ¼ cup sugar and 1 tablespoon cornstarch or cherry pie filling can be used.

Marilyn Cooper, Delhi H. S.
Delhi, Louisiana

STRAWBERRY GLAZE PIE

Number of Servings — 6

1 qt. strawberries
¾ c. water
2 T. cornstarch
¾ c. sugar
¼ t. salt
Few drops red food coloring
1 baked 9" pie shell
Whipped cream

Crush 1 cup red ripe strawberries, add water and bring to boil. Simmer 3 minutes. Strain. Add water if necessary to make 1 cup liquid. Combine cornstarch, sugar, and salt and add to liquid. Stir until smooth. Bring to a boil and stir constantly until mixture thickens. Cool and add red food coloring. Place remaining whole strawberries in baked pie shell. Pour the glaze over the berries. Top the pie with whipped cream.

Martha McNatt, Beech-Bluff H. S.
Beech Bluff, Tennessee

BUTTERSCOTCH PIE

Number of Servings — 6

⅓ c. sifted flour or ¼ c. cornstarch
1 c. brown sugar
¼ t. salt
2 c. milk scalded
3 slightly beaten egg yolks
3 T. butter or margarine
½ t. vanilla
1 baked 9" pastry shell
3 egg whites (beaten stiff)
6 T. sugar

Mix flour, brown sugar, and salt. Gradually add milk. Cook over moderate heat, stirring constantly, until mixture thickens and boils. Cook 2 minutes, remove from heat. Add small amount to egg yolks, stir into remaining hot mixture, cook 1 minute stiring constantly. Add butter, and vanilla, cool. Cover with meringue made of egg whites and 6 tablespoons sugar. Bake in moderate oven 350°F. 12 to 15 minutes.

Mrs. Nell Albrecht, Blum H. S.
Blum, Texas

BUTTERSCOTCH PIE

Number of Servings — 12

2 c. sugar
2 T. cornstarch
1 c. butter
3 c. milk
5 eggs, separated
1 t. vanilla
1 baked pastry shell

Brown sugar, cornstarch and butter together in skillet. Scald 2½ cups milk, separate eggs, beat yolks. Add ½ cup cold milk to yolks. Combine scalded milk to yolks. Gradually add to butter and sugar mixture. Cook until thick, making sure lumps are out. Cool. Add vanilla. Place in cooked pastry shell and add beaten egg whites to top and brown.

Mrs. Fred Herron
Houston, Texas

BUTTERSCOTCH-DATE CREAM PIE

1 baked 9" pastry shell
2½ c. milk, diluted evaporated milk or liquefied
    non-fat dry milk
6 T. butter or margarine
2 egg yolks
1 c. light-brown sugar, packed
¼ c. cornstarch
Dash of salt
½ c. sliced, pitted dates
1 t. vanilla extract
1 c. heavy cream, whipped
¼ c. chopped pecans

Early in day: In double boiler, heat 2 cups milk with butter. Beat yolks, stir in combined sugar, cornstarch, and salt. Blend in remaining ½ cup milk, add to heated milk in double boiler. Cook over hot, not boiling, water, stirring until thick and smooth. Add dates and vanilla. Refrigerate until cold. Turn into baked pastry shell. Refrigerate at least 6 hours. To serve, garnish pie with whipped cream, making swirls, and sprinkle chopped pecans around inside of rim.

Myrtis L. McAlhany, Saint George H. S.
Saint George, South Carolina

BUTTERSCOTCH BROWNIE PIE

Number of Servings — 8
3 egg whites
1 c. sugar
1 c. ground pecans
18 sq. ground graham crackers
½ pt. cream
1 T. sugar

Beat the egg whites until creamy. Add the sugar a little at a time and beat until the whites are very stiff or stand in stiff peaks. Add the ground pecans and the ground graham crackers and mix well. Bake in an 8" pie plate that has been very well greased for 30 minutes at 350°F. When the pie has cooled, top with whipped cream to which 1 tablespoon of sugar has been added, garnish with a few graham cracker crumbs. Refrigerate until used. *Patti Ljungdahl, Carrizo Springs H. S.*
Carrizo Springs, Texas

CARAMEL OR BUTTERSCOTCH PIE

Number of Servings — 6
1⅓ c. brown sugar
7 T. cornstarch
Pinch of soda
2 T. butter
2 c. milk
3 eggs, separated
1 t. vanilla

Mix sugar, cornstarch, soda, butter, and milk in top of double boiler. Cook until thick. Add a little hot mixture gradually to beaten egg yolks, stirring constantly. Then add egg yolk mixture to filling in double boiler. Cook 2 minutes. It is done when the mixture will hold a peak. Put in baked shell. Beat egg whites until stiff but not dry. Gradually add 6 tablespoons sugar and beat until firm. Put on pie and brown meringue.

Mrs. Roy Cousins, Hogansville H. S.
Hogansville, Georgia

CHERRY PIE

Number of Servings — 6-8
1 c. granulated sugar
3 T. cornstarch
¼ t. salt
¾ c. cherry juice
1½ t. fresh lemon juice
¼ t. almond extract
½ t. red food coloring
2 T. butter
3 c. drained red tart cherries

In saucepan place ¼ cup granulated sugar, cornstarch, and salt, mix. Add cherry juice and cook until thick. Add remaining sugar and cook until glossy. Remove from heat and stir in lemon juice, almond extract, food coloring, and 1 tablespoon butter. Add cherries and mix gently. Let cool while preparing crust.

Crust:
2 c. flour
1 t. salt
⅔ c. plus 1 T. shortening
3-4 T. ice water

Sift and measure flour with salt in a large mixing bowl. In 1⅓ cup ice water measure shortening. Drain water from shortening and cut shortening into dry ingredients. Sprinkle 3 or 4 tablespoons ice water in dry ingredients. Mix dough together and press into a ball on a piece of wax paper. Divide dough in half and roll half on floured pastry cloth to fit a 9" pie pan. Place in dish, being careful not to stretch. Roll remainder of dough and cut into strips with an edger. Arrange strips in lattice design on cookie sheet, sprinkled with sugar. Pour filling into pie crust and dot cherries with 1 tablespoon butter before placing lattice top in place. Wet edges of pie crust and slide the lattice top into place. Flute the edges and fit pieces of aluminum foil over. Bake at 450°F. for 10-15 minutes, remove foil bake at 350°F. for 25-30 minutes.

Patricia A. Chwierut, Sunny Hills H. S.
Fullerton, California

BING CHERRY PIE

Number of Servings — 8
11" graham cracker pie crust
1 No. 2 can bing cherries
1 pkg. cherry Jello
1-6 oz. can evaporated milk
¼ t. almond extract
2 egg whites
3 T. sugar

Drain juice from cherries. Add enough water to make 1 cup, bring to boil, pour over gelatin in bowl. Stir until gelatin dissolves. Cool slightly. Combine gelatin mixture, milk, and extract and chill until it coats a spoon. Meanwhile beat egg whites until foamy. Add sugar slowly and beat until it forms soft peaks. Beat gelatin mixture until thick and fluffy. Fold egg whites and cherries into gelatin. Spoon into pie crust. Garnish with cherries and chopped nuts if desired.

Mrs. Margaret Ledbetter, Black Rock H. S.
Black Rock, Arkansas

COBBLER A' LA CHERRY
Number of Servings — 6

1 c. flour
1 c. sugar
1 t. baking powder
½ t. salt
2 T. melted fat
½ c. milk
1 No. 303 can cherries
⅔ c. sugar

Sift together the first four ingredients. Add melted fat and milk, and mix until well blended. Place the can of cherries (with juice) and sugar in saucepan and bring to a boil. Place the first mixture in a greased baking dish and pour the cherry mixture over it. Bake 35 minutes at 400°F. (The batter will rise to the top as it bakes.) Serve with whipped cream or ice cream.

Mrs. Loretta McKnight, Justin F. Kimball H. S.
Dallas, Texas

GLAZED CHERRY PIE

1 baked 9″ pastry shell or graham cracker crust
1 No. 2½ can (3½-4 c.) cherries, drained
¾ c. juice from cherries (add water to complete amount)
¾ c. sugar
3 T. cornstarch
¼ t. salt
½ c. cream for whipping
1 T. sugar for cream

Prepare shell (either pastry or graham cracker). Strain juice from cherries. Place juice in small saucepan, add sugar, cornstarch and salt. Bring to boiling, stirring constantly. Cook 3 minutes, or until thick and clear. Remove from heat. Cool slightly. Spoon glaze over cherries, being sure to carefully coat each one. Arrange on pie shell. Chill pie. Just before serving, whip cream, sweeten, spoon in rings on top of pie.

Mrs. Doris J. Combs, Central H. S.
Woodstock, Virginia

RED CHERRY PIE

Cold water pastry
3½ c. (two 16 oz. cans) water
Packed sour cherries, drained
1¼ c. sugar
½ t. salt
¼ c. cornstarch
1⅓ c. cherry juice
½ t. almond extract
1 t. red food coloring
1 T. lemon juice

Divide pastry in half. Roll pastry for bottom crust and place in 9″ pie pan. Mix sugar, salt, and cornstarch in saucepan. Slowly blend in cherry juice. Boil over medium heat, stirring until thick. Remove from heat. Add extract, coloring, and lemon juice. Mix in 3½ cups cherries. Cool. Pour into pastry lined pie pan. Moisten pastry rim. Place top crust over pie. Flute edge. Bake at 425°F. for 35 minutes.

Mary B. Lewis, Gilbert H. S.
Gilbert, South Carolina

CHERRY COBBLER
Number of Servings — 6-8

1 can cherries
½ c. water
1 c. sugar
1 c. flour
½ c. sugar
2 t. baking powder
½ t. salt
½ c. milk
½ cube margarine

Heat cherries, water and 1 cup sugar to boiling. Combine and mix well the flour, ½ cup sugar, baking powder, salt, and milk. Melt margarine in baking dish. Pour in batter, spread evenly. Pour in cherry mixture (boiling hot). Bake in 375°F. oven until golden brown, about 20-25 minutes.

Thelma Vogel, McAlester H. S.
McAlester, Oklahoma

CHERRY PIE
Number of Servings — 6-8

1½ c. sugar
5 T. flour
¼ t. salt
1 T. oleo, melted
½ c. cherry juice
¼ t. red food coloring
¼ t. almond extract
3 c. drained canned cherries

Combine sugar, flour, and salt. Stir in the melted oleo, then cherry juice, food coloring and almond extract. Add cherries and let stand while making the pastry. Line a 9″ pie plate with pastry, fill with cherry mixture. Cover with top crust or lattice top, flute edges. Cut a 2½″ strip of foil and fold it loosely around edge of pie. Bake at 425°F. about 40 minutes, removing foil about 10 minutes before the end of baking time.

Almond Glaze for Cherry Pie:
1 c. confectioners' sugar (sifted)
½ t. almond flavoring
2 T. cream

Mix sugar, almond flavoring and enough cream to make spreading consistency. Immediately after taking 2-crust pie from oven, spread with glaze.

Barbara H. Thompson, Bovina H. S.
Bovina, Texas

CHERRY-PINEAPPLE PIE
Number of Servings — 6

2 c. drained pie cherries
1 c. crushed pineapple
1 c. sugar
2 T. cornstarch
2 T. flour
¼ t. salt
2 T. butter

Drain fruit. Mix sugar, flour and cornstarch. Combine with fruit and mix well. Place in uncooked pastry shell. Cover with strips of pastry. Bake at 425°F. 20-25 minutes.

Mrs. Inez P. Curvin, Benjamin Russell H. S.
Alexander City, Alabama

CHERRY (Red) BANANA PIE

1 can (1 lb., 4 ozs.) pitted red cherries
1 c. sugar
3½ T. cornstarch
1 T. butter
½ t. cinnamon
1 t. almond flavoring
2-3 medium bananas
1 c. whipping cream, whipped stiff
1 baked 9" pastry shell

Boil cherries, juice, sugar, and cornstarch together 1 minute, or until clear and thick, stirring constantly. Add butter and cool. Blend in cinnamon and almond flavoring. Place layers of sliced bananas in pastry shell. Pour filling over bananas and chill. Spoon wreath of whipped cream on pie and garnish with banana slices (dipped in lemon, pineapple or grapefruit juice), if desired.

Martha Sue Purvis, Joshua H. S.
Joshua, Texas

JUBILEE CHEESE CHERRY PIE

Number of Servings — 8-10

9" unbaked pie shell
No. 2 can pie mix, cherries
1½ pkg. 8 oz. cream cheese
2 eggs
1½ c. sugar
½ t. vanilla
1 c. sour cream
Nutmeg

Pour cherries into unbaked pie shell. Bake 15 minutes in 425°F. oven. Mix cream cheese, eggs, sugar, and vanilla until smooth and creamy. Reduce heat of oven to 350°F. Pour above mixture over cherries. Bake 30 minutes 350°F. Cool. Spread sour cream over pie. Sprinkle with nutmeg. Refrigerate.

Mrs. Ouida T. Hicks, Sidney Lanier H. S.
Montgomery, Alabama

MRS. PARK'S CHERRY CREAM PIE

Number of Servings — 6

1 baked 9" pastry shell
⅔ c. sugar
3 T. cornstarch
½ t. salt
3 c. milk
3 egg yolks, slightly beaten
1 T. butter
1½ t. vanilla
1 jar cherry pie filling
1 c. whipped cream, sweeten to taste

Mix sugar, cornstarch and salt. Gradually pour milk over them in saucepan. Cook over medium heat, stirring constantly, until mixture coats spoon. Cook 1 minute. Remove from heat. Beat some of hot mixture into egg yolks. Return to pan. Cook 1 minute more, stirring. Add butter, vanilla. Pour into baked shell. Cool. Ring around outer edge with cherry filling. Top each slice with whipped cream.

Mrs. Rebecca Park Malone, Alvord H. S.
Alvord, Texas

CHERRY PECAN PIE

Number of Servings — 6

4 egg yolks
1 whole egg
1½ c. sugar
4 T. flour
Juice from 1 lemon
1 can cherries
Red food coloring
½ c. chopped nuts

Combine slightly beaten eggs, sugar, flour, and lemon juice. Cook in double boiler, stirring constantly until thickened. Add food coloring, cherries, and nuts. Pour into baked pie shell. Serve plain or add whipped cream topping.

Betty Johnson, Petersburg H. S.
Petersburg, Texas

CHERRY BLOSSOM PIE DESSERT

Number of Servings — 6

Cherry filling:
¼ c. flour
1 c. sugar
Juice drained from 1 can pie cherries

Cook flour, sugar and cherry juice together until thick and clear.

Crumb top and crust:
1½ c. flour
½ t. soda
1 t. salt
1 c. brown sugar
1 c. 3-minute oats
1 stick margarine

Blend dry ingredients. Cut in margarine with pastry blender until moist and crumbly. Press half of crumb mixture into a greased baking dish. Pour in cherry filling. Top with remaining crumb mixture. Bake 25 minutes at 350°F.

Gladys Vickers, Oakwood H. S.
Oakwood, Texas

CHESS PIE

Number of Servings — 12

5 eggs
1½ c. sugar
1 T. flour
1 T. cornmeal
¼ t. salt
1 t. vanilla
½ c. butter
1 c. milk

Beat egg yolks until light yellow. Add sugar, flour, cornmeal, salt and vanilla. Add melted butter and milk. Pour into 2 unbaked shells and bake 10 minutes at 400°F. Reduce heat to 300°F. and bake until done (silver knife test). Cover with meringue and bake in 300°F. oven for 10 minutes until golden brown. Makes two pies.

Mrs. Ruth L. DeFriese, Young H. S.
Knoxville, Tennessee

CHESS PIE
Number of Servings — 6
3 eggs
1½ c. sugar
1 stick melted butter
1 t. vanilla

Beat eggs, stir in sugar, add melted butter and flavoring. Mix well. Pour into 8" unbaked pie shell. Bake at 350°F. for 30-40 minutes or until done.

Eloise Bayer Hawkins, Walterboro Sr. H. S.
Walterboro, South Carolina

CHESS PIE
2 whole eggs
1½ c. sugar
1 T. flour
1 T. meal
¼ c. milk
¼ c. butter
½ t. vinegar
½ t. vanilla
Dash of salt

Beat eggs real good. Add sugar and beat until thick. Add other ingredients and stir. Pour into unbaked crust and bake at 350°F. 45 minutes.

Mrs. Don Kreitzer, Dickson H. S.
Dickson, Tennessee

CHESS PIE
Number of Servings — 8
2 T. cornstarch
½ c. sugar
3 eggs, slightly beaten
1 c. white corn syrup
⅛ t. salt
½ t. vanilla
1 T. lemon juice
2 T. melted butter

Mix cornstarch and sugar. Beat eggs. Add corn syrup, then all other ingredients. Pour in pastry-lined pie pan that has been baked 5 minutes. Bake at 425°F. until silver knife inserted 1" from edge of filling will come out clean.

Marie C. Hill, Karns H. S.
Knoxville, Tennessee

CHESS PIE
1 stick butter (oleo)
1 c. sugar
3 eggs
1 t. vanilla
Nutmeg, sprinkle
2 t. vinegar (not full)
2 t. cornmeal

Cream butter and sugar. Add eggs, 1 at a time, and beat well each time. Add vanilla, sprinkle of nutmeg, cornmeal, and vinegar. Fold in with spatula. Pour over favorite uncooked pastry shell. Sprinkle little nutmeg on top. Bake 15 minutes at 450°F., then 40 minutes at 350°F.

Mary Lee Hartley, Crisp Co. H. S.
Cordele, Georgia

CHESS PIE
Number of Servings — 6
1 stick margarine
1½ c. sugar
1 T. vinegar
3 eggs, beaten
1 t. vanilla
Pinch salt

Melt margarine. Add sugar and vinegar. Bring to boil. Add this mixture to beaten eggs, salt, and vanilla. Beat good. Pour into unbaked shell. Bake at 325°F. for 40 minutes.

Anne Davis, Westmoreland H. S.
Westmoreland, Tennessee

CHESS PIE
Number of Servings — 6
1 stick butter or margarine
1 c. sugar
3 eggs
2 T. cornmeal
1 T. vinegar
1 t. lemon flavoring
1 t. vanilla

Combine butter and sugar. Cream well. Add all the other ingredients and mix thoroughly. Pour into unbaked 8" pastry shell. Bake at 325°F. 45 minutes to 1 hour. Variation: Add ½ cup coconut flakes to the uncooked ingredients.

Georgia Matthews, Oliver Springs H. S.
Oliver Springs, Tennessee

CHESS PIE
Number of Servings — 6
2 c. sugar
2 T. meal
Salt to taste, very little
3 eggs, slightly beaten
¼ c. butter or margarine, softened
5 T. buttermilk
1 t. vanilla

Mix dry ingredients, add eggs and other ingredients, mix well. Pour into unbaked pastry shell and cook about 1 hour or until firm when shaken, in oven heated to 300°F.

Mrs. Margaret J. Perry, Christiana H. S.
Christiana, Tennessee

CHESS PIE
Number of Servings — 6
1 unbaked 8" pie shell
1 c. light brown sugar
½ c. granulated sugar
1 T. flour
2 eggs, well beaten
2 T. sweet milk
1 t. vanilla
½ c. butter or margarine (melted)

Mix the 2 kinds of sugar and flour thoroughly. Beat in eggs, milk, and vanilla. Add melted butter. Pour into pastry-lined pie pan and bake at 375°F. until set, approximately 35 to 45 minutes. Good served slightly warm, with whipped cream.

Mrs. Ola Lee W. Robinson, North H. S.
North, South Carolina

CHESS PIE

3 eggs (1 whole, 2 yolks)
1 c. sugar
1 T. cornmeal
1 T. butter
1 T. vinegar
2-3 T. sweet milk
1 t. vanilla

Mix ingredients together in a bowl. Pour in a 8" or 9" pie pan lined with uncooked pie crust. Bake at 375°F. approximately 30 minutes or until the top is brown. Use 2 egg whites left from filling to make meringue if desired.

Mrs. Marion Sebastian, Arkadelphia H. S.
Arkadelphia, Arkansas

CHESS PIE

Number of Servings — 6

½ c. oleomargarine or butter, melted
1½ c. sugar
1 t. cornmeal (heaping)
1 t. vanilla
1 t. vinegar
3 eggs
¾ c. coconut

Mix all ingredients and pour into unbaked pie shell. Bake at 350°F. about 45-50 minutes.

Mrs. Minta Skaggs, M. C. Napier H. S.
Hazard, Kentucky

CHESS PIE

Number of Servings — 6

½ c. butter
1¼ c. sugar
1 T. cornmeal
2 T. flour
2 eggs
Juice of ½ lemon
1 t. vanilla
½ c. milk (heat to luke warm)

Melt butter, mix in sugar, cornmeal and flour. Beat in eggs 1 at a time. Mix in lemon juice and vanilla. Add milk and pour into unbaked pastry shell. Bake at 425°F. 10 minutes. Reduce heat to 350°F. and bake about 30 minutes.

Mrs. Jeanine Williams, Meade Memorial School
Williamsport, Kentucky

CHESS PIES (Individual Pies)

Number of Servings — 12

3 eggs
1 c. sugar
½ c. melted butter
1 c. dates, cut up
1 c. raisins
1 c. nuts, chopped

Beat eggs until light. Add sugar and melted butter. Beat again. Stir in dates, raisins, and nuts. Line muffin tins with pastry rounds, spoon filling into them. Bake 25 minutes at 375°F. Makes its own meringue.

Mrs. Vivian Johnson, Junior H. S.
Willmar, Minnesota

CHESS-NUT PIE

Number of Servings — 18

½ c. margarine
¾ c. brown sugar
¾ c. granulated sugar
1 t. vanilla
3 eggs, separated
1 c. nuts
½ c. raisins

Cream margarine and sugars together. Add vanilla and egg yolks. Mix well. Beat egg whites until stiff. Fold into sugar mixture. Add nuts and raisins. Bake in individual pie shells, at 400°F. for 25 minutes. For individual pie shells, make a recipe for a 2-crust pie. Roll out small portions at a time and place in muffin tins.

Constance Huffman, Virgin Valley H. S.
Mesquite, Nevada

COCONUT-CHESS PIE

Number of Servings — 6

½ c. butter
2 c. sugar
5 eggs, separated
2 T. cornstarch
1 c. sweet milk
1½ c. coconut

Eggs, milk and butter should be at room temperature. Cream butter, add sugar gradually. Beat egg yolks and add to butter and sugar mixture. Add cornstarch and blend. Add milk and coconut. Bake at 350° in an unbaked 8" pie shell until brown on top (about 45 minutes). Top with a meringue made from the 5 egg whites. Brown meringue in a slow oven 250°F.

Virginia Bryant, Milan H. S.
Milan Tennessee

LEMON CHESS PIE

2 c. sugar
1 T. flour
1 T. meal
4 eggs
¼ c. melted butter
¼ c. milk
2-4 T. grated lemon rind
¼ c. lemon juice

Combine sugar, flour, and meal in large bowl. Toss lightly with a fork. Add remaining ingredients. Beat with rotary or electric mixer until smooth and thoroughly blended. Pour into unbaked 9" pie shell and bake 35 to 40 minutes at 350°F. or until top is a golden brown.

This recipe submitted by the following teachers:
Mrs. Katye R. Pugh, Treadwell H. S.
Memphis, Tennessee
Mrs. Delma Walden
Tompkinsville, Kentucky
Mrs. Betty Addison, Lipan H. S.
Lipan, Texas
Mrs. Leon Potts, Kossuth H. S.
Kossuth, Mississippi
Mrs. Martha Cervenka, Granger H. S.
Granger, Texas

SOUTHERN CHESS PIE
Number of Servings — 6
3 eggs
1½ c. sugar (½ c. brown sugar and 1 c. granulated
  sugar may be used)
½ c. butter or margarine (melted)
2 T. milk
1 T. flour
1 t. vanilla
1 c. nuts (if desired)
1 pastry shell

Beat eggs. Add sugar, butter, milk, flour, and flavoring. Fold in nuts. Pour in unbaked pie shell. Cook at 375° F. 40-50 minutes. May be served plain or with whipped cream.

This recipe submitted by the following teachers:
Dorothy G. Pruitt, Oxford H. S.
Oxford, North Carolina
Betty B. Belue, Deshler H. S.
Tuscumbia, Alabama

OLD FASHIONED CHESS PIE
Number of Servings — 6-8
2 c. sugar
2 T. flour, heaping
1 T. yellow cornmeal, heaping
1 stick melted butter
3 eggs, beaten
½ c. buttermilk
2 t. vanilla
1 12" unbaked pastry shell

Combine sugar, flour and meal. Mix well. Add stick of melted butter and mix well. Add beaten eggs and mix well. Add buttermilk and vanilla and mix well. Pour mixture into unbaked pastry shell and bake in pre-heated oven of 425°F. for 10 minutes. Reduce temperature to 325°F. and bake 30 minutes. When pie begins to brown, cover with a sheet of aluminum foil to prevent deep browning or burning.

Geneva Franklin, Powderly H. S.
Powderly, Texas

SOUTHERN CHESS PIE
Number of Servings — 6
1 c. white sugar
1 level T. flour
¼ t. salt
2 egg yolks (save the whites for meringue)
1 whole egg
3 T. water
1 t. white vinegar
¼ lb. or ½ c. melted butter

Mix sugar, flour and salt together. Beat the 2 egg yolks and the 1 whole egg together, adding water and vinegar and melted butter. Beat together well. Add the sugar-flour mixture, mix well. Pour into an unbaked pastry shell and bake at 350°F. until set. Usually bakes in 35 minutes and makes a 9" pie. Use the 2 egg whites from the 2 eggs, add 2 tablespoons of sugar, and beat until the meringue will hold its shape well. Spread on top of the pie and brown for 12 minutes in a 350°F. oven.

Mrs. Dorothy Burd, Oldham Co. H. S.
LaGrange, Kentucky

SOUTHERN PIRATES CHESS PIE
Number of Servings — 6
¼ c. butter
1½ c. sugar
3 eggs
1½ t. vinegar
2 T. cornmeal
½ c. cream (not milk)
1 pastry shell

Cream butter and sugar. Add beaten eggs. Mix well. Add vinegar, cornmeal, and cream. Mix well. Pour into unbaked pastry shell and bake at 350°F. 30 to 45 minutes.

Mrs. Irene Henderson, Englewood H. S.
Jacksonville, Florida

LEMON CHESS PIE
Number of Servings — 6-8
4 eggs
2 c. sugar
1 T. flour
Juice of 2 lemons
1 t. lemon extract
⅛ lb. butter

Beat whole eggs well. Add sugar, flour, juice of 2 lemons, lemon extract and melted butter. Mix thoroughly. Pour into unbaked pie shell. Place in oven pre-heated to 425°F. Turn heat to 275°F. as pie is put in oven. Bake 1 hour.

Emma L. Flake Van Laningham,
Walnut Springs H. S.
Walnut Springs, Texas

CHOCOLATE PIE
2 egg yolks
½ c. milk
½ c. sugar
1½ T. flour (heaping)
½ c. white syrup
¼ c. cocoa with water
1 T. butter
1 baked pastry shell
2 egg whites
Sugar for meringue

Beat egg yolks slightly and add milk. Mix sugar and flour separately and then add to egg mixture gradually. Blend syrup in next and then chocolate paste (fairly thin) and butter. Cook in double boiler until thick. Pour into baked 8" pie crust and add meringue.

Anita W. Hall, West Union H. S.
West Union, Ohio

CHOCOLATE PIE
Number of Servings — 6-8
6 T. flour
1½ c. sugar
3 T. cocoa
2 egg yolks
Use whites for meringue
1½ c. evaporated milk
1 t. vanilla
3 T. butter
1 baked pastry shell
4 T. sugar
Pinch baking powder

(Continued on Next Page)

Mix flour, sugar, and cocoa together. Add beaten egg yolks. Add evaporated milk. Add flavoring and butter. Cook in double boiler until thick. Pour into a baked pie shell. For meringue, beat egg whites until stiff. Add sugar and baking powder. Spread on pie and bake at 250°F. for 15 minutes.

Elizabeth Gatewood Moseley,
George Washington H. S.
Danville, Virginia

CHOCOLATE PIE

Number of Servings — 6-8

1¼ c. sugar
½ c. flour (lightly packed)
3 T. cocoa (heaping)
2 c. water
3 eggs, separated
½ stick butter
Dash of salt
1 t. vanilla
1 9″ baked pastry shell

Mix sugar, flour, and cocoa together. Add enough of the water to make a paste. Beat in egg yolks well. Heat remaining water with butter and salt until butter is melted. Add water mixture to first mixture and cook until thick. Remove from heat. Add vanilla. Cool and pour into baked 9″ pie crust. Cover with meringue and brown.

Mrs. Herbert Parker, Sand Rock H. S.
Leesburg, Alabama

CHOCOLATE CREAM PIE

Number of Servings — 6

¼ c. flour
⅔ c. sugar
⅛ t. salt
2 T. cocoa
2 c. milk
3 egg yolks, beaten
1 T. butter
½ t. vanilla
3 egg whites
Sugar
1 baked pastry shell

Combine flour, sugar, salt, cocoa, and milk. Cook over low heat until thick. Beat egg yolks. Stir small amount of hot mixture into eggs. Pour back into saucepan and cook until thick. Add butter and vanilla. Pour into baked pastry shell and top with meringue. Brown in 375°F. oven 10 minutes or until golden brown.

Mrs. Betty M. Albers
Aragon, Georgia

CHOCOLATE CHIFFON PIE (Baked)

Number of Servings — 6

½ c. butter or margarine
1 c. sugar
1 t. vanilla
2 egg yolks
2 sq. unsweetened chocolate
⅓ c. sifted flour
2 egg whites
⅛ t. salt

Cream butter, add sugar gradually and cream together until light and fluffy. Add vanilla and blend thoroughly. Add egg yolks, one at a time, beating well after each addition. Add unsweetened chocolate, melted, and flour, and mix well. Beat egg whites with salt until stiff but not dry and fold them into chocolate mixture. Turn the filling into unbaked pie shell or graham cracker crumb crust. Bake in moderate oven 350°F. for 45 minutes. Cool. Top with whipped cream and shaved chocolate.

Mrs. Mary Light, King H. S.
Kingsville, Texas

CHOCOLATE ICING PIE

Number of Servings — 8

2 eggs, separated
1 c. sugar
¼ c. thin cream
1 t. vanilla

Separate eggs and beat yolks. Add sugar, cream and vanilla to yolks. Then add beaten egg whites. Cook at 400°F. in uncooked crust until done. Cool and cover with your favorite chocolate frosting.

Mildred Tate, Henderson City H. S.
Henderson, Kentucky

CHOCOLATE MERINGUE PIE

Number of Servings — 6

4 T. cocoa
1 c. sugar
6 T. flour
½ t. salt
2½ c. milk
3 egg yolks, slightly beaten
2 T. butter
1 t. vanilla
3 egg whites
6 T. sugar
1 baked 9″ pastry shell

Combine cocoa, sugar, flour, salt and milk and heat in double boiler. Cook until thickened. Stir often. Stir in beaten egg yolks. Cook 2 minutes and add butter and vanilla. Cool. Turn into pie shell. Beat egg whites until foamy. Add sugar, 2 tablespoons at a time, beating until blended. Then beat until mixture stands in peaks. Spread on filling. Bake in oven at 300°F. for 20 minutes.

This recipe submitted by the following teachers:
Mrs. Mary S. Overman, Harmony H. S.
Harmony, North Carolina
Mrs. Loretta Sykes
Mathews, Alabama

CHOCOLATE PRETZEL PIE

Number of Servings — 6-8

1¼ c. fine pretzel crumbs
1 t. sugar
½ c. melted butter or margarine
⅔ c. sugar
4 T. cornstarch
2½ c. milk

(Continued on Next Page)

3 sq. unsweetened chocolate (cut in small pieces)
3 egg yolks, slightly beaten
1 t. vanilla
1 T. crushed toasted almonds
Pretzel thin sticks and bow-knots

Combine first 3 ingredients. Press evenly into 9″ pie pan, covering bottoms and sides completely. Bake about 8 minutes at 325°F. Cool thoroughly. Combine next 4 ingredients in top of double boiler. Cook over boiling water until thickened, stirring constantly. Cover, cook 15 minutes longer. Stir a little of the hot mixture into egg yolks. Add to remaining mixture in double boiler. Cook and stir 2 minutes over hot water. Cool. Add vanilla. Pour into pretzel crust. Decorate with pretzels. Sprinkle with almonds. Chill.

Claudia G. Whitmire, Carolina H. S.
Greenville, South Carolina

FUDGE PIE

Number of Servings — 6-8

2 c. sugar
3 T. flour
3 T. cocoa
2 c. milk
3 egg yolks, beaten
¼ c. butter
1 pastry shell
2 egg whites
Sugar

Mix dry ingredients in saucepan. Gradually stir in milk. Cook over moderate heat until mixture thickens and boils. Boil 1 minute. Stir half of this mixture into egg yolks, then blend into hot mixture in saucepan. Add butter, boil until very thick. Pour into pastry-lined pan. Prepare meringue and spread on pie.

Gail Epperson, Slidell H. S.
Slidell, Louisiana

NO-CRUST FUDGE PIE

Number of Servings — 6

¼ c. butter or margarine
3 sq. unsweetened chocolate
2 c. sugar
4 eggs, well beaten
¼ t. salt
1 t. vanilla
⅝ c. chopped walnuts or pecans
1 pastry shell

Melt butter and chocolate together in medium weight utensil over low heat. Stir in sugar. Blend beaten eggs with chocolate mixture. Add salt, vanilla, and walnuts. Pour into a well greased 9″ glass pie plate. Bake in 350°F. oven for 45 minutes. Serve topped with vanilla ice cream or whipped cream.

This recipe submitted by the following teachers:
Esther Darst Minton, Nogales H. S.
Nogales, Arizona
Mattie Youngblood Miller, Newton H. S.
Newton, Texas

COCONUT PIE

Number of Servings — 12

2 c. sugar
½ t. baking powder
2 T. flour
3 eggs
½ c. melted butter or margarine
1 t. vanilla flavoring
½ t. almond flavoring
1 can flaked coconut
2 unbaked pastry shells

Mix sugar, baking powder, and flour. Add eggs and beat well, then add the rest of the ingredients. Mix well and pour immediately into pastry shells. Bake at 375° F. for 35 minutes. This pie freezes well.

Mrs. Bertha P. Coates, John D. Bassett H. S.
Bassett, Virginia

COCONUT PIE

Number of Servings — 12

4 eggs
2½ c. sugar
2 T. flour
1 c. grated coconut (fresh or dried)
1 T. vanilla
2 c. milk
2 T. butter

Beat eggs until light. Add milk. Mix flour with sugar, add to milk and egg mixture. Stir in coconut and flavoring. Pour into 2 unbaked 9″ crusts. Dot with butter. Bake at 400°F. for 35-40 minutes.

Mrs. Annie Ruth Millikin, Deep River H. S.
Sanford, North Carolina

COCONUT CREAM PIE

Number of Servings — 6

⅔ c. sugar
½ t. salt
2½ T. cornstarch
1 T. flour
3 c. milk
3 egg yolks, slightly beaten
1 T. butter
1½ t. vanilla
¾ c. moist shredded coconut
Meringue:
3 egg whites, beaten
¼ t. cream of tartar
6 T. sugar
½ t. vanilla

Mix sugar, salt, cornstarch, and flour. Stir in milk gradually. Cook over moderate heat, stirring constantly until mixture thickens and boils. Boil 1 minute. Slowly stir half the mixture into egg yolks. Then blend into hot mixture in saucepan. Boil 1 minute more, stirring constantly. Remove from heat and blend in butter, vanilla and coconut. Pour into baked pie shell. Cover with meringue. Bake 8 to 10 minutes at 400°F.

Mrs. Pauline R. Cook, Vernon H. S.
Vernon, Florida

COCONUT PIE (With Orange Juice)
Number of Servings — 6
3 eggs, well beaten
1¼ c. sugar
¼ c. orange juice
½ stick margarine, melted
1 c. coconut

Make your favorite pastry recipe for 1 pie. Blend all ingredients together. Pour into a 9″ pastry-lined pan. Bake at 400°F. for 10 minutes. Reduce heat to 325°F. and continue baking until done.

Euna Anderson, Paris H. S.
Paris, Texas

CRUSTY COCONUT PIE
Number of Servings — 6
½ c. milk
1½ c. coconut
¼ c. butter or margarine
1 c. sugar
3 eggs
1 t. vanilla

Pour milk over coconut and set aside while creaming butter and sugar. Add eggs, and beat mixture well. Then add milk and coconut and flavoring. Pour into unbaked pie shell. Bake at 350°F. for about 30 minutes, or until pie is golden brown and firm.

This recipe submitted by the following teachers:
Mrs. Nelle McLellan, Smithville H. S.
Smithville, Texas
Mrs. Minnie Ella C. Montgomery, Gibsonville H. S.
Gibsonville, North Carolina

OLD FASHIONED COCONUT PIE
Number of Servings — 8
1 c. coconut
1 c. milk
1 pinch of flour
3 eggs, beaten
1 c. sugar
1 pinch of salt
½ stick butter (browned)

Mix above ingredients in order and pour into uncooked pie shell. Dust nutmeg over the top if desired. Bake at 350°F. until set, about 30 minutes.

Mrs. Dorothy B. Byrd, South Gwinnett H. S.
Snellville, Georgia

COCONUT PIE (With Buttermilk)
Number of Servings — 6
Pastry for 1 lge. pie
1 can angel flake coconut
2 c. sugar
2 T. flour
4 eggs, beaten
¼ lb. butter, melted
1 t. vanilla
⅛ c. buttermilk

Line pan with pie crust. Butter crust. Spread coconut on buttered crust. Mix sugar, flour, beaten eggs, melted butter and vanilla. Pour over coconut. Bake at 375°F. until middle is set.

Mrs. Lottie Belle Parker, Bainbridge H. S.
Bainbridge, Georgia

COCONUT KARO PIE
Number of Servings — 12
5 eggs
3 c. white Karo
3 T. flour
¾ c. melted margarine
1 c. coconut
3 t. vanilla

Beat eggs, add flour to melted margarine. Combine eggs and margarine mixture. Add Karo, coconut, and vanilla to the egg mixture. Pour into 2 unbaked pie shells. Bake at 450°F. for 10 minutes, lower oven to 350°F. and bake about 25 minutes longer.

Floy Jones, Taylor H. S.
Taylor, Texas

FRESH COCONUT PIE
Number of Servings — 12
1 fresh coconut
3 eggs (separate yolks and whites)
2 heaping T. flour
2 c. sugar
3 T. melted butter
1½ c. milk or coconut milk plus enough sweet milk to make 1½ c.

Puncture the eyes of the coconut and drain off the milk. Save this to use in pie filling. Bake coconut at 300°F. for 30 minutes, cool, and break open. The meat will then peel out very easily. Leave the brown tissue around the white meat since it adds flavor and color. Grind with a fine cutter on the food chopper. This ground coconut may be stored in the refrigerator a day or two. Mix together the ingredients as listed. Lastly stir in the 3 egg whites which have been beaten stiff. Pour into 2 unbaked pie shells. Bake at 350°F. until golden brown. This pie freezes well, or may be baked the day before serving.

Mrs. Charline White, Guymon H. S.
Guymon, Oklahoma

COCONUT MACAROON PIE
Number of Servings — 6
A crunchy, macaroon-like mixture rises to the top, leaving a delicate custard layer below. Very, very rich. Looks pretty without whipped cream topping.
3 eggs, separated
¼ t. salt
1½ c. white sugar
¼ c. milk
2 T. butter or margarine
1 t. lemon juice
¼ t. almond extract
1½ c. shredded coconut, cut
1 unbaked 9″ pastry shell

Prepare pie crust or use pie crust mix. Make decorative fluted edge. Beat egg yolks and salt until thick and lemon colored. Add sugar, ½ cup at a time, beating well after each addition. Add milk, butter, lemon juice and almond extract. Blend well. Beat egg whites until stiff. Fold coconut and stiffly beaten egg whites into the yolk

(Continued on Next Page)

mixture. Turn into shell. Bake at 375°F. 50 minutes or until knife inserted comes out clean. Garnish in center or around edge with whipped cream and toasted coconut, if desired.

Edith Minnix Atcheson, Colonial H. S.
Orlando, Florida

COCONUT-PINEAPPLE PIE
Number of Servings — 8-10

4 eggs
1 T. cornmeal
1 can crushed pineapple (small)
2 c. sugar
1 can flaked coconut
½ stick butter or margarine

Combine and mix all ingredients well. Pour into an unbaked pastry shell. Cook 30 to 40 minutes at 300°F.

Patricia Champion, Chilton County H. S.
Clanton, Alabama

DATE PIE
Number of Servings — 6

14 graham crackers, crushed
¼ t. salt
1 t. baking powder
3 egg whites, stiffly beaten
1 c. sugar
½ c. chopped walnuts
½ c. dates, chopped fine
1 t. vanilla

Crush graham crackers, add salt and baking powder. Beat egg whites stiff, gradually add sugar and beat well after each addition. Fold cracker mixture into egg whites and beat smooth. Fold in dates, nuts, and vanilla. Pour into greased pie plate and bake at 350°F. about 30 minutes. Serve plain or with whipped cream, lemon sauce or vanilla ice cream.

Ann L. Walsh, Lathrop H. S.
Fairbanks, Alaska

DATE NUT PIE
Number of Servings — Two 9 Inch Pies

½ pkg. sliced dates (small pkg.)
½ lb. English walnuts or pecans
2 c. sweet milk
5 or 6 eggs or 4 eggs plus 2 T. flour
2 c. sugar

Mix together sugar, milk, dates, yolks of eggs thoroughly beaten. Place over slow fire until the dates become well cooked. Add nuts, place in baked pie shells and cover with meringue, to which ½ cup of sugar has been added. To make richer, add butter (size of egg) to each pie.

Mrs. Emma Frances McCluskey,
Cotton Center School
Cotton Center, Texas

DATE NUT PIE
Number of Servings — 6

3 egg whites
1 c. sugar
½ t. almond extract
½ t. baking powder

12 crumbled soda crackers
15 chopped dates
1 c. chopped nuts

Beat egg whites, add sugar gradually. Add baking powder and flavoring. Fold in cracker crumbs, dates, and nuts. Bake in pie pan 30 minutes at 350°F.

Marlowe Davis, South Hall H. S.
Gainesville, Georgia

DATE PECAN PIE

1 c. sugar
1 T. flour
1 egg
1 c. chopped dates
1 c. whipping cream (not whipped)
1 c. pecans

Beat egg, sugar, and flour. Fold in cream, dates, and pecans. Pour in pie shell and bake about 1 hour at 300°F.

Barbara Massengale, Crosbyton H. S.
Crosbyton, Texas

DATE PECAN PIE
Number of Servings — 12

1 c. butter or margarine
2 c. sugar
4 eggs
½ c. cold water
1 c. chopped pecans
1 c. chopped dates
1 t. vanilla

Roll pecans and dates that have been chopped in 4 tablespoons of flour. Cream butter and sugar well. Separate eggs, beat yolks well, and add to butter and sugar mixture. Beat well. Add cold water, stirring well. Add dates, nuts, and flour mixture. Add vanilla. Fold in stiffly beaten egg whites. Pour into 2 pastry-lined pans and bake at 275°F. for 1 hour.

Mrs. Argent Thomas, East Limestone School
Athens, Alabama

DOUBLE-DATE PIE
Number of Servings — 6

1 unbaked 9" pie shell
½ c. butter or margarine
1⅛ c. sugar
1 T. flour
¼ t. salt
1 t. cinnamon
½ t. allspice
5 eggs, beaten
1 c. chopped nuts
1 c. chopped dates

Cream butter and 1 cup sugar. Sift ⅛ cup sugar, flour, salt, and spices together. Add to creamed mixture. Add beaten eggs. Fold in chopped pecans and dates. Pour in pie shell. Sprinkle some pecan halves over top. Bake 10 minutes at 425°F. Lower temperature to 300°F. and bake for 1 hour. Cool before serving.

Mrs. Ola Maye Veley, Waynoka Public School
Waynoka, Oklahoma

EGG CUSTARD PIE
Number of Servings — 8 Inch Pie
3 eggs or 6 yolks
½ c. sugar
⅛ t. salt
¼ t. nutmeg
2 c. scalding hot milk (use part cream for an
extra rich pie)
¾ t. vanilla, if desired
Beat slightly 3 eggs or 6 yolks. Then beat in sugar, salt, nutmeg, scalded milk, and vanilla. Make pastry for 1-crust pie. Line pie pan and lightly coat with oil. Pour into pastry-lined pie pan. Bake just until a silver knife inserted into side of filling comes out clean. Bake at 450°F. for 15 minutes, then at 350°F. to finish (25 to 30 minutes). The center may still look a bit soft but will set later. Caution: Too long baking makes custard "watery." Serve slightly warm or cold.
Mrs. Thelma L. Fowler, South Side H. S.
Counce, Tennessee

EGG CUSTARD PIE
Number of Servings — 6
1 c. sugar
2 T. flour
¼ t. salt
3 eggs, well beaten
3 T. butter (melted)
1½ c. milk
1 t. vanilla
Combine sugar, flour, and salt. Beat eggs until lemon colored, and blend in dry ingredients. Add melted butter and milk and mix well. Pour into a pastry shell and bake in a 375°F. oven for 30 minutes. Allow to set before serving.
Mary Frances Kennedy, Humes H. S.
Memphis, Tennessee

EGG CUSTARD PIE
¾ c. sugar
2 c. sweet milk
1 t. vanilla
Pinch salt
3 eggs
Nutmeg or allspice
Over direct heat, bring sugar, sweet milk, vanilla, and salt to a boil. Beat eggs and pour the first mixture, slowly, over the eggs, beating constantly. Prepare your own pastry or use mix. Line pie pan and flute crust edges. Pour egg mixture into pie shell and sprinkle with nutmeg or allspice. Bake at 350°F. about 30 minutes or until a knife comes out clean. Do not over cook.
Mrs. Audra Rasco, Monahans Senior H. S.
Monahans, Texas

EGG CUSTARD PIE
Number of Servings — 8
¼ lb. butter or margarine
1 c. sugar
Pinch salt
5 eggs
2 c. milk
1 t. vanilla
Nutmeg

Cream butter with sugar and salt. Add eggs and mix well. Add milk and vanilla. Pour into 9" partially baked pie shell. Sprinkle nutmeg over top. Bake at 350°F. for 25 minutes, or until filling is firm. Note: Be sure milk and eggs are room temperature.
Helen M. Scott, Fairmont H. S.
Fairmont, North Carolina

CREAM PIE
Number of Servings — 6
¼ c. cornstarch
⅔ c. sugar
¼ t. salt
2 c. milk, scalded
3 slightly beaten egg yolks
2 T. butter
½ t. vanilla
1 pastry shell
3 stiff-beaten egg whites
6 T. sugar
Mix cornstarch, sugar (⅔ cup), and salt. Gradually add milk. Cook in double boiler until thick, about 10 minutes, stirring constantly. Slowly add small amount of hot mixture to egg yolks, stir into remaining hot mixture. Cook 5 minutes. Cool. Add butter and vanilla. Pour into cooled baked crust and spread with meringue made of egg whites and 6 tablespoons of sugar. Bake in 350°F. oven 12-15 minutes.
Variations of cream pie
Butterscotch: Substitute 1 cup brown sugar for ⅔ cup granulated sugar, increase butter to 3 tablespoons. Coconut: Add 1 cup coconut to filling. Sprinkle ½ cup over meringue before browning. Chocolate: Increase sugar to 1 cup. Melt 2 squares unsweetened chocolate in scalded milk.
Mrs. Margaret Campbell, Chumuckla H. S.
Milton, Florida

CREAM PIE (With Variations)
Filling:
⅔ c. sugar (fill remaining cup with 6 T. flour)
3 c. milk
3 egg yolks
1 t. vanilla
Combine sugar, flour, and milk in top of double boiler. Cook until thick. Beat egg yolks. Beat 5 tablespoons of mixture gradually into yolks. Add all yolks to mixture. Continue to cook until thick, stirring constantly. Cool. Add vanilla. Pour into 10" pastry shell. Top with meringue.

Meringue:
3 egg whites
3 T. sugar
1 t. vanilla
Beat egg whites until stiff. Add sugar a tablespoon at a time beating constantly. Add vanilla. Top pie with meringue. Bake at 350°F. until brown.

Filling Variations:
Chocolate—use 2 tablespoons cocoa or 1 square chocolate (melted), added to sugar, flour, and milk mixture. Coconut—add 1 cup or more grated coconut to cooked filling. Butterscotch—use an extra ¼ cup sugar, brown in skillet with 2 table-

(Continued on Next Page)

spoons butter, add 2 tablespoons water, add this syrup to hot sugar, flour and milk mixture. Pineapple—drain a small can of crushed pineapple, substitute juice for part of milk, add drained pineapple to cooked filling.

Pastry:
2 c. flour
⅔ c. shortening
1 t. salt
3-6 T. water

Mix flour, salt, and shortening (except 2 tablespoons shortening). Cut shortening into flour with pastry blender until it looks like corn meal. Cut 2 tablespoons fat into mixture until it is about the size of peas. Sprinkle water (about a tablespoon at a time) and mix with a fork until all flour is mixed. Shape into balls with hands, warmth from hands will help work in any extra flour. Roll on floured wax paper. Bake at 450°F. 15 minutes.

Mrs. Ola Mae Hawkins, Santa Fe H. S.
Alvin, Texas

CREAM PIE WITH VARIATION

Number of Servings — 6-8

¼ c. cornstarch
⅔ c. sugar
¼ t. salt
2 c. milk, scalded
3 slightly beaten egg yolks
2 T. butter
½ t. vanilla extract
1 9" baked pastry shell
3 stiffly-beaten egg whites
6 T. sugar

Mix cornstarch, ⅔ cup sugar, and salt, gradually add milk. Cook in double boiler until thick, about 10 minutes, stirring constantly. Slowly add small amount of hot mixture to egg yolks, stir into remaining hot mixture. Cook 5 minutes. Cool. Add butter and vanilla. Pour into cooled baked shell and spread with meringue made of egg whites and 6 tablespoons sugar. Bake in moderate oven 350°F. 12 to 15 minutes. Coconut variation: Add 1 cup moist, shredded coconut to filling. Sprinkle ⅙ cup coconut over meringue before browning.

Naomi M. Vaught, Manatee H. S.
Bradenton, Florida

OLD FASHIONED CREAM PIE

Number of Servings — 6

⅓ c. butter, melted
⅓ c. flour
1 pt. milk, scalded
½ c. sugar
1 t. vanilla
1 egg white, well beaten
1 9" unbaked pastry shell

Add flour to melted butter in saucepan. Mix well. Add hot milk, stirring constantly and mix well. Add sugar and vanilla. Fold in beaten egg white. Pour into unbaked pie shell and bake at 400°F. as quickly as possible. Precaution: Never let this pie cook after filling begins to rise.

Sereen N. Taylor, Waterville H. S.
Waterville, Maine

LEMON PIE

Number of Servings — 6

¾ c. sugar
4 T. flour, heaping
2 egg yolks, beaten
½ t. salt
2 c. milk or water
2 T. butter
Juice of 1 lemon
Grated peel of 1 lemon
1 baked 9" pastry shell

Combine in the top of double boiler sugar, and flour, mix well. Add water or milk, stirring constantly. Cook in double boiler until mixture begins to cloud or form white circles on top of mixture. Add egg yolks, and cook until mixture coats spoon, desired thickness. Add lemon juice and grated peel. Mix well. Remove from fire. Pour into cooled baked shell, spread meringue over filling, sealing edges to pastry shell. Brown meringue in moderate oven 350°F. 12-15 minutes, or until golden brown. Cool before serving.

Lettie Ruth Hunter, Douglass H. S.
Lawton, Oklahoma

OLD FASHIONED LEMON PIE

Number of Servings — 6-8

1½ c. sugar
3 T. cornstarch
1 c. water
Grated rind of 1 lemon
Juice of 1½ lemons
3 egg yolks
3 egg whites
Sugar

Combine sugar and cornstarch thoroughly in heavy boiler. Add water, grated rind and lemon juice to mixture. Cook over low heat until the mixture begins to thicken. Beat egg yolks slightly, add hot mixture a little at a time to the beaten egg yolks. Return the mixture to boiler and continue to cook over low heat until mixture thickens to consistency desired. Pour cooled mixture into a 9" pastry shell. Top with meringue. Brown meringue in pre-heated oven at 350°F.

Sammy G. Waldrip, Bastrop H. S.
Bastrop, Louisiana

CREAMY LEMON PIE

1 c. sugar
1⅓ c. cake flour
1½ c. boiling water
3 egg yolks
⅛ t. salt
6 T. lemon juice
2 T. butter
1½ t. grated lemon rind
1 egg white
¼ c. sugar

Mix sugar, flour and boiling water. Cook on low heat until the mixture thickens. Beat egg yolks, add salt, and lemon juice. Combine with cooked mixture. Add butter. Cook for several minutes over low heat. Cool. Add lemon rind. Beat the 1 egg white until stiff and beat in the ¼ cup of sugar.

(Continued on Next Page)

Fold into the cooked mixture. Pour into a baked pastry shell and spread with meringue. Bake in a 325°F. oven for 20 minutes.

Meringue:
2 egg whites
4 T. sugar

Beat egg whites until stiff. Beat in sugar. Spread on pie and bake in 325°F. oven for 20 minutes.

Margaret Henderson, Walters H. S.
Walters, Oklahoma

GRANDMA'S OLD TIME LEMON CREAM PIE

Number of Servings — 6

1 c. sugar
2 T. cornstarch
¼ t. salt
2 c. milk
3 egg yolks, beaten
3 T. butter
1 t. grated lemon rind
⅓ c. lemon juice
1 8″ pastry shell

Mix sugar, cornstarch, and salt. Add milk gradually and stir until smooth. Cook over low heat, stirring constantly, until thickened, about 10 minutes. Stir a small amount of hot mixture into beaten yolks, stirring constantly. Combine with remaining hot mixture. Continue cooking, stirring constantly, about 5 minutes. Remove from heat. Add butter, lemon rind, and juice. Blend thoroughly. Pour into baked pie shell. Top with meringue. Bake at 350°F. until light golden brown.

Mildred H. Morris, Reeltown H. S.
Notasulga, Alabama

LEMON CHIFFON PIE (Baked)

5 T. sugar
2 T. water
3 egg yolks
Grated rind of 1 lemon
3 T. lemon juice
⅛ t. salt
3 egg whites (stiffly beaten, but not dry)
3 T. sugar
1 baked 9″ pastry shell

Mix first 5 ingredients and cook in top of double boiler until of custard consistency. Fold sweetened egg whites lightly into custard, add salt. Fill pie shell. Brown at 400°F. for 10 minutes or brown under broiler.

Shirley McCain, Lee Road Jr. H. S.
Covington, Louisiana

LEMON CRUMBLE PIE

Number of Servings — 8

Lemon crumble filling:
1¼ c. sugar
6 T. cornstarch
½ t. salt
2 c. hot water
1 egg, beaten
⅓ c. fresh lemon juice

1 t. grated lemon peel
2 T. margarine or butter

Combine sugar, cornstarch, and salt. Add hot water gradually and cook over direct heat, stirring constantly for 6 to 8 minutes, or until thick and clear. Add about ¼ cup hot mixture gradually to beaten egg, stir in. Pour back into pan. Cook at low heat 6 minutes longer, stirring constantly. Remove from heat. Add lemon juice, grated peel and butter. Allow to cool.

Lemon crumble crust:
¾ c. crushed cornflakes
¾ c. brown sugar
¾ c. flour
¾ c. shredded coconut
½ t. soda
½ c. melted butter or margarine

Mix cornflakes, sugar, flour, coconut, and soda together, blending well. Stir in melted butter. Cover bottom of a 9″ round cake pan with ⅔ of this mixture. Pour in lemon filling. Sprinkle remaining mixture on top. Bake in moderate oven 350°F. 20 to 30 minutes, or until mixture bubbles up. Cool. Cut in pie shaped pieces. May be served with whipped cream.

Mrs. Ira Black, Sulphur Springs H. S.
Sulphur Springs, Texas

LEMON CUSTARD PIE

Number of Servings — 6

3 eggs
2 c. sugar
2 T. cornmeal
1 T. flour
¼ c. milk
¼ c. lemon juice
½ stick butter
1 unbaked pastry shell

Combine eggs, sugar, mix well. Add cornmeal and flour, stir well. Add milk, lemon juice, and melted butter. Bake in an unbaked pie shell until done at 375°F. 40-50 minutes.

Bernice M. Baker, Cobb Memorial H. S.
Ruffin, North Carolina

LEMON FLUFF PIE

Number of Servings — 8

3 eggs
1 c. sugar
Juice of 1 lemon
¼ t. grated rind
3 T. hot water

Separate eggs. Beat yolks with a spoon. Add ½ cup sugar, lemon juice, lemon rind, hot water and cook in a double boiler until it is like custard. Beat egg whites stiff, add the remaining ½ cup sugar to make a meringue. Fold the egg white mixture into the egg yolk mixture and pour into a baked pie shell (9″). Brown in the oven 15-20 minutes at 325°F. Cool and serve.

Dorothy F. Kingsbury, Keene Teachers College
Keene, New Hampshire

LEMON CUSTARD PIE
Number of Servings — 6

2 c. sugar
2 T. cornmeal
1 T. flour
4 eggs, unbeaten
¼ c. melted butter
½ t. salt
¼ c. milk
¼ c. lemon juice
4 t. grated lemon rind
Unbaked pastry shell

Mix sugar, cornmeal and flour. Add eggs, 1 at a time and beat well after each. Stir in butter, salt, milk, lemon juice and rind and mix well. Pour mixture into pie pan lined with unbaked pastry. Place on lower shelf of oven and bake at 350°F. for 45 minutes or until firm. Allow to cool before cutting.

Laura Ann Martin, Orrum H. S.
Orrum, North Carolina

LEMON MERINGUE PIE
Number of Servings — 6

1¼ c. sugar
⅓ c. cornstarch
¼ t. salt
1¼ c. hot water
3 egg yolks, beaten slightly
3 T. butter
⅓ c. lemon juice
1 T. lemon rind
3 egg whites
Sugar

Bake and cool 9" pastry shell. Blend together in saucepan first 3 ingredients. Stir in gradually 1¼ cups of hot water. Cook over medium heat, stirring constantly, until mixture boils and thickens. Stir a small amount of custard into egg yolks. Put egg yolks into custard and stir until it boils 2 minutes. Remove from heat, add butter, juice and rind. Cool and pour into shell. Top with meringue.

Mrs. Jean Foreman, Eureka Springs H. S.
Eureka Springs, Arkansas

LEMON MERINGUE PIE
Number of Servings — 6-7

1½ c. sugar
¼ c. cornstarch
3 T. flour
¼ t. salt
4 egg yolks
1½ c. water
½ c. lemon juice
¼ t. grated lemon peel
2 T. butter or margarine
1 baked 9" pastry shell

In top of a double boiler, combine sugar, cornstarch, flour and salt. Beat egg yolks until lemon color and add to sugar mixture along with the water. Cook, stirring constantly until the mixture begins to thicken. Add lemon juice and lemon peel and cook 5 minutes longer or until it thickens. Remove from heat. Add butter and stir until melted. Cool. Pour into cooled pastry shell.

Meringue:
4 egg whites
8 T. sugar
1 t. vanilla

Beat egg whites stiff but not dry. Add sugar gradually, add vanilla last. Spread over cooled filling, sealing to edges of pastry. Bake at 350°F. 13 to 15 minutes, until lightly browned.

Mrs. Mamie A. Foust, Jordan-Matthews H. S.
Siler City, North Carolina

LEMON MERINGUE PIE
Number of Servings — 8

4 T. cornstarch plus 3 T. flour or 7 T. cornstarch
2 c. water or milk
1 c. sugar
¼ t. salt
3 egg yolks, slightly beaten
2 T. butter
5 T. lemon juice
2 t. grated lemon rind
1 9" baked pastry shell

Mix flour and cornstarch with ½ cup cold water in top of double boiler, blend in sugar and salt. Add remainder of water and when well blended, stir constantly over low heat until mixture boils. Cover and cook over boiling water 15 minutes. Gradually pour hot mixture over beaten egg yolks, stirring constantly. Return to double boiler and cook 5 minutes longer. Remove from heat, add butter, lemon juice, and rind. Mix well. Cool, pour into pie shell.

Meringue:
3 egg whites
6 T. sugar

Beat egg whites until stiff. Gradually beat in sugar. Pile on top of pie. Bake at 350°F. 15 minutes.

This recipe submitted by the following teachers:
Mrs. Eva Griebel, Stockton Rural H. S.
Stockton, Kansas
Loronia M. Haynes, Madison H. S.
Las Vegas, Nevada

LEMON MERINGUE PIE
Number of Servings — 6

2 c. sugar
½ c. cornstarch
2½ c. boiling water
1 t. butter or margarine
½ t. salt
4 egg yolks
6 T. lemon juice
2 t. lemon rind, grated
4 egg whites
Sugar

Mix the sugar and cornstarch, add water, stirring constantly. Add the fat and salt. Cook, stirring, until the mixture is very thick. Beat the egg yolks and add some of the above mixture. Return to the saucepan and cook 2 minutes. Cool. Add the lemon juice and rind, mixing it well, and pour the mixture into a baked crust. Make meringue. Spread on pie and bake until lightly browned.

Mrs. Joyce Morehead, Malvern Jr. H. S.
Malvern, Arkansas

LEMON MERINGUE PIE
Number of Servings — 6
½ c. cold water
7 T. cornstarch
1½ c. hot water
1½ c. sugar
3 egg yolks, slightly beaten
1 lemon (grated rind and juice)
1 T. butter
1 baked 9″ pastry shell

Mix ½ cup cold water and cornstarch to thin paste. Combine 1½ cups hot water and sugar in top of double boiler and bring to boil over direct heat. Add cornstarch paste and cook until mixture begins to thicken. Return to double boiler and cook until thick and smooth (15 minutes), stirring constantly. Stir a small amount of mixture into beaten egg yolks, return to double boiler and cook a few minutes longer. Add lemon rind, juice, and butter and blend. Cool, stirring occasionally. Pour into baked pastry shell. Top with meringue.

Meringue:
3 egg whites
6 T. sugar
1 t. lemon juice

Beat egg whites until they hold a stiff peak. Add sugar gradually, 1 tablespoon at a time, beating constantly. Add lemon juice and beat until thoroughly mixed. Spread on filling in baked pastry shell and bake at 325°F. 25-30 minutes, or until delicately browned.

Mrs. Mary Dickey Gill, West Lincoln Voc. H. S.
Brookhaven, Mississippi

SLICED LEMON PIE
Number of Servings — 6
½ c. butter
1½ c. sugar
¼ t. salt
2½ T. flour
4 eggs
2 t. lemon rind (grated)
2 lemons, peeled, white membrane removed,
    and sliced very thin
¼ t. cinnamon
9″ pie — 2 unbaked crusts

Blend soft butter, sugar, flour, and salt. Add eggs, reserve a little of whites to brush on top crust. Add grated lemon rind, prepare and add lemons. Mix and pour it in crust. Add top crust and brush with egg white. Sprinkle with cinnamon and sugar. Bake in preheated oven 400°F. for 35 minutes.

Mrs. Rebecca Drone, College Grove H. S.
College Grove, Tennessee

HONEYMOON LEMON MERINGUE PIE
Number of Servings — 6
¼ c. cornstarch
1½ c. milk
¾ c. sugar
½ t. salt
2 egg yolks, beaten well
1 T. butter or margarine
1 t. shredded lemon peel
6 T. lemon juice

Dissolve cornstarch in a little of the milk. Add remaining milk, sugar, and salt. Cook over low heat until thick, stirring constantly. Gradually stir a little of the hot mixture into the beaten egg yolks. Add the egg mixture to the rest of the hot mixture. Stir constantly, and cook 2 minutes longer. Add butter, lemon peel, and lemon juice. Cool while making meringue. Pour into baked 8″ pie crust.

Meringue:
¼ t. salt
2 egg whites
4 T. sugar
1 t. shredded lemon peel

Sprinkle salt over egg whites. Beat until soft peaks form when the beater is lifted. Sprinkle sugar a little at a time over the whites, beating until meringue forms definite peaks. Fold in shredded peel. Spoon over pie, making sure the meringue touches the crust all the way around. Bake at 300°F. 15 to 20 minutes.

Mrs. Theora M. S. Whelchel,
Hudson Community School
Hudson, Iowa

TWO CRUST SLICE O'LEMON PIE
Pastry:
2 c. sifted flour
1 t. salt
⅔ c. homogenized fat
6-7 T. cold water
Sugar
Cinnamon

Cut fat into flour and salt. Add water to moisten, and form into 2 balls. Roll half of pastry and fat into 8″ pie pan. Roll remaining pastry and place over filling. Cut slits to allow escape of steam. Brush with egg whites. Sprinkle with sugar and cinnamon. Bake filling and crust together 400°F. 30-35 minutes.

Filling:
1¼ c. sugar
2 T. flour
⅛ t. salt
¼ c. butter
3 eggs
1 t. lemon rind
1 medium-size lemon, peeled and cut into
    thin slices
½ c. water

(Continued on Next Page)

Combine sugar, flour, and salt. Blend in softened butter. Add beaten eggs (reserve 1 teaspoon egg white for crust). Add water, lemon rind, and lemon slices to sugar mixture.

This recipe submitted by the following teachers:

Meredith Whitaker, Andrews H. S.
Andrews, North Carolina

Mrs. Nadine Hull, Hopkins H. S.
Hopkins, Michigan

LEMON FLUFF FILLING

Number of Servings — 6

3 egg yolks, beaten
½ c. sugar
1 grated rind and juice of lemon
3 T. boiling water
3 egg whites (beat until firm)
½ c. sugar

Combine egg yolks, ½ cup of sugar gradually, lemon juice and rind, and add water slowly. Cook in top of double boiler to thin custard stage. Mix egg whites and ½ cup sugar. Fold meringue mixture into the custard. Fill pie crust, previously baked. May be browned in oven if desired.

Mrs. Virginia Folker, Princess Anne H. S.
Lynnhaven, Virginia

LEMON PIE FILLING

Number of Servings — 6-8

1 c. sugar
½ t. salt
4 T. lemon juice
3 egg yolks
1½ c. water
⅓ c. flour
1 t. butter or oleo

Beat egg yolks in top of double boiler, gradually stir in the sugar, flour, salt, water and lemon juice. Cook in double boiler until mixture thickens, then add butter. Cool and pour into baked pie shell, top with meringue and brown lightly in moderate oven 325°F.

Margaret T. Rayfield, Weogufka H. S.
Weogufka, Alabama

EASY PEACH PIE (Batter Crust)

Number of Servings — 8

1 No. 2½ can sliced peaches
⅓ c. sugar
1 stick margarine or butter
1 c. sugar
1 c. sifted flour
1½ t. baking powder
¼ t. salt
½ c. milk

Heat peaches and ⅓ cup sugar, Melt margarine. Pour over bottom of pyrex dish 12x7x1½. Make batter of 1 cup sugar, sifted flour, baking powder, salt, and milk. Pour batter over melted butter (do not stir). Place sliced peaches on top of batter (do not stir). Bake 350°F. (45 minutes or until golden brown).

Ann Giles, Dixie Heights H. S.
S. Fort Mitchell, Kentucky

PEACH PIE (Butter Crust)

Number of Servings — 6

1 stick (¼ lb.) oleomargarine
1 qt. fresh, frozen or canned peaches, sweetened to taste
1 c. self-rising flour
⅔ c. sugar
⅔ c. milk

Melt 1 stick of oleomargarine in a baking dish. Slice and sweeten 1 quart peaches. Make a batter with flour, sugar, and milk. Pour batter over melted oleomargarine in baking dish. Place peaches evenly on top of batter mixture. Bake for 45 minutes at 350°F. Serve with a topping of whipped cream or ice cream. An easy, inexpensive, delicious and quick dessert.

Mrs. Elsie Evans, Loris H. S.
Loris, South Carolina

LAZY MAN'S PEACH PIE

Number of Servings — 8

⅔ stick margarine
1 c. sugar
1 c. flour
1 T. baking powder
¼ t. salt
¾ c. milk
1 can peaches

Melt margarine in 8" square baking dish. Make a batter of sugar, flour, baking powder, salt, and milk. Pour batter over margarine. Then add fruit and juice. Bake at 350°F. until dough is brown and cooked through fruit for 50-60 minutes. (Cherries may be substituted for peaches. Add ½ cup sugar to syrup from cherries. Cook until sugar is dissolved.)

Mrs. Sandra Sumrall, East Union H. S.
Blue Springs, Mississippi

PEACH OF A PIE

Number of Servings — 6

1 baked 9" pastry shell
1-8 oz. pkg. cream cheese
½ c. sugar
¼ t. salt
1 T. milk
½ t. vanilla extract
2 T. cornstarch
1-10 oz. pkg. frozen strawberries
1 T. lemon juice
1 No. 2½ can peach halves

Mix cream cheese until soft and creamy. Add ¼ cup sugar, salt, milk, and flavoring. Blend thoroughly. Spread mixture on bottom and sides of cooled pie shell. In a saucepan, mix remaining sugar and cornstarch. Add strawberries and lemon juice. Cook until thickened. Cool. Spoon half the mixture into the pie shell. Arrange drained peach halves, rounded side down in pie and spoon remaining strawberry mixture over peaches. Refrigerate until firm.

Mrs. Barbara Wahrmund, Comfort H. S.
Comfort, Texas

FRESH PEACH PIE
Number of Servings — 5
1 small (6 oz.) can fresh frozen orange juice
1 c. sugar
4 T. cornstarch
1 t. almond flavoring
3 fresh peaches (not canned)
1 baked pastry shell
½-1 c. whipping cream flavored to taste with
    sugar and vanilla

Dilute orange juice with 2 cups water, add sugar and cornstarch. Cook until thickened and bubbling. Add almond flavoring. Remove from heat and cool slightly. Slice fresh peeled peaches into pre-baked pie shell. Cover with filling and let stand for about 1 hour. Cover with whipped cream and serve. Garnish top with sliced peaches if desired.

Madge H. Tuckett
American Fork, Utah

PEACH PIE (Crumbly)
Number of Servings — 5
½ recipe plain pastry
1 c. sugar
¼ c. flour
⅛ t. nutmeg
½ c. butter
6-8 large, fresh peach halves
¼ c. water

Mix sugar, flour, and nutmeg. Cut in butter until crumbly. Sprinkle half the crumb mixture in 9" pastry-lined pie pan. Arrange peach halves, cut side down over crumbs, and cover with remaining crumb mixture. Add water and bake in hot oven 450°F. 10 minutes, then in moderate oven 350°F. about 30 minutes.

Mrs. Eleanor Milner, Knox H. S.
Knox, Indiana

PEACH PECAN PIE
Number of Servings — 6
¼ c. soft butter or margarine
¼ c. sugar
2 T. flour
½ c. light corn syrup
¼ t. salt
3 eggs
1½ c. fresh diced peaches
¼ c. chopped pecans
1 unbaked 9" pastry shell
Nut crumb topping

Cream together butter, sugar, and flour, stir in syrup and salt, mix well. Beat in eggs, 1 at a time, until just blended, add peaches. Pour into pie shell. Sprinkle with topping. Bake in hot oven 400°F. about 35 minutes or until knife comes out clean when inserted half way between center and edge of pie. Serve chilled.

Nut crumb topping:
¼ c. flour
¼ c. brown sugar
2 T. butter
½ c. pecans, coarsely chopped

Combine flour, and brown sugar. Work in soft butter until crumbly. Add chopped pecans.

Mrs. Anna Mae Ogle, Sevier County H. S.
Sevierville, Tennessee

LAZY DAISY PIE (Batter Crust)
Number of Servings — 4-6
½ c. milk
½ c. flour
½-¾ c. sugar
1 t. baking powder
1 pinch of salt
1 pt. cooked peaches or blackberries

Mix flour, sugar, baking powder, salt and milk in the order given. Pour mixture into well greased casserole. Add fruit. Bake 45 minutes.

Mrs. Fred Hathorn, Crowley H. S.
Crowley, Louisiana

FRESH PEACH COBBLER
Number of Servings — 10
1 stick butter
1 c. all-purpose flour
2 t. baking powder
1 c. sugar
¾ c. milk
4 or 5 lge. peaches
8 T. sugar
½ c. water

Melt butter in baking dish. Mix flour, baking powder, sugar, and milk and pour into the butter. Peel and slice fresh peaches and spread over mixture. Sprinkle sugar over fruit. Pour water over top of fruit. Bake at 350°F. for 50 minutes.

Mrs. James Hilderbrand, Acorn School
Mena, Arkansas

DRIED PEACH-EGG PIE (Two Pies)
Number of Servings — 12
1-11 oz. box dried peaches
1 c. sugar
1 tall can evaporated milk
1 c. whole milk
1 stick oleo
5 eggs
1 c. sugar
1 t. vanilla
Few grains salt

Cook peaches until tender, mash, add 1 cup sugar. Scald milk, add oleo. Beat eggs, add 1 cup sugar, vanilla, and salt. Add scalded milk mixture to egg mixture. Place stewed peaches in unbaked pie shell. Pour egg mixture on top. Bake at 400°F. for 10 minutes, turn oven to 350°F. and bake 35 minutes or until firm.

Mrs. Wilma Tucker, Marion H. S.
Marion, Louisiana

FRESH PEACH PRALINE PIE
1½ T. quick cooking tapioca
⅔-¾ c. sugar
4 c. sliced fresh peaches
1 t. lemon juice
Pastry for 1 crust, 9" pie

Combine tapioca, sugar, peaches, and lemon juice. Roll pastry ⅛" thick. Line a 9" pie pan. Trim pastry 1" larger than pan and fold edge to form a standing rim. Flute or shape as de-

(Continued on Next Page)

sired. Sprinkle a third of praline crumb topping over bottom of pie shell. Fill with peach mixture and sprinkle with remaining topping. Bake at 425°F. for 45 minutes or until syrup boils in heavy bubbles that do not burst. Serve warm. Vanilla ice cream on top of this warm pie is elegant.

Praline Crumb Topping:
½ c. brown sugar, firmly packed
¼ c. flour
3 T. butter or margarine
½ c. chopped pecans
Combine sugar, flour, and butter until crumbs are size of large peas. Add pecans.

Mrs. Dale Miller, Detroit H. S.
Detroit, Texas

PEACH COBBLER

Number of Servings — 6

1½ c. sliced peaches (raw)
¼ c. water
1 c. sugar
1 egg
1 T. shortening
1 T. milk
½ c. flour
½ t. baking powder
¼ t. salt
Light cream

In saucepan combine peaches, water and ½ cup sugar, bring to a boil. Keep hot. Beat egg, ½ cup sugar and shortening until fluffy. Add milk. Stir in flour, baking powder and salt. Spread batter in greased baking dish. Pour hot peaches over the batter. Bake at 350°F. for 25 to 30 minutes or until fruit is tender. Serve with cream. (Fresh or thawed frozen berries may be used instead of peaches).

Mrs. Betty Dillard, Marion Jr. H. S.
Marion, Virginia

PEACH COBBLER

Number of Servings — 6

2 c. fresh sliced peaches
1 c. sugar
Let this stand while mixing batter. Melt ¼ lb. butter or oleo in a large casserole (2 qt.)
Batter:
1 c. sugar
¼ t. salt
1 t. baking powder
¾ c. flour
1 c. sugar
¾ c. milk
Mix the dry ingredients, beat in the milk until lumps are gone. Pour batter into the melted oleo. Do not stir. Spoon the sliced peaches over the top of the batter. Do not stir. Bake 45 minutes in a 350°F. oven, or until top is brown. Serve with fresh or sour cream. May be reheated if preferred warm. Note: Cherries or blueberries may be used (canned, fresh, or frozen).

Mrs. Ida Belle A. Dowdell, Boone H. S.
Orlando, Florida

PEACH COBBLER

Number of Servings — 8

1 c. milk
1 c. sugar
1 c. self-rising flour
1 t. cinnamon
1 T. butter
1 No. 2½ can sweetened peaches
Combine milk, sugar, and flour. Dot pyrex dish or small baking pan with butter and pour batter in. Arrange drained peached on batter. Bake in 375°F. oven for 25-30 minutes. Serve hot with whipped cream or ice cream.

Mrs. Robert T. Thompson, Branchville H. S.
Branchville, South Carolina

EASY PEACH COBBLER

Number of Servings — 6-8

1 qt. (4 c.) peeled, sliced peaches
¾ c. sugar
2 T. cornstarch
1 T. butter
½ c. sugar
½ c. milk
1 c. flour (sifted or spooned into cup)
2 t. baking powder (double acting)
½ t. salt
¼ c. sugar
1 T. water

Mix sugar and cornstarch and stir into peaches. Put in a 2½ quart baking dish. Cream butter and sugar and a small amount of milk together by hand or with the mixer set at medium speed. Combine flour, salt and baking powder and add alternately with remainder of milk. Spoon over peach mixture (should be enough to cover completely). Sprinkle the ¼ cup sugar over batter and dampen with the water. Bake at 375°F. until well browned (about 15 minutes) and reduce heat to 325°F. to complete baking (about 30 minutes). Test with toothpick or spoon to see that batter is done. Fresh raspberries, blueberries, or blackberries work equally well in this recipe varying the amount of sugar and cornstarch to suit each. This dish freezes well. Just heat to serve.

Mrs. Iris S. Nelson, Franklin H. S.
Franklin, West Virginia

QUICKIE PEACH COBBLER

Number of Servings — 6

1 c. flour
1 c. sugar
3 t. baking powder
½-1 stick butter (depending on richness desired)
1 can sliced peaches
⅔ c. juice from peaches (add water to complete measure if necessary)
Combine flour, sugar, and baking powder. Add juice from peaches and mix. Melt butter in baking dish. Pour batter into baking dish. Place peach slices over batter. Bake at 350°F. for about 45 minutes or until light brown.

Mrs. Wanda Montgomery, Paxon Jr. H. S.
Jacksonville, Florida

QUICK PEACH COBBLER
Number of Servings — 4

1 stick butter
1 No. 303 can sliced peaches
1 c. sugar
Dash of salt
¾ c. flour
¾ c. sugar
3 t. baking powder
1 c. milk (approximate)

Melt butter in baking dish. Put peaches and 1 cup sugar in bowl. In another bowl mix flour, ¾ cup sugar, salt, and baking powder, add milk and stir until smooth. Pour batter over melted butter. Pour peaches over batter. Do not stir! Bake in 350°F. oven for 1 hour. Note: Other fruits and berries may be used in place of peaches.

Mrs. Thomas Carruthers, Buna H. S.
Buna, Texas

QUICK PEACH COBBLER
Number of Servings — 6

4 T. margarine
1 No. 2 can peaches
½ c. sugar
½ c. water
½ c. flour
1½ t. baking powder
½ t. salt
½ c. sugar
½ c. milk

Place margarine in baking dish and melt in oven. Heat peaches, ½ cup sugar, and ½ cup water in saucepan until the sugar is dissolved. Bring to a boil. Mix flour, baking powder, salt, ½ cup sugar, and milk together in mixing bowl and stir until smooth. Remove baking dish from oven when the margarine has melted. Add flour mixture, then peach mixture. Bake 20 to 30 minutes at 375°F. Crust will rise to the top and brown.

Mrs. Marian L. Carpenter, Farmersville H. S.
Farmersville, Texas

DEEP DISH FRESH PEACH PIE
Number of Servings — 4

6 sliced fresh peaches
1 c. sugar
¼ t. salt
1½ T. quick cooking tapioca
2 T. butter
Pastry strips for cover

Combine peaches, sugar, salt, and tapioca. Turn into a casserole and dot with butter. Cover with pastry strips rolled to ⅛" thick, cutting gashes in pastry if a full topping is used. Bake at 425°F. 30-40 minutes.

Patsy Ann Hewston, Jinks Junior H. S.
Panama City, Florida

PECAN PIE (Dark Syrup)
Number of Servings — 6

¼ c. oleo or butter
1 c. brown sugar
3 eggs
1 c. broken pecans
1 c. dark Karo
1 t. vanilla

Cream butter, add sugar and syrup. Add eggs and beat well. Add vanilla and nuts. Pour into a 9" unbaked crust. Bake 350°F. for 50 minutes.

Grace Smith, North Whitfield H. S.
Dalton, Georgia

PECAN PIE (Dark Syrup)
Number of Servings — 6

¾ c. sugar
¾ c. dark corn syrup
1 t. vanilla
2 T. margarine (melted)
3 eggs, slightly beaten
1 c. broken pecans
1 pastry shell (9")

Add sugar, syrup, vanilla, and melted margarine to the slightly beaten eggs. Mix well. Pour the mixture into a pastry shell, lined with the pecans. Bake in a moderate oven 350°F. for 50 minutes, or until brown and firm. Cool and serve.

Mrs. Betty S. Turner, Chicod H. S.
Greenville, North Carolina

PECAN PIE (Light Syrup)
Number of Servings — 6

4 eggs, slightly beaten
1 c. sugar
1 c. white Karo syrup
1 t. vanilla
1 c. chopped pecans
2 T. butter
Pastry:
1¼ c. flour
½ t. salt
7 T. Crisco
3 T. cold water

Combine pastry ingredients together. Mix slightly beaten eggs, sugar, Karo syrup, vanilla, pecans, and butter. Pour into a 9" pie pan lined with unbaked pastry shell. Bake in the oven at 300°F. until a silver knife inserted in center of filling comes out clean.

Tina Butler, Brantley H. S.
Brantley, Alabama

PECAN PIE (Light Syrup)
Number of Servings — 6

½ c. sugar
¼ c. butter
1 c. light corn syrup
¼ t. salt
3 eggs
1½ c. pecans
1 recipe plain pastry

Cream sugar and butter, add syrup and salt, beat well. Beat in eggs, 1 at a time, add pecans. Pour into 9" pastry-lined pie pan. Bake in a moderate oven 350°F. 1 hour and 10 minutes or until knife comes out clean.

Mrs. Myrtle Deranger, Sunset H. S.
Sunset, Louisiana

PECAN PIE (Light Syrup)
Number of Servings — 6

3 eggs
1 c. brown sugar
⅛ t. salt
⅛ c. butter, melted
1 c. white corn syrup
1 c. pecan halves

Beat together with a rotary beater, eggs, brown sugar, salt, melted butter, and corn syrup. Mix in pecan halves. Pour into pastry lined pan. Bake 40 to 50 minutes at 375°F. or until set and pastry is nicely browned. Cool. Serve cold or slightly warm.

Pastry:
1 c. flour
½ t. salt
⅓ c. shortening
2 T. water

Mix together flour, and salt. Cut in shortening and water. Gather dough together and press firmly into a ball. Roll out in a circle 1" larger than pan all around. Fit into pan and flute.

Mrs. Ollie Lee Arter, Kiowa H. S.
Kiowa, Oklahoma

PECAN PIE (Light Syrup)
Number of Servings — 6

1 unbaked 8" pastry shell
½ c. sugar
2 eggs
2 T. water
¾ c. white syrup
4 T. melted butter
½ c. pecans (halves)
1 t. vanilla

Beat together the 2 whole eggs, stirring constantly. To this mixture add the water, sugar, syrup, melted butter, vanilla and nuts (not chopped). Stir thoroughly, add to the pie crust shell. Bake at 350°F. for 25 to 30 minutes.

Mildred Williams, Austin H. S.
El Paso, Texas

PECAN PIE (Light Syrup)
Number of Servings — 6

3 T. flour
4 T. butter
3 eggs
1 c. sugar
½ t. vanilla
1 c. white syrup
1 c. pecans

Mix flour and butter first, add the other ingredients and vanilla. Pour into unbaked pie shell. Bake at 425°F. for 10 minutes, then reduce heat to 300°F. and bake for 30 minutes.

Mrs. Nancy Simonton, Wade Hampton H. S.
Greenville, South Carolina

COWBOY PECAN PIE (Light Syrup)
Number of Servings — 6

1 unbaked 8" pastry shell
⅓ c. margarine
⅓ c. white syrup
1½ c. sugar
3 eggs, beaten
1 c. pecans
½ t. vanilla

Combine in saucepan, margarine, syrup, and sugar. Heat until margarine is melted and sugar is dissolved, stirring frequently. Remove from heat and slowly add eggs and vanilla, mix in thoroughly. Pour pecans in unbaked pie shell and pour egg mixture on top. Bake at 375°F. for 10 minutes and then turn down to 300°F. for 40 minutes.

Mrs. Colleen Stevenson, Ripley H. S.
Ripley, Oklahoma

SOUTHERN PECAN PIE (Light Syrup)
Number of Servings — 6

⅓ c. butter
½ c. brown sugar, firmly packed
1 c. light corn syrup
1 t. vanilla
3 eggs, slightly beaten
1 c. chopped pecans

Prepare pastry for 1-crust pie. Fit into 9" pie pan. Cream butter, gradually add brown sugar, cream well. Blend in corn syrup and vanilla, mix thoroughly. Add slightly beaten eggs, chopped pecans. Turn into pastry-lined pan. Bake in hot oven 450°F. 10 minutes. Reduce temperature to 350°F. for 25 minutes.

Mrs. Rachel A. Brim, Mitchell County H. S.
Camilla, Georgia

PARTY PECAN PIE (Light Syrup)
Number of Servings — 6

3 eggs
¾ c. white syrup
⅔ c. sugar
2 T. butter
1 t. vinegar
1 t. vanilla
1 c. pecans

Place the 3 eggs in a bowl and beat slightly. Add syrup and sugar and mix well. Add butter, vinegar, vanilla, and pecans. Place in an 8" unbaked pie shell and bake for 30 minutes at 325°F.

Evelyn Maughon, Westbrook H. S.
Westbrook, Texas

ALABAMA PECAN PIE (Dark Syrup)
Number of Servings — 6

4 whole eggs
3 T. melted butter
2 T. flour
⅛ t. salt
½ c. sugar
1½ c. dark corn syrup
1½ c. finely chopped pecans
1 t. vanilla

Sprinkle nuts over bottom of an unbaked pastry shell. Pour syrup mixture over unbaked shell. Add the nuts and bake in a hot oven 425°F. for 10 minutes then reduce heat and bake at 325°F. until pie is firm (about 40 minutes).

Mrs. Dow Sport, Dozier H. S.
Dozier, Alabama

SOUTHERN PECAN PIE (Dark Syrup)
Number of Servings — 6

Flake pastry
½ c. granulated sugar
1 c. dark corn syrup
3 eggs
4 T. melted butter or margarine
1 t. vanilla
1 c. broken pecan meats

Line a 9″ pie plate with pastry having a fluted edge. Cook sugar and syrup to 228°F. or boil 10 minutes. Beat eggs well and add hot syrup slowly while continuing to beat. Next add the melted butter, vanilla, and nuts. Pour into unbaked pie shell, bake in hot oven of 450°F. for 10 minutes, and then in a slow oven of 300°F. for 35 minutes. Cool, and serve with whipped cream or ice cream.

Esther L. Harbison, Mountain Home H. S.
Mountain Home, Arkansas

SOUTHERN PECAN PIE (Dark Syrup)
Number of Servings — 6

3 eggs, beaten
1 c. dark corn syrup
1-2 t. vanilla
¾ c. sugar
2 T. melted butter or margarine
1 c. pecans

Line 9″ pie plate with pastry, combine beaten eggs, corn syrup, vanilla, sugar, and melted butter. Blend thoroughly, stir in ½ of the pecans. Pour the mixture into the unbaked pastry shell, put the remainder pecans on top of pie. Bake in moderate oven 350°F. from 45 minutes to 1 hour.
This recipe submitted by the following teachers:
Georgia Matthews, Oliver Springs H. S.
Oliver Springs, Tennessee
Mrs. Ruth C. Humphrey, Wheeler Co. H. S.
Alamo, Georgia

SOUTHERN PECAN PIE
Number of Servings — 6

1 c. sugar
½ c. corn syrup
¼ c. margarine, melted
3 eggs, well beaten
1 c. shelled pecans
1 9″ pastry shell

Combine sugar, syrup, and melted butter. Add beaten eggs and pecans to syrup mixture, mixing thoroughly. Pour filling into pie shell. Bake in oven 375°F. for 40-45 minutes. Cool. Serve.

Mrs. Jean Shwadlenak, Knox City H. S.
Knox City, Texas

CHOCOLATE PECAN PIE
Number of Servings — 6-8

2 sq. unsweetened chocolate
3 T. butter
¾ c. sugar
1 c. light corn syrup
3 eggs slightly beaten
1 t. vanilla
1 c. coarsely chopped pecans
1 unbaked 9″ pastry shell
½ c. cream, whipped

Melt chocolate and butter over hot water. Combine sugar and syrup in saucepan. Bring to a quick boil, boil 2 minutes, add chocolate mixture. Pour slowly over eggs, stirring constantly. Add vanilla and nuts. Mix well. Pour into unbaked pie shell. Bake in 375°F. oven for 45-50 minutes. Cool. Top with whipped cream.

Mrs. Betty Wilson, Panama H. S.
Panama, Oklahoma

CRUSTY PECAN PIE
Number of Servings — 6

1 c. pecans, finely cut
20-24 Ritz crackers, finely ground
1 t. vanilla flavoring
1 c. sugar
3 lge. egg whites, stiffly beaten
½ pt. whipping cream, stiffly beaten

Combine pecans, sugar and Ritz crackers. Blend thoroughly. Add vanilla. Beat egg whites and fold into above ingredients. Blend until all ingredients are moist. Pour into ungreased 9″ pie plate. Bake at 350°F. for 25-30 minutes. Pie will have crusty appearance. Cool. May use whipped cream as a topping with grated bittersweet chocolate sprinkled over cream.

Mrs. Sylvia Kinder, Briarcliff H. S.
Atlanta, Georgia

DATE PECAN PIE
Number of Servings — 5-6

2 eggs
½ c. butter or margarine
1 c. sugar
1 c. dates
1 c. pecans
2 T. wine or orange juice
⅛ t. salt

Cream together egg yolks, butter, and sugar. Add dates, pecans, and wine, mix well. Lastly fold in well beaten egg whites and salt. Bake in uncooked pastry shell at 350°F. for 25 to 30 minutes.

Mrs. Lucille Jordan, Cary H. S.
Cary, North Carolina

PECAN-GINGER SNAP PIE
Number of Servings — 6

3 eggs
1 c. sugar
¾ c. ginger snap crumbs
½ c. fine cut or ground pecans

Beat eggs for 1 minute in electric mixer, add sugar and beat at medium speed until thick. (Do not underbeat.) Fold in ginger snap crumbs and pecans. Pour into well buttered 9″ pie pan. Bake in 325°F. oven for 40 minutes. Cool and serve with whipped cream.

Mrs. Isabel M. Bright, Ashland H. S.
Ashland, Mississippi

PECAN PIE IMPERIAL
Number of Servings — 6
1 unbaked 10″ pastry shell
¾ c. shelled pecans
1¼ sticks butter or margarine
1 lb. brown sugar
4 eggs
½ c. light cream
1½ t. vanilla extract

Pour pecans into unbaked pie shell, distribute evenly. Cream butter, add sugar and blend. Add eggs, one at a time, blending thoroughly. Add cream and vanilla. Pour into pie shell over pecans and bake one hour at 350°F. Note: This pie serves best and tastes best after all heat has cooled out, allowing filling to set properly. Test by feeling side or bottom of pan for remaining warmth.

Mrs. Ina Deere, Rocky Mount H. S.
Shreveport, Louisiana

PECAN RUM PIE
Number of Servings — 6
1 unbaked 9″ pastry shell
¾ c. brown sugar (light)
4 T. butter
¾ c. light corn syrup
¼ c. rum
3 eggs (unbeaten)
⅛ t. salt
1 t. vanilla
1 c. pecan meats

Cream butter and sugar together thoroughly. Add rum and vanilla to corn syrup. Add salt to eggs. Add corn syrup and egg mixtures to the creamed butter sugar mixture, and mix well. Add pecans. Pour into the pie tin lined with pastry. Bake at 350°F. for 45 or 50 minutes.

Mrs. Georgia Short, Moulton H. S.
Moulton, Texas

UPSIDE-DOWN APPLE PECAN PIE
Number of Servings — 6
2 T. soft butter
⅓ c. brown sugar, packed
30 pecan halves
Pastry for 9″ two-crust pie
6 c. sliced apples
¾ c. granulated sugar
2 T. flour
1 t. cinnamon
½ t. nutmeg

Preheat oven to 450°F. Line 9″ pie pan with 13″ circle of aluminum foil, leaving 1″ extending beyond the pan. Spread butter over bottom and around sides, add brown sugar, pat gently into the butter. Prepare pastry, roll one part into 11″ circle. Ease into pan, covering butter, pecans, sugar completely. Combine remaining ingredients and pile into crust. Cover with top crust, seal flute. Prick top with fork. Brush lightly with milk and sprinkle lightly with granulated sugar. Bake 10 minutes at 450°F, reduce heat to 375°F. and bake 35-40 minutes longer. Remove from oven let stand 5 minutes, invert on serving plate, remove foil.

Elizabeth K. Booth, Sherrard H. S.
Sherrard, West Virginia

PINEAPPLE PIE
⅓ c. sugar
1 T. cornstarch
9 oz. can crushed pineapple
½ lb. cream cheese
½ c. sugar
½ t. salt
2 eggs
½ c. milk
½ t. vanilla
¼ c. chopped pecans
9″ unbaked pastry shell

Blend ⅓ cup sugar, cornstarch, and pineapple. Cook until thick and clear, cool. Blend cream cheese with ½ cup sugar and salt. Add eggs one at a time. Blend in milk and vanilla. Spread pineapple mixture in unbaked shell. Pour cream cheese mixture on top. Sprinkle pecans on top of this. Bake in 400°F. oven for 50 minutes. Chill 1½ hours.

Mrs. Carolyn Johnson H. S.
Van Buren, Arkansas

PINEAPPLE CREAM PIE
Number of Servings — 6-8
¾ c. sugar
¼ c. flour
¼ t. salt
2 c. milk
3 egg yolks
2 T. butter or margarine
1 c. crushed pineapple°
1 t. vanilla

°Bananas may be substituted for pineapple, or combine half bananas and half pineapple.
Combine sugar, flour, and salt, add milk gradually, then slightly beaten egg yolks, and butter. Cook over low heat until thickened. Add pineapple and vanilla. Pour into a 9″ baked pie crust. Top with meringue and bake 20-25 minutes at 325°F.

Meringue:
3 egg whites
9 T. sugar
½ t. vanilla

Beat egg whites until stiff and add sugar and vanilla.

Inez Calame Bennett, George West H. S.
George West, Texas

PINEAPPLE-COCONUT PIE
Number of Servings — 6
3 eggs slightly beaten
1 c. sugar
½ c. white corn syrup
¼ c. crushed pineapple, well drained
Juice of ½ lemon
¼ c. melted butter
1 unbaked 9″ pastry shell

Add all ingredients to beaten eggs and blend. Pour into unbaked shell and bake in slow oven, 325°F., until set, about 45-60 minutes.

Mrs. D. E. Slay, Gibsland H. S.
Gibsland, Louisiana

PINEAPPLE MERINGUE PIE

Number of Servings — 6

2¼ c. (No. 2 can) crushed pineapple
½ c. sugar
2½ T. cornstarch
¼ t. salt
3 egg yolks
1 T. lemon juice
1 baked 9″ pastry shell

Heat pineapple in saucepan. Mix ¼ cup sugar thoroughly with cornstarch and salt. Add all at once to hot pineapple and cook stirring until thick and clear. Beat egg yolks with remaining ¼ cup sugar. Stir into hot mixture and cook, stirring one minute. Remove from heat, stir in lemon juice. Cool. Pour into a baked pie shell. When cold spread roughly with meringue.

Meringue:
Dash of salt
3 egg whites
6 T. sugar

Add salt to egg whites, beat until stiff, then gradually beat in sugar. Bake 30 minutes in 300°F. oven.

Mrs. Adeline H. Kirk, Central H. S.
San Angelo, Texas

PUMPKIN PIE

Number of Servings — 6

1½ c. pumpkin
½ c. sugar
1 T. cinnamon
1½ t. salt
2 t. ginger
2 T. molasses
1¼ c. milk
2 T. melted butter
2 egg yolks, beaten
2 egg whites, whipped

Steam pumpkin, drain and put through sieve or use canned pumpkin. Separate eggs. Combine other ingredients. Add to beaten egg yolks. Fold in beaten egg whites. Bake in unbaked pie shell, 45 minutes to 1 hour at 400°F.

Mildred Summerlin, Lineville H. S.
Lineville, Alabama

PUMPKIN PIE

1 c. pumpkin
⅔ c. brown sugar
½ t. cinnamon
¼ t. ginger
¼ t. nutmeg
2 t. molasses
2 eggs (well beaten)
1¼ c. rich milk
1 T. butter
¼ t. salt

Mix ingredients and bake in unbaked pie shell at 450°F. and bake for 15 minutes, reduce heat to 300°F. and bake for 50-60 minutes or until a silver knife comes out clean when inserted in filling.

Mrs. Edith H. Good, Broadway H. S.
Broadway, Virginia

PUMPKIN PIE

Number of Servings — 6

1 c. cooked mashed pumpkin
1 c. milk
1 c. sugar
1 or 2 eggs, beaten together
2 T. flour
1 t. cinnamon
2 T. butter

Mix all ingredients together well in a saucepan and bring to a slow boil, stirring well to keep smooth. Pour in crust. Bake at 350°F. or 400°F. until golden brown.

Marlene Cloud, North Whitfield H. S.
Dalton, Georgia

AUTUMN PUMPKIN PIE

Number of Servings — 8

2 egg yolks, slightly beaten
3 c. pumpkin
1 c. sugar
¼ c. flour
½ t. salt
½ t. cinnamon
½ t. ginger
½ t. allspice
½ t. cloves
1 t. nutmeg
1 t. vanilla flavoring
1½ c. evaporated milk

Mix ingredients in order given. Pour into baked pastry shell. Bake at 400°F. 35 minutes. Top cooled pie with whipped cream and well drained orange sections or with ice cream, sprinkled with brown sugar.

Sue S. Locklear, Fairgrove H. S.
Fairmont, North Carolina

COLONIAL PUMPKIN PIE

Number of Servings — 8

1½ c. cooked pumpkin
1 c. brown sugar
½ t. salt
1 t. cinnamon
1 t. ginger
⅛ t. allspice
2 T. molasses
3 eggs, slightly beaten
1 c. undiluted evaporated milk

Combine pumpkin, sugar, salt, spices, and molasses, and mix. Add eggs and milk, mix thoroughly. Pour mixture into unbaked pie shell. Bake in hot oven 425°F. 40 to 45 minutes, or until knife inserted comes out clean. For lighter color and more delicate flavor, omit molasses.

Mrs. Lola Belle Smith, Williston H. S.
Williston, Florida

CREAMY PUMPKIN PIE

Number of Servings — One 9 Inch Pie

2 c. canned pumpkin
⅔ c. firmly packed brown sugar
½ t. ginger
½ t. nutmeg
1 t. cinnamon
⅛ t. ground cloves

(Continued on Next Page)

½ t. salt
2 eggs, slightly beaten
1 c. cream

Prepare pastry for 1 crust, 9" pie. Bake at 450°F. for 10 minutes. Combine pumpkin, brown sugar, ginger, nutmeg, cinnamon, ground cloves, and salt. Combine slightly beaten eggs and cream and add to pumpkin mixture, mixing well until smooth. Fill crust and bake at 350°F. 50 to 60 minutes, or until pie tests done. Serve topped with sweetened whipped cream.

Pat Carson, Stilwell H. S.
Stilwell, Oklahoma

HONEY PUMPKIN PIE

Number of Servings — 6

1½ c. pumpkin
½ c. honey
½ t. cinnamon
½ t. vanilla
½ t. salt
2 eggs, beaten slightly
1 c. evaporated milk
1 unbaked pastry shell

Combine pumpkin, honey, cinnamon, vanilla, and salt. Add eggs and milk. Pour into pie shell and bake in a 425°F. oven for 40 to 45 minutes.

Mildred Callahan, Thomas Jefferson School
Miami, Florida

PECAN-PUMPKIN PIE

½ c. chopped pecans
¼ c. brown sugar
¼ c. melted butter
2 eggs
¾ c. brown sugar
1¾ c. pumpkin
½ t. salt
1 t. cinnamon
½ t. nutmeg
½ t. ginger
1 tall can evaporated milk (1⅔ c.)
1 9" unbaked pastry shell

Combine pecans, ¼ cup brown sugar, and melted butter in small bowl, reserve. Beat eggs slightly in large bowl. Add ¾ c. brown sugar, pumpkin, salt, and spices, mix well. Stir in evaporated milk. Pour into pastry shell. Bake in hot oven 425°F. for 15 minutes. Reduce heat to 350°F. for 20 minutes. Arrange hot mixture around edge and in center of pie. Bake an additional 10 minutes.

Mrs. E. G. Bryant, Cosby H. S.
Cosby, Tennessee

SPECIAL PUMPKIN PIE

Number of Servings — 6-8

1½ c. cooked or canned pumpkin
½ c. brown sugar
½ t. salt
2 t. cinnamon
½ t. ginger
¼ t. each nutmeg and mace
2 T. butter
1½ c. evaporated milk (undiluted)
1 T. unflavored gelatin
¼ c. cold water

Mix together in top of double boiler all ingredients except gelatin and water. Heat over hot water, stirring frequently. When hot, add gelatin softened in water 5 minutes. Mix well. Cool before putting into crumb crust.

Mrs. Eloise W. Gilreath, Wilkes Central H. S.
North Wilkesboro, North Carolina

RAISIN PIE

Number of Servings — 6-8

1 c. raisins
3 eggs
1 c. sugar
¼ lb. butter
1 T. flour

Cook raisins in a small amount of water until tender. Separate egg yolks and whites (use whites for meringue). Mix sugar and flour with beaten yolks. Pour egg mixture into raisins and cook until thick. Pour into baked pastry shell and cover with meringue. Bake in moderate oven 350°F. about 12 minutes. (Makes 1 9" pie.)

Mrs. Edith Osborne, Sonora Union H. S.
Sonora, California

RAISIN CREAM PIE

Number of Servings — 6

1 c. raisins
½ c. water
1 c. cream
¾ c. granulated sugar
3 egg yolks
2 T. flour
1 t. cinnamon
3 egg whites
6 T. granulated sugar
1 pastry shell

Combine raisins and water. Simmer 5 minutes. Add next five ingredients which have been mixed into a smooth paste. Cook over direct heat, stirring constantly until thick. Pour into pre-baked pastry shell. Beat egg whites until frothy, add granulated sugar gradually. Beat until stiff peaks are formed. Top pie filling with meringue and bake at 400°F. until lightly browned.

Mrs. Irma Haley, Castleford H. S.
Castleford, Idaho

SOUR CREAM RAISIN PIE

Number of Servings — 5

2 eggs
1 c. sugar
1 c. thick sour cream
1 c. raisins, chopped
¼ t. nutmeg
⅛ t. salt
1 T. lemon juice
1 9" unbaked pastry shell

Beat eggs. Add sugar and beat until light. Whip sour cream and fold into egg mixture. Add raisins, nutmeg, salt, and lemon juice. Mix. Pour mixture into pastry shell. Bake at 450°F. 10 minutes. Reduce temperature to 350°F. and bake 20 minutes longer.

Mrs. Ethel A. Nale, Indianola H. S.
Indianola, Oklahoma

RAISIN CREAM PIE
Number of Servings — 6
3 eggs
1 c. sugar
½ t. cinnamon
½ t. nutmeg
½ t. cloves
2½ T. lemon juice
2 T. margarine (melted)
1½ c. seedless raisins
½ c. chopped pecans
1 recipe plain pastry 8″ size

Beat eggs until thick and fluffy. Add sugar, cinnamon, nutmeg, cloves, lemon juice, and melted margarine. Blend well. Fold in raisins and chopped pecans. Pour mixture in an 8″ pastry-lined pie plate. Garnish top with pecan halves (approximately 7). Bake 30-35 minutes in moderate oven 350°F.

Mrs. Jean Jordan, Spurger H. S.
Spurger, Texas

RAISIN CUSTARD PIE
Number of Servings — 4-5
2 eggs
1 c. sugar
½ c. milk
2 T. butter
1 c. raisins
1 t. vanilla
½ c. nuts, chopped

Beat eggs well, add sugar all at once, beat, add milk and butter. Stir in raisins, add vanilla. Pour into 8″ unbaked shell. Sprinkle nuts on top. Bake at 400°F. for 15 minutes. Turn oven to 350°F. and bake until set, about 45 minutes in all.

Country pie crust:
3 c. flour
1¼ c. shortening
1 t. salt
1 egg
5½ T. water
1 t. vinegar

Work flour, shortening, and salt until very fine. Beat egg, water, and vinegar. Make a little well in the flour mixture, add liquid. Roll on floured board. Makes 4 1-crust pie shells.

Mrs. Freda H. Montgomery, Central Union H. S.
Fresno, California

PINEAPPLE RHUBARB COBBLER
Number of Servings — 6
3 T. butter or margarine
3 T. enriched flour
½ c. brown sugar
⅛ t. nutmeg
Dash salt
1 c. water
1½ c. rhubarb (cut in 1″ pieces)
1½ pineapple chunks

Melt butter or margarine in saucepan. Stir in flour, sugar, nutmeg, and salt. Add water and cook until thickened, stirring constantly. Add rhubarb and pineapple. Remove from heat. Pour into ungreased 2-quart casserole. Top with scone swirls.

Scone swirls:
1½ c. sifted enriched flour
2 t. baking powder
½ t. salt
¼ c. sugar
⅛ c. shortening
⅓-½ c. milk

Sift together flour, baking powder, salt, and sugar. Cut or rub in shortening until mixture is crumbly. Add milk to make a soft dough. Turn out on lightly floured board or pastry cloth and knead gently 30 seconds. Roll out into long, narrow strip, 5x12x½. Cut into 6 equal strips of dough about ¾″ wide. Coil loosely, leaving about a 2″ end. Arrange on top of pineapple-rhubarb mixture with the ends meeting at the center. Bake in moderately hot oven 400°F. 35 minutes. Serve warm with cream.

Mrs. Mildred H. Beck, Fairhope H. S.
Fairhope, Alabama

SWEET POTATO PIE
Number of Servings — 8
2 c. mashed potatoes
1 c. thin cream or whole milk
½ c. sugar
2 eggs
2 T. butter
1 t. salt
1 t. grated lemon rind or 1 t. vanilla
1 pastry shell

Put potatoes through ricer or sieve. Beat in eggs and add other ingredients. Pour into pie pan lined with pastry and bake in moderate oven until firm. If desired, cover with meringue and brown.

Mrs. Tressa Costley, Montebello Jr. H. S.
Natchez, Mississippi

SWEET POTATO PIE
Number of Servings — 6
2 eggs
¾ c. sugar
1 c. milk
1 c. mashed, boiled, sweet potato
1 t. lemon flavoring
1 pastry shell

Mix well and pour in unbaked pie shell and bake at 350°F. for 1 hour.

Martha B. Godwin, Windsor H. S.
Windsor, Virginia

SWEET POTATO PIE
Number of Servings — 8
3 lg. sweet potatoes
1 c. sugar
1 T. flour
2 eggs
1 stick margarine
1 t. orange rind
1 t. allspice, if desired
1 pastry shell

Cook sweet potatoes in water until tender. Drain and mash. While hot, add margarine and other ingredients. Beat well. Turn into a 10″ unbaked pie crust. Bake 45 minutes to 1 hour at 375°F.

Mary Sue Smith, Hico H. S.
Dubach, Louisiana

SWEET POTATO PIE
Number of Servings — 8

3 egg yolks
1 c. sugar
1 c. strained sweet potatoes
1 t. cinnamon
1 t. pumpkin spice
½ c. milk
½ t. nutmeg
3 egg whites
1 T. gelatin
¼ c. cold water
1 baked 9″ pastry shell

Beat in top of double boiler egg yolks. Add potatoes, ½ cup sugar, milk, and spices. Soften gelatin in ½ cup cold water. Cook potato mixture in top of double boiler until thick. When thick add dissolved gelatin. Let cool 10 minutes. Fold in egg whites (beaten) to which the other ½ cup sugar has been added. Pour into baked pie shell. Chill. Serve with whipped cream, if desired.

Mrs. Mildred F. Gauthier, Cottonport H. S.
Cottonport, Louisiana

SWEET POTATO PIE
Number of Servings — 6

2 c. mashed, cooked, sweet potatoes
1 stick of butter or margarine, softened
2 egg yolks
1 c. brown sugar
¼ t. salt
½ t. each of ginger, cinnamon, nutmeg
½ c. milk
2 egg whites, beaten stiff with ¼ c. sugar (white)
1 pastry shell

Mix first 6 ingredients. Add milk. Fold in beaten whites. Pour into unbaked pie shell. Bake at 400°F. for 10 minutes. Reduce heat to 350°F. and bake until firm. Nutmeg and a little white sugar may be sprinkled on top before baking if desired.

Nina Swindler, Newbern H. S.
Newbern, Tennessee

SWEET POTATO PIE
Number of Servings — 8

1 small sweet potato (cooked, mashed while hot))
1½ c. sugar
3 whole eggs, beaten together
1 stick oleomargarine
½ tall can evaporated milk, chilled, beaten
Few grains salt
Dash cinnamon
Dash allspice
Dash nutmeg
1 pastry shell

Cook and mash sweet potato while hot. Add sugar. Stir. Add beaten eggs, melted oleomargarine, salt, spices and fold in evaporated milk, chilled and whipped. Pour into unbaked pastry shell. Bake 35-45 minutes at 375°F.

Mrs. Maurice Templeton, Junction City H. S.
Junction City, Arkansas

ALMOND PIE
Number of Servings — 8

3 egg whites
½ c. sugar
3 egg yolks
½ c. sugar
½ c. pecans
2 T. almond flavoring
Pinch of salt
1 c. rolled graham crackers
½ pt. whipping cream

Beat egg whites until frothy. Add ½ cup sugar, gradually. Beat egg yolks. Add ½ cup sugar, pecans, almond flavoring, salt, and rolled graham crackers. Fold egg white mixture into other mixture. Bake at 350°F. for approximately 25 minutes. Serve with whipped cream.

Mrs. Thelma Aguillard, Eunice H. S.
Eunice, Louisiana

TOASTED ALMOND PIE
Number of Servings — 6

1 baked 9″ pastry shell
⅔ c. sugar
3½ T. cornstarch
½ t. salt
2½ c. milk
3 egg yolks (slightly beaten)
1 t. almond extract

Combine sugar, cornstarch, and salt in the top of double boiler. Stir in cold milk. Cook until thickened, stirring constantly. Cover and cook 15 minutes longer. Stir a little of hot mixture into slightly beaten egg yolks. Add into remaining mixture, cook 2 minutes longer, stirring constantly. Cool and add almond extract. Pour into baked shell. Cover with meringue. Sprinkle with almonds. Brown at 350°F. about 15 minutes.

Meringue:
3 egg whites
Dash of salt
3 T. sugar
½ c. almonds (slivered, toasted)

Mrs. Martha H. Melvin, Harrisburg H. S.
Harrisburg, North Carolina

APPLE CRISP
Number of Servings — 6

4 c. sliced apples
½ c. sugar
1 T. lemon juice
½ c. flour
¼ c. brown sugar
¼ t. salt
¼ c. butter
¼ c. nut meats (if desired)

Spread apple slices in shallow baking dish, sprinkle with sugar and lemon juice. In a bowl, mix flour, brown sugar and salt and work in the butter as for biscuits, making a crumbly mixture. Spread evenly over apples and bake at 375°F. 30 to 40 minutes, or until apples are tender and crust crisply browned. Serve warm with whipped cream.

Mrs. Dorothy M. Duncan, Valley Point H. S.
Dalton, Georgia

APPLE NUT COBBLER

Number of Servings — 6

1 can sliced apples
1 c. raisins
½ c. chopped pecans
½ c. granulated sugar
¼ c. brown sugar
2 T. butter

Combine apples, raisins, nuts and sugar and place in baking dish. Crumble butter on top of mixture.

Topping:
1 c. self-rising flour
2 T. shortening
5 T. cold water

Cut shortening into flour until mixture is like meal. Sprinkle water on mixture and stir until it follows the fork around the bowl. Roll dough out and place on top of the apple-raisin combination. Bake at 375°F. 25 to 30 minutes.

Mrs. LaDonna O'Nan, Richardsville H. S.
Richardsville, Kentucky

APPLE STRUDEL

1 can apples
¾ c. sugar
1 c. flour
½ c. sugar
1 t. cinnamon
1 egg, beaten
2 T. butter

Grease an 8x10x2 pan well with butter. Pour in a layer of canned apples sweetened with ¾ cup sugar. Mix together flour, ½ cup sugar, cinnamon. Add beaten egg and mix until crumbly. Sprinkle crumbled mixture over fruit and dot with butter. Bake at 350°F. 30-40 minutes or until brown. Serve warm with cream or ice cream.

Mrs. Joyce Nance, Nixon H. S.
Nixon, Texas

BUTTERMILK PIE

Number of Servings — Two 9 or 10 Inch Pies

3¾ c. sugar
½ c. flour
½ t. salt
6 eggs
1 c. buttermilk
1 t. vanilla
2 sticks oleo
1 t. butter extract
2 unbaked pastry shells

Blend together, sugar, flour, salt, and eggs. Stir just enough to blend egg and ingredients together. Add buttermilk, vanilla and stir until blended. Do not overbeat. Melt the oleo. Add melted oleo and butter extract. Stir quickly and pour into 2 unbaked pie shells. Heat the oven to 350°F. and bake 40 to 60 minutes, or until center of custard is set. Allow to cool before cutting. Bake a day ahead if possible. If only 1 pie is needed half of the recipe may be used.

Elizabeth Heard, Central H. S.
Jackson, Mississippi

BUTTERMILK PIE (Filling)

Number of Servings — 12 (2 Pies)

3 c. sugar
6 T. flour
1½ c. buttermilk
5 eggs
1 c. butter or 1½ sticks margarine, melted
2 t. vanilla

Mix sugar, flour, and ½ of milk. Add beaten eggs. Add rest of milk and fold in melted butter. Add vanilla. Pour in unbaked pie shells and bake at 425°F. for 10 minutes. Then turn oven to 350°F. and bake until knife comes out clean.

Ivah Lou Ashley, Irvin H. S.
El Paso, Texas

BUTTERMILK PIE

Number of Servings — 6

2 c. sugar
½ c. butter or margarine
3 T. flour (rounded)
3 beaten eggs
1 c. buttermilk
1 t. vanilla
Dash of nutmeg

Cream sugar and butter. Add flour and eggs. Beat well. Add buttermilk and flavorings. Pour into a 9″ unbaked pie shell. Bake at 350°F. for 45-50 minutes or until sufficiently browned.

Judy Barnes, Odem H. S.
Odem, Texas

COOKIE SUNDAE PIE

Number of Servings — 6

½ c. soft butter
¼ c. sifted powdered sugar
½ t. vanilla
1 c. sifted flour (plain)
⅛ t. salt

Mix butter, sugar, and vanilla thoroughly. Sift flour and salt together. Add to butter mixture and blend. Chill 30 to 45 minutes. Heat oven to 400°F. Pat dough evenly into greased 9″ pie pan. Flute edge and prick. Bake 10 to 12 minutes or until light brown. Cool. Just before serving. fill with ice cream and top. For tarts, divide in 6 tart pans (4x1).

Mrs. Lera F. Auberry, East Fannin H. S.
Morganton, Georgia

CORNMEAL PIE

Number of Servings — 6

½ c. butter
1 c. sugar
1 small egg, separated
½ c. sweet milk
3 T. cornmeal
1 unbaked pie crust

Melt butter, add sugar, beat egg yolk until creamy and add to butter mixture. Stir in sweet milk. Beat egg white until stiff and fold in above mixture. Fold in the cornmeal last, working quickly. Pour in unbaked pie crust. Bake 40 minutes 375°F.

Betty Jean Wade, Unadilla H. S.
Unadilla, Georgia

CORNMEAL PIE
Number of Servings — 6-8
3 egg yolks
1 stick oleo (melted)
1 c. sugar
3 T. cornmeal
1 t. vanilla

Beat egg yolks. Add oleo and ½ cup sugar, mix cornmeal with remaining sugar. Mix well. Add vanilla. Bake in 9″ pie shell 350°F. for 15 minutes. Reduce heat to 325°F. until filling thickens and crust browns. Stir filling as needed while baking.

Meringue:
3 egg whites
½ t. cream of tartar
5 T. sugar

Beat egg whites and cream of tartar until stiff. Add sugar gradually. Spread on pie, bake 350°F. until brown.
Mrs. Mary C. Harbour, Philadelphia H. S.
Philadelphia, Mississippi

CORNMEAL PIE
½ c. milk
½ c. corn oil margarine
2 eggs
1½ c. sugar
⅓ c. yellow cornmeal (stone ground if possible)
1 t. vanilla or 1 t. coconut flavoring
1 unbaked 9″ hot water pie crust

Preheat oven to 450°F., scald milk, add margarine and let cool to room temperature. Add remaining ingredients. Stir just until blended. Pour into unbaked pie crust and bake at 450°F. for 10 minutes. Reduce heat to 300°F. bake 30 minutes longer. Silver knife blade inserted in center will come out clean when pie is done.

Hot Water Pie Crust:
¼ c. boiling water
⅓ c. shortening
1½ c. sifted all-purpose flour
¼ t. salt

Pour water over shortening, beat until creamy. Cool. Sift flour and salt, add to shortening, mix to soft dough with fork. Roll out between two layers of wax paper. Makes crust for one 9″ single crust pie.
Mrs. Edna Falls Swatsell, Paul H. Pewitt H. S.
Omaha, Texas

FRUIT PIE
Number of Servings — 8
¾ c. butter
¾ c. milk
¾ c. self-rising flour
¾ c. sugar
1 can of fruit (No. 3) (apples, peaches, blueberries, etc.)

Melt butter in an 8x12 pan. Mix flour and sugar, add milk (makes thin batter). Pour into pan with melted butter. Add fruit. Bake 350°F. for 30 minutes, or until brown. Serve with ice cream.
Mrs. Tom Haley, Lumber City H. S.
Lumber City, Georgia

FRUIT COBBLER
Number of Servings — 12
1 c. flour
1 c. sugar
1 c. milk or fruit juice
1 t. baking powder
¼ t. salt
2 c. drained fruit

Mix all ingredients together except fruit and pour into buttered pan. Add fruit and dot with butter. Sprinkle sugar over the top. Bake at 350°F. until brown (about 40-45 minutes). If you use apples, brown sugar and cinnamon are a nice addition.
Mrs. L. S. Coers, Buda Ind. Co. Line
Buda, Texas

MIRACLE FRUIT COBBLER
Number of Servings — 6
1 c. milk
1 c. sugar
1 c. flour
½ t. salt
3 T. butter
1½ t. baking powder
2 c. drained canned fruit such as peaches, cherries or berries (save juice for sauce)

Melt butter in deep pie pan in oven. Make batter of milk, sugar, flour, salt and baking powder. Place in pan with butter. Dip drained fruit over top of batter. Bake in 350°F. oven until firm (30 minutes) and at 425°F. for 10 minutes to brown.

Sauce:
Juice drained from fruit
½-¾ c. sugar
3 T. flour
¼ t. cinnamon
Salt to taste

Make sauce of juice, sugar, flour, cinnamon, and salt. Boil until thickened. Pour over cobbler after it is served into dessert dishes.
Mrs. Josephine S. Loyd, Oneonta H. S.
Oneonta, Alabama

CHERRY COBBLER
1 No. 2 can red pitted sour cherries
¾ c. sugar
3 T. quick cooking tapioca
2 T. butter
Pinch of salt
2 egg yolks
6 T. sugar
¼ t. salt
2 egg whites
¼ t. cream of tartar
½ c. cake flour

In a saucepan mix cherries, ¾ cup of sugar, tapioca, butter, and pinch of salt. Stir until well blended. Bring to a boil and cook 5 minutes, stirring constantly. Pour into an 8″ square pan. Beat egg yolks until thick and lemon colored. Gradually add 6 tablespoons sugar, beating well after each addition. Add ¼ teaspoon salt to the egg whites and beat until foamy. Add cream of tartar and beat until stiff but not dry. Fold beaten

(Continued on Next Page)

egg whites into the egg and sugar mixture. Then fold in lightly flour. Pour over hot cherry mixture and bake at 350°F. for 35 minutes or until the sponge topping springs back lightly from the touch. Serve warm.

Mrs. Loretta S. Homan, South Hagerstown H. S.
Hagerstown, Maryland

FRUIT COCKTAIL MERINGUE PIE

Number of Servings — 6

1 envelope gelatin
½ c. sugar
¼ t. salt
¾ c. syrup from fruit cocktail
2 beaten egg yolks
1 c commercial sour cream
2 t. lemon juice
1½ c. drained fruit cocktail (large can)

Combine in top of double boiler, gelatin, sugar, and salt. Stir in fruit cocktail syrup and egg yolks. Cook over boiling water, stirring often, 15 minutes, until slightly thickened. Remove from heat. Stir in commercial sour cream, and lemon juice. Cool until thickened. Fold in drained fruit cocktail. Turn into 9″ baked pie shell. Top with marshmallow meringue.

Marshmallow meringue:
16 marshmallows
1 t. lemon juice
1 t. syrup from fruit cocktail
2 egg whites
½ t. salt
¼ c. sugar

Melt marshmallows with lemon juice and syrup from fruit cocktail over low heat, stirring often. Cool. Beat egg whites with salt until stiff. Gradually beat in sugar. Fold into marshmallow mixture.

Mrs. Judy Mirka, West Jefferson H. S.
West Jefferson, Ohio

TEN DOLLAR FRUIT PIE

Number of Servings — 12

1 c. flour
1 c. sugar
3 t. baking powder
1 c. milk
½ c. butter
1 qt. fruit, sweetened to taste

Melt butter in bottom of 9x13x2 pan. Heat fruit to boiling. Make a batter of flour, sugar, baking powder, and milk and pour this over the melted butter. Do not stir. Pour the hot fruit over the batter. Do not stir. Bake at 375°F. for 25 minutes.

Mrs. Thelma C. Higgins, Madison Heights Jr. H. S.
Madison Heights, Virginia

GRAPEFRUIT PIE (Pink)

Number of Servings — 8

1 9″ baked pastry shell
32 marshmallows, regular size
½ c. grapefruit juice
1 c. heavy cream

2 c. fresh pinkmeat grapefruit sections, drained (2-3 grapefruits)
⅓ c. toasted coconut

Cut marshmallows in quarters with scissors. Melt marshmallows in ¼ cup grapefruit juice. Cool to room temperature. Add remaining ¼ cup of juice to grapefruit sections. Whip cream. Fold cooled marshmallows, grapefruit and cream together. Pour into cooled pastry shell. Allow to set about 3 hours. Just before serving, sprinkle toasted coconut 1″ in from edge of pie.

Mrs. Wilma B. Russell, Sterling H. S.
Somerdale, New Jersey

CONCORD GRAPE PIE

Number of Servings — 6

3 c. concord grapes
1 c. sugar
2 T. flour
¼ t. salt
½ t. lemon rind
Juice of ½ lemon

Slip skin from grapes. Bring pulp to boil. Press through sieve to remove seeds. Add skins to pulp mixture. Mix sugar, flour, salt, and lemon peel, add to grapes. Pour into unbaked pie shell. Cover with lattice work of crust. Bake at 400°F. 40 to 50 minutes.

Mrs. Edward Felknor, White Pine School
White Pine, Tennessee

GREEN GRAPE PIE

Number of Servings — 6

1 pt. canned green grapes
2 egg yolks
1 T. cornstarch
½ c. sugar
Pinch of salt
1 baked 8″ pastry shell
2 egg whites (stiffly beaten)
4 T. sugar

Drain liquid from canned grapes. Add water to make ½ cup liquid. Mix egg yolks, slightly beaten, with sugar, cornstarch, salt, and liquid from grapes. Bring to boil over direct heat, stirring constantly. When thickened, pour over grapes in your favorite baked pastry shell. Top with meringue made with egg whites and sugar. Bake until golden brown.

Ida Mae Niebuhr, Gonzales H. S.
Gonzales, Texas

ICE CREAM PIE

Number of Servings — 6

1 baked 9″ pastry shell
1 c. sugar
4 T. cornstarch
1 c. boiling water
2 egg whites, stiffly beaten
1 t. vanilla
1 carton whipping cream

Mix sugar and cornstarch together until well blended. Add the boiling water slowly, mixing until sugar is dissolved. Cook over medium heat until mixture is thick and clear, stirring constantly.

(Continued on Next Page)

Cool. Beat egg whites stiff and fold into cooled cornstarch mixture. Add vanilla. Pour into 9" baked pie shell. Whip the cream and spread evenly over cornstarch mixture. Chill. Garnish as desired.

Mrs. Nancy Susedik, Saybrook-Arrowsmith H. S.
Saybrook, Illinois

JEFF DAVIS PIE

Number of Servings — 12

3 c. granulated sugar
1 c. butter or margarine
1 T. flour
¼ t. salt
1 t. vanilla
4 eggs
1 c. sweet milk

Cream sugar and butter or margarine. Blend flour, salt and vanilla into mixture and beat well. Add eggs, then stir milk into mixture. Line 2 9" pie pans with pie crust. Pour in the filling and bake at 275°F. for approximately 1 hour or until filling sets and top is light golden brown.

Mrs. Essie L. Stanley, Saltillo H. S.
Saltillo, Texas

SOUTHERN SEAFOAM LIME PIE

Number of Servings — 6

1 baked 8" pastry shell
1½ c. sugar
6 T. flour
Dash of salt
¾ c. water
½ c. fresh lime juice
3 drops green vegetable coloring
3 egg yolks, well beaten
3 T. butter or margarine
¼ c. grated coconut
3 egg whites
¼ c. sugar
¼ c. grated coconut

In top of double boiler, mix sugar, flour, and salt. Add water and lime juice. Cook over hot water, stirring constantly until thick and smooth. Tint with coloring. Add egg yolks to lime mixture. Cover, cook over hot water 10 minutes, stir in butter and coconut. Cool. Pour into pie shell. Make meringue by beating egg whites until foamy, adding sugar and beating until stiff. Put on top of pie. Sprinkle on coconut and bake until brown in a moderate oven 325°F. about 20 minutes.

Dr. Evelyn S. Simpson, Bearden H. S.
Knoxville, Tennessee

HILO PIE

Number of Servings — 9 Inch Pie

1½ c. graham cracker crumbs
⅓ c. melted butter
¼ c. sugar
¼ c. cornstarch
¼ t. salt
1 c. evaporated milk
1 c. cold water
3 egg yolks, beaten
1 t. vanilla extract
½ c. shredded coconut
½ c. crushed pineapple, drained

Blend crumbs and butter, press onto bottom and sides of pie plate, chill. In saucepan, mix sugar, cornstarch, salt. Mix 1 cup evaporated milk with 1 cup water. Add gradually to dry ingredients. Stir over medium heat until thickened. Remove from heat. Stir small amount into beaten egg yolks. Add to remainder in pan. Heat 3 minutes, stirring constantly. Cool quickly. Add vanilla, coconut, pineapple. Pour into crust. Chill.

Topping:
⅔ c. evaporated milk
1 T. lemon juice
⅔ c. powdered sugar
Pineapple wedges
½ c. shredded coconut, toasted

Chill evaporated milk in ice cube tray until icy. Whip until stiff in chilled bowl with chilled rotary beater. Add lemon juice, whip. Fold in sugar. Spoon onto pie just before serving. Garnish with pineapple and coconut.

Jeanne Mackie, Milwaukie H. S.
Milwaukie, Oregon

MAPLE NUT PIE

Number of Servings — 6

1 8" pastry shell (crumb or baked)
1 can sweetened condensed milk
½ c. maple syrup
½ c. chopped pecans
½ c. toasted coconut
1 c. whipping cream, whipped

Put milk and syrup in a saucepan. Cook over medium low heat, stirring constantly, until thick. Cool slightly. Add nuts. Pour into prepared pie shell. Top with whipped cream and coconut.

Mrs. Marlene Wesselman, Lee H. S.
Midland, Texas

MARTHA WASHINGTON PIE

Number of Servings — 6

2 sq. bittersweet chocolate
2½ c. milk
¾ c. sugar
6 T. flour
½ t. salt
3 egg yolks, slightly beaten
2 T. butter
1 t. vanilla
1-9" layer yellow cake

Add chocolate to milk. Heat in double boiler until chocolate melts. Beat to blend. Combine sugar, flour and salt. Add gradually to chocolate mixture and cook until thick, stirring. Put lid over it and cook for 10 minutes over double boiler. Add half of the hot mixture to the beaten eggs stirring rapidly. Return to the pan and cook 2 minutes longer. Add butter and vanilla. Cool. Split the cake making 2 round thin layers. Spread half of the chocolate between the layers and put the remainder on the top. Serve with sweetened whipped cream.

Mrs. Lucile Horton, Del Rio H. S.
Del Rio, Texas

MOCK APPLE PIE
Number of Servings — 6

1 stack pack Premium crackers
2 c. water
2 c. sugar
2 t. cream of tartar
2 T. lemon juice
1 t. grated lemon rind
Butter or margarine
Cinnamon
Pastry for 2-crust pie

Roll out bottom crust of pastry and fit into 9″ pie pan. Break saltines coarsely into pastry-lined pan. Combine water, sugar and cream of tartar in saucepan. Boil gently for 15 minutes. Add lemon juice and rind, cool. Pour syrup over crackers. Dot generously with butter and sprinkle with cinnamon. Cover with top crust. Trim and flute edges together. Cut slits in top crust to let steam escape. Bake at 425°F. 20 to 30 minutes. Serve warm with cheese apples if desired.

Mrs. Elizabeth C. Jackson, Hobbton H. S.
Newton Grove, North Carolina

OLD FASHIONED COUNTRY PIE
Number of Servings — 8

4 eggs (save 2 whites for meringue)
2 c. granulated sugar
2 T. flour
¼ t. salt
1 small can evaporated milk
1 small can water
1 stick margarine
2 t. orange extract
Unbaked pastry shell

Combine sugar, flour, and salt, mix well. Add all other ingredients, except orange flavoring. Mix well in saucepan. Place over medium heat and cook, stirring constantly, until thick. Remove from heat and add flavoring. Pour into unbaked pastry shell. Bake at 350°F. for 60 minutes. Remove from oven and spread with meringue and brown in oven. This pie is delicious warm or cold.

Meringue:
2 egg whites
4 T. sugar (heaping)
¼ t. salt
2 t. orange extract

Beat egg whites very stiff, add sugar and salt. Beat on high speed of mixer until very stiff. Add orange extract and mix well.
Variations of Old Fashioned Country Pie: For chocolate pie, add 2 tablespoons cocoa and omit the 2 tablespoons flour. For coconut pie, add 1 cup angel flake coconut.

Mrs. Gladys McDaniel, Broaddus H. S.
Broaddus, Texas

ORANGE PIE
Number of Servings — 6-8

1 baked pastry shell
¾ c. sugar
¼ c. cornstarch
⅛ t. salt
1 c. orange juice
½ c. cold water
1 T. lemon juice
3 egg yolks, slightly beaten
1 T. grated orange rind
1 T. butter

Combine sugar, cornstarch and salt in saucepan. Slowly blend orange juice, water and lemon juice into this mixture. Cook and stir over medium heat until mixture is thickened and clear. Stir a little of the hot mixture into egg yolks, add this to remaining hot mixture. Blend in orange rind and butter. Mix well. Cool. Spoon into cooled baked pie shell.

Meringue:
3 egg whites
¼ t. salt
6 T. sugar

Beat egg whites and salt until frothy. Beat in sugar. Beat until stiff and glosssy. Spread over pie, sealing to edge of pastry. Bake at 350°F. until delicately browned, 12-15 minutes.

Pat Duncan, Haltom Jr. H. S.
Ft. Worth, Texas

ORANGE CRUMB PIE
Number of Servings — 6

¼ c. melted shortening
½ c. sugar
1 t. cinnamon
2 c. graham cracker crumbs

Mix well. Press ⅔ of mixture into bottom and against sides of pan. Bake 10 minutes in slow oven.

Filling:
3 egg yolks, beaten well
½ c. flour
¾ c. sugar
⅛ t. salt
1½ c. milk
1 c. fresh orange juice
1 t. grated orange rind

Mix first four ingredients together well. Add milk and orange juice, next, then orange rind. Cook in double boiler 15 minutes until thick. Pour into crust. Cover with meringue made of 3 egg whites and 2 tablespoons sugar. Sprinkle remaining crumbs over meringue. Bake at 150°F. 20 minutes in slow oven. Chill before serving.

Marguerite K. German, Copper Basin H. S.
Copperhill, Tennessee

ORANGE-LEMON FUNNY CAKE PIE
Number of Servings — 6

½ c. orange juice
¾ c. sugar
2 T. butter or margarine
1 t. grated orange rind
Pastry for 1-crust pie
1¼ c. sifted cake flour
1 t. double-acting baking powder
½ t. salt
¾ c. sugar
¼ c. shortening° (room temperature)
    (°Butter or margarine may be substituted for
    the ¼ c. shortening: use 1T less milk)

(Continued on Next Page)

2 t. grated lemon rind
½ c. milk°
1 t. vanilla
1 egg, unbeaten
3 T. chopped nuts or flaked coconut (for topping)

Combine ¼ cup of the orange juice with ¾ cup sugar in a saucepan. Place over low heat. Cook and stir until mixture comes to a boil. Boil 1 minute. Add remaining ¼ cup orange juice, 2 tablespoons butter, and grated orange rind. Mix well. Set aside to cool. Roll pastry on lightly floured board to fit a 9″ or 10″ glass pie plate. Line plate with pastry, letting it extend beyond the edge of the pie plate. Turn edge of pastry under and make a high fluted rim. Measure sifted flour, add baking powder, salt, and ¾ cup sugar. Place shortening in a mixing bowl. Sift in dry ingredients. Add lemon rind, milk, and vanilla and mix until all flour is dampened. Then beat 2 minutes in a mixer at low speed, or 300 vigorous strokes by hand. Add egg and beat 1 minute longer, or 150 strokes by hand. Pour batter into pastry-lined pie plate. Pour lukewarm sauce gently over cake batter. When cake is baked, sauce will form a layer between cake and pie shell. Sprinkle with chopped nuts or coconut. Bake at 350°F. for 50 to 55 minutes. Serve warm. May be topped with whipped cream.

Betty Pate, Clinton H. S.
Clinton, Arkansas

OSGOOD PIE
Number of Servings — 8

2 c. sugar
1 c. butter or margarine
4 eggs
1 c. raisins
1 c. apples (chopped)
1 c. pecans
1 T. vinegar
2 unbaked pastry shells

Cream sugar and butter. Beat eggs. Boil raisins until tender. Mix all ingredients and pour into unbaked pastry shells. Bake at 375°F. for 45 minutes.

Myrtle Stevens, Gracemont H. S.
Gracemont, Oklahoma

OSGOOD PIE
Number of Servings — 6

4 eggs
2 c. sugar
1 c. chopped raisins
1 c. chopped nuts
3 T. vinegar
1 t. butter, melted
1 t. cinnamon
1 t. cloves

Beat egg yolks and add sugar, continue beating until well blended. Add remaining ingredients except egg whites. When mixture is well mixed, fold in the well-beaten egg whites. Bake in unbaked crust until firm. Serve cold with whipped cream.

Peggy M. Ivey, Hudler Jr. H. S.
Monahans, Texas

OSGOOD PIE
Number of Servings — 8

1 t. ground cloves
1 t. ground allspice
1 c. sugar
½ c. butter or oleomargarine
5 egg yolks
1 c. chopped raisins
1 T. water
1 unbaked pastry shell
5 egg whites
10 T. sugar

Mix spices with 1 cup sugar. Cream butter and sugar, add well beaten egg yolks, mix well. Add raisins and tablespoon of water. Pour into uncooked 9″ pastry shell. Bake at 350°F. until firm and golden brown. Make meringue with egg whites and 10 tablespoons sugar. Place meringue on pie and bake until golden brown.

Dena L. Eidson, Roy Miller H. S.
Corpus Christi, Texas

OSGOOD PIE
Number of Servings — 6

1 unbaked 9″ pastry shell
1 c. sugar
1 T. butter
3 eggs (beaten)
½ c. raisins or dates
¾ c. apples, finely chopped
1½ T. cornstarch
½ t. each, cinnamon, cloves, and nutmeg
½ c. chopped nuts
½ pt. whipping cream

Soak raisins in water while mixing other ingredients. Cream butter, add sugar and well beaten eggs. Stir in apples, cornstarch, spices, nuts, and raisins. Bake in an uncooked 9″ pie shell for 45 minutes or until set, at 350°F. Serve with whipped cream.

Mrs. D. W. Fleming,
A & M Consolidated Jr. H. S.
College Station, Texas

OSGOOD PIE
Number of Servings — 6

½ c. butter or oleo
2 c. sugar
4 eggs (separated)
1 t. cinnamon
1 t. nutmeg
1 c. raisins
1 T. vinegar
1 unbaked pastry shell

Cream the butter and sugar. Separate the eggs and beat whites stiff. Add the yolks to creamed mixture and beat well. Blend in the spices, raisins and vinegar. Mix well. Fold in the beaten egg whites. Pour into unbaked pastry lined pie tin and bake at 425°F. for 10 minutes, reduce the heat to 350°F. and continue baking for about 45 minutes longer or until it tests done as for custard pie with a clean silver knife.

Mrs. Margaret Thornton, Thorndale H. S.
Thorndale, Texas

PEANUT STREUSEL PIE

Number of Servings — 6-8
⅓ c. peanut butter
¾ c. sifted confectioners' sugar
1 baked 9" pastry shell
⅓ c. all-purpose flour
½ c. sugar
⅛ t. salt
2 c. scalded milk
3 egg yolks, slightly beaten
2 T. butter or margarine
½ t. vanilla

Blend peanut butter with confectioners' sugar until mealy. Sprinkle two-thirds of mixture over baked pie shell. Combine flour, ½ cup sugar and salt in the top of a double boiler. Stir in scalded milk. Cook over boiling water, stirring constantly, until thickened. Stir a small amount of cooked filling into the egg yolks. Combine with remaining hot mixture and cook several minutes longer. Add butter or margarine, and vanilla. Pour into pie shell. Top with meringue.

Meringue:
3 egg whites
¼ t. cream of tartar
½ c. sugar
1 t. cornstarch

Beat egg whites until stiff, add cream of tartar. Gradually add sugar mixed with cornstarch. Beat until stiff and shiny. Pile on pie and sprinkle with remaining peanut butter mixture. Bake. Cool before serving.

Mrs. Kathryn Jeska, Springfield Local H. S.
Holland, Ohio

ALABAMA PEAR PIE

Number of Servings — 6
Pastry for 2-crust pie
¾ c. sugar
½ t. nutmeg
½ t. cinnamon
½ t. allspice
2 T. cornstarch
6 c. sliced pears (pre-cooked)
½ c. syrup from pears
2 T. butter
2 T. sugar

Line pie pan with pastry. Mix sugar, nutmeg, cinnamon, allspice, and cornstarch together. Make a paste with pear syrup. Mix lightly through pears and pour into pan. Cover with top crust and slit. Dot with butter and sprinkle 2 tablespoons sugar over top. Bake at 425°F. until golden brown (about 35 minutes). Serve cool with ice cream, whipped cream, or cheese.

Mrs. Annette E. Smith, Ranburne H. S.
Ranburne, Alabama

PEAR CRUMBLE PIE

Number of Servings — 8
6 medium pears, pared, cored and cut in eighths
 (4 c.)
1 t. grated lemon peel
½ c. sugar
3 T. lemon juice
1 unbaked 9" pastry shell,

Mix pears, sugar, lemon peel, and juice, arrange in pastry shell.
½ c. enriched flour
½ t. ginger
¼ t. mace
½ c. sugar
½ t. cinnamon
⅓ c. butter or margarine

Combine flour, sugar, and spices, cut in butter until crumbly, sprinkle over pears. Bake in hot oven 400°F. about 45 minutes or until pears are tender. Serve warm with whipped cream.

Mrs. Billie Nowlin, Rising Star H. S.
Rising Star, Texas

STACKED PRUNE CAKE PIE

1 c. butter
1 c. sugar
2 eggs
1 t. vanilla extract
4 c. sifted all-purpose flour
2 t. baking powder
½ t. salt
¼ c. milk

Cream butter well, add sugar continually and continue mixing until very creamy. Add slightly beaten eggs and flavoring. Sift flour, baking powder and salt together, alternately with milk to butter mixture. Chill dough in the refrigerator.

Start your oven at 350°F. or moderate. Divide dough into 7 equal portions. Roll out each portion very thin on a lightly-floured bread board to fit an 8" cake pan. Turn cake pan upside down, place dough on ungreased top of pan and trim edges tidily; bake 20 minutes or until edges turn a delicate brown. Remove from oven and slide cake off bottom of pan with a spatula. Cool on wire rack until all 7 layers are baked. Bake as many layers at a time as possible. The baked layers should not be more than ¼" in thickness and will be very hard.

Filling:
2 lbs. dried prunes, cooked
½ c. prune liquid
1 c. sugar
½ t. cardamon seeds
1 t. vanilla extract
¼ t. salt

Wash prunes (soak prunes for 2 hours if bulk or untenderized; with packaged tenderized prunes, soaking is not necessary). Cover fruit with water and cook slowly about 45 minutes or until tender, drain, saving the liquid. Remove pit, put prunes through a food grinder or cut into fine pieces with scissors. Add prune liquid, sugar and cardamon seeds, split in half and cook until filling is about as thick as jam, cool. Add vanilla extract and salt. Set aside until cake layers are baked. Spread a generous amount of prune filling between each layer and press the many layers of cake to blend with the fruity filling. Wrap the cake tightly in a dry cloth so moisture from the filling mellows the cake. Let it stand at least overnight before cutting. It may age for several days.

Mrs. Zenoba Cumbie, Ralls H. S.
Ralls, Texas

RACHEL'S PIE
Number of Servings — 6
¾ c. chopped nuts
¾ c. chopped dates
¾ c. raisins
2 eggs
1 c. sugar
1 t. vanilla
½ t. rum flavoring
½ t. cloves
½ t. allspice
½ t. cinnamon
Beat eggs well, add sugar flavorings and spices. Add nuts, dates, and raisins, mix well. Bake in uncooked pastry shell for 30 minutes at 400°F. May be served with whipped cream.

Mrs. Rachel Nicholson, Union School
Union, Mississippi

RUSK PIE
Number of Servings — 6
8 rusk (rolled fine)
½ c. sugar
½ c. melted butter
Mix together and pack lightly into baking pan.
Caramel filling:
2 egg yolks
2 c. milk
2 T. cornstarch
¼ t. salt
½ c. sugar
1 t. vanilla
Place ingredients in double boiler. Cook until thick, pour over rusk crust.
4 egg whites
4 T. powdered sugar
Beat egg whites stiff, add powdered sugar. Spread over filling.
4 rusks (rolled out)
½ c. chopped nut meats
Mix together and put this on top. Bake at 350°F. for 35 minutes.

Elaine Kirkpatrick, Handy H. S.
Bay City, Michigan

SOUR CREAM PIE (Nut Topped)
Number of Servings — 6-8
2 eggs
1 c. sugar
1 t. flour
¼ t. salt
¼ t. cinnamon
1 c. dairy sour cream
1 unbaked 9″ pastry shell
½ c. finely chopped walnuts or pecans
Beat eggs, gradually beat in the sugar, add flour, salt, cinnamon and dairy sour cream, mix well. Pour into an unbaked pastry shell. Scatter the finely chopped nuts over the top. Bake at 425°F. for 10 minutes to set the pastry. Reduce the heat to 350°F. and continue baking until the filling is set, about 35 to 45 minutes. Cool before serving. Shredded or grated coconut may be substituted for the nuts as the topping.

Mrs. Carol Johnson, North Junior H. S.
Rapid City, South Dakota

SHOO-FLY PIE
Number of Servings — One Pie
Mix together:
¾ c. table molasses
1 egg
½ t. soda dissolved in 1 c. boiling water
Make crumbs of:
½ c. light brown sugar
¼ t. salt
½ t. cinnamon
⅛ t. nutmeg
⅛ t. ginger
⅛ t. cloves
¾ c. flour
½ t. baking powder
2 T. shortening
Crumb to consistency of cornmeal. Alternate in layers, the molasses mixture and the crumb mixture on unbaked pie crust having the last layer on top of crumbs. Bake 15 minutes at 450°F. then 350°F. until done.

Julia Simpson, Troutman H. S.
Troutman, North Carolina

SKILLET-FRUIT COBBLER
Number of Servings — 6
1 cup flour
¾ c. milk
1¼ c. sugar
1 T. baking powder
1 stick butter
1 qt. canned fruit (cherries, peaches, apples or berries)
Melt butter in skillet, sift flour, sugar, and baking powder together. Stir milk into dry ingredients to make a batter. Pour batter into skillet on top of melted butter. Add fruit to skillet. Bake in 325°F. oven for 45 minutes or until well browned.

Mrs. Zula Rowland, Mackville School
Mackville, Kentucky

SUGAR PIE
Number of Servings — 6
½ c. butter
2 c. sugar
3 eggs
3 lemons (juice)
¼ c. flour
Cream butter and sugar, beat in eggs, add lemon juice and flour. Pour into unbaked pie crust and bake at 350°F. until brown and filling is set.

Jane L. Jones, Summerville H. S.
Summerville, South Carolina

SUNSHINE PIE
Number of Servings — 8
4 eggs
1½ c. granulated sugar
¾ c. citrus juice (3 T. lemon juice plus orange juice to make ¾c)
⅛ t. salt
1 tart apple, peeled and grated
1 unbaked 9″ pastry shell
Beat eggs slightly with fork, add next 4 ingredients and mix well. Pour into pie shell. Bake at 400°F. about 35 minutes or until custard is done. Serve cold.

Estelle Cherry, Granbury H. S.
Granbury, Texas

SURPRISE PIE

Number of Servings — 6

3 egg whites
1 t. baking powder
1 c. sugar
1 c. chopped nuts
1 c. graham cracker crumbs

Add baking powder to egg whites and beat until stiff. Fold in sugar. Add nuts and cracker crumbs. Pour into greased pie pan. Bake 300°F. 30 minutes. Store over night in refrigerator. Serve with whipped cream or ice cream.

Mrs. Frances Willis, Senior H. S.
Denison, Texas

UPSIDE DOWN PIE

Number of Servings — 6

3 T. butter
½ c. sugar
1 c. flour
Pinch salt
1 t. baking powder
Milk to make batter (about ¾ c.)
1 lg. can fruit, cherries, peaches, or
    crushed pineapple
1 c. sugar

Mix together thoroughly butter, ½ cup sugar, flour, salt and baking powder. Add enough milk to make a batter, beat 1 minute, pour into a buttered casserole. Make topping by using canned fruit, fresh fruit or frozen fruit. Mix with sugar and bring to boiling point. Pour over batter and bake in a 400°F. oven for 30 minutes. Serve hot or cold.

Mrs. Gladys Hackney, Arnold Junior H. S.
Cleveland, Tennessee

VINEGAR PIE

Number of Servings — 6-8

3 eggs, beaten
1½ c. melted butter or margarine
3 T. dark vinegar
1 c. sugar
1 unbaked pastry shell

Beat eggs thoroughly, add melted butter, vinegar, sugar. Mix well. Pour into uncooked pie crust. Start in oven 450°F. for 10 minutes, reduce heat to 300°F. and cook until pie is set or knife comes out clean when inserted.

Mrs. Willene West, DeLand Sr. H. S.
DeLand, Florida

COFFEE WALNUT PIE

Number of Servings — 6

½ c. light brown sugar, packed
½ c. soft butter
1 c. granulated sugar
3 eggs
¼ t. salt
¼ c. heavy cream
½ c. strong coffee
1 c. coarsely chopped walnut meats
1 t. vanilla
½ c. broken walnut meats
1 9" unbaked pastry shell

Cream brown sugar and butter until well blended, add granulated sugar and mix well. Add eggs, beating well after each, add salt, cream and coffee and mix well. Cook over boiling water, stirring for 5 minutes. Remove from water and stir in 1 cup walnuts and vanilla, pour into pastry shell. Bake at 350°F. for 1 hour. Scatter broken walnuts on top and bake 5 minutes longer, cool. Note: Pie will puff during making and shrink slightly as it cools.

Mrs. Margaret Fagot, Fairbury-Cropsey H. S.
Fairbury, Illinois

FRUIT PIE TOPPING

Number of Servings — 6

1 c. sugar
¼ c. melted shortening or lard
½ c. milk
1 c. flour
3 t. baking powder
4 c. any fresh fruit or berries
Sugar to sweeten the particular fruit used

Mix the above ingredients together and pour over sweetened fresh fruit. Bake at 350°F. for 45-50 minutes.

Mrs. Frances S. Conway, Walla Walla H. S.
Walla Walla, Washington

PASTRY FOR FRIED PIES

Number of Servings — 6

3 T. butter or margarine
3 T. shortening
½ t. salt
½ t. baking powder
1¼ c. flour
3 T. plus 2 t. ice water

Blend all ingredients together and let stand overnight in refrigerator. Take from refrigerator next morning and let set until it reaches room temperature. Roll out for pies. Fill pies with 2½ tablespoons of favorite fruit pie filling. Dip in sweet milk, prick for fork. Fry in deep fat.

Mrs. Carolyn Rice, McCaulley H. S.
McCaulley, Texas

PERFECT PIE MERINGUE

9 inch
3 egg whites
¼ t. cream of tartar
6 T. sugar
½ t. vanilla
8 inch
2 egg whites
¼ t. cream of tartar
4 T. sugar
⅓ t. vanilla

Too long baking and incomplete blending in of sugar causes "weeping." Beat egg whites with cream of tartar until frothy. Gradually beat in the sugar. Continue beating until stiff and glossy, seal the edges of pie, swirl the top of the pie. Bake at 400°F. 8-10 minutes.

Mary Ulrich, Edison Junior H. S.
San Angelo, Texas

PIE CRUST

Number of Servings — Two, 2 Crust Pies

2½ c. sifted flour
1 c. shortening
1 t. salt
1 whole egg
¼ c. water (cold)
1 T. vinegar

Sift flour and salt, cut shortening into flour until resembles coarse cornmeal. Beat egg with wire whip and combine with vinegar and water. Combine with flour tossing lightly with fork. Make 2 2-crust pies. Bake at 475-450°F. for 8-10 minutes.

Patricia Davison, Bountiful H. S.
Bountiful, Utah

NEVER FAIL PIE CRUST

Number of Servings — Two Double Crusts

3 c. flour
1¼ c. shortening
1 t. salt
1 egg, well beaten
5 T. water
1 T. vinegar

Cut shortening into flour and salt. Combine egg, water, and vinegar. Pour liquid into flour mixture all at once. Blend with a spoon just until flour is all moistened. This is an easy crust to handle and can be re-rolled without toughening. It also keeps in refrigerator for up to 2 weeks.

Mrs. Mina F. Robinson, Perry H. S.
Perry, Kansas

QUANTITY PIE CRUST MIX

Number of Servings — 10-11 Crusts

7 c. sifted flour
1 lb. lard
1 T. salt

Cut lard into flour and salt mixture. Store in tightly covered container. To make 1 crust, measure 1 cup of mix. Pour ¾ of mix in bowl. To remainder of mix in cup, add 2 tablespoons warm water, make a paste. Add to mix in bowl and form soft dough, roll.

Mrs. Irene Timm, Cottonwood H. S.
Cottonwood, Minnesota

PIE CRUST

Number of Servings — 6

2 c. all-purpose flour
1 t. salt
2 T. confectioners' sugar
⅔ c. vegetable shortening
½ c. cream
1 T. butter

Sift flour, salt and sugar into a mixing bowl. Cut in the shortening with a pastry blender until mixture has the appearance of fine bread crumbs. Add cream gradually by sprinkling 1 tablespoonful at a time over the mixture and tossing it lightly with a fork. Shape the dough into a smooth ball by placing it on a sheet of wax paper and then pressing it lightly with the hands. Cut the dough in 2 pieces, one slightly larger for the bottom

crust. Roll out dough and place in pie pan, trim dough to leave ½" hanging over edge of pie pan, flute edge. Brush this bottom lightly with melted butter, set aside while top crust is rolled. Bake at 450°F. for 10 minutes, reduce heat to 400°F. and bake 30 minutes longer or until golden brown.

Mrs. Vivian Nanny, Riviera Schools
Riviera, Texas

TASTY CRUNCH CRUST

½ c. margarine
¼ c. brown sugar, packed
1 c. flour, sifted
½ c. pecans, chopped

Preheat oven to 400°F. Mix all ingredients with pastry blender, spread in oblong pan 13x9½x2. Bake 15 minutes, take from oven, stir with spoon. Immediately press mixture against bottom and sides of 9" pie pan, cool. Fill.

Mary Nicolella, Peters Twp. H. S.
Cenonshbury, Pennsylvania

FOR ADDITIONAL CRUSTS AND TOPPINGS RECIPES REFER TO PIE RECIPES

TASSIE PASTRY

Number of Servings — 12

1 3-oz. pkg. cream cheese
1 stick margarine
1 c. flour

Let cream cheese and margarine soften to room temperature, mash together with a fork. Add sifted flour gradually, blend with fork. Divide into 12 portions, roll into balls, press into muffin tins or small tart shells. Fill with favorite filling or pre-bake at 450° F. until golden brown. Wonderful filled with chicken salad too.

Betty Herrin, Albany H. S.
Albany, Texas

APPLE DUMPLINGS

Number of Servings — 6

2 c. water
2 c. sugar
¼ t. cinnamon
¼ t. nutmeg
¼ c. butter
6 apples
2 c. flour
1 t. salt
2 t. baking powder
¾ c. shortening
½ c. milk

Make syrup of sugar, water, cinnamon, nutmeg. Add butter. Pare and core apples, cut in fourths. Make pastry, roll ¼" thick. cut in 6 parts. Arrange 4 pieces of apples, dot with butter. Fold corners to center and pinch edges together. Place on greased baking pan. Pour over syrup. Bake in moderate oven 375°F. 35 minutes. Serve hot with cream.

Cleota Bolling, Franklin Co. H. S.
Frankfort, Kentucky

PUSHARATA'S (Creation Pastries)
Number of Servings — 4 Dozen
1¼ c. self-rising flour
4 t. baking powder
1 t. nutmeg
1 t. cinnamon
1 t. vanilla extract
1 t. almond extract
1½ c. milk
3 lemon rinds, grated
3 orange rinds, grated
3 apples, grated (peeling and meat)
2 c. pecans, chopped
Cooking oil
Powdered sugar

Grate lemons, oranges, and apples, set aside. Combine dry ingredients, sift into combined liquid ingredients, mix well. Add lemon, orange, and apple gratings and nuts to this mixture. Form into 1" balls and fry in deep fat (2") until light brown. Roll in powdered sugar while hot. Especially good for Christmas when sprinkled with brandy and stored in a tight container for 1 week.

Mrs. Helen H. Bullock, East Central H. S.
Pascagoula, Mississippi

APPLE DUMPLINGS
Number of Servings — 4
Pastry for 8" 2-crust pie
4 medium tart, juicy apples
⅔ c. sugar
1½ c. water
2 T. butter
¼ t. cinnamon

Heat oven to 425°F. (hot). Roll out pastry a little less than ⅛" and cut into 7" square. Pare and core an apple for each dumpling. Boil next 4 ingredients together for 3 minutes. Place apple on each square of pastry. Fill cavities of apples with mixture of ⅓ cup sugar and 1 teaspoon cinnamon, dot each apple with butter. Bring opposite points of pastry up over the apples, overlap, moisten and seal. Lift carefully, place a little apart in baking dish, pour hot syrup around dumplings. Bake immediately 40 to 45 minutes, or until crust is nicely browned and apples are cooked through (test with fork). Serve warm with the syrup and with cream.

This recipe submitted by the following teachers:
Mrs. L. R. Boyter, St. Bernard H. S.
St. Bernard, Louisiana
Mrs. Dorothy L. Maxwell, Westville H. S.
Westville, Illinois
Joyce Meek, Sugar Grove H. S.
Sugar Grove, Virginia

CHEESE APPLE DUMPLINGS
Number of Servings — 4-6
4-6 apples, peel and core
½-1 t. cinnamon
¼ c. sugar
Combine sugar and cinnamon.
Pastry:
1½ c. flour
1 t. salt

½ c. shortening
½ c. grated Kraft American cheese
Cold water

Sift flour and salt together, work in shortening and grated cheese; then add enough cold water to make a firm dough. Roll out and cut in squares large enough to cover a medium-sized peeled and cored apple. Fill cavity of the apple with a mixture of sugar and cinnamon, draw corners of the crust to the top and pinch together. Bake in moderate 350°F. oven until the apples are tender and the crust slightly browned. Serve garnished with additional grated cheese, and the following sauce.
1 c. granulated sugar
2 T. butter
¾ c. water
1 t. cinnamon
Mix all ingredients and boil 5 minutes. When cool, serve around dumplings.

Mrs. Helen Larabee, Central H. S.
Elizabeth City, North Carolina

CREAM PUFFS
Number of Servings — 6
1 c. water
½ c. butter
1 c. flour
¼ t. salt
4 eggs

Put water and butter in a saucepan and heat until the water boils. Pour flour and salt into the hot mixture and beat thoroughly. Stir and cook over a low heat until the mixture forms a stiff ball. Remove from heat and add the unbeaten eggs, 1 at a time, beating thoroughly after addition of each egg. Drop by teaspoonfuls for small puffs and by tablespoonfuls for large puffs on a greased baking sheet. Bake at 450-500°F. for 15 minutes and at 325°F. for 25 minutes. (May be baked at 450°F. 35 minutes for small puffs and 40 minutes for large puffs.) Fill with cream or pie filling or with ice cream.

This recipe submitted by the following teachers:
Mrs. Jacqueline Hoffman, LaPaz H. S.
LaPaz, Indiana
Biffiel Glenn, Skiatook H. S.
Skiatook, Oklahoma
Mrs. Mary Frances Radius, Brownsville H. S.
Brownsville, Texas

CHOCOLATE CREAM PUFFS
Number of Servings — 8
Puff Shells:
½ c. water
¼ c. butter
Dash salt
½ c. sifted flour
2 eggs

Combine and bring to a boil the water, butter, and salt. Add the flour, and eggs, and stir until the mixture forms a smooth ball. Drop 8 heaping tablespoons on ungreased cookie sheet. Bake at 450°F. for 15 minutes. Reduce heat to 350°F. for 20 minutes. Remove with spatula immediately. While hot, split puffs around top to let cool.

(Continued on Next Page)

Filling:
1 pkg. semi-sweet chocolate morsels
1 c. heavy cream

Melt chocolate over hot water, let cool. Beat the cream until stiff. Fold into the melted chocolate. Fill cooled puff shells.

Glaze:
½ c. chocolate morsels
2 T. shortening
2 T. white corn syrup
2 T. milk

Melt chocolate morsels, add remaining ingredients and blend. Pour on top of puffs while warm. Chill until ready to serve.

Cleo Codas, Northern H. S.
Durham, North Carolina

CREAM PUFFS WITH FILLING

Number of Servings — 12

¼ lb. stick butter (½ c.)
1 c. boiling water
1 c. flour
¼ t. salt
4 eggs

Add butter to boiling water. Stir to melt butter. Add flour, and salt all at once. Cook, stirring vigorously, until mixture is smooth and forms soft ball that does not separate. Cool mixture slightly, add eggs, 1 at a time. Beat vigorously after each egg is added. Beat until mixture is smooth. Drop batter onto greased cookie sheet. Bake in very hot oven 450°F. 15 minutes, then in a slow oven 325°F. 25 minutes. Fill cream puffs with filling.

Cream Filling:
⅓ c. enriched flour
½ c. sugar
½ t. salt
2 c. milk
2 slightly beaten eggs
1 t. vanilla

Mix flour, sugar, salt. Slowly stir in milk, cool and stir until mixture boils, then 2 minutes longer. Stir a little of hot mixture into eggs. Return to hot mixture. Stir and bring just to boil. Add vanilla and cool. Variation - Butterscotch Filling: Add ¼ cup butter or margarine and use ⅔ cup brown sugar in place of granulated sugar.

Mrs. Harold Bartlett, Dubberly H. S.
Dubberly, Louisiana

HORNS (Apricot)

Number of Servings — 11 Dozen

1 lb. butter or margarine
1 lb. creamed cottage cheese
4 c. sifted flour (approx.)

Blend above ingredients together with hands to form a dough. Add more flour if cheese is watery. Shape into 1" ball and refrigerate overnight. (Dough may be kept under refrigeration for 1 month).

Filling:
1 lb. dried apricots
2 c. sugar

Cook apricots until tender, drain and puree. Add sugar while still hot. Cool.

Coating:
1½ c. ground almonds (or other nuts)
1¼ c. sugar
2 egg whites, slightly beaten
Confectioners' sugar

Mix nuts and sugar, roll each doughball into a 3" round (make only 10 horns at a time so dough will remain cold). Place a teaspoon of apricot filling in center, roll up in the shape of a horn. Dip into egg white and then roll in nut and sugar mixture. Place on a greased baking sheet. Bake at 375°F. for 12 minutes or until lightly browned. Sprinkle with sugar.

This recipe submitted by the following teachers:

Mrs. Jo Frances Weimar, Alto H. S.
Alto, Texas

Mrs. Johann Spalding, Dundee H. S.
Dundee, Michigan

CUERNITOS (Little Horns)

Number of Servings — 24

2½ c. all-purpose flour
¾ c. butter or margarine
2-3 T. cold water
⅓ c. nuts (finely chopped)
1 t. salt
2 egg yolks
1 egg, beaten
Thick jam or preserves

Measure flour, salt, and butter into mixing bowl. Work butter into flour until finely divided, as for pie crust. Add egg yolks and water and mix to a stiff dough. Divide dough into 24 pieces, shape into balls. Roll each ball on floured board into small rounds about 2½"-3" in diameter. In center of each, place about 1 teaspoon jam or preserves, fold over and press edges together to prevent jam from running out. Place on ungreased baking sheets. Shape filled rolls into small horns. Bake 12-15 minutes at 375°F. Remove from sheets and dust in powdered sugar. Cool before storing.

Sandra M. Woods, Tamassee DAR School
Tamassee, South Carolina

HORNS (Luechow's Almonds)

Number of Servings — 2 Dozen

¼ lb. soft butter (½ c. or 1 stick)
½ c. sugar
5 eggs, slightly beaten
2 pkgs. active dry yeast
⅓ c. warm water
⅔ c. milk, scalded
5½-6 c. sifted flour
¼ lb. butter (½ c. or 1 stick), firm but not brittle cold
Almond filling, and sliced almonds
Almond filling: Thoroughly mix 1½ lbs. (1 c.) almond paste, ⅔ c. sugar and 1 egg

Thoroughly mix the soft butter, sugar and eggs. Soften yeast in the water. Cool milk to lukewarm, then stir into egg mixture along with softened yeast. Last, add enough flour to make a soft dough, mixing well, then refrigerate 3 hours to chill. On lightly floured surface, roll dough to a 14" square, about ½" thick. Now roll in remaining butter this way: Dot the butter over half the

(Continued on Next Page)

dough, then fold other half of dough over butter-dotted area, seal edges. Now roll the dough to a 20x12 rectangle, ¼" thick, fold in thirds; seal edges and repeat this step 3 more times, chilling dough after each rolling if it softens. Put the dough back in refrigerator until next day (or until well chilled). Divide dough in fourths and on lightly floured surface, roll each piece to a 15" circle, about ⅛" thick. Cut each circle in 6 wedges like a pie. Along side opposite point, put 1 table-spoon almond filling. Roll up toward point. Place point down on greased baking sheet, cover and let rise in warm place until almost double, about 30 to 45 minutes. Just before placing in oven, brush tops of horns with 1 slightly beaten egg yolk mixed with 1 tablespoon water. Sprinkle with almonds. Bake in moderate oven 350°F. 20 to 25 minutes or until done. Serve warm.

Mildred Bullard, Fike Sr. H. S.
Wilson, North Carolina

BUTTER TARTS
Number of Servings — 24 Tarts
1½ c. sifted flour
¾ t. salt
½ c. plus 2 T. shortening
3 T. water
½ c. brown sugar (packed)
¼ c. granulated sugar
½ T. flour
1 egg
1 T. milk
½ t. vanilla
¼ c. butter, melted
½ c. pecans or walnuts
Make pastry of first 4 ingredients. Divide into 24 parts and line tart pans or muffin pans. Mix next 3 ingredients, beat in thoroughly egg, milk, vanilla, and butter, fold in nuts. Divide filling mixture evenly into each pastry shell. Bake 425°F. 15-20 minutes or until set.

Joan Swearingen, Lost Nation Community School
Lost Nation, Iowa

CHERRY TARTS
Number of Servings — 15
1 recipe baked pastry in tart-shaped shells
1 3 oz. pkg. cream cheese (room temperature)
½ c. confectioners' sugar
1 c. whipping cream
1 can pie filling cherries (sweetened)
Place the above ingredients in mixing bowl and beat with mixer until the consistency of whipped cream. Spoon creamed mixture into baked tart shells, leaving enough room to top with generous portion of pie-cherries. Chill and serve.

Mrs. Ann Schroeder, Dickinson H. S.
Dickinson, Texas

SURPRISE CHERRY TARTS
Number of Servings — 5-6
1 T. tapioca
¼ c. sugar
⅛ t. salt
½ c. cherry juice and water
⅓ T. margarine, melted
⅛ t. grated orange rind
1 c. cherries (drained, pitted)
1 drop almond extract
Few drops red food coloring
½ c. cottage cheese
2 T. confectioners' sugar
Baked 4" pastry shells
Combine tapioca, sugar, salt, and cherry juice and water in a saucepan. Cook and stir until mixture comes to a full boil, remove from heat, stir in margarine and grated orange rind. Cool to room temperature, stirring occasionally, add cherries, almond extract, and red food coloring. Combine cottage cheese with confectioners' sugar, place about 1 tablespoon cheese mixture in each tart shell. Fill tart shells with the cooled cherry mix-ture and garnish with the remaining cottage cheese mixture, as desired.

Mrs. Betty M. Jackson, Charles B. Aycock H. S.
Pikeville, North Carolina

FRUIT TARTS
Number of Servings — 2 Dozen
1 3 oz. pkg. cream cheese
¼ lb. butter
1½ c. plain flour
Cream butter and cheese together, mix with sifted flour. Roll out pastry on a floured wax paper and cut out small pieces with a biscuit cutter. Place the cut pastry into a small greased muffin pan, fill with fruit filling.

Fruit filling:
¼ lb. butter
1 c. sugar
2 eggs
1 c. nuts
1 c. raisins or chopped dates
Cream butter and sugar, add eggs 1 at a time. Add fruit and nuts and mix thoroughly, place in muffin pans. Bake 15-20 minutes in 350°F. oven. Remove from muffin pan whlie still hot, sprinkle with confectioners' sugar.

Erma E. Holland, Richard Arnold Jr. H. S.
Savannah, Georgia

FRUIT TARTS
Number of Servings — 24
¾ c. butter or margarine
¾ c. granulated sugar
1 egg
1 t. vanilla
2 T. sweet cream
2 t. baking powder
3 c. bread flour
Fat should be room temperature, beat until light and fluffy. Add sugar gradually, add egg, flavor, and cream, beat after each addition. Add sifted dry ingredients. Beat well, chill dough 24 hours. Knead on floured board, roll ⅜" thin, cut with biscuit cutter. Place tarts on plain baking sheet. Add a preserved fruit to each tart. Cover with another tart, pinch edges, prick top. Bake 15-20 minutes at 475°F.

Mrs. Valerie S. Trahan, Abbeville H. S.
Abbeville, Louisiana

FAVORITE TARTS
Number of Servings — 16
Pastry:
1 pkg. cream cheese
1 stick butter
1 c. flour
Pinch of salt
Roll and fill muffin tins.

Filling:
1 stick butter
1 c. sugar
2 eggs
1 c. seeded raisins
1 c. pecans
Cream butter and sugar and add egg yolks, raisins, and egg whites slightly beaten. Pour in crust. Bake 25 minutes at 350°F.

Mrs. Gladys R. Gordner, Southwest School
Greensboro, North Carolina

LIME CHEESE TARTS
Number of Servings — 8-12 Three Inch Tarts
½ c. butter or margarine
⅛ c. sugar
2 egg yolks
1¼ c. flour
2 t. milk
¾ c. finely chopped nuts
Cream butter and sugar, add egg yolks, beat well. Stir in flour, milk, and nuts. Divide dough into 8 pieces and press each evenly on bottom and sides of 3″ tart pan. Prick dough well with fork. Bake 10 minutes at 350°F., cool.

Filling:
1 8 oz. pkg. cream cheese
⅓ c. sugar
2 eggs
1 t. grated lime rind
1 T. lime juice
Green food coloring
Soften cream cheese, blend in sugar and add eggs 1 at a time. Beat until smooth after each addition. Stir in lime rind and juice, tint pastel green with food coloring. Pour into cooled baked tart shells. Bake at 350°F. for 20 minutes or until filling is firm, cool and chill several hours. Garnish with whipped cream and grated lime rind if desired.

Mrs. Theda Ashley, Roosevelt H. S.
Emporia, Kansas

PECAN TARTS (Nancy's)
Number of Servings — 24
1-3 oz. pkg. cream cheese
½ c. margarine
1 c. flour
⅔ c. pecans, chopped
1 egg, beaten
¾ c. light brown sugar
1 T. margarine
1 t. vanilla
Dash of salt
Make pastry of the first 3 ingredients. For ease in mixing, have cheese and margarine at room temperature. Mix well. Chill 1 hour or longer. Divide into 24 parts. Shape into balls. Press

each ball into one part of a miniature muffin tin forming a crust with a roll around top. Leave no holes. Partially fill the 24 tart shells with the pecans portioning them evenly. Make filling of remaining ingredients. Dip by teaspoon and pour over the pecan filled shells. Bake 20 minutes at 400°F. or until brown. Cool slightly. Remove from tins.

Mrs. Hazel Kimbrough, Spade H. S.
Spade, Texas

PECAN TARTS (California Miniature)
Number of Servings — 4 Dozen Tarts
1 small pkg. cream cheese
½ stick butter or margarine
1 c. plain flour, sifted
Cream the butter and cream cheese together, add the flour and mix well. Chill the dough. Roll out very thin. Cut with medium biscuit cutter and fit inside very small party muffin tins.

Filling:
1 stick butter
1 c. sugar
2 eggs, separated
1 t. vanilla
1 c. chopped pecans
1 c. chopped dates or raisins
Cream butter with sugar and egg yolks, add vanilla, chopped nuts and dates (or raisins). Fold in beaten egg whites and pour into uncooked pastry shells. Bake at 350°F. for 20 minutes or until brown. Makes 4 dozen tarts. Adaptable to freezing.

Mrs. Thelma W. LeGette, Rains-Centenary H. S.
Rains, South Carolina

PINEAPPLE DAINTIES (Tarts)
Number of Servings — 2-2½ Dozen
3 T. sesame seed
½ c. chopped pecans
1 c. butter
2¼ c. sifted flour
½ t. salt
1 t. lemon flavoring
½ c. buttermilk
1-9 oz. can crushed pineapple
⅔ c. sugar
3 T. cornstarch
2 egg yolks, slightly beaten
1½ c. sifted powdered sugar
3-4 T. milk
Toast and set aside sesame seed. Blend together until smooth and chill thoroughly butter, flour, salt, flavoring, and buttermilk. Cook pineapple, sugar, cornstarch, and egg yolks until thick. Cool. Roll chilled dough to ¼″ thickness. Sprinkle and press in sesame seeds. Cut dough into 3″ squares. In center of each square place 1 teaspoon of pineapple filling. Bring 4 corners to center over lapping each slightly, dampen each corner to insure sealing. Bake at 350°F. for 25-30 minutes. While warm dribble with glaze of powdered sugar and milk and sprinkle with chopped pecans.

Mrs. Carol Lorene, Lorena H. S.
Lorena, Texas

RASPBERRY TURNOVERS

Number of Servings — 12

Basic French pastry recipe:

1 lb. (4 sticks) butter or margarine, well chilled

4¼ c. sifted flour

1 c. ice water

2 T. lemon juice

Cut ½ pound butter into flour in large bowl until mixture is crumbly and pale yellow. Use a pastry blender (keep remaining butter chilled). Stir in ice water and lemon juice at once into crumbly mixture, continue stirring with a fork until mixture is completely moistened and pastry is very stiff. Wrap in wax paper, chill 30 minutes. Chilling is necessary each time to give a puffy, flaky, crisp pastry. Unwrap pastry and roll out to a rectangle 18x12, on a well floured pastry cloth. Roll straight, lifting the rolling pin each time as you reach the edge, so pastry will be evenly thick, (should be ¼" thick). Slice saved ½ pound butter (chilled) into thin even pats over ⅔ of pastry to form a square 12x12. Fold uncovered ⅓ of pastry over middle third, fold opposite end over top. Then fold pastry in thirds crosswise to make a block. Now you have 9 layers of pastry with pats of butter between each. Roll out again to an even rectangle 18x12, repeat folding as above; chill 30 minutes. Repeat rolling, folding, and chilling 3 more times. Pastry is stiff and cold, so first pound firmly with your rolling pin to flatten, keeping thickness even. After rolling and folding the last time, wrap and chill pastry overnight, or several days, then shape for turnovers or may be used for other pastries.

Turnovers:

1 recipe basic French pastry

¾ c. raspberry jam

1 egg, slightly beaten

Sugar

Roll out pastry evenly to a rectangle, about 21x16, on floured pastry cloth. Pastry should be ⅛" thick. Trim sides to make rectangle, use a ruler. Cut lengthwise into thirds, then crosswise into quarters to make 12 5" squares. Spoon 1 tablespoon raspberry jam into middle of each square; brush edges with beaten egg; fold dough over to make a triangle. Press edges together firmly with thumb or pinch edges with a fork to seal; brush top with beaten egg. Place on ungreased cookie sheets; chill 30 minutes. Bake in very hot oven 450°F. 15 minutes; reduce heat to 350°F. and bake 30 minutes or until turnovers are pugged and a rich brown color. Remove at once from cookie sheets to wire racks; sprinkle tops lightly with sugar, let cool about 10 minutes before serving.

Mrs. Diana Herman Grosz, Bowman Public H. S.
Bowman, North Dakota

TEA-TIME TASSIES

Number of Servings — 24

1 3 oz. pkg. cream cheese

½ c. butter or margarine

1 c. sifted enriched flour

Let cream cheese and butter soften at room temperature, blend. Stir in flour. Chill at least 1 hour. Roll on lightly floured board to about ⅛" thick. Cut with 3" cutter and place in tiny ungreased 1¾" muffin tins. Press dough on bottom and sides of cups.

Pecan filling:

1 egg

¾ c. brown sugar

1 T. soft butter or margarine

1 t. vanilla

Dash of salt

⅔ c. coarsely chopped pecans

Beat together egg, sugar, butter, vanilla and salt until just smooth, stir in pecans. Put 1 teaspoon filling in each pastry cup. Bake at 325°F. 20-25 minutes until filling is set. Remove from cups and place on paper towels to cool.

This recipe submitted by the following teachers:
Mrs. John T. Pendergrass, A. L. Miller Sr. H. S.
Macon, Georgia
Mrs. Mary Hull, Pickens H. S.
Pickens, South Carolina
Mrs. Howard Yarbrough, Cherokee H. S.
Canton, Georgia
Mrs. Billie Crawford, Jacksboro H. S.
Jacksboro, Texas

APPLE TWISTS

Number of Servings — 16

4 medium apples

2 c. sifted all-purpose flour

1 t. salt

⅔ c. shortening

5-7 T. cold water

2 T. soft butter

½ c. sugar

1-1½ t. cinnamon

½ c. melted butter

¾ c. water

Pare, core, and quarter apples. Sift together dry ingredients. Cut in shortening until the size of small peas. Add water until mixture is moist. Roll out on a lightly floured surface to a 12" square. Spread with 2 tablespoons soft butter. Fold sides lengthwise and crosswise, so that the sides lap at the center. Roll out to a 16x10 rectangle. Cut into 16 1" strips. Twist 1 strip of pastry around each quarter of apple. Place in an ungreased 13x9x2 pan, sides not touching. Brush with melted butter, using all. Sprinkle with sugar and spice mixture. Pour ¾ c. water into pan, to prevent sticking. Bake at 425°F. for 20-30 minutes.

Mrs. Elsie C. Dolin, Newberry H. S.
Newberry, Florida

Puddings & Custards

BAKED CUSTARD
Number of Servings — 10
4 eggs, well beaten
½ c. sugar
¼ t. salt
4 c. milk, scalded
½ t. vanilla
Nutmeg

Combine eggs, sugar and salt; slowly add milk and vanilla. Pour into custard cups, sprinkle with nutmeg. Bake in pan of hot water at 350°F. 30 or 40 minutes, or until silver knife inserted into center comes out clean. Serve warm or chill and serve cold.

Jewell West, Crowder H. S.
Crowder, Oklahoma

BOILED CUSTARD
1 qt. milk
1 c. milk
3 egg whites
3 egg yolks
1 c. sugar
2 t. vanilla flavoring

Heat 1 quart sweet milk until nearly boiling, add 3 egg yolks, beaten with 1 cup cold milk. Bring to a boil, being careful not to scorch. Add sugar to the stiffly beaten egg whites and beat with a wire beater while cooking 1 minute. Set aside to cool, add flavoring.

Mrs. Sara Helen McPeake, Central H. S.
Camden, Tennessee

BOILED CUSTARD
Number of Servings — 8
1 qt. sweet milk
5 eggs
1 c. sugar
1 t. vanilla (or any desired flavoring)

Into a double boiler put the milk to get hot, but not boil. Beat the eggs together until light. Add sugar and mix well. Pour a small portion of hot milk into the eggs and sugar to warm and thin this portion. Pour slowly into hot milk. Cook, stirring constantly until it will coat a spoon. Do not over cook. Add flavoring. Chill in refrigerator before serving. Whipped cream makes this custard especially delicious. Use cherries, crystallized fruit or any desired garnish.

Mrs. Joe M. Poston, West Fannin H. S.
Blue Ridge, Georgia

SOUTHERN BOILED CUSTARD
Number of Servings — 12-15
½ gal. sweet milk
3 c. white sugar
6 whole eggs
1 t. vanilla
1½ T. butter

Combine first 3 ingredients, beating eggs well. Cook in top of double boiler until mixture coats a spoon. Remove from heat. Stir in vanilla and butter. Strain through small mesh sieve. Chill well. Top with whipped cream.

Mrs. Colleen Marshall, Lebanon H. S.
Lebanon, Tennessee

BROWN SUGAR CUSTARD
Number of Servings — 6
3 c. brown sugar
3 eggs
½ c. butter, melted

Beat eggs until well mixed, but not foamy. Add brown sugar and melted butter, mix well. Pour into pastry shell and bake until set. Use oven temperature of 325°F. to 350°F.

Martha E. Dorsey, Fleming County High
Flemingsburg, Kentucky

COCONUT CUSTARD
Number of Servings — 6
3 eggs, slightly beaten
¼ c. sugar
¼ t. salt
2 c. milk, scalded
½ t. vanilla
Nutmeg
1 c. coconut

Combine eggs, sugar, and salt; slowly add scalded milk, vanilla, nutmeg and coconut. Pour into custard dishes or a small casserole dish. Place in pan of hot water and bake at 325°F. 30-40 minutes or until mixture does not stick to a clean knife. Serve warm or cooled.

Mrs. Betty Kirschten, Rosebud H. S.
Rosebud, Montana

TRANSPARENT CUSTARD
Number of Servings — 12
2 c. sugar
2 T. flour
4 eggs, beaten separately
⅜ c. butter, melted
1 c. whole milk
⅛ t. salt
1 t. vanilla or 1 t. vanilla and ¼ t. lemon

Mix sugar and flour. Add to well beaten egg yolks. Add melted butter, milk, salt, and well beaten egg whites. Flavor. Bake in two 9″ pastry lined pans. Temperature: 450°F. for 10 minutes then 350°F. for 25 to 30 minutes or until a knife inserted in center comes out clean.

Frances Rast, Byars-Hall H. S.
Covington, Tennessee

LEMON DELICIOUS
Number of Servings — 4
2 T. butter
¾ c. sugar
2 egg yolks (well beaten)
1 lemon, juice and grated rind
1 T. flour
1 c. milk
⅛ t. salt
2 egg whites (stiffly beaten)

Combine first 2 ingredients and cream well. Add next 3, beat well. Add milk and salt. Fold in stiffly beaten egg whites. Bake 350°F. for 30-40 minutes with container set in a pan of water.

Sammie Saulsbury, Crockett Jr. H. S.
Odessa, Texas

LEMON-COCONUT CUPS

Number of Servings — 6-8

1 c. sugar
¼ c. sifted enriched flour
Dash salt
2 T. melted butter or margarine
2 T. grated lemon peel
⅓ c. lemon juice
1½ c. milk, scalded
3 egg yolks, beaten
3 egg whites, beaten stiff
½ c. shredded coconut

Preheat oven to 325°F. Combine sugar, flour, salt, and butter, add lemon peel and juice. Slowly stir scalded milk into beaten egg yolks, add to the first mixture. Fold in egg whites with the shredded coconut and pour into ungreased custard cups, filling ⅔ full. Set custard cups in a shallow pan, filling pan to 1" with hot water. Bake in slow oven 325°F. 45 minutes, or until sponge cake (atop the sauce) is done. Serve warm or chilled.

Caroline W. Timberlake, Newport Jr. H. S.
Kensington, Maryland

LEMON CUPS

Number of Servings — 8

1 c. sugar
4 T. flour
⅛ t. salt
2 T. butter, melted
5 T. lemon juice
Grated rind of 1 lemon
3 egg yolks, well beaten
1½ c. milk
3 egg whites, stiffly beaten

Add blended sugar, flour, and salt to butter, add lemon juice and rind and blend well. Add to egg yolks and milk and stir well, fold in egg whites and pour into greased custard cups, and place in pan of hot water. Bake in moderate oven 350°F. for 45 minutes. When baked, each dessert will have custard on the bottom with sponge cake on top.

This recipe submitted by the following teachers:

Mrs. Eleanor Beyer Brunski, Olney H. S.
Philadelphia, Pennsylvania
Mrs. Arlene Bazzoon, Tarkington H. S.
Cleveland, Texas
Sister M. Del Rey, St. Mary H. S.
Dell Rapids, South Dakota
Joyce F. DeVivo, Lee County. H. S.
Leesburg, Georgia
Mrs. Erma H. Little, H. S.
Creswell, Oregon
Eunice A. Pietila,
Naperville Community H. S.
Naperville, Illinois
Augusta Richardson, Caddo H. S.
Caddo, Oklahoma

LEMON SPONGE CUPS

Number of Servings — 6

1½ T. butter or margarine
⅔ c. sugar
2⅔ T. flour (plain)
Small pinch of salt
3-4 T. lemon juice
Grated rind, 1 or 2 lemons
2 eggs, separated
1 c. milk

Cream shortening, add sugar, flour, salt, lemon juice, and rind. Separate eggs. Beat egg yolks, add milk to yolks. Add to first mixture. Fold in stiffly beaten egg whites. Pour into greased custard cups. Place in a pan of water. Bake about 40-45 minutes at 300°F.

Mrs. Gertrude McRae, Rockingham H. S.
Rockingham, North Carolina

MAGIC ORANGE CUPS

Number of Servings — 5

¾ c. sugar
1½ T. shortening
1 T. grated orange peel
2 egg yolks
3 T. flour, sifted
⅓ c. orange juice
1 scant c. milk
2 egg whites, beaten

Cream sugar and shortening, add orange peel and egg yolks, beat well. Add flour alternately with milk and juice, fold in egg whites. Put into greased custard cups or a 4x8 pan. Bake in pan containing 1" hot water at 350°F. for 20 minutes.

Mrs. Willa Dailey, Gibbon Public School
Gibbon, Nebraska

PINEAPPLE-BANANA DELIGHT

Number of Servings — 8

1 c. sugar
1¼ c. pineapple juice
2 eggs, beaten
2 T. flour
1 T. cornstarch
1 No. 2½ can pineapple cubes (drained)
4 bananas
½ c. chopped nuts
10 marshmallows, quartered

Cook the first 5 ingredients together, stirring constantly until smooth and thick, chill. Just before serving, add rest of ingredients. Top with meringue.

Mrs. Grace L. Hallen, Turner Ashby H. S.
Dayton, Virginia

DELUXE APPLE PUDDING

Number of Servings — 6-8

5-6 c. diced apples
2 T. flour
½ c. sugar (more if apples are sour)

Mix all together and put into flat 9x12 baking pan.

Filling:

1 c. flour
1 c. oatmeal or rolled wheat
½ c. brown sugar
1 t. soda
1 t. baking powder
½ c. shortening (butter preferred)

(Continued on Next Page)

Rub together or blend well all ingredients. Lay over first part, bake at 350°F. to 375°F. until apples are done. Serve hot or cold with plain or whipped cream. Other fruits as fresh or canned peaches or pears may be used for interesting changes.

Mrs. Laura Anderson, Sutherlin H. S.
Sutherlin, Oregon

SPICY APPLE PUDDING
Number of Servings — 6

¼ c. butter
¾ c. sugar
1 egg
¼ t. salt
1 t. soda
¼ t. nutmeg
1⅛ c. flour
½ t. cinnamon
1 T. cream
1½ c. finely chopped apple
Orange sauce:
1 c. sugar
2 T. cornstarch
1 c. water
2 T. butter
1 c. orange juice

Cream butter, add sugar and blend well. Beat in egg until mixture is light and fluffy. Sift together dry ingredients, add to butter mixture. Add apple and cream and mix well, pour into greased and floured 9″ square pan and bake 40 minutes at 350°F. Serve with orange sauce made by cooking together until thick and clear, sugar cornstarch, and water. Then add butter and orange juice and serve warm.

Elaine Goldsmith, Avon H. S.
Avon, Ohio

APPLE DUMPLING PUDDING
Number of Servings — 6-8

2 c. cubed apples
½ c. shortening
1 c. sugar
1½ c. flour
1 egg
2 t. nutmeg
1 t. cinnamon
1 t. soda
½ t. vanilla
Pinch of salt

Mix wet ingredients, mix dry ingredients and mix together. Bake in cube pan at 375°F. for 30 to 35 minutes. Serve with whipped cream or ice cream.

Betty Jan Anderson, Wilder Jr. H. S.
Savannah, Georgia

APPLE-CARROT-HEALTH PUDDING

2 c. flour
2 c. sugar
1 t. soda
1 t. cinnamon
1 t. cloves
¼ t. salt
⅔ c. shortening
2 c. chopped apples
2 c. grated carrots
1 c. raisins
½ c. nuts or coconut

Mix and sift dry ingredients, add shortening and blend. Then add the apples, carrots, raisins, and coconut or nuts, mix well. Bake in an 8x12x2 pan at 350°F. for 30 minutes. This may be served hot or cold, plain or topped with whipped cream and garnished with a cherry or coconut.

Allyene Gregory, Southern Jr. H. S.
Owensboro, Kentucky

APPLE NUT PUDDING
Number of Servings — 6-8

2 eggs
1 c. sugar
¾ c. sifted flour
¼ t. salt
¾ t. baking powder
½ t. cinnamon
¼ t. nutmeg
1 t. almond extract
¾ c. chopped nuts
1½ c. diced raw apples

Beat eggs until light, gradually adding sugar and beating after each addition. Sift flour, measure, and sift with salt, baking powder, cinnamon and nutmeg. Add dry ingredients to egg mixture and then add extract, nuts, and chopped apples. Mix well. Pour batter into a well greased 8″ square cake pan. Bake at 325°F. for 40-45 minutes. Serve with whipped cream or ice cream.

Mrs. Mary Elizabeth Watkins, Lily H. S.
Lily, Kentucky

OZARK PUDDING (Apple-Nut)
Number of Servings — 6-8

1 egg
¾ c. sugar
¾ c. sifted flour
1½ t. baking powder
⅛ t. salt
1 c. raw apples, chopped fine
1 c. nuts, chopped

Beat egg until fluffy, add sugar gradually. Sift flour, add baking powder and salt and add to egg mixture and blend. Add chopped apples and nuts and mix well. Place in a greased pyrex pie pan (or a greased 9x9x1 cake pan) and bake at 350°F. for 35 minutes or until done, cool. Remove from pan. Slice and top with whipped cream.

This recipe submitted by the following teachers:
Rachel Bruner, Westminster H. S.
Westminster, South Carolina
Mrs. Wm. L. Jackson, Camden H. S.
Camden, South Carolina

OZARK PUDDING (Apple-Nut)
Number of Servings — 4

1 egg
¾ c. sugar
2 T. flour (⅛-½ c. may be used)
1¼ t. baking powder (1½ t. may be used)

(Continued on Next Page)

½ c. chopped nuts
½-1 c. chopped apples, peeled or unpeeled
1 t. vanilla
⅛ t. salt

Combine egg and sugar and beat together until smooth, mix flour, baking powder and salt and add to egg mixture. Add nuts, apples, and vanilla. Bake at 350°F. about 30 to 40 minutes or until done. Bake in a pyrex dish allowing plenty of room for this mixture to rise. When done, it is brown and crunchy in appearance and will fall. Serve with whipped cream or ice cream (the whipped cream may be sweetened and salted slightly if desired).

This recipe submitted by the following teachers:
Mrs. Jeanne Plonk Beam, Holbrook H. S.
Lowell, North Carolina
Bernice C. Forester, Oxford H. S.
Oxford, Alabama
Frances J. Williams, Newton-Conover H. S.
Newton, North Carolina
Delores S. Barber, Laurel Hill School
Laurel Hill, North Carolina
Mrs. Emily T. Duley, Frederick Sasscer H. S.
Upper Marlboro, Maryland

BREAD PUDDING (With Orange Sauce)
Number of Servings — 8-10
5 c. stale bread, biscuits or rolls (small pieces)
5 c. milk
¼ c. sugar
2 eggs, well beaten
1 t. vanilla
⅛ c. raisins (1 indiv. box.)

Using a 2-quart casserole, pour milk over bread crumbs and allow to stand at room temperature until all bread is moist and chill is gone from milk. Add sugar, eggs, flavoring and stir well, fold in raisins. Wipe edge of casserole and bake uncovered at 350°F. for approximately 1½ hours, until delicately browned and knife inserted in center comes out clean. While still warm, serve with lemon or orange sauce.

Orange sauce:
½ c. sugar
1 T. cornstarch
1 c. boiling orange juice
2 T. butter
1½ T. lemon juice
Few grains nutmeg
Few grains salt

Mix sugar and cornstarch, add juice gradually, stirring constantly. Cover and boil 5 minutes, stirring occasionally. Remove from heat, add other ingredients. Makes 1 cup.

Margaret Allen Shanks, Orrville H. S.
Orrville, Alabama

BREAD PUDDING DELUXE
Number of Servings — 6
2¼ c. fresh bread cubes
1 13 oz. can evaporated milk (undiluted)
3 egg yolks
1 c. sugar
¼ t. salt

1 t. vanilla
3 T. melted butter
3 egg whites
Jelly or jam, any flavor

Cut crusts off bread, cut bread in cubes and place cubes in greased baking dish. Scald milk, pour scalded milk over well-beaten egg yolks to which ½ cup sugar and salt have been added, mix. Add flavoring and butter and pour mixture over cubes. Place baking dish in pan of warm water and bake 1 hour at 350°F. Remove from oven and spread with jam or jelly. Make meringue of egg whites and remaining sugar, brown in oven. Serve warm or cold.

Nancy Jane Mearig, High Point H. S.
Beltsville, Maryland

QUEENS PUDDING
Number of Servings — 6
2 c. milk
2 c. bread crumbs (or sponge cake crumbs)
¼ c. sugar
Grated rind of 1 lemon
1 T. butter
3 eggs, separated
1 small jar of raspberry or apricot jam or jelly (about 1 c.)

Bring milk to boil, pour over bread crumbs, sugar, lemon rind, and butter which have been mixed together. Let cool for a few minutes. Stir in beaten egg yolks, pour in shallow buttered baking dish about 8x8x2 and bake in 375°F. oven approximately 10 minutes. Remove from oven and spread jam or jelly evenly over the top.
Beat egg whites until stiff but not dry, spread over jam-covered pudding, dredge with a bit of granulated sugar, return to oven and bake until meringue is slightly browned. Serve hot or cold.

Isla C. Painter, Stanley H. S.
Stanley, North Carolina

SUZANNE'S BREAD PUDDING
Number of Servings — 6-8
8 bread slices, diagonally cut
3 c. scalded milk
⅛ c. butter, melted
¾ c. granulated sugar
3 eggs, slightly beaten
½ t. salt
1 t. vanilla

Meringue topping:
3 egg whites, beaten into peaks
¼ t. cream of tartar
6 T. sugar
½ t. vanilla
1 c. chocolate tidbits

Fit bread pieces into buttered 6x12 baking dish, blend in milk, butter, sugar, eggs, salt, and vanilla. Bake at 350°F. for 45 to 60 minutes until pudding tests done. Sprinkle chocolate tidbits over top of pudding. Combine egg whites, cream of tartar, sugar and vanilla into a meringue. Spread on pudding and brown at 350°F.

Mrs. Suzanne Cass, Mansfield Sr. High
Mansfield, Ohio

BREAD AND BUTTER PUDDING
(Ambrosia for the Angels)

8 slices white bread, toasted dry in oven
  (golden brown Melba toast)
2 sticks margarine or butter, melted
4 eggs
2 c. sugar
2 t. vanilla
4 c. milk
Raisins
Nutmeg

Break toasted bread into bite size pieces and put into pan of melted butter. Stir and simmer slowly until all butter has soaked into the bread. Beat eggs, add sugar and blend well. Add vanilla and milk and stir until all ingredients are well mixed. Put buttered bread into baking dish and pour liquid mixture over it. Keep mashing the bread down into the milk for a few minutes so that it may soak up some of the milk. Sprinkle raisins and nutmeg over the top. Again push down into milk a few times. Bake at 400°F. until firm. May be served hot or cold. Variation: Add 1 package melted chocolate chips to milk-egg mixture; substitute chopped nuts for raisins and nutmeg.

Mrs. Evelyn A. Kee, Stell Jr. H. S.
Brownsville, Texas

OLD FASHIONED INDIAN PUDDING
Number of Servings — 12-15

2 qt. milk
5 T. flour
3 T. cornmeal
¾ c. light molasses
1 c. granulated sugar
1 t. ginger
½ t. cinnamon
¼ t. allspice
½ t. salt
1 egg, well beaten
1 c. seedless raisins

Scald 1 quart milk and add the flour mixed with a little cold water. Put in a shallow 4-quart baking pan and add cornmeal, molasses, sugar, spices, and salt. Let stand until cold and add the well beaten egg, raisins and remaining quart of milk. Bake in a 375°F. oven until mixture is hot, then reduce oven to 300°F. and bake about 2 hours or until the liquid is nearly absorbed. Stir occasionally during the first hour and a half of baking. Let brown during last half hour. Serve plain or with whipped cream or vanilla ice cream.

Nancy L. Suydam, Hale-Ray H. S.
Moodus, Connecticut

CHERRY PUDDING
Number of Servings — 6

1 c. flour
1 t. baking powder
¼ t. salt
1 c. sugar
4 T. melted shortening
½ c. milk
½ t. vanilla
2 c. (No. 2½ can) pitted cherries
1 c. hot cherry juice (if not enough juice, add
  water to make 1 cup.

Grease 8x8x2 cake pan. Sift flour, baking powder, sugar into a bowl. Add shortening, milk, and vanilla, and beat vigorously with a spoon or electric mixer. Pour batter into pan, cover with cherries, and sprinkle with ½ the above cup of sugar. Heat cherry juice and pour over top of cherries and sugar. Bake in 375°F. oven for 40 to 45 minutes. May be served plain, with whipped cream, or with ice cream. Best served warm.

Mrs. Bertie L. McDaniel, Sanderson H. S.
Sanderson, Texas

CHERRY PUDDING
Number of Servings — 9

2 T. butter
1 c. sugar
1 c. flour
½ c. milk
1 t. baking powder
2 c. canned cherries
¾ c. sugar

Make a batter of butter, sugar, flour, baking powder and milk. Heat cherries and ¾ cup sugar until sugar is dissolved. Pour batter into utility dish. Pour cherries on top. Bake 25 minutes at 375°F. When done cherries will be underneath. May serve with whipped cream or ice cream.

Ella Mae Broyles, Edmond H. S.
Edmond, Oklahoma

CHERRY PUDDING

2 c. flour
2 c. sugar
1 c. cherry juice
1 c. whole cherries
1 c. nuts, chopped
½ t. soda
2 eggs

Mix together and bake at 350°F.

Sauce:
2 c. brown sugar
2 c. hot water
1 T. butter
1½ T. cornstarch
1 t. vanilla

Mix and cook over low heat until thick. Pour over baked pudding. Keep in refrigerator until cool. Serve with whipped cream on top

Mrs. Joe Branstetter, Hiseville H. S.
Hiseville, Kentucky

CHERRY PUDDING
Number of Servings — 8-10

Fruit Mixture:
1½ c. cherries (or any fruit)
1 c. sugar
⅓ c. water
Heat fruit until sugar dissolves. Cool.
Batter:
1 T. butter
1 c. sugar
1 c. flour
1 t. baking powder
½ c. milk

(Continued on Next Page)

Mix butter and sugar, sift flour and baking powder together, add to butter and sugar mixture alternately with milk. Butter glass baking dish, pour batter into it. Pour fruit mixture on top without stirring. Bake at 350°F. for 30 minutes.

Mrs. Juanita Patton, Achille H. S.
Achille, Oklahoma

QUICK 'N EASY CHERRY PUDDING

Number of Servings — 6-8

1 small can prepared cherry pie filling
2 c. sugar (if filling is sweetened, decrease sugar ½-1 c.)
1 c. flour
1½ t. baking powder
1½ c. milk
½ c. butter or margarine

Empty fruit into bowl and sprinkle over it 1 cup sugar, mix flour, baking powder, remaining sugar gradually with milk to make batter. Melt butter in 8x10x2 baking dish, pour in batter, do not stir. Pour fruit and sugar mixture onto batter, do not stir. Bake at 375°F. until well browned on top (about 30 minutes). Serve hot or cold with milk. Other fillings may be used, such as peach or apple.

Mrs. Estelle S. Dobbins, Auburn H. S.
Riner, Virginia

CHOCOLATE PUDDING

Number of Servings — 6

1 c. flour
¼ t. salt
¾ c. sugar
2 t. baking powder
1½ T. cocoa
½ c. milk
2 T. melted butter
1 t. vanilla
½ c. pecan meats, chopped
¾ c. sugar
3 T. cocoa
1 c. water

Sift together flour, salt, ¾ cup sugar, baking powder, 1½ tablespoons cocoa. Add ½ cup milk, butter, vanilla, and nuts. Pour this mixture into 9″ baking pan and cover with remainder of sugar, cocoa and water, do not stir. Bake at 325°F. until cake part is done. This makes a pudding with its ready made sauce, serve warm.

This recipe submitted by the following teachers:
Jane Kiker, Allison H. S.
Allison, Texas
Frances Shipley, Coon Rapids H. S.
Coon Rapids, Iowa

CHOCOLATE TART (Pudding)

1¾ c. flour
2 T. cocoa
1 pkg. chopped dates
1 c. boiling water
1 t. soda
½ t. salt
½ c. oleo
1 c. sugar

2 eggs
1 t. vanilla
1 c. nuts
1 pkg. chocolate chips

Sift flour, cocoa, and salt. Mix dates with boiling water and soda. Cool. Cream shortening and sugar. Beat well. Add eggs. Alternate flour and date mixture. Add vanilla. Pour in greased pan. Sprinkle wtih nuts and chocolate chips. Bake at 350°F. for about 45 minutes.

Florence Spinks, Raymondville H. S.
Raymondville, Texas

BAKED DEVIL'S FLOAT

Number of Servings — 6

½ c. sugar
1½-2 c. water
12 marshmallows, quartered
2 T. shortening
½ c. sugar
1 t. vanilla
1 c. flour
½ t. salt
1 t. baking powder
3 T. cocoa
½ c. milk
⅛-½ chopped nuts

Cook ½ sugar and water together for 5 minutes, pour into baking dish, top with marshmallows. Cream shortening and remaining ½ cup sugar, add vanilla. Add flour sifted with salt, baking powder and cocoa, alternately with milk, add nut meats. Drop from spoon over marshmallow mixture, cover. Bake in moderate 350°F. oven for 45 minutes. Garnish with whipped cream if desired.

This recipe submitted by the following teachers:
Mrs. Gladys H. Frye, Chilhowie H. S.
Chilhowie, Virginia
Sister M. Dolorita O.S.B., Mt. Marty
Yankton, South Dakota
Mrs. Ruth Lathrope, Wonewoc-Center H. S.
Wonewoc, Wisconsin

FUDGE PUDDING

Number of Servings — 8

2 eggs
1 c. granulated sugar
½ c. butter or margarine
3 T. cocoa
3 T. flour
1 c. pecans
1 t. vanilla

Beat eggs until fluffy, add sugar gradually, continuing beating. Melt margarine and add cocoa, stir cocoa mixture into eggs and sugar. Add the remaining ingredients. Pour into an 8x8 greased pan and place this pan in a larger pan which has hot water in it and bake in a 350°F. oven for 40 minutes. When serving, turn the squares upside down as this pudding forms a gelatinous sauce on the bottom. Serve with whipped cream or a dip of vanilla ice cream.

Mrs. Dorothy Boen, Central H. S.
Muskogee, Oklahoma

BAKED FUDGE OR BROWNIE PUDDING
Number of Servings — 6

1 c. flour
2 t. baking powder
½ t. salt
⅓-¾ c. granulated sugar
2 T. cocoa
½ c. milk
1 t. vanilla
2 T. shortening, melted
¾-1 c. chopped walnuts
¾ c. brown sugar
¼ c. cocoa
1¾ c. hot water

Sift together flour, baking powder, salt, granulated sugar, and cocoa, add milk, vanilla, and shortening, mix until smooth, then add nuts. Pour into greased 8" square cake pan. Mix brown sugar and cocoa, sprinkle over batter. Pour hot water over entire batter and bake in moderate oven 350°F. 40 to 45 minutes.

This recipe submitted by the following teachers:
Mrs. Lee Roy Snapp, Lamar H. S.
Jonesboro, Tennessee
Zelma Goben, Antelope Valley H. S.
Lancaster, California
Mrs. Elene Whetten, Sanders H. S.
Sanders, Arizona
Bonnie Dickinson, Fort Sumner H. S.
Fort Sumner, New Mexico

CHOCOLATE SUNDAE PUDDING
Number of Servings — 6

1 c. flour
2 t. baking powder
½ t. salt
¾ c. sugar
1 egg
½ c. milk
2 T. melted shortening
1 c. chopped nuts
6 T. cocoa
1 c. brown sugar
1¾ c. hot water

Sift together dry ingredients. Add egg, milk, and shortening, mix until smooth. Blend in nuts. Spread into a 9x9x2 pan. Combine sugar and cocoa and sprinkle over batter. Pour hot water into a tablespoon and let flow over sugar mixture. Bake 45 minutes at 350°F. Serve plain or with whipped cream.

Dorotha Prowell, Hereford Sr. H. S.
Hereford, Texas

CHOCOLATE FUDGE PUDDING
Number of Servings — 6-8

1 c. sifted flour
2 t. baking powder
¼-½ t. salt
⅔-¾ c. granulated sugar
2 T. cocoa (or 1 sq. melted chocolate)
½ c. milk
2 T. melted butter or shortening
1 t. vanilla

½ c. chopped pecans
1 c. brown sugar (packed)
4 T. cocoa
1½ c. boiling water
(Additional sugar may be added if desired)

Sift flour, baking powder, salt, sugar and 2 tablespoons cocoa together. Add milk, shortening and vanilla. Mix only until smooth. Add pecans, spread in greased, shallow 1 quart baking dish. Mix brown sugar and 4 tablespoons cocoa. Sprinkle over top of mixture. Pour boiling water over top. Bake at 350°F. for 40 minutes. Serve warm or cold with ice cream or whipped cream.

This recipe submitted by the following teachers:
Kathleen Burchett, Flatwood H. S.
Jonesville, Virginia
Mrs. Jerry Barton, W. B. Atkins Jr. H. S.
Lubbock, Texas

HOT FUDGE PUDDING
Number of Servings — 6

Sauce:
⅓ c. sugar
3 T. cocoa
½ c. water (boiling)
¾ c. milk

Mix in a bowl the sugar, cocoa, boiling water and milk. Set aside.

Pudding:
⅔ c. flour
½ c. sugar
1½ t. baking powder
2 T. cocoa
¼ t. salt
⅔ c. milk
6 T. milk
2 T. melted shortening
¾ t. vanilla

Sift together the dry ingredients. Add the milk, shortening, nuts, and vanilla. Mix quickly. Spread in a greased 6x9x2 pan. Pour cocoa mixture over top of batter. Do not mix. Sauce will be on bottom when pudding is done. Bake 350°F. 30 minutes. Good plain or may be topped with whipped cream or ice cream.

Mrs. Ann Corlew, Greenwood Jr. H. S.
Clarksville, Tennessee

DATE-NUT PUDDING
Number of Servings — 8

½ c. sifted all-purpose flour
½ t. soda
⅛ t. salt
1 c. sugar
3 eggs, beaten together
½ c sweet milk
1 c. dates, chopped
1 c. nuts, broken

Mix the sugar, flour, soda, and salt. Beat the eggs until light, mix with the flour and sugar, add the milk, the dates and the nuts. Blend carefully. Bake in a lightly greased 8" square pan at 325°F. for about 45 minutes. Serve warm or cool (may be topped with whipped cream).

Mrs. Agnes B. LeBlanc, Washington H. S.
Washington, Louisiana

DATE-NUT PUDDING
(With Coconut Topping)
Number of Servings — 8-10

½ lb. chopped dates
1 c. boiling water
1 t. soda
1 egg
1 c. sugar
1 stick (½ c.) melted margarine
1 t. salt
1 t. vanilla
1½ c. sifted enriched flour
½ c. chopped nuts

Add chopped dates and soda to boiling water and let stand about 5 minutes. Mix egg, sugar, melted margarine, salt, and vanilla. Add flour and blend. Add date mixture and nuts. Pour in greased and floured pan (9x12). Bake about 25 minutes at 350°F. Remove from oven and top with icing. Place about 3-4" from broiler and broil about 2 minutes. Remove from oven and cover with foil to moisten. May be served with ice cream.

Icing (optional):
¼ c. melted margarine
1 c. brown sugar
1 c. coconut
5 T. milk

This recipe submitted by the following teachers:
Mrs. Robinette M. Husketh, South Granville H. S.
Creedmoor, North Carolina
Mrs. Ruth Fishburn, Adair H. S.
Adair, Oklahoma

UPSIDE-DOWN DATE PUDDING
(Date-Nut Cake Atop, a Butterscotch Sauce Beneath)
Number of Servings — 9

1 c. pitted dates, cut up fine
1 c. boiling water
½ c. granulated sugar
½ c. brown sugar
1 egg
2 T. butter or margarine, melted
1½ c. enriched flour
1 t. soda
½ t. baking powder
½ t. salt
1 c. chopped nuts

Combine dates and water, blend sugars, egg, and butter. Sift together dry ingredients, add to sugar mixture. Stir in nuts and cooled date mixture. Pour into 11x7x1½ baking dish. Top with brown-sugar sauce.

Brown-sugar sauce:
1½ c. brown sugar
1 T. butter or margarine
1½ c. boiling water

Combine brown sugar, butter or margarine, add boiling water. Bake in moderate oven 375°F. 35 to 40 minutes. Cut in squares, invert on plates. Serve slightly warm with whipped cream.

Mrs. Kathryn Lotz, Riverdale H. S.
Mt. Blanchard, Ohio

DATE-NUT PUDDING
Number of Servings — 10

1 c. sugar
1 c. flour
1 t. baking powder
1 t. salt
1 t. vanilla
¾ c. dates (cut in fourths)
½ c. chopped nut meats (more if you desire)
1 c. milk
Syrup:
1½ c. brown sugar
2 c. hot water

Put the syrup ingredients into the 12" baking pan and simmer while you mix the batter by combining all ingredients and stirring well. Pour the batter into the hot syrup (do not stir). Bake 45 minutes at 375°F. Serve hot or cold with cream, whipped cream, or ice cream.

Mrs. Katherine Porter, San Jon H. S.
San Jon, New Mexico

HEAVENLY DATE PUDDING
Number of Servings — 6-8

2 eggs
¾ c. milk
4 T. flour, level
2 t. baking powder
⅛ t. cinnamon
½ c. sugar
1 pkg. (1 c.) chopped dates
1 c. broken nut meats

Beat the eggs and add milk. Sift together the flour, baking powder, cinnamon and sugar. Add the liquid to the dry ingredients and beat until well mixed. Add the broken nut meats and chopped dates to the mixture. Stir lightly to mix. Pour into a greased mold (1 quart size) and steam for 1 hour.

Ruby C. Irvine, Coalton H. S.
Coalton, West Virginia

DATE-NUT PUDDING (Lemon Sauce)
Number of Servings — 8

1 c. dates, chopped
½ c. bread crumbs, coarse
⅔ c. chopped walnuts
1 t. salt
1 c. sugar
2 t. baking powder
2 eggs, well beaten
1 t. vanilla

Mix in order given, pour into well-buttered loaf pan 9x3x2. Bake 30 minutes in 350°F. oven. Serve warm with sauce.

Sauce:
1 c. sugar
2 T. cornstarch
2 c. boiling water
2 T. butter
1 lemon, juice and rind

Bring sugar, cornstarch and boiling water to boil, cook until slightly thickened. Remove from heat, add butter and lemon.

Mrs. Nellie H. Bennett, Wasatch H. S.
Heber, Utah

GRAPENUT PUFF PUDDING
Number of Servings — 4-6

¼ c. butter
1 c. sugar
2 egg yolks
2 T. flour
3 T. grapenuts
1 c. milk
1 lemon, juice and rind
2 egg whites, stiffly beaten

Cream butter and sugar, mix in next 5 ingredients, fold in egg whites. Pour into 1-quart greased dish, place in pan of hot water and bake at 350°F. 60 minutes.

Peta Jarceau, Hopkinton High
Contoocook, New Hampshire

LEMON CAKE TOP PUDDING
Number of Servings — 6

1 c. sugar
4 T. flour
2 egg yolks, beaten
1 c. milk
¼ t. salt
3-4 T. lemon juice
Grated rind of 1 lemon
1 T. butter
2 egg whites, beaten

Add ingredients in order given, adding butter to milk. Fold in egg whites and cook in covered casserole in pan of water for 25 to 30 minutes at 350°F.

This recipe submitted by the following teachers:
Vades Koonst, Sherman H. S.
Moro, Oregon
Mrs. Lola S. Peruhouse, Tascusa H. S.
Amarillo, Texas
Mable H. Whisnant, Rock Springs H. S.
Denver, North Carolina

LEMON CAKE PUDDING
Number of Servings — 8

1 c. sugar
¼ c. sifted flour
Dash of salt
3 egg yolks, beaten
1½ c. scalded milk
2 T. cooking oil (such as Wesson)
5 T. lemon juice
3 egg whites, stiffly beaten
2 t. grated lemon rind

Sift dry ingredients together. Combine egg yolks, milk, oil, lemon juice and rind. Add to flour mixture. Fold in egg whites. Pour into oiled custard cups. Set cups in pan of hot water. Bake 45 minutes at 325°F. Cool.

Joyce Real, Judson H. S.
Converse, Texas

STEAMED CRANBERRY PUDDING
Number of Servings — 8

Pudding:
1 egg
¼ c. molasses
¼ c. white Karo
1½ c. flour
1 t. baking powder
2 c. cranberries, halved
⅛ c. boiling water with 1 t. soda

Shake cranberries and ½ cup of the measured flour in a paper bag or mix well in a bowl. Mix the other ingredients in the order given and add cranberries. Steam for 2½ hours in a mold. Serve warm with butter sauce.

Butter sauce:
1 c. white sugar
1 c. thin cream
½ c. butter
1 T. flour
1 t. vanilla

Mix the flour with the sugar. Mix all ingredients except vanilla in top of double boiler and cook covered for 30 minutes, add vanilla.

Mrs. Nora Estrem, Battle Lake H. S.
Battle Lake, Minnesota

STEAMED CHOCOLATE PUDDING AND FOAMY SAUCE
Number of Servings — 8

1 egg
½ c. sugar
1 c. milk
2 c. sifted flour
3 t. baking powder
½ t. salt
2 sq. unsweetened chocolate

Beat egg, sugar and melted chocolate with rotary beater, sift together dry ingredients and add alternately with milk. Pour into greased 1-quart mold and steam 1½ hours. Serve warm with foamy sauce. Family recipe for 43 years.

Foamy sauce:
2 T. butter
1 c. powdered sugar
1 egg
1 t. vanilla
1 c. whipping cream

Cream together butter and sugar, add egg and beat until smooth, add vanilla. When ready to serve blend in whipped cream.

Margaret M. Taylor, Irving Jr. H. S.
Pocatello, Idaho

STEAMED FRUIT PUDDING (Using Suet)
Number of Servings — 8-10

1 c. suet (chopped fine)
2 c. flour, heaping
½ c. sugar
1 c. fruit, chopped raisins, currants, nuts or mixed fruit cake fruit
¼ t. salt
¼ t. cinnamon
¼ t. cloves
¼ c. molasses
1 t. soda dissolved in molasses
Hot water

Sift dry ingredients together, combine with cut fruit and nuts and suet. Add hot water to ¼ cup of molasses to make 1 cut. Dissolve soda in this and combine with dry ingredient mixture. Stir

(Continued on Next Page)

only until all dry ingredients are moistened. Steam 1 hour. Serve with a dip sauce.

Dip sauce:

1 c. sugar
¼ c. flour
1½ c. water
2 T. butter
1 t. vanilla

Combine sugar and flour, add to water that has been brought to a boil, stir continually. When thickened, add butter and vanilla.

Mrs. Mary Ellen Hoadley, University H. S.
Laramie, Wyoming

ENGLISH PLUM PUDDING

6 eggs, beaten very light
2 c. brown sugar
¾ lb. beef suet
¾ lb. flour
½ c. sweet milk
¼ lb. bread crumbs
½ c. marachino cherries
Juice from cherries
¼ t. cloves
2 T. fresh lemon juice
1 lb. seedless raisins
1 lb. seeded raisins
1 lb. currants
½ lb. pecans
1 lb. citron, pineapple and cherries mixed
1 t. nutmeg
2 t. cinnamon

Beat eggs, add sugar gradually, then add cherry juice and milk. Dredge chopped fruit with flour to which spices and bread crumbs have been added. Add liquid mixture to dry ingredients, when thoroughly mixed, add suet, nuts and lemon juice. Put in well-greased molds and steam 3½ to 4 hours. Serve with hard sauce.

Hard sauce:

½ c. butter
2 c. confectioners' sugar
1 t. vanilla

Cream butter until very light, gradually add confectioners' sugar, then vanilla.

Faye S. Sutherland, La Rue County H. S.
Hodgenville, Kentucky

SUGAR PLUM PUDDING

Number of Servings — 12-20

2 c. flour
1½ t. soda
1½ c. sugar
1 t. nutmeg
1 t. allspice
1 t. cinnamon
¾ c. oil
3 eggs
1 c. buttermilk
1 c. cooked chopped prunes
1 c. chopped pecans

Sift together dry ingredients. Mix oil, eggs, and sugar in a large bowl. Add dry ingredients alternately with buttermilk to the egg mixture. Fold in

the prunes and nuts. Line a 13x9x2½ pan with wax paper, grease and flour the paper and sides of pan. Bake at 350°F. 35-40 minutes.

Topping:

1 c. sugar
½ c. buttermilk
1 T. corn syrup
½ c. butter

Prepare topping while cake bakes. In a saucepan place the sugar, buttermilk, syrup and butter. Bring to a boil and when pudding is done, pour the topping over the top. Cool and serve. Good when cold too.

Ialeen S. Mode, Franklinton H. S.
Franklinton, North Carolina

RICE PUDDING

Number of Servings — 6-8

3 T. rice (do not use pre-cooked)
3 T. sugar
2 T. butter or Crisco
¼ t. salt
Few grains nutmeg
4 c. milk
½ c. raisins

Place rice, sugar, butter, salt, and nutmeg into a 2-quart casserole or baking dish. Add milk and stir well. Bake in a slow oven, 275°F. for 1½ to 2 hours, or until rice is done. (Do not over-cook.) Stir often during the first hour of cooking. Serve hot or cold.

Mrs. W. D. Worthington, Mena H. S.
Mena, Arkansas

BUTTERSCOTCH RICE

Number of Servings — 4

⅔ c. packaged pre-cook rice
2 c. milk
¼ t. salt
3 T. butter
⅓ c. brown sugar, packed
1 t. vanilla
½ c. snipped dates

In large saucepan, combine rice, milk, and salt, cover loosely. Bring to boil, boil gently 15 minutes, fluffing rice occasionally with fork. Meanwhile, in small saucepan, melt butter, add sugar, cook until sugar dissolves. Add sugar mixture and cooked rice, with vanilla and dates. Serve warm with whipped cream.

Jo Ann Willis, Cotaco H. S.
Somerville, Alabama

STRAWBERRY MERINGUE PUDDING

Number of Servings — 4

¾ c. cake flour
1 t. baking powder
⅛ t. salt
2 eggs
½ c. sugar
½ t. vanilla
1 pt. strawberries, sliced and sweetened to taste
2 egg whites
Dash salt
Custard sauce

(Continued on Next Page)

Sift flour, measure and resift 3 times with baking powder and salt. Beat whole eggs until light and lemon colored, add ¼ cup of the sugar gradually, beating constantly. Add vanilla, sift the dry ingredients into the egg mixture gradually, and fold in carefully. Turn batter into a greased 8″ layer cake pan and bake in a moderate oven 350°F. for 20 to 25 minutes. Place cake on large flat baking sheet and spread berries over top. Cover completely with a meringue.

Meringue: Add a dash of salt to the egg whites and beat until stiff but not dry. Gradually beat in the remaining ¼ cup sugar until thick and smooth. Pile on pudding and bake 15 minutes at 350°F. or until meringue is golden brown. May be served warm or cold with a custard sauce (the 2 remaining egg yolks may be used with the custard sauce).

Mrs. Jimmie Rae Hankins, Lexington H. S.
Lexington, Alabama

SWEET POTATO PUDDING (Grated)

Number of Servings — 8

4 eggs
2 c. milk
3 c. grated sweet potato (raw)
4 T. melted butter
2 c. brown sugar
½ t. cinnamon
¼ t. nutmeg
¼ t. salt

Beat eggs slightly, add remaining ingredients. Pour into buttered baking dish, bake in slow oven 300°F. for approximately 30 minutes or until well browned. Serve warm with whipped cream.

Mrs. Jean G. Sands, Rocky Gap H. S.
Rocky Gap, Virginia

GRATED POTATO PUDDING

Number of Servings — 8

1 c. sugar
¾ c. butter
4 eggs, well beaten
2 c. grated sweet potatoes (raw)
1 c. corn syrup
2 c. milk
1 t. vanilla

Blend sugar and butter, add beaten eggs and mix thoroughly. Add grated potatoes, milk, corn syrup, and flavoring. Blend. Bake at 300°F. for 1 hour. Serve warm or cold with whipped cream or ice cream.

Mrs. Yvonne McCoy, Pewitt H. S.
Naples, Texas

SWEET POTATO PUDDING
(Mashed Potatoes)

Number of Servings — 6

2 c. mashed sweet potatoes
½ c. butter (melted)
1 c. sugar
2 eggs
¼ t. nutmeg
¼ t. cinnamon
⅛ t. cloves

½ c. raisins (optional)
¼ c. coconut (optional)
1 c. evaporated milk
½ c. shredded coconut

Blend potatoes, butter and sugar, add eggs singly, beating after each. Add spices (raisins and coconut if desired) and milk, mix thoroughly. Bake in buttered pan in moderate oven 375° 35 minutes, remove from oven, sprinkle top with ½ cup coconut. Return to oven, bake 10 minutes longer.

Mrs. Carolyn C. Burton, Doyline H. S.
Doyline, Louisiana

BANANA PUDDING

Number of Servings — 6-8

½ c. sugar
2 T. flour
¼ t. salt
2 c. milk
3 eggs, separated
1 t. vanilla
1 medium size box vanilla wafers
4-6 bananas
6 T. sugar

Make a custard by combining the first 3 ingredients and add the milk to which has been added the slightly beaten egg yolks. Cook in top of double boiler until the consistency of custard, add vanilla. Line a baking dish with vanilla wafers, slice bananas over the wafers. Pour over this ½ the custard, repeat with another layer of wafers and bananas. Cover with remaining custard, make meringue of egg whites whipped with 6 tablespoons of sugar added. Beat until stiff and put on top of pudding. Bake at 425°F. 5 minutes or until delicately browned. Serve hot or cold.

Mrs. Ruby C. Phillips,
District Supervisor, Home Economics Education
Montevallo, Alabama

BROWN SUGAR PUDDING

Number of Servings — 6-8

1 c. brown sugar
2 c. water
3 T. butter
½ c. raisins
½ c. walnuts or pecans
1 c. flour
2 t. baking powder
1 t. cinnamon
½ c. granulated sugar
¼ t. salt
1 T. butter
½ c. milk

Simmer brown sugar, water, butter (3 tablespoons) and raisins for 15 minutes, add nuts and pour into 9x13 glass baking dish, let cool. Sift flour, baking powder, cinnamon, sugar and salt into a mixing bowl, add melted butter and milk. Pour batter over sauce. Bake 40 minutes at 350°F. Serve warm with whipped cream or ice cream.

Kathryn Davis, Community H. S.
Pinckneyville, Illinois

CARAMEL DUMPLINGS
Number of Servings — 6

1½ c. plus 3 T. sugar
5 T. butter
½ T. salt
2 c. hot water
1½ c. flour
2½ T. baking powder
½ c. chopped walnuts
¾ c. milk

Heat ½ cup of the sugar in a heavy skillet until it melts to a golden brown syrup. Add 2 Tablespoons of butter, ⅛ tablespoon of salt, and 1 cup of sugar, add the hot water very gradually while stirring constantly. Bring to a boil and cook until sugar is dissolved, about 10 minutes, stirring frequently. Meanwhile sift together flour, baking powder and remaining 3 tablespoons of sugar and salt. Mix in remaining 3 tablespoons of butter until mixture is like coarse cornmeal. Add walnuts, stir in milk all at once mixing ony enough to moisten flour. Drop by tablespoons into gently boiling caramel sauce. Cook covered for 12 to 15 minutes. Serve hot with sauce.

Mrs. George Hersha, Camden-Frontier H. S.
Camden, Michigan

CINNAMON PUDDING
Number of Servings — 8

1 c. granulated sugar
2 t. cinnamon
2 t. baking powder
2 c. flour
½ t. salt
2 T. butter or oleo
1 c. milk
1 t. vanilla
½ c. nut meats

Cream sugar and oleo slightly, sift dry ingredients together and add alternately with milk, add nuts to last flour to coat. Put batter in greased 9″ baking dish. Pour cooled sauce over it and bake 35 to 40 minutes at 350°F. Serve with milk, whipped cream or ice cream.

Sauce:
2 c. brown sugar, packed
3 T. butter
1½ c. butter
Boil 1 minutes, cool, pour over batter.

This recipe submitted by the following teachers:
Dorothy Heidlebaugh, Mendon Union H. S.
Mendon, Ohio
Mrs. Mary Stockslager, Farmersville H. S.
Farmersville, Ohio

CRACKER PUDDING
Number of Servings — 6

1 qt. milk
⅔ c. cracker crumbs
½ c. butter or oleo
1 c. sugar
2 eggs
1 c. seeded raisins

Scald milk and pour over cracker crumbs and raisins. Add butter, sugar and beaten egg. Bake ¾ hour at 350°F. Stir several times during the baking.

Glenna A. Starbird, Oxford Hills District H. S.
Norway, Maine

CHOCOLATE DUMPLINGS
Number of Servings — 6

Chocolate sauce:
¾ c. brown sugar
¼ c. cocoa
1 T. cornstarch or flour
Dash of salt
2 c. water
2 T. butter or margarine

Combine sugar, cocoa, cornstarch, and salt in heavy skillet. Stir in water and cook until mixture begins to boil and thicken slightly, stirring constantly. Add butter and mix well. Remove from heat while making dumplings.

Chocolate dumplings:
1 c. flour
2 t. baking powder
½ t. salt
½ c. sugar
2 T. cocoa
3 T. shortening
1 egg
½ c. milk
1 t. vanilla

Sift together flour, baking powder, salt, sugar, and cocoa, add shortening, egg, milk, and vanilla. Stir to blend ingredients. Beat thoroughly for 1 minute. Return skillet to heat and bring chocolate sauce to boil, drop dumplings by spoonfuls on sauce. Reduce heat, cover and simmer gently for 20 minutes. Serve warm with cream if desired.

Mrs. M. C. Montgomery, McKinney H. S.
McKinney, Kentucky

CHOCOLATE DUMPLINGS
Number of Servings — 6

¼ c. vegetable shortening
½ t. salt
1 t. cinnamon
¼ c. sugar
2 sq. chocolate, melted
1 c. flour
2 t. baking powder
½ t. soda
¾ c. milk

Cream together shortening, salt, cinnamon, and sugar. Add melted chocolate and blend. Sift together flour, baking powder and soda. Add to the creamed mixture alternately with milk. Drop by spoonfuls on hot syrup.

Syrup:
⅔ c. sugar
2 c. water
⅛ t. salt
1 sq. chocolate

Mix sugar, water, salt, and chocolate. Bring to a boil. Pour into casserole and add dumplings. Bake at 350°F. for 45 minutes.

Mrs. Ruby Bundy, Bush H. S.
Lida, Kentucky

RED CHERRY DUMPLINGS
Number of Servings — 4

1 can pie cherries
½ c. honey
⅛ t. almond extract
1 T. butter
3 T. top milk or coffee cream
2 T. sugar
1 c. biscuit mix
Few drops red food coloring

Combine cherries, honey, and almond extract in deep saucepan. Heat to boiling and add butter. Add cream and sugar to biscuit mix, mix well, the dough should be soft enough to be dropped by spoonfuls. Drop dumplings onto the bubbling cherry mixture. Cover tightly and steam about 20 minutes. Serve warm topped with ice cream or whipped cream.

Mrs. Celeste T. Prugel, Sonora H. S.
Sonora, Texas

MARY LASSWELL'S FRUIT DUMPLING
Number of Servings — 4

1 qt. blueberries, cherries, raspberries or tart apples, diced
1 recipe biscuit dough made with buttermilk, adding 2 T. sugar to dry ingredients and 1 egg beaten into buttermilk.

Using a deep, heavy saucepan with close-fitting lid, cook fruit in pint of water and sweeten to taste. Turn biscuit dough out on a floured board and form into a large doughnut, leave a big hole in the middle. Have fruit boiling hot, drop dough on top, cover pot tightly. Simmer 20 minutes. Do not lift lid until time is up. Turn dumpling out, upside down on a deep hot plate. Serve with cream.

Mrs. Marie M. Mingledorff, Coffee County H. S.
Douglas, Georgia

FRUIT COCKTAIL PUDDING
Number of Servings — 8-10

1 c. flour
1 c. sugar (less may be used if preferred)
½-1 t. salt
1 t. soda
1 egg, well beaten
1 No. 303 can fruit cocktail (well drained)
½-1 c. brown sugar
½ c. nuts, chopped
½ t. cinnamon (optional)

Sift together flour, sugar, salt, and soda, add well-beaten egg. Add fruit cocktail, mix well. Pour into well-greased large oblong pan, sprinkle well-mixed brown sugar and nuts over top. Bake in a 350°F. oven 45 minutes or at 300° F. for 1 hour. Serve warm or cold with whipped cream or sauce.

Sauce:
1 c. evaporated milk
1½ c. sugar
¾ c. butter
½ t. rum flavoring, almond, or other flavoring

Mix ingredients in saucepan. Boil 1 minute, add flavoring desired.

This recipe submitted by the following teachers:
Mrs. Louise Tucker, Fox H. S.
Fox, Oklahoma
Mrs. Marilouise Hurley, Central Union H. S.
El Centro, California
Ruth C. Peabody, Sunnyside Jr. H. S.
Sunnyside, Washington
Dixie Lee Golden, Hobson H. S.
Hobson, Montana
Madeline Johnson, Pinehurst Jr. H. S.
Pinehurst, Idaho
Mrs. Margaret Olson, Gaylord Public H. S.
Gaylord, Minnesota
Mrs. Elizabeth S. Watson, Clark County H. S.
Winchester, Kentucky
Ruth Morris, Ajo H. S.
Ajo, Arizona

GRAHAM CRACKER PUDDING
Number of Servings — 9

3 eggs
¾ c. sugar
1 t. vanilla
½ t. baking powder
1 c. graham cracker crumbs
½ c. nuts

Beat eggs. Add sugar and vanilla. Mix baking powder and graham cracker crumbs and add to the sugar mixture. Add nuts. Bake in greased and floured 8x8 pan 350°F. 25 minutes, until brown. Serve with the following orange sauce.

Orange Sauce:
1 egg
½ c. butter
1 c. brown sugar
½ c. orange juice

Beat egg. Add butter, sugar, and orange juice. Cook over low heat or in double boiler until slightly thick. Serve hot.

Mrs. Arthur Deffebach, Ranger H. S.
Ranger, Texas

GRAHAM CRACKER PUDDING
Number of Servings — 6

1 pkg. (20) graham crackers, crushed
1 c. sugar
3 T. flour
½ c. ground nuts
½ c. coconut
¼ c. cooking oil
1 egg, beaten
1 c. buttermilk
1 t. soda

Mix the sugar, flour, nuts, and coconut and make a well in the center. Dissolve the soda in the buttermilk. Add buttermilk, beaten egg and oil in the well of dry ingredients and mix well. Pour into a deep pie pan and bake 10 minutes at 350°F. and 20 minutes at 300°F. Serve warm or cold, with or without whipped cream or ice cream.

Verdie B. Jones, McAlester Jr. H. S.
McAlester, Oklahoma

GRAHAM CRACKER PUDDING
Number of Servings — 10-12

½ c. butter
1 c. granulated sugar
2 eggs
2 t. baking powder
2 c. graham crackers (rolled fine, measure after rolling)
Few grains salt
1 c. sweet milk
1 c. chopped nuts

Cream butter and sugar, add well-beaten egg, beat. Flour nuts slightly, mix with remaining ingredients and add all at once, beat thoroughly. Bake in a square layer pan, or 9x12 pan, which has been well buttered at 350°F. for 30 minutes. Serve warm or cold with lemon-caramel sauce.

Lemon-caramel sauce:
2 c. medium brown sugar
2 T. flour
1 c. boiling water
Grated rind and juice of 1 lemon
2 T. butter

Mix sugar and flour, add butter. Pour over this mixture, the cup of boiling water and cook until creamy. Add lemon rind and juice, and serve warm over the graham-cracker pudding.

Mrs. Frances S. McDonough, Morrison H. S.
Morrison, Tennessee

LINCOLN AND LEE PUDDING
Number of Servings — 8

1 c. flour
⅛ t. salt
1 t. baking powder
½ c. sugar
½ c. milk
½ c. chopped nuts
½ c. raisins
Syrup:
1 c. brown sugar
2 c. water
1 T. butter

Sift flour and resift with salt and baking powder. Reserve 4 tablespoons of flour mixture to dredge raisins and nuts. Add sugar to flour mixture and then add milk gradually. Mix well and add nuts and raisins. Drop by spoonfuls into syrup made of sugar, water and butter which was brought to the boiling point. Bake in oven at 400°F. 30 minutes. Serve warm with whipped cream.

Mrs. O. K. Vorthmann, Sumner Community School
Sumner, Iowa

MAGIC PUDDING
Number of Servings — 5

2 c. sponge cake pieces
½ t. salt
1½ t. vanilla
1 9-oz. can crushed pineapple
3 eggs
2 T. sugar
¼ t. almond extract
1 c. milk

Distribute cake pieces evenly into five lightly buttered 5-ounce custard cups. Beat eggs until fluffy and light, beat in salt, sugar, and extracts. Blend in undrained pineapple and milk, spoon liquid over cake and set cups in pan of water to bake. Bake at 350°F. 40 to 45 minutes until set, cool on wire rack. Turn out on serving plate and spoon additional crushed pineapple or thin red jelly over top of each serving.

Alice L. Atkins, Central H. S.
Manchester, New Hampshire

ORANGE PUDDING

3 oranges
Juice of ½ lemon
1 c. sugar
1 T. cornstarch
1 pt. milk
2 eggs, separated
¼ t. salt

Peel oranges, section, and cut into bite-size pieces. Squeeze lemon juice over oranges, add ½ cup sugar, set aside while the rest of the pudding is being prepared. Beat egg yolks, stir in 2 teaspoons milk, add same quantity of milk to cornstarch and beat the 2 mixtures together. Heat the rest of the milk to boiling, add the eggs and cornstarch mixture, cook for 5 minutes. Add salt and rest of the sugar. Remove from the fire and put in dish over the oranges by spoonfuls. Beat egg whites stiff, add 1 tablespoon of sugar and spread on top of the pudding and brown in a 325°F. oven. Serve warm or cold.

Mrs. Anna Wheeler Phillips,
Enterprise Vocational H. S.
Brookhaven, Mississippi

ORANGE CAKE PUDDING
Number of Servings — 4-6

⅓ c. sifted all-purpose flour
⅔ c. sugar
¼ t. salt
2 eggs, separated
2 small cans evaporated milk

(Continued on Next Page)

⅔ c. orange juice
1 T. orange rind
½ c. nuts

Sift together sugar, flour and salt, beat egg yolks and add milk and orange juice. Blend into dry ingredients. Beat egg whites until peaks form, fold into mixture. Pour mixture into custard cups. Sprinkle with nuts and orange rind. Bake in water at 325°F. for 45 minutes. Serve chilled with whipped cream. May keep custards in refrigerator several days before serving.

Leacy Newell, Wilcox County H. S.
Camden, Alabama

PEACH PUDDING
Number of Servings — 6

¾ c. sugar
½ c. milk
4 T. butter
½ t. salt
1 t. baking powder
1 c. flour
2 c. peaches, sliced

Combine sugar and butter, then add other dry ingredients, alternating milk. Pour batter over sliced peaches placed in bottom of 8x2 pan.

Topping:
1 c. sugar
1 T. cornstarch
¼ t. salt
1 c. boiling water

Mix dry ingredients and sift over batter. Pour 1 cup boiling water over this. Bake at 325°F. for 50-60 minutes. Serve warm with cream.

This recipe submitted by the following teachers:
Glenda Flanagan, Ferguson H. S.
Ferguson, Kentucky
Mrs. Margaret Helton, Harrodsburg H. S.
Harrodsburg, Kentucky

PERSIMMON PUDDING

4 c. flour
2 t. baking powder
1 t. salt
1 t. soda
4 c. persimmon pulp
3 eggs
3 c. sugar
3 T. butter
4½ c. sweet milk
1 t. vanilla extract

Mix dry ingredients. Mix wet ingredients. Combine dry and wet ingredients. Fill greased loaf pan ⅔ full. Bake at 325°F. for a little more than an hour. Serve plain or with whipped cream.

Edith P. Broyles, Silk Hope H. S.
Siler City, North Carolina

PERSIMMON PUDDING
Number of Servings — 20

1 qt. persimmon pulp
2 c. milk
3 c. sugar (1 brown, 2 white)
3 eggs
3½ c. plain flour
2 t. baking powder

Mix ingredients in the order given, add eggs one at a time, beating well after each addition. Add flour to which baking powder has been added. Melt butter, Use a portion to grease two baking dishes. Add remainder to pudding mixture. Add vanilla. Mix and pour into baking dishes. Bake 30-45 minutes at 350°F. Serve with whipped cream.

Mrs. Frances S. Sharpe, Central H. S.
Statesville, North Carolina

PANN KAKA (Rennet Pudding)
Number of Servings — 12-15

2½ qts. whole milk
1 c. sugar
1 c. flour
½ t. salt
5 lge. eggs
2 t. vanilla
1 rennet tablet (such as Hansen's)

Scald 2 quarts milk. Sift sugar, flour and salt together. Slightly beat the eggs. Stir the sifted flour-sugar mixture into eggs. Add the 2 cups of unscalded milk and the vanilla. Add scalded milk, stirring as you add it. Pour into baking pan. Dissolve the rennet tablet in 2 tablespoons of luke warm water. While slowly stirring the egg-milk mixture, gradually add the dissolved rennet. Slowly stir, about 1 minute or until waves in the milk slow down and set themselves. Care must be taken not to stir too long. Carefully place pan in 350°F. oven. After 10 minutes, check pudding. If bubbling, lower heat to 300°F. and continue baking until pudding is firm, custard-like consistency. May sprinkle sugar over top a few minutes before removing from oven. Carefully handle until pudding has cooled.

Edith M. Anderson, S. F. Austin H. S.
Austin, Texas

RASPBERRY SQUARES
Number of Servings — 16

Pastry:
1 c. sifted flour
1 t. baking powder
½ c. butter or margarine
1 egg
1 T. milk
½ c. raspberry jam

Heat oven to 350°F. Grease an 8″ square pan. Sift flour and baking powder together in a bowl. Cut in butter or margarine with 2 knives or a pastry blender until mixture looks mealy. Beat the egg slightly and stir into flour mixture along with milk. Mix well. Spread dough over bottom of baking pan, cover with a layer of jam.

Topping:
2 T. butter or margarine
1 egg
1 c. sugar
1 can (4 oz.) shredded coconut
1 t. vanilla

Melt butter, beat the egg until frothy. Add sugar and melted butter to egg, mix thoroughly. Chop coconut, mix into sugar-egg mixture. Add vanilla and spread on top of the raspberry jam. Bake 30 minutes.

Mrs. Ruby Maynard, Angleton H. S.
Angleton, Texas

Cheese Cakes

BESTEVER CHEESE CAKE
(Without Sour Cream)
Number of Servings — 12
Crust:
1 c. sifted enriched flour
¼ c. sugar
1 t. grated lemon peel
½ c. butter or margarine
1 slightly beaten egg yolk
¼ t. vanilla

Combine flour, sugar and lemon peel, cut in butter until mixture is crumbly. Add egg yolk and vanilla, blend. Pat ⅓ of dough on bottom of 9" spring-form pan (sides removed). Bake in hot oven at 400°F. about 6 minutes, cool. Butter sides of pan and attach to bottom. Pat remaining dough evenly on sides to a height of 2".

Cheese filling:
2½ 8 oz. pkg. cream cheese
⅛ t. vanilla
½ t. grated lemon peel
⅞ c. sugar
1½ T. enriched flour
⅛ t. salt
2½ eggs (½ c.)
1 egg yolk
2 T. heavy cream

Stir cream cheese to soften, beat until fluffy, add vanilla and peel. Mix sugar, flour and salt, gradually blend into cheese. Add eggs and yolks, 1 at a time, beating well after each. Gently stir in cream. Turn into crust-lined pan and bake at 500°F. 5 to 8 minutes or until top edge of crust is golden. Reduce heat to 200°F. and bake 1 hour longer. Remove from oven, cool in pan about 3 hours, remove sides of pan, serve.

Mrs. Juanita M. Rogers, Paul G. Blazer Sr. H. S.
Ashland, Kentucky

CHEESE CAKE PIE (Without Sour Cream)
Number of Servings — 6-8
1 c. graham cracker crumbs, fine
¼ c. sugar
¼ c. butter, melted
2-8 oz. pkg. cream cheese
2 eggs
⅔ c. sugar
½ c. evaporated milk
1 t. vanilla
Pineapple or other fruit preserves

Press on bottom and sides of 9" pie pan the first 3 ingredients. Chill until needed. Beat cream cheese until fluffy. Add unbeaten eggs and sugar and beat until smooth. Add milk and vanilla, a little at a time, beating until smooth each time. Pour mixture into crumb crust and bake in 300°F. oven for 45 minutes. Cool at room temperature. Pie settles as it cools. Spread preserves over cooled pie. Serve chilled.

Mrs. Doris B. Lutz, Westdale Jr. H. S.
Baton Rouge, Louisiana

CHEESE CAKE
Number of Servings — 12
Crust:
2 c. rolled graham cracker crumbs
½ c. sugar
1 t. cinnamon
½ c. melted butter (or use half shortening)
Mix all ingredients well, reserve ½ cup for top of cake. Pat remainder onto bottom and sides of glass baking dish 8½x11 (grease sides of pan first).

Filling:
1½ lb. cream cheese
Scant c. sugar
3 whole eggs
Pinch of salt
1 t. vanilla
1 c. dairy sour cream

Mix all ingredients except sour cream, beat with electric mixer for 10 minutes (will be "liquidy" when ready). Add sour cream and beat for 2 more minutes. Pour into crumb-lined pan and bake for 20 minutes at 350°F. Remove and sprinkle top with crumbs. Bake 10 more minutes, do not bake more than 30 minutes in all. Turn off oven, leave door ajar and leave cake in oven for at least 1 hour. Refrigerate thoroughly before serving.

Nancy L. Beyer, Metamora H. S.
Metamora, Illinois

CHEESE CAKE
Number of Servings — 8
¾ pt. sour cream
¾ lb. cream cheese
1 c. sugar
2 eggs
1 t. vanilla
½ pt. whipping cream

Cream together sour cream and cream cheese. Gradually add sugar, eggs one at a time, and vanilla. Pour into a pie pan lined with a graham cracker crust. Bake 25 minutes at 350°F. Cool. Add whipped cream to top. Sprinkle top lightly with cracker crumbs.

Frieda C. Black, Walterboro H. S.
Walterboro, South Carolina

CHEESE CAKE
Number of Servings — 6
2-3 oz. pkg. cream cheese
½ c. sugar
2 eggs
1 t. vanilla
½ pt. sour cream
8 t. sugar
½ t. vanilla

Cream cheese and ½ cup sugar together, beat in eggs and add vanilla. Place in baked graham cracker crust. Bake in 350°F. oven for 20 minutes. Cool 5 minutes. Mix sour cream, 8 teaspoons sugar and vanilla. Spread on top of filling and bake 5 minutes. Cool. Place in refrigerator.

Freda C. Richey, Marshall Co. H. S.
Guntersville, Alabama

CHEESE CAKE

Number of Servings — 12

¾ c. Zwieback crumbs or chocolate wafer crumbs
⅛ c. sugar
3 T. melted butter
½ t. cinnamon
2 eggs, beaten fluffy
½ c. sugar
4-3 oz. pkg. Philadelphia cream cheese
⅓ t. vanilla
1 pt. sour cream
½ c. sugar

Mix first 4 ingredients together. Press into a loaf pan. Add ½ cup sugar to the beaten eggs. Whip cream cheese with vanilla. Mix together. Pour into crust and bake in preheated oven 325°F. for 10 minutes. Add topping, sour cream mixed with ½ cup sugar. Sprinkle top with ground nuts and bake again at 375°F. for 10 minutes. Chill.

Mrs. Merle G. Hail, Eunice H. S.
Eunice, Louisiana

CHEESE CAKE

Number of Servings — 8

1 box Holland Rusk
½ c. sugar
1 t. cinnamon
¼ lb. butter
4 eggs
1 t. vanilla
1 c. sugar
1½ lb. cream cheese
½ pt. sour cream
½ t. vanilla
2 T. sugar

Roll Holland Rusk to fine crumbs. Mix sugar and cinnamon with Holland Rusk. Pour melted butter over mixture and form crust in 10" pan. Cream cheese and beat eggs in one at a time. Add sugar and vanilla. Beat until well mixed. Pour into 10" crust and bake 25 minutes at 375°F. Cool 10 minutes and put sour cream, vanilla and sugar on top. Bake 470°F. for 5 minutes. Cool in refrigerator for 24 hours.

This recipe submitted by the following teachers:
Peggy St. Clair, Horse Branch H. S.
Horse Branch, Kentucky
Linda Melton, Centertown H. S.
Centertown, Kentucky

CINNAMON CHEESE CAKE

Number of Servings — 8

Crust:
20 graham crackers
½ c. melted butter
¼ c. sugar

Mix together the ingredients for crust, press into the bottom of a round 9" cake pan. Bake for 5 minutes at 350°F.

Filling:
1 lb. (2 8 oz. pkg.) cream cheese, soft
½ c. sugar
3 eggs

Beat cream cheese until fluffy, add sugar, beat in eggs until very smooth. Bake at 350°F. 15-20 minutes until firm in center.

Topping:
1½ c. sour cream (12 oz.)
1 c. sugar
1 t. vanilla
½ t. cinnamon
½ c. almonds

Mix together the sour cream, sugar and vanilla, spoon on top. Sprinkle with cinnamon and slivered almonds. Bake 10 minutes at 350°F., cool and refrigerate.

Mrs. Lynne Wise, Howard H. S.
Howard, Ohio

GOURMET CHEESE CAKE

Number of Servings — 12

6 egg yolks
¾ c. sugar
1½ lb. cream cheese
8 T. sifted flour
1½ c. sour cream
1½ T. lemon juice
1 t. vanilla
6 egg whites
¾ c. sugar
1 box zwieback, crushed
3 T. sugar
3 T. butter
1 T. cinnamon

Mix egg yolks, sugar, cream cheese, flour, sour cream and lemon juice, beat until smooth. Beat egg whites until frothy, add sugar gradually and continue beating until peaks form. Fold into cheese mixture. Mix last 4 ingredients and press into greased pan, bottom and sides, reserving some for top. Bake at 325°F. for 1 hour. Let cool in oven 1 hour.

Mrs. Mary Ann Yelovich, Union H. S.
Union, Wisconsin

CHEESE PIE

Number of Servings — 10-12

2 c. graham cracker crumbs
½ c. sugar
½ c. melted butter
2 8 oz. pkgs. cream cheese
2 eggs
⅔ c. sugar
1 t. vanilla
1 c. commercial sour cream
2 T. sugar
1 t. vanilla

Roll enough graham crackers to make 2 cups or use package crumbs. Mix with ½ cup sugar and melted butter. Press into the bottom and sides of a 9" spring form pan to form a crust. Cream until smooth the softened cream cheese and blend in eggs, ⅔ cup sugar and 1 teaspoon vanilla. Pour into crust and bake in a moderate hot oven 375°F. for 20 minutes. Remove from oven and let pie stand 15 minutes. Meanwhile combine sour cream with 2 tablespoons sugar and 1 teaspoon vanilla. Carefully spread over baked filling. Return pie to a very hot oven 425°F. and bake 10 minutes. Cool pie, then chill over night before serving.

Mrs. Joseph S. Klimczak, Bogalusa H. S.
Bogalusa, Louisiana

BLACKBERRY CHEESE PIE
Number of Servings — 6-8
1¼ c. graham cracker crumbs
½ c. melted margarine
½ c. sugar
8 oz. pkg. cream cheese
½ c. sugar
2 eggs, (well beaten)
1 can blackberry prepared pie mix

Mix cracker crumbs with margarine and ½ cup sugar. Spread on bottom of 9x9 pan, blend cheese, ½ cup sugar and beaten eggs. Pour over cracker mixture and bake at 350°F. 20 minutes, cool. Pour 1 can blackberry (or your favorite pie filling). Mix over cooled mixture, top with whipped cream or topping if desired.

Mrs. Ruth McLaughlin, New London Local H. S.
New London, Ohio

CHERRY CHEESE CAKE
Number of Servings — 6
Crumb crust:
1½ c. graham cracker crumbs
2 T. butter
2 T. sugar
Blend above ingredients, press on bottom and sides of 9″ pan to a height of 3″.

Filling:
2 8 oz. pkg. cream cheese
4 eggs
1 c. sugar
1 t. vanilla
Soften cheese, beat until smooth, adding eggs, sugar, and vanilla. Pour into crumb-lined pan. Bake 30 minutes in 325°F. oven, it will be quivery when done, reset oven at 470°F.
1 c. sour cream
1½ t. lemon juice
1 t. sugar
Mix above ingredients, spread on top of cheese cake and return to oven for 5 minutes. Cool and top with cherry topping.

Cherry topping:
½ c. cherry juice
1 c. sour pitted cherries
¾ c. sugar
2 T. cornstarch
½ t. almond flavoring
Mix cherry juice, cornstarch, and sugar, cook over medium heat until thick. Add cherries and flavoring. Pour over cheese cake, chill five hours, serve.

Mrs. Eileen Blake, Thomas Jefferson H. S.
El Paso, Texas

CHERRY CHEESE PIE
Number of Servings — 6
Crust:
½ box cinnamon crisp graham crackers
1 stick butter or margarine
Make crust by combining melted butter with fine cracker crumbs. Press into a pie plate (8″). Place in refrigerator while making pie filling.
Filling:
4 3 oz. pkgs. cream cheese
½ c. sugar

3 eggs, beaten
1½ t. lemon flavoring

Cream well together the cream cheese and sugar. Add beaten eggs and flavoring. Blend well. Pour filling into cracker crust and bake. Start in cold oven. Bake 45 to 55 minutes at 275°F.

Topping:
1 No. 2 can tart red cherries
3 T. cornstarch
½ c. sugar
Red coloring

While pie is baking, place ingredients for topping in saucepan and cook until thickened, adding red coloring to achieve bright red color. Top baked pie with thickened cherry mixture. Cool. Slice and serve topped with whipped cream.

Frances M. Kearse, St. Johns H. S.
Darlington, South Carolina

CHEESE CAKE WITH CHERRY TOPPING
Number of Servings — 12

1½ c. graham cracker crumbs (16 crackers)
1 stick melted butter or margarine
½ c. sugar
Combine crumbs, butter, and sugar. Press on the bottom and sides of a 12″ spring form pan. Chill.
Filling:
8 oz. Philadelphia cream cheese
1 pt. creamed cottage cheese
1 T. lemon juice
2 eggs
½ c. sugar

Blend cheese until creamy, add lemon juice. Lightly beat eggs. Add to mixture. Add sugar and vanilla. Beat until smooth. Pour into crust. Bake at 375°F. for 25 minutes.

Topping:
1 can cherry pie filling or 1 can frozen cherries
    (drained)
½ c. sugar
2 T. cornstarch

Mix sugar and cornstarch with cherry juice. Cook until thick. Mix in cherries. Chill. Serve over top of cake.

This recipe submitted by the following teachers:
Dorothy Miller, Miami East H. S.
Casstown, Ohio
Mrs. Berniece Gorsuch, Bellingham H. S.
Bellingham, Washington
Mrs. Frances Eldridge, Central H. S.
Clifton, Illinois
Mrs. Minnie Lou Huneycutt, Piedmont School
Monroe, North Carolina

CRANBERRY CHEESE PIE
Number of Servings — 12-16

2 8 oz. pkg. cream cheese, softened
3 eggs
⅔ c. sugar
⅛ T. almond extract
1 pt. sour cream mixed with 3 T. sugar and 1 T.
    vanilla

(Continued on Next Page)

Cranberry glaze:
1 can No. 1 whole cranberry sauce
2 T. sugar
1 T. cornstarch
1 T. grated lemon rind
1 T. lemon juice

Beat softened cream cheese until smooth and creamy, add eggs, 1 at a time, beating well after each addition. Thoroughly blend in almond extract and the ⅔ cup sugar, pour into lightly greased 9″ pie pan and bake in slow oven 325°F. for 50 minutes. Set aside to cool for 20 minutes. Spread sour cream mixture over baked cheese layer and return to oven for another 15 minutes, chill. Before serving, cover pie with cooled cranberry glaze made by heating together cranberry sauce, sugar, cornstarch, lemon rind, and lemon juice. Cook over low heat, stirring constantly until thick and clear, cool. Spread on top of pie leaving ½″ sour cream showing on sides.

Janice Bell, Perris Union H. S.
Perris, California

PINEAPPLE CHEESE CAKE
Number of Servings — 12
Crust:
1¾ c. graham cracker crumbs
¼ c. sugar
½ c. soft butter

Mix and press into 9″ round layer cake pan, graham cracker crumbs, sugar and soft butter. Bake 5 minutes at 375°F.

Filling:
12 oz. cream cheese
½ t. vanilla
½ c. sugar
⅛ t. cinnamon
2 eggs, slightly beaten
1 No. 2 can crushed pineapple, drained

Blend together the cream cheese and vanilla, add gradually, blending until smooth after each addition, the sugar, cinnamon, eggs, and pineapple. Pour into crust and bake at 325°F. for 35 minutes.

Topping:
1 c. sour cream
1 t. vanilla
3 T. sugar

Mix together sour cream, vanilla and sugar to spread over cake when it is done. Chill about 3 hours in refrigerator before serving.

Mrs. Delaine Blankenship, Elk Garden H. S.
Elk Garden, West Virginia

CHEESE CAKE EXTRAORDINAIRE
(Strawberry)
Number of Servings — 8
Cheese cake:
4 3 oz. pkg. cream cheese
¾ c. sugar
3 eggs
½ t. vanilla
Sour cream topping:
½ pt. sour cream
½ c. sugar
½ t. vanilla

Strawberry topping:
1 pkg. frozen strawberries
2 T. cornstarch
⅛ c. sugar

Combine the softened cream cheese and sugar and beat until smooth. Add eggs, 1 at a time, beating well after each addition, add vanilla. Pour into a 9″ unbaked graham cracker crust and bake 30 minutes at 350°F., cool for 10 minutes. Pour sour cream topping on top of cheesecake and bake 15 minutes more at 350°F. When cheese cake cools, prepare strawberry topping. Cook the 3 ingredients in a saucepan over medium heat until thickened. Spread on cheese cake, chill thoroughly.

Mrs. Sandra Walters, Channelview H. S.
Channelview, Texas

ICE BOX CHEESE CAKE
Number of Servings — 15
Crust:
2½ c. graham crackers
1 stick butter or oleo
½ c. sugar

Melt butter, blend with sugar and graham crackers. Press ⅔ of this mixture in bottom of 12x8½ baking dish. Chill.

Filling:
1 pkg. lemon gelatin
1 c. boiling water
1 can evaporated milk (chilled)
¾ c. sugar
1 8 oz. pkg. cream cheese
2 T. lemon juice

Dissolve gelatin in boiling water. Chill until it starts to thicken. Soften cream cheese and beat in gelatin mixture. Beat chilled milk to whip-cream consistency. Gradually add sugar, the cream cheese mixture and lemon juice. Pour over graham crackers. Sprinkle remaining crackers on top. Chill at least 4 hours.

Mrs. Marjorie Rendulic, Edgewater H. S.
Orlando, Florida

CHIFFON CHEESE CAKE
Number of Servings — 12
1 pkg. lemon Jello
1 c. boiling water
4 T. lemon juice
1 c. sugar
1 8 oz. pkg. cream cheese
1 lge. can evaporated milk
2½ c. graham cracker crumbs
½ c. granulated sugar
¾ stick margarine

Dissolve Jello in boiling water and set aside. Cream lemon juice, sugar, and cheese until smooth. Add Jello mixture and cool. Chill milk and whip until stiff. Fold into cheese mixture. Blend crumbs, sugar, and melted margarine until entire mixture is moist. Spread half of the crumbs on bottom of 9x15 cake pan. Add first mixture. Sprinkle remainder of crumbs on top. Chill.

Mary Lykins Holman, North Warren H. S.
Smiths Grove, Kentucky

CHEESE CAKE

Number of Servings — 12

1 box lemon Jello
1 c. hot water
¾ c. sugar
1 lemon
1 t. grated lemon rind
½ t. vanilla
1 8 oz. pkg. cream cheese
1 lge. can evaporated milk
4-5 T. melted butter
20-24 graham crackers

Mix Jello, hot water and ½ cup sugar, chill in refrigerator until partially congealed. Mix ¼ cup sugar, vanilla, juice of 1 lemon and grated lemon rind with 1 package cream cheese. Chill and whip evaporated milk, add Jello mixture and beat, add cream cheese mixture. Mix melted butter with graham crackers, line large loaf pan or 2 pie pans with this crust and pour in the cheese cake mixture. Sprinkle a few cracker crumbs over top, decorate with cherries if desired and chill overnight.

This recipe submitted by the following teachers:
Carolyn M. Holley, Heflin H. S.
Heflin, Louisiana
Mrs. Irene Long, Canton South H. S.
Canton, Ohio

CHEESE CAKE

Number of Servings — 15

1 pkg. lemon Jello
1 c. hot water
3 T. lemon juice
1 8 oz. pkg. cream cheese
1 c. sugar
1 t. vanilla
1 tall can evaporated milk, chilled
½ lb. graham crackers (35-40 crackers)
½ c. butter or oleo, melted

Dissolve lemon Jello in hot water, add the lemon juice and cool. Cream the cream cheese, add sugar and vanilla and mix well. Add the cream cheese mixture to the Jello mixture. Whip the evaporated milk and fold into the Jello-cheese mixture. Crush the graham crackers and add the melted butter. Line a 9x13 pan with the crumbs, pour in the mixture and sprinkle top with graham cracker crumbs. Refrigerate for 12 hours or more, may be frozen. Vary by adding 1 can of well-drained crushed pineapple or fruit cocktail.

This recipe submitted by the following teachers:
Mrs. Carl Taylor, Augusta H. S.
Augusta, Arkansas
Mrs. Velma Crosby, Carlisle Consolidated School
Carlisle, Iowa
Mrs. Norma W. Parton, Estacado Jr. H. S.
Plainview, Texas

CHEESE CAKE

Crust:
2 c. graham cracker crumbs
5 T. melted butter
¼ t. gelatin
2 T. sugar

Blend well. Pack remainder into a 9" cake pan. Chill. Reserve ⅓ cup of crumb mixture for topping.

Filling:
1 pkg. lemon Jello
1 c. hot water
1 8 oz. pkg. cream cheese
¾ c. sugar
1 t. grated lemon rind
2½ T. lemon juice
1 pkg. whip mix (such as Dream)
½ c. cold milk
2 t. vanilla

Combine the Jello and hot water and stir until Jello dissolves. Cool until partially congealed. Whip. Cream cheese and sugar well. Blend in lemon juice and rind. Combine with whipped Jello. Combine whip mix, cold milk and vanilla and whip to peak stage. Fold into cream-cheese mixture. Turn into crust. Garnish top with reserved crumbs. Chill.

Mary D. Vincent, Bremen Consolidated School
Bremen, Kentucky

NO-BAKE CHEESE CAKE

Number of Servings — 10-12

2 envelopes unflavored gelatin
1 c. sugar, divided
⅛ t. salt
2 eggs, separated
1 c. milk
1 T. lemon juice
1 t. grated lemon rind
1 t. vanilla

Mix gelatin, ¾ cup of sugar and salt thoroughly in top of a double boiler. Beat egg yolks and milk together. Add to gelatin mixture. Cook over boiling water, stirring constantly until gelatin is dissolved, about 5 minutes. Remove from heat and stir in lemon juice, rind and vanilla. Chill, stirring occasionally, until mixture mounds slightly when dropped from a spoon. While mixture is chilling, prepare crumb topping.

Topping:
2 T. melted butter
1 T. sugar
½ c. graham cracker crumbs
¼ t. cinnamon
¼ t. nutmeg
3 c. (24 oz.) creamed cottage cheese
1 c. heavy cream, whipped
1 c. crushed pineapple

Mix butter, sugar, cracker crumbs, cinnamon and nutmeg. Sieve or beat cottage cheese on high speed of electric mixer, about 3 minutes. Stir into gelatin mixture. Beat egg whites until stiff. Beat in remaining ¼ cup sugar. Fold into gelatin mixture. Fold in whipped cream. Add crushed pineapple. Turn into 8" spring form pan. Sprinkle with crumb mixture and chill until firm.

This recipe submitted by the following teachers:
Mrs. Joan Hays, Lincoln H. S.
Lincoln, Arkansas
DeWayne Law, Valley H. S.
Hot Springs, Virginia

SOUR CREAM CHEESE PIE

Number of Servings — 6-8

Crust:

1½ c. graham crackers, crushed
¼ c. oleo or butter
2½ T. sugar

Mix crust ingredients and press into pie pan, bake at 325°F. for 10 minutes. Remove and press with cup around edges and bottom of pan.

Filling:

1 can sweetened condensed milk
⅛ c. lemon juice
2 egg yolks
2 T. sugar
¾ c. sour cream
2 egg whites, beaten

Mix milk, lemon juice, egg yolks and sugar together thoroughly. Fold in sour cream and egg whites. Pour filling in crust, sprinkle remaining crumbs on top, chill thoroughly, cut and serve.

Mildred Taylor Marsh, Colonial H. S.
Orlando, Florida

APRICOT CREAM CHEESE PIE

Number of Servings — 8

1 can (1 lb., 14 oz.) apricot halves
¼ c. apricot syrup
1½ t. unflavored gelatin
1 pkg. (3 oz.) soft cream cheese
¼ c. sugar
1 can (6 oz.) evaporated milk or ¾ c., chilled icy cold
2 T. lemon juice
1 baked 9" pastry shell
Red food coloring
Mint sprigs

Drain apricots, reserving ¼ cup syrup, set aside 6 halves for garnish and cut remaining apricots in small pieces. Soften gelatin in syrup and dissolve over hot water, beat cheese until creamy. Gradually beat in sugar and gelatin, whip chilled milk until fluffy, add lemon juice, and beat until stiff. Blend into cheese mixture, and fold in diced apricots. Pour into baked pastry shell, give each reserved apricot half a red "cheek" by brushing a little red food coloring on each, arrange on pie. Chill until firm, just before serving, garnish with mint.

Sara McMahan, Brackett H. S.
Brackettville, Texas

BLUEBERRY PIES

Number of Servings — 12

1 8 oz. pkg. cream cheese
½ pt. commercial sour cream
½ c. sugar
1 can blueberry pie filling (1 lb., 6 oz.)

Soften cream cheese. Add sour cream and sugar. Blend well. Pour into cooled baked graham cracker crust. Top with blueberry pie filling and chill thoroughly before serving (this dessert may be stored in freezer).

Graham cracker crust (2 pies):
40 graham cracker squares

½ c. or 1 stick butter
½ c. sugar

Roll crackers to fine crumbs. Pour into bowl, add soft butter and sugar. Blend well. Press into 8" or 9" pie pans. Bake at 375°F. for 8 minutes. Cool before filling.

Frances C. Patin, Poydras H. S.
New Roads, Louisiana

BLUEBERRY CREAM CHEESE PIE

Number of Servings — 8

1 3 or 4 oz. pkg. Philadelphia cream cheese.
½ c. powdered sugar
½ t. vanilla
½ pt. whipping cream
1 T. lemon juice
1 baked 9" pastry shell
1 can prepared blueberry pie filling

Cream together softened cream cheese, powdered sugar and vanilla. Whip cream until stiff, not dry, Fold cream into cheese mixture. Spread in pastry shell. Stir lemon juice into berry filling. Spoon over cream filling. Chill (any fruit pie filling may be used).

Mrs. Marjorie W. Browning, Pensacola H. S.
Pensacola, Florida

CHERRY CHEESE DELIGHT PIE

Number of Servings — 6

1 3 oz. pkg. cream cheese
½ pt. whipping cream (or a whip cream substitute)
½ c. powdered sugar
1 can instant cherry pie filling
1 9" crumb crust

Make a 9" graham cracker or vanilla wafer crumb crust. Soften 1 small package cream cheese. Whip ½ pint whipping cream until stiff. Add softened cream cheese. Beat until very stiff. Add powdered sugar. Beat. Pour into crumb crust. Top with cherry pie filling. Chill. Note: A whip cream substitute may be used instead of the ½ pint whipping cream (strawberry pie filling may be used).

Sarah Pfeifer, Norphlet H. S.
Norphlet, Arkansas

LEMON CREAM CHEESE PIE

1 can Eagle brand milk
½ c. lemon juice
2 8 oz. pkg. cream cheese
2 egg yolks
1 t. vanilla

Whip cream cheese until smooth, blend milk, lemon juice, and egg yolks. Combine with the cream cheese and beat until smooth, add vanilla flavoring. Pour into pastry shell, use whipped cream for icing or sprinkled vanilla crumbs on top. May use a vanilla wafer crust.

Mrs. Yvonne Hansen,
Pearland Independent School District
Pearland, Texas

PINEAPPLE CHEESE CAKE

Number of Servings — 12

1 pkg. lemon Jello
1 c. hot water
1 tall can evaporated milk
1 8 oz. pkg. cream cheese
1 c. sugar
1 t. vanilla
½ lb. graham crackers
¼ lb. margarine
1 heaping T. powdered sugar
1 c. crushed pineapple (drained)

Dissolve Jello in the hot water and chill until syrupy. Beat the milk, which has been chilled for several hours, until it forms stiff peaks. Beat the syrupy Jello until foamy, then beat it into the milk. Cream the cheese with the sugar and vanilla. Fold into the beaten milk. Fold in the crushed pineapple. Crush crackers fine, add powdered sugar, then melted margarine. Sprinkle ½ crumbs in a large rectangular pan. Pour in the cake mixture and top with remaining crumbs. Chill at least 4 hours.

Suzie Kelly, Union H. S.
Broken Arrow, Oklahoma

PINEAPPLE CHEESE CAKE

Number of Servings — 16

Crust:
1½ c. graham cracker crumbs
¼ c. sugar
1 t. cinnamon
½ c. butter or margarine, melted

Combine graham crackers, sugar and cinnamon, blend in butter and press half of mixture in 9" pan.

Filling:
2 envelopes unflavored gelatin
1 No. 2 can crushed pineapple
4 slightly beaten egg yolks
1 c. sugar
2 t. grated lemon rind
1 T. lemon juice
¼ t. salt
2 12 oz. small curd cottage cheese
1 T. vanilla
2 c. heavy cream, whipped
4 egg whites, stiffly beaten

Drain pineapple, soften gelatin in ½ cup of pineapple juice. In double boiler, combine egg yolks, sugar, lemon peel, salt and 2 tablespoons pineapple juice, cook 5 to 8 minutes, remove from heat, add gelatin and mix. Add lemon juice, crushed pineapple, cottage cheese and vanilla. Fold in whipped cream and stiffly beaten egg whites, pour into crumb pan. Sprinkle remaining crumbs over the top, chill 5 hours (better 24 hours).

Wilma A. Talkington, Wheeler H. S.
Wheeler, Texas

FROZEN PINEAPPLE-CHEESE CAKE

Number of Servings — 12

1-8 oz. pkg. cream cheese
1 stick oleo
1 c. sugar
1 pkg. lemon gelatin
1 c. boiling water
1 small can crush pineapple (juice included)
1 lge. can evaporated milk, whipped
⅓ lb. crushed graham crackers

Cream the cheese and oleo well. Add sugar. Dissolve the gelatin in boiling water. Add pineapple and juice. Let chill until it begins to thicken. Whip well chilled evaporated milk. Add the cream cheese mixture to the gelatin. Fold this mixture into the whipped evaporated milk. Sprinkle half of the crushed graham crackers into two 8x8 cake pans. Divide the mixture into these pans and sprinkle the remaining crumbs on top.

Mrs. Byrle J. Daugherty, Bessemer H. S.
Bessemer, Alabama

YAM CHEESE CAKE

1⅔ c. graham cracker crumbs
1 t. nutmeg
1½ T. gelatin
½ c. cold water
3 eggs, separated
¾ c. sugar
½ t. salt
3 T. melted butter
1-3 oz. pkg. cream cheese
1-8 oz. pkg. cream cheese
1 c. whipping cream
2 c. mashed canned yams
2 t. vanilla
2 T. orange juice
⅛ c. milk

Reserve ½ cup crumbs for topping. Mix remaining crumbs, cinnamon, nutmeg and butter. Press into bottom of a 9" cake pan with removable bottom or a spring form pan. Soften gelatin in water. Place egg yolks, ½ cup sugar, salt, and milk in saucepan. Mix thoroughly after sugar is added to yolks (you may have to use a rotary beater). Cook over low heat until mixture thickens. Mix cheese, yams and orange juice together until smooth. Add gelatin to egg mixture and mix. Add cheese-yam mixture to gelatin-egg mixture. Beat until well blended. Chill until firm. Beat egg whites until foamy, adding remaining ¼ cup sugar. Whip cream. If mixture is too firm, beat with mixer until smooth. Fold egg whites, cream and vanilla into yam mixture. Pour into crumb-lined pan. Top with remaining crumbs and chill until firm. Run spatula around pan and lift out cake by pushing bottom of pan up when ready to serve.

Virginia Crossno, Newellton H. S.
Newellton, Louisiana

Frozen Desserts

To Make Ice Cream With an Ice Cream Freezer

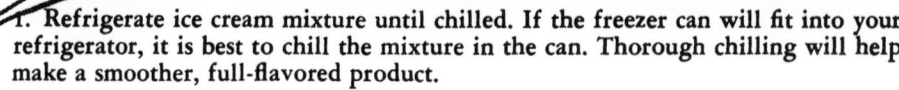

1. Refrigerate ice cream mixture until chilled. If the freezer can will fit into your refrigerator, it is best to chill the mixture in the can. Thorough chilling will help make a smoother, full-flavored product.

2. Fill the freezer can no more than ⅔ full. This will allow plenty of room for expansion of the mixture when air is beaten in by the revolving dasher. We call this the "overrun."

3. Ice cream freezes as heat is absorbed from it by the ice and salt. Salt is used to lower the temperature of the ice, since ice alone is not cold enough to freeze desserts by this method.

4. To freeze the ice cream use 8 parts of ice to 1 part ice cream salt. Finely crushed ice melts faster and hastens freezing so it is best to crush larger pieces.

5. Turn the freezer slowly at first. After a few minutes you will feel a resistance which means the mixture is beginning to freeze. Then turn more rapidly until the dessert is frozen. This helps to produce a smooth product.

6. Drain all the water from the freezer tub before removing the cover, to prevent the brine from entering the can, but do not lift can from ice. Remember to thoroughly wipe the cover before taking it off so that salt will not get into the ice cream.

7. Scrape the ice cream from the dasher and quickly pack it down with a spoon or rubber scraper.

8. As a safety measure, cover the can with a double thickness of waxed paper before replacing the cover. Plug hole of freezer can cover with folded waxed paper as a cork!

Be sure that all the water has been drained from the tub so ice cream will freeze firmly.

9. Now repack the freezer, but this time use a mixture of 4 parts of ice to 1 part ice cream salt. With these proportions the temperature will drop quickly and the ice cream will harden faster. Cover the freezer with a heavy cloth or newspapers and allow to stand at least 2 hours. In this time the ice cream will "ripen" and greatly improve in flavor as well as become a harder, more desirable consistency.

Types of Frozen Desserts

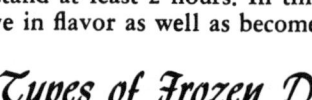

1. ICE CREAM

A. Plain or Philadelphia Ice Cream

Evaporated milk, cream or milk is sweetened, flavored and frozen. It may or may not contain either gelatin or eggs.

B. French or New York Ice Cream

Evaporated milk or cream is folded into a custard containing many egg yolks and the mixture is frozen.

C. American Ice Cream

Similar to French ice cream except that flour or cornstarch is substituted for part or all of the egg yolks.

D. Parfait

Whipped cream or whipped evaporated milk and flavoring are folded into a foundation of beaten egg whites or yolks cooked with hot syrup, and the mixture is frozen. However, the modern version of a parfait is alternate layers of ice cream and various sauces or syrups. It is usually topped with whipped cream and chopped nuts or cherries.

2. FROZEN CUSTARD

Similar to French ice cream, but is distinguished by the liberal amount of egg yolks. It sometimes has a lower fat content than is required by law for ice cream.

3. COMMERCIAL FROZEN DESSERTS

Similar to frozen custard, but without egg yolks. It usually contains a low fat content. Another type of commercial frozen dessert resembles plain ice cream, except that vegetable fat is substituted for butterfat.

4. ICE

Fruit juice, sweetened with sugar, diluted with water and frozen.

5. SHERBET

A frozen mixture of fruit juice, sugar and milk, cream or ice cream, which is used in place of part or all of the water. It may contain a stabilizer such as gelatin.

6. MOUSSE

Still-frozen dessert with a sweetened, flavored whipped cream base. It may or may not contain fruits.

7. BISQUE

A plain ice cream base is frozen with the addition of candies, marshmallows, macaroons, or ladyfingers.

BAKED ALASKA
Number of Servings — 8
1 qt. brick ice cream (regular ice cream if round
    cake is used)
Thin sheet sponge cake (or 9″ round)
Meringue:
4 egg whites
4 T. powdered sugar
½ t. cream of tartar
½ t. vanilla

Meringue: Beat whites until stiff, add sugar gradually, and continue beating, add flavoring.
Cover a board with white paper, arrange cake on
paper and ice cream on cake, having cake extend
½″ beyond cream. Cover entirely with meringue
and spread smoothly. Brown quickly in hot oven
450°F.-500°F. Board, paper, cake and meringue
are poor conductors of heat and prevent cream
from melting. Slip from paper on serving platter.
This recipe submitted by the following teachers:
Margaret Augustine, Tunkhannock Joint H. S.
Tunkhannock, Pennsylvania
Mrs. Delma Hunt, Yazoo City H. S.
Yazoo City, Mississippi

BAKED ALASKA
Number of Servings — 20
1 9″ yellow cake layer
1 qt. vanilla ice cream
1 qt. raspberry sherbet
8 egg whites
1 c. granulated sugar

A few days ahead, cut out piece of heavy brown
paper at least ½″ larger than cake layer. Place on
14x10 cookie sheet, center cake on paper. Place in
freezer to chill. Line 1½ quart mixing bowl with
wax paper or foil, along bottom and sides, pack
vanilla ice cream. Fill center with raspberry sherbet as directed. On top, place sheet of wax paper,
then, with palms of hands, press top flat. Freeze
until firm. When ice cream is firm, make meringue,
beating egg whites until they stand in moist,
drooping peaks when beater is raised. Slowly add
sugar, 2 tablespoons at a time, beating until stiff
and glossy. Quickly invert ice cream on cake
layer, peel off paper. Quickly cover ice cream and
cake completely with meringue, return to freezer.
About 15 minutes before serving, heat oven to
500°F. Remove Alaska from freezer and promptly
bake 4 to 5 minutes or until delicate brown. Remove from oven, transfer to chilled serving plate
and serve immediately.
Mrs. Miriam Tollett, Istrouma Jr. H. S.
Baton Rouge, Louisiana

BAKED ALASKA PIE
Number of Servings — 6
2 c. coconut
¼ c. melted butter
8 lge. marshmallows
1 pkg. (¼ lb.) Bakers German sweet chocolate
¾ c. evaporated milk
½ t. vanilla
3 pts. strawberry ice cream
3 egg whites
⅛ t. salt
6 T. sugar

Mix coconut and melted butter. Press into 8″ or
9″ pie pan. Bake at 300°F. until brown, 30 to 35
minutes. Melt marshmallows and chocolate in milk
over hot water. Remove from heat. Add vanilla.
Cool. Pack ice cream into crust rippling with
chocolate sauce. Freeze until firm. Beat egg whites
and salt until foamy. Gradually beat in sugar. Beat
until meringue will stand in peaks. Spread over
filling, sealing to crust. Sprinkle with coconut.
Place pie on board. Bake at 500°F. until lightly
browned, about 2 minutes. Serve immediately or
return to freezer until ready to serve.
Mary E. Bishop, Vina H. S.
Vina, Alabama

ALASKAN COOKIE PIE
Number of Servings — 7
Crust:
½ c. butter
¼ c. powdered sugar
½ t. vanilla
1 c. flour
¼ t. salt
⅓ c. chopped nuts

Mix by conventional method in mixing bowl. Turn
into buttered pie pan, and press into shape of pie
crust. Bake in 400°F. oven, 10-12 minutes, cool,
freeze.

Filling:
1 qt. ice cream, any flavor
Press into cookie crust, Keep frozen until ready
to serve.

Meringue:
3 egg whites
½ c. sugar
¼ t. cream of tartar

When ready to serve, pile meringue on top of ice
cream, being sure it covers ice cream completely
and adheres to crust. Set pie pan on square board
which has been soaked in water, place in 500°F.
oven until meringue is nicely browned, about 3-5
minutes. Serve immediately, or return to freezer
until ready to serve.
Martha Wreath Streeter, Wamego Rural H. S.
Wamego, Kansas

MILE HIGH MOCHA ALASKA
Number of Servings — 12-14
2 pt. chocolate ice cream
2 pt. coffee ice cream
1 9″ layer, cake type brownie

Line 1½ quart bowl with foil, extending foil over
the edges of the bowl. Soften chocolate ice cream
and pack into bowl, leaving a cavity in the center.
Place in freezer. Soften the coffee ice cream and
finish filling bowl of chocolate ice cream, packing
ice cream firmly. Freeze until hard. To assemble
Alaska: Place cooled brownie layer on a board on
a baking sheet, invert bowl of ice cream over
cake. Remove bowl, tear away foil. Cover cake
and ice cream with meringue, sealing meringue to
board for air tight seal. Bake on lowest rack of
a 500°F. oven for 3 minutes or just until meringue
is a golden brown. Remove dessert to serving
platter.

(Continued on Next Page)

Meringue:
6 large egg whites
1 c. sugar

Beat egg whites until frothy. Gradually beat in sugar. Continue beating until whites are stiff and glossy.

Helena Tidrow Raine, Mission H. S.
San Luis Obispo, California

MINCEMEAT PIE ALASKA

Number of Servings — 6
8" baked pie shell
1 pt. vanilla ice cream
¼ c. chopped candied cherries
½ t. vanilla extract
1 c. mincemeat
3 egg whites
6-8 T. sugar

Have pie shell well chilled. Soften ice cream slightly and stir in cherries and vanilla extract. Spoon ice cream into cold pie shell, top with layer of mincemeat. Wrap and freeze in disposable pie plate until ready to serve, no longer than 2 months. Just before serving, beat egg whites until stiff, gradually beating in the sugar. Remove pie from freezer, transfer to regular pie plate. Pile meringue on top of pie, spreading to seal edges well. Bake in a hot oven 450°F. 5 to 8 minutes or until browned. Serve immediately.

Beatrice Clark, Keller H. S.
Keller, Texas

RIBBON ALASKA PIE

Number of Servings — 8
2 T. butter
2 1 oz. sq. unsweetened chocolate
1 c. sugar
1 6 oz. can (⅔c.) evaporated milk
1 t. vanilla
2 pt. vanilla ice cream, softened
1 9" baked pastry shell
½ pkg. (packet) meringue mix
¼ c. crushed peppermint-stick candy

To make fudge sauce, mix butter, chocolate, sugar, and evaporated milk in saucepan, cook and stir over low heat until thick and blended. Remove from heat, add vanilla, cool thoroughly. Spread 1 pint ice cream in pastry shell, cover with half the cooked fudge sauce, freeze; repeat layers, freeze firm. Prepare meringue following package directions for pie meringue. Reserve 2 teaspoons candy, fold remainder into meringue, spread over pie, sealing to edges. Top with candy. Bake at 475°F. about 4 minutes or until lightly browned. Serve at once or freeze.

Naomi P. Schumacher, Maplewood Jr. H. S.
Maplewood, Louisiana

SUNFLOWER BAKED ALASKA

Number of Servings — 4-6
    (Used as the dessert for a garden party)
4-6 3½" tall florist flower pots
Aluminum foil
Brown and yellow construction paper
Glue
4-6 green colored toothpicks

1 layer of cold white cake
3 egg whites
⅛ t. salt
½ t. vanilla extract
6 T. granulated sugar
1 pt. hard-frozen vanilla ice cream

Cleanse flower pots in hot, soapy water. Dry well and line pots with aluminum foil. Cut out sunflowers from yellow construction paper and glue a circle of brown construction paper in the center of each sunflower. Glue a green toothpick to each sunflower representing the stem. Cut small circles of the cold white cake and place in the bottom of each flower pot.

Prepare the meringue by adding salt and vanilla extract to egg whites, beat to a coarse foam. Add sugar in 1-tablespoon portions, beating well after each addition. Beat until mixture has good piling quality. Quickly add frozen ice cream to each flower pot and pile meringue atop ice cream to form the "dirt" for the sunflower. Bake immediately in an extremely hot oven 500°F. 3-5 minutes or until peaks are delicately browned. Remove from oven and quickly place a sunflower in the center of the meringue in each flower pot and serve immediately.

Other decorations for the garden party: Use brown and yellow as your color scheme for tablecloth, napkins, favors, etc. Construct a triangular centerpiece for the serving table from large wild sunflowers picked from the surrounding fields and roadsides, add a few stems of colored wheat to the arrangement, and you have an original and unusual centerpiece. With the dessert serve mint tea with lemon slices.

Frances Walton, Lazbuddie H. S.
Lazbuddie, Texas

STRAWBERRY ICE CREAM PIE

Number of Servings — 8
1 baked 10" pastry shell
16 marshmallows
1 lge. pkg. frozen strawberries (drain and save 2 T. juice)
2 egg whites
4 T. sugar
Few drops red food coloring
2 T. strawberry juice
1 qt. vanilla ice cream

Melt marshmallows in double boiler with strawberry juice. Cool. Beat egg whites until stiff, adding sugar while beating. Fold into marshmallow mixture, add red coloring, set aside. Put ice cream into shell. Cover with strawberries. Top with meringue, being sure that meringue seals the ice cream. Place in broiler 5 minutes, until meringue browns quickly. Serve at once.

Helen Hester Burnside, Robt. E. Lee H. S.
Baton Rouge, Louisiana

HOMEMADE CHERRY ICE CREAM

Number of Servings — 15-20
4 eggs, separated
1 c. sugar
½ c. powdered milk

(Continued on Next Page)

1 can sweetened condensed milk
½ gal. homogenized milk
1 8 oz. jar maraschino cherries and juice
Cracked ice
Ice cream salt

Separate egg whites and yolks, beat each until fluffy. Beat sugar, powdered milk, and condensed milk into egg yolks, add homogenized milk to egg yolk mixture, beat thoroughly. Add chopped cherries and juice to egg and milk mixture. Fold in the beaten egg whites, freeze in electric or hand-operated freezer.

Mrs. Tillie Gandy, Weatherford Jr. H. S.
Weatherford, Texas

CHOCOLATE ICE CREAM
Number of Servings — 12

4 c. milk
4 c. cream
½ t. salt
3 eggs
2 c. sugar
3 T. vanilla
1 T. flour
3 sq. chocolate
4 c. cream

Heat 2 cups milk. Beat together eggs and flour and ½ cup milk. Add to heated milk. Cook until custard, add 3 squares chocolate. Stir until melted and add 4 cups cream and rest of ingredients, stir well and pour in freezer.

Mrs. Peter Alberda, Manhattan H. S.
Manhattan, Montana

CHOCOLATE MARBLE ICE CREAM
Number of Servings — 6-8

16 marshmallows
1½ c. milk
1 c. heavy cream, whipped
1 T. pure vanilla
½ c. chocolate syrup, such as Hershey's

Heat marshmallows and milk until they are blended. Chill until partially set, add whipped cream flavored with vanilla, chill in freezing unit. Add chocolate syrup, such as Hershey's to partially frozen mixture. Stir just enough to get desired marbleized effect. Freeze quickly and serve in chilled sherbet dishes.

Lou Hampson, Antlers H. S.
Antlers, Oklahoma

HAND FREEZER ICE CREAM (Uncooked)
Number of Servings — One Gallon

4 eggs
1½ c. sugar
1 lge. can evaporated milk
2 qts. whole milk (approximately)
⅛ t. salt

Separate and beat yolks and whites of eggs separately. To the yolks, add sugar and canned milk and beat. Fold in beaten whites to which salt has been added. Pour into freezer can. Add enough fresh milk to cover top of dasher. Do not overfill, allow room for expansion in freezing.

Mrs. Frank Grace, Dardanelle H. S.
Dardanelle, Arkansas

FREEZER ICE CREAM (Uncooked)
Number of Servings — 12

3 eggs
2½ c. sugar
1 t. salt
2 tall cans evaporated milk
½ gal. homogenized milk
2 t. vanilla

Beat eggs until light, beat in sugar and salt. Stir in evaporated milk, homogenized milk and vanilla. Pour into gallon-size ice cream freezer canister. Pack freezer with crushed ice and ⅛ part ice cream salt. Turn hand freezer until hard, or use electric freezer. Recipe may be varied by adding crushed fruit before freezing, or toppings may be used.

Mrs. Don McMahen, Emerson H. S.
Emerson, Arkansas

ICE CREAM (Uncooked)
Number of Servings — 1 Gallon

3 can condensed milk
1½ qt. milk
1 lg. can chocolate syrup or 2 pkg. frozen
    strawberries, mashed

Combine ingredients and freeze in ice cream freezer. Makes a rich, well-flavored cream.

Norma O. Meyers, Sulphur H. S.
Sulphur, Louisiana

FREEZER ICE CREAM
Number of Servings — 16

1 envelope gelatin, plain
¼ c. cold water
1 c. milk
6 eggs
½ t. salt
1⅔ c. granulated sugar
1 pt. thick whipping cream
Ice cream salt

Soak gelatin in cold water, heat milk to scalding, pour over gelatin. Beat eggs and salt until creamy. Gradually add sugar and beat until very thick, similar to whipped cream. Add whipping cream and gelatin mixture and mix carefully. Pour into sterilized 1 gallon freezer can and add milk to within 2″ of top of can. Assemble freezer and start motor and run for 2 minutes without ice or salt. Add ice to fill freezer ½ full then add 2 cups ice cream salt. Then more ice until freezer is filled, add 1 more cup salt. Keep freezer filled with ice but do not add more salt. When ice cream is frozen, remove dasher, cover can, replace lid and add 1 cup ice cream salt over ice. This packs it until serving time.

Mrs. Naomi Mounsey, Booker H. S.
Booker, Texas

LEMON ICE CREAM (Crunchy)
Number of Servings — 4-6

¾ c. evaporated milk
6 T. (½ can) frozen lemonade concentrate
¼ c. sugar
Few grains salt

(Continued on Next Page)

Crumb mixture:
1 T. melted margarine
¼ c. crushed cornflakes
¼ c. finely cut nuts
2 T. brown sugar

Chill milk until ice crystals form around edges. Whip until fluffy, gradually add the mixture of lemonade, sugar and salt, whip until stiff. Put into 1 quart ice tray. Sprinkle the crumb mixture (made by combining last 4 ingredients) over top. Freeze without stirring at coldest temperature until firm.

Mrs. Angeleta T. Cottle, North Duplin H. S.
Calypso, North Carolina

PEACH ICE CREAM (Or Other Fruit)
Number of Servings — 1 Gallon

1 qt. milk plus 1 c. (or more depending on
    amount of fruit to be used)
1 can sweetened condensed milk
1 small can evaporated milk
1 pt. whipping cream
1 c. sugar
3 T. vanilla flavoring
3 c. (or less) mashed peaches (fresh), or straw-
    berries mixed with ¾ c. sugar and juice of
    1 lemon (other fruit may be substituted such
    as 6 well-ripened bananas or 1 2½ can
    crushed pineapple. If pineapple is used,
    reduce the amount of sugar ½ c.)

Combine first 6 ingredients and freeze to a mush in an electric or hand-turned freezer. Add peaches (or other fruit) mixture and freeze hard. Remove dasher and pack with ice and salt until ready to serve. Keeps well in deep freeze without getting icy.

Ruth Stovall, State Dept. of Education
Montgomery, Alabama

PEACH RHUBARB ICE CREAM
Number of Servings — 6

2 c. unpeeled diced rhubarb (fresh or frozen)
½ c. water
1 c. sugar
2 T. lemon juice
½ t. grated lemon rind
1 (1 lb.) can peach slices drained
1 pt. whipping cream
⅛ t. almond extract
⅛ t. salt
Red food coloring

Cook rhubarb in water until tender, add ¾ cup sugar and cook 2 or 3 minutes. Stir in lemon juice rind, cool. Freeze to a mush, chop peaches fine, or crush coarsely. Beat cream with almond extract, salt, and remaining ¼ cup sugar until stiff. Beat partially frozen rhubarb until smooth, stir in peaches and fold in stiffly beaten cream. If a deeper pink color is desired, stir in a drop or 2 of red vegetable coloring. Return to freezer, stir once or twice until firmly frozen.

Marie A. Kelley, Dudley M. Hughes H. S.
Macon, Georgia

FRESH PEACH ICE CREAM
Number of Servings — One Gallon

2 cans sweetened condensed milk
4 c. fresh peaches
1 T. flour
1 T. vanilla
2 qts. milk

Put condensed milk in large bowl and mix fresh peaches that have been mashed or chopped. Add flour and beat. Add vanilla and remaining milk, mix well. Pour in hand freezer and freeze.

Mrs. Bennie D. Pendley, Hildebran H. S.
Hildebran, North Carolina

FROZEN PLUM PUDDING
Number of Servings — 16

For 1 gallon:
2½ qt. milk
7 eggs
2½ c. sugar, caramelize half
1 pt. whipping cream
½ t. salt
2½ t. vanilla
1 medium bottle cherries
1 c. raisins
1 flat can crushed pineapple, well drained
Grated rind of 1 orange
1 slice green candied pineapple, chopped
½ c. wine
1 c. nuts

Soak fruits (but not nuts) in the wine overnight. Beat eggs and add half the sugar, heat milk to scalding, add caramelized sugar, and stir until dissolved. Pour 2 cups of the hot mixture over eggs and sugar, stirring constantly, then pour back into milk. Stir and cook over low heat until mixture coats a spoon, cool. Before freezing, add salt and cream, and the friuts and nuts.

Augusta Jannett, Yoakum H. S.
Yoakum, Texas

STRAWBERRY ICE CREAM
Number of Servings — One Gallon

6 eggs, well beaten
1¾ c. sugar
2 t. vanilla
Dash of salt
Pkg. strawberry ice cream mix
Tall can of evaporated milk
10 oz. pkg. frozen strawberries (thawed)

Combine the above ingredients and place in a 1 gallon ice cream freezer can. Finish filling the can with whole milk to 2" from the top. Freeze.

Mrs. Olga Masch Decker, Gunter H. S.
Aubrey, Texas

TUTTI-FRUTTI ICE CREAM (Hand Freezer)
Number of Servings — 1 Gallon

3 mashed bananas
Juice of 3 oranges
Juice of 3 lemons
1 small can crushed pineapple
3 c. sugar
3 c. evaporated milk

(Continued on Next Page)

3 c. milk
¼ c. chopped cherries
Few drops red food coloring (if desired)
Mix all ingredients together, pour in freezer can.
Pack ice and salt around can, freeze.

*Audrey Bailey, Northfield Jr.-Sr. H. S.
Northfield, Minnesota*

APRICOT-ORANGE SHERBET
Number of Servings — 6-8
18 lge. marshmallows, cut
1 c. orange juice
1 c. apricot syrup or juice
1 c. apricot pulp
Dash salt
2 c. light cream, whipped
½ c. sugar
Combine marshmallows, orange juice, apricot juice
and salt in saucepan, stir over low fire until marshmallows melt. Add apricot pulp, cool, pour into
large refrigerator tray. Freeze until mushy, add
whipped cream with sugar in it, fold in until
mixed well. Freeze, nice with fresh peaches also.

*Mrs. Coral McCune Hawkins, Tehachapi H. S.
Tehachapi, California*

AVOCADO SHERBET
Number of Servings — 6-8
1 t. grated lemon rind
½ c. lemon juice
½ c. orange juice
1 c. sugar
¾ c. mashed avocado (medium ripe)
1 c. heavy cream, whipped
Combine lemon rind, fruit juices, sugar and avocado. Blend until sugar dissolves, pour into large
refrigerator tray and freeze for 30 minutes, stir
well, fold in whipped cream. Return to freezer
and freeze until firm without stirring.

*Mrs. Frances Baker Bishop, Senior H. S.
Denton, Texas*

BANANA SHERBET
Number of Servings — 6-8
4 oranges (small wedges)
4 lemons (juice)
2 ripe banans, mashed
3 c. water
2 c. granulated sugar
1 T. gelatin
Soak gelatin 5 minutes in 1 cup water, heat rest
of water with sugar to make syrup. Dissolve gelatin mixture in syrup, cool. When cooled, add fruits,
place in ice cube tray and freeze.

*Helen A. Wilson, Newport Jr. H. S.
Kensington, Maryland*

BUTTERMILK SHERBET
Number of Servings — 6
2 c. buttermilk
1 c. crushed pineapple (drain off most of the
   juice)
½ c. sugar
Few grains salt
1 unbeaten egg white
Mix together buttermilk, crushed pineapple, sugar

and salt, pour into refrigerator tray. Freeze quickly
at lowest temperature. When almost frozen, remove from tray, break up using electric beater
and add unbeaten egg white, whip until light
and fluffy. Return to refrigerator tray, serve when
firm.

*Kathryn Lynch, West H. S.
Bremerton, Washington*

CREAMY BUTTERMILK SHERBET
Number of Servings — 8
3 eggs
¾ c. sugar
½ c. light corn syrup
2 c. buttermilk
⅓ c. lemon juice
2 T. lemon rind
Beat eggs until foamy, gradually add sugar and
continue beating until thick. Fold in remaining
ingredients, turn mixture into refrigerator tray.
Freeze until almost firm, turn into chilled mixing
bowl and whip at high speed with electric mixer
until creamy, about 4 minutes. Pour into 1 quart
mold and freeze until firm. To unmold, turn upside
down on platter and wrap with warm towels for
a few seconds. Spoon a strawberry sauce or preserves over individual servings.

*Mrs. Allan P. Cobb, Mosinee H. S.
Mosinee, Wisconsin*

CRANBERRY SHERBET
4 c. cranberries
1 t. gelatin
2 c. sugar
2 c. boiling water
¼ c. cold water
1 pt. gingerale
Cook cranberries in water until the skins break,
press through a strainer. Soften gelatin in cold
water and add to the pulp, add sugar, stir until
dissolved, cool. Add gingerale, fast freeze to mush
consistency. Turn into mixing bowl and beat, freeze
until firm. Makes an excellent accompaniment for
fowl.

*Helen M. Lee, J.E.B. Stuart H. S.
Falls Church, Virginia*

CRANBERRY SHERBET
Number of Servings — 8
1 c. sugar
1 c. water
2 c. cranberries
½ c. grapefruit juice
Cook first 3 ingredients 15 minutes, cool. Pour into
electric blender, blend 1 minute, add grapefruit
juice and blend ½ minute more. Pour into refrigerator tray and freeze (you do not have to stir
while freezing). Serve in sherbet or small sauce
dishes.

*Mabel L. Jones, Snow Hill H. S.
Snow Hill, Maryland*

FRUIT ICE
Number of Servings — 6-8
3 c. sugar
3 c. water, boiling
1 c. orange juice

(Continued on Next Page)

½ c. lemon juice
1 T. grated lemon rind
1 T. grated orange rind
1 c. crushed pineapple
¼ c. crushed strawberries

Add sugar to water in saucepan, stirring until sugar dissolves, boil for 5 minutes, cool. Add juices, rinds, pineapple, and strawberries to sugar mixture. Put fruit mixture into refrigerator tray, freeze to mush consistency. Remove fruit mixture to chilled bowl, beat quickly with rotary beater until smooth. Return to tray and continue freezing.

Mrs. Louise P. Shelnutt, Armuchee H. S.
Armuchee, Georgia

FRUIT SHERBET
Number of Servings — 4
1 c. water
1 c. sugar
¼ t. salt
1 banana, mashed
4 T. lemon juice
1 orange, juice and pulp
1 egg white

Stir sugar and water over low heat until sugar is dissolved, boil rapidly for 5 minutes, cool. Add fruit (pulp and juice). Freeze to a mush, stir 2 or 3 times while freezing. Add beaten egg white at the mushy stage. Freeze until firm.

Mrs. Jimmie Cain, Thrall H. S.
Thrall, Texas

PEGGY'S FRUIT SHERBET
Number of Servings — 20
6 ripe bananas, mashed
3 c. sugar
1 lge. can apricots, cut up
1 No. 2 can crushed pineapple
Juice of 3 lemons
2 small cans of frozen orange juice plus 2 cans of water

Combine all ingredients and freeze in 4 ice trays. Fill tall glasses ½ full of sherbet and fill glass remainder of the way with gingerale. It takes 3 quarts of gingerale for recipe and serves 20.

Mrs. Adeline Scarborough, Edmunds H. S.
Sumter, South Carolina

FRUIT AND MILK SHERBET
1½ qt. milk (chilled)
2½ c. sugar
5 lemons, juice
½ envelope Knox gelatin
½ qt. water
1½ T. vanilla
1 lb. can shredded pineapple
1 jar. maraschino cherries

Mix juice, sugar and gelatin (dissolved in ½ cup cold water). Pour remainder of water over lemon rinds, bring to boiling quickly and pour over sugar. When cold, add pineapple and cherries (chopped). Add slowly to very cold milk, stirring constantly. Freeze.

Mrs. Nelle B. Underwood, Flomaton H. S.
Flomaton, Alabama

GRAPE SHERBET
Number of Servings — 20
1 pt. grape juice
Juice of 3 lemons
3½ c. sugar
1 pt. whipping cream
1 can crushed pineapple (small size)
Add enough milk to make 1 gal. ice cream

Mix sugar, grape juice, lemon juice and pineapple, whip cream, add to the mixture. Finish with the required amount of milk, freeze in a gallon ice cream freezer.

Mrs. Alton D. Lewis, Lexington H. S.
Lexington, Tennessee

JELLO SHERBET
Number of Servings — 10
1 pkg. Jello dissolved in 1 c. boiling water
1½ c. sugar
Juice of 2 lemons
1 qt. milk

Mix well, put into refrigerator freezing trays. Freeze until it is solid for ½" or slightly more from the edges of the tray. Return to chilled bowl, beat until blended and creamy. Return to freezing trays and freeze until right consistency to eat. If sherbet becomes too hard, it will soften if allowed to set in refrigerator about 10 minutes.

Ruth Marshall, Borger Sr. H. S.
Borger, Texas

LEMON ICE
Number of Servings — 6
2½ c. sugar
3 c. water
¼ t. salt
3 t. grated lemon rind (3 lemons)
1 c. lemon juice (5½ lemons)

Place sugar, salt and water over low heat, stir until sugar is dissolved. Boil 5 minutes, cool, add lemon rind and juice, pour into freezing tray and freeze until mushy. Scrape into a well chilled bowl, beat with chilled rotary beater until smooth, but do not allow ice to melt. Return promptly to freezing tray, stir 2 to 3 times during freezing. Freeze firm, serve in sherbet dishes which have been chilled.

Mrs. J. W. Garner, Hay Long H. S.
Mt. Pleasant, Tennessee

LEMON SHERBET
Number of Servings — 1 Quart
2 eggs, beaten
½ c. sugar
¾ c. corn syrup
2 c. buttermilk
½ c. lemon juice
1 T. grated lemon peel

Mix in order listed. Pour in freezing tray or small electric ice cream freezer. Freeze until almost firm, about 1 hour. Turn into chilled bowl, cut apart and beat until smooth. Return to tray and freeze until firm, about 3 hours.

Anita Smith, Edinburg H. S.
Edinburg, Texas

LEMONADE SHERBET
Number of Servings — 1 Quart

1 lge. can evaporated milk
2 T. lemon juice
½ c. sugar
1 6 oz. can frozen lemonade

Chill 1 large can evaporated milk in refrigerator tray until icy. Whip until stiff and add 2 tablespoons lemon juice and whip until very stiff. Fold in ½ cup sugar and 1 (6 ounce) can of softened lemonade. Freeze until firm, stirring occasionally.

Mrs. Ray Mofield, Benton H. S.
Benton, Kentucky

LEMON SHERBET

2 qt. sweet milk
3 c. sugar
Juice of 6 lemons
Grated rind of 1 lemon
2 beaten egg whites

Dissolve sugar in milk, add lemon juice very gradually to milk while stirring milk. Do not add milk to lemon juice. Add lemon rind, fold in beaten egg whites. Freeze in 1-gallon hand turning type freezer.

Mrs. Mary R. Abney, Bay Springs H. S.
Bay Springs, Mississippi

LEMON SHERBET
Number of Servings — 6

1 c. sugar
Pinch salt
1 c. water
½ c. thin cream
½ c. lemon juice
2 egg whites

Combine ¾ cup sugar, salt and water. Cook for 5 minutes and cool. When syrup is cooled, add the cream. Mix well and add the lemon juice. Freeze until mushy in the refrigerator tray. Turn in a chilled bowl, beat thoroughly. Beat egg whites stiff, slowly add ¼ cup sugar and fold carefully until the sugar is dissolved. Then fold into mixture. Freeze until firm.

Agnes I. Howell, Andrew Jackson H. S.
Jacksonville, Florida

LEMON MINT ICE
Number of Servings — 12

5½ c. water
3 c. granulated sugar
¼ t. salt
Rind of 1 lemon, grated
1⅛ c. lemon juice
Green coloring
Few drops peppermint flavoring
2 egg whites, stiffly beaten

Boil sugar and water together 5 minutes, add lemon rind, salt and cool. Add lemon juice, green coloring and peppermint flavoring. Pour into freezer trays and freeze until partially frozen. Fold in stiffly beaten egg whites, continue freezing until ready to serve.

Mary Jane Elliott, Centreville H. S.
Centreville, Michigan

LEMON CREAM SHERBET
Number of Servings — 6

1 pt. milk
1 c. sugar
Grated rind of 1 lemon
Juice of 2 lemons
2 egg whites
2 T. sugar
½ pt. whipping cream

Add sugar to milk and dissolve, add lemon rind and juice. Stir while adding juice, pour mixture into ice cube tray and freeze until firm. Beat egg whites until stiff, add the 2 tablespoons of sugar and continue beating until sugar is well blended. Whip the cream and combine with the egg whites. Remove frozen mixture from tray to large mixing bowl and add the cream and egg white mixture. Stir until smooth, return to ice tray and freeze until ready to serve (may be served in 30 minutes).

Mrs. Opal Wood, Navasota H. S.
Navasota, Texas

LIME JELLO SHERBET
Number of Servings — 6-8

1 pkg. lime Jello
1 c. boiling water
1 c. sugar
3 lemons, juice and rind
1 qt. milk

Dissolve Jello in boiling water. Add sugar. Cool. Add other ingredients. Freeze (stir 3 or 4 times during freezing). When soft frozen, beat with rotary beater. Return to refrigerator tray until ready to serve.

Ella S. Harrell, Victoria H. S.
Victoria, Virginia

ORANGE DELICIOUS
Number of Servings — 8

2 c. sugar
1 c. water
2 c. orange juice
1 c. cream (thin)
2 egg yolks
1 c. heavy cream

Boil sugar and water 5 minutes, add orange juice. Scald thin cream, add egg yolks, and cook in double boiler until mixture thickens. Cool, add to orange mixture, with heavy cream beaten stiff, freeze.

Mrs. George K. Rheney, Hephzibah H. S.
Hephzibah, Georgia

ORANGE SHERBET
Number of Servings — 4
1 small can frozen orange juice
   or 1 c. fresh orange juice
¼ c. lemon or lime juice
1 c. sugar

Chill 1 large can of evaporated milk in the refrigerator tray until partially frozen. Whip until it stands in peaks, or 1 cup whipping cream may be used. Mix fruit juices and sugar, heat until sugar is dissolved. Pour into freezing tray and freeze until mushy. Add frozen fruit juice mixture to whipped cream or whipped evaporated milk. Beat until thoroughly blended (light beating, more folding). Return to trays and freeze until mushy and partially frozen. Beat the mixture until smooth.

Mrs. Dixie E. Stafford, Charlotte H. S.
Charlotte, Texas

ORANGE-PINEAPPLE SHERBET
  (Low Calorie)
Number of Servings — 20
1-6 oz. can frozen orange juice concentrate
1-6 oz. can frozen pineapple juice concentrate
3½ c. cold water
2 T. Sucaryl solution
1 c. non-fat dry milk solid

Mix ingredients into a large metal mixing bowl in order listed. Beat just enough to blend. Set bowl in deep-freeze or pour into ice cube trays in freezer. Freeze 1 to 2 hours until half frozen. Beat on low speed until softened. Then beat on high speed 3 to 5 minutes until creamy but not liquid. Pour into freezer containers or ice cube trays. Freeze. *Mrs. Alice Blakeney, Runge H. S.*
Runge, Texas

PARTY SHERBET
Number of Servings — 10
2 c. whole milk
1 small can evaporated milk
½ c. heavy cream
1 egg, slightly beaten
1½ c. sugar
1½ lemons, approximately ½ c. juice
Salt
1 small can crushed pineapple

Combine whole milk, evaporated milk, cream and egg, set aside. Combine sugar, lemon juice, salt, and crushed pineapple. Slowly combine milk mixture to pineapple mixture to prevent curdling. Scald freezer can, pour in mixture, freeze using 6 parts ice to 1 part salt. Turn slowly to start freezing process, about 3 minutes, then turn fast to whip the sherbet, about 5 minutes. Remove beaters, cover tightly, pack with ice.

Donna Mae Hurst, Box Elder H. S.
Brigham City, Utah

FROZEN RAINBOW DELIGHT
Number of Servings — 10-12
1 pt. whipping cream
3 T. white sugar
1 t. vanilla
18 coconut macaroons

1 c. chopped walnuts
3 pints sherbet (1 orange, 1 lime, 1 raspberry)

Whip cream and add sugar and vanilla. Crush or grind (with coarse food chopper) the macaroons, mix with chopped nuts. Fold macaroons and nuts into the whipped cream. Put ½ of mixture into a 9x13 pan, spread evenly. Put small spoonful of sherbets alternately over the top so that some of each color will be in each serving, use all the sherbets. Top with the rest of the whipped cream mixture, cover, and freeze.

Mrs. Gladys M. Myers,
Anoka-Isanti School District No. 15
St. Francis, Minnesota

SHERBET DESSERT
Number of Servings — 12-15
1 pt. whipped cream
1 pt. lime sherbet
1 pt. lemon sherbet
1 pt. orange sherbet
3 c. vanilla wafers (crushed)

Line the bottom of a 9x13 pan with whipped cream and sprinkle half of crumbs over the cream. Spoon each kind of sherbet alternately, by teaspoonful over the crumbs. Place these close together, sprinkle remainder of crumbs over sherbet. Top with rest of cream and sprinkle with finely ground nuts, freeze.

Mrs. James H. Witt, Williston Jr. H. S.
Williston, North Dakota

THREE-OF-A-KIND SHERBET
Number of Servings — 10
3 oranges
3 lemons
3 bananas
3 c. sugar
3 c. water
3 egg whites

Prepare juice from oranges and lemons, mash bananas, put all through a strainer, add the water and sugar, and stir constantly until dissolved. Put into freezer and freeze until the consistency of mush, then open the top carefully and quickly and stir in the egg whites beaten stiff. Repack and finish freezing. Same procedure would be followed if frozen in the refrigerator.

This recipe submitted by the following teachers:
Lillian Mattson, Moses Lake H. S.
Moses Lake, Washington
Melba D. Stoffers, Hermiston Sr. H. S.
Hermiston, Oregon

TROPICAL FROZEN DESSERT
Number of Servings — 10
3 c. sugar
3 c water
3 oranges
3 lemons
3 bananas
7-Up

Bring water and sugar to a boil for 5 minutes, cool and add the juice of the oranges, lemons and the bananas, mashed with a fork. Pour into trays

(Continued on Next Page)

and freeze. When ready to serve, break into pieces with a fork and place in individual sherbet dishes and fill for 7-Up. This is also delicious as a fruit cocktail if used when slushy.

Mrs. LeArta Hammond, West Side H. S.
Dayton, Idaho

FROZEN BANANA PIE
Number of Servings — 6
1 regular size can evaporated milk (chilled in freezing compartment)
2 eggs
1 c. sugar
2 bananas, mashed
¼ t. salt
Juice of 2 lemons
About 10 graham crackers
Whip chilled milk until it will stand in peaks. Beat egg, add sugar, and mashed bananas, add salt and lemon juice, add to whipped milk. Roll graham crackers out until fine. Place in pie plate as a crust, (no butter is mixed with the crumbs). Pour mixture gently into pie crust, freeze.

Mrs. Alletta Gould, Seymour Jr. H. S.
Seymour, Connecticut

FROZEN BANANA ICE CREAM PIE
Number of Servings — 6
1¼ c. finely crushed chocolate cookies or vanilla wafers or graham crackers
2 T. sugar
⅛ c. melted butter or margarine
2 ripe medium sized bananas (mashed)
1½ pt. vanilla ice cream (ice milk for low calories)
½ c. coarsely chopped nuts
Blend thoroughly cookie crumbs, sugar and butter. Press mixture firmly on bottom and sides of 9" pie plate. Chill in freezer. Mix together bananas, ice cream and nuts until thoroughly blended. Mixture should be thick enough to hold its shape. Pour and spread evenly over the chilled prepared crust. Garnish top of pie with 2 tablespoons of cookie crumbs. Store in freezer until ready to serve.

Mrs. Edna Crow, Hollis Schools
Hollis, Oklahoma

CHERRY PIE DESSERT
Number of Servings — 10-12
Crust:
½ pkg. lemon thin wafers
1 stick oleo or butter
½ c. sugar
1 c. pecans, chopped
Filling:
1 can sweetened condensed milk
¼ c. lemon juice
½ pt. whipping cream
½ t. almond flavor
1 pkg. frozen red tart cherries
Mix crushed wafers, sugar, and pecans, add melted butter. Press into 9x15 pan, chill. Mix condensed milk with lemon juice, let stand while whipping cream. Add whipped cream, flavor and cherries. Pour onto crust, freeze for several hours.

Mrs. Viola Gracey, Hermleigh H. S.
Hermleigh, Texas

CHOCOLATE ICE CREAM SUNDAE PIE
Number of Servings — 8
Crust:
1 egg white
¼ t. salt
¼ c. sugar
1¼ c. finely chopped nuts
Beat egg white with salt until stiff, fold in sugar and nuts. Place in greased pie plate, spreading well on sides, and prick with fork. Bake at 400°F. about 10 minutes, cool well.
Filling:
1 pkg. chocolate instant pudding
1 c. coffee cream
1 pt. vanilla ice cream
Dissolve 1 package chocolate instant pudding in coffee cream, fold mixture into softened vanilla ice cream. Pour into cooled crust and put into freezing compartment of refrigerator or freezer.

Mrs. Ivy West Cross, Patrick Henry H. S.
Ashland, Virginia

CHOCOLATE PEPPERMINT PIE
Number of Servings — 6-7
2 T. butter
1¼ c. marshmallow creme
¼ t. salt
3 c. corn flakes
1 pt. chocolate ice cream
1 pt. vanilla ice cream
½ c. chopped peppermint candy
Combine butter, marshmallow creme, and salt in a large fry pan, place over low heat. Stir constantly until mixture is smooth and hot, add cereal. Stir carefully until all cereal flakes are coated, press mixture gently over sides and bottom of buttered 9" pie pan, chill. Fill with a layer of chocolate ice cream, top with a layer of vanilla ice cream, smooth top. Place in freezer to become firm, garnish with chopped peppermint stick candy, place in freezer.

Mrs. Dorothy Jean Keller, Cobden Unit School
Cobden, Illinois

COFFEE PIE
Number of Servings — 8
2 1 oz. sq. unsweetened chocolate
2 T. margarine
2 T. hot evaporated milk
¾ c. sifted confectioners' sugar
1½ c. shredded angel flake coconut
½ gal. vanilla ice milk
4-5 T. instant coffee
½ c. chopped pecans or brazil nuts
Set ice milk in bowl to soften enough to stir instant coffee into it, melt chocolate and margarine over hot water. Stir milk into confectioners' sugar, add to chocolate mixture, stir in coconut. Press onto bottom and sides of lightly buttered 9" pie plate. Thoroughly stir coffee into ice milk and place into pie plate, sprinkle with chopped nuts. Place in freezer until serving time, this is thick enough to cut 8 servings. (The amount of instant coffee used can be adjusted to individual taste).

Mrs. Glenda Ballinger, Kirkman Technical H. S.
Chattanooga, Tennessee

FROSTY CRANBERRY PIE
Number of Servings — 8
1 qt. vanilla ice cream
1 c. cranberry-orange relish (can use ready frozen)
¼ c. drained crushed pineapple
1 baked 9″ pastry shell (or crumb crust)
½ c. sweetened whipped cream (if desired)
Toasted almonds

Combine pineapple with relish, soften ice cream just enough to blend with the cranberry-orange relish. Spoon into baked and cooled pastry shell or crumb crust, set in freezer until ice cream is firm. Garnish top with crumbs or whipped cream and toasted almonds just before serving.

Mrs. Kathryn McCardle, New Salem H. S.
New Salem, North Dakota

CREME DE MENTHE PIE
Number of Servings — 8
¾ pkg. chocolate wafers
¼ c. butter, melted
24 marshmallows
⅔ c. creme de menthe
1 c. whipping cream

Roll chocolate wafers into crumbs, put into a 9″ pie pan and add the melted butter. Pat out into a pie crust and place into deep freeze until filling is ready. Melt in a double boiler 24 marshmallows, after they are melted add ⅔ cup creme de menthe and cool. Whip cream until very stiff, fold in marshmallow mixture, pour into frozen pie crust and place in the freezer until served. Allow at least 2 hours before serving. Cut into at least 8 pieces as pie is very rich.

Eileen Whitfield, Stanford H. S.
Stanford, Montana

GRASSHOPPER PIE
Number of Servings — 6-8
2 T. butter
14 crushed Hydrox cookies
24 marshmallows
½ c. milk
4 T. green creme de menthe
2 T. white creme de cacao
1 c. whipped cream

Melt butter and stir it into crushed Hydrox cookies, press into an 8″ pie tin and use for crust. Melt marshmallows in milk. Stir in green creme de menthe and white creme de cacao, fold in whipped cream and pour all into pie crust, freeze, serve frozen.

Mrs. Shirley Hansen, Abraham Lincoln H. S.
San Jose, California

ICE CREAM PIE
Number of Servings — 4-6
2 pts. vanilla ice cream
3 c. finely crumbled ginger cookies
6 T. finely chopped pecans
6 T. sugar
½ c. melted butter
¼ c. light cream

Keep ice cream in freezer until needed. Mix cookie crumbs with nuts, sugar, melted butter and cream.

Take out ¾ cup and set aside. Pat the rest firmly into bottom and around sides of an 8″ pie plate and chill thoroughly. Just before serving, fill with ice cream (let ice cream stand at room temperature 10 minutes to soften slightly). Sprinkle reserved crumbs over top and serve immediately. Or line ice cream tray with crumb mixture, fill with ice cream, sprinkle crumbs on top of ice cream and put filled tray into freezer to keep frozen until ready to serve.

Mary Jane Bevins, Belfry H. S.
Belfry, Kentucky

DATE-NUT ICE CREAM PIE
Number of Servings — 8
1 7¼ oz. pkg. pitted dates
½ c. water
½ c. sugar
1 t. lemon juice
1 T. plain gelatin
½ c. cold water
¼ c. chopped pecans
1 4¾ oz. pkg. vanilla wafers
⅛ c. butter, melted
1 qt. vanilla ice cream

Cut dates into fourths, combine with sugar, water, and lemon juice in a small saucepan. Cover and cook slowly until dates are soft, remove from heat and add the gelatin which has been dissolved in the cold water. Add nuts and let mixture cool. Meanwhile, crush vanilla wafers and mix with the melted butter, press mixture into bottom and on sides of a 9″ pie plate. Spread 1 pint of vanilla ice cream over the crust. Spread the cooled date mixture on the ice cream. Top with the last pint of vanilla ice cream which has been slightly softened at room temperature. Place in freezing compartment of refrigerator to harden. Just before serving, let pie stand at room temperature for 5 to 10 minutes to make cutting easier.

This recipe submitted by the following teachers:
Mrs. Betty Knowles, Whiteface H. S.
Whiteface, Texas
Selma Sailors, Diller Community Schools
Diller, Nebraska

FROZEN LEMON DESSERT
Number of Servings — 8-10
2 egg yolks
1 c. sugar
1 lemon, juice and rind
2 egg whites
1½ c. thick cream
1½ c. crushed vanilla wafers

Cook together until thick the egg yolks, sugar and lemon juice and rind. Cool. Beat the egg whites until stiff. Add lemon mixture to this. Whip cream, then add to above mixture. Mix well. Pour into freezer trays that have been sprinkled generously with the crushed vanilla wafer crumbs. Top with crumbs. Freeze. Cut into squares or wedges for serving.

Mrs. Helen C. Borders, Waco School
Waco, North Carolina

FROZEN LEMON PIE
Number of Servings — 10-12
2 eggs
¾ c. sugar
2 lemons
1 lge. can evaporated milk
1 box vanilla wafers

Chill milk, beat 2 eggs, add sugar and juice of 1 lemon and rind of 1 lemon. In another bowl, beat chilled milk until stiff adding juice of 1 lemon. Fold in egg and sugar mixture into whipped milk, then pour into a pie plate lined with vanilla wafers, freeze.

Mrs. Mack G. Rogerson, Chowan H. S.
Tyner, North Carolina

FROZEN LEMON PIE
Number of Servings — 6
4 egg yolks
½ c. sugar
2 lemons (juice and rind)
4 egg whites
1 c. whipping cream
3 T. sugar
Vanilla wafer crumbs

Cook egg yolks, sugar, lemon juice and rind in a double boiler until thick, cool. Add stiffly beaten egg whites, and whipped cream (to which 3 tablespoons of sugar has been added). Put a layer of vanilla wafer crumbs on bottom of freezing tray. Pour in mixture, cover top with more crumbs, freeze.

Mrs. Lee Burnett, Iraan H. S.
Iraan, Texas

FROZEN LEMON PIE
Number of Servings — 8
3 eggs
½ c. plus 1 T. sugar
⅛ t. salt
¼ c. lemon juice
Grated rind of ½ lemon
½ pt. whipping cream
1 c. cookie or graham cracker crumbs

Separate eggs, beat yolks slightly and cook in double boiler with ½ cup sugar, salt, lemon juice and rind until a little thick. Cool slightly and fold into the 3 stiffly beaten egg whites plus 1 tablespoon sugar. Fold this into the whipped cream, make a layer of cracker crumbs in 8x8 square pan, pour mixture on top and add remaining crumbs on top, freeze.

This recipe submitted by the following teachers:
Mrs. Amy Crain, Orosi H. S.
Orosi, California
Mrs. Sarah Dueitt, Spring H. S.
Spring, Texas
Hilda B. Cassell, Blackstone H. S.
Blackstone, Virginia

ICE CREAM LEMONADE PIE
Number of Servings — Two Pies
½ gal. vanilla ice cream
1 can lemonade concentrate
½ c. chopped toasted pecans

Crust:
1 box. vanilla wafers
1 stick margarine

Make crust first and let it be cooling. Crush or crumble vanilla wafers. Melt margarine. Mix margarine with wafer crumbs. Press and shape crust to fit pie pan. Brown slightly in oven. Cool. This will make 2 crusts. Soften slightly the half gallon of ice cream in a large bowl. Add lemonade concentrate. Mix well. Divide mixture and put equal amounts into each pie crust. Top each pie with toasted pecans. Wrap in Saran wrap and place in the freezer.

Mrs. T. W. Saterfiel, Noxapater H. S.
Noxapater, Mississippi

LEMONADE ICE BOX PIE
Number of Servings — 12
1 lge. can frozen lemonade
½ gal. vanilla ice cream
1 pkg. graham crackers

Mix lemonade with ice cream in a large mixing bowl (do not dilute lemonade with water). When thoroughly mixed, pour in a large pyrex baking dish which has been lined with crushed graham cracker crumbs. Sprinkle more crumbs over top. Place in freezing section and keep frozen, serve by slicing in sections.

Mrs. Clyda Phillips, Star City H. S.
Star City Arkansas

FROZEN FRESH LEMON TARTS
Number of Servings — 12
3 eggs, separated
¼ c. fresh lemon juice
⅔ c. granulated sugar
¼ t. salt
1 t. grated lemon rind
1 t. pure vanilla extract
1 c. heavy cream, whipped
½ c. fine vanilla wafer crumbs

In double boiler, combine well-beaten egg yolks, lemon juice, sugar and salt. Cook over hot, not boiling water until custard coats metal spoon, chill. Stir in rind and vanilla, beat egg whites stiff. Fold into custard, fold in whipped cream. Place No. 5 fluted baking cups in each of 12 2½" muffin tins, sprinkle bottom of each with 1 teaspoon crumbs. Fill with lemon mixture, sprinkle remaining crumbs over top. Freeze until firm.

Mrs. Evelyn B. Fontenot, Church Point H. S.
Church Point, Louisiana

LIME ICEBOX PIE
Number of Servings — 6
½ c. lime juice
1 can sweetened condensed milk
2 egg yolks, beaten slightly
Green cake coloring, if desired
2 egg whites
4 T. sugar
12-16 graham crackers
4 T. butter

Mix the juice, milk, egg yolks, and the coloring. Make a meringue of the egg whites and the sugar.

(Continued on Next Page)

Fold the meringue into the lime mixture. Make a crumb crust of the graham crackers and the melted butter. Line a refrigerator tray with the crust and fill with the lime mixture. Sprinkle a few crumbs over the top and freeze. It takes several hours or over night to freeze well.

Mrs. Flo Perry Brame, Lake Air Jr. H. S.
Waco, Texas

FROZEN LIME PIE

Number of Servings — 18

4 eggs
2 cans sweetened condensed milk
½ c. lime juice
Graham crackers
Green food coloring

Make a crust of graham crackers, sugar and butter. Press into 3 refrigerator ice cube trays. Separate eggs and beat yolks, add condensed milk and lime juice to egg yolks. Add green food coloring for the desired shade of green. Beat egg whites and fold into the yolk mixture. Pour into the refrigerator trays, sprinkle top with graham cracker crumbs. Put in freezer overnight, serve frozen.

Evelyn B. McDonald, Coosa County H. S.
Rockford, Alabama

FROZEN LIMEADE PIE (Or Lemon)

Number of Servings — 12-15

1 can sweetened condensed milk
1 can frozen limeade
1 can evaporated milk (whipped)
3 egg yolks
3 egg whites (stiffly beaten)

Combine the sweetened condensed milk with the egg yolks and limeade, fold in whipped milk and then the whipped egg whites. Add green color and pour into 2 9" pie pans lined with graham cracker crust. Garnish with slices of lime or cracker crumbs if desired. To make a lemon pie, substitute the lemonade for the lime and use yellow coloring. Freeze and wrap until ready to serve.

Mrs. Neal Prisock, Louisville H. S.
Louisville, Mississippi

FROZEN LIME PIE

Number of Servings — 20

1 c. crushed vanilla wafers
1 T. grated lime rind
⅛ c. fresh lime juice
6 eggs
1 c. sugar
1 pt. whipping cream
Green food coloring

Separate egg yolks from whites. Beat egg yolks until thick. Add grated rind, sugar to beaten egg yolks (use double boiler). Cook until thick. Cool. Beat egg whites separately until stiff. Beat cream until thick but not dry. Fold egg whites into cream and custard. Color to pleasing green with cake coloring. Pile in pan on top of crushed vanilla wafers. Freeze.

Mrs. Lelia V. Matthews, Burton H. S.
Burton, Texas

PUMPKIN ICE CREAM PIE

Number of Servings — 7

¼ c. honey or brown sugar
¾ c. canned or cooked mashed pumpkin
½ t. cinnamon
¼ t. ginger
Dash nutmeg
Dash cloves
¼ t. salt
1 qt. vanilla ice cream
⅓ c. broken pecans, if desired
1 baked 9" pastry shell

Combine honey, pumpkin, spices and salt, bring just to a boil, stirring constantly, cool. Beat into softened vanilla ice cream and add nuts if desired. Spread in baked pastry shell, freeze until firm. Trim with whipped cream and pecan halves if you like. For a change, try this filling in a flavorful graham cracker crust.

This recipe submitted by the following teachers:
Lydia Lou Roper, Jefferson H. S.
Lakewood, Colorado
Evelyn B. Willey, Gates County H. S.
Gatesville, North Carolina

MILE HIGH STRAWBERRY PIE

Number of Servings — 6-8

1 pkg. (10 oz.) frozen strawberries
1 c. sugar
2 egg whites
1 T. lemon juice
⅛ t. salt
½ c. whipping cream
1 t. vanilla
1 baked 10" pastry shell

Place defrosted strawberries, sugar, egg whites, lemon juice and salt in large bowl of electric mixer. Beat at medium speed for 15 minutes or until mixture is stiff and holds its shape. Whip cream, add the vanilla and fold into strawberry mixture. Pile lightly into baked pastry shell. Freeze several hours or over night. Garnish with strawberries if desired. Note: Make sure beaters are free from slightest amount of grease or the first mixture will not be fluffy.

Mrs. Betty Tipton, Everman H. S.
Everman, Texas

FROZEN STRAWBERRY DELIGHT

Number of Servings — 12

1 lge. can evaporated milk
½ c. sugar
2 T. lemon juice
1 pt. sweetened frozen strawberries

Place evaporated milk in container and chill for 1 hour or until ice crystals form. Add sugar and lemon juice to strawberries and beat until strawberries are beaten into a fine pulp. Whip milk. Add strawberry mixture to milk, and whip until well mixed. Place into two 9" pie plate lined with crumb crust. Place in freezer for 2 hours. Take out 5 to 10 minutes before serving.

Gail Shackelford, Baker School
Mobile, Alabama

STRAWBERRY ICE CREAM PIE

Number of Servings — 6

16 marshmallows
2 T. crushed strawberries
Red food coloring
2 egg whites
¼ c. sugar
¼ t. salt
3 c. vanilla ice cream
1 9" baked pastry shell or graham cracker crust
1 c. fresh sliced strawberries

Heat marshmallows with the crushed strawberries, folding over and over until marshmallows are half melted. Remove from heat and continue folding until mixture is smooth and spongy. Add a few drops of red food coloring and cool, beat egg whites until nearly stiff, then beat in sugar slowly, add salt. Fold into cooled marshmallow mixture, place ice cream in a pastry shell or graham cracker crust. Cover with 1 cup fresh, sliced strawberries, top with marshmallow meringue. Brown quickly under broiler for 30 seconds. This may be served immediately or stored in the freezer until ready for use.

Mrs. Shirley Hannes, Giddings H. S.
Giddings, Texas

FROZEN STRAWBERRY PIE

Number of Servings — 8

1 pkg. whip mix (such as Dream)
1 small box frozen strawberries
2 egg whites, beaten stiff
1 t. vanilla
1 small pkg. vanilla wafers
Whipping cream or another pkg. of whip mix

Line pyrex pie plate with vanilla wafers. Beat whip mix according to instructions. Fold in thawed strawberries until well blended. Fold in beaten egg whites. Place mixture in vanilla wafer crust. Freeze. Top with whipped cream or another package of whip mix. Cut in small wedges. Serve immediately.

Mrs. Dorothy T. Rabb, Lowe Jr. H. S.
Minden, Louisiana

STRAWBERRY-PINEAPPLE ICE CREAM PIE

Number of Servings — Two 8 Inch Pans

1 T. lemon juice
1 c. marshmallow creme
1 pkg. defrosted strawberries
1 can partially defrosted pineapple cubes (can use canned pineapple as well)
½ pt. whipping cream
2 graham cracker pie crusts

Blend lemon juice and marshmallow creme, add strawberries (drain slightly), and pineapple and fold in whipped cream. Partially freeze this mixture, pour into graham cracker pie shell and return to freezer until firm. Remove from freezer and let set a few minutes before serving. Other types of berries may be used besides strawberries.

Nevaleen Selmat, Wakita H. S.
Wakita, Oklahoma

FROZEN OZARK PUDDING
(Mrs. Truman's)

1 egg
¾ c. sugar
3 T. flour
1¼ t. baking powder
⅛ t. salt
1 t. vanilla
½ c. chopped nuts
½ c. chopped pared apples
Whipped cream

Beat egg. Add sugar gradually, beating thoroughly after each addition. Sift flour, baking powder, and salt together. Blend with egg-sugar mixture and mix well. Pour into buttered 9" shallow pie plate. Bake at 350°F. for 20-25 minutes. Line a 9x5x3 loaf pan with wax paper. Pack ½ quart coffee ice cream into pan. Break cooled pudding into pieces. Place evenly over ice cream. Cover with another half quart of ice cream. Freeze until ready to serve.

Sue Dawson, Northwest District Supervisor,
Home Economics Education
Montevallo, Alabama

FROZEN CHRISTMAS PUDDING

Number of Servings — 8

1½ c. vanilla wafers (23 wafers)
½ c. chopped nuts
8 oz. jar candied fruit
1 No. 2 can crushed pineapple (drained)
¼ t. cinnamon
¼ t. nutmeg
8 marshmallows
¼ c. hot pineapple juice
1 c. whipping cream

Dissolve marshmallows in hot pineapple juice, add all other ingredients but cream, mix well. Whip cream until stiff and fold into mixture. Line pan with vanilla wafers, leaving some crumbs to sprinkle on top. Add mixture and sprinkle vanilla crumbs over top, freeze until firm. Remove from pan, slice and serve.

Mrs. Helen S. Roberts, Alvin H. S.
Alvin, Texas

FROZEN ENGLISH TOFFEE PUDDING

Number of Servings — 6-8

¼ lb. vanilla wafers
2 c. powdered sugar
2 T. cocoa
¼ t. salt
½ c. butter or oleo
1 T. butter or oleo
1 c. chopped pecans
2 eggs, separated
½ t. vanilla

Crumb vanilla wafers and mix in a tablespoon butter which has been melted. Use ¾ of mixture to cover bottom of 8" square pan or 2 long refrigerator trays. Sift the sugar, cocoa and salt together and cream into softened butter, add egg yolks, vanilla and pecans, mix well. Fold in beaten egg whites and spoon over crumbs. Top with remaining crumbs and freeze.

Vera Murphy, Atchison County Community H. S.
Effingham, Kansas

FROZEN LEMON CUSTARD

Number of Servings — 6-8

5 T. orange juice
3 T. lemon juice
3 eggs (5 if small)
½ c. sugar
½ pt. whipping cream
Pinch salt
24 vanilla wafers
½ envelope gelatin

Mix egg yolks, sugar, and fruit juices in top part of double boiler (save enough juice to dissolve gelatin), cook until thick. While hot stir in ½ envelope of gelatin that has been dissolved in the fruit juice, add grated lemon rind. Fold in beaten egg whites and whipped cream, line tray with vanilla wafer crumbs, pour in mixture and top with crumbs. Freeze, serve.

Frances Bailey,
State Supervisor, Home Economics Education
Little Rock, Arkansas

FROZEN LEMON CUSTARD

Number of Servings — 4

1 egg yolk
⅛ c. sugar
¼ t. grated lemon rind
3 T. lemon juice
1 egg white
⅛ c. water
⅛ c. instant dry milk
Few grains salt if desired

Mix together egg yolk, sugar, grated lemon rind and lemon juice in small bowl. Place egg white in water and dry milk in large bowl. Beat until it stands in peaks. Gradually fold lemon mixture into egg white, pour into quart tray and freeze without stirring. Tray may be lined with crumb mixture using ¾ cup of graham cracker crumbs to ¼ cup melted butter. Crumbs may be sprinkled on top.

This recipe submitted by the following teachers:

Mary Kay Ketter, Askov H. S.
Askov, Minnesota

Joy Kay Hillhouse, Mathiston H. S.
Mathiston, Mississippi

Emma Lois Stephens, Elm City H. S.
Elm City, North Carolina

LEMON ICEBOX PUDDING

Number of Servings — 8

1 tall can evaporated milk
¼ c. lemon juice
¾ c. sugar
15 vanilla wafers

Chill evaporated milk over night. Whip milk until thick like whipped cream. Add lemon juice and sugar. Mix well. Crush vanilla wafers and sprinkle over bottom of loaf pan (reserve small amount to sprinkle over top). Pour pudding into pan and sprinkle crumbs over top. Freeze until firm. Drained, crushed pineapple and/or nuts may be added to this.

Vera Faye Elledge, Mabank H. S.
Mabank, Texas

LEMON CUSTARD FROZEN DESSERT

Number of Servings — 6

3 egg yolks
½ c. sugar
1 t. lemon rind
3 T. lemon juice
3 egg whites
⅓ c. sugar
1 6 oz. can (⅔ c.) evaporated milk, chilled and whipped or 1 c. cream (whipped)
Vanilla Wafers

In top of double boiler, beat egg yolks until thick and lemon colored. Gradually beat in the ½ cup sugar, lemon juice and rind. Cook and stir over simmering water until thick. Cool thoroughly. Beat egg whites until soft peaks form, gradually add the ⅓ cup sugar, beating until stiff peaks form. Fold into cooled lemon mixture. The fold in whipped milk or cream. Line bottom and side of pie pan or baking dish with whole vanilla wafers. Pour in lemon mixture and freeze until firm.

Mildred Hart, Andalusia H. S.
Andalusia, Alabama

FROZEN LEMON PUDDING

Number of Servings — 8

¾ c. evaporated milk
2 egg yolks, well beaten
6 T. sugar
½ t. grated lemon rind
¼ c. lemon juice
2 egg whites
2 T. sugar
¾ c. graham cracker crumbs

Chill milk until icy cold, mix egg yolks, sugar, lemon rind and lemon juice in the top of a double boiler. Cook and stir over boiling water until thickened, cool. Beat egg whites until stiff, gradually add 2 tablespoons sugar. Fold egg whites into lemon mixture and chill. Rub the bottom and sides of a refrigerator tray with butter or margarine, spread half of the cracker crumbs in the bottom of the tray. Whip the chilled milk until stiff. Fold into the lemon mixture and put into tray. Sprinkle with remaining crumbs, freeze without stirring. Makes about 1 quart.

Mrs. Gloria S. Moore, Hall Summit H. S.
Hall Summit, Louisiana

RUM PUDDING

Number of Servings — 8

1 pt. heavy cream
3 eggs, separated
8 T. sugar
4 T. rum flavoring
1 t. vanilla
1 t. nutmeg

Beat cream until stiff, set aside. Separate eggs and beat yolks until foamy. Add 4 tablespoons sugar, rum favoring, vanilla and nutmeg to beaten yolks. Beat egg whites stiff, forming peaks, add 4 tablespoons sugar to egg whites. Lightly blend the egg yolks mixture and whipped cream into beaten egg whites. Pour into individual cups and freeze, serve frozen.

Jacqueline Hardee, University H. S.
Los Angeles, California

BANANA NIPS

Number of Servings — 5

1 pkg. butterscotch bits
¼ c. peanut butter
5 bananas
¾ c. flaked coconut

Melt butterscotch bits and peanut butter in saucepan over low heat, stir slightly. Roll freshly peeled bananas in the melted butterscotch bits and peanut butter, cool thoroughly. Sprinkle each banana with coconut and place bananas on cookie sheet which has been covered with wax paper and place in freezer. Simulated banana ice cream. Banana nips should be eaten frozen but not frozen very hard.

Mrs. Naomi F. Stock, Lakota H. S.
West Chester, Ohio

BISCUIT TORTONI

Number of Servings — 6

¾ c. sugar
¾ c. strong coffee
3 egg yolks
1 T. butter
1 pt. whipping cream
25 coconut macaroons

Boil sugar and coffee until mixture threads. Add butter and cool. Beat in egg yolks. Freeze this mixture, stirring once or twice during the freezing process. Roll macaroons into crumbs. Line refrigerator pan with crumbs. Save ¾ cup of crumbs for top. Whip cream and beat in frozen mixture slowly. Pour in pan, top with crumbs and freeze. Cut in blocks to serve.

Helen Sergent, Gate City H. S.
Gate City, Virginia

FROZEN CHOCOLATE JUBILEE

Number of Servings — 9-12

¾-1 box vanilla wafers
4 T. melted butter
2 c. powdered sugar
½ c. butter or margarine
2 sq. chocolate
1 t. vanilla
3 egg yolks
3 egg whites
1 qt. vanilla ice cream
1 c. chopped nuts (optional)

Line 9x12 pan with vanilla wafers or graham crackers crushed and mixed with 4 tablespoons butter, press firm. Cream sugar, butter, add melted chocolate, vanilla and beaten egg yolks. Fold in stiffly beaten egg whites and spread on wafer crust and chill until firm. Spread softened vanilla ice cream over top of chocolate mixture, sprinkle with nuts (optional), freeze.

This recipe submitted by the following teachers:
Ruth Ferguson, Belle Plaine Community H. S.
Belle Plaine, Iowa
Sylvia I. Evavold, Hawley Jr. H. S.
Hawley, Minnesota

CRANBERRY CHIFFON FREEZE

Number of Servings — 1½ Quarts

¼ lb. (about 16) marshmallows
½ c. water
2 t. grated lemon rind
1 lb. can whole cranberry sauce or cranberry jelly
2½ c. whipped instant milk°

Dice marshmallows, place in saucepan with water. Heat until marshmallows melt, add lemon rind and cranberries. Blend until smooth, cool thoroughly. Fold chilled cranberry mixture into whipped instant milk, spoon into refrigerator trays, freeze until firm.

°To whip instant milk mix ½ cup ice water and ½ cup instant milk. Whip until soft peaks form, add ¼ cup lemon juice. Continue beating until stiff peaks form (3-4 minutes). Fold in ¼ cup sugar.

Nella Ramsey, Navarro H. S.
Geronimo, Texas

CREME DELIGHT

Number of Servings — 20

2 small pkg. chocolate covered graham crackers
2 c. sweet milk
1 lge. pkg. marshmallows
½ gal. chocolate ripple ice cream
¾ c. creme de menthe
½ c. whipping cream

Crush crackers, line bottom of 2 large dishes. Heat milk and marshmallows until marshmallows have melted. Remove from heat and cool to lukewarm. Add ice cream and creme de menthe, stirring until ice cream is dissolved, fold in cream which has been whipped. Spoon mixture into pans lined with crushed crackers, sprinkle a few crushed crackers on top, freeze. Will keep 2 weeks.

Alice Kernodle, East H. S.
Memphis, Tennessee

FROZEN DESSERT

Number of Servings — 6-8

1 c. pineapple juice
½ c. orange juice
24 lge. marshmallows
Pinch salt
1 pt. cream (whipping)
Vanilla wafer crumbs

Heat juices and dissolve marshmallows and pinch of salt. When cool, whip in pint of cream until semi-jelled and put half in pan 4x10. Add layer of crumbs, spoon in rest of mixture, and add another ⅛" layer of wafers and place in freezer.

Janelle Hammonds, County Line H. S.
Branch, Arkansas

FROZEN DESSERT

Number of Servings — 8-10

2 c. brown sugar
¾ c. flour
2 eggs
1 c. chopped nuts
1 t. soda
1 t. vanilla
1 pt. whipping cream or 1 qt. vanilla ice cream (softened)

(Continued on Next Page)

Sift flour and soda, beat eggs and add sugar, add flour mixture and vanilla, add nuts. Pour into 1 very large pan or 2 small lightly greased pans. Bake at 350°F. for exactly 25 minutes. It will look very peculiar. Cool in pan and break into small pieces, fold into whipped cream or softened vanilla ice cream, freeze firm, serve.

Dionetta K. Talley, Demopolis H. S.
Demopolis, Alabama

ICEBOX FRUIT CAKE (Frozen)

Number of Servings — 12-15

2 c. cookie or graham cracker crumbs
1 lb. marshmallows
2 c. thin cream or 1 c. milk and 1 c. cream
2 c. frozen strawberries, sweetened and drained
2 c. diced or crushed pineapple (drained)
2 c. pitted and chopped dates
2 c. chopped walnuts
1-6 oz. can lemonade concentrate (undiluted)

Butter a 5x9x3 loaf pan. Sprinkle with most of crumbs, leaving some for top. Heat marshmallows with cream, stirring at intervals until half dissolved. Remove from heat and beat until smooth. Cool. Add drained strawberries, pineapple, dates, nuts and lemonade concentrate to the cooled marshmallows, stirring gently. Pour into crumb lined pan, topping with remaining crumbs. Freeze in compartment or freezer. If to be stored for more than a day or two, use vapor-proof wrap. Slice for serving as for oven-baked cake.

Mrs. Loretta Qualls, Livingston Academy
Livingston, Tennessee

FROZEN FRUIT CAKE

Number of Servings — 8-10

1 c. whipping cream or evaporated milk
2 c. milk
½ c. sugar
¼ c. flour
¼ t. salt
2 eggs, beaten
1 t. vanilla
1 c. white raisins
1 c. broken pecans
2 c. cake crumbs, white cake, vanilla wafers, or macaroons
½ c. candied red cherries, halved
¼ c. chopped candied green fruit, or other colors if desired

Chill cream or evaporated milk for whipping. Scald milk in top of double boiler. Mix together sugar, flour, salt, and add to milk all at once. Cook over hot water about 3 minutes, stirring constantly, add vanilla, cool. Reserve a few whole red and green fruits and nuts. Stir raisins, crumbs, and remainder of chopped fruits and nuts into mixture. Whip chilled cream and fold into mixture, pour into 1¼ quart loaf pan, or any other desired container (bottom greased and lined with wax paper on which fruits and nuts have been arranged). Freeze in refrigerator or freezer overnight. Slice as desired.

Letha Thomas, Mt. Pleasant H. S.
Mt. Pleasant, Texas

FROZEN FRUIT CAKE

Number of Servings — 12

2 c. milk
½ c. sugar
½ c. flour
¼ c. flour
¼ t. salt
2 eggs
1 c. white raisins
1 c. broken pecans
2 c. crumbled macaroons
½ c. chopped candied cherries
1 t. vanilla
1 c. whipping cream

Scald milk. Blend sugar, flour, and salt. Add to milk. Stir until smooth. Cook on low heat 10 minutes. Add beaten eggs slowly. Cook until thick, stir constantly. Cool. Add other ingredients folding in whipped cream last. Freeze in tray of refrigerator.

Mrs. Agnes Foster, Hartford H. S.
Hartford, Kentucky

FROZEN FRUIT DELIGHT

Number of Servings — 8-10

1 c. diced pineapple
Juice from 2 oranges
2 bananas (mashed smooth)
⅔ c. sugar
1 c. nuts (chopped)
10 marshmallows (cut fine)
2 c. cream (whipped)
1 small bottle maraschino cherries (cut fine)

Soften marshmallows in juice drained from pineapple, add orange juice, sugar, pineapple, nuts, marshmallows. Fold in whipped cream and freeze.

Mary D. Thompson,
Montgomery-Wabash-Twp.-Owensville H. S.
Owensville, Indiana

FROZEN FRUIT DESSERT

2 c. sugar
1 c. water
1 qt. apricots (cut up) plus ½ of juice
1 pt. frozen strawberries
1 small can chunk pineapple
4 sliced bananas
Pinch of salt

Cook sugar and water and cool, add apricots and half the juice, strawberries, pineapple, bananas, and salt. Freeze above mixture until solid, then spread on topping.

Topping:
1 egg
⅔ c. sugar
Juice of 1 orange
Juice of 1 lemon
1 c. whipped cream

Mix together egg, sugar, orange juice, lemon juice, add whipped cream. This dessert may be kept in the freezer until ready to serve. It should be served frozen, not thawed.

Mrs. Frances M. Whited, Toledo H. S.
Toledo, Oregon

FROZEN FRUIT DESSERT

Number of Servings — 12

2 c. miniature marshmallows
1 No. 2 can crushed pineapple
½ c. heavy cream, whipped
⅓ c. salad dressing
4 bananas, diced
1 c. diced peaches (fresh or frozen)
1 c. sliced strawberries (fresh or frozen)

Heat marshmallows and pineapple together until marshmallows are melted. Cool until slightly thickened. Fold in whipped cream, salad dressing and fruit, blend. Freeze to firm stage and cut in squares for serving.

Mrs. Louise Brame, South Hopkins H. S.
Nortonville, Kentucky

FROZEN LIME PIE

Number of Servings — 6

1¼ c. fine graham cracker crumbs
2 T. sugar
¼ c. melted margarine
2 eggs, unbeaten
½ c. sugar
½ c. light corn syrup
⅜ c. fresh lime juice
2 c. light cream
Green food coloring
1 envelope (1 T.) unflavored gelatin
¼ c. water

Mix graham cracker crumbs and sugar. Add butter. Blend thoroughly. Press mixture evenly and firmly on bottom and sides of 9″ pie plate. Beat eggs until thick and lemon-colored, gradually add sugar and corn syrup, continuing to beat until blended. Add lime juice and cream. Tint a delicate green. Soften gelatin in water 5 minutes in medium saucepan. Dissolve gelatin over low heat, stirring constantly. Remove from heat, add egg mixture and blend. Pour into ice tray. Freeze firm. Set temperature control at coldest point. Place frozen mixture in mixing bowl. Beat at low speed until broken up. Beat at high speed until smooth. Work quickly, do not allow mixture to melt. Pour into graham cracker pie shell. Freeze firm.

Mrs. Joe D. Gamble, Ropes H. S.
Ropesville, Texas

MOTHER'S FROZEN FRUIT DESSERT

Number of Servings — 10

1 can fruit cocktail
1 small can evaporated milk, chilled
1 small bottle maraschino cherries
2 T. flour
2 T. sugar
2 T. lemon juice
3 T. mayonnaise

Drain juice from fruit cocktail and cherries. Mix juice, flour, sugar and cook until thick. Chill. Whip chilled milk and add lemon juice. Beat 1 minute. Fold in mayonnaise, then chilled fruit cocktail. Freeze.

Carolyn Stroup, Dallas County H. S.
Plantersville, Alabama

FRUIT MARSHMALLOW DELIGHT

Number of Servings — 6

1 lge. can fruit cocktail
½-¼ lb. marshmallows
1 glass pimento cream cheese
½ pt. whipping cream
2 T. mayonnaise

Drain fruit, cut marshmallows and add to drained fruit. Add creamed cheese and whipping cream. Mix together and freeze.

Mrs. Lynn R. Kiehl, South San Antonio H. S.
San Antonio, Texas

FROZEN FRUIT MOLD

Number of Servings — 6

2 c. fruit cocktail
4 T. chopped green or red cherries
1 small can evaporated milk or 1 c. whipping cream
1½ T. lemon juice
½ c. chopped pecans
8 marshmallows
2 T. mayonnaise

Drain fruit cocktail and cherries. Whip chilled evaporated milk or cream until very stiff. Fold in drained fruit, lemon juice, mayonnaise, chopped nuts and marshmallows (cut in eighths). Pour into ring mold or individual molds. Freeze until firm.

Mrs. Clova Bryson, Rochelle H. S.
Rochelle, Texas

FROZEN FRUIT SALAD OR DESSERT

Number of Servings — 8-10

2 3 oz. pkg. cream cheese
1 c. mayonnaise
1 c. heavy cream, whipped
½ c. red maraschino cherries, quartered
½ c. green maraschino cherries, quartered
1 No. 2 can (2½ c.) crushed pineapple, drained
2½ c. diced marshmallows
   (about 24 marshmallows)

Combine cheese and mayonnaise, blend until smooth. Fold in whipped cream, fruit, and marshmallows. Pour into 1-quart refrigerator tray, freeze firm.

Kathryn Seal, Dixie County H. S.
Cross City, Florida

GOLDEN FROZEN FRUIT SALAD OR DESSERT

Number of Servings — 12-15

1 No. 2½ can sliced pineapple, drained and diced
1 No. 2½ can apricots, drained and diced
2½ c. miniature marshmallows
1 c. nuts, chopped
Dressing:
4 T. vinegar
4 egg yolks or 2 whole eggs, beaten
4 T. sugar
1 T. water
½ pt. whipping cream

Combine vinegar, egg yolks, sugar and water and cook over low heat until thick, cool and add to fruit nut mixture, add whipped cream. Place in pyrex or aluminum pan (8x12), freeze.

Virginia Riddel, Spencer H. S.
Spencer, West Virginia

FROZEN FRUIT SALAD
Number of Servings — 6-8

½ pt. whipping cream
1 2½ can fruit cocktail

Whip cream, adding sugar and vanilla to taste. Fold in drained fruit cocktail. Put in pans (ice trays or molds), and place in freezer. Before removing and serving, let stand several minutes to soften.

Mrs. Portia H. Wilkins, Mathias 12-yr. School
Mathias, West Virginia

GRAHAM CRACKER MOUSSE
Number of Servings — 18

1 pt. whipping cream
⅔ c. sugar
1 t. vanilla
1 envelope gelatin
¼ c. cold water
1 box graham crackers
Strawberries or maraschino cherries

Whip chilled cream, add sugar and vanilla. Stir gelatin into cold water and dissolve over hot water. Add to whipped cream and beat until thoroughly mixed. Line bottom of a square or rectangle pan with graham crackers, then top with whipped cream mixture. Alternate layers of crackers and cream, having cream mixture on top. Garnish with fruits. Place in freezing unit for about 3 hours before slicing to serve.

Novell H. Berry, Douglas H. S.
Douglas, Alabama

GRAPE MARLOW
Number of Servings — 6

24 lge. marshmallows
1½ c. grape juice
4 T. orange juice
1 c. cream whipped with 2 T. sugar

Melt marshmallows in grape juice over low heat, cool, add orange juice. Put in tray in refrigerator (freezer). In a few minutes it will begin to thicken, when it does, fold in whipped cream, return to tray and freeze. Serve as you do ice cream in dessert dishes.

Joyce Gandy Garrison, Chesnee H. S.
Chesnee, South Carolina

ICE CREAM CAKE
Number of Servings — 12

20 standard-size ladyfingers
2 qt. vanilla ice cream
1 (6 oz.) can frozen orange juice concentrate
2 pkg. frozen raspberries
2 (9 oz.) cans crushed pineapple
1 T. frozen lemon concentrate
1 t. almond flavoring
1 t. rum flavoring
6 chopped maraschino cherries
3 T. chopped blanched pistachio nuts
Sweetened whipped cream
Sugared strawberries
Mint leaves (optional)

Line the bottom and sides of a 9″ springform pan with ladyfingers, split in half. Mix 1 quart vanilla ice cream with the frozen undiluted orange juice. Pour into mold over bottom layer of ladyfingers, work quickly to prevent ice cream from becoming too soft. Freeze firm. Meanwhile, buzz raspberries and pineapple in a blender with lemon concentrate or puree through food mill. Strain to remove seeds and freeze until partially frozen, place in chilled bowl and beat slightly. Spoon over orange layer and refreeze. To the other quart of ice cream add almond and rum flavoring, cherries and nuts. Pour this over the raspberry layer and freeze overnight. Remove from freezer 2 hours before serving. Garnish with sweetened whipped cream, sugared fresh strawberries, and if you like, mint.

Shirley Mae Griffiths, Wilson Borough H. S.
Easton, Pennsylvania

LEMON ICE CREAM SANDWICH
Number of Servings — 12-14

4 eggs
4 lemons
1 c. sugar
Few grains of salt
1 lge. can evaporated milk, chilled and whipped
Vanilla wafers
Grated rind of lemon

Cook egg yolks, sugar, lemon juice, and salt to form custard. Add lemon rind. Cool. Add to whipped milk, fold in well-beaten egg whites (2 tablespoons sugar added to egg whites). Line refrigerator trays with crackers, pour in filling. Cover with cracker crumbs. Put in freezer. Freeze slightly.

Kay W. Holland, Dexter H. S.
Dexter, Georgia

MINT DAZZLER
Number of Servings — 12-15

2 c. vanilla wafer crumbs
¼ c. melted butter
½ c. butter
1½ c. sifted powdered sugar
3 eggs, slightly beaten
3 sq. unsweetened chocolate, melted
1½ c. whipping cream, whipped
1 pkg. (8 oz.) miniature marshmallows
½ c. crushed peppermint stick candy

Blend together crumbs and melted butter, press firmly in bottom of greased 8″ square pan. Cream together butter and sifted sugar thoroughly, add eggs and melted chocolate and beat until light and fluffy. Spoon over crumbs and set in freezer while whipping cream. Gently fold marshmallows into whipped cream, and spread over chocolate layer, Sprinkle with crushed candy, garnish with additional whipped cream if desired, freeze.

This recipe submitted by the following teachers:
Blanche Stroup, Tipton H. S.
Tipton, Indiana
Mrs. Kathryn Whitten, Hanford H. S.
Hanford, California
Mrs. J. C. Sutton, Delavan-Darien H. S.
Delavan, Wisconsin
Nancy Capell, Lowndes County H. S.
Fort Deposit, Alabama

FROZEN PEACHES 'N' CREAM
Number of Servings — 8
1½ c. crushed vanilla wafers
¼ c. melted butter or margarine
2 T. orange juice
1 T. lemon juice
½ lb. marshmallows (about 20)
1 c. crushed fresh peaches
1 c. heavy cream, whipped
Combine wafer crumbs and melted butter, pat evenly over sides and bottom of 8" square cake pan or 9" pie pan. Combine fruit juices, heat to boiling. Add marshmallows and stir until dissolved, cool, add peaches. Fold in whipped cream, pour into wafer crust. Freeze 3 to 4 hours or until firm.
This recipe submitted by the following teachers:
Mary Ada Parks, Anna-Jonesboro H. S.
Anna, Illinois
Mrs. Hazel Hasty, Urbana Sr. H. S.
Urbana, Illinois

FROZEN ORANGE PECAN MOLD
Number of Servings — 6-8
1 pkg. cream cheese (8 oz.)
¼ c. orange juice
½ c. pecans
1 can crushed pineapple (9 oz.)
½ c. pitted dates
¼ c. maraschino cherries
½ t. grated orange peel
1 c. cream, whipped
Combine cheese and orange juice, beat until fluffy. Fold in fruits and nuts and cream, freeze.
Mrs. Reva Wilson, Drummond H. S.
Drummond, Montana

PECAN ROLL
Number of Servings — 8
30 graham crackers
1 c. whipping cream, whipped
½ lb. (16) marshmallows, diced
1 small bottle cherries
1 c. nuts, chopped
Roll crackers to fine crumbs and reserve ½ cup. Mix crackers, cream marshmallows, cherries and nuts. Shape into a roll using reserved crumbs. Wrap in foil and freeze. Slice and serve with whipped cream.
Runette Davis, Glynn Co. Jr. H. S.
Brunswick, Georgia

PINEAPPLE MARSHMALLOW PUFFS
Number of Servings — 24
1 pkg. miniature marshmallows
1 c. crushed pineapple
1 c. whipping cream
½ c. walnuts, broken
¾ c. graham cracker crumbs
Drain pineapple, add to marshmallows, let stand 30 minutes in refrigerator. Fold this into whipped cream, add walnuts. Chill several hours, place some cracker crumbs on wax paper, use ice cream scoop to measure marshmallow mixture, drop mounds 1 at a time on crumbs and roll for individual servings, freeze. Remove 15 minutes before serving.
Mrs. Janice Ruelle, Colman H. S.
Colman, South Dakota

PINK ARCTIC FREEZE
Number of Servings — 8-10
2 3 oz. pkg. cream cheese
2 T. mayonnaise or salad dressing
2 T. sugar
1 lb. can (2 c.) whole cranberry sauce or 2 c. frozen strawberries
9 oz. can (1 c.) pineapple, crushed or pineapple tidbits, drained
½ c. chopped California walnuts
1 c. whipping cream, whipped
Soften cheese, blend in mayonnaise and sugar, add fruits and nuts, fold in whipped cream. Pour into 8½x2½x2½ loaf pan, freeze firm 6-8 hours or overnight. When ready to serve, let stand at room temperature about 15 minutes, turn out on lettuce, slice.
Mrs. Norma S. Brady, Martin H. S.
Laredo, Texas

PEPPERMINT-CHOCOLATE CREAM ROLL
Number of Servings — 8
½ pt. whipping cream
1 pkg. soft (white with pink strikes) peppermint candy
1 pkg. plain chocolate wafers
Crush about 10 peppermint candies between layers of wax paper with rolling pin. Whip cream until it forms peaks, sweeten to taste. Add crushed candy to the whipped cream. A small amount of red food coloring will give it more of a pink coloring. Roll out a sheet of wax paper, place approximately 1 tablespoon of cream mixture on top of 1 chocolate wafer. Continue this procedure making a short stack on the wax paper. As soon as the stack begins to tumble, tip it on its side and continue adding cream topped wafers so that it makes a long roll. Wrap the roll in the paper twisting the ends. Gently squeeze from both ends so that the cream will squeeze out to the edges of the wafers making an even roll. Place in freezer for 1 hour before serving. When serving, slice the roll diagonally about ¾" thick, creating a layered appearance. (Peppermint extract and green food coloring may be substituted for the candy).
Marjorie Peterson, Pacific H. S.
San Bernardino, California

SNOWBALLS
Number of Servings — 20
⅛ c. butter
⅔ c. sugar
2 egg yolks
1 c. drained pineapple
1 c. nuts
½ pt. whipping cream
Coconut (angel flake)
1 pkg. vanilla wafers
Mix butter, sugar, egg yolk, add pineapple and nuts, spread between vanilla wafers and freeze. Remove frozen cookies from freezer and cover with whipping cream. Sprinkle with coconut and freeze until ready to serve.
Mrs. Maxine Bottoms, Holdenville H. S.
Holdenville, Oklahoma

TARRAGON FROZEN DESSERT

Number of Servings — 6

1 lge. can crushed pineapple
1 pkg. marshmallows
1 c. walnuts or pecans
4 T. tarragon vinegar
4 egg yolks (beaten)
3 T. sugar
½ pt. whipping cream

Put pineapple in mixing bowl, cut marshmallows and pecans into small pieces, add to pineapple. Place in refrigerator to cool. Mix in double boiler vinegar, egg yolks and sugar, cook at medium heat until mixture is thick, cool. Whip cream, add fruit and cooked mixture to whipped cream. Place in ice tray and freeze. (May be made day before.)

Vickie C. Howard, Miami Jackson H. S.
Miami, Florida

FROZEN PINEAPPLE TORTE

Number of Servings — 9

3 egg yolks
Dash of salt
½ c. sugar
1 9 oz. can crushed pineapple
2 T. sugar
2 T. lemon juice
3 egg whites
1 c. heavy cream, whipped
2 c. vanilla wafer crumbs

Beat egg yolks, salt and ½ cup sugar, add syrup from pineapple and lemon juice. Cook over hot, not boiling water, until mixture coats the spoon, stirring constantly. Add pineapple, cool, make meringue of egg whites and 2 tablespoons sugar. Fold in whipped cream and custard mixture, coat sides of refirgerator tray with wax paper. Cover bottom of tray with half of the wafer crumbs. Pour in custard mixture and cover with remaining crumbs, freeze firmly about 3 to 4 hours. Can be made day before using.

This recipe submitted by the following teachers:
Mrs. Miriam Bobo Templeton,
Hickory Tavern H. S.
Gray Court, South Carolina
Mrs. Dorothye Hansen, Marshall H. S.
Marshall, Michigan

FROZEN PINEAPPLE TORTE

Number of Servings — 6-8

3 egg yolks
Dash of salt
½ c. sugar
1-9 oz. can crushed pineapple, drained
2 T. lemon juice
3 egg whites, beaten stiff
2 T. sugar
1 c. heavy cream, whipped
2 c. vanilla wafer crumbs

Beat egg yolks, salt, and ½ cup sugar. Add syrup from pineapple and lemon juice. Cook over hot, not boiling water until mixture coats spoon, stirring constantly. Add pineapple. Cool. Make meringue of egg whites and 2 tablespoons of sugar. Fold in whipped cream and custard mixture. Coat sides of oiled refrigerator tray with wafer crumbs. Spread half the remaining crumbs over bottom. Pour in custard mixture. Cover with remaining crumbs. Freeze firm, about 3 to 4 hours.

Neva T. Bailey, Hicks Memorial H. S.
Autaugaville, Alabama

FROZEN LEMON TORTE

Number of Servings — 8

¾ c. vanilla wafer crumbs
3 egg yolks, well beaten
¼ c. lemon juice
Grated rind of 1 lemon
⅛ t. salt
½ c. sugar
3 egg whites, beaten stiff
½ c. evaporated milk

Line greased refrigerator tray or dish with half the wafer crumbs. Combine egg yolks and lemon juice, rind, salt, and sugar. Cook in double boiler until thick. Cool. Whip the chilled milk, add beaten egg whites, and then the cooled lemon mixture. Pour over crumbs in tray and cover with remaining crumbs. Cover with Saran wrap or aluminum foil and freeze. Serve in finger width slices or cut in squares. Can be stored 1 month.

This recipe submitted by the following teachers:
Mrs. Florene Gipson, Benton H. S.
Benton, Arkansas
Ruth Finley, Alexandria H. S.
Alexandria, Alabama

LUSCH TORTE

Number of Servings — 12

½ lb. butter or margarine
1 lb. powdered sugar
½ lb. vanilla wafers
1 c. broken pecans
6 egg yolks
4 egg whites
1 t. vanilla

Crush wafers into crumbs, saving ½ cup to top torte. Add 3 tablespoons pecans, 2 tablespoons sugar, 2 tablespoons butter. Press into the bottom of 8x8x2 square glass pan. Bake in 300°F. oven until slightly browned, then cool. Take out ½ cup sugar for meringue. Then take remaining sugar and butter and put in electric mixer. Start at slow speed and increase to fast speed gradually. Add egg yolks, 1 at a time, whipping thoroughly. Fold in remaining pecans. Beat egg whites until stiff. Add sugar reserved for meringue. Gradually add meringue to butter mixture. Pour over wafer crust. Top with remaining crumbs and nuts. Cover with aluminum foil and place in freezer for 12 hours. Cut in small squares to serve.

Mrs. Oleta Moore Smith, O'Donnell H. S.
O'Donnell, Texas

Tortes & Meringues

ALMOND TORTE

Number of Servings — 8

⅞ c. flour, sifted
2 t. baking powder
¼ t. salt
⅓ c. butter
½ c. sugar
4 egg yolks
1 t. vanilla
¼ c. milk

Sift flour, baking powder, and salt together. Cream butter, add sugar gradually and cream well. Add unbeaten egg yolks and beat thoroughly. Add vanilla. Add sifted ingredients alternately with milk. Pour into 2 loose bottom layer cake pans and cover each with meringue. Pile meringue in the center of each layer. Spread to within 1" of side of pan. Place almond halves on edge into meringue. Bake in moderate oven, 350°F. for 35 minutes. When cool serve with whipped cream, fresh berries, or ice cream between layers.

Meringue:
4 egg whites
1 c. sugar
½ c. blanched almond halves

Beat egg whites until stiff but not dry, and add sugar gradually.

Eileen Anderson, Wells H. S.
Wells, Minnesota

AMBER FRUIT TORTE

Number of Servings — 8-9

1 c. sugar
1 egg, beaten
1 can fruit cocktail mix (lge. No. 2½ size can) well drained
1 c. flour
½ t. salt
¾ t. soda
4 T. brown sugar
¼ c. chopped walnuts

Blend sugar and beaten egg, add the drained cocktail mix and the sifted dry ingredients. Spread in square 9" pan. Mix the brown sugar and nuts and sprinkle on the top. Bake at 325°F. for 15 minutes then reduce to 300°F. and bake for another 45 minutes. Serve with whipped cream or ice cream on top.

Mrs. Avis Thompson, Tigerton H. S.
Tigerton, Wisconsin

APPLE-DATE TORTE

Number of Servings — 6

4 c. diced tart apples
1 c. sugar
½ c. sifted enriched flour
2 t. baking powder
1 egg
1 T. melted butter or margarine
1 t. vanilla
½ c. coarsely chopped nuts
½ c. chopped dates (may be omitted if desired)

Wash apples. Pare if skins aren't tender. Cut in 8 sections. Remove core and cut each section in 4 or 5 pieces. Combine ingredients in bowl. Stir until thoroughly mixed. Do not beat. Turn into greased 8x8x2 pan. Bake in moderate oven 350°F. about 40 minutes until apples are tender (test with fork). Cut in generous squares and serve hot or cold with cream, whipped cream or vanilla ice cream.

This recipe submitted by the following teachers:
Mrs. Steve Nickisch, Napoleon, Public H. S.
Napoleon, North Dakota
Mrs. Gladys Helm, Milford H. S.
Milford, Nebraska

APPLE TORTE

Number of Servings — 6

1 egg
¾ c. sugar
¾ c. apples
½ c. flour
1 t. baking powder
Pinch of salt
¼ t. almond extract
¼ c. walnut meats

Beat egg lightly. Add sugar and apples. Stir in flour, baking powder, salt, almond extract, walnut meats. Mix well. Pour into greased pie tin. Bake 25 minutes at 350°F. oven. Serve with whipped cream or ice cream. Caramel ice cream makes a good topping.

This recipe submitted by the following teachers:
Janet King, Hastings Public School
Hastings, Minnesota
Nancy Kimbrell, Florida High FSU Univ. School
Tallahassee, Florida

BUTTERSCOTCH NUT TORTE

Number of Servings — 12

6 eggs, separated
1½ c. sugar
1 t. baking powder
2 t. vanilla
1 t. almond extract
2 c. graham cracker crumbs
1 c. broken nut meats
1 pt. whipping cream

Beat egg yolks well, add sugar, baking powder and flavoring. Beat egg whites enough to hold a peak. Fold into yolks. Add crumbs, then nuts. Line two 9" layer pans with wax paper. Pour in cake batter. Bake at 325°F. 30 or 35 minutes. Cool. Whip whipping cream sweetened with 3 tablespoons powdered sugar, and put between layers, on top and sides.

Sauce:
1 c. brown sugar
¼ c. butter
¼ c. water
1 T. flour
¼ c. orange juice (1 medium orange)
1 well beaten egg
½ t. vanilla

Mix well and boil until thick enough to pour. When cool, pour over whipped cream.

This recipe submitted by the following teachers:
Mrs. Jo Anne Sandager, Stillwater Jr. H. S.
Stillwater, Minnesota
Bobbie Jean Pope, Holly Pond H. S.
Holly Pond, Alabama

BLUEBERRY TORTE
Number of Servings — 6-8

2 c. or 20 graham crackers, crushed
½ c. melted butter
½ c. brown sugar, firmly packed
8 oz. cream cheese
½ c. granulated sugar
2 eggs
2 T. lemon juice
1 No. 2 can blueberry pie filling

Mix crumbs with melted butter and brown sugar. Pack sugar, butter, and crumbs firmly in 11x13 baking dish. Mix in bowl the cream cheese and granulated sugar until smooth. Add eggs one at a time, beat after each addition. Add lemon juice. Pour mixture over crumb mixture. Bake 20 minutes at 350°F. Cool. Spoon blueberry pie filling over top of mixture. Serve with ice cream or whipped cream.

Jo Ann Kreidler, Three Rivers H. S.
Coshocton, Ohio

CHARME TORTE
Number of Servings — 8

4 egg whites
1 c. sugar
2 t. baking powder
Pinch of salt
1 t. white vinegar
1 t. vanilla

Sift together 2 or 3 times the sugar, baking powder, and salt. Beat egg whites until stiff. Add sugar mixture a tablespoon at a time, and continue to beat. Add vinegar and vanilla. Pour into shallow baking dish. Turn oven off and leave dish in oven over night or at least 8 hours without opening oven door. Cut into squares. Serve with fresh, frozen or canned fruit or ice cream. Or use ice cream topped with fruit.

Alma Keys, Director, Home Economics Education
State Department of Education
Little Rock, Arkansas

CHERRY TORTE
Number of Servings — 6-8

4 egg whites
¼ t. salt
¼ t. cream of tartar
1 c. sugar

Have egg whites at room temperature. Beat whites until frothy, add salt and cream of tartar. Beat until soft peaks form. Add sugar slowly, continue beating for 10-15 minutes. Add extract. Pour in buttered 9″ pie pan. Spread evenly over bottom of pan, and pile high on sides. Place in hot oven, 450°F. Close door turn off heat. Let stand in closed oven 5 hours or over night.

Filling:
½ c. sugar
2 T. cornstarch
Dash of salt
⅗ c. cherry juice
1 (1 lb.) can pie cherries
1 c. heavy cream
1 T. butter extract

Combine sugar, cornstarch, and salt. Add cherry juice, cook until clear and thick, stirring constantly. Add butter extract and cherries. Chill. Pour into torte shell. Top with whipped cream to which sugar and extract have been added. Chill before serving.

Topping:
1 c. heavy cream (whipped)
2 T. sugar
¼ t. almond extract

Mrs. Blanche Gavin Sims,
Waynesboro-Central H. S.
Waynesboro, Mississippi

CHERRY TORTE DELIGHT
Number of Servings — 8-10

3 egg whites
1 c. sugar
½ t. cream of tartar
1 c. soda cracker crumbs
⅛ c. nuts, chopped
1 pkg. whip mix (such as Dream)
½ t. vanilla
1 can cherry pie mix

Mix and beat egg whites, sugar, cream of tartar. Add to soda crackers and nuts. Mix well and spread on well greased cookie sheet. Bake at 325°F. for 25 minutes. Cool well. Whip, whip mix according to directions on package, add vanilla. Spread on cake mixture alternately with cherry pie mix. Refrigerate.

Elaine Roberts, Mt. Iron H. S.
Mt. Iron, Minnesota

CHOCOLATE CHIP DATE TORTE
Number of Servings — 15-18

1 c. finely chopped dates
1 c. boiling water
1 t. baking soda
1¾ c. sifted flour
½ t. salt
1 c. shortening or butter
¼ c. cocoa (may use less)
1 c. sugar
2 eggs
1 t. vanilla
½-1 c. finely chopped nuts
1 (6 oz. pkg.) semi-sweet chocolate chips

Mix together dates, water and soda. Cool. Sift flour and salt together. Cream shortening, cocoa and sugar together until fluffy. Add eggs and vanilla and continue beating. Add the flour alternately with the date mixture, beating after each addition. Do not over beat. Pour the batter into a 13x9x2 pan which has been thoroughly greased and floured. Sprinkle nuts and chips over the top and press lightly into the batter. Bake at 350°F. 40-45 minutes. Serve as a dessert, plain or with whipped cream. May be cut into bars.

This recipe submitted by the following teachers:
Bertha Hundley, Red Bank H. S.
Chattanooga, Tennessee
Mrs. Ramona Flanum, Anoka Sr. H. S.
Anoka, Minnesota
Ethel Bettencourt, Artesia H. S.
Artesia, California

CHOCOLATE TORTE ROYALE
Number of Servings — 8-10

Cinnamon Meringue Shell:
2 egg whites
¼ t. salt
½ t. vinegar
½ c. sugar
¼ t. cinnamon

Cover cookie sheet with piece of heavy paper. Draw an 8″ circle in center. Beat egg whites, salt, and vinegar until soft peaks form. Blend sugar and cinnamon. Gradually add to egg whites, beating until very stiff peaks form and all sugar is dissolved. Spread within circle making the bottom ½″ thick and mounting around edge, making it ¾″ high. For trim form ridges on outside with teaspoon. Bake in very slow oven 275°F for 1 hour, turn off heat and let dry in oven (door closed) about 2 hours. Peel off paper.

Twin Cream Filling:
1-6 oz. pkg. (1 c.) semi-sweet chocolate pieces
2 beaten egg yolks
¼ c. water
1 c. heavy cream
¼ c. sugar
¼ t. cinnamon

Melt the chocolate over hot, not boiling water. Cool slightly. Spread 2 tablespoons of the chocolate over bottom of cooled meringue shell. To remaining chocolate, add egg yolks and water. Blend. Chill until mixture is thick. Combine cream, sugar, and cinnamon. Whip until stiff. Spread half over chocolate in shell. Fold remainder into chocolate mixture and spread on top. Chill several hours or over night. Garnish with whipped cream and pecans.

This recipe submitted by the following teachers:
Mary L. Robison, Nappanee H. S.
Nappanee, Indiana
June Lawrence, Fremont H. S.
Fremont, Michigan
Mrs. Hollis Williams, Cooper H. S.
Cooper, Texas

DATE-NUT TORTE
Number of Servings — 8

½ c. flour
1 t. baking powder
½ t. salt
3 eggs
1 c. sugar
1 c. dates, chopped
1 c. English walnuts, chopped
2 T. lemon juice

Sift together flour, baking powder, and salt. Beat eggs until light. Add sugar, dates, and nuts. Stir in flour. Spread the batter evenly in a well greased jelly roll pan. Bake 30 minutes at 350°F. Spread lemon juice over baked torte. Serve cold with ice cream or whipped cream. (Mellows in 24 hours.) It is good cut in small strips and served as a bar cookie.

Mrs. Mary Sprague, Parksley H. S.
Parksley, Virginia

COCONUT CRUNCH TORTE
Number of Servings — 6-8

1 c. graham cracker crumbs
½ c. chopped moist coconut
½ c. chopped walnuts (or pecans)
4 egg whites
⅛ t. salt
1 t. vanilla
1 c. sugar
1 pt. butter-brickle ice cream (optional)

Combine cracker crumbs, coconut, and nuts. Beat egg whites with salt and vanilla until foamy. Gradually add sugar and continue beating until stiff peaks are formed. Fold crumb mixture into egg white mixture. Spread in well greased 9″ pie plate. Bake about 30 minutes at 350°F. Cut in wedges, Serve hot or cold, with or without ice cream.

This recipe submitted by the following teachers:
Mrs. Edith Conner, Hooks H. S.
Hooks, Texas
Manona Brewer, Orestimba Union H. S.
Newman, California
Blanche Maxwell, Spring Valley Public Schools
Spring Valley, Wisconsin
Mrs. Barbara Williams, Catlin Twp. H. S.
Catlin, Illinois
Mrs. Richard P. Hempel, Lennox H. S.
Lennox, South Dakota

DATE-NUT SODA CRACKER TORTE
Number of Servings — 12-16

1 c. white sugar
1 t. baking powder
14 soda crackers (rolled)
12 dates
½ c. nuts
4 egg whites

Mix sugar, baking powder, dates (cut fine) and chopped nuts. Add the mixture to the crackers and blend. Beat egg whites stiff into the above mixture. Pour into an 8x8x2 pan and bake 30 minutes at 350°.

Florence M. Stewart, Wilder H. S.
Caldwell, Idaho

DATE-NUT TORTE
Number of Servings — 12

4 eggs
1 c. sugar
1 c. fine dry bread crumbs
1 t. baking powder
2 c. finely cut pitted dates
1 c. cut up walnuts

Beat eggs thoroughly. Gradually beat in sugar. Mix bread crumbs and baking powder, stir into egg mixture. Mix in dates and walnuts. Spread in greased pan (9x9x1¾). Bake at 350°F. 35 minutes or until set. Cut in oblongs, 3x2. Serve cool with whipped cream or ice cream.

Agnes Falkowski, Southern Door H. S.
Brussels, Wisconsin

GRAHAM CRACKER TORTE
Number of Servings — 6
24 crushed graham crackers
¼ c. sugar
½ c. melted butter (or margarine)
⅛ c. flour (or ¼ c. cornstarch)
⅔ c. sugar
¼ t. salt
2 c. scalded milk
3 beaten egg yolks
2 T. butter
½ t. vanilla
3 stiffly beaten egg whites
6 T. sugar

Mix crackers, ¼ cup sugar, and ½ cup melted butter and save ¼ of it. Pat the rest in bottom and on sides of pan. Make a white sauce of flour, ⅔ cup sugar, salt, 2 tablespoons butter and scalded milk. Add vanilla and egg yolks and pour into cracker crumb crust. Make a meringue of the egg whites and 6 tablespoons sugar and spread on top. Sprinkle top with remaining crumbs. Bake for ½ hour at 350°F. Cool and serve.

Mrs. Helen Bell, South Jr. H. S.
Grants Pass, Oregon

HEATH TORTE
Number of Servings — 12
4 egg whites
¼ t. cream of tartar
¼ t. salt
⅔ c. granulated sugar
⅔ c. confectioners' sugar
½ t. vanilla

Have ingredients at room temperature. Beat egg whites until foamy. Add cream of tartar and salt. Beat to distribute evenly. Add granulated sugar very gradually. Continue beating while adding confectioners' sugar gradually. Continue beating, add vanilla, and beat until mixture is thick, and stands in stiff peaks. Requires 10 to 15 minutes. Bake two 8″ shells 1 hour in slow oven. Turn off heat. Cool 1 hour. Bake on aluminum foil or brown paper.

Filling:
Whip 1 cup cream. Sweeten with 2 tablespoons confectioners' sugar, or to taste. Spread on meringue layer with whipped cream. Sprinkle with ½ crushed Heath candy bar. Add second torte layer. Spread with remaining whipped cream. Sprinkle with remaining ½ crushed Heath candy. Chill before serving. May be kept in refrigerator 1 or 2 days.

Sara Thompson, Wallins H. S.
Wallins, Kentucky

HUGUENOT TORTE
Number of Servings — 16
4 eggs
3 c. sugar
8 T. flour
5 t. baking powder
½ t. salt
2 c. chopped tart cooking apples
2 c. chopped pecans or walnuts
2 t. vanilla

Beat whole eggs until very frothy and lemon colored. Add other ingredients in above order. Pour into 2 well butterd baking pans about 8x12. Bake at 325°F. about 45 minutes or until crusty and brown. To serve, scoop up with pancake turner (keeping crusty part on top) and cover with unsweetened whipped cream.

This recipe submitted by the following teachers:
Mrs. Mary C. Williamson, Hallsboro H. S.
Hallsboro, North Carolina
Mrs. Betty Q. Weathers, Bowman H. S.
Bowman, South Carolina
Marthanne Limehouse, St. Paul's H. S.
Yonges Island, South Carolina
Lenda Boozer, Bennettsville H. S.
Bennettsville, South Carolina

LEMON ANGEL TORTE
Number of Servings — 8
4 egg whites
¾ c. sugar
¼ t. salt
¼ t. cream of tartar
1 c. heavy cream, whipped

Preheat oven to 450°F. Place egg whites, sugar, salt, and cream of tartar in a small mixing bowl. Beat at high speed until stiff peaks form (15 minutes). Spread in well buttered 9″ pie plate. Place in oven and turn off heat. Let stand in oven 5 hours or over night. (Do not peek.) Fill torte with half of the whipped cream, then lemon filling, then remaining cream. Chill at least 5 hours or put in freezer.

Lemon Filling:
4 egg yolks
½ c. sugar
Dash of salt
1 T. grated lemon rind
3 T. lemon juice

Beat egg yolks until thick in double boiler. Gradually beat in sugar, salt, lemon rind, and juice. Cook until thick, about 5 minutes. Cool.

This recipe submitted by the following teachers:
Donna G. Bennett, Elmira H. S.
Elmira, Oregon
Mrs. Winifred E. Leutz, Ephrata H. S.
Ephrata, Pennsylvania

NUT TORTE (Roll or Stack)
Number of Servings — 6
1 c. sugar
½ t. vanilla
1 c. nuts, chopped fine
1 c. soda crackers, rolled fine
4 eggs, separated

Add sugar, vanilla, nuts, and crumbs to well beaten egg yolks. Fold in stiffly beaten whites. Line shallow pan 10x15 with oiled, floured wax paper. Bake torte 15 minutes at 350°F. Roll as for jelly roll or cut into oblongs and stack with rich chocolate-butter-confectioners' sugar frosting between layers or on top.

Mrs. Mildred Williams, Mt. Washington H. S.
Mt. Washington, Kentucky

MAHOGANY TORTE
Number of Servings — 16
1 c. sugar
3 T. margarine
1 egg
1 c. buttermilk
2 sq. chocolate, melted
1 t. soda
1 t. baking powder
1¼ c. flour

Mix in order given. Sift soda and baking powder with flour. Bake in pan 8x12 at 400°F. Spread on the following mixture as soon as cake is removed from the oven.

1 c. dates, cut fine
1 c. sugar
1 c. water
1 c. pecans

Boil dates, sugar, and water until thick and add pecans. Spread on hot cake. Cut in squares and top with whipped cream.

Leah Hamilton, Mercedes H. S.
Mercedes, Texas

MOCHA TORTE
Number of Servings — 10-12
1-1 lb. pkg. brownie mix
2 eggs
¼ c. water
¾ c. coarse walnuts
2 c. whipping cream
½ c. brown sugar
2 T. instant coffee
¼ c. chopped walnuts

Stir brownie mix, eggs, water, coarse walnuts together and pour into two 9″ well greased cake pans. Bake 20 minutes at 350°F. Whip cream until thick. Gradually add brown sugar (packed) and instant coffee. Continue beating cream until it is of spreading consistency. Spread between and on top of cooled brownies which have been cut into 2 layers. Dot top with walnuts. Chill at least 6 hours before serving.

Mrs. Marilyn Telander, Ellsworth H. S.
Ellsworth, Illinois

RASPBERRY TORTE
Number of Servings — 8
1 qt. berries
1 c. water
1½ c. sugar
2 T. cornstarch
2 c. flour
1 c. brown sugar
¾ c. butter

Boil the water, sugar, and cornstarch until clear and then pour over uncrushed fruit. Cool. Mix the flour, brown sugar, and butter as for a pie crust. Set aside 1 cup of this mixture. Line an 8x8x2 pan with the remaining mixture. Add the fruit mixture and sprinkle the 1 cup of the mixture on top. Bake at 375°F. for 30-35 minutes. Apples and rhubarb are also very good.

Mrs. Beverly Wruck, Clintonville Sr. H. S.
Clintonville, Wisconsin

STRAWBERRY TORTE CAKE
Number of Servings — 12
1 pkg. white cake mix
2 egg yolks
1½ t. almond flavoring
4 egg whites
¼ t. cream of tartar
1 c. sugar
½ t. nutmeg
2 c. heavy cream, whipped or dessert topping mix
Few drops red food coloring
1 qt. strawberries, washed and hulled

Mix the cake according to package directions, except use 2 egg yolks instead of egg whites. Add 1 teaspoon almond flavoring. Place batter in three 9″ layer cake pans which have been lined with wax paper. Refrigerate until the meringue is ready. Beat egg whites with cream of tartar until frothy. Gradually add sugar, 2 tablespoons at a time, beating well after each addition, until all sugar is dissolved and a very stiff meringue is formed. Fold in the nutmeg and spread the meringue evenly over the tops of the 3 layers. Bake at 325°F. for 40 minutes. Cool slightly, loosen edges and turn out of pans. Cool completely. Whip the cream with the remaining ½ teaspoon almond flavoring and a few drops of red food coloring. Cut berries in half and sugar lightly. Spread a little of the pink whipped cream on the top of a layer. Add a few berries, then place the next layer on top. Repeat. When the third layer is in place, frost the sides of the cake with the rest of the whipped cream and make a crown effect on top with small spoonfuls of cream. Mound the remaining berries in the center top of the cake.

Mrs. J. C. Jones, Jr., Greene County H. S.
Eutaw, Alabama

TORTION TORTE
Number of Servings — 6-8
7 egg whites
1 c. sugar
1 T. vinegar
1 t. vanilla
1 c. whipping cream
½ c. sugar
½ c. chopped pecans
Cherries if desired

Beat eggs very stiff. Add sugar gradually, then vinegar and vanilla last. Continue until mixture is very stiff. Have ready 2 rectangles of heavy wax paper, 12x9. Wet the paper with water and place on a greased cookie sheet. Divide egg mixture into 2 equal parts and shape in twin rectangles on the wet wax paper. Bake 325°F. for 1 hour. When baked, place one meringue on a platter, peel off paper, put other meringue on another platter. Cool. Put together with whipped cream mixture. Whip cream, add sugar and pecans and vanilla. Place half between meringues and remaining on top. Decorate with cherries.

Mrs. Lee Durham, Lincoln H. S.
Philadelphia, Pennsylvania

ZWIEBACK TORTE

Number of Servings — 12

6 eggs
2 c. sugar
1 pkg. Zwieback (crushed)
2 t. baking powder
½ t. salt
1½ c. chopped nuts
1 t. vanilla extract
2 t. brandy extract

Cream eggs and sugar well. Add Zwieback, baking powder, salt, chopped nuts, vanilla, and extracts. Bake at 350°F. 25 minutes. Use a long baking pan. Cut into squares and serve with ice cream or top with whipped cream.

WadeDelle Squires, Bamberg H. S.
Bamberg, South Carolina

MERINGUE SHELLS

Number of Servings — 12

6 egg whites
2 c. granulated sugar
1 T. vinegar
1 t. vanilla

Beat egg whites very stiff, add sugar sifting it in gradually, add vinegar and vanilla. Beat 15 minutes, with electric mixer on high, after all ingredients are added. Shape on unoiled brown paper (may use the inside of a paper sack). Hold teaspoon vertically and make depression on each shell. Bake at 200-225°F. for 1 hour. Turn off heat but allow shells to remain in the oven. Turn heat on again and bake another hour. Turn off this time and allow to cool in the oven. Fill with favorite filling, lemon, pineapple, or fill with ice cream or fresh fruit.

Mrs. Evelyn W. Newsom, Mt. Vernon H. S.
Mt. Vernon, Texas

MERINGUE TORTE—MERINGUES

Number of Servings — 12

6 egg whites (¾ c.)
2 c. sugar
1½ t. lemon juice or vinegar

Beat egg whites until stiff (hold a point), gradually beat in half of sugar, beat in the lemon juice or vinegar a little at a time (adding alternately with the remaining sugar). Beat until very stiff and glossy. Bake in 275°F. oven (very slow oven) using two 9" round layer cake pans lined with brown paper. Drop lightly by spoonfuls onto paper lined pans. Bake layers 60 minutes or until lightly or delicately browned and crusty. Cool. Remove from pan by using a spatula to lift from paper. Serve filled with ice cream and fresh berries or cut up fruit. Individual meringues may be baked by using a baking sheet lined with brown paper, drop by small spoonfuls in circles or heart shapes on the paper (draw pattern on brown paper of circles or hearts). Fill in outlines with meringue.

Mary R. Cole, North Marshall H. S.
Calvert City, Kentucky

ALMOND ANGEL PIE

Number of Servings — 6

3 egg whites, beaten slightly
1 t. baking powder
½ c. sugar
½ c. nuts, chopped
1 t. almond flavoring
Vanilla cracker crumb crust
1 c. whipping cream

Mix baking powder, sugar and flavoring into stiffly beaten egg whites. Pour into crumb crust and bake at 325°F. until light brown. Cool. Add whipped cream on top and sprinkle nuts over cream generously.

Mrs. Elizabeth L. Bateman, Alice Drive Jr. H. S.
Sumter, South Carolina

ANGEL FOOD PIE

Number of Servings — 6

1½ c. crushed graham crackers
½ c. or ¼ lb. butter
⅓ c. powdered sugar

Mix together until mass sticks together. Pack in pie pan and smooth with back of spoon. Do not let crust extend to the top rim of pan.

Filling:
4 egg whites
½ c. granulated sugar
1 t. vanilla

Beat egg whites until stiff. Add sugar gradually and beat until very thick. Add vanilla. Pour into graham cracker crust. Bake at 300°F. for 30 minutes or until lightly brown. After pie cools, put in refrigerator. These pies are best made the day before they are to be served. Just before serving, whip 1 cup cream and add 3 tablespoons sugar and 1 teaspoon vanilla. Spread over top of pie and sprinkle with ground or finely chopped pecans.

Zona Beth Cates, Tempe Union H. S.
Tempe, Arizona

ANGEL PIE

Number of Servings — 4-6

4 egg whites
¼ t. salt
¼ t. cream of tartar
1 c. sugar
½ t. vanilla
1 c. whipping cream
4 T. sugar
¼ t. vanilla

Beat egg whites until stiff enough to peak. Add cream of tartar and salt. Add sugar gradually beating slowly: Add vanilla. Pile on brown paper in the desired shape. Bake 1 hour at 375°F. Turn upside down. Carefully remove paper. Cool thoroughly. Cover with whipped cream, to which has been added sugar and vanilla. Refrigerate 12-24 hours. Garnish with fresh fruit when served. (Strawberries, raspberries, etc.)

Mrs. Geraldine Peery, Edison H. S.
San Antonio, Texas

ANGEL FOOD PIE

2 egg whites
½ c. sugar (or less)
1 t. vanilla
1 baked pastry shell

Beat egg whites until almost stiff, add sugar and vanilla. Beat until mixture stands alone. Pour into baked pastry shell. Place in slow oven 300°F. and bake until the whites are slightly browned, about 30 minutes. Remove from oven and allow to cool.

Topping:
1 c. whipping cream
¼ c. sugar
½ t. vanilla
1 c. nut meats (black walnuts are best)

Whip cream, add sugar and vanilla. Spread evenly over the cooled pie, sprinkle with nuts.

Janiece Helm, Walkerton H. S.
Walkerton, Indiana

ANGEL FOOD PIE

Number of Servings — 6

Crust:
4 egg whites
¼ t. cream of tartar
1 c. sugar

Beat egg whites until frothy, add cream of tartar and beat until stiff. Gradually add sugar and beat until stiff and glossy, spread in greased pie pan. Bake 1 hour at 275°F. for first 20 minutes, then 300°F. for rest of time, cool.

Filling:
4 egg yolks
1 whole egg
½ c. sugar
3 T. lemon juice
2 t. grated rind
1 c. cream (whipped)

Beat egg yolks and whole egg until lemon colored. Beat in sugar, lemon juice and grated rind. Cook in double boiler, stir constantly, cool. Place filling in baked shell over top, add whipped cream. Place in refrigerator overnight, serve cold.

Mrs. Anna B. Whitescarver, Flemington, H. S.
Flemington, West Virginia

ANGEL COCONUT PIE ALA MODE

Number of Servings — 6

4 egg whites
1 t. vanilla
1 c. sugar
¼ t. salt
1 c. graham cracker crumbs
½ c. coconut
½ c. nuts, coarsely chopped
Vanilla ice cream

Beat egg whites until foamy, add vanilla and continue beating, gradually adding sugar and salt, beat until stiff. Fold in other ingredients (except ice cream). Pour into a greased pie pan and bake for 30 minutes at 325°F. Cut in wedges and serve with ice cream.

Claudia Tharpe, Bunker Hill H. S.
Claremont, North Carolina

CHOCOLATE ANGEL PIE

Number of Servings — 6-8

Meringue shell:
2 egg whites
⅛ t. cream of tartar
½ c. sugar
½ c. finely chopped pecans
⅛ t. vanilla

Combine egg whites, salt, cream of tartar in mixing bowl, beat until foamy. Add sugar 2 tablespoons at a time, beating after each addition until sugar is blended. Beat until mixture stands in very stiff peaks, fold in finely chopped pecans and vanilla. Spoon into lightly greased 8" pie pan, make a nest like shell, building up ½" above edge of pan. Bake in slow oven 300°F. 50-55 minutes. Cool to room temperature.

Chocolate angel filling:
1 4 oz. cake semi-sweet chocolate
3 T. water
1 t. vanilla
1 c. whipping cream

Place chocolate and water in saucepan over low heat, stir until chocolate is melted. Cool until thickened, add vanilla. Whip cream, fold chocolate mixture into whipped cream, pile into meringue shell. Chill at least 2 hours before serving. Optional: Garnish with ¼ cup whipped cream, 1 tablespoon shaved bitter chocolate, and ¼ cup chopped pecans.

This recipe submitted by the following teachers:
Mrs. Velma Shaffer,
State Supervisor, Home Economics Education
Little Rock, Arkansas
Katie Jackson, Cass City H. S.
Cass City, Michigan
Mrs. Lillian Pursley, Rush Springs H. S.
Rush Springs, Oklahoma
Mrs. Sara Edge, Lafayette H. S.
Lafayette, Alabama
Ruth Averitt, Lafayette Sr. H. S.
Lexington, Kentucky
Mildred Snell, Fitch H. S.
Youngstown, Ohio
Marjorie Scott, Bethany H. S.
Bethany, Illinois

CHOCOLATE MERINGUE PIE

Number of Servings — 3

Crust:
3 egg whites
⅛ t. cream of tartar
1 c. sugar
1 t. vanilla
1 c. chopped nuts
18 soda crackers (crushed)

Beat egg whites until stiff, add cream of tartar. Gradually add sugar and beat, add vanilla. Fold in chopped nuts and soda crackers. Grease pie plate with oleo and spread mixture into the plate. Bake 35 minutes at 325°F.

Filling:
½ pt. whipping cream
4 T. sugar
2 T. cocoa
½ t. vanilla

(Continued on Next Page)

1 can coconut

Mix ingredients together (except vanilla), and leave in refrigerator for 1 hours or longer, then beat. Add vanilla, put in cooled crust, sprinkle with 1 can coconut, chill and serve.

Mrs. Edith C. McMahan, Goodwater H. S.
Goodwater, Alabama

ANGEL LEMON PIE
Number of Servings — 6

Crust:
4 egg whites
1 c. sugar
¼ t. cream of tartar or ½ t. baking powder
Beat egg whites until frothy, add cream of tartar. Add sugar gradually, beating until stiff but not dry, turn into a well oiled 9″ pie pan. Bake at 250°F. for 50-60 minutes, cool on wire racks, (Note: Crust puffs up, then as it cools it drops back down.)

Filling:
3 T. cornstarch
1 c. sugar
1½ c. boiling water
3 egg yolks, well beaten
Juice and grated rind of 1 lemon (rind may be omitted)
1 T. butter

Mix cornstarch and sugar thoroughly in a saucepan, add boiling water. Mix well and put on to boil, cook 2 minutes, add well beaten egg yolks and lemon, add butter. Add to cornstarch mixture, remove from heat and cool. Pour in baked pastry shell and top with whipped cream if desired.

Dorene Nehr, Three Rivers H. S.
Three Rivers, Texas

ANGEL MERINGUE CAKE
Number of Servings — 10-12

4 eggs, separated
¼ t. salt
1½ c. sugar
1 t. vinegar
1 t. almond flavoring
¼ t. cream of tartar
Whipped cream
Cream pie filling (your favorite)

Add salt to egg whites. Beat until foamy. Add cream of tartar. Blend until it forms a peak, but not stiff. Add sugar gradually. Continue beating until stiff. Add flavoring and vinegar. Beat until thick, stiff and dry. Line three 9″ cake pans with wax paper. Fill pans half full. Bake at 275°F. for 1½ hours. Make your favorite cream pie filling. Alternate layers of meringue, pie filling and whipped cream until all layers are covered. Cover with whipped cream. Chill. This cake may be frozen for later use.

Mrs. Lillian Wise, Rabun Gap H. S.
Rabun Gap, Georgia

ANGEL NUT PIE
Number of Servings — 6-8

3 egg whites
1 c. sugar
½ t. baking powder
20 Ritz crackers
1 c. chopped nuts
1 t. vanilla

Beat egg whites until stiff. Add sugar and baking powder to beaten egg whites. Crush the crackers, add to above mixture with nuts and vanilla. Pour into well greased or buttered 9″ aluminum pie pan and bake 30 minutes at 350°F. Cool.

Topping:
½ pt. whipping cream
2 t. sugar
1 t. vanilla
¼ c. (or less) chopped nuts

Whip the cream with sugar and vanilla. Spread over pie and sprinkle with chopped nuts. Refrigerate at least 3 hours before serving.

Ruth Hanegan, Hope H. S.
Hope, Arkansas

ANGEL PECAN PIE
Number of Servings — 6

3 egg whites
¼ t. cream of tartar
1 c. sugar
16 (2″ sq. crackers broken up)
1 t. vanilla
1 c. chopped pecans

Beat egg whites until foamy and add cream of tartar. Beat until stiff or holds peak. Gradually add sugar. Add vanilla and chopped pecans. Fold in cracker crumbs. Pour into slightly buttered pie pan. Bake at 325°F. 35 minutes. Cool and cover with whipped cream topping.

Topping:
1 c. whipping cream
3 T. sugar
½ t. vanilla

Whip cream until it thickens. Add sugar and vanilla. Continue whipping until thick and holds peak. Spread on top of pie and sprinkle with coconut.

Mrs. Mary Sallee, Pocahontas H. S.
Pocahontas, Arkansas

ANGEL STRAWBERRY PIE
Number of Servings — 6

6 egg whites
¼ t. salt
1 c. sugar
1 t. vanilla
1 c. sugar
1 t. vinegar
1 c. cream, whipped
2 T. sugar
1 box fresh strawberries

Beat egg whites to which salt has been added. Beat until stiff but not dry and add the cup of sugar gradually, beating after each addition. Add vanilla and second cup of sugar very gradually, alternating with the vinegar and beating as you add. Spread in greased and floured pyrex pie plate. Spread higher in middle. Bake 1½ hours at 275°F. and 30 minutes at 300°F. Cool. Spread

(Continued on Next Page)

top with the cream, to which the 2 tablespoons of sugar have been added. Cover this with strawberries, cut in half.

Mrs. R. A. Moore, Breckenridge H. S.
Breckenridge, Texas

CHERRY PUFF
Number of Servings — 8-10
4 egg whites
½ t. cream of tartar
¼ t. salt
1 c. granulated sugar
½ t. vanilla

Beat egg whites until frothy. Add cream of tartar and salt, beat until stiff. Add sugar and vanilla. Pile into a well buttered 9″ pie plate. Bake at 275° F. for 1 hour.

Filling:
4 egg yolks
1 c. sugar
Rind of 1 lemon and 2 T. juice
1 c. red tart cherries (water packed)
1 t. red food coloring

Combine all ingredients for filling except food coloring. Cook on low heat, stirring constantly, until custard consistency. Add food coloring. Cool. If too thick to spread well add a little lemon juice. Spread in thin layer all over the top of the meringue.

Topping:
¾ c. heavy cream
1 T. sugar

Whip cream and add sugar. Spread over top of filling. Place in refrigerator for 24 hours. Top with nuts.

Mrs. Sally Kmon, Manchester Memorial H. S.
Manchester, New Hampshire

MERINGUE CRUNCH BARS
Number of Servings — 9
14 graham crackers
3 egg whites
1 c. granulated sugar
1 t. baking powder
¼ t. salt
½ to 1 c. chopped nuts
1 t. vanilla

Crush the graham crackers between wax paper until they resemble coarse meal. Beat egg whites until foamy throughout. Add sugar gradually, beating well after each addition. Continue beating well after each addition. Continue beating until stiff peaks form. Bake in greased 8x8x2 pan at 325°F. 25 to 30 minutes. While still warm cut into bars. Remove from pan and cool. Serve topped with whipped cream.

Mrs. Carolyn Younk Ferguson, Sparkman H. S.
Sparkman, Arkansas

COFFEE CREAM PIE IN NUT CRUST
Number of Servings — Two 8 Inch Pies
2 egg whites
½ c. sugar
¼ t. salt
3 c. finely chopped pecans

Grease well two 8″ pie tins. Beat egg whites until stiff but not dry. Add sugar and salt gradually. Beat until stiff and satiny. Fold in nut meats. Press onto bottom and sides (not rim) of pie tins. Prick well with fork. Bake at 400°F. about 12 minutes. Cool.

Filling:
2 T. instant coffee
½ c. water
½ lb. marshmallows
2 slightly beaten egg yolks
½ pt. heavy cream, whipped
½ t. almond extract

Combine coffee, water, and marshmallows. Cook over medium heat, stirring constantly until melted. Add coffee mixture slowly to beaten egg yolks, stirring constantly. Chill until mixture begins to set. Beat at medium speed until mixture is smooth. Fold in whipped cream and almond extract. Pour into cooled crusts. Chill several hours. Garnish with mounds of additional whipped cream and sprinkle with grated chocolate.

Mrs. Billie M. Mackey, Blythewood School
Blythewood, South Carolina

FOOD FOR THE ANGELS
Number of Servings — 9
3 egg whites
¾ c. sugar
25 Ritz crackers, crushed
1 t. vanilla
½ c. chopped walnuts
1 c. cream, whipped
2 T. sugar
Grated coconut

Beat the egg whites stiffly. Gradually add ¾ cup sugar. Fold in the crackers, vanilla, and nuts. Put into 8x8 greased pan and bake at 350°F. for 20-30 minutes. Cool well. Whip the cream. Add 2 tablespoons sugar. Spread on the baked layer and sprinkle with coconut. Chill over night.

Alfrieda Jacobson, Granite Falls H. S.
Granite Falls, Minnesota

FOOD FOR THE GODS
Number of Servings — 12
1 lb. English walnut pieces
1 lb. dates, cut up (½ lb. may be used)
Pinch of salt
2 c. sugar
½ c. cracker crumbs
2 t. baking powder
6 eggs (whites and yolks beaten separately)

Mix walnuts, dates, salt, and sugar together. Mix cracker crumbs, baking powder and beaten egg yolks together. Combine wet and dry mixtures. Fold in stiffly beaten egg whites. Place in lightly greased 8x12 cake pan. Bake 20 minutes in moderate oven 350°F. or 375°F. Serve warm or cold with whipped cream.

This recipe submitted by the following teachers:
Mrs. Vera Troyer, Bennett County H. S.
Martin, South Dakota
Ida Lou N. Holmes, Calvin Coolidge H. S.
Washington, D. C.

FORGOTTEN MERINGUE
Number of Servings — 15
5 egg whites
½ t. cream of tartar
1½ c. sugar
1 t. vanilla
¼ t. salt

Preheat oven to 450°F. while assembling materials. Beat eggs and salt until foamy. Add cream of tartar and beat until stiff but not dry. Add sugar gradually. Add flavoring. Turn into well greased pan, about 8x12. Put in oven. Turn off heat as soon as torte is in oven. Do not open oven until morning. Serve with ice cream and fruit or chocolate sauce.

Jean Stokes, Batesville H. S.
Batesville, Arkansas

GRAHAM CRACKER PIE
Number of Servings — 6
1 c. graham cracker crumbs
1 c. sugar
½ c. chopped pecans
½ t. baking powder (1 t. may be used)
Pinch of salt
3 eggs, separated

Mix together dry ingredients. Add beaten egg yolks and mix together thoroughly. Add stiffly beaten egg whites and fold into above mixture. Pour into greased pie pan. Bake at 325-350°F. for 15 or 20 minutes. Served warm, topped with ice cream or whipped cream.

This recipe submitted by the following teachers:
Joyce H. Marks, Escambia H. S.
Pensacola, Florida
Mildred R. Buck, Linden H. S.
Linden, Alabama

HEATH MERINGUE DESSERT
Number of Servings — 12
7 egg whites (stiffly beaten)
1¾ c. sugar
9 Heath bars, ground
1 pt. whipping cream
Vanilla

Make a meringue of egg whites and sugar. Bake at 300°F. in 2 well greased and paper lined cake pans for 1 hour. Grind heath bars. Whip whipping cream and flavor with vanilla and a little sugar. Place 1 meringue on a cake plate. Ice with whipped cream and sprinkle half the Heath bars on the cream. Place other meringue on this. Ice with cream and put the rest of the Heath bars on top. Refrigerate 10 hours before serving.

Mrs. Gavin G. Craig, Jr., Alvaton H. S.
Alvaton, Kentucky

HEAVENLY PIE
Number of Servings — 8
3 egg whites (stiffly beaten)
2 t. baking powder
1 c. sugar
1 t. vanilla
1 c. chopped pecans
1 c. graham cracker crumbs
Whipped cream

Beat egg whites until stiff. Add baking powder, sugar, and flavoring. Beat slowly until well blended. Fold in pecans and crumbs. Bake in greased pie plate 25 minutes at 350°F. Cool. Refrigerate. Serve with whipped cream.

Mrs. Ray N. McEachern, Chireno H. S.
Chireno, Texas

MACAROON PIE
Number of Servings — 8
16 saltine crackers
12 dates (chopped)
½ c. chopped nuts
¼ c. coconut
4 egg whites (stiffly beaten)
¾ c. sugar

Crush crackers, add chopped dates, nuts, and coconut. Beat egg whites until stiff. Add sugar and flavoring. Fold cracker mixture into egg whites. Bake 30 minutes in 300°F. oven. Top with whipped cream or ice cream before serving.

Dorothy S. Darby, Winder-Barrow H. S.
Winder, Georgia

MACAROON PIE
Number of Servings — 6
12 dates, chopped
½ c. nuts
12 soda crackers, rolled fine
1 c. sugar
1 t. almond extract
3 egg whites

Beat egg whites until stiff. Add extract to egg whites. Combine all dry ingredients. Fold into beaten egg whites. Bake in well greased pie pan 30 minutes at 350°F. Top with whipped cream. Serve while hot. (No pie shell is used.)

Mrs. Kay Waters, South H. S.
Knoxville, Tennessee

MYSTERY PIE
3 egg whites
1 c. sugar
23 Ritz crackers (rolled)
1 c. pecans (chopped)
1 t. vanilla

Beat egg whites scantly, add sugar, a small amount at a time and beat until stiff but not dry. Mix cracker crumbs and pecans and fold into egg mixture. Add vanilla and pour into buttered casserole. Bake in 350°F. oven for 30 minutes. Let cool and top.

Topping:
3 T. instant chocolate
1 c. whipping cream

Whip cream and just before finished whip into it instant chocolate. Add some sugar if desired. Refrigerate until ready to serve.

This recipe submitted by the following teachers:
Mrs. Janette Knox, Falkville H. S.
Falkville, Alabama
Lola T. St. Romain, Bunkie H. S.
Bunkie, Louisiana

PARADISE PIE
Number of Servings — 6

4 egg whites
1 c. sugar
¼ t. salt
½ t. cream of tartar
½ t. vanilla

Prepare meringue shell by beating egg whites until stiff. Fold in sugar gradually. Add next three ingredients. Place into a greased 9" pie pan. Put in oven (which has been heated to 400°F but is now off). Let remain over night. Don't peek!

Filling:
1 c. whipping cream
1 T. sugar
½ t. vanilla
2 oranges, diced
2 bananas, diced
½ c. coconut
1 t. grated orange rind

Whip cream, add sugar and vanilla and divide in equal portions. Add diced fruit and ½ of coconut to one portion. Fill shell and garnish with remaining whipped cream, coconut and orange rind. Refrigerate until chilled.

Mrs. Beverly J. Burcham, Olympia H. S.
Olympia, Washington

PARADISE PIE
Number of Servings — 6

4 egg whites
⅛ t. salt
1 c. and 2 T. sugar
1 t. vinegar
1 t. vanilla

Beat egg whites with salt until foamy. Add vinegar and vanilla. Gradually add sugar and beat 20 minutes with rotary beater or 10 minutes with electric mixer. Place in lightly greased pie pan, shaping crust up the sides. Bake at 200°F. for 1 hour.

Fluffy Fruit Filling:
½ pt. whipping cream
2 T. powdered sugar
½ c. crushed pineapple
½ c. ground pecans

Whip cream until stiff. Fold in sugar, nuts, and well drained pineapple. Fill pie shell and place in refrigerator for 4 or 5 hours until ready to serve. (Fresh crushed strawberries sugared and well drained may be substituted for pineapple.)

Marguerite Goldsworthy, Sarasota Jr. H. S.
Sarasota, Florida

PARTY PIE
Number of Servings — 6

3 egg whites
1 c. sugar
1 t. vanilla
1 pt. whipping cream
10 white soda crackers
1 t. baking powder
1 c. dates
1 c. walnuts

Beat egg whites stiffly. Fold in sugar and vanilla. Roll crackers fine, add baking powder. Mix with egg whites. Add nuts and cut up dates. Place in a greased pan 8x8x2 at 325°F. for 30 minutes. When cool, cover with whipped cream. Let stand in refrigerator a few hours before serving.

Mrs. A. M. Sowder, Sherwood H. S.
Sandy Spring, Maryland

PEACHES AND CREAM PIE
Number of Servings — 5-6

3 egg whites
1 c. granulated sugar
24 Ritz crackers, crushed fine
¼ t. baking powder
½ c. chopped pecans
½ pt. whipped cream, sweetened or whip mix
1 lge. can (or frozen) sliced peaches

Beat egg whites until stiff. Slowly add sugar, beating until sugar is dissolved. Fold crackers, baking powder, and chopped pecans into beaten egg whites mixture and pour into buttered pie pan, 9". Bake 30 minutes in 325°F. oven. Cool. Fill with sweetened whipped cream and sliced peaches. Refrigerate 1 to 2 hours. Cut into pie wedges, serve.

Mrs. Suzanne Morris, W. C. Pryor Jr. H. S.
Fort Walton Beach, Florida

RED RASPBERRY MERINGUE PIE
Number of Servings — 8

3 egg whites
1 c. sugar
1 t. vanilla
½ t. baking powder
14 Ritz crackers, crushed
¾ c. chopped nuts
1 carton frozen red raspberries
½ pt. whipping cream

Drain red raspberries thoroughly. Beat egg whites until stiff. Gradually add sugar and vanilla. Mix together baking powder, crushed Ritz crackers and nuts. Fold into egg white mixture. Bake in a well greased 9" pie pan for 45 minutes at 325°F. Cool thoroughly. Whip cream and fold in red raspberries. Fill meringue shell with whipped cream mixture. Chill for an hour before serving.

Mrs. Jean H. Teale,
Bentleyville-Ellsworth Area Joint H. S.
Ellsworth, Pennsylvania

RHUBARB MERINGUE
Number of Servings — 15

1 c. cake flour
5 T. powdered sugar
½ c. butter
3 eggs
2 c. sugar
½ c. flour
1 t. baking powder
3 c. rhubarb, cut up

Beat together 1 cup cake flour, powdered sugar, and butter. Put in pan 9x13 and bake at 350°F. for 15 minutes. Beat the eggs, sugar, flour, baking

(Continued on Next Page)

powder, and rhubarb. Spread on top of first mixture and bake at 350°F. for 45 minutes. Top with whipped cream.

Mrs. Lois Lovas, Mayville H. S.
Mayville, North Dakota

RITZ CRACKER PIE

Number of Servings — 6

20 Ritz crackers
½ o. sugar
1 c. chopped pecans
3 egg whites
½ c. sugar
1 t. vanilla
1 c. whipped cream

Crush Ritz crackers, add ½ cup sugar and chopped pecans. Beat egg whites until stiff, add sugar (½ cup) and vanilla. Beat. Fold in egg whites to cracker mixture. Pour into heavily buttered 9″ pie pan. Bake at 325°F. or 350°F. 30-35 minutes. Cool. Serve with whipped cream. Garnish with fruit if desired. Keep chilled until serving time. For variation ½ can coconut and ¼ cup candied cherries may be folded in with the nuts.

This recipe submitted by the following teachers:
Gertrude Louise Green, Cedar Bluff H. S.
Cedar Bluff, Alabama
Mrs. H. D. Wilkinson, Ector H. S.
Odessa, Texas
Mrs. H. C. Black, La Porte H. S.
La Porte, Texas
Mrs. E. V. Bravenec, La Porte H. S.
La Porte, Texas

RITZ CRACKER PIE

Number of Servings — 6

3 egg whites, well beaten
½ t. cream of tartar
1 c. white sugar
20 Ritz crackers, rolled fine
¾ c. pecans, chopped
1 t. vanilla
½ pt. cream, whipped
¼ c. brown sugar
¼ c. pecans, chopped

Beat egg whites well with cream of tartar, adding white sugar as you beat. Fold in the Ritz crackers, rolled fine, the ¾ cup pecans and vanilla. Mix well and pour into a greased pan, size 8x8 (pie tin is nice). Bake at 350°F. for 25 to 30 minutes. Cool. Cover with whipped cream and brown sugar mixture. (Sprinkle ¼ cup chopped pecans on top.) Spread cream mixture on top. Refrigerate for several hours (4-5 hours). Cut and serve.

Verdonna F. Graham, Sapulpa Sr. H. S.
Sapulpa, Oklahoma

RITZ CRACKER PIE

Number of Servings — 8

3 egg whites
½ t. baking powder
1 c. sugar (granulated)
½ t. vanilla
¼ t. salt
¾ c. broken walnut meats
14-20 crumbled Ritz crackers
1 c. whipping cream
Sugar to sweeten whipping cream

Beat egg whites until stiff. Add baking powder, sugar, vanilla, and salt. Then add nut meats and crumbled Ritz crackers. Bake at 325°F. or 350°F. for ½ hour in well greased pan. Cool. Cover with whipped cream and place in freezing unit of refrigerator for 1 hour. Leave in refrigerator until served.

This recipe submitted by the following teachers:
Pat Oglesby, Fort Vancouver H. S.
Vancouver, Washington
Mrs. Velma McWhirter, Wilson H. S.
Wilson, Texas

RITZ CRACKER PIE

Number of Servings — 6

18 Ritz crackers
1 c. sugar
1 t. baking powder
½ c. chopped walnuts
4 egg whites
½ t. vanilla

Roll out crackers so they are a fine crumb mixture. Mix sugar, baking powder, and walnuts with cracker crumbs. Beat egg whites until very stiff. Fold in dry ingredients. Add vanilla. Pour into well buttered pie plate. Bake 325°F. 40 minutes. Serve with whip cream.

Mrs. George Raboin, Carney H. S.
Carney, Michigan

RITZ CRACKER PIE

Number of Servings — 6-8

24 Ritz crackers
½ c. sugar
1 c. chopped nuts
3 egg whites
½ c. sugar
1 t. vanilla

Crush Ritz crackers, add ½ cup sugar and chopped nuts. Beat egg whites until stiff. Add ½ cup sugar and vanilla. Fold cracker and sugar mixtures into egg white mixture. Spread into well greased 9″ pie tin (do not use glass). Bake at 325°F. 35-40 minutes. Slice and serve when cool. May top with whipping cream or ice cream. Variation: ½ cup chopped angel flake coconut. ½ cup chopped dates.

Jeanette Phillips, Bridgeport H. S.
Bridgeport, Texas

RITZ CRACKER PIE

Number of Servings — 6

3 egg whites
1 c. sugar
1 t. baking powder
Pinch of salt (optional)
1 t. vanilla
20 Ritz crackers, crumbled (crumble by hand so they will not be too fine)
1 c. pecans, broken in pieces
Whipped cream

Beat the egg whites until stiff. Add the sugar, baking powder, vanilla, crumbs and pecans. Pour into a lightly greased 9″ pie pan. Bake for 30 minutes at 325-350°F. Serve with whipped cream. This pie can be made the day before it is to be served. Keep chilled until serving time. Garnish with shaved chocolate if desired.

This recipe submitted by the following teachers:
Mrs. Mary Eula Cowles, Newkirk H. S.
Newkirk, Oklahoma
Elizabeth Curry, Marianna H. S.
Marianna, Florida
Mrs. Kathryn Leischner, DeLand-Weldon H. S.
DeLand, Illinois
Mrs. Frances Stewart, Klamath Union H. S.
Klamath Falls, Oregon

SODA CRACKER PIE

Number of Servings — 6

12 soda crackers, rolled fine
1 c. chopped nuts
1 t. baking powder
3 egg whites
1 c. granulated sugar
1 t. vanilla
1 c. cream, whipped
Frozen or fresh fruit (optional)

Mix crackers, nuts, and baking powder together and set aside. Beat egg whites until stiff and slowly add sugar and vanilla. Fold together with cracker mixture. Put into well greased pie dish. Bake at 330°F. for 30 minutes. Cool. Whip cream and spread over pie. Place in refrigerator 2 hours before serving. For color or variety sweetened fruit may be used to garnish this dessert.

Mrs. Claudia Thomsen, Madison Jr. H. S.
Rexburg, Idaho

SODA CRACKER MERINGUE

Number of Servings — 6-8

3 egg whites
1 c. sugar
1 t. vanilla
¼ t. baking powder (if desired)
14-20 soda crackers
½-¾ c. nuts

Beat egg whites. Add sugar slowly. Add vanilla. Mix nuts and cracker crumbs. Add to beaten egg whites. Butter pie tin and spread mixture. Bake 20 minutes at 350°F. or 30 minutes at 325°F.

This recipe submitted by the following teachers:
Helen O'Dea, Le Sueur H. S.
Le Sueur, Minnesota
Marla Jackson, Nashwauk-Keewatin H. S.
Nashwauk, Minnesota

YAM-PECAN DELIGHT

Number of Servings — 4

2 egg whites
½ c. sugar
⅛ t. cream of tartar
½ c. chopped pecans
⅛ t. vanilla flavoring

Beat egg whites until light and foamy. Gradually add cream of tartar and sugar (1 tablespoon at a time) beating after each addition. Fold in pecans and vanilla. Heap in mounds on brown paper placed on a baking sheet. Use spoon to form cups. Bake at 250°F. until lightly browned.

Yam Mixture:
5 small yams, cooked and mashed
¼ c. oleomargarine or butter
1 egg yolk
¼ c. chopped pecans
¼ c. grated coconut
¼ t. cinnamon

Combine all ingredients and cook over low heat, stirring until well blended. Fill cooled meringue cups with yam mixture. Top with whipped cream and a cherry.

Mrs. Ruth H. Armand, Marksville H. S.
Marksville, Louisiana

Jiffy Desserts

BUTTER PECAN FRUIT RING

Number of Servings — 12-14

¼ c. butter
½ c. pecans
½ c. brown sugar
1 white cake mix
1 c. whipping cream
3 T. powdered sugar
1 t. vanilla
2½ c. cut up fruit

Break pecans and butter into a greased 10″ ring mold, sprinkle with sugar, mix cake and place on top. Bake at 350°F. 35-40 minutes, remove at once and cool. Whip cream, add powdered sugar and vanilla. Fold in fruit, pile in center of cake ring and serve.

Eunice M. Steiner, Bangor H. S.
Bangor, Wisconsin

CHERRY-CHOCOLATE UPSIDE-DOWN CAKE

Number of Servings — 9

4 T. (½ stick) butter or margarine
¾ c. firmly packed light brown sugar
⅛ t. salt
1 can (1 lb., 4 ozs.) unsweetened red tart pitted
    cherries
1 pkg. devil's food cake mix

Melt butter or margarine in 9x9 baking pan, stir in brown sugar and salt, heat slowly, stirring constantly just until bubbly, remove from heat. Drain cherries, saving liquid for cake. Spoon cherries over sugar mixture in pan. Prepare devil's food cake mix, following label directions, using liquid from cherries as part of liquid called for on package. Pour over cherries in pan. Bake at 350°F. 1 hour, or until center springs back when lightly pressed with fingertip. Cool on wire rack 5 minutes. Cover pan with serving plate, quickly turn upside down, then carefully lift off baking pan. Cut into squares, serve warm, plain or with milk, cream, or ice cream.

Mrs. Lois Witt, Heber Springs H. S.
Heber Springs, Arkansas

MAJESTIC CHERRY COCONUT CAKE

Number of Servings — 8-10

1 small bottle maraschino cherries
1 box light brown sugar
1 white cake mix
1 can coconut
3 T. butter or margarine

Grease and flour oblong baking pan. In large saucepan, mix cherries, juice, coconut, brown sugar, and margarine. Heat until sugar dissolves. While heating, mix white cake mix according to directions. Pour cherry coconut mixture in bottom of floured pan, smooth evenly. Pour cake mix over mixture, shake gently to remove excess bub-

bles. Bake 25 minutes at 375°F., cool 15 minutes after removing from oven. Turn upside down on serving platter and decorate with whole cherries.

Mrs. Bonnye Gage, Talco H. S.
Talco, Texas

BROILED COCONUT CAKE

Number of Servings — 10-12

1 box orange-coconut cake mix
½ c. cooking oil

Beat cake mix and cooking oil following directions for cake mix on the box (add any ingredients to the mix stipulated on the box). Bake in an oblong pan according to directions for cake mix.

Topping:

1 c. pecans
1 c. coconut
½ c. firmly packed light brown sugar
1 stick melted butter
2 egg yolks
2 T. milk

Blend pecans, coconut, sugar, butter, egg yolks, and milk. When the cake is done, spread on the topping and broil until the topping is light brown. Cool and cut in squares.

Emily J. Bonds, Hillcrest H. S.
Simpsonville, South Carolina

CHOCOLATE ORANGE DESSERT

Number of Servings — 12

Cake:

1 pkg. chocolate cake mix

Prepare cake as directed on package and bake in individual Mary Anne cake form pans. Remove from pans and cool.

Filling:

5 T. flour
¾ c. granulated sugar
¾ c. orange juice
1 T. lemon juice
2 T. orange rind
3 egg yolks
½ t. butter

In a saucepan, combine flour, sugar and juices and cook until thick and clear. Remove from heat, add egg yolks, orange rind and butter. Cook over hot water 2 minutes longer. Thoroughly cool the filling and fill the cake.

Meringue:

3 egg whites
6 T. granulated sugar

Beat egg whites until stiff, add sugar gradually. Cover cake filling with the meringue and bake in a 375°F. oven until brown.

Sally Rhoads Parks, Audubon H. S.
Audubon, New Jersey

EASY RIBBON CAKE
Number of Servings — 6-8

1 lb. pound cake (loaf)
(a good bought cake may be used)
1 (8 oz.) pkg. cream cheese
2 bananas
Juice of ½ lemon (more if preferred)

Mix cream cheese, bananas, and lemon juice until very creamy. Slice cake crosswise into very thin slices. Spread mixture on slices as for sandwiches, stack as for a layer cake. Do not put any of the mixture on the top. Wrap tightly in wax paper or aluminum foil, put in refrigerator. Slice very thin when ready to serve. This keeps for several days when wrapped tightly.

Elizabeth D. Parish, Geneva H. S.
Geneva, Alabama

FRUIT CAKE
Number of Servings — 7 Pound Cake

2 c. boiling water
½ lb. butter
2 c. sugar
½ lb. raisins
½ lb. currants
½ lb. dates
1 lb. pecans and black walnuts
1 pkg. candied pineapple
1 pkg. red and green pineapple
1 pkg. candied cherries
3½ c. flour
2 t. soda
1 t. cloves
1 c. wine
1 t. cinnamon

Mix first 5 ingredients together and boil 3 minutes, cool. Dredge with 1 cup flour next 5 ingredients. Mix all ingredients together. Bake at 275°F. 3 to 5 hours.

Mrs. Patricia Nixon, St. Louis H. S.
St. Louis, Oklahoma

GOLDEN RICH CAKE

1 19 oz. pkg. yellow or lemon cake mix
4 eggs
⅔ c. soft shortening
¼ c. water
2 t. vanilla
1 pkg. (8 oz.) softened cream cheese
½ c. finely chopped nuts

Place all ingredients except the nuts in the large mixer bowl. Beat 4 minutes on medium speed. Fold in finely chopped nuts, bake in greased and floured 10″ tube pan at 350°F. 50 to 60 minutes or until a tooth pick stuck into cake comes out clean. Cool and remove from pan.

Mrs. Frances Dailey,
Greater Greensburg Salem Sr. H. S.
Greensburg, Pennsylvania

JELLO CAKE
Number of Servings — 12

1 box yellow or white cake mix
1 box Jello (lemon or pineapple)
⅔ c. water

⅔ c. salad oil
4 eggs

Put all ingredients in a large mixing bowl and beat with electric mixer, medium speed, until thoroughly blended and smooth. Pour batter into a greased and floured tube pan and bake 1 hour at 350°F. Serve plain or with a sauce.

Mrs. Agnes ʌɪ. Jones, Sedalia H. S.
Sedalia, Kentucky

JELLO CAKE

1 pkg. Jello
¾ c. hot water
4 eggs
¼ c. salad oil
1 pkg. white cake mix

Mix Jello and water. Cool. Beat in eggs, 1 at a time. Add salad oil, mix with cake mix, beat at medium speed 3 minutes. Line angel loaf pan with wax paper, grease and flour sides of pan. Bake cake at 325°F. 35-40 minutes.

Louise Ferguson, Violet Hill H. S.
Violet Hill, Arkansas

APRICOT JELLO NECTAR CAKE
Number of Servings — 8-10

1 pkg. white or yellow cake mix (2 layer size)
1 pkg. lemon Jello
¾ c. (5 oz. can) apricot nectar
¾ c. cooking oil
2 t. lemon juice or 1 t. lemon flavoring
4 egg yolks

Mix all ingredients in mixing bowl. Beat egg whites and fold into cake batter (egg whites may be beaten in 1 at a time). Bake in tube or loaf pan at 350°F. for 1 hour or until done.

Glaze:
¾ c. powdered sugar
Juice of 1 lemon

Combine powdered sugar and lemon juice and pour on top of cake when taken from oven, while in pan. Let cool in pan before removing.

This recipe submitted by the following teachers:
Parma Bohls, Galena Park Ind. Schools
Galena Park, Texas
Norma Piboin, Madisonville H. S.
Madisonville, Texas
Mrs. Fran Pratt, Wm. Adams H. S.
Alice, Texas
Mrs. Carrie Hoffman, Hamilton H. S.
Hamilton, Texas
Miriam Gaines, Iuka H. S.
Iuka, Mississippi
Irene Clanton, Fairview Jr. H. S.
Memphis, Tennessee

LEMON JELLO CAKE
Number of Servings — 16

1 box yellow or white cake mix (lemon cake mix may be used)
1 box lemon Jello (lemon, pineapple or other flavors may be used)
¾ c. water

(Continued on Next Page)

¾ c. Wesson oil
4 eggs
1 t. lemon flavoring (if desired)

Combine cake mix, Jello, water, oil and eggs. Mix well and pour in greased loaf pan or angel food cake pan. Bake at 350°F. 30 minutes. Use a glaze or butter icing on top.

This recipe submitted by the following teachers:
Mrs. Elden Brunet, Oakdale H. S.
Oakdale, Louisiana
Mrs. Margaret Ransone, Lancaster H. S.
Kilmarnock, Virginia
Ruth M. Thompson, Neptune H. S.
Neptune, New Jersey
Patsy Clodfelter Bowers, Morganton H. S.
Morganton, North Carolina
Audrey W. Newman, Los Banos H. S.
Los Banos, California
Madine Moss, Plumerville H. S.
Plumerville, Arkansas
Mrs. Irene Knudsen, Del Norte County H. S.
Crescent City, California
Mrs. Thelma Moore, Parlier H. S.
Parlier, California

LEMON JELLO CAKE
Number of Servings — 12

1 pkg. lemon gelatin
1 c. boiling water
1 box yellow, white or lemon cake mix
4 eggs
¾ c. cooking oil
1 T. lemon extract (if desired)

Dissolve gelatin in water and let cool slightly, add this to the cake mix, then add eggs and cooking oil. After this mixture has cooled, pour into tube pan and bake in 350°F. oven for 1 hour.

Lemon Glaze:
¼ c. lemon juice
1½ c. confectioners' sugar
  or 1 c. confectioners' sugar
Juice of 1-2 lemons

Mix together lemon juice, and confectioners' sugar until smooth. Ice hot cake.

This recipe submitted by the following teachers:
Carol Willbanks, Newnan H. S.
Newnan, Georgia
Mrs. Janice Wikoff, Lemoore Union H. S.
Lemoore, California
Mrs. Lanona Stewart,
Haltom High-Birdville-Fort Worth, Texas
Fort Worth, Texas
Mrs. Carolene Wood, Perkins H. S.
Perkins, Oklahoma
Jo Hatcher, Tahlequah Sr. H. S.
Tahlequah, Oklahoma
Mrs. Wilmuth McBeth, Santa Paula Union H. S.
Santa Paula, California

LEMON JELLO CAKE
Number of Servings — 18-20

½ c. Wesson oil
½ c. powdered sugar
⅓ c. lemon juice
4 eggs

1 pkg. lemon Jello
⅔ c. warm water
1 box lemon cake mix

Dissolve Jello in the warm water. Mix Wesson oil, powdered sugar, lemon juice and beaten eggs. Combine Jello with above ingredients and mix. Add lemon cake mix and beat well, pour into 2 9" cake pans and bake 20-25 minutes at 350°F. Let cool and fill with a lemon icing.

Mrs. Louise Simpson, New Site H. S.
Alexander City, Alabama

TASTY LEMON "QUICKIE"
Number of Servings — 15-20

1 box lemon cake mix
1 box instant lemon pudding
¾ c. cooking oil
¾ c. water
4 eggs

Combine ingredients in the order listed. Bake in tube cake pan at 325°F. 45-50 minutes. Remove cake from oven and let remain in pan. Insert ice pick in cake, making many "openings."

Sauce:
½ c. orange juice
2 T. butter
2 c. confectioners' sugar

Combine sauce ingredients and pour over cake. Let cake cool before removing from pan.

Nell M. Arnold, Russellville Sr. H. S.
Russellville, Alabama

LEMON INSTANT PUDDING CAKE
Number of Servings — Large Cake

1 pkg. yellow cake mix
⅓ c. cooking oil
4 eggs
1 c. plus 2 T. water
1 pkg. lemon instant pudding

Combine cake mix, pudding mix, and cooking oil, add water and beat 2 minutes. Add eggs 1 at a time, beating well after each. Bake in greased pan 30 minutes at 350°F.

Frosting:
1 small can concentrated lemonade
1 lb. pkg. confectioners' sugar

Combine sugar and lemonade. Punch holes in top of cake and drizzle mixture over cake. Place under boiler until sugar melts.

Mrs. June Dawson, Eudona H. S.
Eudona, Arkansas

ORANGE JELLO CAKE
Number of Servings — 12

1 pkg. yellow cake mix
Dash of salt
1 pkg. lemon Jello
½ c. boiling water
⅔ c. salad oil
4 eggs
¼ c. orange juice

Place cake mix in electric mixer, add salt, turn to low speed. Dissolve Jello in boiling water and add slowly. Add the salad oil, the eggs, 1 at a time,

(Continued on Next Page)

then the orange juice. Cut brown paper to fit the bottom of a tube cake pan, grease pan and paper and flour well. Bake for 1 to 1½ hours at 325°F., let cool in pan. While still warm add topping.

Topping:
2 c. powdered sugar
½ c. orange juice
Combine powdered sugar and orange juice. Let stand, stirring occasionally while cake is baking. Put this over the cake while still warm, so it will soak in well.
Mrs. M. Anding, Madisonville Jr. H. S.
Madisonville, Louisiana

ORANGE JELLO CAKE
Number of Servings — 16
1 pkg. orange Jello
¾ c. boiling water
1 pkg. yellow cake mix
4 whole eggs
¾ c. cooking oil
½ t. orange extract
½ t. almond extract
¼ t. grated orange rind
Grease tube pan. Dissolve Jello with boiling water, cool. Add cake mix and beat with rotary beater until batter is smooth, add 1 egg at a time, beating after each addition. Slowly add cooking oil, beating slowly as addition is made. Fold in extract and rind and bake 50 minutes at 350°F.
Mrs. LaVerne Stokes, Westwood H. S.
Palestine, Texas

STRAWBERRY JELLO CAKE
Numsber of Servings — 8
1 pkg. white cake mix
1 pkg. strawberry Jello
4 eggs
¾ c. cooking oil
1 c. well drained strawberries
Line three 8" cake pans with wax paper, preheat oven to 350°F. Combine all ingredients in mixing bowl and mix thoroughly, beat for 2 minutes. Bake for 25-30 minutes. Frost with strawberry cream frosting.

Strawberry Cream Frosting:
½ c. butter
1 box powdered sugar
½ c. drained strawberries
Mix together and frost layers and top of cake.
Mary Finley, Baker County H. S.
Macclenny, Florida
Mrs. Willie Ruth Atchley, Lanier H. S.
Maryville, Tennessee
Mrs. Roberta Brooks, Dimple H. S.
Clarksville, Texas
Mrs. Jerry McCool, Central H. S.
Moss Point, Mississippi

MINUTE MAKER CAKE
Number of Servings — 8-10
1 T. butter
1 c. brown sugar
1 egg
Pinch salt
1 c. flour

2 T. boiling water
1 t. soda
1 t. vanilla
1¼ c. diced apples
¾ c. nuts, chopped
Combine ingredients in order listed. Bake at 350°F. in a square pan 7½x7½x2 for 30 minutes.
Sauce:
½ c. brown sugar
2 T. flour
½ c. boiling water
4 T. butter
1 t. vanilla
Combine first 4 ingredients and cook until thick, add vanilla.
Mrs. Betty Jean Flocco, West Allegheny Sr. H. S.
Imperial, Pennsylvania

MINUTE-MIX CITRUS CAKE
Number of Servings 12-16
4 eggs, separated
¾ c. cooking oil
¾ c. apricot nectar or orange juice
1 pkg. yellow cake mix
3 t. lemon extract
10 T. lemon juice
2 c. powdered sugar
2 t. grated lemon rind
2 t. grated orange rind
Beat egg whites until stiff. In a separate bowl, combine egg yolks, cooking oil and fruit juice, beat in cake mix, mix well. Add lemon extract, fold stiffly beaten whites into above mixture. Pour into oiled stem pan, bake at 325°F. for 45 minutes to 1 hour. Cool in pan 5 minutes, then remove from pan. While still hot, punch holes all through cake (use an ice pick for this). Spoon over the cake a mixture of lemon juice, powdered sugar and citrus rind. Allow to soak in for several hours.
Margery M. Stratton, Germantown H. S.
Germantown, Tennessee

MOCHA SPICE CAKE WITH PISTACHIO
1 pkg. devils' food cake mix
½ t. cinnamon
¼ t. allspice
¼ t. nutmeg
4 t. instant coffee
1 pkg. fluffy frosting mix
¼ t. almond extract
4 drops green food color
2 drops yellow food color
½ c. chopped pistachio nuts
Line two 8" cake pans with wax paper. To cake mix in bowl, add cinnamon, allspice, nutmeg and coffee. Prepare batter according to label directions. Pour into prepared pans, bake 35 to 40 minutes at 350°F., cool. Split each layer in half, making 4 layers. Prepare fluffy frosting according to package directions. Add almond extract, green and yellow food coloring, and fold in pistachio nuts. Spread between layers and on top and sides of cake.
Alberta Ball Bickerdike, East Pike School
Griggsville, Illinois

ORANGE BABA'S

Number of Servings — 10

1 pkg. yellow cake mix

Mix cake according to directions, fill well greased paper cups (hot drink) half full. Bake at 375°F. for 25 minutes or until done.

Sauce Baste:

¾ c. water
¾ c. orange juice
¾ c. sugar
3 T. orange peel (cut fine)

Mix ingredients together and cook 5 minutes. Pour over baba's until absorbed, chill and serve with whipped cream flavored with rum flavoring. Top with a pecan.

Alice S. Clements, Indiana Joint H. S.
Indiana, Pennsylvania

ORANGE DATE-NUT CAKE

1 box yellow cake mix (or 1-2-3-4 cake)
1 c. nuts (pecans or walnuts)
1 box dates or raisins
1 c. fresh orange juice
1½ c. white sugar
3 orange rinds (grated fine)

Use 1-2-3 recipe or mix, add raisins and nuts. Bake in two 9″ cake pans. Combine orange juice, white sugar and grated orange rind, mix and let melt. Take cake out of pans and remove paper, turning bottom layer of cake upside down. Pour juice over layer and turn right side up, pour juice on top. Have cake hot and let sit over night or 2 days.

Mrs. Hazel G. Tripp, Madison-Mayodan H. S.
Madison, North Carolina

SAD CAKE

Number of Servings — 12

3 eggs
1 lb. brown sugar
2 c. Bisquick
1 c. chopped pecans

In large bowl, slightly beat 3 eggs. Add brown sugar, mix well, breaking up all lumps. Add the Bisquick and pecans, mix until well moistened. Bake in heavy pan 9x12x2 or iron skillet. Bake 25 to 30 minutes at 350°F. This cake falls in the center.

Mrs. Sue Shields, Hedley H. S.
Hedley, Texas

SPICE CAKE (Baked Icing)

Number of Servings — 18

2 eggs whites
1 c. brown sugar
1 c. broken nut meats
1 pkg. spice cake mix

Beat egg whites until they hold a peak. Add brown sugar, beating it in. Spread on top of cake batter, sprinkle on the nuts and bake at 350°F. until cake is done (35 to 40 minutes).

Mrs. Jane Osborn Shipway, Flintstone H. S.
Flintstone, Maryland

ANGEL SQUARES

Number of Servings — 3-4 Dozen

1 medium angel cake
1 lb. box confectioners' sugar
Strong instant coffee
1 lb. pkg. salted peanuts

Cut angel cake into 1″ squares. Grind peanuts fine. Sift confectioners' sugar into medium bowl. Make strong coffee and add gradually to sugar until a slightly thinner than frosting consistency is reached. Spoon mixture over cake, roll in peanuts.

Ruth Adams, Claymont H. S.
Claymont, Delaware

BANANA FUDGE COOKIES

Number of Servings — 3 Dozen

1 ripe banana
1 egg
2 T. water
1 pkg. chocolate cake mix
1 c. chocolate chips

Mash banana, add egg, water, cake mix, and mix thoroughly, mix in chocolate chips. Drop by spoonfuls on cookie sheet. Bake at 350°F. for 10 minutes. For variety, mint chocolate chips may be added or ½ t. mint flavoring.

Betty Welty, Gervais Union H. S.
Gervais, Oregon

CAKE MIX DROP COOKIES

1 box cake mix
½ c. nuts
¼ c. shortening
1 egg
3 T. water

Mix cake mix with nuts and shortening, blend thoroughly with electric mixer, add egg and water and mix thoroughly. Dough will be quite stiff. Drop by teaspoonfuls on ungreased baking sheet and bake 10-12 minutes at 350°F. Variations: Add chocolate chips to white cake mix, decorate with sprinkles or walnut halves. To make a rolled cookie, add only 1 tablespoon of water, shape into roll and chill for 1 hour. Slice and bake as directed above.

Mrs. Eva Malerich, Colfax H. S.
Colfax, Washington

GLORIFIED BROWNIES

Number of Servings — 24 Squares

1 pkg. brownie mix
1 c. chopped nuts
1 pkg. miniature marshmallows
1 pkg. fudge mix

Use brownie mix and add ½ cup chopped nuts. Bake in pan in oven as stated on package, when done, cover with marshmallows and melt under broiler carefully, as it burns easily. Cook fudge by package directions, add nuts and pour over brownies. When cold, cut into small squares.

Mrs. Edith L. Barker, Allendale-Fairfax H. S.
Fairfax, South Carolina

JIFFY BROWNIES

2 c. graham crackers or vanilla wafers
1 can Eagle Brand milk
1 t. salt
1 8 oz. pkg. chocolate chips
1 c. broken nuts
1 t. vanilla

Mix all ingredients and pour in a greased and lightly floured pan (8x14). Bake 25 minutes at 350°F. Cut while hot.

Alliene Allen, Fairfield H. S.
Fairfield, Texas

CANDY DANDIES

Number of Servings — 36
¼ c. soft butter
¾ c. brown sugar (packed)
1 egg
1¼ c. Bisquick
½ c. chopped nuts
1 chocolate covered coconut bar

Mix well the butter, brown sugar and egg. Stir in Bisquick, chopped nuts and cut up candy bar. Drop with teaspoon 2 inches apart on ungreased baking sheet. Bake until lightly browned (about 10 minutes) at 375°F.

Mrs. Linnie Mae Sharkey, Woodland H. S.
Amite, Louisiana

CHERRY ROLL SQUARES

Number of Servings — 8
1 c. unsifted flour
1 c. sugar
1 c. drained sour cherries
1 c. nut meats
1 egg
1 t. baking soda

Mix all ingredients together well. Spread in a pan 8x8x2 that has been well greased and floured. Bake at 350°F. for 25-30 minutes. Cut into squares and top with sweetened whipped cream, serve.

Mrs. Virginia Slough, Northwestern H. S.
Springfield, Ohio

CHOCOLATE MOUND BARS

Number of Servings — 24
2 c. crushed graham crackers
¼ c. powdered sugar
½ c. melted butter

Mix ingredients and pat into a 9x12 pan. Bake at 350°F. 10 minutes.

Topping:
1 can sweetened condensed milk
2 c. angel flake coconut
1 t. vanilla

Mix ingredients and spread over crust. Bake 10 minutes at 350°F. Melt 1 giant milk cholocate bar and 1 square baking chocolate. Spread over the top, cut in squares at once. Put in refrigerator to set.

This recipe submitted by the following teachers:
Mrs. Vivian Harwood, Harbor Beach Community
Harbor Beach, Michigan
Deloris Sandbeck, Dilworth H. S.
Dilworth, Minnesota

CHOCOLATE WHEAT GERM BARS

Number of Servings — 16 Pieces
2 c. graham cracker crumbs
½ c. wheat germ
1 6 oz. pkg. chocolate bits
1 15 oz. can sweetened condensed milk
1 t. vanilla

Mix all ingredients together, spread mixture evenly in a greased 8″ pan. Bake in a moderate oven 350°F. 30 to 35 minutes. Cool and cut into bars or small squares.

Mrs. Eileen Krody, Bethel-Tate H. S.
Bethel, Ohio

EASY BARS

Number of Servings — 21
1 pkg. chocolate chips (12 oz.)
1 c. peanut butter (smooth or crunchy)
½ pkg. miniature marshmallows
1 c. salted peanuts (more if desired)

Mix peanut butter and chocolate in top of double boiler and heat until chips have melted. In a buttered 9x12 cake pan, spread marshmallows, add peanuts. Pour first mixture over marshmallows and peanuts, refrigerate. Cut into squares.

Clinette L. Wolf, West Concord H. S.
West Concord, Minnesota

CRUMB MACAROONS

Number of Servings — 2 Dozen
1 c. fine dry bread crumbs
1 c. sugar
1 c. chopped walnuts
2 eggs, well beaten
¼ t. vanilla

Mix all ingredients thoroughly. Drop by teaspoonfuls onto greased cookie sheet. Bake at 350°F. for 15 minutes. Remove from cookie sheet immediately.

Mrs. Elizabeth Enders,
Watsonville Joint Union H. S.
Watsonville, California

ICE BOX GINGERBREAD

Number of Servings — 15
1 c. shortening
1 c. sugar
3 eggs
2 t. ginger
¼ t. allspice
¼ t. cinnamon
1 c. sorghum
1 t. soda
1 c. milk
3 c. flour

Cream shortening and sugar. Add eggs one at a time beating well after each addition. Add spices and sorghum. Dissolve soda in milk and add alternately with flour. Put in refrigerator and dip out as needed, but don't stir. (Use cup cake liners.) Bake 45 minutes at 350°F.

Mrs. Winifred Robinson, Homedale H. S.
Homedale, Idaho

JIFFY FINGERS

Number of Servings — 3-30
Day-old bread
Sweetened condensed milk
Brown sugar
Coconut

Cut crust away from edges of day-old bread and cut into 3 ladyfinger slices. Brush each with a liberal amount of sweetened condensed milk and sprinkle with brown sugar and/or coconut. Place on generously greased cookie sheet. Bake until coconut begins to brown in a 350°F. oven.

Polly Powell, Nordhoff H. S.
Ojai, California

MACAROON TOFFEES

Number of Servings — 4 Dozen

1 coconut macaroon mix
½ c. chocolate chips
½ c. chopped nuts

Heat oven to 375°F. Bake coconut macaroon mix in special baking paper lined 9" square pan for 15 minutes. Top with ½ cup semi-sweet chocolate chips. Return to oven for several minutes to melt chocolate. Spread over top. Sprinkle with chopped nuts.

Mary M. Mueller, Augusta H. S.
Augusta, Wisconsin

1-MINUTE COOKIES

Number of Servings — 3 Dozen

2 c. sugar
½ c. cocoa
½ c. milk
1 stick margarine
2 c. quick oatmeal
½ c. peanut butter
½ c. coconut
1 t. vanilla

Mix sugar, cocoa, milk, and margarine. Boil one minute after mixture begins to boil. Mix in oatmeal, peanut butter, coconut and vanilla. Drop on wax paper by teaspoonfuls.

Mildred S. Whiteside, Milton Consolidated
Milton, Delaware

COCONUT DATE BALLS

Number of Servings — 20

1 pkg. dates, cut fine
1 stick margarine
2 eggs, slightly beaten
¾ c. sugar
2 c. Rice Krispies
1 c. pecans, chopped
Coconut

Put cut up dates and margarine in skillet over low heat. When margarine melts, add eggs and sugar and stir constantly while cooking for 15 minutes. (It will pull away from sides of pan.) Mix in Rice Krispies and pecans. Cool. Roll into marble sized balls and roll in coconut.

Mrs. Nola Warwick, DeKalb H. S.
DeKalb, Texas

PRALINE TOAST

Number of Servings — 12

½ c. melted butter
1 c. brown sugar
½ c. finely chopped nuts (pecans)
12 thin slices white bread

Mix brown sugar with butter. Add pecans, blend thoroughly. Spread mixture on bread. Brown in oven at 450°F. Crust may be trimmed and bread cut into shapes. Makes a very nice accompliment to coffee, tea or brunch.

Jean Higginbotham Smith, Richardson H. S.
Richardson, Texas

CARAMEL NUT CLUSTERS

Number of Servings — 2 Dozen

1 pkg. butterscotch pudding mix
1 c. sugar
1 T. butter
½ c. evaporated milk
1½ c. chopped nuts

Mix pudding powder, sugar, butter, and milk in a saucepan until smooth. Cook slowly to a soft ball stage. Remove from the heat. Cool slightly. Beat until mixture begins to thicken. Add nuts and drop from teaspoon onto wax paper.

Ardis Williams, Yuba City H. S.
Yuba City, California

PECAN ROLLS

Number of Servings — 24

1 jar marshmallow creme
1 box powdered sugar
1 t. almond flavoring
1 pkg. Kraft caramels
Grated pecans

Mix marshmallow creme, powdered sugar, and flavoring. Shape into fingerlike pieces. Place on platter. Let set over night. Melt Kraft caramels (in double boiler), add small amount of milk as needed. Dip finger shaped pieces in caramel mixture. Roll in grated pecans. Cool.

Mrs. Gayle D. Lee, Forest Hill H. S.
Forest Hill, Louisiana

SWEDISH FRUIT BALLS

½ c. butter (1 stick)
1 c. dates (cut up)
1 c. sugar
2 eggs
2 c. Rice Krispies
Pinch of salt
¼ c. candied cherries or mixed fruits
1 c. chopped nuts
½ t. vanilla
½ t. almond flavoring
Coconut

Turn electric fry pan control to 220°F. Melt butter, add dates. Cream eggs and sugar. Add to butter mixture in fry pan. Cook until thick, stirring constantly. Cool, add other ingredients. Form into balls, roll in coconut. Store in refrigerator in tin. Will keep a month.

Mrs. Evelyn C. Mann, Gretna H. S.
Gretna, Virginia

1 MINUTE FUDGE FROSTING
Number of Servings — 1 Large Cake

2 sq. chocolate
2 c. sugar
4 T. white syrup
½ c. salad oil
¾ c. milk

Melt chocolate over hot water. Remove from heat. Add sugar, syrup, salad oil and milk. Boil one minute after it has come to a rolling boil, stirring constantly. Remove from heat. Beat and cool until of spreading consistency. (May be cooled in pan of cold water.)

Daisymae Eckman, Pawnee City H. S.
Pawnee City, Nebraska

A QUICK APPLE PIE
Number of Servings — 8

2 cans apple pie filling (spiced)
½ box yellow cake mix
¾ stick butter or margarine (melted)
¼ to ½ c. broken pecans

Grease lightly, bottom and sides of 1½-2 quart pyrex baking dish. Cover bottom with apples. Sprinkle dry cake mix (½ box) over apples. Pour melted margarine or butter over cake mix. Sprinkle nuts on top. Bake 350°F. for 45 minutes (take out before nuts get parched). Cut in squares. Serve with vanilla ice cream.

Mrs. Mary Alice Hendrix, Rose H. S.
Greenville, North Carolina

ANGEL CARAMEL TARTS
Number of Servings — 6

1 can of sweetened condensed milk
½ pt. whipping cream
¼ t. vanilla
6 patty shells

Remove the label from a can of sweetened condensed milk, place in a pan of water and boil for 1½ hours, keeping covered all the time. Remove can from water, cool, open can, stir, and put into baked patty shells. (Pie crust baked on back of custard cups.) Whip cream, add vanilla and use as topping for dessert. Caramel filling may be made day before it is used.

Marjorie Bullard Turner, Miss. School for the Blind
Jackson, Mississippi

BROWNIE PIE
Number of Servings — 4-6

½ c. margarine, melted
½ c. sugar
½ c. flour
¼ c. cocoa
2 eggs, beaten
1 t. vanilla

Melt margarine in pie pan. Sift dry ingredients together into margarine. Add eggs and vanilla. Stir until thoroughly mixed. Bake at 350°F. for 25 minutes. (It will not be firm when done.) Serve while warm with ice cream or whipped cream.

Gaynelle C. James, Gardner H. S.
Gardner, Illinois

CHERRY-PINEAPPLE CRUMBLE
Number of Servings — 8-12

1 (16 oz.) can pitted cherries
1 (16 oz.) can crushed pineapple
1 box regular yellow cake mix
½ c. butter
½ c. chopped nuts

Mix cherries and pineapple in 9x13 cake pan. Sprinkle cake mix over, evenly. Melt butter and drizzle over cake mix. Top with nuts. Bake at 350°F. for 40-45 minutes. Serve warm with ice cream or cold with whipped cream. Variations: Use cherries and peaches or fruit cocktail. Spice cake with pears or peaches. Chocolate cake with cherries.

Laura Kiel, Badger H. S.
Lake Geneva, Wisconsin

CRUMB PIE
Number of Servings — 8

Broken bread crumbs (rolls, biscuits, cake, etc., enough to partially fill 9" pie plate)
2 eggs
1½ c. milk
1 c. sugar
2 T. butter or margarine

Separate eggs. Mix yolks thoroughly with sugar. Scald milk with butter in it. Add milk mixture to the egg yolk-sugar mixture and mix completely. Pour over bread crumbs making sure to soak all crumbs. Bake at 350°F. for 25 minutes. (Do not let it cook dry.) Remove from oven and spread preserves, jam, jelly, raisins, etc. over the crumbs. Cover with meringue. (2 egg whites, ¼ cup sugar, few grains salt and cream of tartar.) Brown meringue in 350°F. oven.

Mrs. June S. Haddock, Grimesland H. S.
Grimesland, North Carolina

QUICK FRUIT CRUMBLE
Number of Servings — 6

1 can fruit pie filling
1 box white cake mix (loaf size)
½ c. chopped nuts
¼ c. melted butter

Put pie filling in 8x8 pan. Sprinkle with the cake mix, then nuts and melted butter. Bake at 350°F. for 30 minutes. Excellent served with whipped cream or ice cream.

Mrs. Willetta R. Wallace, Whiteville H. S.
Whiteville, North Carolina

QUICK FRUIT COBBLER
Number of Servings — 6

1 stick oleo
¾ c. sugar
¾ c. flour
1 t. baking powder
¾ c. milk
1 can fruit or 1½ pt. frozen fruit

Melt oleo in an 8x8 pan. Mix together the sugar, flour, baking powder, and milk. Pour over melted oleo. Then pour in the fruit. Do not mix this together. Bake at 350°F. for 35-40 minutes.

Mrs. Dorothy Vacek, New Braunfels Sr. H. S.
New Braunfels, Texas

JIFFY FRUIT COBBLER
Number of Servings — 6-8
1 stick butter or oleo
1 c. flour, sifted
1 c. sugar
2 t. baking powder
Few grains of salt
1 t. nutmeg (optional)
1 c. sweet milk (may use ⅔ c.)
1 No. 2 can your favorite fruit, heated, or 1 lge. pkg. frozen fruit thawed and heated

Melt stick of oleo or butter in large casserole. Mix flour, sugar, baking powder, salt and milk until smooth. Pour into melted butter, stirring gently. Add favorite fruit without stirring again. Bake at 350°F. for 1 hour or at 375°F. 30-40 minutes. If fruit is not sweetened, heat 1 cup of sugar with the fruit.

This recipe submitted by the following teachers:
Mrs. Mary A. Campbell, Fort Necessity H. S.
Fort Necessity, Louisiana
Mrs. Hazel Jeane, Bloomington H. S.
Bloomington, Texas

QUICK FRUIT PIE
Number of Servings — 6
2 sticks pre-mixed pastry
½ c. sugar
¼ t. cinnamon
¼ t. nutmeg

Mix ingredients together. Grease pie pan and place 1 can cherry pie mix or 1 can apple pie mix into pan. Sprinkle topping over fruit. Bake at 375°F. for 20 minutes or until brown. Serve with whipped cream or ice cream.

Helen Cade, Marengo County H. S.
Thomaston, Alabama

PEACH COBBLER
Number of Servings — 8
1 No. 2½ can sliced peaches
½ t. cinnamon or nutmeg
3 T. butter
½ box white or yellow cake mix

Pour peaches into pan or baking dish. Sprinkle with cinnamon or nutmeg and dot with butter. Spread dry cake mix over the top, stir slightly to partially dampen cake mix. Bake at 350°F. for 25-30 minutes.

Mrs. Frances Alsup, Kopperl H. S.
Kopperl, Texas

QUICK PEACH PIE
Number of Servings — 8
1 c. sugar
2 c. self-rising flour
½ c. oleo or butter
1 c. milk
1 can sliced peaches

Mix sugar, flour and milk, melt butter in baking dish. Put part of batter into baking dish, then add peaches and most of the juice. Cover with remaining batter. Bake at 350°F. for 45 minutes.

Mrs. Winona L. Walker, Baker H. S.
Baker, Florida

JIFFY PEACH COBBLER
Number of Servings — 4-6
1 pkg. frozen sliced peaches (1 qt.)
½ c. brown sugar
½ c. white sugar
½ c. flour (plain)
½ stick butter
1 c. water
⅛ t. salt
⅛ t. nutmeg

Blend brown sugar, white sugar, flour, salt, and nutmeg. Make batter by adding water. Oil baking dish, pour batter over peaches, stir, add melted butter, stir. Bake 1 hour at 325°F., stir occasionally.

Ruth Parker, Corbin H. S.
Corbin, Kentucky

DELUXE SUNDAES
Number of Servings — 6-8
1 qt. vanilla ice cream
1 c. sugar cookie crumbs
¼ c. chopped pecans
1 pt. frozen strawberries, partially thawed
½ c. sugar
Whipped cream for garnish

Using an ice cream dipper, shape balls of vanilla ice cream. Roll each in a mixture of cookie crumbs and chopped pecans. As each ball is rolled, place it in a refrigerator tray in the freezer, allow balls to harden. Reserve a few nice berries for garnish. Combine remaining partially thawed strawberries and sugar, mix well and store in refrigerator. At serving time, place ice cream ball in sherbet dish. Top with strawberries and garnish with whipped cream and whole berries. Note: Other flavors of ice cream and other toppings may be used.

Mrs. Mary Jo Clapp, Jamaica Consolidated H. S.
Sidell, Illinois

DELICIOUS DESSERT
Number of Servings — 15
20-24 graham crackers
½ stick butter or margarine
¼ c. sugar
Mix and bake 5-8 minutes at 350°F.
Filling:
1 box lemon pie filling
2 egg whites
½ c. sugar (⅛ c. more if desired)
2½ c. water
1 c. whipping cream
1 c. crushed pineapple

In a saucepan mix together egg yolks and sugar, add contents of lemon pie filling box and gradually stir in 2½ cups water. Cook, stirring constantly until the mixture boils (5 to 8 minutes), cool. Beat egg whites until they stand in peaks, Fold in lemon mixture, fold in stiffly beaten whipped cream and pineapple (drained). Pour in graham cracker shell, freeze until firm.

Nadine Calvin, Ravenna H. S.
Ravenna, Nebraska

CRANBERRY-ORANGE DELIGHT
Number of Servings — 6
1 bottle cranberry juice
1 pt. orange sherbet

Spoon the sherbet into sherbet glasses. Pour the cranberry juice on top. This makes a delightful end to a dinner featuring fowl.

Mrs. Carol Zwolanek, Stanley-Boyd Area Schools
Stanley, Wisconsin

LEMON ICE CREAM PIE
Number of Servings — 8
½ gal. vanilla ice cream
1 can frozen lemon juice (or orange juice)
Graham cracker crust

Beat the frozen juice into the ice cream. Put into the graham cracker crust and freeze.

Mrs. Joel Ferrell, Brinkley H. S.
Brinkley, Arkansas

MAPLE ICE CREAM
Number of Servings — 8
2 eggs, separated
½ c. maple syrup (pure)
1 pt. vanilla ice cream
¼ c. chopped nut meats
½ t. salt

Beat egg yolks until thick and lemon colored in top of double boiler. Add maple syrup and beat until smooth. Place over hot water, stir constantly and cook until mixture thickens. Remove from hot water and cool. Place 1 pint vanilla ice cream in refrigerator until mushy, fold maple mixture and ¼ cup nut meats into egg whites, which have been stiffly beaten with salt. Fold into ice cream and mold in large colored paper muffin cups. Set in empty ice cube tray, refreeze.

Joan M. Hughes, Southern Area H. S.
Catawissa, Pennsylvania

ORANGE COLA SHERBET
Number of Servings — 1½ Gallons
9 orange cola drinks
2 cans Eagle Brand milk

Add carbonated drinks to Eagle Brand milk. This may be mixed in the metal freezer container to avoid dish washing. Freeze in electric or hand freezer until firm. The flavor may be changed by adding grape or lemon carbonated drinks.

Mrs. Juanita Cochran, Holly Ridge H. S.
Holly Ridge, Louisiana

RASPBERRY LUSH
Number of Servings — 8
1 c. raspberries (fresh or frozen)
1 c. sugar
2 egg whites
½ pt. whipping cream

Beat first 3 ingredients together and whip, whip, and whip. Then whip cream, fold into above mixture and freeze. Note: You may like to use a vanilla wafer crust with this.

Roberta Bosch, Mandan Jr. H. S.
Mandan, North Dakota

QUICK ICE CREAM
Number of Servings — 4-6
1 tall can evaporated milk
1 can (small) concentrated lemon or orange juice
½ c. sugar

Chill the evaporated milk, whip to full fluff. Add sugar and fruit juice and place in freezer tray and serve in a couple hours.

Idilla I. Alfson, Woonsocket Public H. S.
Woonsocket, South Dakota

VIENNESE VELVET
Number of Servings — 6
1 qt. vanilla ice cream
6 c. hot, double strength coffee
Whipped cream

Place 1 large scoop of vanilla ice cream in each of 6 tall glasses. Pour hot, double strength coffee carefully over ice cream until glass is about ⅔ full. Add a second scoop of ice cream and fill glass with coffee. Garnish with whipped cream and add a sprinkle of nutmeg if desired. You will need long spoons for the first half of this dessert-beverage, but you will drink the latter half.

Mrs. Elizabeth R. Whisnant, East Rutherford H. S.
Forest City, North Carolina

ANGEL'S DELIGHT
Number of Servings — 6
1 box chocolate cookies
1 c. milk
38 lge. marshmallows (1 bag)
1 t. peppermint extract
1 pt. whipping cream

Roll cookies and save half for topping. Place in bottom of 8x8 pyrex dish, place milk in top of double boiler. Add marshmallows, when dissolved, beat until smooth, cool. Add peppermint extract. Whip cream in separate bowl, add to marshmallow mixture, add food coloring if desired. Pour on top of crumb layer. Top with remaining crumbs. Cover with wax paper and chill 24 hours.

Sally Hildebrand, Enumclaw H. S.
Enumclaw, Washington

ANGEL FOOD LEMON-COCONUT SQUARES
Number of Servings — 6
1 c. sweetened condensed milk
6 T. lemon juice
1 t. grated lemon peel
1 10x5 loaf angel cake
2 c. toasted, shredded coconut
1 No. 2 can (2½ cups) sliced peaches, drained
Mint leaves

Combine the sweetened condensed milk and lemon juice, stir until thickened, add the grated lemon peel. Cut angel cake in 1¾" slices. Turn each slice on its side and frost with the lemon mixture. Sprinkle slices with coconut, chill. Place 3 canned peach slices on each. Garnish with mint.

Florence Wentz, Bakerhill H. S.
Bakerhill, Alabama

AMBROSIA PUDDING

Number of Servings — 6

1 pkg. instant vanilla pudding
⅔ c. orange juice (fresh, canned, or frozen)
1 can (9 oz.) crushed pineapple
1 c. heavy cream, or whipped dried or evaporated milk
18 vanilla wafers
½ c. flaked coconut

Prepare pudding according to package directions using orange juice for liquid. Add pineapple, fold in whipped cream, pile in sherbet glasses. Tuck wafers around side, chill. Top with coconut.

Mrs. Leon Wigginton, Wynne H. S.
Wynne, Arkansas

APPLESAUCE SURPRISE

Number of Servings — 10

1 No. 2 can applesauce
1 lge. can evaporated milk
¾ c. sugar
1 t. vanilla flavoring
1 lge. box vanilla wafers
2 lemons, juice

Chill cream overnight, beat until thick, add lemon juice. When standing in peaks, add sugar, flavoring and applesauce. Stir with spoon until well mixed. Line bottom of deep dish with vanilla wafer crumbs. Add layer of cream applesauce mixture. Alternate with cream mixture and crumbs until all is used. Refrigerate for 30 minutes before serving.

Annette Braswell, Monroe Area H. S.
Monroe, Georgia

APRICOT TREAT

Number of Servings — 4

1 4 oz. pkg. instant lemon pudding
1 c. apricot nectar
1 c. dairy sour cream

With rotary beater, blend instant lemon pudding with apricot nectar and dairy sour cream. Serve in dessert glasses.

Bethany E. Radtke,
Marine City Ward-Cottrell H. S.
Marine City, Michigan

BUTTERSCOTCH SURPRISE

Number of Servings — 6

1 box butterscotch pudding mix
1 box whip mix (such as Dream)
½ c. pecans, chopped

Cook butterscotch pudding mix according to box directions. Cool. Prepare whip mix according to box directions. Fold into partially cooled butterscotch pudding, the prepared whip mix, reserving a small amount. Stir in pecans and spoon mixture into dessert dishes. Top with reserved whip mix and sprinkle with pecan bits.

Nancy J. Ross, Del Rio H. S.
Del Rio, Texas

BUTTERSCOTCH PARFAITS

Number of Servings — 12

2 c. oats
1 c. brown sugar
⅔ c. butter

Heat oven to 350°F. For butterscotch crunch, combine oats, brown sugar, and butter. Mix well. Place in shallow pan and bake in preheated oven about 10 minutes. Stir occasionally. Chill. Crumble.

Filling:

2 c. cottage cheese
2 c. milk
2 pkg. instant lemon pudding
½ c. lemon juice

Cream cottage cheese. Add milk, instant pudding, and lemon juice. Beat 1 minute. Alternate layers of crunch and filling in parfait glasses. Store in refrigerator until served.

Mrs. Patsy Reaves, WB Atkins Jr. H. S.
Lubbock, Texas

CAKE OR COOKIE PUDDING

Number of Servings — 6

1 pkg. ready-to-mix chocolate or vanilla pudding
2 c. stale cake or cookie crumbs
½ c. whipping cream or 1 pkg. whip mix (such as Dream)
6 cherries
6 nut halves or 6 t. chopped nut meats

Mix package of pudding according to directions on box. Cool. Crumb cake or cookies. Place layer of crumbs in square shallow pan or ice tray, using 1 cup or half of cake crumbs. Cover crumbs with ½ of cool pudding. Make another layer of crumbs with remaining crumbs. Top crumbs with remaining custard, chill ½ to 1 hour. Cut in squares. Serve topped with whipped cream or topping. Garnish with cherries or nuts.

Mrs. Catherine Richard, Destrehan H. S.
Destrehan, Louisiana

CHERRY DESSERT

2 c. graham or vanilla wafer crumbs
1 stick oleo or butter (melted)
1-8 oz. pkg. cream cheese
1 c. powdered sugar
Chopped nuts
1 pkg. whip mix (such as Dream)
1 can cherry pie filling

Combine graham or vanilla wafer crumbs and melted oleo or butter and press into square cake pan. Bake 10 minutes. Spread with mixture of cream cheese and powdered sugar. Sprinkle with chopped nuts. Whip, whip mix and put on top of mixture. Refrigerate. When ready to serve add cherry pie filling (or it may be added before dessert is refrigerated.)

This recipe submitted by the following teachers:
Frances Baltz, O'Fallon Township H. S.
O'Fallon, Illinois
Mrs. Carol Hedges, Fort Recovery H. S.
Fort Recovery, Ohio

CHERRY CREAM PIE
Number of Servings — 6

1 graham cracker crust
3 oz. cream cheese
½ c. powdered sugar
½ pt. whipping cream
1 can instant pie cherries

Make graham cracker crust. Cream together the cream cheese and powdered sugar. Whip your whipping cream separate until very stiff. Combine with cream cheese mixture and whip 1 minute more. Pour into graham cracker pie shell. Top with can of instant pie cherries. Chill until firm.

Mrs. Elizabeth Ferguson, Dollarway H. S.
Pine Bluff, Arkansas

CHERRY DESSERT
Number of Servings — 8-10

40 marshmallows
1¼ c. milk
1½ c. whipping cream
1⅓ c. graham cracker crumbs
⅜ c. melted butter
3 T. sugar
1 can cherry pie filling (blueberry pie filling can
    also be used)

Dissolve marshmallows in milk in double boiler, stirring as needed. Cool. Whip cream, fold into marshmallow mixture. Crush graham crackers, mix in butter and sugar. Pack into pan lightly, saving part of crumbs for top of dessert. Pour ½ of marshmallow mixture over crumbs. Spoon cherry pie mix over marshmallow mixture. Add remainder of marshmallow mixture over cherries. Sprinkle crumbs on top. Refrigerate in 7½x12 pan.

Ann Held, Horicon H. S.
Horicon, Wisconsin

CHOCOLATE REFRIGERATOR LOAF

2 T. cocoa (add more if desired)
½ pt. whipping cream (sweetened to taste)
12 2 section graham crackers

Add cocoa to sweetened cream. Frost each cracker separately with whipped cream mixture making a stack. Frost top and sides of loaf. Chill over night. Slice and serve.

Mrs. Katherine Hoar, South Jr. H. S.
Rapid City, South Dakota

FRENCH SILK CHOCOLATE PIE
Number of Servings — 6

1 stick butter or oleo
¾ c. sugar
1 sq. melted chocolate
2 eggs
½ t. vanilla
Vanilla wafer pie shell

Cream oleo and sugar, add cooled chocolate. Add one egg and beat five minutes. Add second egg and beat five minutes. Add vanilla. Pour into shell which has been made by putting whole vanilla wafers around sides and bottom of small pie tin. Chill at least 6 hours.

Eloise Hearin, Thomas Edison Jr. H. S.
Springfield, Illinois

COCONUT CRUMB SQUARES
Number of Servings — 9

12 sugar honey graham crackers
1 T. sugar
2 T. melted butter
1 pkg. Jello coconut pudding
2 c. milk
1 t. vanilla
1 T. sugar
1 T. butter
½ c. whipping cream
1 T. confectioners' sugar
¼ t. vanilla

Crush graham crackers, add 1 tablespoon sugar and 2 tablespoons melted butter, mix well. Spread and pack in bottom of 8" square cake pan. Bake 5 minutes at 350°F. Cook Jello pudding with milk as directed on package, cool. Add 1 teaspoon vanilla and 1 tablespoon sugar and 1 tablespoon butter. Spread on crumbs in pan, chill until set. Before serving, spread with whipped cream to which confectioners' sugar and vanilla have been added. Cut into 9 squares and remove carefully with large spatula.

Elizabeth A. Blackman, Fremont H. S.
Fremont, North Carolina

INSTANT DATE NUT ROLL
Number of Servings — 8

2 c. vanilla wafer crumbs
1 c. chopped dates
½ c. chopped pecans
½ c. sweetened condensed milk
2 t. lemon juice

Mix crumbs, dates and pecans, add milk mixed with lemon juice. Knead well. Shape into a 3" roll. Wrap in wax paper and store in the refrigerator for 12 hours. Serve with whipped cream.

Mrs. Dolores Q. Parks, R. B. Worthy H. S.
Saltville, Virginia

FRUIT COCKTAIL EGG NOG PIE
Number of Servings — 6-7

1 No. 2½ can fruit cocktail
1 envelope unflavored gelatin
1½ c. commercially prepared eggnog
⅛ t. salt
¼ t. almond flavoring
1 c. whipping cream
1 baked 9" pastry shell

Drain fruit cocktail thoroughly. Measure ½ cup of the syrup. Stir gelatin into syrup. Place over boiling water and stir until gelatin is dissolved. Remove from heat. Stir into eggnog. Add salt and flavoring. Chill until mixture mounds when dropped from spoon. Whip cream. Fold into gelatin mixture along with 1½ cups well drained fruit cocktail. Chill again 5 to 10 minutes, until mixture mounds. Heap into baked and cooled pastry shell. Chill 2 to 4 hours. Decorate with remaining fruit cocktail.

Carolyn Attebery, Turrell H. S.
Turrell, Arkansas

HEAVENLY HASH
Number of Servings — 6

16 marshmallows
1 No. 2 can crushed pineapple
1 small bottle maraschino cherries
½ pt. heavy whipping cream

Cut marshmallows in small pieces, drain juice from pineapple (do not use juice). Cut cherries in small pieces and use cherry juice. Whip the cream and add to other ingredients. Chill in refrigerator 3 hours before serving. Delicious served on squares of angle food cake.

Mrs. Verna I. Boyd, Pisgah H. S.
Sand Hill, Mississippi

GINGERED HEAVENLY HASH
Number of Servings — 8

1 can (1 lb.) fruit cocktail
1½ c. miniature marshmallows
1 c. dairy sour cream
2 T. finely chopped crystallized ginger
3 T. chopped pecans or sliced walnuts

Drain fruit cocktail, combine drained fruit with marshmallows, sour cream and ginger. Chill over night or at least 4 hours. Sprinkle with nuts just before serving. Garnish with maraschino cherries or mint leaves. May be spooned into sherbet glasses accompanied by sugar cookies.

Mrs. Willye P. Mdodana, San Luis Obispo Jr. H. S.
San Luis Obispo, California

LEMON PUDDING - CHEESE PIE
Number of Servings — 6

16 graham crackers
⅛ c. melted butter
2 T. sugar
1 pkg. instant lemon pudding
2 c. milk
1 8 oz. pkg. cream cheese

Roll graham crackers into fine crumbs. Combine with butter and sugar and form into crust. Bake at 375°F. for 5 minutes, cool. Soften cream cheese in ½ c. milk, beat pudding into 1½ cup milk. Add softened cream cheese and continue beating until it begins to thicken. Pour into crust and chill 1 hour.

This recipe submitted by the following teachers:
Helen J. Rothermel, Overbrook Regional H. S.
Clementon, New Jersey
Mrs. Clara Ferguson, Spurgeon School
Spurgeon, Indiana
Mrs. Winifred C. Hobart, Akron-Fairgrove H. S.
Fairgrove, Michigan
Ruby L. Meis, Mt. Pleasant Sr. H. S.
Mt. Pleasant, Michigan

INSTANT PUDDING PIE
Number of Servings — 5

1 pkg. instant pudding mix
¾ c. milk
1 c. whipping cream
1 t. flavoring (harmonious with flavor of pudding)
1 8" vanilla wafer crust

Mix pudding and milk and let set without moving. (Note: It is important that the pudding be allowed to set before folding in the whipped cream.) Fold in flavored whipped cream, pour into vanilla crumb crust and let set over night in refrigerator. Garnish with toasted almonds or shaved chocolate or whipped cream.

Mrs. Louise S. Murphy, Irving H. S.
Irving, Texas

ORANGE CHIFFON DESSERT
Number of Servings — 10

1 orange chiffon cake
1½ c. powdered sugar
¼ lb. oleo or butter
3 eggs, separated
1 c. whipping cream

Slice the cake in thin slices and break and arrange until ½ of the slices cover the bottom of a loaf pan 12x16. Beat together thoroughly the butter, powdered sugar and egg yolks. Fold in the whipped cream, and the beaten egg whites. Spread over the cake, arrange the other half of the cake slices on top, refrigerate. Cut into squares to serve. Top with spoonful of filling or whipped cream.

Mrs. Floyd King, Molden H. S.
Molden, Illinois

PEPPERMINT WHIP
Number of Servings — 8

14 thin chocolate wafers
½ pt. whipping cream
1¼ c. miniature marshmallows
½ c. crushed peppermint candy

Crush wafers until fine crumbs. Put ½ the crumbs in a 9x9 buttered pan, whip cream and fold in marshmallows and crushed candy. Carefully spoon onto crumb mixture, top with remaining crumbs. Cover with wax paper. Chill in refrigerator several hours or over night.

This recipe submitted by the following teachers:
Carolyn L. Marquand, Blaine Jr. Sr. H. S.
Blaine, Washington
Mrs. Annette B. Tramm,
Bradley-Bourbonnais Community H. S.
Bradley, Illinois

PINEAPPLE BAKELESS CAKE
Number of Servings — 8

Juice from 2 lemons
1 can Eagle Brand milk
1 No. 2 can drained, crushed pineapple
1 pkg. vanilla wafers

Combine lemon juice and milk, add drained, crushed pineapple and stir. Place layer of mixture in ungreased 8x12 baking dish. Over this mixture, place 1 layer of vanilla wafers, continue alternating until all the lemon juice, milk, and pineapple is used. Top with vanilla wafers, add red cherries for decoration. Refrigerate until ready to serve.

Elizabeth Fox, Gustine Independent School
Gustine, Texas

TOFFEE SURPRISE
Number of Servings — 6
1 can sweetened condensed milk
6 pineapple slices
6 maraschino or candied cherries
Whipping cream
Put unopened can of sweetened condensed milk in large pan of water, cover and simmer for 6 hours (additional water may have to be added so can will be completely covered at all times). Cool in refrigerator overnight. A few minutes before serving time, open both ends of can and push contents through. Slice into 6 slices, laying each slice on a pineapple slice. Top with sweetened whipped cream and garnish with red and/or green cherries. Note: Several cans may be 'cooked' at once and stored in the refrigerator for company treats.
Mrs. Emely Sundbeck, Manor H. S.
Manor, Texas

WAFER- PUDDING DESSERT
Number of Servings — 6
1 pkg. chocolate pudding mix (not instant)
¼ lb. vanilla wafers
½ pt. whipping cream
1 c. pecans
2 T. sugar
1 t. vanilla
Make pudding according to directions (for added nutrition, a whole egg may be added. Beat egg well. Add small amount to hot liquid, mix well and add to remaining pudding). Cool. Whip cream, adding 2 tablespoons sugar and 1 teaspoon vanilla. Line casserole with vanilla wafers, add ½ of pudding, add ½ of whipped cream. Sprinkle nuts, add layer of wafers, add remaining pudding, cream, and sprinkle with nuts. Chill.
Mrs. Marie L. Fuller
Texarkana, Texas

QUICK BANANA PUDDING WITH MERINGUE TOPPING
Number of Servings — 8
Pudding:
1 box instant vanilla pudding
1 small pkg. vanilla wafers
3 lge. bananas, sliced
Mix pudding according to directions on box, arrange wafers, sliced bananas, and pudding in layers in a 2 quart casserole, ending with a layer of pudding on top. Pudding may be served as is or made extra special by adding the following quick topping.
Meringue Topping:
2 egg whites
¼ t. salt
4 T. sugar
¼ t.. vanilla flavoring (if desired)
Beat eggs and salt until frothy, beat in sugar, 1 tablespoon at a time and beat until meringue is stiff and glossy. Spread topping on pudding, gently swirling it into peaks. Bake at 350°F. for 12-15 minutes.
Mrs. Ella Jo Adams, Allen Sr. H. S.
Allen, Texas

JIFFY BREAD PUDDING
Number of Servings — 6
3 slices dried bread
2 c. hot milk
⅛ t. salt
⅓ c. sugar
3 slightly beaten eggs
2 t. vanilla
Break bread into hot milk and allow bread to absorb milk while other ingredients are being measured. Add rest of ingredients and beat slightly with an egg beater. Cook in a preheated heavy bottom kettle that has about 1 teaspoon of melted butter in it. Cook over low heat, stirring occasionally. When liquid has been absorbed, remove from heat and add vanilla. If chocolate bread pudding is desired, add about ⅓ cup of chocolate chips to the hot pudding and stir until chips are almost melted. Serve plain pudding with whipped cream topped with fruit, strawberries, cherries, canned apricots, or fruit cocktail, etc. Garnish chocolate pudding with shredded coconut.
Lily Carlson, Mora H. S.
Mora, Minnesota

CAKE 'N PUDDIN'
Number of Servings — 15-20
1 c. brown sugar
½ c. cocoa
2 c. water
12 marshmallows (regular size)
1 pkg. devil's food cake mix
½ c. chopped nuts
In an oblong pan 13x9x2, mix brown sugar and cocoa, stir in 2 cups water. Snip marshmallows into quarters and scatter over this mixture. Prepare cake mix according to package directions and spoon over the above mixture, spread nuts over top. Bake according to the cake mix directions. This will have a rich pudding under the cake, marshmallows will blend, some will rise to top. Have plenty of whipped cream or ice cream to use as topping.
This recipe submitted by the following teachers:
Janet Oyler, Glasco H. S.
Glasco, Kansas
Mildred Lee Bozeman, Groveland H. S.
Groveland, Florida

DEVIL'S FOOD PUDDING CAKE
Number of Servings — 20
1 pkg. devils food cake mix
⅔ c. cooking oil
2 eggs
1 t. baking powder
9 oz. chocolate chips
1½ c. pecan meats, broken
1 pkg. chocolate pudding
Prepare pudding according to instructions on the package. Cool. Into a large mixing bowl, combine the cake mix, cooking oil, baking powder, eggs and cooled pudding mix, beat well. Pour into well oiled 13½x9½x1½ pyrex pan. Sprinkle with chocolate chips and nuts. Bake at 350°F. for 40 minutes on the lowest shelf of the range.
Rose Richmond, Mooreland H. S.
Mooreland, Oklahoma

JIFFY FRUIT DESSERT
Number of Servings — 6
1 can prepared fruit pie mix (apple, peach, cherry)
1 t. almond extract
1 t. lemon extract
1 small box "Jiffy" white cake mix
½ c. melted butter

Empty fruit mix into buttered baking dish, mix almond and lemon extracts into fruit mix in dish. Sprinkle dry cake mix over fruit mixture. Pour melted butter over ingredients in dish and bake at 350°F. for 1 hour. Serve immediately. If desired, garnish with whipped cream.

Mrs. Bonnie Sampson, Sulphur Springs H. S.
Jonesboro, Tennessee

PEACH CAKE PUDDING
Number of Servings — 12-15
1 pkg. lemon pie filling mix (not instant)
1 can (29 oz.) drained, sliced peaches
1 pkg. marble cake mix
Whipping cream

Prepare lemon pie filling mix as directed on package. Spread in an ungreased oblong pan 13x9½x2, or a shallow 3-quart casserole. Arrange peaches over pudding, prepare cake mix as directed on package. Pour over peaches, bake in a moderate oven 350°F. 50 to 60 minutes (with knife, test in center for doneness). Serve either warm or cold, topped with whipped cream. Refrigerate leftover dessert.

Shirley Hash Underwood, LaRue County H. S.
Hodgenville, Kentucky

AMBROSIA (Sour Cream)
Number of Servings — 6
1 can mandarin orange sections and juice
1 c. pineapple cubes and juice
1 c. finely grated coconut
1 c. miniature marshmallows
1 c. dairy sour cream

Combine and chill all ingredients. Note: May be served as a salad if the juice is drained from the fruit. A cup of chopped pecans may be added.

This recipe submitted by the following teachers:
Mrs. Lois H. Nicholson, Saluda H. S.
Saluda, South Carolina
Mrs. Mary Gorrell Moser,
Mechanicsburg Area Sr. H. S.
Mechanicsburg, Pennsylvania

APPLE DESSERT QUICKIE
Number of Servings — 6
1 c. sifted enriched flour
1 c. brown sugar
1 t. cinnamon
⅛ c. butter
3 c. sliced peeled apples

Mix together flour, brown sugar, and cinnamon. Cut or rub in the butter and place the apples in a greased 8″ square pan. Sprinkle with the flour mixture. Bake in a moderate oven 350°F. for 30 minutes. Serve with plain or whipped cream.

Mrs. Shirley C. McCulley, North Dorchester H. S.
Hurlock, Maryland

APPLE COOGAN
Number of Servings — 8
1 egg
¼ cup oil
½ c. milk
1¼ c. flour, all purpose
¼ c. whole wheat flour
2 t. baking powder
½ c. granulated sugar
½ t. salt
1 c. raw apples cut in slices or chunks
¼ c. brown sugar
1 t. cinnamon

Mix the egg, oil and milk in a bowl. Sift the flour, whole wheat flour, baking powder, sugar and salt into the bowl of liquids and stir. Put in greased pan and poke the apples into the dough. Sprinkle the brown sugar and cinnamon on top and bake in 400°F. oven for 35 minutes. Serve warm or cold.

Mrs. Sylvia Haapala, Winlock H. S.
Winlock, Washington

FRESH UNCOOKED APPLESAUCE
Number of Servings — 4-6
3 red skinned apples
½ t. salt
1 qt. water
1 T. lemon juice
¼ t. cinnamon or nutmeg
¼ c. honey (or more, to taste)

Thinly slice cored, peeled (or unpeeled preferred) apples into salted water. Let stand 15 minutes to prevent discoloration. In blender, combine lemon juice, spice and honey with ½ of apple slices. Run blender to mix, adding balance of apples and mixing until all has been blended to as smooth a sauce as wished. Chill before serving. Note: Uncooked applesauce may be prepared using a medium grater. Also, a tasty pear sauce may be made by substituting ripe hard type pears for apples.

Mrs. Gwen Bayer, Summerville Union H. S.
Tuolumne, California

APPLE SURPRISE
Number of Servings — 8
1 No. 2 can prepared apple pie filling
1 No. 303 can applesauce
1 box spice cake mix
1 stick oleomargarine

Empty apple pie filling into 9″ square cake pan. Empty applesauce in with the apple pie filling and mix these 2 together. Open package of cake mix and spread contents evenly over the apple mixture. Cut oleomargarine into squares and dot the top of cak mix, it should completely cover the mix. Bake at 350°F. 50 to 60 minutes. Cut in squares and serve warm with ice cream for a delicious surprise. This recipe may be varied using any of the prepared fruit fillings and white or yellow cake mix, omitting the applesauce.

Pollyanna Rogers, Howe H. S.
Howe, Oklahoma

CHERRY CRISP
Number of Servings — 9
1 c. flour
1 T. sugar
⅛ t. salt
1 stick oleo
1 box vanilla pudding
1 can prepared pie cherries
½ pt. whipping cream

Mix or blend all ingredients, pat into an 8x10 ungreased loaf pan. Bake at 350°F. 20 minutes. Add a layer of vanilla pudding, next the prepared pie cherries. Whip and sweeten cream, spread on top of dessert, chill and serve.

Mrs. Rhea Adgate, Fenton H. S.
Fenton, Michigan

CHERRY COCONUT DELIGHT
Number of Servings — 8
1¾ c. shredded coconut
1 c. granulated sugar
1½ c. flour
½ c. margarine
1 can cherries

Combine ingredients (except cherries) into crumbs. Put half of crumbs in a greased 9x9 baking dish. Cover with cherries, cover with remaining crumbs. Bake for 30 minutes at 375°F. Can be served with whipped cream on top.

Bette Jo Switzer, Salem-Oak Harbar H. S.
Oak Harbor, Ohio

CHERRY DELIGHT
Number of Servings — 25
2 No. 2 cans (5 c.) sour red pie cherries
　　and juice
1 c. sugar
½ t. red food coloring
2 pkg. white cake mix

Mix cherries, sugar and food coloring, pour into pans. Mix the cake, doubling the amount of eggs and water and using 1½ the mixing time. Pour this cake mixture over cherries, dividing between 2 oblong baking pans size 13x9½x2. Bake 45 to 50 minutes in moderate oven 350°F., cool slightly. Invert on large serving plate. Serve warm, plain or with whipped cream.

Oma Nadean Waldron, Webber Township H. S.
Bluford, Illinois

CHERRY SUPREME
Number of Servings — 9
1 can pie cherries
1 9 oz. box cake mix
¾ c. sugar
1 T. cornstarch
1 stick margarine

Add sugar and cornstarch to cherries, mix thoroughly. Cook, stirring constantly until thickened. Pour into 9″ cake pan, crumble dry cake mix over cherries. Melt margarine and pour over mixture. Bake 40 minutes at 375°F. Other fruit, fresh or canned, may be used instead of cherries.

Helene Arnold, Franklin County H. S.
Frankfort, Kentucky

COOKIE SANDWICHES
Number of Servings — 2 Dozen
1 roll slice 'n bake cookies (⅛″ thin)
24 solid chocolate wafers (peppermint-rum)
Slice the roll of slice 'n bake cookies, place half the slices on cookie sheet. Top each with a chocolate wafer, cover with remaining cookie slices. Bake at 375°F. for 10-12 minutes.

Elaine A. Petrik,
South Winneshiek Community School
Calmar, Iowa

FRUIT BOWL
Number of Servings — 12
In glass bowl, arrange layers of different colored fruits in season or canned fruit (well drained).
Sauce:
½ c. sugar
¾ c. water
2 T. cornstarch
Juice and rind of 1 lemon
Juice of 1 orange

Mix cornstarch and sugar, add water, rind, lemon juice, orange juice and cook until thickened. Pour hot over fruit and chill.

Esther F. Intermill, Chassell H. S.
Chassell, Michigan

FRUIT DESSERT (Five In One)
Number of Servings — 6-8
1 c. bananas, sliced
1 c. mandarin oranges
1 c. coconut
1 c. sour cream (commercial)
1 c. pineapple chunks

Combine all ingredients just enough to blend with the cream. Serve immediately.

Ann Eddington, Waldport H. S.
Waldport, Oregon

HEAVENLY GRAPES
Number of Servings — 8
4 c. green seedless grapes
1 c. sour cream
Brown sugar

Wash grapes, drain well. Combine grapes and sour cream. Put into a large bowl or individual dishes. Sprinkle top generously with brown sugar.

Mrs. Suzanne Lockard, United H. S.
New Florence, Pennsylvania

JIFFY DESSERT
Number of Servings — 4
16 graham crackers
⅔ c. Jello, jam or preserves
½ c. whipped cream

Put jelly, jam or preserves between layers of graham crackers (3-4) and top with whipped cream.

Mrs. Sharlene Swann, Columbus H. S.
Columbus, Wisconsin

PARTY PEACH MELBA

Number of Servings — 6

6 peach halves
½ c. toasted almonds
8 oz. can red raspberries or 1 pkg. thawed frozen
    raspberries or 1 c. sweetened fresh raspberries
1 pt. vanilla ice cream
Rum flavoring
¾ c. water
1½ c. sugar

Wash and peel fresh peaches, cook until tender in syrup of water and sugar. If canned peaches are used, place 1 peach half in 6 individual dessert dishes. Stud peach halves with almonds. Spoon raspberries over peaches, chill. Whip ice cream with electric beater at medium speed or with wooden spoon until it reaches pouring consistency. Blend in flavoring, pour over peaches.

Mrs. Pat Botner Feiler, Chiefland H. S.
Chiefland, Florida

PEACH DELIGHT

Number of Servings — 8

1 toasted coconut cake mix
1 stick butter or oleo
1 small carton of sour cream
8 peach halves
½ c. sugar
2 T. cinnamon

Grease 2½ quart baking dish or pan 2″ high. Cut in butter and cake mix, press into rectangular pan. Spread sour cream over mixture evenly, arrange peach halves on top. Sprinkle with sugar and cinnamon mixture, bake as directed on cake mix box. Serve hot.

Shirley Gott, Venice Public School
Venice, Illinois

BAKED PEARS

Number of Servings — 6

6 pears
1 c. sugar
Grated rind and juice of 1 lemon
Grated rind and juice of 1 orange
Butter or oleomargarine

Peel and core pears, combine other ingredients and pour over pears. Dot with butter or oleomargarine. Bake at 350°F. for 1 hour.

Charline Webb, Gaylesville H. S.
Gaylesville, Alabama

QUICK PINEAPPLE DESSERT

Number of Servings — 9

1 c. flour
1 c. brown sugar
1 t. soda
½ t. salt
1 egg
1 small can (8½ oz.) crushed pineapple

Place all ingredients in bowl and mix, pour into greased 8x10 pan.

Topping:
¼ c. brown sugar
¼ c. chopped nuts

Sprinkle topping over surface. Bake at 350°F. 30 to 40 minutes. Serve with whipped cream or ice cream.

Mrs. Lois Myers, Vassar H. S.
Vassar, Michigan

RHUBARB CRISP

Number of Servings — 6

3 c. rhubarb (cut)
¾ c. sugar
2 t. cinnamon
1 c. flour
1 c. sugar
½ c. butter

Mix rhubarb, sugar and cinnamon together. Place in a 9x9 square pan. Place flour, sugar, and butter in bowl. Blend until crumbly, cover top of rhubarb. Bake at 375°F. for 25-30 minutes.

Mrs. Audrey Jacobs, Fruitland H. S.
Fruitland, Idaho

SINGED ANGEL WINGS

Brush cut sides of wedges of angel food or chiffon cake with melted butter. Lightly brown both sides under broiler, about 1 minute on each side. Serve with orange butter sauce.

Orange Butter Sauce (1½ c.):
¼ c. butter, softened
¾ c. sugar
2 egg yolks, beaten
1½ t. grated orange rind
⅛ c. orange juice
⅓ c. milk

Cream butter with sugar, stir in beaten egg yolks, grated orange rind, orange juice and milk. Cook over hot water 10 to 15 minutes.

Virginia Martell, Johnston City H. S.
Johnston City, Illinois

QUICK DESSERT

Number of Servings — 4-6

1 pkg. instant vanilla pudding
½ c. coconut
1 small can fruit cocktail

Mix coconut and fruit cocktail with the instant pudding, chill.

Hazel E. Schaad, Fulton Community H. S.
Fulton, Illinois

Refrigerator Desserts

AMBROSIA CAKE

Number of Servings — 12-16

2 10 oz. commercial angel cakes
1 small can crushed pineapple
1 can southern style coconut
½ pt. whipping cream
Juice of 3 oranges
Juice of 3 lemons

Break cakes in bite sizes in large bowl, add coconut and pineapple and mix well. Pour juice over mixture and work well, press into a flat container about 1½" thick. Ice top with sweetened whipped cream. Allow to stand in refrigerator overnight or at least 6 hours. Cut in squares and serve. Around Christmas add red and green maraschino cherries with pineapple, freezes well.

Elizabeth P. Hiht, Sylacauga H. S.
Sylacauga, Alabama

ANGEL CAKE DELUXE

Number of Servings — 12-14

1 angel cake
1 qt. ice cream (2 flavors desired)
1 pkg. lemon pie filling
1 c. whipped cream

Prepare pie filling as directed on package, cool (do not prepare meringue). Fold whipped cream into lemon mixture, slice angel cake into 3 horizontal slices. Place ice cream on 2 layers, frost sides and top with lemon mixture. Chill until serving time, this may be successfully frozen.

Variations: Cut center out of cake leaving about 1" around edge, pack with 2 flavors of ice cream. Place center on top and fill with more ice cream, making a 2 tiered cake. Frost with whipped cream or lemon cream filling.

Suggestions: Banana chiffon cake filled with pistachio nut ice cream and raspberry sherbet. Frost with green colored whipped cream. Angel food cake with vanilla ice cream and strawberry ice cream and frost with pink whipped cream. Angel cake with maple nut ice cream and vanilla ice cream, frost with chocolate whipped cream.

Mrs. Winifred S. Elliott, Rockville H. S.
Rockville, Connecticut

ANGEL DELIGHT CAKE

Number of Servings — 16

1 No. 2 can crushed pineapple
1 4 oz. box marshmallows, cut
1 8 oz. bottle maraschino cherries
1 envelope plain gelatin
1 c. milk
1 c. chopped blanched almonds
1 pt. heavy cream, whipped
1 10" angel food cake

Combine pineapple, marshmallows and cherries, including juice, let soak 6 hours or overnight. Soften gelatin in ½ cup cold milk for 5 minutes, add ½ cup hot milk. Chill until slightly thickened, add fruit mixture and almonds. Fold in whipped cream and cut cake in 2 layers. Put layers together with the mixture and frost the top and sides, drop remaining mixture in the hole. Chill cake before serving, decorate with cherries and almonds.

Verna Buerge, Turlock Union H. S.
Turlock, California

ANGEL'S DELIGHT

Number of Servings — 12

3 egg yolks
1 c. sugar
1 c. milk
Pinch of salt
1 t. vanilla
1 envelope plain gelatin
¼ c. cold water
½ pt. cream
3 egg whites, beaten stiff
1 small angel food cake
Coconut
Nuts
Maraschino cherries for top

Combine egg yolks, sugar, salt, and milk, cook 6 to 8 minutes until spoon coats. Dissolve gelatin in cold water, add to hot custard mix, cool. Fold into mixture whipped cream and beaten egg whites. Grease cake pan with butter lightly (9x13 pan). Make alternate layers of broken angel cake with above mixture, begin with cake, finish with mixture, chill for 12 hours. Serve with whipped cream, top with nuts, coconut or cherries as desired.

Mrs. Lettie G. Weinberg, Ravenswood H. S.
Ravenswood, West Virginia

ANGEL CAKE SURPRISE

Number of Servings — 12

1 10" angel food cake
1 c. whipping cream
3 T. sugar
½ t. vanilla
¼ c. chopped maraschino cherries
1 c. drained (crushed) pineapple
1½ pt. whipping cream
4 T. sugar
¼ lb. marshmallows, chopped
1 c. pecans, chopped

Combine 1 cup heavy cream (whipped) with 3 tablespoons sugar and vanilla, fold in chopped maraschino cherries, drained crushed pineapple, chopped marshmallows, and pecans, chill. Cut cake with serrated knife, 1" slice from top of a 10" cake. Cut out a ring 2" wide and 2" deep, spoon in chilled filling. Replace slice cut from top and frost top and sides with sweetened whipped cream, chill. Decorate with pineapple tidbits and maraschino cherries.

Mrs. Don E. Brown, Grayville H. S.
Grayville, Illinois

ANGEL FLUFF DESSERT

Number of Servings — 5

½ c. whipping cream, whipped
1 c. marshmallow fluff
⅓ c. maraschino cherry halves, drained
1½ c. drained crushed pineapple
2 ripe bananas, peeled and diced
3 c. broken pieces angel food cake

Combine whipped cream and marshmallow fluff, fold in remaining ingredients. Pile into dessert dishes, chill before serving.

Rosalie Osowski, Buffalo H. S.
Buffalo, Minnesota

ANGEL CAKE DESSERT

Number of Servings — 16-18

1 pt. milk
1 c. sugar
2 beaten egg yolks
¼ t. salt
1 pkg. lemon Jello
2 egg whites, stiffly beaten
1 No. 2 can crushed pineapple, drained
½ pt. whipping cream
1 lge. angel food cake, cut in 24 or more slices

Combine egg yolks, sugar, salt and milk in top of double boiler, cook over boiling water until mixture coats the spoon. Sprinkle in, slowly, the dry Jello powder, stir until dissolved, remove from heat. Set aside to cool, then chill until slightly jelled. Line bottom of a very large pan with thinly sliced angel food cake. Combine Jello mixture with stiffly beaten egg whites, add the drained pineapple and whipped cream. Cover cake with ½ of Jello mixture, cover with another layer of thinly sliced cake, spread remaining mixture over top. Sprinkle toasted coconut evenly over top, chill in refrigerator overnight.

Mrs. Jean Harris, Highland H. S.
Cowiche, Washington

ANGEL CUSTARD ROYAL

Number of Servings — 15-18

6 egg yolks, beaten
¾ c. sugar
¾ c. lemon juice
1½ t. grated lemon rind
¼ c. cold water
1 T. unflavored gelatin
6 egg whites, beaten
¾ c. sugar
Few drops yellow food coloring
1 angel food cake

Trim crust from cake, tear into pieces, combine egg yolks, ¾ cup sugar, lemon juice, and lemon peel, cook over hot, not boiling water, until mixture coats the spoon, remove from the heat, add gelatin softened in cold water, cool until partially set. Fold in whites beaten with remaining ¾ cup sugar. Arrange ⅓ of cake pieces loosely in the bottom of a 10″ tube pan, pour over half of custard, continue for 3 layers, chill until firm. Invert on platter and fill center with whipped cream or frost with whipped cream.

Mrs. Charlene Kersten, Marion H. S.
Marion, Wisconsin

ANGEL CAKE MOLD

Number of Servings — 16-18

¾ c. sugar
1 T. lemon juice
6 eggs, separated
1 envelope unflavored gelatin
¼ c. cold water
¾ c. crushed pineapple and juice
1 t. salt
1 T. grated lemon rind
Angel food cake

Whipping cream
Coconut

Cook sugar, lemon juice and egg yolks in double boiler until thick. Soak gelatin in ¼ cup water. Add to lemon mixture. Add lemon rind. Beat 6 egg whites until stiff. Add ¾ cup of sugar. Turn electric beater on low and add lemon mixture to beaten egg whites. Break up small angel food cake in small chunks. Grease angel food pan with cooking oil. Put a layer of cake chunks, then a layer of lemon mixture and cake chunks, etc. Place in refrigerator to mold. May be made a day before. Unmold and fill center and cover top and sides with whipped cream and coconut.

Mrs. Ruth Bell, Trinity H. S.
Trinity, Texas

BRIDE'S DELIGHT

Number of Servings — 20-25

2 c. crushed pineapple
1 c. chopped pecans
3 c. diced marshmallows
¾ c. diced maraschino cherries
2 pt. whipping cream
Angel food cake

Combine the first 4 ingredients and place in refrigerator to chill for at least an hour (may be chilled longer if desired). Approximately 30 minutes before serving time, whip the cream and fold it into the above mixture, place in refrigerator until ready to serve. Serve on angel food cake squares.

Mrs. Annie Fred Wright, Blacksburg H. S.
Blacksburg, Virginia

CHERRY CAKE ROLL

Number of Servings — 16

1 pkg. angel food cake mix
2 cans cherry pie filling
Whipped cream

Mix angel food cake as directed on box, divide batter evenly and spread in 2 jelly-roll pans. Do not grease pans. Bake in 375°F. oven for 15 to 20 minutes until it tests done. Dust tea towel with powdered sugar and use 4 Jello molds to hold up each corner of cake pan. Invert cake pan over tea towel and have corners rest on molds, cool. When cool, carefully run knife tip around edge of cake, freeing sides of cake from pan. With cake upside down, gentle ease cake from pan onto towel. Place 2 fairly long strips of Saran wrap (edges overlapping, on table next to cake, place cake on Saran wrap. Spread filling over cake (a little less than 1 can if desired), roll as a jelly roll. Wrap tighty in the Saran wrap and place on tray for freezer. Make sure the end of each cake roll are tucked under when placed on the trap, freeze. To serve, remove from freezer and slice immediately, each cake roll will make 8 servings. Serve on plates and let stand 1½ hours before serving, serve with whipped cream.

Mrs. Ethel D. Finley, Montgomery Blair H. S.
Silver Spring, Maryland

ANGEL DESSERT
Number of Servings — 25

1 white angel food cake, broken in small pieces
1 qt. drained crushed pineapple
1 small jar maraschino cherries, drained
3 c. milk
4 egg yolks
1 c. sugar
2 envelopes gelatin
½ c. cold water
½ t. salt
4 egg whites
2 c. cream or evaporated milk
2 T. lemon juice
1 c. chopped walnuts
1 small can shredded coconut

Place ½ of the angel food cake pieces in the bottom of oblong cake pan, next cut up maraschino cherries, then the drained, crushed pineapple, and the remaining cake pieces. Cook next 3 ingredients (custard) until it coats a knife, add the gelatin, softened in cold water with the salt. Cool, then add the egg whites, stiffly beaten, the cream, and lemon juice. Pour over cake and cover with chopped nuts and shredded coconut. Chill overnight.

Mrs. Jean B. Gilleece, Lamar H. S.
Lamar, Colorado

CHOCOLATE ANGEL FOOD DESSERT
Number of Servings — 16

2 pkg. chocolate chips
4 beaten egg yolks
Pinch of salt
1 t. vanilla
4 beaten egg whites
2 T. sugar
1 pt. whipping cream
1 c. chopped nuts
1 loaf or cone-type angel food cake
Cherries or chocolate decors (may be used for
    decorations)

Melt chocolate chips in double boiler, slowly add beaten egg yolks and pinch of salt, beat well, add vanilla. Fold in beaten egg whites to which 2 tablespoons of sugar have been added, fold in whipped cream and nuts. Slice (the long way) 1 loaf angel food cake into equal slices, or tear a cone-type angel food cake in small pieces. Line the bottom of a 12x8x2 cake pan with angel food slices or bits, saving half of the angel food for top layer. Pour half the chocolate mix over angel food. Cover with remaining pieces of cake and pour last of the chocolate mix over this. Chill 6 hours or longer. Serve with whipped cream topped with a cherry (may sprinkle chocolate cake decors and whipped cream).

This recipe submitted by the following teachers:
Mrs. Bernice Anderson, Central Jr. H. S.
Reno, Nevada
Bernice Duncan, Gould H. S.
Gould, Oklahoma
Mrs. Margaret Morgan, Austin H. S.
Austin, Minnesota
Marianne Olson, Paynesville H. S.
Paynesville, Minnesota
Georgia M. Johnson, Southeast H. S.
Bradenton, Florida

GOOD CHOCOLATE DESSERT
Number of Servings — 10-12

1 pkg. chocolate tid-bits
4 T. water
2 eggs, separated
1 pinch salt
1½ pts. whipping cream
½-1 c. chopped nuts
1 medium angel food cake

Melt chocolate tid-bits with water in top of double boiler. Beat egg yolks and add hot mixture to eggs a little at a time. Add salt. Cool. Beat egg whites and fold in. Beat and fold in 1 pint of whipping cream. Fold in nuts. Break cake into bite size pieces and form layer in large rectangular pyrex dish. Pour mixture over cake and repeat layers. Top with ½ pint whipped cream. Chill and cut in squares.

Mrs. Doris Crawford Hodgson, Baldwin Co. H. S.
Bay Minette, Alabama

WALDORF ANGEL FOOD (Chocolate)
Number of Servings — 12-16

10" angel food cake
6 T. sugar
⅛ t. salt
6 T. cocoa
3 c. whipping cream
⅛ c. toasted almonds, cut up
⅛ c. shaved toasted almonds

Place angel food cake upside down on plate or wax paper, slice entire top from cake about 1" down. Lift off top and lay to one side. Cut down into the cake 1" from outer edge, and 1" from middle hole, leaving a substantial "wall" of cake about 1" thick and a 1" base at the bottom. Remove center with a curved knife or a fork, being careful to leave a "wall" of cake at bottom. Place on serving plate. Completely fill cavity with the chilled filling. To prepare filling, mix together sugar, salt, cooca and whipping cream, chill 1 hour or more, whip until stiff. Fold into about half of cream mixture the cut-up toasted almonds, use this part to fill cake cavity. Replace top of cake and press gently, spread remaining cream mixture on top and sides of cake. Sprinkle with shaved, toasted almonds. Chill 3 hours or more before serving, cut into generous pieces.

Radora Massey, Sterling H. S.
Sterling City, Texas

CHRISTMAS DESSERTS

Dissolve each box of Jello in 1½ cup hot water.
1 box cherry Jello
1 box lime Jello
1 box orange Jello
1 pt. whipping cream
1 angel food cake
1 envelope gelatin soaked in:
¼ c. cold water
¼ c. hot water
½ c. orange or pineapple juice

Put Jello into 3 ice trays, when set, cut into small cubes. Combine ingredients and add gelatin mix-

(Continued on Next Page)

ture to whipped cream slowly while beating. Place ½ of an angel food cake in a 9x12 pan. Pour ½ of mixture over it and place ½ of Jello cubes on top, repeat until mixture and Jello cubes are used up.

Opal M. Brouillard, Barnard Independent School
Barnard, South Dakota

FLOWER GARDEN BOUQUET

6 beaten egg yolks
1½ c. sugar
¾ c. lemon juice
1½ t. grated lemon peel
1 envelope gelatin
¼ c. cold water
6 stiffly beaten egg whites
1 lge. angel food cake

Make custard of egg yolks, ¾ cup sugar, lemon juice, and lemon peel. Cook over hot, not boiling, water until mixture coats spoon. Remove from heat and add gelatin softened in cold water. Fold in egg whites beaten with remaining ¾ cup of sugar. Tear angel food cake in bite size pieces and place in angel food cake pan oiled with salad oil. Pour custard over cake pieces and chill until firm. Unmold and garland with spring flowers.

Mrs. Judy C. Hall, Seagoville H. S.
Seagoville, Texas

ICE CREAM CAKE

Number of Servings — 12

1 angel food loaf cake
2 pts. brick ice cream (use 2 colors, for instance cherry and vanilla)
½ pt. cream
Food coloring for tinting cream

Slice angel food cake in 3 lengthwise slices. Slice each brick ice cream in 3 slices. Place 3 slices of ice cream on first slice of angel food cake. Place a slice of cake on top of ice cream, followed by another layer of cake, another layer of ice cream and finally the cake. Frost with tinted whipped cream. Freeze.

Mrs. Ross Wilson, Coalfield H. S.
Coalfield, Tennessee

FROZEN DELIGHT

Number of Servings — 6

1 loaf angel food cake
1 No. 2 can crushed pineapple
1 Pt. whipping cream
4 T. sugar

Slice cake lengthwise in order to obtain two slices ½" thick. Whip cream and add sugar. Place 1 slice of cake in an ice tray, cover with layer of crushed pineapple and top with whipped cream. Repeat layers of cake, crushed pineapple, and whipped cream. Freeze. Slice into 6 servings.

Mrs. Martha K. Mercer, Cass H. S.
Cassville, Georgia

LEMON ANGEL DESSERT

Number of Servings — 16

⅔ c. butter or margarine
1⅓ c. sugar
1 t. vanilla
1 t. grated lemon rind
¼ c. lemon juice
5 egg yolks
5 egg whites
⅔ c. heavy whipping cream
1 angel food or chiffon cake

Thoroughly mix butter and sugar. Add vanilla, grated lemon rind and lemon juice. Mix well. Add 5 egg yolks, 1 at a time. Beat well after each addition. Fold in stiffly beaten egg whites and whipped cream. Line a 13x9x2 baking pan with wax paper. Cut cake in 16 slices. Arrange 8 slices on bottom of baking pan, spread half of filling over these. Place remaining 8 slices on top. Finish with remaining filling. Freeze immediately.

Mrs. Beulah Holt, Chester H. S.
Chester, Texas

LEMON ANGEL DELIGHT

Number of Servings — 12

1 10" angel food cake
6 egg yolks, beaten
¾ c. sugar
¾ c. lemon juice
1 envelope gelatin
¼ c. water
6 egg whites, stiffly beaten
¾ c. sugar

Soften gelatin in ¼ cup water, combine egg yolks, ¾ cup sugar, lemon juice, and lemon rind. Cook over hot water until mixture coats spoon, remove from heat and add softened gelatin, cool until partially set. Beat egg whites stiff, add ¾ cup sugar and small amount of yellow food color to custard mix. Fold egg whites into custard mixture. Fold in angel food cake that has been broken into small bite-size pieces. Pour in oblong pan and chill until firm, slice and serve with whipped cream.

Mrs. Aline N. Melton, Suttle H. S.
Suttle, Alabama

MANDARIN ORANGE CAKE

Number of Servings — 12

1 baked angel food cake
1 11 oz. can mandarin orange segments, drained (reserve juice)
½ c. walnuts, finely chopped
2 c. heavy cream
⅓ c. granulated sugar
⅛ t. salt
¼ t. orange extract

With a 2-tined fork, poke about 10 holes 1" apart around the top of the cake. Slowly pour ⅛ cup mandarin orange liquid over top of cake, set aside 12 orange segments and 2 tablespoons of finely chopped walnuts for decorations. Coarsely chop remaining orange segments and drain well. Combine cream, sugar, salt, and orange extract in mix-

(Continued on Next Page)

ing bowl, beat until cream just holds its shape. Fold in chopped oranges and walnuts. Frost sides and top of cake with cream mixture. Decorate top with reserved orange segments and nuts, chill before serving.

Addie Jo Curry, LaPoynor H. S.
LaRue, Texas

PINEAPPLE ANGEL DESSERT
Number of Servings — 20

2 T. gelatin (unflavored)
½ c. cold water
3 egg yolks
2 c. milk
1 c. sugar
1 No. 1 can crushed pineapple, drained
2 c. whipped cream
3 egg whites, beat stiff
½ c. chopped nuts
1 angel food cake (crumbled)
1 small bottle maraschino cherries

Soften gelatin in water, beat egg yolks, add milk and sugar. Mix well and cook over hot water until it coats spoon. Add softened gelatin and stir until dissolved, cool. Drain pineapple and add to cool mixture, fold in whipped cream and egg whites, add nuts. Line bottom of oiled pan with crumbled cake, pour half of mixture over cake. Mix remaining cake crumbs and mixture and pour into pan, chill until firm. Cut into squares and garnish with whipped cream and cherries.

This recipe submitted by the following teachers:
Mrs. Robert Cook, Desha Central School
Rohwer, Arkansas
Mrs. Betty Jenness,
Linesville-Conneaut-Summit H. S.
Linesville, Pennsylvania

PINEAPPLE SUPREME
Number of Servings — 8-10

1 c. sugar
1 c. pineapple juice
2 eggs
1 pkg. lemon Jello
1 tall can Pet milk (very cold)
1 angel food cake

Beat eggs, add sugar, then juice, and cook in double boiler until consistency of custard. Remove from fire, add Jello dissolve, and let cool. Beat chilled milk and fold into custard. Pour over broken angel food cake pieces.

Mrs. Marvolin Stephens, Thompson H. S.
Siluria, Alabama

RASPBERRY ANGEL RING
Number of Servings — 6

1 pkg. raspberry Jello
Dash of salt
1½ c. hot water
1 10 oz. pkg. frozen raspberries
1 c. heavy cream, whipped
1 angel food cake

Dissolve Jello and salt in the boiling water, add berries and stir until thawed. Chill until partially

set, whip cream, then whip Jello mixture until fluffy and fold into whipped cream. Tear cake into small pieces and place a layer in bottom of angel food pan, cover with Jello mixture and continue with alternate layers until pan is full. Chill until set, unmold and cover with whipped cream.

Malta O. Ledford, Jupiter H. S.
Jupiter, Florida

STRAWBERRY ANGEL FOOD CREAM CAKE
Number of Servings — 16

Bake an angel food cake, using your favorite
    mix, cool thoroughly
1 pkg. strawberry Jello
1 10 oz. pkg. frozen strawberries
½ c. whipping cream
1 c. boiling water
4 T. sugar

Thaw strawberries and strain juice. Make Jello, using 1 cup boiling water and 2 tablespoons sugar. Add strawberry juice to Jello. There should be ½ cup juice. If not, add enough water to make ½ cup. Cool in refrigerator until partially set. Whip Jello. Whip cream and add 2 tablespoons sugar. Fold together Jello, whipped cream and drained strawberries. Set in refrigerator until stiff enough to stay on cake, about 5 minutes. Cover angel food cake with mixture. Make it thick. Refrigerate until ready to serve.

Gladys Crawford, McDaniel Jr. H. S.
Denison, Texas

STRAWBERRY BAVARIAN
Number of Servings — 8

1 3 oz. pkg. strawberry gelatin
1 9 oz. can crushed pineapple and juice
¼ c. non-fat dry milk crystals
¼ c. ice water
2 c. coarse angel food cake crumbs (tear angel food
    cake into bite-size pieces)

Dissolve strawberry gelatin according to directions on package. Chill until mixture is as thick as unbeaten egg whites. Fold in pineapple and juice. Whip dry milk crystals and ice water until stiff. Fold into gelatin-pineapple mixture. Pour over cake crumbs which have been placed in a 1½ quart casserole or loaf pan. Chill until firm. Spoon into individual dessert dishes.

Mrs. Harriet Krause, Pasadena Sr. H. S.
Pasadena, Texas

STRAWBERRY REFRIGERATOR DESSERT
Number of Servings — 6

1 pkg. strawberry gelatin
1 c. hot water
¼-⅛ c. cold water
2 10 oz. pkg. frozen strawberries
2 c. heavy cream, whipped
1 10″ angel food cake (broken up)

Dissolve strawberry gelatin in hot water, add cold water and chill until partially set. Beat until light and fluffy. Drain the frozen strawberries, reserve juice. Fold berries and the whipped cream, into the gelatin. Using the 10″ angel cake, break cake in small pieces. Alternate layers of cake and

(Continued on Next Page)

gelatin mixture in a 9x11 oblong pan. Chill until firm (preferably overnight). Unmold and cut, drizzle glaze over top.

Glaze:
1 c. strawberry juice
1 T. cornstarch
3 drops red food coloring
1 t. soft butter

Mix all the ingredients except the butter and cook until clear, from 3 to 7 minutes, add butter last and cool.

Mrs. Joan DeLaet, Barneston Consolidated School
Barneston, Nebraska

TIPSY PUDDING
Number of Servings — 10
Candied figs
Candied pineapple
Raisins
Candied dates
Candied cherries
Rum, brandy, whisky or sherry
2 c. milk
⅛ t. salt
4 T. sugar
3 T. flour
3 eggs, slightly beaten
1 angel food cake
Whipped cream
Chopped nuts
Finely chopped red and green cherries
Frosted grapes

Cut the first 5 ingredients into very small pieces, enough to make 2 cups. Soak overnight in rum, brandy, whisky or sherry, enough to barely cover. Next day, make custard by mixing milk, salt, sugar, and flour in a double boiler and stir constantly for 15 minutes, add 3 beaten eggs and cook 5 minutes more, cool. Slice angel food cake in 3 horizontal layers with a long thin knife, a silk thread works well, too. Gently mix the cool custard and the fruit and use the mixture as a filling for the cake. Ice the hole with whipped cream, sprinkled with chopped nuts and finely chopped red and green cherries. Garnish with frosted grapes. Put a compote in the hole in the center of the cake and pile high with frosted red and green grapes. To frost grapes: Dip the fruit in a sugar-water syrup, just before it dries, dip again in sugar. You get a sparkling, crystal effect.

Mrs. Anne Dodenhoff Nelson, J. E. B. Stuart H. S.
Falls Church, Virginia

STUFFED ANGEL FOOD CAKE
Number of Servings — 12-14
1½ envelopes plain gelatin
1 c. water
⅔ c. sugar
1 c. pineapple juice
Juice of 1 lemon
1 lge. angel food cake
1 pt. whipping cream
1 c. nuts, almonds or pecans, cut
1 small bottle cherries, cut
1 lge. can crushed pineapple, drained

Dissolve gelatin in ¼ cup cold water. Add sugar. Heat remaining water and pineapple juice to boiling point and add to gelatin. Add lemon juice. Congeal slightly. Cut off top of cake, about ½" thick. Take crumbs out of cake, leaving about ½" wall on side and bottom. When mixture begins to congeal, add stiffly whipped cream, crumbs, nuts, pineapple, and cherries (will fill cake center hole and cover top and sides). Chill in refrigerator.

Mrs. Nettie C. Herring, East Duplin H. S.
Beulaville, North Carolina

APPLESAUCE ICE BOX CAKE
Number of Servings — 6
Vanilla wafers
½ c. sweetened condensed milk
¾ c. applesauce
1 T. lemon juice

Line refrigerator tray with wax paper, arrange a layer of vanilla wafers on paper. Cover with other ingredients mixed together. Top with another layer of vanilla wafers. Put in freezing unit for 12 hours. Serve with or without whipped cream.

Bettie Lou Horton, Tanner H. S.
Tanner, Alabama

BAKELESS CAKE
Number of Servings — 12
1 No. 2 can crushed pineapple
2 eggs, separated
1 c. water or juice from pineapple
½ c. butter
½ c. sugar
1 box coconut bars (cookies)
1 box lemon Jello

Beat egg yolks and mix with water, sugar and butter. Bring to boil, add Jello and cool. Beat egg whites and fold in mixture. Add pineapple. Put layers of coconut bars and layers of mixture, alternately. Chill.

Dorothy G. Burford, Blacksburg H. S.
Blacksburg, Virginia

COOKLESS CAKE
(May Also Be Used As A Pudding)
Number of Servings — 6
1 stick butter or oleo
2 c. sugar
3 egg whites
19 oz. can crushed pineapple
¼ can shredded coconut
1 c black walnut meats
1 t. vanilla
1 pkg. vanilla wafers

Cream butter and sugar until light and fluffy. Add beaten egg whites and combine with nut meats, coconut, pineapple and vanilla. Place an even layer of wafers in bottom of casserole. Add a thin layer of filling on top of wafers. Repeat until all of filling is used. Place in refrigerator over night. Remove from casserole by placing in warm water for a few minutes.

Beda Sue Hogue, Green Forest H. S.
Green Forest, Arkansas

CHERRY SNOW CAKE

Number of Servings — 10-15

2 c. sifted cake flour
1¼ c. sugar
3½ t. baking powder
½ t. salt
⅞ c. milk or pineapple juice
2 T. shortening
1 t. vanilla
3 egg whites, unbeaten

Sift flour, sugar, baking powder, and salt into mixing bowl. Drop in shortening, add ⅔ cup liquid, then flavoring, beat 200 strokes (2 minutes by hand or with a mixer at low speed). Add egg whites and remaining liquid, beat 2 minutes longer. Bake in 2 square 8" greased pans at 350°F. for 25 to 30 minutes. Chill layers, split in half, spread cherry almond filling between layers and on top of cake. Chill in refrigerator several hours before serving. Serve in 1" slices.

Cherry almond filling:
1 T. gelatin
¼ c. cold water
1 8 oz. jar maraschino cherries, finely cut (juice also)
½ c. sugar
⅛ t. salt
2 c. heavy cream
⅓ c. blanched almonds, finely cut
¼ t. vanilla
½ t. almond flavoring

Soften gelatin in cold water for 5 minutes. Place over boiling water, stir until dissolved, add finely cut maraschino cherries plus the juice, sugar, and salt. Chill until slightly thickened, whip heavy cream, add blanched almonds, vanilla, almond flavoring and fold into gelatin mixture.

Carolyn Mae Horky, Fremont Jr. H. S.
Fremont, Nebraska

CHOCOLATE ICE BOX PARTY CAKE

Number of Servings — 18

1 lb. butter
1 doz. eggs
4 oz. bitter chocolate (4 blocks)
2 doz. almond macaroons
1½ doz. lady fingers
½ c. bourbon
1 lb. sugar
1 lb. pecans

Cream butter and sugar 20 minutes. Beat egg yolks 6 minutes with an electric beater. Add egg yolks to sugar and butter. Add melted chocolate and pecans. Fold in beaten egg whites. Soak macaroons in ½ cup bourbon from 1 to 2 hours. Line spring cake pan with lady fingers (standing up around edge). Put half of macaroons on bottom of pan, then a layer of chocolate mixture. Add rest of macaroons, then rest of chocolate. Leave over night in refrigerator. Serve with sweetened whipped cream.

Mrs. Lucille Weaver, West Jr. H. S.
Gulfport, Mississippi

CHOCOLATE-MINT ICE BOX CAKE

Number of Servings — 15

1 lb. cream-filled chocolate cookies, such as Oreo's
¾ c. butter
3 c. confectioners' sugar
3 eggs
3 sq. chocolate, melted
1½ c. cream, whipped
16 marshmallows, cut
1 9 oz. pkg. after dinner mints
½ c. pecans or other nuts
1 t. vanilla

Grind cookies and press into a 7x11 cake pan or flat casserole dish. Reserve ½ cup for topping, combine butter, sugar, eggs, and chocolate. Mix thoroughly and spread over cookie layer, fold marshmallows, mints, and nuts into whipped cream and spread over second layer. Top with reserved ½ cup crumbs. Place in refrigerator and leave 2 days.

Mrs. Mary K. Hutton, Elkton H. S.
Elkton, Virginia

DATE ICE BOX CAKE

Number of Servings — 12

½ lb. graham crackers
1 pkg. (10 ozs.) dates
2 T. orange juice
¼ t. salt
¼ lb. miniature marshmallows
½ c. nut meats, chopped coarsely
1 c. sweet cream, whipped

Crush graham crackers with rolling pin. Cut dates into eighths with wet scissors. Pour orange juice over dates, add salt. Fold the dates, nuts and marshmallows into the whipped cream. Fold in cracker crumbs, reserving about 3 tablespoons. Sprinkle the unused crumbs on a sheet of wax paper and shape the mixture on this into a roll about 3" in diameter. Cover with the paper and place in refrigerator for at least 12 hours. Cut into ½" slices and serve plain, with whipped cream, with vanilla ice cream or with a favorite sauce.

Mrs. Ina Mae Perry, Lexington H. S.
Lexington, Texas

REFRIGERATOR FRUIT CAKE

1 pkg. rolled graham cracker crumbs (3 c.)
½ t. cinnamon (powdered)
1 c. dried dates
½ c. candied pineapple
½ c. candied orange peel
1 c. small gumdrops
½ c. candied cherries
1 c. shredded coconut
1 small can sweetened condensed milk
1 c. pecans or walnuts

Roll graham cracker crumbs until fine, mix cinnamon well with crumbs. Cut dates, pineapple and orange peel into medium size pieces, add to cracker mixture and stir with a wooden spoon. Cut gumdrops into fourths and add, a few at a time, to the graham cracker mixture, add the whole

(Continued on Next Page)

candied cherries and stir into the graham cracker fruit mixture. Add shredded coconut and pecans or walnuts (whole or broken pieces). Add ⅓ of the sweetened condensed milk, stir well and add the second portion, stir and add the remainder. Place ½ of this mixture in a 4x8 rectangular pan lined with wax paper or foil. Place wax paper or foil over the top and press firmly. Remove the top paper and add the rest of the mixture. Cover and press with the hand as hard as possible. Place the pan in the refrigerator to chill for several days. Remove the pan as soon as the cake is molded, this is better when it is made 3 or 4 weeks before serving. Cut into thin slices for serving as it is very rich.

Mrs. Daisy Massey, Fredericksburg H. S.
Fredericksburg, Texas

ICE BOX FRUIT CAKE

Number of Servings — 8

1 pkg. lemon Jello
1 c. water
1 small pkg. marshmallows
½ c. coconut
1 c. juice from the fruits
1 can crushed pineapple (small)
1 lge. can fruit cocktail
1 c. nuts
½ c. cherries
½ pt. cream, whipped
Crushed vanilla wafers

Dissolve lemon Jello in water, put in double boiler and dissolve marshmallows. Cool until syrupy. Add pineapple, fruit cocktail, nuts, cherries, whipped cream, juice and coconut. Put a layer of crushed vanilla wafers in loaf pan, a layer of fruit mixture, another layer of wafers, and a layer of the fruit mixture. Place in refrigerator until firm.

Mary Jane Henderson, Egypt School
Walnut Ridge, Arkansas

NO-BAKE FRUIT CAKE

Number of Servings — 12

2 c. miniature marshmallows
⅔ c. evaporated milk
6 T. undiluted frozen orange juice
4 c. honey graham crackers, crushed
½ t. cloves
1 t. nutmeg
1 t. cinnamon
1 c. walnuts
¼ c. candied cherries
¾ c. dates
1 c. candied fruit
¾ c. raisins

Melt the marshmallows, milk, and orange juice in a 3-quart double boiler. Mix the crackers, cloves, nutmeg, and cinnamon, pour over candied fruit, nuts, and raisins. Mix well with liquid, wrap in wax paper, mold into pyrex dish and chill for 2 days in the refrigerator.

Margaret Sue Thomas, Atoka H. S.
Atoka, Oklahoma

UNCOOKED FRUIT CAKE

Number of Servings — 15

1 lb. graham crackers
¼ t. cinnamon
¼ t. cloves
¼ t. allspice
¼ lb. butter or margarine
1½ c. pecans, chopped fine
1 lb. crystallized mixed fruits and peels, chopped
1 lb crystallized pineapple
½ lb. crystallized cherries
1 c. white raisins
1 c. grated coconut
1 c. honey

(If crystallized mixed fruits are not available substitute the following:)

¼ lb. crystallized citron
¼ lb. crystallized figs or dates
¼ lb. crystallized orange peels
9 crystallized cherries and 10 pecan halves
¼ lb. crystallized lemon
3 slices of crystallized pineapple

Crush graham crackers to near powder form, add spices and mix well. Add softened butter or margarine and mix well, add chopped nuts and chopped crystallized fruits and mix well. Add white raisins, coconut, then honey, mix thoroughly. Place slices of pineapple, cherries and pecan halves in the bottom of a greased loaf pan. Press ingredients firmly in pan, refrigerate 24 hours before serving. Serve plain or with whipped cream.

Mrs. Frances D. Daniel, Central Gwinnett H. S.
Lawrenceville, Georgia

UNCOOKED REFRIGERATOR FRUIT CAKE

Number of Servings — 60-80

1 lb. candied cherries (½ lb. each red and green)
1 lb. pecans
1 lb. dates
1 lb. candied pineapple slices
2 cans Eagle brand milk
3 (9 oz.) pkg. vanilla wafers

Chop candied fruit and pecans and mix, crush vanilla wafers and add to fruit mixture. Add milk and mix well, divide mixture into 4 equal parts and shape each into rolls about 10" long and 2" thick. Wrap each roll in foil and store in refrigerator until well chilled. With sharp knife, slice each serving from roll at desired thickness (about ½").

Mrs. Mary Carroll, Greenville Jr. H. S.
Greenville, Texas

ICE BOX CAKE

Number of Servings — 12

¾ c. sugar
½ c. butter
2 egg yolks
1½ c. drained crushed pineapple
4 bananas (sliced)
½ c. nut meats
2 boxes lemon gelatin
Vanilla wafers

Cream sugar and butter, add egg yolks, crushed

(Continued on Next Page)

pineapple, bananas, and nut meats. Place layer of vanilla wafers in bottom of large cake pan. Cover wafers with mixture. Cover with lemon gelatin which is partially congealed and place in refrigerator until it sets.

Mrs. Jan Rodacker, Fessenden H. S.
Fessenden, North Dakota

LEMON ICE BOX CAKE
Number of Servings — 6
4 eggs
½ c. sugar
1 orange, juice and grated rind
Juice of 1 lemon
1 c. whipping cream
Vanilla wafers to line tray and top mixture

Combine egg yolks, sugar, orange juice and grated rind and lemon juice in top of double boiler and cook until thick. Beat egg whites until stiff, then beat into custard while custard is hot. Cool until lukewarm, whip cream until stiff, fold into mixture. Line refrigerator ice tray with vanilla wafers, pour in custard and top with layer of wafers. Cover with aluminum foil to prevent ice crystals forming on dessert. Place in freezer until firm. May be made several days ahead as the flavor improves with age.

Mrs. Jas. E. Britt, Maiden H. S.
Maiden, North Carolina

MACAROON ICE BOX CAKE
Number of Servings — 12
1 pkg. unflavored gelatin
2 c. milk
4 eggs, separated
1 c. powdered sugar
1 t. vanilla
1 small bottle maraschino cherries
1 pkg. or box macaroon cookies

Dissolve gelatin in 2 cups of milk. Separate eggs. Beat the yolks to which sugar has been added. Add this mixture to the milk and gelatin in the top of a double boiler. Heat until thick. Stir frequently. Beat egg whites until stiff but not dry. Add the flavoring and fold into the custard mixture. Line an 8x12 pan with either foil or wax paper. Cut up 1 bottle maraschino cherries and place on bottom of pan. Add layer of cookies, then layer of mixture until pan is full. Store over night in the refrigerator.

Joyce Niedenthal, Parkway Jr. H. S.
Fort Lauderdale, Florida

ORANGE REFRIGERATOR CAKE
Number of Servings — 10
12 whole ladyfingers
4 egg yolks
1 c. sugar
½ t. salt
½ c. orange juice
1 t. grated orange rind
1 T. gelatin softened in ¼ c. cold water
4 egg whites
2 T. lemon or lime juice
½ c. whipping cream
Orange sections

Line a 9″ loaf pan, sides and bottom, with split ladyfingers. Beat egg yolks and add ½ cup sugar, fruit juices, grated rind and salt. Cook in double boiler until thick, add gelatin and stir until dissolved. Chill this mixture until quite thick, then add egg whites which have been beaten stiff which has other ½ cup sugar added. Pour into lined pan and chill 24 hours if possible, unmold and slice. Garnish with whipped cream and orange sections. For a richer dessert, fold in ½ cup whipped cream and orange sections before chilling.

Mrs. Christine C. Risher, Noxubee County H. S.
Macon, Mississippi

PINEAPPLE ICE BOX CAKE
Number of Servings — 12
½ c. butter
1 c. sugar
3 egg yolks
1 c. vanilla wafer crumbs
¾ c. boiling water
1 pkg. lemon gelatin
1 small can crushed pineapple
1 c. chopped nuts
3 stiffly beaten egg whites
Additional cracker crumbs to cover bottom of dish

Combine butter and sugar, cream, add egg yolks and cracker crumbs. Dissolve gelatin in hot water, add to first mixture. Add pineapple and nuts and fold in egg whites. Butter a 9x12 dish, cover bottom with cracker crumbs, pour in mixture. Chill 48 hours before serving. Serve with whipped cream and cherry.

This recipe submitted by the following teachers:
Mrs. Georgia Mitchell, Blacksburg H. S.
Blacksburg, South Carolina
Katherine M. Simons, Cross H. S.
Cross, South Carolina

PINEAPPLE ICE BOX CAKE
Number of Servings — 10
1 can sweetened condensed milk
1 c. crushed pineapple, drained
3 T. lemon juice
2 small boxes vanilla wafers

Drain juice off pineapple. To condensed milk, add lemon juice. When thickened, add pineapple. Line refrigerator pan or pyrex dish with wax paper. Put a layer of vanilla wafers, a layer of pineapple mixture, another layer of wafers (broken), another of mixture until all of mixture has been used. Let set in refrigerator over night. Slice and serve. Top with whipped cream, if desired.

Betty Sudduth, Westminster H. S.
Westminster, South Carolina

PINEAPPLE ICE BOX CAKE
Number of Servings — 8-12
4 eggs
1¼ c. sugar
1 can (No. 2) crushed pineapple
2 T. butter
1 pkg. lemon Jello
1 c. chopped nuts
1 lb. vanilla wafers

(Continued on Next Page)

Beat egg yolks and sugar and ½ cup pineapple juice. Cook until thick. Remove from heat and add butter, Jello, pineapple and rest of juice. Let cool and add nuts. Fold in stiffly beaten egg whites. Roll or grind vanilla wafers until fine. Put a layer in bottom of long pyrex dish, then pineapple mixture. Top with rest of crumbs. Serve with whipped cream.

Mrs. Melvin Sullivan, Gillham H. S.
Gillham, Arkansas

PINEAPPLE CHIFFON CAKE

Number of Servings — 8-10

1 envelope unflavored gelatin
¼ c. cold water
3 eggs, separated
1 c. crushed pineapple
2 T. lemon juice
¼ t. salt
⅓ c. sugar
⅔ c. evaporated milk, chilled
1 pkg. lge. thin chocolate cookies

Soften gelatin in cold water, combine slightly beaten egg yolks, pineapple and syrup, 1 tablespoon lemon juice and salt. Cook over hot water, stirring constantly until of custard consistency, stir in softened gelatin, cool. Slowly beat sugar into stiffly beaten egg whites, fold in. Whip icy cold evaporated milk until triple in volume, add 1 tablespoon lemon juice and beat until very thick, fold in. Spoon ¼ of mixture into wax paper lined 9x5 loaf pan, add a layer of large thin chocolate cookies. Repeat 3 times, add remaining chiffon as last layer. Chill overnight, unmold.

Mrs. Virginia C. Miller, Winecoff School
Concord, North Carolina

PINEAPPLE REFRIGERATOR CAKE

Number of Servings — 8-12

2 sticks butter
1 box powdered sugar, sifted
4 eggs
1 can crushed pineapple
1 t. vanilla flavoring
1 pkg. vanilla wafers
1 c. nuts

Cream butter, add sifted sugar, cream. Add eggs 1 at a time, beat well after each addition. Add well-drained pineapple. Add vanilla flavoring. Put in dish in alternate layers, mixture, vanilla wafers and nuts. Refrigerate 24 hours before serving.

Magda West McCormick, Negreet H. S.
Negreet, Louisiana

RAINBOW 'PRISIM' CAKE

Number of Servings — 15-16

1 pkg. orange Jello
1 pkg. cherry jello
1 pkg. lime Jello
3 c. hot water
1½ c. cold water
1 c. pineapple juice
¼ c. sugar
1 pkg. lemon Jello
½ c. cold water

1 c. graham cracker crumbs
¼ c. butter or margarine, melted
2 c. heavy cream

Prepare first 3 packaegs of Jello separately using 1 cup hot water and ½ cup cold water for each, chill until firm in separate 8x8x2 pans. Combine pineapple juice and sugar, heat until sugar is dissolved. Remove from heat and dissolve lemon Jello in hot mixture, add ½ cup cold water, chill until syrupy. Mix crumbs with melted butter, Press crumb mixture over the bottom of a 9" spring form pan. Whip the 2 cups of cream and pour into the syrupy lemon Jello mixture. With knife dipped into hot water, cut the orange, cherry, and lime Jello into ½" bits, fold the cubed Jello into the whipped cream mixture. Pour into spring form pan, chill 8 hours in refrigerator before serving.

Mrs. James Swaffar, Hughes H. S.
Hughes, Arkansas

REFRIGERATOR CAKE

3 c. vanilla wafer crumbs
1½ c. powdered sugar
½ c. butter
2 eggs, well beaten
1 c. cream, whipped
¾ c. pecans, chopped
1 c. crushed pineapple, drained

Add beaten eggs to well creamed butter and sugar. Beat until fluffy. Place in bottom of pan a layer of vanilla wafer crumbs. Pat firmly. Add the creamed mixture, pineapple, whipped cream, and nuts. Add the remaining wafer crumbs. Refrigerate over night. Serve with whipped cream on top with a cherry.

Mary Denton Pierce, Clinton County H. S.
Albany, Kentucky

STRAWBERRY REFRIGERATOR CAKE

Number of Servings — 8

1 pkg. strawberry Jello
1 c. water
1 c. sugar
1 pt. frozen strawberries
1 14 oz. can condensed milk
2 T. lemon juice
1 9 oz. pkg. vanilla wafers

Chill milk and whip with lemon juice. Mix Jello, water, and sugar. Heat and mix with frozen strawberries. Fold mixture into whipped milk. Line pan 8x11x2 with wax paper. Begin with layer of vanilla wafers and alternate with mixture until it is all used. Place in freezer until firm. Cut in blocks and serve.

Matha L. Taylor, Algoma H. S.
Algoma, Mississippi

MILE-HIGH CHERRY CHIFFON PIE

Number of Servings — 6-8

1¼ c. finely crushed graham crackers
2 T. sugar
6 T. soft butter or margarine
1 14½ oz. can evaporated milk

(Continued on Next Page)

1 No. 303 can sour pitted red cherries
1 pkg. cherry flavored gelatin
2 3 oz. pkg. softened cream cheese
2 T. granulated sugar
½ t. almond extract
½ t. lemon juice

Combine graham cracker crumbs, sugar and butter. Press all but ¼ cup into a 9″ buttered pie plate, bake crust 8-10 minutes in a 350°F. oven. Chill thoroughly (almost freezing) all but ¼ cup evaporated milk, chill bowl and beater. Meanwhile drain juice from cherries, add enough water to make 1 cup. Bring juice to boil, pour hot juice over gelatin. Stir until gelatin is dissolved, add flavoring. Chill until gelatin is consistency of unbeaten egg whites. While gelatin chills, fluff cheese with ¼ cup reserved evaporated milk and sugar, then beat chilled gelatin until frothy. When milk is ready, beat to consistency of whipped cream. Fold milk and cut-up cherries into gelatin mixture along with almond extract. Place ⅓ cherry mixture in pie shell, spoon on half cheese mixture, top with half of remaining cherry filling. Spoon on rest of cheese and top with rest of cherry pie filling. Sprinkle on remaining crumbs, chill.

Mrs. Duane Torguson, Bristol H. S.
Bristol, South Dakota

CHOCOLATE SUNDAE CREAM PIE

Number of Servings — 6-7

1¼ c. evaporated milk
½ t. nutmeg
3 egg yolks
½ c. granulated sugar
⅛ t. salt
¾ T. gelatin
3 T. cold water
½ t. vanilla
3 egg whites, beaten stiff
¼ c. grated chocolate
1 c. sweetened whipped cream

Heat milk with nutmeg, beat egg yolks with sugar and salt and mix with the milk and boil until consistency of thick cream. Cook slowly and stir constantly to prevent scorching. Add gelatin which has been hydrated in water, add vanilla. When cool, fold in beaten egg whites, pour into baked pastry shell (9″) and place in refrigerator. When cold, cover with whipped cream and sprinkle top with grated chocolate.

Mrs. Ann Hohman, Juniata Valley H. S.
Alexandria, Pennsylvania

CHOCOLATE SUNDAE PIE

Number of Servings — 6

1 c. condensed milk (Eagle brand)
½ c. water
⅛ t. nutmeg
3 egg yolks mixed with ½ c. sugar and ⅛ t. salt
1 T. gelatin dissolved in 3 T. water
3 egg whites, beaten
1 t. vanilla

Heat milk, water and nutmeg in double boiler. When hot add 3 egg yolks, sugar and salt and cook until it begins to thicken. Add the gelatin dissolved in water and fold in beaten egg whites and vanilla. Pour in baked pie crust, when cool, top with ½ cup sweetened whipped cream and sprinkle with ¼ cup grated chocolate.

Mrs. Blanche Ivanish, Malta H. S.
Malta, Montana

NESSLERODE PIE (Chocolate)

Number of Servings — 8

1 baked 9″ pastry shell
1 T. plain gelatin
¼ c. cold water
2 c. light cream
2 eggs, separated
Pinch of salt
¼ c. plus 6 T. granulated sugar
1 T. rum flavoring
Chocolate shavings

Dissolve gelatin in cold water for 5 minutes, scald cream in top of double boiler. Beat egg yolks with fork, then stir in salt and ¼ cup sugar. Add scalded cream to egg yolks. Return mixture to double boiler and cook over boiling water, stirring constantly, about 5 minutes. Remove from heat, add gelatin and stir until dissolved. Pour into a bowl and chill until it begins to thicken. Beat egg whites stiff, gradually add 6 tablespoons sugar, while beating. Fold into chilled custard with rum flavoring, pour into shell, chill, add shaved chocolate.

Mrs. Bertha Hale, North Phoenix H. S.
Phoenix, Arizona

COCONUT CLOUD PIE

Number of Servings — 6-8

1 T. unflavored gelatin
⅛ c. cold water
4 egg yolks
⅔ c. sugar
1¼ c. milk
⅛ t. salt
4 egg whites, stiffly beaten
⅔ c. coconut
1½ t. vanilla
1 t. lemon extract
½ pt. whipping cream

Soften gelatin in cold water. Combine egg yolks and sugar. Add milk and cook in double boiler, stirring constantly, until custard coats a spoon. Add softened gelatin to hot custard. Stir until dissolved. Add salt and cool. When mixture begins to thicken, fold in stiffly beaten egg whites, coconut, vanilla, and lemon extract. Pour into baked pastry shell. Chill. To serve, sprinkle pie with coconut and make wreath of whipped cream.

Rose Marie Willis, Calico Rock H. S.
Calico Rock, Arkansas

GRAPE CHIFFON PIE

Number of Servings — 6

1 baked pastry shell
1 envelope unflavored gelatin
¼ c. cold water
3 eggs, separated
⅛ t. salt
⅔ c. sugar

(Continued on Next Page)

½ c. milk
1½ t. vanilla extract
1½ c. seeded tokay grapes
1 T. sugar
½ pt. whipping cream
Grapes for garnish

Soften gelatin in cold water, set aside. Beat egg yolks in top of a double boiler, add salt and ¼ cup of sugar, blend in milk. Stir and cook over hot water until the mixture coats a metal spoon, add softened gelatin, mix well. Cool over ice water until the mixture begins to thicken, fold in vanilla extract and grapes. Beat egg whites until they stand in soft peaks, into which gradually beat in remaining ¼ cup sugar, fold in custard. Turn into a cold baked 9″ pastry shell, chill until firm and ready to serve. Sweeten cream with the 1 tablspoon sugar spread over pie, garnish with Emperor grapes.

Laurel J. Willcox, Oscar Frommel Smith H. S.
South Norfolk, Virginia

LEMON CHIFFON PIE
Number of Servings — 9 Inch Pie
½ c. sugar
1 envelope unflavored gelatin
⅔ c. water
⅛ c. lemon juice
4 egg yolks, slightly beaten
1 T. grated lemon rind
4 egg whites
½ t. cream of tartar
½ c. sugar

Blend ½ cup sugar, gelatin, water, lemon juice and egg yolks in saucepan. Cook over medium heat, stirring constantly, until mixture comes to a boil. Stir in lemon rind, place pan in cold water and cool until mixture mounds slightly when dropped from spoon. Beat egg whites, cream of tartar and sugar to stiff peaks. Fold lemon mixture into meringue. Pile into cooled baked pastry shell or graham cracker crust and chill several hours.

Gay Linthicum, Damacus H. S.
Damascus, Maryland

HEAVENLY LEMON PIE
Number of Servings — 6
9″ baked pastry shell
4 eggs, separated
¾ c. sugar
¼ c. lemon juice
1 t. grated lemon rind
½ t. gelatin
1 T. cold water
½ c. whipping cream

Blend egg yolks, sugar, lemon juice, and rind. Cook over hot water, stirring constantly until thick, about 20 minutes. Dissolve gelatin in water and stir into hot mixture. Cook another 2 minutes. Cool. Beat egg whites until very stiff and fold into lemon mixture. Pour into baked pastry shell. Chill in refrigerator. Top with sweetened whipped cream if desired.

Alice Ruth E. Blackburn,
District Supervisor, Home Economics Education
Montevallo, Alabama

LEMONADE CHIFFON PIE
Number of Servings — 6
1 c. evaporated milk
1 envelope unflavored gelatin
¼ c. cold water
½ c. boiling water
1 pinch of salt
⅔ c. sugar
6 oz. can frozen lemonade concentrate
Juice of 1 lemon
1 baked 9″ pastry shell or graham cracker crust

Chill milk in ice tray until frozen around edges. In a 3-quart bowl soften gelatin in cold water. Add boiling water. Stir until gelatin is dissolved. Add salt, sugar, lemonade concentrate and lemon juice. Stir until lemonade thaws. Chill until mixture is very thick but not set. Put ice cold milk into cold 1-quart bowl. Whip with a cold beater at high speed until stiff. Fold into chilled gelatin mixture. Put mixture into graham cracker crumb crust or baked pie shell (cooled). Chill until firm, about 3 hours.

Bernice Marshall, Texas Sr. H. S.
Texarkana, Texas

LEMON CHIFFON PIE
Number of Servings — One 9-Inch Pie
Crust:
1 c. crushed graham crackers
4 T. melted butter

Mix melted butter with graham cracker crumbs. Pat firmly into pie plate on bottom and sides, forming a pie shell. Chill thoroughly.

Filling:
5 T. sugar
2 T. water
3 egg yolks
Grated rind of 1 lemon
3 T. lemon juice
⅛ t. salt
3 egg whites
3 T. sugar

Combine first 5 ingredients. Cook over boiling water, stirring until thick. Cool. Beat egg whites and salt until stiff, but not dry. Fold in sugar. Fold egg whites into custard. Fill pie shell. Chill and serve (may be wrapped and frozen 2 to 3 months).

Mary R. Ruble, Cocke Co. H. S.
Newport, Tennessee

MILE HIGH LEMONADE CHIFFON PIE
Number of Servings — 6
Crust:
3 T. butter
1½ c. coconut (4 oz.)

Melt butter in skillet, add coconut and stir over medium heat until coconut is golden brown. Press mixture firmly on bottom and sides of 9″ pie pan, cool at room temperature.

Filling:
1 c. evaporated milk
1 envelope unflavored gelatin
¼ c. cold water

(Continued on Next Page)

½ c. boiling water
⅔ c. sugar
1 6 oz. can frozen lemonade concentrate

Chill milk in ice tray until almost frozen, soften gelatin in ¼ cup cold water, add ½ cup boiling water, stir until dissolved. Add sugar and frozen lemon concentrate. Stir until lemonade thraws, chill until mixture is thick. Whip iced milk until stiff, fold into chilled gelatin. Put into coconut crust, chill 3 hours.

Mrs. Bonnie Shaw, Clarkfield Public School
Clarkfield, Minnesota

FROSTED DAIQUIRI PIE
Number of Servings — 8
1 envelope unflavored gelatin
½ c. lime juice (fresh or frozen)
3 egg yolks
¼ c. cold water
½ t. salt
⅔ c. sugar

Mix ingredients in double boiler, beat with rotary beater until well blended. Cook over low heat until mixture coats spoon. Cool slightly and add 1 tablespoon lime rind and tint with 3 drops green food coloring, cool. Add ⅓ cup light rum, refrigerate until slightly thicker than unbeaten egg whites. In a bowl large enough to hold complete mixture, beat 3 egg whites until they form firm, moist peaks. Add ⅔ cup sugar, 1 tablespoon at a time until very stiff. Then fold in first mixture until well blended. Pour in baked pastry shell and refrigerate, garnish with whipped cream topped with red or green colored sugar.

Genevieve Dillon, Rio Grande H. S.
Albuquerque, New Mexico

ORANGE CHIFFON PIE
1 t. grated orange rind
4 lge. Florida oranges cut in sections and well drained (seedless and well ripened preferred)
1 envelope unflavored gelatin
1 c. sugar plus 1 T.
½ t. salt
1¼ c. milk
3 egg yolks, slightly beaten
1 pkg. (3 to 4 oz.) cream cheese
½ c. fresh orange juice (usually this amount will drain from orange sections)
1 t. undiluted frozen orange juice
3 egg whites

Grate the rind from 1 of 4 oranges and reserve for later. Pare 4 oranges beyond the white part, section out with all membrane removed and put in wire strainer to drain. Sprinkle 1 tablespoon sugar over sections while draining. Combine gelatin, ¾ cups sugar, and salt in top of double boiler (save remaining ¼ cup sugar). Stir in milk and egg yolks, cook over boiling water, stirring constantly until mixture thickens slightly and coats a spoon. Divide mixture between 2 small bowls (about 1 cup in each). Beat cream cheese into mixture in 1 bowl, blending until smooth, slowly stir in ¼ cup fresh orange juice and 1 teaspoon of undiluted frozen orange juice. Then stir re-

maining ¼ cup fresh orange juice and 1 tablespoon undiluted frozen juice into mixture in second bowl, chill both until they begin to thicken. Pour thickened cheese-gelatin mixture into baked pastry or crumbs shell. Save 8 most perfect sections of oranges and place rest over top of cheese-gelatin layer, chill while making the 2nd layer. Beat egg whites until foamy in large bowl, add remaining ¼ cup sugar, 1 tablespoon at a time, beating well after each addition, until meringue stands in stiff peaks. Fold in thickened orange-gelatin mixture and 1 teaspoon grated orange rind. Swirl on top of layer in shell, chill. Chill 2 hours before serving, may be refrigerated overnight.

Mrs. Margaret Mofield, Mainland Sr. H. S.
Daytona Beach, Florida

ORANGE FLUFF PIE
Number of Servings — 6-8
1 envelope plain gelatin
¼ c. cold water
4 eggs, separated
1 c. sugar
½ c. orange juice
½ t. salt
1 T. grated orange peel
2 T. toasted coconut

Soften gelatin in water, beat egg yolks and ½ cup of sugar in top of double boiler. Add juice and salt and blend well. Heat and stir over hot, not boiling water until mixture coats spoon, about 20 minutes. Remove from heat and add gelatin and orange peel. Cool until mixture begins to thicken, stirring occasionally. Beat egg whites until foamy and add remaining sugar gradually while beating until stiff peaks form. Fold in custard, spoon into coconut crust or patty shells. Top with toasted coconut and chill 3 to 4 hours.

Coconut crust
¼ c. butter
1 c. marshmallow creme
½ c. shredded coconut
3 c. bite-size shredded rice biscuits, crushed to measure 1½ c.

Butter a 9″ pie plate, heat and stir butter and marshmallow creme over hot water until syrupy. Stir in vanilla, coconut, and crushed cereal, press into pie plate, add orange fluff filling.

Mrs. Grace Callaway,
Alexander Stephens Institute
Crawfordville, Georgia

PINEAPPLE ORANGE CHIFFON PIE
Number of Servings — 6
2 eggs
1 c. sugar
1 box orange Jello
1½ c. pineapple juice
1 lge. can evaporated milk (cold)

Beat the eggs together, add sugar, Jello and juice. Bring to a boil. Cool. Whip evaporated milk chilled in freezing unit, preferably over night. Stir into pineapple mixture, pour into vanilla wafer crust. Chill.

Emma Ruth Everett, Decatur Atl. Center
Decatur, Mississippi

PINEAPPLE CHIFFON PIE

Number of Servings — Two Pies

1 can evaporated milk or 1¾ c. cream
1 pkg. lemon Jello
1 c. white sugar
1½ c. pineapple juice
1 egg, well beaten
1 box vanilla wafers

Chill milk or cream. Mix thoroughly the lemon Jello, sugar, pineapple juice and the egg, bring to a boil. Set aside to cool. Whip milk or cream and fold in cooled syrup. Line 2 pie plates with vanilla wafers and fill with filling. Place in refrigerator.

Mrs. Lois O. Crabtree, Ceres School
Ceres, Virginia

PEPPERMINT CHIFFON PIE

Number of Servings — 6

1½ c. crushed peppermint stick candy
¼ c. sugar
1 envelope unflavored gelatin
1¼ c. milk
3 egg yolks, slightly beaten
¼ t. salt
3 egg whites
¼ c. sugar
½ c. heavy cream, whipped
1 3½ oz. can (1⅓ c.) flaked coconut, toasted

Mix candy, ¼ cup sugar, gelatin, milk, egg yolks, and salt. Cook and stir over low heat until gelatin dissolves and candy melts. Chill until partially set. Beat egg whites until soft peaks form, gradually add ¼ cup sugar, beating to stiff peaks, fold into gelatin mixture. Fold in whipped cream and chill until mixture mounds slightly when spooned. Pile into coconut crust, chill until firm, top with whipped cream if desired. Coconut crust: Press coconut over bottom and sides of buttered 9″ pie plate.

Mrs. Kathryn Lumpkin, Randolph County H. S.
Wedowee, Alabama

PUMPKIN CHIFFON PIE

Number of Servings — 6

1 T. unflavored gelatin
¼ c. orange juice
3 egg yolks
1 c. sugar
1¼ c. cooked or canned pumpkin
½ c. milk
½ t. salt
½ t. cinnamon
½ t. nutmeg
½ t. ginger, optional
3 egg whites

Soften gelatin in orange juice. In top of double boiler, beat the egg yolks until bubbly, stir in ½ cup sugar, pumpkin, milk, salt, cinnamon and nutmeg. Cook over boiling water, stirring constantly until thickened. Stir in softened gelatin, continue to stir until gelatin is dissolved. Remove from heat, chill until slightly thicker than unbeaten egg white consistency. Beat egg whites until stiff peaks, gradually beat in ½ cup sugar, about 1 tablespoon at a time. Gently mix pumpkin mixture into egg whites, pour into baked pastry shell, chill until firm. Serve garnished with whipped cream, add slivered candied ginger for a special touch. Gingersnap crust may be used instead of pastry shell.

This recipe submitted by the following teachers:
Mrs. Ellen D. Feagan, Las Cruces H. S.
Las Cruces, New Mexico
Mrs. Elizabeth Hayton, Huntington Jr. H. S.
Kelso, Washington
Pauline K. Fish, Mt. Lebanon H. S.
Pittsburgh, Pennsylvania

PUMPKIN CHIFFON PIE

Number of Servings — 6

1½ T. gelatin
¼ c. cold water
3 eggs (separated)
½ c. brown sugar
½ c. white sugar
1¼ c. canned pumpkin
½ c. milk
¾ t. ginger
¾ t. cinnamon
¾ t. nutmeg
½ t. salt
¼ c. sherry
1 c. heavy cream

Soften gelatin in cold water. Beat egg yolks, add brown sugar, pumpkin, milk, seasonings and sherry. Cook over low heat until thick, stirring constantly. Add softened gelatin to hot mixture. Stir until dissolved. Cool. Beat egg whites until stiff. Add remaining sugar and fold into filling. Pour into baked pastry shell and chill. Serve topped with whipped cream.

Margaret H. Holloway, Groves H. S.
Savannah, Georgia

PUMPKIN-CHIFFON PRALINE PIE

1 stick pie crust mix
⅓ c. butter or margarine
⅓ c. firmly packed brown sugar
⅓ c. chopped walnuts or pecans
¾ c. granulated sugar (for filling)
1 envelope unflavored gelatin
1½ t. pumpkin pie spice
½ t. salt
4 egg yolks, slightly beaten
1 can (about 1 lb.) pumpkin
¾ c. milk
4 egg whites
¼ c. granulated sugar (for meringue)
½ c. cream, whipped

Prepare pie crust mix, follow recipe on package. Bake in very hot oven 450°F. for 10 minutes. While crust bakes, cream butter, or margarine, and brown sugar well in bowl, stir in nuts, spread on bottom of partly baked crust. Bake 5 minutes longer or until golden brown. Combine ¾ cups granulated sugar, gelatin, pumpkin pie spice, and salt in top of double boiler. Stir in egg yolks, pumpkin and milk. Cook 15 minutes. Chill. Beat egg whites until foamy in large bowl, beat in ¼

(Continued on Next Page)

cup granulated sugar. Set bowl in pan of ice. Beat pumpkin-gelatin mixture until fluffy. Fold in chilled meringue (still over ice). Spoon into pastry shell. Serve with whipped cream (keep refrigerated).

Mary Beth Tuck, Longview Sr. H. S.
Longview, Texas

RUM CHIFFON PIE

Number of Servings — 6

4 eggs, separated
1 c. sugar
½ c. milk
1 envelope unflavored gelatin
¼ c. cold water
⅛-¼ c. rum
1 9″ crumb crust or pastry shell

Dissolve envelope of gelatin in ¼ cup of cold water, beat the egg yolks lightly, add ½ cup of sugar and milk to egg yolks. Cook in double boiler until mixture thickens. While mixture is hot, add gelatin. When this mixture is cold add rum, then the stiffly beaten egg whites to which the other ½ cup sugar has been added. Pour custard into a cold pastry shell and place into refrigerator until it sets. Before serving, pie may be topped with whipped cream and grated chocolate. Cream may be swirled around pie using pastry tube and then decorate with silver dragees or bits of crystallized fruit, sprigs of fresh mint stuck in cherries.

This recipe submitted by the following teachers:
Evelyn Cotney, Assistant State Supervisor
State Department of Education
Montevallo, Alabama
Marie S. Griffin, Thomasville H. S.
Thomasville, Alabama

RUM PIE

Number of Servings — 6

1 envelope unflavored gelatin
¼ c. cold water
3 egg yolks
½ c. milk
¼ t. salt
½ c. sugar
6 macaroons
4 T. rum
3 egg whites
2 T. sugar
½ pt. whipping cream

Soften gelatin in cold water. Beat egg yolks. Add milk, salt and ½ cup sugar. Cook, stirring constantly until thick. Remove from heat, add softened gelatin and stir until dissolved. Add crumbled macaroons and beat until dissolved. When almost cool, add rum. When this begins to stiffen, fold in stiffly beaten egg whites to which 2 tablespoons of sugar has been added. Fold in cream. Turn into baked pastry shell and chill. Serve with whipped cream and toasted almonds.

Mrs. Ruth H. Hughes, Abbeville H. S.
Abbeville, South Carolina

STRAWBERRY JELLO PIE

Number of Servings — Two Pies - 12

3 eggs
¾ c. sugar
1 No. 1 flat can (1 c.) crushed pineapple
1 pkg. strawberry Jello
1 tall can evaporated milk
Two 9″ graham cracker pie crusts

Chill the evaporated milk. Combine eggs, sugar and crushed pineapple and mix well. Bring to a boil. Remove from the heat and add 1 package strawberry Jello (lime or raspberry can be substituted). Stir until Jello is dissolved. Cool thoroughly. Whip the evaporated milk until stiff (the consistency of whipped cream). Fold the Jello mixture into the whipped milk, then pour into the 2 pie crusts. Chill. The pies are firmer if made the day before serving.

Mrs. Mary Belle Nutt, Cotulla H. S.
Cotulla, Texas

APRICOT PARFAIT PIE

Number of Servings — 6

1 baked 9″ pastry shell
1 pkg. lemon flavored gelatin
1¼ c. apricot juice heated to boiling
(use juice drained from canned apricots, plus enough water to make 1¼ c. liquid)
1 pt. vanilla ice cream
1½ c. canned apricots, drained and crushed to a pulp
½ c. heavy cream, whipped

In 2-quart saucepan, dissolve gelatin in boiling hot apricot juice, add ice cream by spoonfuls, stirring until melted. Refrigerate in pan until thickened but not set, about 15 minutes. Fold in apricot pulp, turn into baked pastry shell. Refrigerate until set, about 25 minutes. Garnish with circle of whipped cream.

Mrs. Harold Poling, Berrien Springs H. S.
Berrien Springs, Michigan

CHOCOLATE LIME PARFAIT PIE

Number of Servings — 6

1 box lime Jello
1 c. boiling water
1 T. chocolate crumbs
1 c. vanilla ice cream
1 8½ oz. can crushed pineapple
½ pt. whipping cream
4 T. melted butter
1 8½ oz. box chocolate wafers

Crush chocolate wafers fine, add melted butter, pat into 9″ pie pan. Bake in hot oven 10 minutes and allow to cool. Dissolve Jello in 1 cup boiling water, add the ice cream and stir until it is melted. Fold in the drained crushed pineapple, chill until almost congealed. Spoon mixture over chocolate wafer crust, spread whipped cream on top. Sprinkle 1 tablespoon chocolate crumbs on top of the whipped cream.

Mrs. Virginia S. Sharbutt, Vincent School
Vincent, Alabama

DATE-NUT PARFAIT PIT

1 pkg. orange Jello
1¼ c. hot water
½ c. chopped dates
1 pt. vanilla ice cream
½ c. chopped nuts
¼ t. cinnamon
Whipped cream for topping
Graham cracker crust or pastry shell

Dissolve orange Jello in hot water, add dates and ice cream, cool until it begins to thicken. Add nuts and cinnamon, pour in graham cracker crust or pastry shell. Top with sweetened whipped cream, seasoned with a dash of cinnamon, chill.

Mrs. Eugene S. Turner, Lexington H. S.
Lexington, Tennessee

LEMON-COCONUT PARFAIT PIE
Number of Servings — 6-8

1 can shredded coconut
3 T. margarine
1 pkg. lemon gelatin
1 c. hot water
1 pt. vanilla ice cream
2 T. lemon juice
1 t. grated lemon rind

Prepare pie crust by heavily coating 1 8″ pie pan with margarine. Press coconut into the margarine. Bake at 350°F. until lightly browned. Dissolve gelatin in hot water. Spoon in ice cream and stir until completely melted. Add lemon juice and rind. Pour into completely cooled pie crust. Allow to chill at least an hour before serving. Garnish with thinly cut lemon slices.

Joella Gartner, Brazosport Sr. H. S.
Freeport, Texas

PEACH PARFAIT PIE
Number of Servings — 6-8

3½ c. sliced peaches, sweetened or 1 No. 2½ can
1 3 oz. pkg. lemon flavored gelatin
½ c. cold water
1 pt. vanilla ice cream
1 baked 9″ pastry shell
½ c. whipping cream, whipped

If using fresh peaches, let stand about 15 minutes after mixing with sugar, drain peaches (fresh or canned), reserving syrup. Add water to syrup to make 1 cup, heat to boiling, add gelatin, stir until dissolved, add cold water. Cut ice cream in 6 pieces, add to hot liquid, stir until melted. Chill until mixture mounds slightly when dropped from a spoon (15 to 20 minutes). Fold in peaches and pour into cooled pastry shell, chill until firm. Top with whipped cream and peaches.

Mrs. Marjorie Bales, Seaman Rural H. S.
Topeka, Kansas

STRAWBERRY PARFAIT PIE

Pastry shell or graham cracker crust
Graham cracker crust:
20 graham crackers (crushed into crumbs)
¼ c. melted butter or margarine
Mix crumbs and butter and form crust in 9″ pie pan, bake at 375°F. for 8 minutes.

Filling:
1 pkg. (3 oz.) strawberry Jello
1¼ c. hot water
1 pt. strawberry ice cream
1½ c. sliced and drained strawberries (fresh or frozen berries may be used; if frozen berries are used, make use of liquid in place of some of the water)

Dissolve strawberry Jello in hot water, add ice cream, mixing by spoonfuls. Chill until mixture thickens (not set), add strawberries. Chill in graham cracker crust, top with whipped cream if desired, top with whole strawberries if available. Variations: Raspberry gelatin, raspberry ice cream and raspberries; cherry gelatin, pitted dark cherries and vanilla ice cream; lemon Jello may be used with any fruit.

This recipe submitted by the following teachers:
Mrs. Patricia Bieber, Bel-Norte County H. S.
Crescent City, California
Mrs. Wylodine Reed, Aberdeen H. S.
Aberdeen, Mississippi
Mrs. Connie Cotter, Middleton H. S.
Middleton, Wisconsin
Jere Lyn Sanders, San Marcos H. S.
San Marcos, Texas

ALMOND CRUST CHERRY CREAM PIE
Number of Servings — 6

1 stick pie crust mix
½ c. slivered almonds, finely chopped
1⅜ c. condensed milk
⅛ c. lemon juice
1 t. vanilla
½ t. almond extract
½ c. whipping cream, whipped

Mix pastry as directed on mix, except add chopped almonds. Prick sides and bottom. Bake and cool. Combine the milk, lemon juice, vanilla and almond extract. Stir until mixture thickens. Fold in the whipped cream and spoon into cooled shell. Top with cherry glaze. Chill 2-3 hours.

Glaze:
2 c. sour cherries (drained)
⅝ c. cherry juice
¼ c. sugar
1 T. cornstarch
2-3 drops red food coloring

Blend cherry juice, with sugar and cornstarch. Cook over low heat, stirring constantly, until mixture is thickened and clear. Add drained cherries and coloring. Spread over cream filling.

Mrs. Otto Bakken, Kerkhoven, Public School
Kerkhoven, Minnesota

AMBASSADOR PIE
Number of Servings — 12-15

1 envelope Knox sparkling gelatin
4 T. cold water
2 c. milk, scalded
1¼ T. cornstarch
1 c. sugar
4 eggs

(Continued on Next Page)

¼ t. cream of tartar
Graham cracker crust:
17 graham crackers, rolled fine
½ c. sugar
½ c. butter

Dissolve gelatin in cold water, combine cornstarch and ½ cup sugar, add the scalded milk, stir while it cooks. Add 4 egg yolks and cook to a soft custard, add the gelatin, stir until dissolved, and cool the mixture. Add the cream of tartar to the egg whites and beat until stiff, add remaining ½ cup sugar. Fold egg whites into the custard and use whatever flavoring desired. Pour into a graham cracker crust in a 8x11 pan, refrigerate until firm. Serve with whipped cream and chopped nuts.

Mrs. Herman H. Hitchcock, Healdton H. S.
Healdton, Oklahoma

BANANA-JEWEL PIE

Number of Servings — 6

1 baked 9" pastry shell
1 pkg. gelatin dessert
⅓ c. cranberry juice or port wine
1 8 oz. pkg. soft cream cheese
1 T. milk
¼ c. granulated sugar
⅛ t. nutmeg
⅛ t. vanilla extract
Dash salt
3 medium bananas
1 c. heavy cream, whipped
Toasted shredded or flaked coconut

Bake the pastry shell, prepare gelatin dessert as package label directs except only 1½ cups water. Stir in juice, cool, stirring occasionally until lukewarm. In a small bowl, blend cream cheese with milk, sugar, nutmeg, vanilla, and salt. With back of teaspoon, carefully spread the mixture over the bottom and well up on the side of pastry shell. Peel and slice bananas into lukewarm gelatin, spoon mixture into cheese-lined pastry shell. Refrigerate. Just before serving, add border of whipped cream and sprinkle with toasted coconut.

Nancy Davis, Mechanicsburg H. S.
Mechanicsburg, Ohio

BLACK BOTTOM PIE

Number of Servings — 8

1 baked pastry shell
½ c. sugar
1 T. cornstarch
2 c. milk (scalded)
4 egg yolks, beaten
1 pkg. chocolate bits
1 t. vanilla
1 T. gelatin
¼ c. cold water
4 egg whites, beaten
¼ c. sugar
2 t. rum
1 c. cream, whipped

Combine sugar and cornstarch. Add scalded milk to egg yolks, add to sugar mixture. Cook until spoon is coated. Add 1 cup to chocolate bits. Add vanilla. Pour in shell. Soften gelatin in cold water

and add to remaining hot custard. Stir until dissolved. Chill. Fold in egg whites to which ¼ cup sugar has been added. Add rum. Pour over chocolate mixture. Garnish with whipped cream and chocolate.

Willie Kathryn Roney, Headland H. S.
Headland, Alabama

BRADOCK PIE

Number of Servings — 18

25 graham crackers
1½ c. butter
3½ c. powdered sugar
6 eggs
3 c. boiling water
2 boxes raspberry Jello
1¾ c. whipping cream
1 No. 2 can crushed pineapple

Roll crackers in crumbs, put about ⅓" deep in bottom of large loaf pan. Cream butter until soft and creamy, add powdered sugar (save ½ cup for egg whites), mix well. Beat egg yolks and whites separately until thick, add ½ cup powdered sugar to whites, add to sugar mixture, mix well and pour on cracker crumbs. With 3 cups boiling water, make 2 boxes Jello, set to whipping stage. Whip Jello and whip cream, mix together, add pineapple, mix well and pour on butter mixture. Sprinkle crumbs on top and let stand at room temperature 2-3 hours. Put in a cool place to set. Note: Any flavor Jello may be used, bottom layer could be colored.

Janice M. DeReu, Pipestone H. S.
Pipestone, Minnesota

BLACK BOTTOM PIE

Number of Servings — 6

Crust:
14 or more crisp ginger snaps or chocolate wafers
5 T. melted butter

Roll snaps out fine, add butter to cookie crumbs and pat evenly into a 9" pan. Bake 10 minutes in 300°F. oven, allow to cool.

Filling:
2 c. milk, scalded
4 egg yolks, beaten
½ c. sugar
1¼ T. cornstarch or 2 T. flour
1½ sq. unsweetened chocolate
1 t. vanilla
1 envelope (1 T.) unflavored gelatin
4 T. cold water
4 egg whites
½ c. sugar
¼ t. cream of tartar
2 T. rum, optional
   1½ t. rum flavoring may be substituted
1 c. heavy cream, whipped and sweetened with
   2 T. confectioners' sugar if desired
½ sq. unsweetened chocolate

Add beaten egg yolks, sugar and cornstarch to scalded milk. Cook in double boiler for about 20 minutes, stirring occasionally until it generously coats a spoon. Remove from heat and take out 1

(Continued on Next Page)

cup, add 1½ squares chocolate to this 1 cup of custard and beat well. As custard cools, add vanilla and pour into pie crust and chill. Soak gelatin in cold water and add to remaining hot custard, let cool, but not until thick. Beat egg whites, sugar and cream of tartar into meringue and fold into custard. Add rum, if used, and as soon as chocolate custard has set, add second mixture, chill again until it sets. Spread the whipped cream on top, shave and sprinkle ½ square chocolate over pie and serve. Pecans may be sprinkled on top instead of chocolate or wafer crumbs may be used.

This recipe submitted by the following teachers:

Mrs. Alice Allison Kealhofer, Satartia H. S.
Satartia, Mississippi

Mrs. Maurine Taylor, East Mountain School
Gilmer, Texas

Louise Crosby Roebuck, Semmes H. S.
Semmes, Alabama

Mrs. Erma Manning, Linn H. S.
Doddsville, Mississippi

Mrs. Janice King, Commerce H. S.
Commerce, Texas

CANDIED FRUIT PIE (Rich)

Number of Servings — 6

1 9" baked pastry shell
1 envelope unflavored gelatin
¼ c. cold water
2 c. light cream
⅔ c. sugar
Few grains salt
2 eggs, separated
1½ t. rum or rum extract
¼ c. finely sliced candied fruit
½ c. heavy cream, whipped
1 sq. (1 oz.) unsweetened chocolate

Prepare your favorite 9" pastry shell. Soften gelatin on cold water. Meanwhile heat cream until a film glistens over the top (do not boil). Add ⅓ cup of sugar, salt, and softened gelatin and stir until dissolved. Beat egg yolks in, stir in the cream-gelatin mixture quickly and cook over boiling water about 5 minutes or until as thick as soft custard. Chill until mixture is like thick syrup. Beat egg whites stiff and beat in the remaining ⅓ cup of sugar very gradually. Mix gently or fold egg whites into chilled egg yolk mixture. Add rum extract and candied fruit and pour into baked pastry shell. Chill until filling sets. Before serving, spread a thin layer of whipped cream over the top and sprinkle with thin curls or slivers of chocolate.

Mrs. Florence Flora, Hull-Daisetta H. S.
Daisetta, Texas

CARAMEL PECAN PIE

Number of Servings — 6

1 envelope gelatin
¼ c. water
½ lb. (28) caramels
¾ c. milk
Dash of salt
1 c. heavy cream, whipped
½ c. chopped pecans
1 t. vanilla

Dissolve gelatin in ¼ cup water, melt caramels in milk over hot water, add gelatin, salt and stir until dissolved. Chill until slightly set, fold in 1 cup heavy cream, whipped, chopped pecans, and vanilla. Fill pie crust and trim with pecan halves. Chill 2 or 3 hours.

Foy Morgan, Alexandria H. S.
Alexandria, Alabama

ALMOND CRUST-CHERRY OR BLACKBERRY CREAM PIE

Number of Servings — 6

Crust:

Add ½ cup slivered almonds, finely chopped to your favorite pastry shell recipe. Prick sides only of pastry shell. Bake and cool.

Cherry Cream Filling:

1⅓ c. (15 oz. can) sweetened condensed milk
⅓ c. lemon juice
½ t. almond extract
½ c. whipping cream, whipped

Mix ingredients, fold in whipped cream. Spoon into crust.

Cherry Glaze:

¼ c. sugar
1 T. cornstarch (more if desired)
⅔ c. cherry juice
2 to 3 drops red food coloring
1 lb. can pitted sour cherries (drained)

Mix sugar, cornstarch, juice and coloring. Cook over low heat until thick. Add cherries. Spread over cream filling and around outer edge of pie. Chill. For blueberry glaze, substitute 2 cups blueberries (drained), and ⅔ cup blueberry juice for cherries and cherry juice.

This recipe submitted by the following teachers:

Mrs. Leon White,
Jonesboro, Texas

Mrs. Glenda Winningham, Pleasant Plains H. S.
Pleasant Plains, Arkansas

Myrtle Little, Hattiesburg H. S.
Hattiesburg, Mississippi

CHERRY CREAM PIE

Number of Servings — 8

1 15 oz. can sweetened condensed milk
¼ c. lemon juice
½ t. almond extract
½ pt. whipped cream
1 1 lb., 6 oz. can cherry pie filling
1 12" crumb crust or pastry shell

Blend condensed milk, lemon juice and almond extract and stir until mixture thickens. Fold in whipped cream. Pour into pie crust and spread evenly. Spoon cherry pie filling over the mixture, completely covering the cream filling. Chill an hour or over night. This is a rich pie, so cut in small slices to serve.

Mrs. Christine Applin, Baker Jr. H. S.
Austin, Texas

CHRISTMAS PIE
Number of Servings — 8

1 can sweetened condensed milk
Juice of 1 lemon
2 c. crushed pineapple, drained
2-3 bananas, sliced
12-16 vanilla wafers
1 c. heavy cream, whipped and sweetened

Line bottom and sides of an 8" or 9" pie plate with vanilla wafers. Combine condensed milk and lemon juice and stir until thickened. Add fruit and pour into wafer lined plate. Spread the sweetened whipped cream over top of pie and chill or serve immediately.

Ruth Riffe, Hobart H. S.
Hobart, Oklahoma

CHOCOLATE PIE (Using Hershey Bars)
Number of Servings — 6-8

4-5-6 Hershey almond candy bars
½ c. milk
16-20 lge. marshmallows
½ pt. whipping cream (or whip mix)
1 graham cracker or vanilla wafer crust
    (½ c. coconut may be added to crust)
1 t. vanilla, if desired

Melt marshmallows, candy bars in milk in a double boiler, cool. Whip cream and fold into cooled mixture, pour into crust and chill.

This recipe submitted by the following teachers:

Mrs. W. C. McManuws, Columbia H. S.
Columbia, Mississippi
Mrs. Ramona Warwick, Castlewood H. S.
Castlewood, South Dakota
Mrs. Nadine Kaiser, Hydro H. S.
Hydro, Oklahoma
Karen Hofer, Beresford H. S.
Beresford, South Dakota
Jane Spring, Falls Church H. S.
Falls Church, Virginia
Mrs. Betty G. Canada, Munford Home Ec. Dept.
Munford, Alabama
Mrs. Marlys Weinman,
Plainview Community School
Plainview, Minnesota
Oleta Hayden, Milford H. S.
Milford, Texas
Marilyn Berkseth Olson, Antioch Township H. S.
Antioch, Illinois
Mrs. Marilyn Deanna Turner, Locust Grove H. S.
Locust Grove, Oklahoma
Noreen Aamoth, Hibbing H. S.
Hibbing, Minnesota
Mrs. Eleanor Johnson, Chetek H. S.
Chetek, Wisconsin
Mrs. Frances Morton, Tallulah H. S.
Tallulah, Louisiana
Mrs. Jonette Dillavou, Kofa H. S.
Yuma, Arizona
Hilda Ann Whiltney, Grand Saline H. S.
Grand Saline, Texas
Mrs. Dorothy Grimes, Jett H. S.
Nicksburg, Mississippi

CHRISTMAS MERINGUE PIE
Number of Servings — 6

Filling:
1 envelope Knox gelatin
½ c. sugar
¼ t. salt
¾ c. syrup from fruit cocktail
2 egg yolks
1 c. commercial sour cream
2 T. lemon juice
1½ c. fruit cocktail (drained)

Combine gelatin, sugar and salt in top of double boiler. Stir in ¾ cup syrup from fruit cocktail and beaten egg yolks. Cook over boiling water, stirring often, 15 minutes, until slightly thickened. Remove from heat. Stir in sour cream, and lemon juice. Cool until thickened. Fold in drained fruit cocktail. Turn into baked 9" pastry shell. Top with marshmallow meringue. Sprinkle with toasted coconut. Chill 2 hours or longer.

Meringue:
16 marshmallows
1 T. lemon juice
1 T. syrup from fruit cocktail
2 egg whites
¼ t. salt
¼ c. sugar

Melt marshmallows with lemon juice and 1 tablespoon syrup from fruit cocktail. Cook over low heat, stirring often. Cool. Beat in 2 egg whites with ¼ teaspoon salt until stiff. Gradually beat in sugar. Fold in marshmallow mixture. Spread on top of pie.

Mrs. Aline Burruss, Bogalusa Jr. H. S.
Bogalusa, Louisiana

WHITE CHRISTMAS PIE
Number of Servings — 6

Filling:
½ c. sugar
¼ c. all-purpose flour
1 envelope unflavored gelatin
½ t. salt
1¾ c. milk
¾ t. vanilla
¼ t. almond flavoring

Blend thoroughly in saucepan the sugar, all-purpose flour, gelatin, salt. Stir in gradually the milk. Cook over medium heat until mixture boils, stirring constantly. Boil 1 minute. Place pan in cold water. Cool until mixture mounds slightly when dropped from spoon. Blend in the vanilla and almond flavoring.

Meringue:
3 egg whites
¼ t. cream of tartar
½ c. sugar

Carefully fold in a meringue made of egg whites, cream of tartar and sugar. Gently fold in ½ cup cream, whipped and 1 cup shredded coconut. Pile into cooled pastry shell. Sprinkle with coconut. Chill several hours. Optional: Top with raspberries or strawberries.

Mrs. Patsy Robertson, Quitman H. S.
Quitman, Arkansas

CHOCOLATE CHIP PIE

Number of Servings — 6

2 eggs, separated
2½ T. sugar
⅜ c. sweet milk
Pinch of salt
1 envelope unflavored gelatin
¼ c. water
1 t. vanilla
2½ T. sugar
½ c. chipped semi-sweet chocolate
1 c. heavy cream

Beat egg yolks and sugar. Add milk and salt. Cook in double boiler until thick, stirring constantly. Soften gelatin in cold water, add vanilla, and then add to hot mixture. Chill. Beat egg whites and add remaining sugar. Fold in chocolate, saving some for garnish. Pour in graham cracker crust and chill until firm. Spread with whipped cream and chipped chocolate just before serving.

Mrs. Dorsey Long, Laverne Public School
Laverne, Oklahoma

CHOCOLATE CREAM PIE

Number of Servings — 6

Chocolate-Coconut Crust:
2 sq. unsweetened chocolate
2 T. butter
2 T. hot water
⅞ c. confectioners' sugar
1⅛ c. coconut

Melt chocolate and butter, stirring in top of double boiler. Combine water and sugar. Add to chocolate mixture. Add coconut, mix well. Spread on greased pie pan. Chill.

Chocolate Filling:
1 pkg. (¼ lb.) sweet cooking chocolate
3 T. water
1 t. vanilla
1 c. whipping cream

Melt chocolate and water over low heat, stirring. Cool until thickened. Add vanilla. Whip cream. Fold chocolate mixture into whipped cream. Pour into crust and chill before serving.

Becky Owens, Glen Alpine H. S.
Glen Alpine, North Carolina

CHOCOLATE FLUFF PIE

Number of Servings — 6-8

3 oz. bitter chocolate
½ c. sugar
3 T. milk
4 egg yolks
1 t. vanilla

Melt and blend together over low heat the bitter chocolate, sugar, and milk. Beat in 1 at a time the egg yolks and vanilla.

Meringue:
4 egg whites
½ c. sugar
¼ t. cream of tartar

Beat egg until frothy, add cream of tartar, continue beating. Add sugar to egg whites gradually

and continue beating until sugar is completely blended. Fold meringue into chocolate mixture. Pour into cooled, baked pastry shell. Chill. Garnish with whipped cream just before serving if desired.

Hazel S. Wilkinson, Carroll H. S.
Ozark, Alabama

CHOCOLATE ICE BOX PIE

Number of Servings — 12 - 2 Pies

2½ c. white sugar
½ c. cornstarch
¼ c. flour
   (Note: In summer use 2 extra T. cornstarch and 2 extra T. flour.)
1 qt. milk
3 sq. chocolate
6 egg yolks, beaten lightly
2 T. butter
1 t. vanilla
½ t. salt
Baked pastry shells
Whipped cream
Chopped nuts

Mix dry ingredients, sugar, cornstarch, flour, and milk. Cook in double boiler until is begins to thicken. Add chocolate squares. Cook until rather thick. Beat eggs, add to mixture. Cook about 5 minutes. Remove from heat. Add butter, vanilla, and salt. Cool. Put filling in pastry shells. Top with whipped cream. Sprinkle with chopped nuts. Keep in ice box.

Mrs. Ray Jean Streetman, College H. S.
Bartlesville, Oklahoma

CHOCOLATE ICE BOX PIE

Number of Servings — 6

1 stick butter (soft)
¾ c. sugar
2 eggs
1 block melted chocolate (cooled)
1 t. vanilla
1 baked pastry shell

Cream butter and sugar. Add 1 egg and beat 5 minutes. Add second egg and beat 5 minutes. Add melted chocolate and vanilla. Pour into baked pastry shell. Top with whipped cream. Garnish with cherries and nuts or shaved chocolate. Chill in refrigerator.

Mrs. Ila S. Williams, New Kent H. S.
New Kent, Virginia

EASY CHOCOLATE PIE

Number of Servings — 6-8

1 pkg. semi-sweet chocolate pieces
3 T. milk
2 T. sugar
4 egg yolks
1 t. vanilla
Pinch of salt
4 egg whites, stiffly beaten

Melt together the chocolate pieces, milk and sugar over low heat. Cool slightly and add the unbeaten egg yolks 1 at a time, beating well after each

(Continued on Next Page)

addition. Add the vanilla and a pinch of salt. Fold the chocolate mixture into the stiffly beaten egg whites. Pour into crumb crust or a cooled baked pastry shell. Chill in the refrigerator for at least 1 hour. May be served with whipped cream if desired.

Ruth Wiman, Roscoe H. S.
Roscoe, Texas

GERMAN CHOCOLATE MARSHMALLOW PIE

Number of Servings — 6-8

½ lb. miniature marshmallows
½ bar (¼ lb.) German sweet chocolate, broken up
¾ c. milk
½ t. salt

Combine ingredients and heat in top of double boiler or over low heat, stirring occasionally, until marshmallows and chocolate have melted, cool.

½ pt. heavy cream, whipped
½ t. vanilla

Fold cooled mixture into whipped cream and vanilla. Turn into a 9″ pastry shell or a chilled 9″ graham cracker crust and chill 2 to 3 hours before serving. If desired, garnish with marshmallow flowers. To make each flower, snip a marshmallow crisscross with a scissors and insert a chocolate chip.

Eleanore Pehlke, Elmwood H. S.
Elmwood, Wisconsin

COFFEE PIE

Number of Servings — 6

1 T. butter
1 c. very strong coffee (hot)
30 marshmallows, quartered
1 c. cream, whipped
½ c. chopped nuts
9″ baked pastry shell

Add butter to hot, strong coffee, fold in marshmallows, cool until quite stiff, fold in whipped cream. Pour into baked pastry shell, top with crushed nuts, chill in refrigerator.

Mrs. Florence D. Sorrell, Benson H. S.
Benson, North Carolina

CREME DE MENTHE PIE

Number of Servings — 6

16 cream cookies, rolled (such as Hydrox)
⅛ c. butter, melted
24 lge. marshmallows
½ c. milk
¼ c. creme de menthe
1 c. whipping cream
2 sq. semi-sweet chocolate

Roll out Hydrox cookies and add them to the melted butter, press into pie pan and let set. In a double boiler, melt the marshmallows, add milk, cool. To this mixture add creme de menthe and whipped cream. Pour into shell, shave chocolate over. Refrigerate 2-3 hours before serving.

Eva Claire Korsmo, Long Prairie H. S.
Long Prairie, Minnesota

GRASSHOPPER PIE

Number of Servings — 6-8

24 marshmallows
¾ c. milk
2 oz. cream de menthe
1 oz. cream de cocoa
1 c. cream
16 Hydrox chocolate cookies
3 T. butter

Melt, then chill marshmallows and milk, add cream de menthe and cream de cocoa. Whip cream and fold mixtures together. Pour into 9″ pie pan lined with crushed Hydrox cookies and melted butter, which is packed into pie pan. Chill several hours. May garnish with grated bitter chocolate, whipped cream, or cherries.

Helen Larson, McGregor H. S.
McGregor, Minnesota

JELLO PIE WITH GRAHAM CRACKER CRUST

Number of Servings — 6

½ c. boiling water
1 pkg. Jello (any flavor)
1 c. sugar
1 lge. can evaporated milk (chilled)

Dissolve Jello and sugar in boiling water. Cool and add to the milk which has been whipped until stiff. Pour into graham cracker crust and chill.

Crust:
1½ c. graham cracker crumbs
½ c. (scant) soft butter
¼ c. powdered sugar

Mix soft butter, graham cracker crumbs and powdered sugar. Pat mixture in pie pan, chill several hours before using.

Mrs. Helen T. Carnes, Walnut Grove S.
Walnut Grove, Alabama

JELLO PIE

Number of Servings — 8

2 eggs
1 c. sugar
1 pkg. orange Jello
1 c. pineapple juice
1 tall can of evaporated milk
½ c. crushed pineapple
1 lge. pkg. vanilla wafers
2 T. melted butter
Cherries for garnish (optional)

Mix in mixer eggs and sugar. Pour in boiler and add orange Jello and pineapple juice. Mix well and bring to a boil. Chill in ice trays. Whip chilled evaporated milk. Fold pineapple into above mixture. Line 2 pie pans with vanilla wafers. Sprinkle crushed wafers in bottoms of pans. Add melted butter. Turn filling into crusts, wrap with aluminum foil and freeze. Use toothpicks to hold up foil. Cherries may be added as a garnish.

Helen Moran, Pass Christian H. S.
Pass Christian, Mississippi

LEMON ICE BOX PIE
Number of Servings — 8-10

3 egg yolks, well beaten
¼ c. lemon juice
½ t. lemon rind, grated
⅛ t. salt
½ c. plus 1 T. sugar
1 c. heavy cream, whipped
3 egg whites, beaten stiff
1 graham cracker crust 8x8 pan

Mix egg yolks, lemon juice, lemon rind, salt, and sugar in a medium size saucepan. Cook until thick, cool. Fold in heavy whipped cream and stiffly beaten egg whites. Add mixture to the top of the graham cracker crust and refrigerate for several hours. Top with a cherry or whipped cream.

Mrs. Ruth Cole, South Junior H. S.
Waco, Texas

LEMON ICE BOX PIE
(Graham Cracker Crust)
Number of Servings — 6

Crust:
1¼ c. graham crackers, crushed
2 T sugar
6 T. butter, melted

Mix crumbs and sugar, stir into melted butter and mix well. Press firmly on bottom and sides of 9" pie pan. Chill 1 hour before filling.

Filling:
1 can sweetened condensed milk
¼ c. lemon juice
3 egg yolks

To the can of condensed milk, add lemon juice, a little at a time, stir. Add egg yolks and mix well.

Topping:
3 egg whites
6 T. sugar
⅛ t. cream of tartar

Beat whites and cream of tartar stiffly, add sugar, beat. Place on filling and bake in 400°F. oven until golden brown, chill and serve.

Mrs. Inez Burgan, Harrison Co. H. S.
Cynthiana, Kentucky

RICH LEMON PIE
Number of Servings — 8

1 stick butter
48 vanilla wafers

Melt butter in a 9" pie plate. Crumble vanilla wafers and add to melted butter. Mix well and shape into pie crust.

Filling:
4 egg yolks
Juice of 4 lemons
1 can Eagle Brand condensed milk

Beat egg yolks until light colored, add lemon juice. Blend well. Add condensed milk and blend well. Pour into crust.

Meringue:
4 egg whites
¼ t. salt
8 T. sugar

Add salt to egg whites and beat at high speed on mixer until frothy. Continue beating while adding the sugar a little at a time. Beat until stiff peaks form. Drop mounds of meringue with spoon around edge of filling. Spread meringue until it touches inner edges of crust all around. Pile rest of meringue in center and spread to meet border. Swirl to make peaks. Bake in 325°F. oven for 12 to 15 minutes or until golden brown. Cool. Refrigerate at least 2 hours before serving.

Clare Morrow, Madison H. S.
Madison, Florida

LEMON JELLO PIE
Number of Servings — 10-12

1 c. sugar
1½ c. pineapple juice
2 eggs, well beaten
1 box lemon Jello
1 lge. can evaporated milk

Bring to boiling point sugar, pineapple juice and eggs. Dissolve Jello in hot mixture and cool. Chill evaporated milk until icy and whip until very stiff. Fold cooled mixture into whipped milk. Fill 2 graham cracker pie crusts. Chill until pie will hold shape when cut.

Mrs. Zella H. Mills, Hancock H. S.
Sneedville, Tennessee

LIME JELLO PIE
Number of Servings — 6

2-10 cent boxes chocolate cookies
½ stick of butter
1 lge. can evaporated milk
1 pkg. lime Jello
½ c. boiling water
¼ c. sugar
¼ c. lemon juice

Place large can of evaporated milk in freezing unit for 1½ hours before ready to use. Dissolve 1 package lime Jello in boiling water. Add sugar and lemon juice, dissolve thoroughly. Whip milk until like whipped cream. Fold in Jello mixture. Pour into crust made of chocolate cookie crumbs mixed with butter. Top with chocolate decors and place in refrigerator.

Mrs. Louella G. Milner, Richton H. S.
Hattiesburg, Mississippi

ORANGE PHILLY PIE
Number of Servings — 8
Crust:
Slice-and-bake cookies

Lightly grease and sugar the bottom, sides and edge of a 9" pie pan, cut slice-and-bake cookies into ⅛" slices. Overlap slices around sides of pan to form scalloped edge, line bottom with more slices (use a half roll per crust). Bake 6-8 minutes at 375°F.

Orange Filling:
3 oz. pkg. orange gelatin
1½ c. hot water
¼ c. sugar
8 oz. pkg. cream cheese
¼ c. orange juice
1 t. lemon juice

(Continued on Next Page)

Dissolve orange gelatin in hot water, blend together sugar and softened cream cheese. Gradually blend in gelatin, orange juice, and lemon juice. Chill until almost firm, whip until fluffy. Pour into cooled crust and sprinkle with grated orange rind, chill until firm.

This recipe submitted by the following teachers:
Ruth Darnell, Brookport H. S.
Brookport, Illinois
Lucille Sherard, Morgan County H. S.
Hartselle, Alabama

PINEAPPLE FLUFF (Low Calorie)
Number of Servings — 6
¼ c. cold water
1 envelope unflavored gelatin
2 T. sugar
½ c. hot water
2 T. lemon juice
½ c. crushed pineapple, cooked
Few grains salt
1 egg white, stiffly beaten
Cherries

Soften gelatin in cold water. Add sugar and hot water. Stir until dissolved. Add lemon juice, pineapple, and salt. When it begins to thicken, beat until light and frothy. Fold in stiffly beaten egg white and beat until thick. Pile into sherbet glasses, decorate with a cherry.

Mrs. Doris Ann Arnold, Halton Jr. H. S.
Fort Worth, Texas

PINEAPPLE TART
Number of Servings — 24
1 box graham crackers, rolled fine
2 T. melted butter
½ c. brown sugar

Melt butter and add to brown sugar and cracker crumbs. Line a pan 10x15 or depending upon desired thickness, with approximately ½ crumb mixture.

Filling:
½ c. granulated sugar
2 T. cornstarch
1 c. water
1 egg, beaten
1 can crushed pineapple

Combine above ingredients in a saucepan. Cook until thick. Pour over crumb mixture in pan. Cover with remaining cracker crumbs. Chill thoroughly in refrigerator until firm or over night. Cut into servings. Top with whipped cream.

Ann D. Holmes, Central H. S.
Fayetteville, North Carolina

UNCOOKED PINEAPPLE PIE
Number of Servings — 8
½ c. margarine
1 c. sugar
Dash of salt
2 eggs, separated
1 c. nuts, (or less)
1 c. drained, crushed pineapple
1 c. cream, whipped
1½ c. shredded coconut
Vanilla wafers

Cream margarine and sugar. Add salt and egg yolks. Mix well, add the beaten egg whites, using folding motion. Add nuts and pineapple. Mix well. Add coconut to whipped cream. Line a 10x7x11 pie plate with vanilla wafers. Spread half of pineapple mixture over wafers, then half of cream mixture. Make another layer of wafers, using same steps. Chill. (Can be frozen.)

Mrs. Betty G. Lowrance, Mooresville Sr. H. S.
Mooresville, North Carolina

PUMPKIN-MALLO PIE
Number of Servings — 6-8
1 c. cooked pumpkin
1 lb. marshmallows (cut in pieces)
¼ t. allspice
⅛ t. nutmeg
1¼ c. whipping cream
1 pastry shell

Combine all except cream in pan, heat and stir until marshmallows are completely melted, chill thoroughly. Beat mixture well with large spoon, gradually add whipped cream and beat until thoroughly mixed and smooth. Pour into baked pastry shell and chill until set.

Mrs. Mabel Jones, Eden H. S.
Eden, Texas

RUM ICE BOX PIE
Number of Servings — 6
Crust:
½ stick melted oleo
1½ c. graham cracker crumbs

Place graham cracker crumbs in pie pan and pour oleo over them, mix and spread.

Filling:
25 marshmallows
2 t. instant coffee
¾ c. boiling water
1 pkg. whip mix (such as Dream)
1 T. rum or rum flavoring

Melt marshmallows in hot water to which the coffee has been added. Place in refrigerator until it begins to set. Prepare whip mix according to directions on package, fold in coffee mixture and rum. Pour filling on crust, chill until set.

Mrs. Kathryn Patrick, Cummings Jr. H. S.
Brownsville, Texas

REAL GOOD PIE
Number of Servings — 6-8
Crust:
⅔ c. pecans
¼ lb. vanilla wafers
¼ c. melted butter

Grind pecans and wafers together, pour melted butter over the mixture. Line pie pan with ¾ of the mixture.

Filling:
½ c. butter
1 c. firmly packed powdered sugar
1¼ t. vanilla
1 sq. unsweetened chocolate

(Continued on Next Page)

¼ pkg. German chocolate (6 small blocks)
3 egg whites, stiffly beaten
Dash of salt
Whipped cream

Cream butter and powdered sugar, add melted chocolate, vanilla, salt. Fold in stiffly beaten egg whites. Pour over crumbs in pan and sprinkle remaining crumbs on top. Place in refrigerator for 12 hours. Top with whipped cream before serving.

Mrs. Leo W. Thames, Robert E. Lee H. S.
Baton Rouge, Louisiana

STRAWBERRY PIE
Number of Servings — 6

1 batch tea cake dough
1 pt. sliced strawberries
1 c. boiled custard
1 c. whipped cream

Make a pie crust from the tea cake dough. Bake until light brown. Cool. Mix berries, custard and whipped cream. Pour in crust. Chill. If all of the filling mixture will not go in crust, it can be heaped full after the crust has been chilled.

Mrs. Pauline B. Commer,
Crowder White Attendance Center
Crowder, Mississippi

STRAWBERRY PIE
Number of Servings — 6

2½ c. strawberries
½ c. hot water
¾ c. sugar
2 t. lemon juice
1 pkg. strawberry Jello
1 c. whipping cream

Mix strawberries, water, and sugar and let come to boil. Remove from heat. Add Jello and dissolve thoroughly. Add lemon juice. Chill until partially congealed, then fold into mixture ½ cup whipped cream. Put into graham cracker crust (or vanilla wafer), and chill. Before serving, add remaining whipped cream on top. Drop whole strawberries in cream on top.

Mrs. Lila Wilkins, Smylie Wilson Jr. H. S.
Lubbock, Texas

STRAWBERRY ICE BOX PIE
Number of Servings — 6-8

¼ c. lemon juice
1 can sweetened condensed milk
1¼ c. strawberries (frozen)

Mix milk, lemon juice and strawberries and pour into a graham cracker crust. Top with whipped cream sprinkled with chopped nuts.

Graham Cracker Crust:
1½ c. graham cracker crumbs
¼ c. sugar
½ stick margarine

Mix graham cracker crumbs, sugar and melted margarine. Shape in a 9″ pie plate and brown in a 350°F. oven until slightly browned. Cool before filling.

Mrs. Nadine H. Shipp, Fyffe H. S.
Fyffe, Alabama

STRAWBERRY ICE BOX PIE
Number of Servings — 6

Vanilla Wafer Crust:
1⅗ c. crushed vanilla wafers
¼ c. margarine (melted)
¼ c. sugar

Combine above ingredients and press into pie pan. Add filling, and chill.

Filling:
24 marshmallows
1 box frozen strawberries
1 c. chopped nuts
1 pt. whipping cream

Melt marshmallows with 7 tablespoons liquid from strawberries, cool. Whip the cream while above mixture cools. Combine melted marshmallows, strawberries, nuts and fold into whipped cream. Pour into vanilla wafer crust, let set for 6 hours in refrigerator.

Dorothy Minton, Littlefield H. S.
Littlefield, Texas

FRENCH STRAWBERRY PIE
Number of Servings — 6

1 cooled 9″ baked pastry shell
1 pkg. (3 oz.) cream cheese
1 qt. fresh strawberries
1 c. granulated sugar
3 T. cornstarch
Few drops of food color

Spread cream cheese, softened with milk or cream, over bottom of cooled, baked pastry shell. Wash berries, cap, drain well, place half of the berries (choicest ones) in the cheese-coated pastry shell. Mash remaining berries well, bring to boiling point, and slowly stir in sugar and cornstarch which have been mixed together. Cook slowly, stirring until thick, add food coloring, cool. Pour over uncooked berries in pie shell. Place pie in refrigerator until very cold. Top with whipped cream or ice cream if desired.

This recipe submitted by the following teachers:
Ellen Webb Massengill, Seminole H. S.
Seminole, Texas
Gail Corbell, Shongaloo H. S.
Shongaloo, Louisiana
Foye Davis, Horatio School
Horatio, Arkansas

STRAWBERRY PIE
Number of Servings — 6

20 marshmallows (large)
1 pkg. strawberries
1 c. evaporated milk (whipped)
1 t. lemon juice
2 t. orange juice

Melt marshmallows in double boiler. Add strawberries and fold in whipped milk and juices. Pour in cracker or vanilla wafer crust and chill or freeze.

Broxie C. Stuckey, Gordo H. S.
Gordo, Alabama

FLUFFY STRAWBERRY PIE

Number of Servings — 6

9" graham cracker crust
1 10 oz. pkg. strawberries (partially thawed)
¾ c. water
⅓ c. sugar
¼ t. salt
2 eggs
2 t. lemon juice
1 pkg. strawberry gelatin
⅔ c. dry milk (instant preferred)

Mix in a 1½-quart saucepan, strawberries, ¼ cup water, sugar, salt, 2 egg yolks, and lemon juice. Cook and stir over medium heat until mixture comes to a full boil, take off heat, stir in gelatin until dissolved. Chill mixture until it is very thick, but not set. Put into a 1-quart bowl 2 egg whites, ½ cup water and dry milk. Whip with electric beater at high speed, or with rotary hand beater until stiff. Fold whipped mixture into strawberry mixture, let stand a few minutes. Put into chilled crust. Chill until firm, about 2 hours or until ready to serve.

This recipe submitted by the following teachers:
Patricia McGee, Conrad H. S.
Conrad, Montana
Ruby Smeadley, Joe T. Robinson H. S.
Little Rock, Arkansas

STRAWBERRY PIE

Number of Servings — 6-7

1 egg white
¼ t. salt
½ c. white sugar
2 T. Karo syrup (white)
½ t. vanilla
1 8" or 9" baked pastry shell
¾ qt. fresh strawberries
½ pt. whipping cream
2 T. powdered sugar

Mix the sugar and Karo in small pan, cook until it forms a medium hard ball in cold water. When mixture has begun to cook rapidly for about 3 or 4 minutes, start beating the egg white with the salt. Pour the cooked syrup into beaten egg whites. Beat until it is quite stiff and has a glazed appearance, add vanilla, beat in well. Line the baked pastry shell with the meringue. Slice strawberries into this lined crust, saving about a dozen large berries for garnishing. Whip the cream, add powdered sugar, spread on top of berries. Garnish, chill 1 hour before serving.

Mrs. Charmiane W. Freeman, Halls H. S.
Halls, Tennessee

STRAWBERRY-PINEAPPLE PIE

Number of Servings — 12

1 c. sugar
11 ozs. (½ can) crushed pineapple or juice
2 eggs, well beaten
1 pkg. strawberry Jello
1 lge. can Pet milk (chilled)
1 pkg. vanilla wafers

Mix sugar, pineapple and eggs. Bring to a boil.

Remove from heat, add Jello. Cool. Whip chilled milk, fold into other mixture. Pour into 2 pie pans lined with vanilla wafers. Let set 30 minutes. Serve.

Laverne Dupree, Bell City H. S.
Bell City, Louisiana

WINE PIE

Number of Servings — 6

½ c. wine (port)
1½ doz. marshmallows
½ pt. whipped cream

Quarter marshmallows, heat wine. Dissolve marshmallows in hot wine. Cool and fold in whipped cream. Put in graham cracker crust. Chill in refrigerator over night.

Mrs. Carrie S. Bolton, Pageland H. S.
Pageland, South Carolina

YUM-YUM PIE

Number of Servings — 8

1 baked pastry shell
1 lge. pkg. cream cheese
½ c. powdered sugar
1 c. whipped cream
1 can cherry pie mix

Mix the Philadelphia cream cheese and the powdered sugar real well. Fold in the whipped cream. Put this mixture into the pie shell and chill to set. Put the cherry pie mix on top and chill (not freeze). When ready to serve, top with whipped cream.

Pastry (especially good):
1 c. all-purpose flour
1 c. cake flour
2 T. sugar
1 t. salt
1 stick margarine (a must)
¼ t. baking powder
5-6 T. ice water

Ella Bang, Yankton H. S.
Yankton, South Dakota

CHERRY PUDDING SUPREME

Number of Servings — 8

1 pkg. cherry Jello
1 c. boiling water
4 eggs, separated
1 c. sugar
1 8 oz. bottle maraschino cherries (juice to be reserved for use, keep several cherries for decoration, chop remainder)
1 c. chopped nuts
3½ doz. vanilla wafers (crushed)

Dissolve Jello with the cup of boiling water and set aside to cool. Beat egg yolks and add sugar and juice from cherries. Cook mixture in a double boiler until it thickens. Remove from heat and stir in vanilla wafer crumbs, Jello, cherries, and nuts. Fold in beaten egg whites. Pour into a pie plate or pyrex dish. Chill. Slice and serve with whipped cream. Garnish with whole cherries.

Daphne Smith, Winnsboro H. S.
Winnsboro, Texas

CALIFORNIA FRUIT PUDDING
Number of Servings — 10

⅛ lb. apricots
¼ lb. prunes
¼ lb. dates
¼ lb. seedless raisins
⅛ lb. fancy eating figs
⅜ lb. marshmallows
½ t. phosphate baking powder
¼ lb. fresh graham crackers, crushed
¼ c. chopped nuts

Wash apricots and prunes, cover with water and cook until tender and practically no water remains. Drain and cut pulp of prunes from pits. Remove pits from dates and any stems from raisins. Mix all fruits together and run through food chopper. Cut marshmallows in small pieces with scissors dipped in cold water. Mix fruits with marshmallows and baking powder and knead thoroughly. (The phosphate baking powder will leaven the cold mixture.) Let stand 2 to 5 hours. Prepare square or rectangular shallow pans. Butter thickly and dust generously with graham cracker crumbs. Knead remaining crumbs into mixture lightly and press into prepared pans about ¾" thick. Press chopped nuts in surface. Allow to ripen at least 24 hours. Cut in squares and serve with whipped cream. This ice-box dessert will keep for several weeks.

Mrs. Virginia O. Savedge, Northampton H. S.
Eastville, Virginia

CHRISTMAS PUDDING

1 T. gelatin
4 T. cold water
2 c. milk (scalded)
½ c. sugar
1½ T. cornstarch
4 egg yolks, beaten
¼ t. salt
4 egg whites, beaten
½ c. sugar
¾ t. vanilla
¼ t. almond extract
¼ t. cream of tartar

Dissolve gelatin in cold water. Mix ½ cup sugar, cornstarch, beaten egg yolks, and salt. Gradually add scalded milk and return to double boiler. Cook to consistency of boiled custard. Add gelatin. While hot, gradually fold in well beaten egg whites to which have been added ½ cup sugar, vanilla, almond extract, and cream of tartar. Spoon over vanilla wafer crumbs which have been crushed for crust in a 9x14 pyrex dish. Chill until set. 1 hour before serving whip ½ pint heavy cream and ¼ cup sugar and spread over top of pudding. On top of this spread fresh grated coconut. Cut in squares. Decorate each square with a small wreath of red cinnamon drops with a gumdrop bow.

Clarice I. Snider, Unicoi Co. H. S.
Erwin, Tennessee

HUNTINGTON PUDDING
Number of Servings — 8-12

2 c. water
2 c. brown sugar
Pinch of salt
3 egg whites
¼ c. cornstarch moistened in water
3 cubed bananas, or 1 c. black walnuts, or 2 c. of clipped or small marshmallows, or a combination of the three

Combine water, brown sugar, and salt. Bring to a boil. Beat egg whites until stiff. Thicken syrup with cornstarch and water. Pour over egg whites. Cool. Fold in bananas or nuts or marshmallows or any combination. Chill. Serve plain or with whipped cream.

Ruth E. Carlson, Donovan H. S.
Donovan, Illinois

LEMON SNOW PUDDING
Number of Servings — 6-8

2 envelopes unflavored gelatin
½ c. cold water
2 c. hot water
1½ c. sugar
½ c. lemon juice, fresh, frozen, or canned
3 egg whites, beaten stiff

Soften gelatin in cold water. Dissolve in hot water. Add sugar, stir until sugar dissolves. Add lemon juice. Chill until partially set. Beat until frothy. Fold in egg whites. Pour into 1-quart mold. Chill until firm. Unmold and serve with vanilla custard sauce. Top with sliced bananas centered with a maraschino cherry.

June Farley Houchins, Tuslaw H. S.
Massillon, Ohio

MACAROON PUDDING
Number of Servings — 12

4 egg yolks, beaten
½ c. sugar
½ c. milk
2 envelopes Knox unflavored gelatin
20 almonds, chopped
1 pt. whipping cream
1 doz. almond macaroons (4 days old)

Cook egg yolks, sugar and milk to custard consistency in double boiler. Remove from heat, add gelatin softened in 3 tablespoons water. Chill until mixture begins to thicken. Add chopped almonds, crumbled macaroons, and fold in whipped cream. Pour into an 8" square pan, mixture should be 1¼" thick. Refrigerate 6 hours. Cut into squares. Top with whipped cream and maraschino cherries.

Mrs. Eleanor L. Miller, Wahama H. S.
Mason, West Virginia

PARADISE PUDDING
Number of Servings — 12

¼ lb. almonds, blanched
1 doz. marshmallows
1 doz. candied cherries
½ doz. macaroons
1 pkg. lemon Jello
1 pt. boiling water
1 c. whipped cream
¼ c. sugar

(Continued on Next Page)

Dissolve Jello in the boiling water. When cold, set dish in ice water and whip to consistency of whipped cream. Cut almonds, marshmallows, cherries, and macaroons in fine pieces and add to Jello mixture. Fold in the whipped cream. Put in a square pan and set in a cold place to harden.

Susie Carlisle, McKinney H. S.
McKinney, Texas

PINEAPPLE PUDDING
Number of Servings — 12

1 lb. confectioners' sugar
¼ lb. butter
3 eggs
No. 2 (size) crushed pineapple
1 pt. cream (whipped)
1 lb. Vanilla Wafers

Sift confectioners' sugar and add butter. Cream until mealy. Add one egg at a time and beat well. Add vanilla if desired. Whip the cream until fairly stiff. Add the drained pineapple and the whipped cream. Line a pan with the wafers. Cover with the mixture. Repeat until all the mixture has been used. Use a few more wafers if necessary. Chill over night. Serve with whipped cream topped with a cherry. (May be frozen.)

Margaret Miller, Henry Co. H. S.
New Castle, Kentucky

PINEAPPLE ICE BOX PUDDING
Number of Servings — 8

¼ lb. butter or margarine
1 c. powdered sugar
3 eggs
½ pkg. lemon Jello
1 c. hot water
½ pt. evaporated milk (chilled)
1 c. drained, crushed pineapple
1 box vanilla wafers (crumbs)

Dissolve Jello in hot water and let partially set. Line an 8½x11 dish with crumbs. Cream sugar and butter. Beat 1 egg at a time into the creamed sugar and butter. Pour this mixture into the lined dish. Whip the partially set Jello. Whip the chilled evaporated milk. Fold the two together. Add drained pineapple. Pour this mixture on top of layer in dish. Sprinkle with more vanilla wafer crumbs. Refrigerate 2 hours.

Mrs. Dorothy Pogue, Pawnee H. S.
Pawnee, Texas

PLUM PUDDING
Number of Servings — 12-15

2 c. water
1 c. raisins
1 pkg. orange Jello
½ c. sugar
1½ c. nuts
1 c. chopped dates
1 c. crushed pineapple
1 c. Grapenuts
½ t. cinnamon
½ t. cloves

Cook raisins in water until tender. Add to Jello and sugar, stir until Jello and sugar are dissolved.

Add other ingredients and stir. Set aside to congeal. Serve with whipped cream.

Mrs. Evelyn Kearns Harris, Seagrove H. S.
Seagrove, North Carolina

RUM PUDDING
Number of Servings — 8

8 eggs
1 c. sugar
2 envelopes gelatin (unflavored)
½ c. cold water
¾ c. rum
1 pt. whipped cream

Beat eggs and sugar together until thick and lemon colored. Soak gelatin in cold water. Heat gelatin mixture in a double boiler until gelatin is dissolved. Whip cream and add to egg mixture. Add gelatin. Add the rum. Pour into a mold and congeal. Unmold and serve with topping of tart thickened fruit juice.

Topping:
2 c. fruit juice (strawberry, cranberry or plum)
2 sticks cinnamon
2 T. cornstarch

Boil together for 5 minutes or until thickened partially. Cool.

Ruth M. Dreyer, Circle H. S.
Circle, Montana

TIPSY PUDDING

5 eggs
¾ c. sugar
½ c. roasted almonds
1 t. vanilla
1 pt. whipping cream
1 qt. milk
1½ envelopes gelatin, soaked in ½ c. cold water
1 lge. sponge cake
1 c. equal parts of brandy and fruit liquor

Make boiled custard of eggs, sugar, and milk. Add gelatin soaked in water. Cook 2 minutes, add vanilla and let cool. Soak cake in liquor-brandy mixture. Place a layer of cake in a spring form pan, then a layer of custard alternating layers. Chill well before serving. Top with whipped cream and nuts before serving.

Beverly Raven, Woodlin School
Woodrow, Colorado

LIME PINEAPPLE SALAD
Number of Servings — 12

1 pkg. lime Jello
2 c. water and pineapple juice
1 small can crushed pineapple
1-3 oz. pkg. cream cheese
16 lge. marshmallows
1 c. pecan meats, chopped

Drain pineapple, add water to make one cup, boil, add marshmallows and Jello and stir until dissolved. Add 1 cup cold water and chill until partially set. Soften cream cheese, stir in pineapple and chopped nuts, add Jello mixture and refrigerate over night.

Alice R. McCreary, Monroe Co. H. S.
Monroeville, Alabama

CROWN JEWEL SALAD

Number of Servings — 14

3 pkg. (3 oz. each) flavored gelatin (1 each, black cherry, lime, and strawberry)
3 c. boiling water
1½ c. cold water
1 c. pineapple juice
¼ c. sugar
1 pkg. (3 oz.) raspberry gelatin
½ c. cold water
1 c. cold milk
1 t. vanilla
2 envelopes whipped topping

Prepare the first 3 flavors of gelatin separately, using 1 cup hot water and ½ cup cold water for each. Pour into separate 8x8x2 pans and chill until firm (or over night). Mix pineapple juice and sugar, heat until sugar dissolves. Remove from heat and dissolve raspberry gelatin in hot liquid. Add ½ cup of the cold water. Chill just until syrupy. Combine milk, vanilla and topping mix in a bowl with narrow bottom. Blend, then beat, until mixture forms soft peaks. Fold into the syrupy gelatin. Cut the firm black cherry, strawberry, and lime gelatin into cubes of about ½". Fold into raspberry gelatin mixture. Pour into a 9" angel food cake pan. Chill 8 hours, unmold. Spread top and sides with additional whipped topping and sprinkle with coconut, tinted pink, if desired.

Mrs. Caroline Baker Watts, Clay-Battelle H. S.
Blacksville, West Virginia

FAVORITE FRUIT SALAD (low calorie)

Number of Servings — 6

1 303 can dietetic fruit salad
1 can (8 oz.) dietetic gingerale
1 envelope unflavored gelatin
2 oranges, sectioned and cut
Juice of 1 lemon
1 banana, diced

Drain juice from canned fruit. Pour gelatin over juice to soften. Stir. Heat until dissolved. Cool. Add gingerale and refrigerate until thickened. Mix all fruits together. Fold into the gelatin mixture. Refrigerate until firm.

Mrs. Enid Beazley, Princess Anne H. S.
Lynnhaven, Virginia

OVER NIGHT SALAD

Number of Servings — 6-8

2 eggs, beaten
1 c. pineapple juice
2 T. flour
3 T. sugar
½ lb. miniature marshmallows
1 No. 2 can pineapple
1 c. cream

Boil and cool eggs, juice, flour and sugar in a double boiler. Cool. Add marshmallows, pineapple, and whipped cream. Chill over night.

Evangeline La Barre, Belt Valley H. S.
Belt, Montana

FROSTED SALAD

Number of Servings — 10

2 pkg. lemon gelatin
2 c. hot water
2 c. 7-Up
20 oz. crushed pineapple
1 c. small marshmallows
2 bananas, sliced

Dissolve gelatin in 2 cups boiling water, add 7-Up. Let partially set. Add marshmallows, pineapple, and bananas. Chill solid.

Topping:
½ c. sugar
2 T. flour
1 c. pineapple juice
1 egg, beaten
2 T. butter
2 c. whipping cream

Cook until thick, the sugar, flour, pineapple juice, and egg. Add butter and cool. When cool, add whipped cream. Spread over gelatin that has set. Sprinkle with grated cheese and maraschino cherries. Use 9x13 pan.

Jean Applegarth, Smith Center H. S.
Smith Center, Kansas

PALM BEACH SALAD DESSERT

Number of Servings — 10

1 c. pineapple juice
2 T. butter
2 egg yolks
⅛ c. sugar
Juice of ½ lemon
2 T. flour
1 pt. whipping cream
1 small can cubed pineapple
1 small can Royal Anne cherries
½ lb. small marshmallows

Heat pineapple juice, and butter until butter melts. Beat egg yolks, sugar, lemon juice, and flour together. Add to hot juice and cook until thick, stirring constantly. Cool. Add whipped cream. Add remaining ingredients. Chill thoroughly, serve on halves of pears or crisp lettuce.

Mrs. E. R. Moss, Biggersville H. S.
Rienzi, Mississippi

PARTY SALAD

Number of Servings — 15

1 pkg. lime Jello
2 pkg. lemon Jello
3 c. hot water
1 No. 2½ can crushed pineapple
2 pkg. cream cheese
32 lge. marshmallows
1 c. cream, whipped

Dissolve Jello in hot water. (A bit of green coloring may be added to the Jello.) Add crushed pineapple. After the mixture begins to set, add the beaten cream cheese and marshmallows. Whip the cream and add to the mixture. Sprinkle grated cheese over the top. Chill and serve.

Mrs. Bess Snyder Mohl, Petersburg H. S.
Petersburg, West Virginia

PARTY SALAD

Number of Servings — 12

2 pkgs. orange Jello
2 pkgs. lemon Jello
2 cans mandarin oranges
1 No. 2 can crushed Pineapple
1 pkg. miniature marshmallows
1 pt. whipping cream
1 c. salad dressing
¼ c. grated sharp cheese

Prepare Jello according to directions on packages. When Jello is thick, fold in fruits. Place a layer of marshmallows on top of above mixture. Whip cream and fold in salad dressing. Spread above mixture on Jello mixture. Sprinkle cheese on top of mixture. Chill.

Mrs. Letitia G. Roberts, Tuscaloosa H. S.
Tuscaloosa, Alabama

24 HOUR SALAD OR DESSERT

Number of Servings — 10

24 lge. marshmallows
1 c. crushed pineapple
½ c. chopped pecans
½ pt. whipping cream
2 T. sugar

Chop marshmallows and pecans, Add the drained pineapple. Whip the cream, add sugar. Mix all together. Chill. Serve on lettuce leaf for salad or serve in bowl for dessert.

Jeannette Reynolds, Crowville H. S.
Crowville, Louisiana

AMBROSIA (Molded)

Number of Servings — 9

1 c. graham cracker crumbs
¼ c. butter or margarine, melted
1-9 oz. can (1 c.) crushed pineapple
1 pkg. orange flavored gelatin
¼ c. sugar
1 c. hot water
1 c. dairy sour cream
¼ t. vanilla
1 c. diced orange sections
½ c. flaked coconut

Combine crumbs and butter, reserve ⅓ cup for topping. Press remaining crumb mixture into an 8x8x2 baking dish. Drain pineapple, reserving syrup. Dissolve gelatin and sugar in hot water. Stir in reserved syrup. Chill until partially set. Add sour cream and vanilla, whip until fluffy. Fold in the pineapple, oranges, and coconut, pour over crumbs in dish. Sprinkle top with reserved crumbs. Chill until firm. Cut in squares. Trim with maraschino cherries.

Mrs. Barbara Rawdon, Grants Sr. H. S.
Grants, New Mexico

APPLE DELIGHT

Number of Servings — 6

1 pkg. apple Jello
1½ c. hot water
1 c. dry cottage cheese
1 c. applesauce
1 T. lemon juice

Dissolve Jello in hot water. Chill until syrupy. Whip cottage cheese until it becomes a smooth paste. Add applesauce and lemon juice and blend thoroughly. Whip the partially conjealed Jello until fluffy. Add cottage cheese and applesauce mixture, blend, and refrigerate until firm.

Mrs. Ora McCarroll, Istrouma Sr. H. S.
Baton Rouge, Louisiana

CINNAMON APPLESAUCE REVEL

Number of Servings — 8

2 pkg. lemon flavored gelatin
½ c. red cinnamon candies
2½ c. boiling water
2 c. unsweetened applesauce
1 T. lemon juice
Dash of salt
½ c. chopped walnuts
½ c. heavy cream, whipped

Dissolve gelatin and candies in boiling water. Stir in applesauce, lemon juice and salt, chill until partially set. Stir in walnuts. Pour into 10x6x1½ dish. Spoon whipped cream atop, swirl through gelatin. Chill until firm.

Mrs. Marian L. Wilson, Hopkins Academy
Hadley, Massachusetts

APRICOT DELIGHT (Congealed)

Number of Servings — 12

1 can apricot nectar
1½ pkg. lemon Jello
1 T. sugar
1 can frozen orange juice
1 c. crushed pineapple
½ c. chopped nuts
1 banana (diced small)
1 c. miniature marshmallows
Dash of salt
1 T. lemon juice

Heat apricot nectar just under boiling point. Add Jello and sugar, let cool. Add frozen orange juice, crushed pineapple, nuts, banana, and marshmallows. Stir in salt and lemon juice to improve flavor. Pour into mold and congeal.

Kitty Barrett, Rock Hill H. S.
Rock Hill, South Carolina

APRICOT SUPREME

Number of Servings — 10-15

1 lge. pkg. Nabisco waffle cream wafers
12 graham crackers
½ c. oleo or butter
1 c. powdered sugar
2 eggs, separated
2 c. dried apricots, cooked
½ pt. whipping cream

Crush cookies and graham crackers. Divide crumbs in half. Spread half in bottom of greased 8x13 pan. Cream butter and sugar. Add beaten egg yolks. Fold in beaten egg whites. Spread this mixture on top of crumbs. Then spread on the cooled cooked apricots. Top with the whipped cream. Add the remaining crumbs. Chill several hours or over night.

Betty Lou Hawks, San Jacinto Jr. H. S.
Pasadena, Texas

APRICOT FLUFF
Number of Servings — 12
1 c. butter
2 c. powdered sugar
4 eggs, well beaten
1 lb. vanilla wafer crumbs
2 c. cream, whipped and sweetened with
    ½ c. sugar
2 c. nuts, chopped fine
1 No. 2½ can apricots

Cream butter and sugar, add eggs and beat well. Cook over hot water until mixture coats a spoon. Let cool. Butter large pan. Spread ⅔ of crumbs over bottom. Pour cooled custard over crumbs, sprinkle 1 cup nuts over custard, add 1 cup whipped cream. Lay apricots over cream. Put the other cup cream over apricots. Sprinkle remaining cup nuts and crumbs on top. Refrigerate 24 hours before serving.

Mrs. Iva Stringer, Shady Grove Attendance Center
Laurel, Mississippi

BANANA MARLOW
Number of Servings — 6
30 medium marshmallows
¾ c. boiling water
1 c. mashed bananas
1 T. lemon juice
1½ c. whipping cream

Melt marshmallows in boiling water. Add the banana pulp and lemon juice. Cool. When quite cool and slightly thickened, combine with the cream, which has been whipped. Pour into trays and freeze without stirring.

Mrs. Melba M. Sanders, Pike Co. H. S.
Brundidge, Alabama

BLUEBERRY DESSERT
Number of Servings — 12
20 graham crackers
¼ c. sugar
¼ c. margarine
Mix well and press into 9x11 pan.
Filling:
2 eggs
½ lb. cream cheese
½ c. sugar
1 t. vanilla

Whip until creamy, pour on crumbs. Bake 15 minutes at 350°F. Cook and top with blueberry pie filling. Put in refrigerator over night. Serve with whipped cream or ice cream.

This recipe submitted by the following teachers:
Mrs. Emogene Tilmon, Paris H. S.
Paris, Arkansas
Mrs. Evelyn Johnson, Bottineau H. S.
Bottineau, North Dakota

BLUEBERRY REFRIGERATOR DESSERT
Number of Servings — 9
1 pkg. or 22 graham crackers
2 T. powdered sugar
½ t. plain gelatin
¼ c. margarine or butter
1 can (No. 2) blueberry pie filling

Roll crackers until fine, place in bowl, add sugar and gelatin. Mix. Add melted margarine and stir well. Press into pan 9x9 to form the bottom layer. Spread the blueberry pie filling over the crust.
Topping:
6 oz. cream cheese, softened
1 pkg. whip mix (such as Dream)
½ c. sugar
½ c. milk
1 T. vanilla

Soften cream cheese, add whip, sugar, milk and vanilla and beat with electric mixer until it has the consistency of whipped cream. Spread topping over the blueberry filling. Refrigerate to set (2 to 3 hours or over night). Cut and serve.

Mrs. Lavaughn F. Bouch, Sand Fork H. S.
Sand Fork, West Virginia

ELEGANT BLUEBERRY DESSERT
Number of Servings — 8
2 c. graham cracker crumbs
1 stick butter, melted
½ c. chopped pecans
½ lb. marshmallows
½ pt. whipping cream (whipped)
½ c. milk
1 can blueberry pie filling
1 T. lemon juice

Mix cracker crumbs and butter, add pecans. Press ½ of mixture into a greased 8x8 pan. Melt marshmallows in milk in double boiler, cool thoroughly, add stiffly whipped cream. Spread ½ of mixture over crust. Spread blueberry pie filling to which lemon juice has been added over marshmallow mixture. Spread rest of marshmallow mixture. Top with rest of crust. Chill over night.

Mrs. Jane Brewer, Cullman H. S.
Cullman, Alabama

CARAMEL MARLOWE
Number of Servings — 12
16 caramels
½ c. milk
24 lge. marshmallows
1 c. whipping cream
¼ c. chopped pecan nut meats
1½ c. crushed graham crackers
4 T. butter, melted
1 T. sugar

Crush graham crackers, add sugar, and melted butter. Mix. Save ¼ cup crumb mixture for topping. Pat crust into 8x12 pan. Melt caramels in milk in top of double boiler. Add marshmallows and heat until melted. Chill. Fold in whipped cream and nut meats. Pour into crust, add crumb topping. Refrigerate 6 hours or over night.

Mrs. Merle Twesme,
Arcadia, Wisconsin

CHARLOTTE RUSSE
6 egg whites (stiffly beaten)
6 egg yolks
1 qt. double or whipping cream
1 envelope unflavored gelatin

(Continued on Next Page)

2 T. cold water
1 c. sugar
2 t. vanilla
Pinch of salt

Soften gelatin in cold water. Add ½ cup boiling water to dissolve gelatin. Beat egg yolks and sugar. Add pinch of salt and vanilla. Add above yolks to gelatin gradually to insure against lumping. Add whipped cream. Fold in egg whites. Line punch bowl or individual compotes with ladyfingers. Pour in whipped cream mixture. Garnish with maraschino cherries. Place in refrigerator until ready to serve.

Mary L. Adams, Danville H. S.
Danville, Kentucky

CHARLOTTE RUSSE (Pineapple)

1 t. vanilla
1½ T. gelatin
¾ c. boiling water or fruit juice
¼ c. cold water
1 c. sugar
3 egg whites
½ pt. cream
½ pt. whipped dry milk
½ pt. cherries
1 small can pineapple
¼ c. marshmallows

Mix gelatin and cold water. Add boiling juice or water to gelatin. Whip cream. Fold other ingredients into cream. Place in oblong pan and chill.

Nanci C. White, Lepanto H. S.
Lepanto, Arkansas

CHARLOTTE RUSSE (Strawberry)

Number of Servings — 10-12

7 or 8 whole ladyfingers
2 (3 oz.) pkg. of strawberry flavored gelatin
2 c. boiling water
1½ c. crushed strawberries
1 T. lemon juice
½ c. sugar
⅛ t. salt
2 c. heavy cream, whipped

Put a 3" strip of wax paper around the inside of an 8" spring form pan. Split ladyfingers. Cut tips from one end of the halves so they will stand. Arrange, rounded ends up around edge of pan lined with wax paper. Put strawberry gelatin in large bowl. Add boiling water and stir until dissolved. Combine strawberries, lemon juice, sugar, and salt. Stir until dissolved. Combine with gelatin mixture, chill until mixture thickens to the consistency of unbeaten egg whites. Fold in whipped cream. Carefully spoon into ladyfinger lined pan. Chill until firm. At least 5 hours or over night. Remove the side of the spring form pan and the wax paper, lift onto a large serving plate. Decorate top with additional whipped cream and whole strawberries. (If spring form pan not available, charlotte may be made in and served from a deep 2½ quart casserole.)

Mrs. Dorothy D. Walker, Bowling Green H. S.
Bowling Green, Kentucky

CHARLOTTE RUSSE

Number of Servings — 6

1 envelope plain gelatin
¼ c. cold water
2 eggs, separated
⅛ c. sugar
1 c. milk
Pinch of salt
1 c. whipping cream
½ t. vanilla
    or
2 T. fresh orange juice
2 T. bourbon, brandy sauce or flavoring

Soak gelatin in water, separate the eggs, beat well, add sugar, milk and salt. Cook over moderate heat until spoon coats. Remove from heat. Add soaked gelatin. Melt, chill until very thick. Beat egg whites until stiff. Whip cream. Combine egg whites and cream, fold in cooked mixture. Add flavoring. Place in refrigerator.

Ethel D. Johnson, Jackson H S.
Jackson, Alabama

CHERRY ALMOND FLUFF

Number of Servings — 6

1 pkg. cherry flavored Jello
½ c. sugar
1 c. boiling water
¼ c. lemon juice
¼ c. water
½ c. chopped toasted almonds
1 tall can evaporated milk, chilled

Mix gelatin and sugar, add boiling water, stir until dissolved. Add lemon juice, water and almonds. Chill the mixture until slightly thickened. Whip the milk until very thick. Fold lightly into the gelatin mixture. Pile into individual serving dishes and chill at least 2 hours before serving. Garnish with whipped milk topping and almond slivers.

Mrs. R. R. Broach, Somerville H. S.
Somerville, Texas

CHERRY CHOCOLATE ICE BOX DESSERT

Number of Servings — 10

½ lb. chocolate covered graham crackers
½ c. melted butter (cooled)
1 pkg. whip mix (such as Dream)
1 (3 oz.) pkg. cream cheese (softened)
1 can ready-mixed cherry pie filling

Cool whole chocolate crackers in refrigerator so the chocolate does not melt. Crush the crackers quite fine. Set aside ¼ cup crumbs for topping. Add the cooled butter to the bulk of the crumbs and press on the bottom of an 8x10 pan. Beat the whip mix until very stiff. Beat in the cream cheese and mix well. Spread mixture carefully over the graham cracker crust. Spread cherry pie filling over the cream cheese mixture, and top with ¼ cup of the reserved crumbs. Refrigerate 12-24 hours before serving. Variations: Use plain graham crackers, use blueberry pie filling, or garnish each piece for serving with a maraschino cherry.

Mrs. Astrid Ahrens, Blue Earth Public School
Blue Earth, Minnesota

CHERRY ICE BOX DELIGHT

Number of Servings — 6

1 can condensed milk
Juice from 2 lemons
1 box. whip mix (such as Dream)
1 can black cherries (drained) (other fruit may be used, such as pineapple or strawberries)
1 can pecans

Combine milk and lemon juice. Fold in prepared whip (prepare using directions on package). Add cherries and pecans. Put in vanilla wafer crust. Chill.

Mrs. Jim L. Miller, State Line H. S.
State Line, Mississippi

CHERRY CREAM MOLD

Number of Servings — 6-8

1 pkg. black cherry gelatin
¾ c. boiling water
¾ c. commercial sour cream
1 can (13½ ozs.) crushed pineapple (undrained)
¾ c. bing cherries (drained)

Dissolve gelatin in boiling water. Stir in sour cream, pineapple and bing cherries. Chill until partially set. Stir lightly. Pour into oiled (1½ quart) mold. Chill until firm.

Patsy K. Myers, Christian Co. H. S.
Hopkinsville, Kentucky

CHERRY-NUT CREME

Number of Servings — 12

1 pkg. instant vanilla pudding
1¾ c. milk
1 envelope unflavored gelatin
¼ c. milk
1 c. whipping cream
¼ c. sugar
½ t. vanilla
½ c. marshmallows (diced)
½ c. maraschino cherries, cut up
½ c. pecans, chopped
1 small box vanilla wafers

Prepare pudding as directed on package using 1¾ cup milk. Dissolve gelatin in ¼ cup milk. Whip cream, adding sugar and vanilla. Add whipped cream to pudding mixture with gelatin. Line square baking dish with vanilla wafers. Pour half mixture over wafers and sprinkle half of nuts, marshmallows and cherries over this. Add the rest of pudding mixture and again sprinkle nuts, cherries, and marshmallows over top. Refrigerate for 2 hours.

Mary L. Lane, San Benito H. S.
San Benito, Texas

CHERRY MARSHMALLOW FLUFF

Number of Servings — 12

1 c. oats (quick or old fashioned, uncooked)
1 c. brown sugar
½ c. melted butter
For base thoroughly mix all ingredients. Pat into bottom of 9x13 pan and chill.
Topping:
1 lb. 14 oz. can pitted, dark sweet cherries

1 pkg. cherry flavored gelatin
2 c. miniature marshmallows
1 c. chopped nut meats
1 pt. whipping cream

Drain cherries, reserving 1½ cup cherry juice. Heat cherry juice, add gelatin and stir until dissolved. Place in refrigerator until partially set. Mix drained cherries, marshmallows and nutmeats, let stand while gelatin is setting. Beat gelatin until frothy. Add cherry mixture. Whip the cream and fold into whipped cream and cherry mixture. Pour over base. Chill until set.

Ermadee Meyer, Sac Community H. S.
Sac City, Iowa

CHOCOLATE DELIGHT

Number of Servings — 9

2 c. powdered sugar
4 T. cocoa
¼ t. salt
¾ c. butter (1½ sticks)
2 eggs
1 c. nuts (chopped)
1½ t. vanilla
1¾ c. vanilla wafer crumbs

Sift sugar, cocoa, and salt. Cream butter. Add sugar mixture, then egg yolks. Mix well. Add nuts and vanilla. Fold in stiffly beaten egg whites. Line pan 7x9 with wax paper. Put ⅔ of vanilla wafer crumbs in bottom of pan. Pour in chocolate mixture and sprinkle remainder of crumbs on top. Refrigerate 12 hours. Cut in squares and serve with whipped cream topped with a cherry.

Mrs. Louis King, Jefferson H. S.
Jefferson, Texas

CHOCOLATE REFRIGERATOR DESSERT

Number of Servings — 6

2 c. vanilla wafer crumbs
1 c. chopped nuts
1 stick butter or margarine (melted)
1 c. whipping cream
1 bar German chocolate
2 T. water
1 t. vanilla flavoring
1 pinch salt
3 T. sugar (granulated or confectioners')

Mix vanilla wafer crumbs, chopped nuts, and melted butter. Pat ½ of mixture into bottom of 9x6 dish or pan. Whip chilled cream, gradually adding sugar and salt. Fold chocolate, which has been melted in water, and vanilla into the whipped cream. Place on crumbs and sprinkle remainder of nut and crumb mixture on top. Chill over night in refrigerator. Cut into squares to serve.

Mrs. Charlotte J. Callihan, Greene Central H. S.
Snow Hill, North Carolina

CHOCOLATE REFRIGERATOR DESSERT

Number of Servings — 8

½ c. pecan meats
¼ lb. vanilla wafers
½ c. butter
1 c. powdered sugar

(Continued on Next Page)

3 eggs, separated
1½ sq. chocolate, melted

Roll vanilla wafers. Mix with finely cut pecans. Spread half of mixture on ungreased pan. Cream butter and sugar. Add egg yolks. Beat well. Add chocolate and egg whites, beaten stiff. Pour over crumbs. Sprinkle top with remaining crumbs. Refrigerate over night.

Mrs. Julian Raburn, Telfair Co. H. S.
McRae, Georgia

JELLIED CHOCOLATE PUDDING
(Mint Sauce)
Number of Servings — 4
2 c. milk
1 sq. unsweetened chocolate
3 T. sugar
¼ t. salt
1 T. gelatin soaked in 2 T. cold water
½ t. vanilla

Scald milk with chocolate in double boiler. Beat until smooth. Add sugar, salt, and gelatin. Stir until gelatin dissolves. Add vanilla and pour into mold. Chill. Serve with marshmallow mint sauce.

Mint Sauce:
½ c. sugar
¼ c. water
8 marshmallows
1 egg white
1 drop oil of peppermint
Green coloring

Boil sugar and water 5 minutes, add marshmallows cut in pieces with wet scissors. Add this syrup mixture gradually to stiffly beaten egg whites. Flavor, color and chill.

Mrs. Agnes F. Beers, Henry Co. H. S.
McDonough, Georgia

LIME CHOCOLATE DELICIOUS
Number of Servings — 12
2 c. crushed chocolate sandwich cookies
1 stick oleo, melted

Mix cookie crumbs and oleo in 9x13 pan and press down firmly to cover bottom.

Filling:
1 box lime Jello
1 c. sugar
1¾ c. boiling water
¼ c. lemon or lime juice
1 (11 oz.) can evaporated milk, chilled and whipped

Mix Jello, sugar, boiling water and lemon or lime juice. Stir to dissolve sugar and Jello. Chill until thick, but not set. Chill milk in ice tray until crystals form on sides of pan. Whip milk. Whip Jello mixture and blend with milk. Pour into crust. Sprinkle more cookie crumbs on top and chill until set.

Mrs. Joel T. Hicks, Siloam Springs, H. S.
Siloam Springs, Arkansas

COFFEE MARLOW
Number of Servings — 6
1 c. boiling hot coffee
24 marshmallows
1 c. whipped cream
1 c. nuts
18 graham crackers, crushed

Pour hot coffee over marshmallows. Stir over low heat until marshmallows dissolve. Cool and chill. Fold whipped cream and nuts into chilled mixture. Cover bottom of 8" or 9" pie pan with half of crushed graham crackers. Pour the marlow mixture over the graham crackers. Cover top with the remaining crumbs. Chill. (May be frozen for later use.)

Guylene Stover, Canyon H. S.
Canyon, Texas

CRANBERRY GELATIN DESSERT
Number of Servings — 16
2 c. sugar
1 c. water
2½ T. gelatin, soaked in ½ c. cold water
4 c. raw cranberries, ground
1 medium sized orange, with rind, chopped
1 c. chopped celery
1 c. chopped nuts
1 c. yogurt

Cook sugar and water to make thin syrup. Add soaked gelatin. Stir until dissolved. Cool. Add remaining ingredients. Pour into mold. Chill. Serve with a dressing of whipped yogurt.

Mrs. Carrie Dickerson, Inola H. S.
Inola, Oklahoma

HAZELNUT CREAM
Number of Servings — 4
½ c. shelled hazelnuts
1 c. milk
2 egg yolks, beaten
¼ c. sugar
1 t. vanilla extract
½ envelope or ½ T. gelatin dissolved in ¼ c. water
¼ c. water
½ c. heavy cream

Heat nuts in oven until brown skins peel. Remove skins, grate nuts. Combine with milk, egg yolks, sugar, and vanilla in top of double boiler. Bring almost to a boil, remove from heat, stir in dissolved gelatin until mixture thickens. Whip cream until stiff, fold into nut mixture. Turn into glass serving dishes. Chill. Decorate with additional whirls of whipped cream to serve.

Lucile B. McGehee, So. West DeKalb School
South Decatur, Georgia

VELVET CREAM
3 c. milk
⅔ c. sugar
4 T. cornstarch
⅛ t. salt
2 eggs, separated
1 t. vanilla
½ c. cream
Fruit and nuts if desired

Scald milk in double boiler. Add cornstarch mixed with sugar and salt. Cook on low heat, stirring constantly until thickened, about 10 minutes. Beat egg yolks, pour mixture over them. Return to

(Continued on Next Page)

heat and cook about 2 more minutes. Remove from heat and add vanilla. Beat as it cools, folding in beaten egg whites and then whipped cream. Serve plain or with cake or cookies. Variations: Add 2 squares melted chocolate to scalded milk. Add nuts and/or fruit folding into cooled velvet cream.

LaVelle M. Leopard, Athens Jr. H. S.
Athens, Alabama

DATE NUT COFFEE DESSERT
Number of Servings — 12-15

1 lb. marshmallows
1 c. strong, hot coffee
1 pt. whipped cream
1 c. chopped dates
½ c. chopped pecans
1 small bottle maraschino cherries, drained and sliced
½ c. graham cracker crumbs

Melt in top of double boiler, marshmallows and coffee. Cool. Add dates, nuts, and cherries, Fold in whipped cream. Prepare graham cracker crumbs. Oil a pan to use as mold. Sprinkls with crumbs. Pour mixture into pan and sprinkle lightly with crumbs. Place in refrigerator over night or until it congeals.

Era King, Lamar H. S.
Lamar, Arkansas

DATE DELIGHT
Number of Servings — 8

1 pkg. dates
½ c. sugar
1 c. water
1 c. nuts, chopped
½ pt. whipping cream
2 T. sherry
1 box graham crackers

Combine chopped dates, sugar, and water. Cook over low heat until thick. Remove and cool. Add nuts. Spread date mixture on graham crackers making three layers. Whip cream and add sherry. Cover top and sides as you would ice a cake. Chill in refrigerator for several hours.

Mrs. Martha McDaniel, Gray Court-Owings H. S.
Gray Court, South Carolina

DATE-NUT LOAF
Number of Servings — 10-12

16 marshmallows
1 lb. dates
1 c. chopped nuts
¾ c. cream
1 t. vanilla
1¼ c. graham cracker crumbs

Chop marshmallows and dates very fine. Blend all ingredients together, saving ¼ cup crumbs. Line 3x7x2½ pan with foil and sprinkle with ¼ cup crumbs. Pack in the blended mixture. Chill for several hours. Unmold and slice. Serve with whipped cream and garnish with a cherry.

Mrs. Virginia H. Culbertson,
Mid-Carolina H. S.
Prosperity, South Carolina

DATE DESSERT (Choc-o-Date)
Number of Servings — 8

12 cream filled chocolate cookies, crushed
1 8 oz. pkg. (1 c.) pitted dates, cut up
¾ c. water
¼ t. salt
2 c. tiny marshmallows or 1 lb. marshmallows
½ c. chopped nuts
1 c. heavy cream
½ t. vanilla

Reserve ¼ cup cookie crumbs, spread remainder in 10x6x1½ baking dish. In saucepan, combine dates, water, and salt, bring to boiling, reduce heat and simmer 3 minutes. Remove from heat, add marshmallows and stir until melted. Cool to room temperature. Stir in chopped nuts. Spread date mixture over crumbs in dish. Combine cream and vanilla. Whip and swirl over dates. Sprinkle with reserved crumbs. Chill over night. Cut in squares.

Margie Morgan, Bishopville H. S.
Bishopville, South Carolina

ENGLISH TOFFEE
Number of Servings — 8

½ c. butter
2 c. powdered sugar
Pinch salt
4 T. cocoa
2 eggs, separated
1 T. vanilla
1 c. nuts
12 vanilla wafers, crumbled

Cream butter and sugar, salt and cocoa. Add egg yolks and beat until smooth and light. Beat egg whites until stiff. Add vanilla. Add to the first mixture and beat until very light. Add nuts. Line an 8x12 pan with wax paper. Sprinkle bottom with vanilla wafer crumbs. Pour in mixture. Put rest of crumbs on top. Refrigerate several hours before serving. Cut in squares. Top with whipped cream or ice cream.

Mrs. J. H. Fields, Chattanooga Valley H. S.
Chattanooga, Tennessee

FRUIT DELIGHT
Number of Servings — 12-15

1 pkg. orange gelatin
1 pkg. lemon gelatin
1 c. boiling water
1 can (No. 2) crushed pineapple
3 cans mandarin orange slices
1 small pkg. marshmallows
1 pt. whipping cream
1 c. salad dressing plus 1 t. prepared mustard
Grated sharp cheese

Dissolve gelatin in boiling water, add juices and fruit. Mix well. Pour in 13x9 shallow dish. Top with marshmallows. Congeal. Top with whipped cream into which was folded salad dressing and prepared mustard. Sprinkle top with grated cheese. Refrigerate until firm.

Mrs. Suan R. Salter, Robert E. Lee H. S.
Montgomery, Alabama

FRUIT COCKTAIL GELATIN DESSERT

Number of Servings — 8

1 No. 2½ can fruit cocktail
2 T. lemon juice
1 T. unflavored gelatin
Dash of salt
3 oz. pkg. cream cheese
½ c. chopped nuts
1 c. whipping cream
½ c. sugar

Drain juice from fruit cocktail. Add lemon juice. Soften gelatin in juices. Dissolve over hot water. Soften cream cheese. Add fruit cocktail, salt, gelatin mixture and nuts. Beat cream until stiff. Add sugar gradually. Fold into the fruit mixture. Place in individual molds or a 1-quart mold and chill. To cut calories, use diet sweet fruit cocktail and 1 tablespoon of Sucaryl in place of ½ cup sugar.

Mrs. Willie Pence, Mauriceville H. S.
Mauriceville, Texas

SNOW FLAKE FRUIT BOWL

Number of Servings — 8

3 lge. oranges, pared and sectioned
2 ripe bananas, peeled and sliced
1 can (13 oz.) frozen pineapple chunks, partly thawed
1 pkg. frozen mixed fruits, partly thawed
½ c. flaked coconut

Arrange fruits in separate mounds in shallow bowl. Drizzle juice from oranges over bananas. Sprinkle coconut over all, chill. To serve, spoon fruits into individual dessert dishes, top with eggnog custard cream.

Eggnog Custard Cream:
2 c. light or table cream
1 c. milk
2 T. sugar
1 T. rum flavoring
½ t. vanilla
1 pkg. vanilla flavor instant pudding mix

Combine the above ingredients. Beat 1 minute with a rotary beater, let stand 5 minutes, or until set, then chill. Stir until creamy before serving. Makes about 3½ cups.

Mrs. Kenneth J. Moore, R. E. Lee Institute
Thomaston, Georgia

TUTTI FRUTTI JELLO SURPRISE

Number of Servings — 6-8

1 regular size box cherry Jello
½ c. chopped nuts
½ doz. macaroons (almond)
1 pt. whipping cream

Dissolve Jello and chill until thickened. Beat in chopped nuts and broken macaroons. Fold in half the whipped cream. Place in dessert dishes or large serving bowl and refrigerate until firm. Serve with whipped cream topping (other half whipped cream) and maraschino cherries.

Mrs. Katherine B. Winfree,
Port Neches-Groves H. S.
Port Neches, Texas

GONE WITH THE WIND

Number of Servings — 8

1 c. milk, scalded
2 egg yolks, beaten
1 pkg. orange Jello
1 c. hot water
Vanilla wafers
Brown sugar
Butter
1 flat can crushed pineapple
½ c. cream, whipped
2 egg whites, beaten
¼ c. sugar added to beaten egg whites

Make a custard of milk and beaten egg yolks. Add hot water to Jello. Cool Jello and add to custard. Set until mixture starts to congeal. During this time place a layer of vanilla wafer crumbs about ¼" to ½" thick in loaf pan. Cover with a thin layer of brown sugar and butter. Place drained, crushed pineapple over brown sugar. Combine beaten egg whites and sugar, add to cream. Add to cooled Jello mixture. Pour over pineapple and set until firm. Sprinkle with cookie crumbs. (1 tablespoon plain gelatin and 1 package orange punch powder may be substituted for Jello.)

Shirlee A. Huskinson, Bonneville H. S.
Idaho Falls, Idaho

GRASSHOPPER SANDWICHES

Number of Servings — 4

Unfrosted chocolate wafers
1½ c. whipped low-calorie topping,
Sugar or other sweetening agent
1 oz. Creme de Menthe
1 oz. white Creme de Cocoa

Whip topping to make 1 cup. Sweeten to taste. Fold in each liquor. Alternate a chocolate wafer with a layer of the topping and top with a small amount of the flavored topping on a chocolate wafer. (Topping becomes green with the addition of the liquors, do not use brown Creme de Cocoa.) May be garnished with a mint leaf, chocolate shot or a green maraschino cherry.

Beverly Anderson, Rolla H. S.
Rolla, North Dakota

HEAVENLY HASH

Number of Servings — 8

1 small box strawberries
1 No. 2 can sliced pineapple
1 c. pecans
½ lb. marshmallows
1 pt. whipped cream
½ c. sugar

Chop fruits and marshmallows very fine and let stand to chill 1 hour. Add whipped cream to which has been added the sugar and nuts, chopping nuts fine. Other fruit combinations may be used if desired. Makes a delectable cake topping with sponge or angel cake or it may be served in compote for desserts.

Mrs. Cora L. Coleman, Coffeeville H. S.
Coffeeville, Alabama

HEAVENLY HASH

Number of Servings — 8

1 No. 2½ can fruit cocktail
1 No. 2 or 303 can crushed pineapple
2 lge. ripe bananas
1 small bottle maraschino cherries
1 small bottle minted green cherries
1 pt. whipping cream
1 lge. pkg. small marshmallows

Mix cocktail and pineapple. Slice bananas into mixture and stir gently to coat bananas with juice to prevent darkening. Drain well. Quarter part of the well drained cherries, leave some whole for garnish. Whip the cream. Fold everything except the garnish together. Chill thoroughly. Garnish with holly and cherries, or as desired.

Mrs. Zelma A. Cromer, Senior H. S.
Lexington, Oklahoma

HEAVENLY HASH

Number of Servings — 8

1 doz. marshmallows
1 No. 2 can crushed pineapple
½ pt. whipping cream
½ c. pecans

Cut up marshmallows and mix with pineapple. Let mixture stand until it becomes soft. Add finely chopped pecans, then whipped cream. Chill before serving.

Mrs. Johnie M. Dismuke, Lytle Ind. School
Lytle, Texas

HEAVENLY HASH

Number of Servings — 6-8

1 pkg. cherry gelatin
⅔ c. (1 small can) evaporated milk
2 T. lemon juice
½ c. confectioners' sugar
1 c. coconut
1 small can well-drained crushed pineapple
¼ c. well-drained chopped maraschino cherries
¼ c. chopped pecans
Angel food cake slices

Mix gelatin according to package directions. Pour into 8" square pan to congeal. Chill evaporated milk in ice tray until crystals form around edges of tray (15-20 minutes). Whip until stiff (about 1 minute). Add lemon juice and whip until very stiff (about 2 minutes longer). Beat in sugar. Cut gelatin into cubes, fold gelatin, coconut, pineapple, cherries, and pecans into whipped cream. Serve over slices of angel food cake.

Mrs. Gladys Truitt, Warren Co. H. S.
Bowling Green, Kentucky

JELLO DESSERT (Colorful)

Number of Servings — 6

1 box whip mix (such as Dream)
1 box cherry Jello
1 box lime Jello
1 pkg. small marshmallows
1 No. 2 can crushed Pineapple

Prepare Jello as on package. Place in refrigerator to congeal. When jelled thoroughly, prepare whip mix. Stir Jello, whip, pineapple, and marshmallows until mixed. Place in bowl and use for dessert when needed. Will keep for 3 or 4 days.

Mrs. Nancy H. King, Chesterfield H. S.
Chesterfield, South Carolina

JELLO DELIGHT (Using Coca-Cola)

Number of Servings — 10

2 pkg. black raspberry Jello
2 c. hot water
1 can black sweet cherries (drained)
1-10 oz. pkg. frozen strawberries (drained)
1 Coca-Cola
1 c. broken nuts
1 c. small or chopped marshmallows

Dissolve the Jello in the hot water. Measure the drained juices and Coca-Cola. Add water, enough to make 2 cups of the cold liquid. Pour this into the Jello and hot water mixture. Add the remaining ingredients, pour into mold. Place in the refrigerator to congeal. Stir occasionally to keep the fruit from settling to the bottom. Top each serving with whipped cream.

Mrs. Floyd Craig, Divide H. S.
Nolan, Texas

LEMON BISQUE

Number of Servings — 12

1 13 oz. can chilled evaporated milk
1 pkg. lemon Jello
1¼ c. hot water
½-¾ c. sugar
¼ t. salt
Juice and rind of 2 lemons
1 lge. pkg. vanilla wafers

Dissolve Jello in hot water and sugar, salt, juice and rind of lemons. Congeal slightly. Whip milk and add to above mixture. Cover bottom of long dish with crushed vanilla wafers. Sprinkle crumbs lightly on top. Refrigerate, cut in squares and serve. (Servings depend on the size of square you cut.)

This recipe submitted by the following teachers:
Mrs. Bernice Britt, West Hardin H. S.
Saratoga, Texas
Mrs. Ruth Yelvington, Mildred H. S.
Corsicana, Texas
Mrs. Anna Elizabeth Davis, Trumann H. S.
Trumann, Arkansas
Louise D. Coldren
Tallulah Falls, Georgia

LEMON BISQUE

Number of Servings — 14

1 pkg. lemon Jello
1 c. hot water
1 lge. pkg. cream cheese
1 c. sugar
1 t. vanilla
1 can evaporated milk (chilled)
Juice of 2 lge. lemons
2 c. graham cracker crumbs
1 stick margarine (melted)
2 t. sugar

(Continued on Next Page)

Mix cracker crumbs, margarine, and 2 teaspoons sugar. Line large pyrex dish with ⅔ of mixture. Dissolve Jello and cheese in hot water. Add sugar, vanilla, and let stand until beginning to set. Whip milk and lemon juice until it stands in peaks. Beat in Jello mixture. Pour lemon mixture in pan lined with crumb mixture. Sprinkle remaining crumbs on top. Chill several hours. Cut in squares to serve.

Brenda Swofford, St. Matthews H. S.
St. Matthews, South Carolina

LEMON BISQUE (Using Honey)
Number of Servings — 14-16
1 can (13 oz.) evaporated milk
1 pkg. lemon Jello
1¼ c. boiling water
¼ c. honey
⅛ t. salt
3 T. lemon juice
Grated rind of 1 lemon
2½ c. vanilla crumbs or graham crackers

Chill can of milk in refrigerator over night. Dissolve gelatin in boiling water, add honey, salt, lemon juice and rind. When slightly congealed, beat milk until stiff and whip gelatin mixture into it. Spread half of crumbs in large pan (10x12) and pour lemon mixture over it. Top with other crumbs. Set in refrigerator to chill 3 hours. Serve with whipped cream if desired.

This recipe submitted by the following teachers:
Leila Cullison, Lakeview H. S.
Decatur, Illinois
Vera Mays, Gillett Jr. H. S.
Kingsville, Texas

LEMON CHIFFON SANDWICHES
Number of Servings — 6-8
1 pkg. lemon gelatin
1½ c. hot water
⅔ c. sugar
1 t. grated lemon rind
4 T. lemon juice
⅛ t. salt
1 lge. can evaporated milk
1 small box vanilla wafers

Dissolve gelatin in hot water. Add sugar, lemon rind, lemon juice and salt. Refrigerate until slightly thickened. Add the milk that has been thoroughly chilled and whipped. Mix well. Pour into buttered pan lined with crushed wafers. Cover top with crushed wafers. Freeze or refrigerate. Serve in slices. Some people prefer it just refrigerated, rather than frozen.

Lois Webb, Elaine H. S.
Elaine, Arkansas

SNOW PUDDING (With Custard Sauce)
1 T. granulated gelatin
¼ c. cold water
1 c. boiling water
1 c. sugar
¼ c. lemon juice
3 egg whites, stiffly beaten

Soak gelatin in cold water. Dissolve in boiling water. Add sugar and strained lemon juice. Set aside in cool place and occasionally stir. When it begins to thicken, beat until frothy. Fold in stiffly beaten egg whites and continue beating until stiff. Chill again. Spoon into sherbet glasses. Serve with custard sauce and top with red cherry.

Custard Sauce:
1 c. milk
¼ c. brown sugar
3 egg yolks
Pinch salt
½ t. vanilla flavoring

Scald milk in top of double boiler. Beat egg yolks well. Gradually add sugar and beat until smooth. Add scalded milk to egg-sugar mixture. Stir until well blended. Return egg-milk to double boiler, cook until thick or coats spoon. Add vanilla and salt. Chill. Serve over snow pudding.

Mrs. Mary S. Hatcher, Brooks Co. H. S.
Quitman, Georgia

MAPLE NUT SPONGE
Number of Servings — 4
1 envelope unflavored gelatin
¼ c. cold water
1½ c. hot milk
2 eggs (separated)
1 c. maple syrup
¼ t. salt
1 t. vanilla
½ c. chopped nut meats

Soften gelatin in cold water 5 minutes. Combine hot milk and beaten egg yolks in the top of a double boiler. Cook until slightly thickened. Remove from heat. Add softened gelatin, stir until gelatin is dissolved. Stir in syrup and salt. Chill until mixture begins to stiffen. Fold in stiffly beaten egg whites, vanilla, and nuts. Chill and serve. Garnish with whipped cream if desired.

Mrs. Olith Hamilton, Wk Kellogg H. S.
Nashville, Michigan

MARSHMALLOW DESSERT
Number of Servings — 6-8
¾ c. milk
½ lb. marshmallows
1 pt. cream
1 T. sugar
½ t. vanilla
1 pt. drained fruit (pineapple, fruit cocktail, strawberries, peaches, maraschino cherries)

Melt marshmallows with milk in double boiler and cool. Whip cream. Add sugar and vanilla. Fold whipped cream into marshmallow mixture. Add fruit. Pour into graham cracker crust. Garnish with crumbs. Chill several hours.

Crust:
2 doz. graham crackers
¼ c. butter
1 T. sugar

Prepare graham cracker crust. Save a few crumbs for garnish

Mrs. Carol Jacobs, Orangeville Comm. H. S.
Orangeville, Illinois

CANDY CANE DESSERT

Number of Servings — 6

16 marshmallows
4 sticks peppermint candy (6")
¾ pt. whipping cream
½ c. chopped nuts
½ lb. (2 c.) vanilla wafers, crushed

Cut marshmallows in eighths. Crush peppermint candy and fold in stiffly whipped cream. Add nuts and marshmallows. Cover bottom of square pan with half of crushed vanilla wafers. Pour in whipped cream mixture. Sprinkle remaining crumbs on top. Place in refrigerator over night or until thoroughly chilled.

Imogene Crosby, Spring City H. S.
Spring City, Tennessee

CHOCOLATE PEPPERMINT SURPRISE

Number of Servings — 6

1½ c. cream, whipped
½ lb. peppermint stick candy
½ c. light cream
½ T. plain gelatin
2 T. cold water
10 oz. box chocolate wafer (NBC)

Dissolve the candy in the light cream over low heat. Add gelatin to cold water. After candy has dissolved in light cream, add the gelatin mixture and stir until dissolved. Cool mixture. Whip cream until very stiff. Fold in the peppermint mixture. Line mold with wafers. Stand up around the edge. Add ½ of the peppermint mixture. Place another layer of wafers and then peppperimnt mixture. Broken wafers may be used to decorate top. Chill and serve with whipped cream.

Mrs. Beatrice K. Irwin, Central H. S.
Knoxville, Tennessee

MOUSSE (Orange)

Number of Servings — 10

1 c. orange juice
2 T. gelatin
3 egg whites
1 c. sugar
2 pt. whipping cream
5 oranges, in sections
Maraschino cherries
Pecans (optional)

Soak gelatin in half of the orange juice 5 minutes. Dissolve over hot water. Add remaining half cup of orange juice. Beat egg whites with half of the sugar to make soft meringue. Whip one pint of cream. Add remaining half cup of sugar. Combine gelatin mixture, meringue and whipped cream. Turn into ring mold. Chill until set. Turn out on large round tray. Fill center with additional pint of cream. Garnish with cherries and nuts. Surround mousse with fresh orange sections. Served at the table.

Lois Pullen, State Dept. of Education
Baton Rouge, Louisiana

MOUSSE (Harlequin)

Number of Servings — 10-12

1 pkg. black cherry Jello
1 c. hot water
½ c. diluted grape juice
1 pkg. strawberry Jello
1 c. hot water
½ c. cold water
1 pkg. lime Jello
1 c. hot water
½ c. cold water
1 pkg. raspberry Jello
¼ c. sugar
1 c. hot water
½ c. diluted grape juice
2 c. cream (whipped)
½ c. crushed pineapple (drained)
1 can coconut

Prepare the first 3 kinds of Jello in separate pans (8x8x2), chill until firm. Prepare raspberry Jello and chill until syrupy. Cut the 3 pans of Jello that are firm into ½" cubes. Whip cream and fold into raspberry mixture. Add crushed pineapple to this mixture, then the Jello cubes. Pour into angelfood cake pan and chill 8 hours. Unmold and sprinkle coconut on top and sides. Serve with whipped cream if desired.

Mrs. Velma Grizzle, Tipton H. S.
Tipton, Oklahoma

ORANGE JUICE DESSERT

Number of Servings — 9

1-6 oz. can frozen orange juice
3-6 oz. cans water
1 lb. marshmallows

Dilute orange juice with water, add marshmallows and heat until marshmallows dissolve. Pour mixture into an 8x8 pan and place in refrigerator to congeal. Serve with whipped cream.

Gladys S. Esslinger, New Hope H. S.
New Hope, Alabama

ORANGE MARSHMALLOW DESSERT

Number of Servings — 4

2 oranges
¼ lb. (16) marshmallows
½ c. orange juice (frozen orange juice may be used)
½ c. heavy cream (whipped)

Chill oranges before preparing. Peel oranges cutting deep enough to remove white membrane. Remove section by section and half sections. Add marshmallows to orang juice. Place over low heat stirring occasionally until marshmallows are melted. Remove from heat. Stir in diced orange sections. Chill until mixture is thick. Fold in whipped cream. Spoon into dessert dishes and chill until firm. If desired, garnish with additional whipped cream and orange sections or a green cherry on whipped cream.

Lucille R. Marker, Robertsdale H. S.
Robertsdale, Alabama

CANTALOUPE A' PARFAIT
Number of Servings — 10-12

1 pkg. lime Jello
1 pt. vanilla ice cream
No. 2 can crushed pineapple
3 cantaloupes
Juice from pineapple plus water to make 1¼ c.

Heat the pineapple juice and water, remove from heat, add lime Jello. Stir until gelatin is dissolved. Cut ice cream into pieces and turn into hot mixture. Blend with fork until all ice cream is softened and smoothly mixed. Place mixture in refrigerator until chilled. When partially congealed, fold 1 cup crushed pineapple into the mixture. While the parfait is chilling, peel 3 cantaloupes, cut off the top and remove the seeds. Spoon the parfait into the hollow of each cantaloupe and replace the top. Return to the refrigerator for complete congealing, allowing 3 hours. The cantaloupes may be frosted with softened cream cheese if desired. When ready to serve, cut into 1″ slices with a sharp knife. Attractive when served on a large ivy leaf.

Mrs. Hazel Edberg, Denair H. S.
Denair, California

KAY'S PARTY PARFAITS
Number of Servings — 6

1 c. sour cream
1 c. flaked coconut
1 c. pineapple chunks
1 c. mandarin oranges
1 pt. orange or lime ice

Combine all ingredients except the ice and chill thoroughly. Spoon into parfait glasses alternating with lime or orange ice.

Marian Barber, Jefferson H. S.
Roanoke, Virginia

PINEAPPLE BISQUE
Number of Servings — 12

1 8 oz. pkg. vanilla wafers, crushed
½ lb. butter
¾ lb. confectioners' sugar
4 egg yolks
1 t. vanilla
4 egg whites
1 No. 2 can crushed pineapple
1 4 oz. bottle cherries
Whipped cream
1 c. chopped nuts

Cream butter and sugar. Add egg yolks and vanilla. Fold in stiffly beaten egg whites. Line 14x16 pan with half the wafer crumbs. Spread beaten mixture on this. Add layer of drained pineapple ½″ thick. Add chopped cherries, pineapple. Spread whipped cream evenly. Sprinkle with chopped nuts. Add remainder of crushed wafers as a crust. Chill 12 hours before serving.

Flora Ward, Newville H. S.
Newville, Alabama

PINEAPPLE DELIGHT
Number of Servings — 4-6

1 c. whipping cream
1 small can crushed pineapple
1½ c. miniature marshmallows

Whip cream, drain pineapple and add to cream, folding in gently. Add marshmallows by folding in. Chill for 2 or more hours before serving.

Virginia Crossno, Newellton H. S.
Newellton, Louisiana

PINEAPPLE ANGEL FLUFF DESSERT
Number of Servings — 8

42 lge. marshmallows
1 c. milk
1-10½ oz. can crushed pineapple, drained
1 c. cream, whipped
1½ t. vanilla
½ c. nuts (if desired)
3 c. crushed honey graham crackers

Melt marshmallows with milk in double boiler, cool. Add the drained pineapple to marshmallow mixture. Mix well. Fold whipped cream into the marshmallow and pineapple mixture. Add vanilla. Cover bottom of dish, 7x11 with 2 cups graham crackers. Add the marshmallow mixture, and top with remaining 1 cup graham crackers. Chill until set, cut and serve.

This recipe submitted by the following teachers:
Mrs. Nancy S. Cully, Northwestern H. S.
Palmyra, Illinois
Marie Slover, Springlake H. S.
Earth, Texas

PINEAPPLE NUT DESSERT
Number of Servings — 10-12

1 pkg. (7½ oz.) vanilla wafers
1 c. butter or margarine
1 c. granulated sugar
2 eggs
1-2 t. vanilla
2 c. crushed pineapple, well drained
1 c. finely chopped walnuts (or other nuts)

Crush vanilla wafers to fine crumbs (makes about 2 cups), reserve 2 tablespoons. Cream butter to consistency of mayonnaise, add sugar gradually. Add eggs one at a time, beating well after each addition. Add vanilla, mix well. Combine pineapple and walnuts, stir until well mixed. Line a loaf pan 8x5x3 with foil, leaving overhang so loaf can be lifted out easily. Press ½ cup crumbs on bottom of pan. Add about ¼ pineapple mixture, spreading evenly. Repeat until crumbs and pineapple mixture are used up, ending with latter. Scatter reserved crumbs on top. Chill 24 hours or longer (or freeze). Garnish with whipped cream and maraschino cherries. Slice to serve.

This recipe submitted by the following teachers:
Mildred Hardy, George Mason H. S.
Falls Church, Virginia
Rosalind Dunham, Hayden H. S.
Hayden, Arizona
Mrs. Luella Robb, Round Valley Union H. S.
Covelo, California

PINEAPPLE ORANGE DELIGHT

Number of Servings — 8-10

Graham Cracker Crust:
1½ c. graham crackers
3 T. granulated sugar
⅛ c. butter, melted
Crush crackers and add sugar and butter. Place in 9x14 oblong pan and bake at 350°F. for 10 minutes. Let cool.

Vanilla Cream Filling:
⅔ c. granulated sugar
3 T. cornstarch
½ t. salt
3 c. milk
3 egg yolks (slightly beaten)
1 T. butter
1½ t. vanilla
Mix sugar, cornstarch, salt and cook for 1 minute with milk. Separate ½ mixture and mix with egg yolks slowly. Combine with rest of mixture and boil for 1 minute longer. Add butter and vanilla, remove from heat and pour on cracker crust. Let cool.

Pineapple-Orange Filling:
1 c. sugar
¼ c. cornstarch
½ t. salt
1 c. orange juice
2 T. butter
2 T. orange rind
2 T. lemon juice
¾ c. crushed pineapple
Mix sugar, cornstarch, salt, and orange juice and bring to boil. Boil for 1 minute. Remove from heat and add butter, orange rind, lemon juice, and pineapple. Cook for 1 minute, cool and pour on vanilla cream filling. Refrigerate dessert for 24 hours. Serve in squares topped with 1 teaspoon of whipped cream.

Sweetened Whipping Cream:
1 c. chilled whipping cream
¼ c. sifted confectioners' sugar
1 t. vanilla
Whip cream until stiff, then add sugar and vanilla.

Mrs. Irene O. Lane, Atascadero Union H. S.
Atascadero, California

PINEAPPLE MARSHMALLOW ROLLS

Number of Servings — 16

3 c. miniature marshmallows
1 No. 2 can crushed pineapple, drained
1 c. whipping cream
½ c. chopped nuts
2 c. graham cracker crumbs
Combine marshmallows and drained pineapple and let stand 1 hour. Whip cream, add nuts and let stand 5 minutes. Combine the pineapple mixture and the cream mixture and shape into oblong rolls. Roll in crushed graham cracker crumbs. Chill several hours before serving. May be frozen to serve later.

Mrs. Stacie O. Houser, Sun Valley H. S.
Monroe, North Carolina

PINEAPPLE PARTY DESSERT

Number of Servings — 9

12 graham crackers, crushed
1 No. 2 can crushed pineapple (heavy syrup)
1½ c. whipping cream or pkg. whip mix
1 envelope gelatin
¼ c. water
½ c. chopped nut meats
¾ c. sugar
½ c. chopped maraschino cherries
Drain pineapple. Heat the juice. Dissolve gelatin in cold water and add to hot juice. Stir until dissolved. Add sugar and cool until slightly congealed. Add pineapple and cream which has been whipped. Fold in nuts and cherries. Line an 8x8 pan with ½ of the crushed crumbs. Pour the mixture into the pan. Top with remainder of crumbs. Refrigerate 6 hours.

Mrs. William B. Keiner, Gen. Beadle H. S.
Madison, South Dakota

PINEAPPLE FLUFF

Number of Servings — 12

2 c. sugar
2 c. crushed pineapple
6 lge. eggs, separated (7-8 eggs if small)
1 pkg. lemon Jello
1½ c. graham cracker crumbs
Combine 1 cup sugar with beaten egg yolks and undrained crushed pineapple in saucepan and cook stirring constantly until mixture thickens. Add the package of lemon Jello. Cool mixture to room temperature. Beat egg whites until stiff and gradually add the additional 1 cup sugar a little at a time and beat until very stiff. Fold this mixture into the cooled pineapple mixture. Spread 1 cup of crumbs on bottom of 9x13 pan. Spread mixture over crumbs. Sprinkle remaining crumbs on top. Chill until set. Cut into squares to serve. Top with dab of whipped cream and cherry if desired.

Mrs. Marlene Westly, Volga H. S.
Volga, South Dakota

PINEAPPLE PARTY CHEESE CAKE

Number of Servings — 16

2⅛ c. fine vanilla wafer crumbs
½ c. butter, melted
1 No. 2 can crushed pineapple
2 T. gelatin
4 egg yolks, slightly beaten
1 c. sugar
2 t. lemon peel
¼ t. salt
2 12 oz. cartons cottage cheese
1 T. vanilla
2 c. heavy cream, whipped
4 egg whites, stiffly beaten
Mix crumbs and melted butter, press on bottom and sides of a buttered 9" spring form pan. Drain pineapple, reserving syrup. Soften gelatin in ½ cup of pineapple syrup. In double boiler combine egg yolks, sugar, salt, lemon peel, and 2 tablespoons pineapple syrup, stirring constantly. **Cook**

(Continued on Next Page)

over simmering water about 8 minutes or until mixture is like smooth custard. Remove from heat and add dissolved softened gelatin in hot mixture. Add crushed pineapple, cottage cheese, and vanilla, fold in whipped cream, then egg whites. Pour into the crumb lined pan, chill about 5 hours or until firm. Garnish with pineapple and maraschino cherries.

Mrs. Mary Meyer, Griggsville H. S.
Griggsville, Illinois

RASPBERRY DESSERT

Number of Servings — 12-15

½ c. butter
1½ c. powdered sugar
2 eggs
1½ c. vanilla wafer crumbs
1 pkg. raspberry Jello
½ c. hot water
1 pkg. frozen raspberries
¾ c. nuts, chopped
1 c. heavy cream, whipped
½ t. vanilla

Cream butter with sugar. Add eggs and beat thoroughly. Line 9x12 pan with 1 cup wafer crumbs and spread the egg mixture over the crumbs. Dissolve Jello in hot water. Mix in raspberries, nuts, whipped cream, and vanilla. Spread with spoon as a layer over the egg mixture. Sprinkle with remaining crumbs and chill over night.

Mrs. Vanora Fry, High School
Little River, Kansas

RASPBERRY JELLO

Number of Servings — 8

1 box raspberry Jello
⅛ t. salt
1 box frozen raspberries
¾ c. chopped nuts
½ pt. whipping cream

Prepare Jello as directed on box.° Add salt. When mixture has cooled, add frozen raspberries and nuts. Chill in individual Jello molds. Top with whipped cream.
°—May use less liquid since raspberries will contain liquid.

Carolyn Smith, Kermit H. S.
Kermit, Texas

RASPBERRY DELIGHT (With Cranberry Sauce)

Number of Servings — 6

1 pkg. raspberry gelatin
1 c. hot water
2 c. crushed pineapple, drained
½ c. cranberry sauce
1 c. chopped pecans
1 small pkg. cream cheese (softened)

Dissolve gelatin in hot water, cool. Add pineapple and remaining ingredients. Turn into mold and chill.

Anna Ruth Rhodes, Ardmore H. S.
Ardmore, Alabama

SAUCY RASPBERRY DESSERT

Number of Servings — 6

1 pkg. raspberry flavored gelatin
1 c. hot water
1 c. canned applesauce
2 T. sugar
1 t. grated lemon rind
1 T. lemon juice
⅔ c. chopped walnuts
¾ c. tiny marshmallows
½ c. heavy cream, whipped

Dissolve raspberry gelatin in hot water. Add applesauce, sugar, lemon rind and juice. Chill over ice water until slightly thickened. Fold in walnuts and marshmallows. Pour into 1-quart mold. Chill until firm. Unmold and serve with whipped cream.

Mrs. Sharron Lykke, Austin H. S.
Austin, Texas

RICE IMPERIAL

Number of Servings — 6-8

1 c. chopped candied fruit
¼ c. brandy
1 c. raw rice
Boiling water
Milk
¼ t. salt
1 envelope unflavored gelatin
4 egg yolks
1 c. sugar
1 t. vanilla
1 c. heavy cream, whipped

Soak fruit over night in brandy. Cook rice in boiling water about 10 minutes. Pour off water and finish cooking rice in 1⅓ cup milk to which salt has been added. Cool. Sprinkle gelatin on ⅔ cup cold milk in top of double boiler. Cook over boiling water adding egg yolks, sugar, and vanilla. Stir constantly and cook until thickened. Mix with rice. Cool and stir in undrained fruit and then the whipped cream. Chill.

Mrs. Mary Davis Faison, Weldon H. S.
Weldon, North Carolina

SPANISH CREAM

Number of Servings — 3-4

1 envelope gelatin
2 T. cold milk
1¼ c. scalded milk
2 egg yolks, well beaten
¾ c. blended syrup
2 egg whites, beaten stiff
⅛ t. salt
1 t. vanilla

Soak gelatin in cold milk, dissolve in hot milk. Pour over yolks, cook in double boiler until thickened. Add syrup, chill until partially set. Beat until foamy and fold in salted, beaten whites, and vanilla. Pour into mold and chill. Top with whipped cream and strawberries or other fruit.

Mrs. Connie Ault, Connellsville Sr. H. S.
Connellsville, Pennsylvania

STRAWBERRY FRUIT PARFAIT

Number of Servings — 8-10

1 pkg. strawberry gelatin
2 c. hot water
1 pt. vanilla ice cream
1 c. strawberries

Dissolve gelatin in hot water. Chill until partially set. Beat in ice cream with beater. Fold in berries. Chill. Garnish with whole strawberries.

Mrs. Jean Bragg, Manor H. S.
Manor, Georgia

STRAWBERRY ICE BOX DESSERT

Number of Servings — 10-12

12 oz. pkg. vanilla wafers
¼ lb. margarine
1½ c. powdered sugar
2 eggs
1 qt. strawberry halves
½ pt. whipping cream

Crush wafers fine. Put more than half in an 8x12 pan. Cream margarine and sugar. Add eggs and beat well. Spread over crumbs. Cover with sliced strawberries, then whipped cream. Cover with remaining crumbs. Chill several hours or over night.

Mrs. Marguerite McGinness, Danbury H. S.
Danbury, Texas

STRAWBERRY SWIRL

Number of Servings — 12

1 c. graham cracker crumbs
1 T. sugar
¼ c. butter or margarine, melted
2 c. sliced fresh strawberries or 10 oz. pkg. frozen strawberries (thawed)
1 3 oz. pkg. strawberry flavored gelatin
1 c. boiling water
½ lb. marshmallows
½ c. milk
1 c. whipping cream, whipped

Mix crumbs, sugar, and butter. Press firmly over bottom of 9x9x2 baking dish. Chill until set. Sprinkle 2 tablespoons sugar over fresh berries, let stand ½ hour. Dissolve gelatin in boiling water. Drain strawberries, reserving juice. Add water to juice to make 1 cup, add to gelatin. Chill until partially set. Meanwhile, combine marshmallows and milk. Heat and stir until marshmallows melt. Cool thoroughly. Fold in whipped cream. Add berries to gelatin, then swirl in marshmallow mixture to marble. Pour into crust. Chill until set. Cut in 9 or 12 squares.

This recipe submitted by the following teachers:
Frances W. Moorman, Sterlington H. S.
Sterlington, Louisiana
Mrs. J. E. Little,
Pearland Independent School District
Pearland, Texas

STRAWBERRY LUSCIOUS
(With Sour Cream)

Number of Servings — 12-15

2 pkg. strawberry gelatin
2 c. boiling water
1 lge. pkg. frozen strawberries
1 can (No. 211) crushed pineapple
2 lge. ripe bananas
½ carton dairy sour cream

Dissolve gelatin in boiling water. Add thawed strawberries with juice, undrained pineapple and bananas which have been mashed and whipped. Pour half mixture into an 8x12 pan and chill until set. Spread sour cream over top of congealed layer. Cover with remaining gelatin. Chill until firm.

This recipe submitted by the following teachers:

Mavis W. Van Beek, Central H. S.
Aberdeen, South Dakota

Mrs. Norman K. Good, Columbia City Joint H. S.
Columbia City, Indiana

TOASTED SNOW SQUARES

Number of Servings — 6

1 envelope unflavored gelatin
4 T. cold water
1 c. boiling water
⅔ c. sugar
3 egg whites, unbeaten
¼ t. salt
¼ t. vanilla
8 graham crackers, crushed

Sprinkle gelatin over cold water and soak five minutes. Add boiling water and stir until dissolved. Stir in sugar and cool the mixture. Add egg whites, salt, and vanilla. Beat very fast until light and resembles thick cream. Pour into a mold and chill. When ready to serve, cut in squares, roll in fine crumbs. Arrange in dessert glasses, and top with butter sauce.

Butter Sauce:
2 egg yolks
⅛ c. sugar
⅛ c. butter, melted
1 T. grated lemon rind
2 T. lemon juice
⅛ c. cream, whipped

Beat egg yolks until thick. Add sugar gradually and continue beating. Add butter, lemon rind, juice and blend well. Fold in cream and chill. Top snow squares and garnish with whipped cream.

This recipe submitted by the following teachers:

Lou Ann Restad, Palmer H. S.
Palmer, Alaska

Mildred Timm Paxson, Brawley Union H. S.
Brawley, California

SNOW BALLS
Number of Servings — Five Dozen

4 eggs, separated
2 c. sugar
1 No. 2 can crushed pineapple
1 stick margarine
1 envelope gelatin
¼ c. water
1 c. pecans
1 t. vanilla
2 pkgs. Mama's Cookies or vanilla wafers
1 can angle flake coconut
3½ pts. whipping cream

Beat egg yolks, add sugar and beat until foamy (about 30 seconds). Add pineapple and cook over moderate heat, stirring occasionally until thick. Add margarine and stir for 5 minutes. Add to this mixture the gelatin that has been dissolved in ¼ cup water. Fold into this mixture the 4 egg whites, beaten stiffly. Add nuts and flavoring. Chill over night. Spread this gelatin mixture between 2 cookies (more cookies can be used if desired and also a larger cookie. Cover these cookies with whipping cream and sprinkle with coconut).

Mrs. Donna Brown, Wolfe City H. S.
Wolfe City, Texas

TOASTED MARSHMALLOWS
Number of Servings — 8

1 T. gelatin
¼ c. cold water
¾ c. boiling water
1 c. sugar
1½ t. vanilla
3 egg whites
1 c. coconut bar cookie crumbs
½ pt. cream, whipped

Soften gelatin in cold water. Dissolve in boiling water, add sugar. Set bowl containing this mixture in ice water. Add vanilla and egg whites and beat with electric mixer until mixture thickens. Turn into shallow pan and refrigerate about 6 hours. Cut into squares. Roll in coconut bar cookie crumbs. Place in dessert bowls. Top with whipped cream.

Mrs. Francys Putnam, Chapel Hill Jr. H. S.
Chapel Hill, North Carolina

TROPICANA
Number of Servings — 8

1½ c. vanilla wafer crumbs
¼ c. margarine
3 egg yolks
1 can sweetened condensed milk
1 small can crushed pineapple
3 egg whites, beaten stiff

Combine crumbs and margarine and line a square 9" pan. Mix egg yolks, add condensed milk and crushed pineapple. Fold in stiffly beaten egg whites. Pour half of mixture over crumbs in pan and top with crumbs, then pour remaining mixture into pan and top with crumbs. Chill several hours and serve. May be topped with whipped cream.

Melba Lee Moore, Harrisburg H. S.
Harrisburg, Arkansas

PEPPERMINT DESSERT
Number of Servings — 12

1 box chocolate wafer cookies
1 lb. marshmallows
1 cup milk
½ c. crushed peppermint candy (add pink coloring for deeper color)
1 pt. whipping cream (whipped)

Crush cookies. Put ½ in bottom of cake pan about 8x12, save ½ for top. Melt marshmallows in milk in double boiler, cool. Add crushed candy and fold in whipped cream. Pour over cookie crumbs. Sprinkle rest of cookie crumbs over top. Refrigerate 8-24 hours.

Marian McKisson, Chaffey H. S.
Ontario, California

TWENTY-FOUR HOUR ICE BOX DESSERT
Number of Servings — 10

2 c. cherries (halved and seeded)
2 c. diced pineapple
2 c. orange sections (cut up)
2 c. marshmallows (quartered)
¼ lb. almonds (blanched and chopped)
2 eggs
¼ c. sugar
¼ c. light cream
Juice of 1 lemon
1 c. heavy cream, whipped

Combine cherries, pineapple, orange, marshmallows, and almonds. Beat eggs until light, gradually add sugar, light cream, and lemon juice. Mix thoroughly, cook in double boiler until smooth and thick, stirring constantly. Remove from heat, cool, fold in the whipped cream. Pour over fruit and mix lightly. Chill 24 hours in refrigerator. Can be served as a dessert topped with a maraschino cherry or as a salad on crisp lettuce.

Mrs. Rosemary Kutchie
Champion Humboldt Community
Champion, Michigan

VANILLA WAFER DESSERT
Number of Servings — 12

1 c. unsweetened orange juice
½ c. unsweetened pineapple juice
(If preferred use 1 c. pineapple juice and ½ c. orange juice)
¼ t. salt
¼ pkg. orange Jello (3 oz. size) (may be omitted)
24 marshmallows, quartered
1 c. cream, whipped
1 lb. vanilla wafers, crushed

Combine fruit juices, salt and bring to a boil. Add quartered marshmallows and Jello. Stir until melted. Chill until slightly thickened. Fold in whipped cream. Spread ⅔ of crushed wafers in bottom of 8x8 cake pan. Gently smooth gelatin cream mixture over wafers. Sprinkle remaining wafers on top. Chill until firm. Cut into squares.

This recipe submitted by the following teachers:

Lora A. Hagglund, Hutchinson H. S.
Hutchinson, Minnesota

Luana Hutchings, Moapa Valley H. S.
Overton, Nevada

Fruit Desserts

RECIPES CONTAINING FRUITS CAN BE FOUND
IN ALL SECTIONS OF THE BOOK

AMBROSIA

Number of Servings — 20-25

1 No. 2 can crushed pineapple
1 doz. oranges
1 medium size fresh coconut (grated)
    or 1 c. angel flake coconut

Obtain fruit pulp and juice from oranges, being careful to remove all membrane and seeds. Remove hull and brown covering of coconut and grate coconut using a fine grater. The coconut milk may be used if desired. Combine grated coconut, coconut milk, orange pulp and juice and crushed pineapple. Sugar may be added if the mixture is not of desired sweetness. Chill and heap into sherbet dishes. Garnish with red or green cherries or mint leaves.

This recipe submitted by the following teachers:
Hazel P. Lowe, Chatham H. S.
Chatham, Virginia
Mrs. Billie C. Carver, Bethel Hill School
Woodsdale, North Carolina

AMBROSIA FRUIT DESSERT

Number of Servings — 8-10

11 oz. can mandarin oranges
13 oz. can pineapple chunks
1 c. Bakers angel flake coconut
½ c. whipping cream, whipped
1 c. cut-up marshmallows

Mix all ingredients. Chill several hours or over night.

Mrs. Donald E. Quattlebaum, Wren H. S.
Pendleton, South Carolina

AMBROSIA DESSERT SALAD

Number of Servings — 6

1 No. 2 can (2½ c.)
Pineapple tidbits
⅜ c. instant rice
1 c. drained Mandarin orange segments
1½ c. tiny marshmallows
1 c. dairy sour cream
2 T. sugar

Drain pineapple and measure ⅔ cup juice. In small saucepan, bring pineapple juice to boiling. Stir in rice. Cover and let stand 5 minutes for rice to steam. Remove cover. Fluff rice with fork. Cool. Combine fruit, marshmallows, rice, sour cream, and sugar. Chill several hours.

Mrs. Cloe Entricken, Norman H. S.
Norman, Arkansas

APPLE-CAKE TREAT

Number of Servings — 6

Bottom Layer:
4-6 apples, pared and sliced
    or 1 can apples
½ c. brown sugar, firmly packed
½ t. cinnamon
½ t. nutmeg
Water to cover

Combine and simmer above ingredients until tender and place in greased (buttered) baking dish.
Topping:
½ c. melted butter or margarine
1 c. sugar (granulated)
1 c. flour
1 c. milk
2 t. baking powder

Mix together until smooth. Pour over apples. Bake at 300°F. for 1 hour.

Angie T. Miller, James Monroe H. S.
Fredericksburg, Virginia

APPLE CRUMBLE

Number of Servings — 4-6

3-4 apples
½ c. brown sugar
6 T. butter
¼ c. graham cracker crumbs or macaroon crumbs
Whipped cream (optional)

Pare and slice apples and place in buttered baking dish. Mix brown sugar, melted butter, and crumbs, and pour over apples. Bake 20 to 30 minutes, or until apples are cooked at 400°F. Serve in glass dishes with whipped cream.

Mrs. Bettye L. Davis, Shady Grove H. S.
Maringouin, Louisiana

APPLE DATE DESSERT

Number of Servings — 6

½ c. margarine
¾ c. sugar
1 egg
1½ c. sifted flour
1 t. baking powder
½ t. soda
2 c. chopped tart apples
1 (8 oz.) pkg. dates, cut up
¼ c. brown sugar (firm pack)
1 t. cinnamon
½ c. chopped nuts

Cream margarine and sugar. Add egg and beat well. Stir in flour, baking powder and soda. To this mixture add apples and dates and mix well. Spread in a well-greased 8x8 pan. Sprinkle the top with the mixture of brown sugar, cinnamon and nuts. Bake at 350°F. for 30 to 35 minutes. Serve warm with vanilla ice cream or whipped cream.

Mrs. Margaret Cepelka, Clarke County H. S.
Berryville, Virginia

APRICOT DESSERT

Number of Servings — 9

1 c. sifted flour
½ t. soda
½ t. salt
⅜ c. margarine
½ c. brown sugar
1 c. quick oats
1 lge. can apricots, drained
1 T. margarine
Cinnamon

(Continued on Next Page)

Sift together the pre-sifted flour, soda and salt. Blend or cut in the ⅓ cup margarine with a pastry blender. Add brown sugar and oats and blend. Melt the 1 tablespoon margarine in an 8" square pan (coat the pan well). Press half of the above mixture into the pan. Lay drained apricot halves on and top with the other half of the mixture. Dot with butter, sprinkle with cinnamon and dribble apricot juice on top. Bake at 350°F. for 30 minutes.

Mrs. Minnie Burke, Los Gatos H. S.
Los Gatos, California

BANANAS HAWAII

Bananas (1 per serving)
Sugar
Whipping cream (½ pt. for 4-6 bananas)
Cherries

Wrap peeled bananas in wax paper and freeze. Just before serving, slice frozen bananas into dessert dishes. Sprinkle with sugar. Pour on enough chilled cream to coat the fruit. (The cream will freeze to the banana slices). Top with a cherry. This may also be served over ice cream or cake.

Mrs. Suanne Lett Black, Sidney Lanier H. S.
Montgomery, Alabama

BLUEBERRY DREAM DESSERT
Number of Servings — 8-10

2 c. quick rolled oats, uncooked
1 c. flour
1 c. firmly packed brown sugar
¾ c. butter, melted
2 c. blueberries
1 T. flour
½ c. sugar
2 T. lemon juice
⅛ t. salt
¾ c. water, or juice from canned blueberries

Mix rolled oats, flour and brown sugar. Add melted butter and mix well (using a fork). Line bottom of 8" square pan with oatmeal mixture. Reserve about ¾ cup for topping. Combine remaining ingredients in a saucepan and simmer about 5 minutes. Remove from heat and pour into oatmeal crust. Sprinkle with remaining crumbs and bake at 350°F. for 35 minutes. Serve topped with whipped cream or ice cream.

Esther Cain, Brodhead H. S.
Brodhead, Wisconsin

BAKED CANTALOUPE
Number of Servings — 4

2 cantaloupes
3 c. sliced peaches
½ c. sugar
Few grains mace
Mint sprigs

Halve cantaloupes. Remove seeds. Combine peaches, sugar, and mace. Fill cantaloupes with peaches, arranging slices in radiating pattern on top. Bake at 425°F. 15 minutes. Garnish with mint. Serve at once.

Jean Passino, Keewatin-Nashwauk Jr. H. S.
Keewatin, Minnesota

CHERRY BLOSSOM DESSERT
Number of Servings — 8

Filling:
¼ c. flour
1 c. sugar
¾ c. cherry juice
¼ t. red food coloring

Combine sugar and flour in saucepan. Drain juice from can of cherries and blend in. Cook over direct heat until mixture thickens. Remove and add coloring and cherries. Set aside to cool.

Crust:
1½ c. flour
1 t. salt
½ t. soda
1 c. brown sugar
1 c. quick cooking oatmeal
½ c. shortening

Sift flour, salt and soda together. Blend in sugar and oatmeal. Cut shortening into dry ingredients until particles are the size of small peas. Press half of this mixture into bottom of ungreased pan 12x8x2. Cover with cooled cherry filling. Cover with remaining oatmeal mixture and press down gently with a spoon. Bake for 25 minutes at 350°F. Cut into squares and serve warm or cold. May be topped with whipped cream if desired.

Mrs. Sudie Lee Nelson, Stark H. S.
Orange, Texas

CHERRY CRUNCH
Number of Servings — 6-8

1 c. brown sugar
1 c. uncooked quick cooking oatmeal
½ c. flour
½ c. butter or margarine
1 No. 2 can pitted cherries

Mix brown sugar, oatmeal, and flour together. Cut in butter until mixture is crumbly. Press half of mixture into a 1½ quart greased baking dish. Place cherries and ¼ cup liquid on top of mixture. Crumble remaining mixture over cherries. Bake at 375°F. for 30 minutes or at 350°F. 40-45 minutes. Cut into squares and serve with whipped cream of vanilla ice cream.

This recipe submitted by the following teachers:
Mrs. Paulita P. Wade, King William H. S.
King William, Virginia
Betty Otteson, Pearl City H. S.
Pearl City, Illinois

CHERRY SURPRISE
Number of Servings — 6

1 c. flour
¼ t. salt
2 t. baking powder
½ c. sugar
¼ c. shortening
½ c. milk
1 (1 lb.) can pitted sour cherries
Red food coloring
½ c. sugar

(Continued on Next Page)

Place flour, salt, baking powder, ½ cup sugar, shortening, and milk in mixing bowl. Mix until batter is smooth. Spread evenly in an 8″ baking pan. Combine cherries, food coloring (if desired), ½ cup sugar. Pour over batter. Bake at 375°F. 40 minutes or until top is brown. Serve plain or top with ice cream.

Bernice Palmer, Lynville H. S.
Preston, Mississippi

CHERRIES JUBILEE

Number of Servings — 10

1 No. 2 can Bing cherries (pitted)
1 c. cherry juice
2 t. cornstarch
⅓ c. cognac or Kirsch

Drain Bing cherries and cook 1 cup juice down to ¾ cup. Mix cornstarch to paste with 2 tablespoons of remaining juice. Add to hot juice and cook until thick and clear, stirring constantly. Cover and hold until needed. Just before serving, heat juice to boiling. Add well drained cherries. Heat through and pour into chafing dish over flame, place before hostess along with ½ cup warm cognac and individual servings of ice cream. Pour warm cognac over cherries, ignite in darkened room and spoon flaming cherries over ice cream.

Phyllis J. Hill, Paradise Valley H. S.
Phoenix, Arizona

CRANBERRY CRUNCH

Number of Servings — 6-8

1 c. uncooked rolled oats (quick cooking)
½ c. flour
1 c. brown sugar
½ c. butter or oleo
1 lb. can jellied or whole cranberry sauce
  (Fresh cranberry jelly or sauce may be used)

Mix oats, flour, and brown sugar. Cut in butter until crumbly. Place half of this mixture in an 8x8 greased baking dish. Cover with cranberry sauce. Top with balance of crumb mixture. Bake 45 minutes at 350°F. or 35 minutes at 375°F. Serve hot in squares topped with scoops of vanilla ice cream.

This recipe submitted by the following teachers:
Mrs. James Whitmore, Cotopaxi H. S.
Cotopaxi, Colorado
Marion McMurrey, Shepherd H. S.
Shepherd, Texas

CRANBERRY ALMOND CRUNCH

Number of Servings — 6

1 c. brown sugar
½ c. butter
½ t. almond extract
1½ c. oatmeal (or bread crumbs)
½ c. flour
½ c. chopped almonds
1 (1 lb.) can whole cranberry sauce or 2 c. cooked
  cranberries with sugar

Cream sugar and butter. Add almond extract. Mix together oatmeal and flour. Add oatmeal and flour

mixture to creamed sugar and butter. Blend ingredients until oatmeal is thoroughly coated. Add chopped almonds. Spread ½ of mixture on bottom of 9x12 glass baking dish. Pour and spread cranberry sauce. On top of the sauce, add remaining oatmeal mix. Bake at 350°F. 15-20 minutes. Serve hot or cold, with or without ice cream. Note: Apples, peaches and other fruits may be substituted. Bread crumbs may be substituted for oatmeal. Flavorings are optional.

Mrs. Mary Sue E. Spencer, Princess Anne H. S.
Virginia Beach, Virginia

FRUIT COMPOTE (Hot)

Number of Servings — 10-12

1 No. 2 or 2½ can purple plums
1 No. 2½ can unpeeled whole apricots
1 No. 2 can pineapple spears
2 T. lemon juice
¾ t. nutmeg
¼ c. honey
1 T. salad oil

Drain fruit, and arrange in large baking dish. Sprinkle with lemon juice, nutmeg, honey, and salad oil. Heat in very slow oven until fruit is warm, occasionally spooning over fruit syrup which is formed. Serve hot over ice cream balls or sponge cake. May serve in compote and allow guests to top their own desserts.

Margaret W. Cyrus, Herndon H. S.
Herndon, Virginia

FRUIT CUP

Number of Servings — 10-12

1 No. 2½ can fruit cocktail
1 orange
2 bananas
1 apple
½ lb. grapes
Marshmallows and red cherries for garnish

Chill fruits. Peel orange and banana and cut up into fruit cocktail. Pare and core apple, cut bite size. Add grapes. Combine. Garnish and return to refrigerator to keep chilled until ready to serve.

Mrs. Marion Butschek, Nordheim Independent
Nordheim, Texas

RASPBERRY-STRAWBERRY PARFAIT

Number of Servings — 4-6

1 pkg. (10 oz.) frozen raspberries or strawberries
1 pkg. vanilla pudding
⅛ t. salt
¼ c. water
1 T. butter
1 c. whipping cream

Strain berries, save juice and pulp. Combine pudding, salt, water, fruit pulp and juice in saucepan. Blend well. Cook slowly until full boil is reached. Remove from heat, add butter. Chill. Stir until creamy. Alternate layers of pudding and whipped cream in parfait glasses. Ice cream may be included in the layers.

Thelma I. Birt, Troy H. S.
Troy, Ohio

FRUIT DESSERT
Number of Servings — 8-10

1 c. pineapple juice
3 T. lemon juice
2 T. flour
1 egg
6 T. sugar
12 marshmallows
½ c. whipping cream
1 c. pineapple
3 bananas

Beat egg, sugar, and flour together. Add pineapple juice, cook in double boiler until thick. Remove from heat, cut marshmallows (different colors add variety) in hot mixture. Cool. Cut bananas and pineapple in small pieces and mix. Stir in cooled fruit dressing. Fold in whipped cream. This dessert is very good, can be made ahead of time except for whipped cream. To lower calories, leave off whipped cream.

Pruda Caudill Prather, Carter H. S.
Carter, Kentucky

FIVE CUP FRUIT DESSERT
Number of Servings — 8

1 c. well drained canned mandarin oranges
1 c. well drained canned pineapple tidbits
    or diced pineapple
(1 No. 2 can fruit cocktail may be substituted for
    the oranges and pineapple)
1 c. flaked coconut
1 c. miniature marshmallows
1 c. sour cream
1 c. green grapes (optional)
8-10 maraschino cherries (optional)
½ c. chopped nuts (optional)

Combine ingredients tossing lightly until well mixed. Cover and chill in refrigerator. May be served as a salad.

This recipe submitted by the following teachers:
Mrs. Ernest Osborn, Friona H. S.
Friona, Texas
Irene Hochstein, Rapidan H. S.
Rapidan, Minnesota
Mary Ann DeVore, Antwerp Local School
Antwerp, Ohio
Margaret G. Holloway, Havre de Grace H. S.
Havre de Grace, Maryland
Mrs. Prudence Sheldon, Airport Community H. S.
Carleton, Michigan
Mrs. Susan Roach, Rome Canaan H. S.
Stewart, Ohio

MEL'S FRUIT DELIGHT
Number of Servings — 6-8

2 apples
4 bananas
1 can coconut
Cherries
2 T. condensed milk (optional)
3 T. mayonnaise
Cherry juice (to thin mayonnaise)

Wash and core apples. Cut in ¼" or ½" cubes. Cut bananas, mix. Add half a can of coconut and a few cherries. Combine mayonnaise with condensed milk (optional), thin with cherry juice. Pour over mixture and toss with 2 forks. Arrange remainder of coconut around edges and dot with cherries (may be used as a salad).

Mrs. Imelda Watson, Leesville H. S.
Leesville, Louisiana

GRAPE JUICE TAPIOCA
Number of Servings — 8

1 pt. grape juice
½ c. tapioca
1 c. sugar
Juice and rind of 1 lge. orange
½ c. chopped nuts
1 small can crushed pineapple
Crushed vanilla wafers
Whipped cream

Cook grape juice and tapioca in double boiler until thick. Remove from heat. Add rest of ingredients and mix well. Arrange in layers alternately with crushed vanilla wafers, ending with grape on top. Chill 1 hour. Top with whipped cream.

Mrs. Gloria Ward, Normangee H. S.
Normangee, Texas

ALMONDROON STUFFED PEACHES
Number of Servings — 6

2¾ oz. finely chopped almonds
½ c. macaroon crumbs
4 T. granulated sugar
1 T. chopped candied pineapple
¼ c. sherry wine or Marsala wine
3 T. fine sugar
6 lge. fresh peaches

Blanch almonds, chop finely. Add macaroon crumbs and mix with electric mixer. Add pulp of peach and 4 tablespoons of granulated sugar and candied pineapple, mix well. Remove pit and part of the peach around stone of peaches and fill halves with mixture but do not pack. Put 2 halves of peaches together and fasten with wooden picks. Place peaches in an 8" pyrex baking dish and pour the wine over the peaches and sprinkle peaches with the fine granulated sugar. Bake at 325°F. 35 minutes. (Optional, but good: Stick whole clove on 1 side of peach half). Increase heat to 350°F. if aluminum pan is used.

Sarah M. Culotta, Northside H. S.
Lafayette, Louisiana

PEACH BETTY
Number of Servings — 8

4 c. peaches (5 lge.)
2 c. soft bread crumbs
¼ c. light brown sugar
½ t. lemon juice
2 T. butter

Put half of peaches in baking dish. Add half of bread crumbs. Then rest of peaches and bread crumbs. Add brown sugar, lemon juice and dot with butter. Cover and bake 30 minutes at 375°F. Uncover the last 10 minutes to brown.

Mildred Few, Blue Ridge H. S.
Greer, South Carolina

OATMEAL PEACH CRUMBLE

Number of Servings — 4-5

2 c. canned peaches
2 T. lemon juice
¼ t. cinnamon
1 T. butter or margarine
¼ c. melted shortening
⅓ c. brown sugar
⅓ c. all-purpose flour, sifted before measuring
⅛ t. salt
¼ t. soda
⅔ c. quick cooking oatmeal
½ t. vanilla

Arrange peaches in greased shallow baking dish, sprinkle with lemon juice and cinnamon and dot with butter or margarine. Combine melted shortening and brown sugar. Sift flour, salt and soda together and mix with the oatmeal. Blend with the sugar mixture, crumbling well. Add vanilla. Spread over peaches and bake in a preheated oven at 350°F. for 45 minutes. Serve with warm custard sauce or top milk.

Mrs. Nan L. Dyer, Mission H. S.
Mission, Texas

PEACHES PAREE

Number of Servings — 8

1½ t. cornstarch
1 c. syrup
1 No. 2½ can peaches
2 t. lemon juice
¼ t. cinnamon
½ t. almond extract

Blend cornstarch, syrup from peaches. Add lemon juice, cinnamon and almond extract. Stir and cook until thickened. Add drained peach slices. Heat 3 minutes. Serve over pound cake.

Mrs. Margaret Fuller, Williamstown H. S.
Williamstown, Kentucky

SUNDAY PEACHES

Number of Servings — 4

1 can peach halves (drained)
1 c. fresh lemon juice
2 c. crushed vanilla wafers

Roll drained peach halves in lemon juice, then roll in vanilla wafers. Chill in refrigerator, serve in dessert dishes.

Mrs. Donna Smith, Fluvanna H. S.
Fluvanna, Texas

OVEN BAKED PRUNES

Number of Servings — 8-10

2 c. dried prunes
1½ c. water
½ c. sugar
¼ t. dry mustard
⅛ t. cinnamon
⅛ t. cloves
1 T. vinegar

Place prunes in casserole or covered pan. Add sugar, spices, and vinegar to water and blend. Pour over prunes. Cover. Bake 1¼ hours at 350°F.

Mrs. Janice M. Kennedy,
Troy Community Joint H. S.
Troy, Pennsylvania

RHUBARB SURPRISE

Number of Servings — 8-10

1½ c. diced rhubarb
8 lge. marshmallows, cut in 4ths
⅓ c. brown sugar
¼ c. butter or margarine
½ c. white sugar
1 egg, well beaten
¾ c. sifted all-purpose flour
⅛ t. salt
1½ t. baking powder
¼ c. finely chopped nuts

Butter or grease a cake pan 12x9x2 (Pyrex preferred). Place diced rhubarb evenly over bottom. Cut marshmallows in small pieces (use knife dipped in water for easy cutting). Put marshmallows over rhubarb in bottom of pan. Sprinkle brown sugar evenly over top. Make a batter by creaming butter and sugar. Add beaten egg. Sift dry ingredients together and add alternately with milk to cream mixture. Carefully pour batter over rhubarb and marshmallows in baking dish. Bake at 350°F. for 1 hour. To serve, cut in squares while warm and serve with fresh cream, or allow to cool and spoon into sherbet glasses. Top with whipped cream. To vary the recipe, substitute 4 cups of apples for rhubarb.

Mrs. Charlotte Clarke, Central H. S.
Aberdeen, South Dakota

RHUBARB CRISP

Number of Servings — 6

2 c. diced rhubarb
1 c. all purpose flour
1 c. granulated sugar (or brown)
1 t. ground cinnamon (optional)
⅓ c. butter or oleo (or ¼ c. vegetable oil and ¼ t. salt) (½ c. oleo may be used)

Place diced rhubarb in a greased shallow pan. Mix flour, sugar and cinnamon. Cut fat into mixture. Sprinkle mixture on rhubarb. Bake in moderate oven 350°F. for 25 minutes. Serve warm.

This recipe submitted by the following teachers:

Mrs. Dorothy J. Clark, Tawas Area H. S.
Tawas City, Michigan

Leah Lackman, Beulah H. S.
Beulah, North Dakota

RHUBARB CREAM DESSERT

Number of Servings — 6

1½ c. sugar
3 T. flour
½ t. nutmeg
1 T. butter
2 beaten eggs
3-4 c. rhubarb

Blend sugar, flour, nutmeg and butter. Add eggs and mix with rhubarb. Bake in greased pan at 450°F. 10 minutes, then at 350°F. 30 minutes. Serve hot or cold with whipped cream.

Marlene Lien, Trempealeau H. S.
Trempealeau, Wisconsin

Foreign Desserts

VIENNESE COCONUT MACAROONS (Austria)

Number of Servings — 36 Cookies

¼ c. butter
½ c. sugar
2 eggs
2 T. heavy cream
¼ t. vanilla
½ c. flour
4 T. cornstarch
½ t. baking powder
1 c. coconut
6 crushed vanilla wafers

Cream butter and sugar. Add the well-beaten eggs, cream and vanilla. Sift the dry ingredients, and add to the first mixture. Add the coconut and wafers. Drop by teaspoonfuls, 1" apart, on a greased cookie sheet and bake in a moderate oven until brown on top (8-10 minutes).

Kathryn Woods, Woodrow Wilson H. S.
Beckley, West Virginia

VIENNESE PEACH TART (Austria)

Number of Servings — 6-8

½ c. butter or margarine
½ c. confectioners' sugar
1 c. sifted enriched flour

Cream butter until soft. Add sugar gradually, continuing to cream. Blend in flour to make a soft dough. Pat evenly into 12" pizza pan, covering bottom and sides. Bake at 350°F. for 20 minutes.

Filling:
1 T. cornstarch
3 T. sugar
½ c. orange juice
½ s. red current jelly (melted)
8 large fresh peaches (about)

Combine cornstarch and sugar. Add orange juice. Cook, stirring until thick and clear. Stir in melted current jelly. Cool slightly. Peel and slice peaches. Arrange in single layer in baked shell. Spoon glaze evenly over peaches. Chill. Garnish with whipped cream.

This recipe submitted by the following teachers:
Mrs. Mildred Wilson, Kennard Dale H. S.
Fawn Grove, Pennsylvania
Mrs. Mary K. Albrittain, Glasva H. S.
Faulkner, Maryland

BOHEMIAN CAKE

Number of Servings — 16-20

¾ c. butter.
1½ c. sugar
4 egg yolks, beaten thoroughly
2 c. sifted cake flour
½ t. soda
½ c. sweet milk
1 t. vanilla extract
¼ t. lemon extract
4 egg whites, beaten stiff
½ t. cream of tartar

Cream butter and sugar until light and fluffy. Add egg yolk. Add sifted dry ingredients alternately with milk. Add extracts. Fold in egg whites beaten with cream of tartar. Grease and dust with flour a 10" tube pan. Line bottom with pecan halves. Pour in batter. Bake 45 minutes in a 350°F. oven. When done, turn out so pecans will be on top. Sprinkle with powdered sugar and no other frosting is needed.

Mrs. Marian G. Craddock, Colorado H. S.
Colorado City, Texas

BOLO DE LARANJA (Brazil Orange Cake)

Number of Servings — 6

5 egg yolks
8 T. orange juice
2 c. flour
2 c. sugar
1 t. baking powder
½ t. vanilla
5 beaten egg whites

Combine and mix egg yolks and orange juice. Mix flour, sugar, and baking powder together and add slowly to the egg yolk mixture. Beat or mix for about 2 minutes. Add vanilla and fold in egg whites. Pour in well greased pan. Bake in moderate oven for 25 minutes. May be served with topping of any choice or just plain orange juice.

Louise Figueiredo, Leonville H. S.
Leonville, Louisiana

ALFAJORES (Sometimes Called National Sweet of Chile)

Number of Servings — 3 Dozen

2 c. cornstarch
½ c. flour
1 t. baking powder
½ t. salt
¾ c. margarine
1 c. sugar
1 egg
2 egg yolks
1 t. vanilla
2 t. grated lemon rind
Coconut

Sift together cornstarch, flour, baking powder, and salt, set aside. Cream margarine. Add sugar and beat until light. Beat in whole egg, egg yolks, vanilla, and lemon rind. Add flour mixture and mix well. Chill 1½ hours. Remove a small amount at a time to a floured board, keeping the remainder chilled. Roll out dough to ¼" thickness with floured rolling pin. Handle the dough lightly and add extra flour to the board as needed. Cut into 1½" rounds with a floured cutter. Place on greased baking sheets. Bake 325°F. about 15 minutes, or until lightly browned around the edges. Remove to cooling racks. Dulce de Leche (North American style). Shake 1 can of Eagle Brand milk. Place can in saucepan and cover completely with water. Boil rapidly for 1½ hours, adding more water as needed to keep can covered. After removing from heat, cool can under water. Fill each pair of cookies with Dulce de Leche. Spread the edges with Dulce de Leche. Roll the edges in coconut.

Mrs. Melba M. Smith, Grandview H. S.
Grandview, Texas

CHEWS (China)

Number of Servings — 16 Bars

¾ c. butter
1½ c. flour
3 T. brown sugar

Cream together the ingredients to make the crust. Pat the mixture into a greased 10x10 pan. Bake at 300°F. for 10 minutes.

Topping:

2 eggs
1 t. baking powder
2 T. flour
1 c. dates, cut up
1 c. nuts, chopped
1 c. coconut

Beat the eggs slightly. Add the dry ingredients which have been sifted together. Add dates, nuts, and coconut. Sprinkle over the baked mixture. Bake at 275°F. for 25 minutes. While hot, frost with frosting made of 1 cup powdered sugar, the juice of 1 lemon and a bit of cream or soft butter if more liquid is needed. When cool, cut in squares.

Mrs. Rita Simones, Lakeville H. S.
Lakeville, Minnesota

NUT CAKE (China)

Number of Servings — 30

1 lb. candied cherries (red)
1 lb. dates (seeded)
1 lb. candied pineapple
2 c. flour (sifted once)
2 t. baking powder
4 eggs, well beaten
1 c. sugar
2 lbs. pecans (not chopped)

Dice pineapple into ¼" chunks, cut cherries and dates in half. Mix fruits with sifted flour and baking powder. Pour beaten eggs and sugar over fruit mixture (use hands to mix well). Add nuts and mix thoroughly. Place in large, well greased tube pan. Pack firmly with hands (this will be thick with little dough). Bake 1 hour and 15 minutes at 250°F. Cool. Remove from pan and slice thin. This cake keeps well and is better served cold. It also freezes well.

Mrs. Margaret Ann Durham, Hereford H. S.
Hereford, Texas

ORIENTAL CHEWS (China)

1 c. sugar
¾ t. baking powder
2 eggs
1 c. pecans
¾ c. flour
¼ t. salt
1 c. dates
3 T. ginger (candied) or ½ t. dry powdered ginger

Mix and sift dry ingredients. Add chopped dates, nuts, and ginger. Beat egg whites. Add beaten yolks. Stir into first mixture. Bake in greased pan in 325°F. oven for 20 minutes.

Darla Wille, Wabasso H. S.
Wabasso, Minnesota

BAR COOKIES (Czechoslovakia)

Number of Servings — 2 Dozen Squares

1 c. white sugar
2 sticks margarine
2 egg yolks
2 c. flour
1 c. pecans
½ c. strawberry or raspberry jam

Cream margarine and sugar. Add egg yolks, flour, and pecans. Mix thoroughly. Divide stiff batter in half and spread half of mixture in a brownie pan. Mash ½ cup strawberry jam fine and spread on top of first layer. Press remaining batter on top of jam layer. Bake 1 hour in a 375°F. oven. Cut in squares.

This recipe submitted by the following teachers:
Mrs. Francis Reeves, Wilmer-Hutchins H. S.
Hutchins, Texas

Mrs. Lucy B. Taylor, Warren H. S.
Warren, Arkansas

APPELSINFROMAGE—ORANGE SNOW (Denmark)

Number of Servings — 16-18

10 egg yolks, separated
1½ c. white sugar
1 envelope gelatin
¼ c. cold water
Juice of 6 oranges (strained)

Beat egg yolks and sugar until lemon-colored. Soak gelatin in cold water, melt over hot water. Combine with eggs and sugar and add the orange juice. Cool until it begins to thicken (like a lemon filling). When thick, beat the egg whites until stiff, fold into the above mixture. Refrigerate. Serve with whipped cream. A spritz cookie is perfect with this dessert after the Christmas dinner. Note: One lemon may be substituted for one orange for juice. This dessert is best when served the day after it is prepared as the egg whites often lose their fluffy texture and liquefy. Makes about a gallon.

Mrs. Edith Jorgensen, Emery Independent H. S.
Emery, South Dakota

APPLE PUDDING (Denmark)

Number of Servings — 8

1½ c. fine dry bread crumbs
⅛ c. butter
2 c. applesauce (1-lb. can)
¼ t. salt
1 T. lemon juice
½ t. cinnamon

Sauté crumbs in butter until evenly browned. Line a greased square pan 8x8x2 with half of crumbs. Mix applesauce, salt, lemon juice and cinnamon. Pour half over crumbs, cover with rest of crumbs, then remaining applesauce. Top with sweetened whipped cream. Chill several hours. Serve in squares decorated with bits of red jelly, if desired.

Mrs. Nelda Joy Lowry, Caddo Mills H. S.
Caddo Mills, Texas

COCONUT CAKE (Denmark)

Number of Servings — 8

1 c. butter
1½ c. sugar
4 eggs, separated
2 c. flour
3 t. baking powder
Pinch of salt
1 c. light cream
1 t. vanilla

Cream sugar and butter and add 1 unbeaten egg yolk at a time. Mix well. Sift flour, baking powder, and salt together, and add alternately with the cream and vanilla. Fold in stiffly beaten egg whites. Bake in 2 layers at 350°F. for 25 to 30 minutes. Frost with Danish coconut frosting or chocolate fudge.

Mrs. Eleanor Weathermon, Wink H. S.
Wink, Texas

FRUIT SOUP (Denmark)

Number of Servings — 8-10

1 c. pearl barley
3 c. water
2½ c. cooked raisins
½ c. cooked prunes
Juice of 1 orange
1 stick cinnamon

Cook pearl barley in water. Mix in boiled fruit and other ingredients. Simmer over low heat 3 to 4 minutes. Serve hot or cold.

Verna J. Barnes, Argyle H. S.
Argyle, Wisconsin

DANISH PUDDING (Denmark)

Number of Servings — 12

1 c. butter
1¾ c. sugar
3 whole eggs
1 T. orange juice
1 T. orange rind (grated)
1½ t. soda
1 t. salt
3 c. sifted flour
1 c. buttermilk
1 lb. pkg. dates
1 c. chopped nuts
1 c. crystallized cherries

Cream butter, sugar, and dates. Add eggs and beat well. Add orange juice and rind. Sift flour, salt, and soda 3 times. Add alternately with buttermilk. Add nuts and cherries. Grease and flour pan. Bake in tube pan at 350°F. for 1 hour.

Glaze:
1 c. sugar
1 c. orange juice
Rind of 1 orange, grated

Mix sugar, orange juice, grated orange rind and let stand while caking is baking. When cake is done, remove from oven and pour sauce over it while hot.

Mrs. Jane Guinn, Townsend H. S.
Townsend, Tennessee

DANISH KRINGLE (Denmark)

Number of Servings — 2 Dozen

Filling:
¼ c. butter
½ c. packed brown sugar
1 c. chopped pecans
Prepare filling by creaming butter and sugar until fluffy. Add nuts and set aside.
Kringle:
2 c. sifted flour
1½ T. sugar
½ t. salt
½ c. soft butter
½ c. milk, scalded
1 egg, separated
¼ c. warm water (110-115°F.)
1 pkg. active dry yeast
Icing:
1 c. sifted confectioners' sugar
½ T. milk
¼ t. vanilla
Prepare kringle by measuring flour, sugar, salt, and butter into bowl, blend well. Cool milk slightly, then stir in egg yolk. Pour into bowl with first ingredients. Add yeast to warm water and let stand a few minutes. Add to other ingredients and mix thoroughly. Scrape dough from sides of bowl (it will be very soft). Cover tightly and chill 2 to 48 hours. Then divide dough into 2 parts. Take 1 part and return other part to refrigerator. Beat egg white. Grease 2 baking sheets. Cover board with cloth and flour well. Roll dough to a 6x18 rectangle. Spread 3″ center strip with half of beaten egg white, then filling. Pinch dough to close fold. Put on baking sheet in ovals, closing ends. Shape second kringle. Cover and let rise 45 minutes. Bake at 400°F. 20 to 30 minutes. Spread with sugar icing while hot.

Nancy Wooten, Lakeview H. S.
Rossville, Georgia

DANISH PASTRY APPLE BARS (Denmark)

2½ c. flour
1 t. salt
1 c. lard or shortening
1 egg yolk
Enough milk to make ⅔ c. with egg yolk
2 handfuls corn flakes
8-10 apples
1 c. sugar
1 t. cinnamon
1 egg white
1 T. water
1 c. powdered sugar
Vanilla

Mix ingredients including milk and egg yolk for pie crust. Roll one-half dough to fill 10½x15½ cookie tray. Sprinkle bottom crust with crushed corn flakes. Peel and slice apples and place over crust and flakes. Sprinkle with sugar and cinnamon. Roll out other half of dough and place on top, pinch edges. Beat egg white stiff and brush over crust. Bake at 400°F. for 60 minutes. While warm, frost with water, powdered sugar, and vanilla. Pour over warm crust.

C. Teloris Helle, Evansville Public School
Evansville, Minnesota

DANISH SAND TARTS (Denmark)
Number of Servings — 4 Dozen

2 sticks oleo
2 c. flour
1 t. vanilla
1 T. ice water
5 T. (heaping) confectioner's sugar

Cream oleo and sugar. Add vanilla and water, mix well. Add flour by cupful, then add by tablespoons, until it holds shape when dropped. Drop by teaspoon on ungreased cookie sheet. Bake 10-12 minutes at 375°F.

Mrs. Karleen J. Moore, Happy Independent School
Happy, Texas

SPONGE CAKE (Denmark)

2 c. sifted all-purpose flour
¼ t. salt
2 t. baking powder
1 c. milk
2 T. butter
4 eggs
2 c. sugar

Sift together flour, salt, baking powder. Scald milk. Melt butter in hot milk. Beat eggs until light and thick, slowly add sugar. Beat with spoon 5 minutes, or with electric mixer 2½ minutes. Fold sifted dry ingredients into the creamed mixture all at one time. Fold in all the hot milk and butter. Blending should take only 1 minute. Line a 13x9½ pan with wax paper and pour in batter. Bake in moderate oven 350°F. about 45 minutes. or until cake pulls away from sides of pan. Turn out on a rack, remove wax paper, and cool cake completely. Split cake carefully into 3 layers. Put together with —

Lemon Filling:
1¼ c. sugar
¼ c. sifted all-purpose flour
¼ t. salt
1 c. hot water
1 T. butter
⅛ c. lemon juice
Grated rind of 1 lemon
3 egg yolks (beaten)

Sift together in top of double boiler sugar, flour, and salt. Stir in water and butter. Add lemon juice and lemon rind. Cook over boiling water until thick and smooth, stirring constantly. Blend in egg yolks. Continue cooking until clear, about 5 minutes. Cool thoroughly. Spread between layers of cake. Top with —

Fruit Topping:
6 pear halves
3 pineapple slices
14 strawberries
1 t. mint jelly

Drain well the pear halves, pineapple slices and strawberries. Arrange over cake. Fill center of each pear with mint jelly.

Glaze:
1 c. fruit juice (pear and pineapple)
¼ c. sugar
1½ T. cornstarch
¼ c. cold fruit juice

Heat the 1 cup of fruit juice. Combine the sugar and cornstarch. Blend in the cold fruit juice. Add to hot fruit juice. Cook until thick and clear, stirring. Spoon over cake. Frost sides with powdered sugar frosting. Decorate edges with swirls from a pastry tube.

Hilma A. Davis, Kansas State College
Pittsburg, Kansas

APPLE TRIFLE (England)
Number of Servings — 4-6

8″ round or square sponge cake
½ c. apricot jam
3 medium size cooking apples
1 c. sugar
Juice of ½ lemon
1 reg. pkg. of ready-to-make vanilla pudding

Split sponge cake through the center with a sharp knife and spread with jam on bottom half. Put top half on. Peel apples, cut in halves, and remove cores. Put in pan with sugar and enough water to cover apples. Simmer until apples are soft but unbroken. Lift out fruit and continue to boil syrup quickly until it is reduced to ½ cup. When cold, arrange apples on sponge sandwich, pour syrup over. Make pudding and pour over top, just enough to run down the sides.

Susan J. Owen, Patricksburg H. S.
Patricksburg, Indiana

TRIFLES (England)
Number of Servings — 16-18

1 c. sugar
¼ c. flour
3 egg yolks
1 c. milk
1 t. vanilla
1 c. red plum jam
½ pt. whipped cream
Cherries
Pecans

Cook sugar, flour, eggs, and milk over double boiler until thick. Add vanilla. Use a day old cake or a pound cake. Slice cake ¼″ thick and line bottom of cake (layer) pan. Spread 1 cup red plum jam over cake. Again add layer of cake and another cup of jam. Spread on thick hot custard. Cool. Add whipped cream, sugar as desired. Dot with cherries and pecans.

Bobbie Lea Clarke, Goliad H. S.
Goliad, Texas

TRIFLE (England)
Number of Servings — 12-14

1 recipe sponge cake (see below)
1½ c. raspberry jam
2½ c. pineapple juice
1 T. lemon juice
½ t. almond extract
1 c. slivered blanched almonds
1 recipe soft custard, chilled (see next page)
1 c. heavy cream
2 T. confectioners' sugar
½ t. vanilla
½ c. glace' cherries

(Continued on Next Page)

Bake sponge cake in oblong pan 13x9½x2. Cut cake into slices about ⅛″ thick and spread slices generously with raspberry jam. Place 1 slice on top of another, sandwich fashion. Cut into 2″ pieces. Place pieces in sherbet dish. Combine pineapple juice, lemon juice, and almond extract. Pour 2 tablespoons juice over cake in each cup (more if necessary to moisten cake). Sprinkle with a few slivered almonds. Add enough soft custard to cover cake, chill. Whip cream and fold in confectioners' sugar and vanilla. Garnish with whipped cream and half of a glace' cherry. Sprinkle a few almonds on top.

Sponge cake:
1 c. sifted cake flour
1 t. baking powder
¼ t. salt
1 c. sugar
4 egg yolks
1 T. lemon juice
1 t. grated lemon peel
2 T. water
4 egg whites

Sift flour, baking powder and salt together 3 times. Sift sugar twice. Beat egg yolks and add ½ cup of the sugar gradually, beating until light and lemon colored. Add lemon juice, grated peel and water. Beat well. Sift flour a little at a time over yolk mixture and fold in carefully. Beat egg whites to frothy stage. Gradually add other ½ cup of sugar and beat to soft peak stage. Fold into yolk mixture just enough to combine both mixtures. Bake in ungreased pan in slow oven 325°F. 45 to 50 minutes or until springy to touch.

Soft custard:
2 eggs
¼ c. sugar
⅛ t. salt
2 c. milk, scalded
½ t. vanilla

Beat eggs slightly. Add sugar and salt. Stir hot milk slowly into egg mixture. Cook in double boiler on low heat, stirring constantly until mixture is thick enough to coat spoon. Remove from heat. Add vanilla. Turn at once into a cold bowl and chill. Note: If cooked too long, the custard may curdle. If this should happen, beat with a rostary egg beater to a smooth consistency.

Mrs. Sanders McWhorter, Roxboro H. S.
Roxboro, North Carolina

PLUM PUDDING (British Isles)

Number of Servings — 12-15

½ c. light molasses
¾ c. brown sugar
1 c. chopped suet (or ¾ c. butter)
1 t. soda
1 c. milk
1 t. cloves
2 t. cinnamon
1 t. salt
3 c. flour
2 c. dates
2 c. raisins
½ c. peel

Mix fruit together. Mix sugar, fat, molasses, soda. Add and blend in milk. Add flour mixture and fruit mixture alternately. Grease three 1 pound shortening cans (with lids). Half fill cans with dough. Place in canner on rack above water-bath and steam for 4-5 hours. To store, refrigerate or freeze in container. Heat before using. Serve with a lemon or hard sauce.

Mary Carlyn Mitchell, Pelican Rapids Public H. S.
Pelican Rapids, Minnesota

MANSIKKATORTTU (Strawberry Tart, Finland)

Number of Servings — 8

5 egg yolks
¾ c. sugar
3 c. crushed strawberries (fresh or frozen)
1 c. cookie or cake crumbs
1 t. almond extract
5 egg whites
Whipped cream

Beat egg yolks until light. Add sugar and beat until yolks and sugar mixture is stiff and lemon colored. Add strawberries. Drain frozen berries. Add cake crumbs and almond extract. Beat egg whites until stiff but not dry. Fold into strawberry mixture. Pour mixture into a buttered baking dish (8x12). Bake in moderate oven 350°F. for 35 minutes. Serve with whipped cream.

Marquita K. Christensen, Marshall H. S.
Marshall, Minnesota

BLENDER POTS DE CREME (France)

Number of Servings — 6

¾ c. milk
1 c. (6-oz. pkg.) semi-sweet chocolate bits
1 egg
2 T. sugar
Pinch of salt

Heat the milk just to the boiling point. Place all the other ingredients in the blender and add the hot milk. Blend at low speed for 1 minute. Pour into 6 pots de créme and chill for several hours (2 will do). Pretty tea cups substitute nicely for pots de créme if filled about half full since the pudding is very rich and very smooth.

Mrs. Penelope Coffin, Seymour Union H. S.
Seymour, Wisconsin

FRENCH CHERRY PIE (France)

Number of Servings — 8

1 c. sifted flour
½ t. salt
⅓ c. shortening
2 T. water

Mix flour and salt. Cut in shortening. Sprinkle with water. Press firmly into a ball. Roll into circle 1″ larger than pan. Place in pan. Flute edges, prick pastry bottom. Bake in 475°F. oven for 8 minutes.

Filling:
¾ c. sugar
⅓ c. cornstarch
⅛ t. salt

(Continued on Next Page)

1 c. boiling water
2 eggs
1 c. evaporated milk
1½ t. unflavored gelatin
1 T. cold water
¼ t. almond extract
1 No. 2 can pitted sour cherries

Blend sugar, cornstarch, and salt. Add water gradually, stirring to prevent lumping. Set over medium heat and cook, stirring constantly, until very thick. Beat eggs, add evaporated milk, slowly stir into cornstarch mixture. Soften gelatin in cold water and stir in. Continue to cook until mixture is smooth and thick, about 5 minutes. Cool. Add almond extract. Turn into cooled, baked pie shell. Drain cherries thoroughly, saving juice for glaze. Spoon cherries over filling. Spoon cherry glaze over cherries. Chill before serving.

Cherry Glaze:
1 T. cornstarch
¼ c. sugar
⅔ c. cherry juice
¼ t. red food coloring

Blend cornstarch and sugar. Slowly stir in cherry juice. Cook over low heat, stirring constantly until clear and slightly thickened. Remove from heat. Add ¼ teaspoon red food coloring and mix well. Cool slightly before spooning over pie.

Mrs. Margaret D. Randall, Tallulah H. S.
Tallulah, Louisiana

CHOCOLATE SUPREME TARTS (France)

Number of Servings — 18

4 egg whites, beaten stiff
1½ c. sugar, added by spoonfuls
¼ t. cream of tartar
¼ t. almond extract

Preheat oven 300°F. From brown paper, cut 18 rounds 3" in diameter. Place on cookie sheet. Beat egg whites until stiff, gradually add sugar by spoonfuls, cream of tartar and almond extract. Spread each round with meringue, making a slight rim around the edges. Bake 10 minutes. Turn off heat and let meringues dry 5 minutes longer.

Filling:
2 egg whites
½ c. sugar
2 T. cocoa
¾ c. butter
4 oz. semi-sweet chocolate (melted)
½ c. ground almonds

Beat the egg whites, sugar and cocoa until smooth in top of double boiler over hot water (not boiling). Still beating constantly, add the butter by spoonfuls and finally add the melted sweet chocolate. Remove from heat, stirring occasionally until the mixture is spreading consistency. Swirl filling into the "nest" of the meringues and sprinkle the tops with ground nuts.

This recipe submitted by the following teachers:
Mrs. Ernestine A. McLeod, Hatfield H. S.
Hatfield, Arkansas
Mrs. Marolyn K. Whitehead, West Miami Jr. H. S.
Miami, Florida

CHOCOLATE ROLL (France)

Number of Servings — 8

2 T. boiling water
1 t. instant coffee
1 pkg. sweet cooking chocolate
5 eggs, separated
1 c. sifted confectioners' sugar
1 t. vanilla
¼ c. cocoa

Stir together water, coffee, and chocolate in pan over low heat until chocolate is melted. Beat egg yolks until thick. Beat in ¾ cup of sugar, a tablespoon at a time, add vanilla. Beat well. Slowly fold in warm chocolate mixture. Beat egg whites until stiff. Fold in chocolate mixture. Turn into 13x9x2 pan that has been lined with greased wax paper. Bake in oven 350°F. 15 to 18 minutes. Mix remaining sugar and cocoa and sprinkle over tea towel. Invert cake in towel and roll loosely. Cool on rack 30 minutes. Carefully unroll cake. Spread with coffee cream filling. Carefully reroll without towel. Chill. Slice like jelly roll for serving.

Coffee cream filling:
½ c. heavy cream
1 T. confectioners' sugar
½ t. instant coffee
¼ t. vanilla

Beat together all ingredients until mixture holds a soft peak.

Mrs. J. C. Embry, Forestburg H. S.
Forestburg, Texas

'CREME DE LA CREME' OF CUSTARDS (France)

Number of Servings — 8

A glorious French dessert baked in a ring mold, filled with whipped cream and strawberries.

⅔ c. sugar
½ c. water
4 whole eggs
4 egg yolks
⅓ c. sugar
⅛ t. salt
1 c. heavy cream
2½ c. milk
1 t. vanilla

Cook the ⅔ cups sugar over low heat, stirring, until caramelized. Add water, stir until smooth. Pour mixture which should be thick as corn syrup, into a 1 quart mold. Rotate to coat bottom and lower sides. Beat together until blended, not foamy, 4 whole eggs, 4 egg yolks, ⅓ cup sugar, and salt. Pour the mixture, a little at a time, into the prepared ring mold. Set the mold into a pan of boiling water and bake in a preheated oven 325°F. until set, about 45 minutes. Immediately set mold in cold water to cool quickly. Chill. To unmold, run the tip of a knife around inner rim of mold. Place serving plate over custard, then invert, holding mold and plate together. Shake gently. Lift off the mold.

Mrs. Myrtle Trice Sands, Ware County H. S.
Waycross, Georgia

COOKIES (France)

Number of Servings — 8-10

3 c. flour
2 c. brown sugar
1 c. hot water
1 t. soda
1 t. vanilla
1 t. baking powder
½ t. salt
2 eggs
1 c. melted shortening
1 c. raisins
½ c. nut meats

Sift flour, soda, baking powder and salt together. Mix in bowl and add hot water, eggs, shortening, vanilla, raisins, and nuts. Stir together and bake on large cookie sheet at 375°F. oven for 15 minutes. Frost with favorite butter frosting.

Betty G. Quick, Barrington H. S.
Barrington, Illinois

FRENCH PUDDING (France)

Number of Servings — 16

2¼ c. confectioners' sugar
¾ c. butter
3 eggs
¾ lb. vanilla wafers
1 pt. whipping cream
1½ c. chopped pecans
1½ pkg. frozen strawberries, **drained slightly**

Cream butter and sugar. Add beaten eggs. Roll wafers and grease pans before lining with a layer of wafer crumbs. Add a layer of batter mixture. Add layer of crushed fruit, nuts and a layer of whipped cream. Repeat layers. Use some of the whipped cream for top and sprinkle with nuts. Refrigerate 24 hours before serving. May be frozen. Makes two 10x6 pyrex or loaf pans.

Doris Strauss, Atlanta Public H. S.
Atlanta, Texas

CREAM PIE (France)

Number of Servings — 12

½ lb. vanilla wafers, crushed
2 c. soft butter or oleo
1 c. confectioners' sugar
2 eggs, unbeaten
½ pt. whipping cream
¾ c. black walnut meats, chopped
(may use other kinds of nuts)
1 small bottle maraschino cherries, chopped fine

First mixture: Cream butter or oleo, confectioners' sugar and unbeaten eggs together. Second mixture: Whip cream, add chopped cherries and chopped nut meats (any kind of nut meats may be used). Place half of wafer crumbs in bottom of two ice cube trays (spread evenly). Spread evenly the first mixture over wafers in 2 trays. Spread the second mixture evenly over the first mixture in both trays. Cover with the remaining crumbs and place in refrigerator for 24 hours. Serve with a dip of whipped cream and a cherry, etc.

Mrs. Betty L. Hill, New Smyrna Beach H. S.
New Smyrna Beach, Florida

CREAM ICING (France)

1 c. milk
¼ c. flour
½ c. butter
½ c. margarine
1-1¼ t. vanilla
1 c. granulated sugar

Place flour into top of double boiler, add milk slowly and cook over boiling water, stirring constantly until very thick. Set aside to cool to room temperature. Cream margarine and butter well at medium speed. Add vanilla and cooled pudding, creaming well. Slowly add the granulated sugar. Beat at No. 3 speed for 10-15 minutes. Store in air tight container in refrigerator. Do not beat after it has been refrigerated. (Delicious on a white or yellow cake topped with well-drained crushed pineapple.)

Mrs. Ella Baker, Martin H. S.
Laredo, Texas

FRENCH PINEAPPLE (Or Uncooked Cake) (France)

Number of Servings — 12-15

1 lb. vanilla wafers
½ c. butter
2 c. powdered sugar
4 eggs
1 T. sugar
1 c. pineapple (well drained)
1 c. pecans (broken)
1 small bottle Maraschino cherries
1 c. whipping cream

Line 8½x13x2 dish with vanilla wafers, cream butter, and sugar. Add eggs one at a time. Beat well. Pour egg mixture over wafers. Add 1 tablespoon sugar to pineapple, cherries, and broken nuts. Pour over egg mixture. Whip cream and pour over fruit mixture. Chill in refrigerator 12 to 24 hours.

Georgia Turner, Fort Worth Technical H. S.
Fort Worth, Texas

FROZEN FRENCH PASTRY

Number of Servings — 16-20

1 lb. vanilla wafers, crushed
½ lb. pecan meats, ground
4 eggs
1 lb. confectioners' sugar
2 qts. whipping cream, whipped
1 box frozen strawberries, slightly thawed
1 lg. can crushed pineapple
1 box frozen raspberries, slightly thawed

Cook sugar, eggs and butter over boiling water for 1½ hours (no need to watch or stir). Mix nuts and wafer crumbs. Cover bottom of large pan with crumb mixture and pour syrup (sugar, egg, and butter mix) over them. Cover with layer of whipped cream. Now add strawberries, layer of cream, raspberries, layer of cream and top with a few crumbs. Freeze. Keeps in deep freeze for a long period very well.

Mrs. Jane Beacham, Clara H. S.
Clara, Mississippi

FROZEN FRENCH PASTRY
Number of Servings — 6 or More
1 lb. Nabisco cookies
½ c. butter
1 c. powdered sugar
2 eggs
1 pt. cream, whipped

Make a custard by cooking in double boiler, the butter, eggs, and powdered sugar. Cook until thick. Roll wafers with rolling pin until pulverized. Put a ½" layer of the crushed cookies in bottom of a freezing tray, then a layer of whipped cream, then a layer of custard and then whipped cream. Top with crushed cookies. Chill. Cut in squares to serve.

Virginia C. Lee, Technical H. S.
Memphis, Tennessee

FRENCH SILK PIE (France)
Number of Servings — 8
1¼ c. graham cracker crumbs
2 T. white sugar
¼ c. melted butter
¼ lb. butter
¾ c. white sugar
2 sq. chocolate, melted
1 t. vanilla
2 eggs

Combine graham cracker crumbs, sugar, and melted butter. Put into pie pan and bake at 400°F. for 8 minutes. Cream butter, sugar, vanilla, and melted chocolate well. Add eggs separately, beating 5 minutes at high speed after adding each egg. Pour into crust. Refrigerate overnight.

Mrs. Kenneth A. Wagner, Watertown Sr. H. S.
Watertown, South Dakota

FRENCH CHOCOLATE SILK PIE
Number of Servings — 6
½ c. butter or oleomargarine
¾ c. sugar
1 sq. unsweetened chocolate, melted
  (2 sq. if desired)
1 t. vanilla
2 eggs
1 baked pastry shell

Cream butter and sugar. Add melted chocolate and vanilla. Add 1 egg, beat 5 minutes at high speed. Add the second egg, beat 5 minutes more. Pour into a baked pie shell and refrigerate. When ready to serve, top with whipped cream (may add finely chopped nuts if desired).

This recipe submitted by the following teachers:
Mrs. Eunice C. Peters, Hopewell Memorial H. S.
Aliquippa, Pennsylvania
Clara M. Dayton, Cokeville H. S.
Cokeville, Wyoming
Molly Dunn Nicholls, Greenup Independent
Greenup, Kentucky
Alice Copenhaver, Ringgold H. S.
Ringgold, Georgia
Mrs. Julia R. Clark, Grundy Co. H. S.
Tracy City, Tennessee
Mrs. Frank S. Driver, Middle River H. S.
Meyers Cave, Virginia

GLACE STRAWBERRY PIE (France)
Number of Servings — 5-6
1¼ c. sifted flour
½ t. salt
⅛ c. plus 1 T. hydrogenated shortening
2-3 T. water

To make plain pastry, mix together the flour, and salt. Cut in with pastry blender hydrogenated shortening. Sprinkle with water. Gather dough together and press firmly into a ball. Roll into a circle 1 " larger than the pan, then fit pastry into pan. Trim off ragged edges, fold pastry back and under and build up a high fluted edge. Prick pastry well to prevent puffing during the baking. Bake at 475°F. for 8 minutes.

Filling:
1 pt. strawberries
3 oz. pkg. cream cheese (white)
1 c. sugar
3 T. cornstarch
1 pkg. frozen strawberries
Whipped cream

Wash, drain and hull the strawberries. Spread the cream cheese, which has been softened over the cooled crust. Cover with the strawberries.

Drain the juice from a package of defrosted strawberries, and, if necessary, add water to juice so it measures 1½ cups. Bring this to boiling and gradually stir in mixture of sugar and cornstarch. Cook over low heat. Stir constantly until boiling, boil 1 minute. Add remaining defrosted strawberries and cool. Pour this cool mixture over the strawberries in the pie shell. Chill about 2 hours. Just before serving, decorate with whipped cream (piped on with a pastry tube) or use the quick canned whipped cream.

This recipe submitted by the following teachers:
Mrs. Loretta Fowler Bennett,
Edgar Allan Poe, Int. School
Annandale, Virginia
Ruth C. Holder, Thorpe Jr. H. S.
Thorpe, Virginia

TIFFIN FAMOUS PUDDING (France)
Number of Servings — 9
½ lb. vanilla wafers, coarsely crushed
¼ lb. butter at room temperature
1 c. powdered sugar
2 eggs
1 c. whipping cream
½ c. chopped walnuts
½ c. maraschino cherries
¼ t. vanilla

Line a buttered 9" square pan with one-half the vanilla wafer crumbs. Cream butter with a mixer, add powdered sugar slowly. Add eggs, one at a time, beating until fluffy after each addition. Spread mixture in wafer lined pan. Refrigerate until stiff. Whip cream, add nuts, cherries, and vanilla. Spread over top of butter mixture. Top with remaining crumbs. Freeze, cut in squares to serve.

Janet Low, Balaton H. S.
Balaton, Minnesota

TORTONI (French Whipped Ice Cream)

Number of Servings — 6

1 c. clear Karo syrup
3 egg yolks
1 dash of salt
½ T. unflavored gelatin
3 T. cold water
1 c. whipping cream (whipped)
Crushed macaroons

Dissolve gelatin in cold water in top of double boiler. Mix syrup, egg yolks, and salt. Beat thoroughly. Keep beating until thickened (5 minutes after water in bottom of double boiler starts boiling). Add dissolved gelatin. Stir all until dissolved. Remove from heat and cool until thick. Add whipped cream. Put in freezing compartment until mixture is cold enough to hold up well when transferred to paper nut cups. Dust tops thickly with macaroon crumbs. Freeze until hard.

Macaroons Francaise:
2 egg whites
¼ t. salt
¾ c. granulated sugar
½ t. vanilla
1⅓ c. coconut

Beat egg whites until stiff but not dry. Add the salt. Beat in the sugar ¼ cup at a time. Add vanilla. Fold in coconut. Drop rounded teaspoonfuls 1" apart on a baking sheet which has been well greased with unsalted fat. Bake at 275°F. for 25 minutes. (When stored in a tightly covered tin, they will keep fresh for weeks.)

Susan Hiatt, Lapeer Sr. H. S.
Lapeer, Michigan

BLITZEN CAKE (Germany)

Number of Servings — 10-12

½ c. shortening
½ c. sugar
4 egg yolks
5 T. milk
1 c. cake flour
1 t. baking powder
½ t. vanilla
4 egg whites
1 c. powdered sugar
½ c. chopped nuts
Filling:
Juice and rind 1 lemon
1 c. sugar
1 egg, beaten

Cream shortening and sugar. Add beaten yolks. Stir in the milk. Beat in sifted flour and baking powder, add vanilla. Put in 2 layer cake pans which have been greased slightly. Beat egg whites until stiff. Add powdered sugar. Beat well and spread on top of each layer. Sprinkle with chopped nuts. Bake in 350°F. oven until browned. Make a filling of the above ingredients by combining and cooking in double boiler until thick. Cool. Spread between the cooled cake layers.

Mrs. Elizabeth Sacker, Triton Regional H. S.
Runnemede, New Jersey

APPLE PIE (Germany)

Number of Servings — 6-8

1-9" pie shell
4-5 c. sliced apples
1¼ c. sugar
⅛ t. nutmeg
½ t. cinnamon
⅛ t. salt
2 slightly beaten eggs
½ c. top milk

Line a 9" pie pan with pastry. Slice apples in thick slices about ¼" thick. Place sliced apples in shell in overlapping position. Sprinkle sugar, nutmeg, cinnamon, and salt over apples. Make a custard of 2 slightly beaten eggs mixed with ½ cup top milk. Pour custard over apples and bake at 400°F. on second rack from bottom for 40 to 45 minutes. If apples are unusually hard, cook them for 5 minutes, drain and then place in crust.

Floyce B. Houeye, Amite H. S.
Amite, Louisiana

BERLINER KRANTZER WREATHS (Germany)

Number of Servings — 4 Dozen

¾ c. butter or margarine
¾ c. shortening.
1 c. granulated sugar
2 T. grated orange peel
2 eggs
4 c. sifted flour
1 egg white
2 T. sugar
Red and green colored sugar

Mix butter, shortening, sugar, orange peel, and 2 eggs thoroughly. Stir in flour. Chill several hours or overnight. Roll small pieces of dough to the size of a pencil and 6" long. Place on ungreased cookie sheet. Form each to a circle, bringing one end over and through in a single knot. Brush tops with meringue (made by beating egg white until stiff, then beating in 2 tablespoons suger). Sprinkle "wreath" with green sugar and "bow" with red. Bake at 400°F. for 9 minutes.

Mrs. Donna Hussung, New Albany Sr. H. S.
New Albany, Indiana

COOKIES (Germany)

Number of Servings — 5 Dozen

4 eggs
1 pkg. light brown sugar
2½ c. sifted flour
1 t. cinnamon
½ t. cloves
Few grains salt
1 c. chopped nut meats

Beat eggs and sugar until thick, using electric beater. Sift flour again with spices and salt. Fold into egg and sugar mixture. Add chopped nuts. Spread on greased pan 12x18x1 or 2 pans 9x12x1. Bake at 375°F. for 20 minutes or until done, but do not overbake. Cool in pan for about 1 minute. While still very warm, spread with glaze. Cool. Cut into squares. These cookies are easily and quickly made.

(Continued on Next Page)

Glaze:
1 c. powdered sugar
2-3 T. water
¼ t. almond extract
Mix powdered sugar, water, and almond extract (should be as thick as cream).

Mrs. JoAnna W. Boyens, Many H. S.
Many, Louisiana

FASTNACTHS—A RAISED DOUGHNUT (Germany)

Number of Servings — 2 Dozen

1 c. milk
1 pkg. dry or compressed yeast
1½ c. sifted flour
¼ c. Crisco
Deep fat or oil for frying
1 t. salt
¼ c. sugar
1 egg
2 c. sifted flour

Heat milk slightly and dissolve yeast. Add 1½ cups flour and beat until smooth. Cover with damp cloth and let rise in warm place until double in bulk, about 2 hours. Cream Crisco, salt, and sugar, add egg and mix well. Stir into yeast sponge. Add 2 cups flour and mix thoroughly. Rub top of dough with Crisco and let rise again, until double in bulk. Roll about ⅜" thick and cut with floured doughnut cutter. Allow to rise about 45 minutes. Fry until brown, 3 to 5 minutes in deep fat heated to 365°F. Drain on absorbent paper. Sprinkle with sugar or use glaze made by adding about 3 tablespoons water to 1 cup confectioners' sugar.

Mary Helen Strong, Cross Plains H. S.
Cross Plains, Texas

GERMAN CRUMB CAKE (Germany)

Number of Servings — One 12 Inch Square

3 c. flour
1 c. lard
1 c. brown sugar
1 c. sour milk
½ t. salt
1 t. nutmeg
1 t. cinnamon
2 t. baking soda
½ t. baking powder
½ c. raisins
2 eggs

Blend first 3 ingredients. Reserve ½ cup of these crumbs for the top of cake. Add the rest of ingredients. Blend well. Pour into a greased deep baking dish. Put remaining crumbs on top, pushing them down slightly into the batter. Bake at 350°F. for 40-50 minutes.

Mrs. Marion R. Hessler, Gov. Mifflin Sr. H. S.
Shellington, Pennsylvania

KRUMEL TORTE (Germany)

Number of Servings — 16

4 eggs
½ c. sugar
1 t. baking powder

1 t. vanilla
8 T bread crumbs
1 lb. dates, chopped
1 lb. walnuts, chopped

Beat eggs. Add sugar, vanilla, and baking powder. Mix. Add remaining ingredients and mix. Pour into a greased square pan. Bake at 350°F. for about 35 minutes. Cut into squares. This makes a good holiday dessert. Wrap in aluminum foil and store.

Mrs. Dorothy Houtz, Elkton Sr. H. S.
Elkton, Maryland

LEBKUCHEN SQUARES (Germany)

Number of Servings — 6 Dozen

1 c. honey
¾ c. brown sugar, firmly packed
1 egg
1 t. grated lemon rind
3 T. lemon juice
2 c. sifted flour
1 T. pumpkin pie spice
½ t. baking soda
¼ t. salt
½ c. golden raisins
½ c. chopped blanched almonds
1 c. sifted confectioners' sugar
18 candied green cherries, halved
18 candied red cherries, halved

Heat honey to boiling in small saucepan. Pour into large bowl, cool completely. Stir in brown sugar, egg, lemon rind, and 1 tablespoon lemon juice. Sift dry ingredients into medium-size bowl, stir in raisins and almonds. Gradually stir into honey mixture, blending well. Chill overnight to blend flavors. Divide dough and spread evenly into 2 greased baking pans, each 9x9x2. Bake in moderate oven 350°F. 30 minutes or until firm. While cookies bake, stir remaining 2 tablespoons lemon juice into powdered sugar until smooth in small bowl. Set pans of hot cookies on wire racks. Press 36 cherry halves, cut side down, in 6 even rows on top in each pan, drizzle frosting over. Cool cookies completely in pans, then cut panful into 36 squares.

Mrs. Georgia Balls, Alameda Jr. H. S.
Pocatello, Idaho

OBST TORTE (Germany)

Number of Servings — 12

⅛ c. butter
⅛ c. sugar
½ t. vanilla
1 egg
1 c. flour
1 t. baking powder
Filling:
3-4 c. fresh, canned, or frozen fruit
Sugar
1 T. cornstarch
1 c. whipping cream

Soften butter. Add sugar, vanilla, and egg. Mix well. Add sifted flour and baking powder. Mix well. Chill 1 hour. Line bottom and sides of spring form pan. Bake at 375°F. 15-20 minutes. Drain canned or frozen fruit reserving juice or crush 1

(Continued on Next Page)

cup fresh fruit to make juice. Sweeten to taste. Boil juice. Mix cornstarch with a little sugar. Stir in, cook until thick. Fill baked shell with fruit. Pour cooled juice over fruit. Chill. Decorate with whipped cream. *Mrs. J. S. Elsner, Hampton H. S.*
Allison Park, Pennsylvania

PEACH CREAM KUCHEN (Germany)
Number of Servings — 8-9
2 c. sifted flour
¼ c. sugar
¼ t. baking powder
1 t. salt
½ c. butter or margarine
1 can (No. 2½) peach slices (could also use apple slices)
½ c. sugar
1 t. cinnamon
2 egg yolks
1 c. dairy sour cream

Sift the flour, ¼ cup sugar, baking powder, and salt together into a bowl. Cut in the butter with a pastry blender or 2 knives until the mixture resembles fine crumbs. Transfer to a lightly greased 9x9x2 baking pan and press crumbs firmly against the bottom and sides. Arrange well-drained peach slices evenly over the bottom. Stir half cup of sugar and cinnamon together and sprinkle over the fruit. Bake is a quick oven 400°F. for 15 minutes. Beat the egg yolks, blend in the sour cream. Spoon over the partially baked kuchen and continue baking for 20 minutes or until golden brown. Serve warm or thoroughly chilled.

This recipe submitted by the following teachers:
Malinda J. Herflicker, Stockbridge H. S.
Stockbridge, Michigan
Mary A. Gallagher, Plainwell H. S.
Plainwell, Michigan
Gail Witherow, Clearfield Area H. S.
Clearfield, Pennsylvania

PLUM KUCHEN
Number of Servings — 9
1½ c. sifted flour
½ t. salt
2 t. baking powder
3 T. sugar
3 T. shortening
1 egg
6 T. milk
4½ plums (fresh and cut in halves)

Sift together pre-sifted flour, salt, baking powder, and sugar. Cut in shortening. Combine the egg and milk. Stir the liquid into the dry ingredients. Spread in a greased pan 8x8. Cover the top with plum halves (cut side up) and sprinkle with streusel topping. Bake at 425°F. 25 minutes.

Streusel Topping:
½ c. sugar
1 t. cinnamon
¼ c. sifted flour
¼ c. butter

Combine the sugar, flour, and cinnamon. Cut in the butter.
Mrs. Shelley Brown, White Cloud H. S.
White Cloud, Michigan

STRUDEL (Germany)
Number of Servings — Two 9x13 Pans
3 c. flour
1 egg
1 T. lard
½ t. salt
1 c. lukewarm water

Mix flour, egg, salt, and lukewarm water. Work this on a board for 20 minutes, kneading and pounding the dough against board. By this time it should not stick. Divide dough into 2 parts, kneading it just a little bit more with a little more flour. Cover with a cloth, let stand about 15 minutes. (This is important to let the dough rest.) Roll dough out to the size of a plate, spread with a little melted fat, which is a combination of lard and butter. Spread and pull dough in the air. Stretch this as fine as tissue paper on the table, which is covered with a large white tablecloth. Again spread with a little of the melted fat. Spread on filling, trim thickened edge all the way around and roll up using the tablecloth. Place in buttered pan, or cut to fit pan. Bake at 350°F. about 45 minutes or until crust is light brown. Serve warm.

Apple Filling:
8-10 apples

Cut apples as for pie. Spread sugar and cinnamon on the apples when on the dough. Raisins, if you like them, may be used. Proportion of sugar as for 1 apple pie.

Cheese Filling:
1 lb. creamed cottage cheese
2 eggs, beaten well
¼ c. sugar
Pinch of salt
Mix well and spread on dough.

Cabbage Filling:
1 small head cabbage, chopped fine
1 T. salt
2 T. lard
Dash black pepper

Chop cabbage, add salt and let stand for 1 hour. Squeeze out cabbage and fry until light brown. Spread on dough. Spread a little more fat on and roll.

Potato Filling:
4 cold boiled potatoes
½ t. salt
1 T. sugar

Sprinkle a little black pepper on potato. Grate cold boiled potatoes into the stretched dough, add the other ingredients. Spread with warm butter, or a mixture of butter and lard that is melted. Roll.
Mrs. Dragica Nerbun, Ladysmith H. S.
Ladysmith, Wisconsin

APPLE-RAISIN STRUDEL
Number of Servings — 12-16
1½ c. sifted flour
1 T. baking powder
¾ t. salt
¼ c. shortening
½ c. milk

(Continued on Next Page)

¼ c. butter or margarine, melted
3 apples
¾ c. raisins
¾ c. sugar
1 t. cinnamon
¼ t. mace

Sift flour with baking powder and salt. Cut in shortening. Blend in milk. Roll very thin on pastry cloth or other smooth, floured cloth, to a rectangle about 10x15. Spread with about ¾ of the butter, leaving about 1" on short side unspread. Peel, core and dice apples. Rinse and drain raisins. Spread apples and raisins over dough, lengthwise, leaving about 2" at unbuttered end. Combine sugar, cinnamon and mace. Sprinkle over fruit. Roll as for jelly roll toward unbuttered end, using cloth to lift end of roll. Moisten all edges and pinch together to seal. Place on greased, shallow baking pan with sealed edges down. Spread outside of roll with remaining butter. Bake at 425°F. for 10 minutes. Reduce temperature to 350° for 30 minutes.

Joan L. Haines, Cle Elum H. S.
Cle Elum, Washington

YULE CAKE (Germany)

½ c. whole Brazil nuts
1 c. English walnut halves
2 c. pecan halves
1 pkg. whole dates
⅜ c. almonds
½ c. whole red maraschino cherries, drained
½ c. whole green maraschino cherries, drained
½ c. seedless raisins
¾ c. sifted flour
¾ c. sugar
½ t. baking powder
½ t. salt
3 eggs
1 t. vanilla

Grease bottom and sides of loaf pan. Line bottom with wax paper, grease paper. Put nuts and fruit in large bowl. Sift dry ingredients together over nuts and fruit, mix well, coating each piece. Beat eggs until light and fluffy. Add vanilla, blend into nut mixture. The dough will be stiff. (The nuts and fruits looks coated. There is only enough batter to hold the fruit and nuts together.) Spoon into pan, spread evenly. Bake in slow oven at 300°F. for 1 hour and 15 minutes. Cool 10 minutes in pan, then turn out of pan.

Sue Farmer, Haughton H. S.
Haughton, Louisiana

ICE BOX CAKE (Greece)

Number of Servings — 6-10

1 c. strong coffee (must be cold)
4 egg yolks
1½ c. confectioners' sugar
1 stick margarine
1 chocolate candy bar (such as Hershey's)
¾ c. blanched sliced almonds (toasted)
1 lg. box vanilla wafers

Beat egg yolk on high speed until stiff, add margarine and beat until creamy. Add the sugar and melted chocolate. Mix until thick.
Dip vanilla wafers in coffee very quickly, and cover the bottom of a cake plate with a layer of the dipped wafers. Spread filling over wafers, then sprinkle with almonds. Continue the layers (one on top of another) until filling is used up, being sure to end with filling and almonds. Place in refrigerator at least 3 hours before serving. Will keep 1 week if stored in refrigerator.

Belva Liles, Tuscaloosa H. S.
Tuscaloosa, Alabama

BAKLAVA (Greek Pastry)
Number of Servings — 20-25
2 lbs. chopped walnuts
1 t. powdered cinnamon
½ t. powdered cloves
¾ lb. butter
1 lb. pastry sheets (purchased at Greek stores)
Syrup:
½ pt. honey
¼ t. lemon extract
1 lb. sugar
Juice of ½ lemon

Combine walnuts and spices. Melt butter, removing salt until butter is clear. Brush bottom of 10x14 pan with melted butter, and place 1 pastry sheet over this. Brush with melted butter. Repeat this process until 4 pastry sheets line the bottom of the baking pan. Brush fourth layer with melted butter and sprinkle with nut mixture. Repeat this until nut and spice mixture is all used. End with 4 top layers brushed with butter. Cut into diamond shapes. Bake at 300°F. until golden brown. While pastry is baking, prepare syrup. Boil syrup ingredients together. Cool, and using a spoon, pour very slowly over baked Baklava.

Niki Sitaras, Wolcott Jr. H. S.
Warren, Michigan

PAXIMADIA—TEA COOKIES (Greece)
½ c. cooking oil
¼ lb. butter
1½ c. sugar
3 eggs
1 t. soda
3 t. baking powder
2 t. ainseed
5½ c. flour

Cream butter and oil. Add eggs one at a time. Beat until creamy. Stir in all ingredients except flour. Knead in flour to form soft dough. Divide into 5 parts. Roll into long loaf 2½" wide, 1" thick. Place on greased cookie sheet 2" apart. Cut into half slices. Bake 375°F. 20 minutes. Slice while warm. Cool slightly. Toast on both sides until light brown. Cool before storing. Excellent keeping qualities.

Paula E. Reeves, Dalton H. S.
Dalton, Georgia

PECAN BARS (Greece)
Number of Servings — 50-55
2 c. butter (1 lb.)
8 T. powdered sugar
4 c. chopped pecans

(Continued on Next Page)

4 c. flour
2 T. vanilla
2 T. ice water
1 lb. powdered sugar

Cream butter thoroughly and add 8 tablespoons sugar and continue creaming until all is blended. Mix nuts and flour and add to cream mixture, adding gradually until well blended. Add vanilla and ice water and mix. Roll pieces of dough with palm of hand into 1" rolls or half moon designs. Bake on cookie sheets for 35 minutes in oven 350°F. until golden brown. Sift powdered sugar generously over rolls and place in cookie jar to preserve. Arrange in layers carefully to avoid breaking.

Mrs. Hazel C. Tassis, Imperial H. S.
Imperial, California

HAWAIIAN CAKE
Number of Servings — 8
½ c. shortening
¼ c. brown sugar
1 egg
1 c. flour
½ t. baking powder
2½ c. crushed pineapple
Topping:
2 eggs
1 c. sugar
3 T. melted butter
1½ c. coconut
½ c. chopped nuts

Cream shortening and sugar. Add beaten egg and dry ingredients. Pat batter in greased 9" pie pan or oblong baking pan. Drain pineapple well. Mix topping as listed. Place drained pineapple over batter, add topping. Bake 40 minutes at 350°F. Cut in squares or wedges. Serve plain or with whipped cream and cherry garnish.

Mrs. Louise S. Barton, Herrin Twp. H. S.
Herrin, Illinois

DUTCH FAMILY CAKE (Holland)
Number of Servings — 8-10
½ c. shortening
2 sq. bitter chocolate
1 c. sugar
2 eggs
1 c. applesauce
1 t. vanilla
½ c. pecans, chopped
1 c. flour
½ t. baking powder
¼ t. soda
¼ t. salt

Melt and blend shortening and chocolate together. Cool. Beat eggs, add sugar, applesauce, vanilla, pecans, and chocolate mixture. Sift flour, baking powder, soda, and salt together. Add to mixture. Pour into greased and floured square pan 8x8 and bake 30-40 minutes at 350°F. To decorate top, use paper mat for stencil. Place on top of cake, dust with powdered sugar. Remove mat carefully. Lift straight up. Cut into squares.

Mrs. J. E. Clowdis, Gordon H. S.
Decatur, Georgia

DUTCH DUMPLINGS (Holland)
Number of Servings — 4
1 c. flour
2 t. baking powder
¼ t. baking soda
¼ t. salt
2 T. white sugar
2 T. shortening
½-¾ c. cooked, sweetened dried peaches

Sift all dry ingredients together in a mixing bowl. Chop in shortening. Add peaches to make a stiff dough. Make into balls about the size of an egg. Roll in flour and drop into ¾ quart boiling water. Cover and steam for 25 minutes. Add 2 tablespoons butter, 1 tablespoon sweet cream, and 2 tablespoons sugar. Cook 1 minute. Serve hot.

Mabel Kitchings Owen, Monticello H. S.
Monticello, Arkansas

APRICOT PASTRIES (Hungary)
Number of Servings — 30-40
½ lb. sweet butter
½ c. plus 1 T. granulated sugar
3 egg yolks
2½ c. flour
Grated lemon rind
Apricot jam

Cream butter, add sugar, grated lemon rind, and cream again. Add egg yolks and mix thoroughly. Add flour slowly. Work into a lump and chill about an hour. Roll, place in pie pans, spread with apricot jam. Reserve a little dough for lattice strips. Twist and criss-cross on top of jam. Bake at 400°F. in a pre-heated oven 18 to 20 minutes. Dough will be browned around edges, bottom will not be browned. Pans are 1x6 and 1x8 aluminum pans. When cool, cut into 1½" squares. Serve. Other fruit jams may be substituted.

Mrs. Margaret Yoder, Upper Perkiomen H. S.
East Greenville, Pennsylvania

NUT ROLLS (Hungary)
Number of Servings — 4 Dozen
1 yeast cake
¼ c. sugar
½ t. vanilla
½ c. sweet cream
3 eggs
6 T. shortening
3 c. sifted flour
1 t. salt
2 lbs. walnuts
3 ozs. honey
¼ lb. butter
1 c. sugar
1 box graham crackers
1 box confectioners' sugar

Dissolve yeast, sugar, and vanilla in warm cream. Beat eggs and add to yeast mixture. Cut shortening, flour and salt as for pie crust. Add yeast mixture and knead. Chill one hour. Grind walnuts and mix with honey, butter and sugar. Roll out dough. Crush graham crackers and mix with confectioners' sugar. Cover dough with this mixture or roll it in mixture. Fill with walnut mixture and roll up in thin rolls (⅛"). Cut to 1" rolls. Bake 400°F. 18-20 minutes.

Anne Marie Potzner, Weatherly Area Joint H. S.
Weatherly, Pennsylvania

BISCUIT TORTONI (Italy)

Number of Servings — 6-8

1 c. heavy cream
¼ c. powdered sugar
1 egg white
½ c. crumbled macaroons
2 t. sherry

Whip 1 cup heavy cream. Gradually fold in powdered sugar, egg white stiffly beaten, alternately with crumbled and seived macaroons and sherry. Pack mixture in individual paper cups, sprinkle tops with extra seived (and crumbled) macaroons, and set in refrigerator tray. Freeze without stirring until firm.

Marguerite H. Buckley, Woodrow Wilson Jr. H. S.
Roanoke, Virginia

COFFEE TORTONI (Italy)

Number of Servings — 8

1 egg white
1 T. instant coffee
2 T. sugar
1 c. whipping cream
¼ c. sugar
1 t. vanilla
⅛ t. almond extract
¼ c. buttered almonds

Beat egg white until it forms peaks. Add instant coffee and sugar. Beat cream in a separate bowl, add ½ cup sugar and vanilla, and almond extract. Fold almonds into this mixture. Fold egg white mixture into cream mixture. Put into cup cake papers, placed in muffin tins. Freeze for 24 hours.

Mrs. Doris Dixon, Monterey Sr. H. S.
Lubbock, Texas

CREAM PUFF ITALIANE (Italy)

⅓ c. butter
1 t. salt
1 c. boiling water
1 c. all-purpose flour
5 eggs

Add butter and salt to boiling water in the top of a double boiler. When the butter melts, add flour all at once until the paste leaves the sides of the pan and forms a ball. Remove from the heat, cool slightly, and beat in whole eggs, one at a time, beating briskly after each addition. Drop paste by demitasse spoon, on buttered baking sheet, and bake in moderate oven 375°F. for 25 minutes or until paste is well puffed and cakes are dry and browned. Cool on rack and fill with Italiane Cream.

Italiane Cream:
1 lb. Ricotta (Italian creamed cheese)
4 T. sifted confectioners' sugar.

Combine sugar with cheese and cream well. Split puffs with sharp knife and fill with cheese mixture. Pile puffs on plate and dust liberally with confectioners' sugar.

Ruth A. Fanelli, East Bay H. S.
Wimauma, Florida

CHRISTMAS MACRONI'S (Italy)

4 c. sugar
½ c. butter
8 eggs
1 t. cinnamon
1 t. cloves
2½ c. flour
Few grains salt
1 t. lemon flavoring
½ c. rich milk
4 c. nuts (preferably black walnuts)

Cream sugar and butter. Add eggs. Sift and measure the flour. Add salt and the spices and sift together. Add the milk and flavoring alternately with the flour mixture. Stir in nuts. Bake on ungreased baking sheet in 375°F. oven, until lightly browned around the edges. Remove from the pan immediately. You may have to return the pan to the oven for a minute to be able to remove the last of the cookies.

Joan McCready, Missouri Valley H. S.
Missouri Valley, Iowa

CREAM ROLLS CANNOLI (Italy)

Number of Servings — 16-18

3 c. flour
¼ c. sugar
1 t. cinnamon
¼ t. salt
3 T. shortening
2 eggs, well beaten
2 T. white vinegar
2 T cold water
½ c. pistachio nuts
Egg white, slightly beaten
Sifted confectioners' sugar

Sift dry ingredients into a bowl. Cut in shortening until size of peas. Stir in eggs. Blend in vinegar and water 1 tablespoonful at a time. Turn dough onto lightly floured surface and knead. Wrap in wax paper and chill for 30 minutes. Set out deep saucepan or automatic deep-fat frier and heat fat to 360°F. Roll chilled dough ⅛″ thick on floured surface. Cut dough into oval shape. Wrap dough loosely around tubes just lapping over opposite edges. Seal edges by brushing with egg white. Fry only as many Cannoli shells as will float uncrowded one layer deep in the fat. Fry about 8 minutes or until golden brown, turning occasionally during frying time. Drain over fat before removing to absorbent paper. Cool slightly and remove tubes. Cool completely. When ready to serve, fill with Ricotta filling. Sprinkle ends of Cannoli with chopped nuts and dust shells with confectioners' sugar.

Filling:
3 c. (about 1½ lb.) Ricotta cheese
1¼ c. sugar
2 t. vanilla extract
½ c. finely chopped candied citron
¼ c. semi-sweet chocolate pieces

Mix the above ingredients thoroughly. Chill in refrigerator until used.

Mrs. John Gudeman, Stanford H. S.
Stanford, Illinois

CREME FROSTING (Italy)
Number of Servings — Large Cake

3 T. flour
½ c. milk
½ c. granulated sugar
¼ c. butter
¼ c. shortening
1 t. vanilla or other flavoring

Shake flour and milk in small jar, cook until thickened in saucepan over medium heat. Cool. In small mixing bowl beat butter and shortening at high speed until fluffy. Add sugar. Beat at high speed until fluffy and smooth. Add thickened mixture (completely cooled). Beat again and add flavoring.

Toni Guast, Lackawanna Trail Joint Schools
Factoryville, Pennsylvania

RICOTTA PIE (Italy)

Crust:
1 c. flour
⅓ c. shortening
¼ t. salt
2-3 T. water

Filling:
1 c. sugar
2 c. Ricotta cheese
½ t. salt
1 T. cornstarch
1 T. lemon juice
1 T. vanilla
2 eggs
1 c. milk
Nutmeg

Cream sugar and cheese well. Add salt, cornstarch, and cream again. Add lemon juice, vanilla and eggs. Mix milk in last. Bake at 375°F. about 45 minutes. Sprinkle nutmeg on top lightly. Lower to 350°F. the last 15 minutes.

Mrs. Lois Borba, Gustine H. S.
Gustine, California

CUSTARD DESSERT "ZABALIONE" (Italy)
Number of Servings — 6

3 eggs
¼ c. sugar
⅛ t. salt
1½ T. lemon juice, wine or vanilla

Put eggs in upper part of double boiler. Beat until light and thick. Add next 3 ingredients, beat. Place over simmering water (upper part of double boiler should not touch water). Beat while cooking over simmering water (6-7 minutes), until thick and fluffy. Serve immediately in sherbet glasses.

Florence Tooke, Reed Custer H. S.
Braidwood, Illinois

JAPANESE FRUIT CAKE
Number of Servings — 12

1 orange
1 lemon
1 c. raisins
1 c. sugar
⅓ c. butter or shortening
1 egg
2 c. sifted all-purpose flour
1 t. soda
1 c. sour or buttermilk
1 c. nuts, chopped if desired

Juice of lemon and orange, add sugar and let stand while mixing and baking the cake. Cream the ⅓ cup butter or shortening and the other cup of sugar, add the egg and mix thoroughly. Add soda to the sour or buttermilk and add alternately to the creamed mixture with the flour. Grind the raisins and the rinds of the orange and lemon. add to the mixture. Bake at 350°F. until done. Add sugar mixture while still warm.

Mrs. Alton McCue, Holly Grove School
Holly Grove, Arkansas

BIZCOCHITOS COOKIES (Mexico)

1 c. sugar
2 c. lard
1 t. anise seed
2 eggs
6 c. sifted flour
3 t. baking powder
1 t. salt
¼ c. water

Cream lard with hand thoroughly, add sugar and anise seed. Beat eggs and add to lard mixture. Blend until light and fluffy. Sift flour with baking powder and salt and add to first mixture. Add water and knead until well mixed. Roll ½" thick and cut into fancy shapes. Roll top of each cookie in a mixture of 1 teaspoon cinnamon to each ½ cup sugar. Bake in a moderate oven until slightly brown.

Catherine Dicks, State Supervisor,
Home Economics Education
University Park, New Mexico

MEXICAN WEDDING CAKES
Number of Servings — 3½ Dozen

1 c. butter or margarine
¾ c. confectioners' sugar
1 t. vanilla
2 c. flour
1 c. finely chopped walnuts
Extra confectioners' sugar

Cream butter, ¾ cup confectioners' sugar and vanilla. With a spoon gradually blend in flour. Mix in walnuts. Shape into ¾" balls, rolling in palms. Place about ½" apart on ungreased cookie sheet. Bake in slow 325° F. oven 30 minutes, cookies should be creamy color. Remove to wire rack until just warm, roll in a little of the extra confectioners' sugar. Cool entirely. Roll again in a little of the confectioners' sugar. Store in tightly covered container. Cookies will be a rounded shape with flat bottoms.

Mrs. Joan Thro, West Hardin H. S.
Stephensburg, Kentucky

FLAN (Caramel Custard) (Mexico)
Number of Servings — 8

1¾ c. sugar
3 egg whites
8 egg yolks
2 tall cans evaporated milk

(Continued on Next Page)

2 t. vanilla
6 T. brandy or rum

Put 1 cup sugar into a deep baking pan (or square loaf pan) in which custard is to be baked, and place over heat. Stir constantly until sugar melts and turns golden. Remove from heat and tip pan back and forth until it is entirely coated with caramel. Let cool while mixing custard. Beat egg whites and egg yolks together well and add milk, remaining sugar and vanilla. Beat until sugar dissolves, then strain custard into caramel coated pan. Cover custard, place pan in a larger pan containing 1" of hot water, and bake in moderate oven 350°F. for 1 hour. While still hot, turn out on serving platter. When ready to serve, pour brandy or rum over pudding and send to the table burning.

Adele Rummel Viales, San Benito County H. S.
Hollister, California

LECHE QUEMADA (Mexico)
(Burned Milk Candy)
Number of Servings — 2 Dozen Small Squares

1 qt. pasteurized milk
2 c. granulated sugar
⅛ t. cream of tartar
½ c. chopped pecans or pecan halves

Place milk, sugar, and cream of tartar in a saucepan. Stir to dissolve. Cook over low flame about 1 hour or until mixture begins to thicken. Stir occasionally and later constantly. When mixture thickens, check by caramel method by dropping a drop of the mixture into a cup of cold water until a soft ball forms or use candy thermometer and let it be 230°F. Remove from heat, add chopped pecans. Pour into wax paper-lined square cake pan and let it cool, cut into squares. Top with pecan halves for decoration. Other suggestions: Do not add chopped pecans. Pour mixture by the spoonful unto wax paper, top with pecan halves on each candy.

Letioia Poz, Rio Grande City H. S.
Rio Grande City, Texas

SPICED PECANS (Mexico)

1 c. sugar
½ c. water
1 t. cinnamon
¼ t. salt
1 t. vanilla
2½ c. pecans (whole)

Combine in saucepan and cook over medium gas flame to 232°F. or thread stage the following, sugar, water, cinnamon and salt. Remove from flame. Add vanilla and pecans. Stir until nuts are well coated and mixture becomes creamy. Pour onto greased platter or baking sheet. With spoons or forks, separate nuts as they cool.

Mrs. Maria Gutierrez Tijerina,
Albert Sidney Johnston H. S.
Austin, Texas

FRUIT SOUP (Norway)
Number of Servings — 4-6

2 c. mixed dried fruit
3 c. water (enough to cover)
½ c. grape juice (if desired)
½ lemon, sliced
2 T. sago or tapioca
¼ t. salt
½-⅔ c. sugar
1 stick cinnamon
¼ t. cloves

Cook fruit in water until tender. Add juice, lemon, cloves, sago (that has been soaked overnight), salt, and cinnamon. Cook until sago or tapioca is clear or translucent. Sweeten to taste. May be served hot or cold. Used by Norse on Christmas Eve and as a gift to the sick.

Juli Ann Gronbeck, Rugby H. S.
Rugby, North Dakota

LACE COOKIES (Norway)

½ c. butter
½ c. dark brown sugar
¼ c. granulated sugar
¾ c. flour
¼ c. ground oatmeal
¼ c. white Karo
½ c. ground nuts
1 t. vanilla
⅛ t. crushed cardamon (optional)

Bring to bubbling point butter, sugar, and Karo. Remove from fire and add the flour, nut and oatmeal mixture. Add flavoring. Grease a cookie sheet generously and drop by teaspoonful about 4" apart. They spread very much. Bake about 10 minutes in a 325°F. oven. Cool about a minute and carefully lift from cookie sheet with a pancake turner. Make only a few at a time. If they get too cold, they will be difficult to remove from cookie sheet. In that case, slip the cookie sheet back into the oven and reheat and proceed as before. These cookies were originally shaped on a broom stick handle. While they are still warm, shape them on a small rolling pin and slip off when cooled. They may be shaped over an inverted muffin tin and into cups, which may be used to hold pudding dessert or ice cream. Store the cookies in an airtight container.

Mrs. Hannah Hoff Brown, Area Supervisor,
Home and Family Life Education
Texas Education Agency
Waco, Texas

KREUMKAKE (Norway)
Number of Servings — 36

1 c. whipping cream
1 c. sugar
2 eggs
2½ c. flour
¼ c. butter
1 t. vanilla

Cream the butter, add sugar and cream well. Add the unbeaten eggs one at a time. Fold in the whipped cream and flour. Last, add the vanilla. Do not stir too much. Bake in a Kreumkake iron on top of the stove.

Mrs. John Kuecker, Seward H. S.
Seward, Nebraska

PRUNE PUDDING (Norway)
Number of Servings — 4-6

2 c. chopped, cooked prunes
1 c. prune juice
½ c. sugar
4 T. cornstarch
Dash of salt
Prune pits, 12 or more
2 T. lemon juice
Whipped cream for topping or Dream Whip

Bring the chopped prunes and juice to a boil in the top of a double boiler. Meanwhile combine the sugar, cornstarch, and salt. Gradually stir this mixture into the hot prunes and prune juice. Blend well. Place over hot, but not boiling water. Cook, stirring constantly for about 10 minutes, or until thickened and glossy. Cover and let cook over the hot water for 10 minutes while preparing the prune pits and lemon juice. Crack the prune pits and chop the kernels coarsely. Add these with the lemon juice to the cooked pudding mixture by stirring in gently. Turn into individual molds or a large ring mold. Chill thoroughly, unmold and serve with whipped cream or low calorie whipped topping. The original calls for custard sauce.

Farah Rust, Radford H. S.
Radford, Virginia

GLORIFIED RICE (Norway)
Number of Servings — 6-8

2 c. rice (boiled)
2 c. pineapple chunks
2 c. whipped cream
½ c. sugar

Boil rice until it is tender. Cool. Add pineapple and sugar to the rice and mix. Whip the cream and fold it into the rice and pineapple. Chill. The Norwegian custom is to serve this dessert on Christmas Eve.

Mrs. Gene Stricklin, Pompano Beach Jr. H. S.
Pompano Beach, Florida

CARROT HALWA (Pakistan)
Number of Servings — 4

1 lb. carrots
½ c. sugar
2 T. butter
1 qt. milk
4 whole cardamons
2 whole cloves
24 almonds
1 T. cornstarch
Pinch of saffron

Scrape and grate carrots. Cook them in milk under the boiling point for approximately 10 minutes. Add cornstarch and simmer for 5 minutes, stirring frequently. In another pan, heat butter, add cloves and cardamons and carrot mixture. Saute until a light brown. Add sugar and continue stirring until sugar is well dissolved and carrots are a golden brown. Add slivered almonds, transfer halwa to a bowl and chill. (Carrots take on a new role in a delicious dessert.)

Janet D. Cooper, Marine City Ward Cottrell H. S.
Marine City, Michigan

RICE PUDDING or FIRNI (Pakistan)
Number of Servings — 4

1 qt. milk
¼ c. cream of rice
1 c. sugar
1 can evaporated milk (small)
1 T. pistachio nuts (if available)
1 T. silver cake dusting

Mix cream of rice with milk in a heavy pan. Bring to boil slowly, stirring constantly. Cook until thick for 15 minutes. Add sugar and can of milk. Stir and cook until thick enough. Pour in small glasses or one big bowl. Chill, and decorate with silver dusting, and finely sliced pistachios. May be served with fruit cocktail and other fruits.

Saeeda Hamid, Gaden County H. S.
Oshkosh, Nebraska

APPLE DESSERT (Russia)
Number of Servings — 6

½ c. granulated sugar
1 c. brown sugar
1 c. flour
¼ c. butter
1 t. cinnamon
½ c. chopped walnuts
Sliced apples

Fill a buttered pan (11x7x1½) ⅔ full of sliced apples mixed with granulated sugar. Mix other ingredients together. Sprinkle on top of apples. Bake 30 minutes at 350°F. Serve with lemon sauce, whipped cream or ice cream.

Mrs. Fern Whitmarsh, Cody H. S.
Detroit, Michigan

SCANDINAVIAN COOKIES
Number of Servings — 40 Cookies

½ c. butter
¼ c. brown sugar
1 egg
1¼ c. sifted flour
½ c. pecans, finely chopped
Grape jelly

Cream butter and sugar. Blend in egg. Add flour and nuts. Roll in balls about the size of a large marble. Place on greased cookie sheet, flatten balls. Bake 5 minutes at 350°F. Remove from oven. Dent center with wooden spoon handle. Bake about 12 minutes longer, Fill dented center with small amount of jelly.

Mrs. Laurena Ward, Ashford H. S.
Ashford, Alabama

SCOTCH SHORTBREAD (Scotland)
Number of Servings — 20-25

4 c. sifted all-purpose flour
1 c. butter
1 c. margarine
1 t. salt
1 c. light brown sugar

Mix together like pie dough. Put into two 2″ rolls. Chill overnight. Line cookie sheets with brown paper. Slice rolls into ½″ thick slices (mark edges with fork if desired). Bake 350°F. for 15-20 minutes, until golden.

Dianne J. MacPherson, Garden Spot H. S.
New Holland, Pennsylvania

CAPIROTADA (Bread Pudding) (Spain)

Number of Servings — 4

1 c. sugar
2 c. water
6 slices toasted bread
1 t. cinnamon
1½ c. grated or sliced American or
  cheddar cheese
1 c. raisins
2 T. butter
1 c. diced fresh apple (optional)
½ c. chopped nuts (optional)

Caramelize sugar, add water and cinnamon and boil until sugar dissolves, stirring occasionally. Place a layer of bread in a casserole, a layer of cheese, raisins, apples, and nuts. Repeat until all the ingredients are arranged in layers. Add butter. Pour syrup over the mixture and bake in moderate oven until the syrup is all absorbed by bread.

Gregorita Pena, Arroyo Grande Union H. S.
Arroyo Grande, California

SPANISH FLAN (Spain)

Number of Servings — 8-10

1½ c. sugar
8 eggs
4 c. milk
1 stick cinnamon
1 t. vanilla

Caramelize ½ cup sugar by cooking in a pan or skillet until melted and a golden brown, stirring constantly. While still hot, spread evenly over bottom of a shallow 2-quart casserole or in individual dishes. Cool. Beat eggs until foamy, gradually add the remaining 1 cup of sugar, beating well after each addition. Meanwhile, scald the milk with the cinnamon stick. Gradually add the hot milk to the egg mixture, stirring constantly until sugar is completely dissolved. Strain the egg mixture. Add the vanilla. Pour into the casserole. Place in hot water and bake 1 hour 10 minutes. Cool.

Janette Swanson, Ainsworth Public Schools
Ainsworth, Nebraska

ANGLEMAT (Sweden)

Number of Servings — 6

1 pt. whipping cream
½ c. raspberry or strawberry preserves
1½ c. butter cookies, crushed fine

Whip the cream until thick. Add the preserves and cookie crumbs and mix well. Serve very cold but not frozen. This is a rich dessert, delicious and quickly made.

Mrs. Eris Terry, San Perlita H. S.
San Perlita, Texas

MAZARIN—SWEDISH COOKIE (Sweden)

Number of Servings — 12-15

½ c. margarine
¼ c. sugar
1 egg
1½ c. flour
1 t. baking powder

Blend sugar and margarine. Add egg and mix well. Sift flour and baking powder together and add to mixture. Chill while making the filling. Grease muffin tins and mash dough to sides and bottom of tins with floured fingers. The dough should be between ⅛"-¼" thick.

Cookie filling:
½ c. margarine
¾ c. sugar
2 eggs
½ c. finely chopped pecans or
½ c. minced almonds

Blend margarine and sugar. Add eggs and mix well. Add nuts to mixture. Place filling in uncooked dough shells until half full. Place in 350°F. oven for 15-20 minutes or until golden brown. Remove from oven and cool 1-2 minutes.

Mrs. Mary Jo Johnson, Adrian Independent School
Adrian, Texas

NUT CRESCENTS (Sweden)

Number of Servings — 9 Dozen

1⅛ c. all-purpose flour
2 t. salt
1 t. baking powder
¼ c. soft shortening
¾ c. granulated sugar
1 egg
2 T. milk
1 t. vanilla extract
1 c. chopped pecans
½ c. granulated sugar

Heat oven. Sift together first 3 ingredients, thoroughly mix shortening with ¾ cup sugar, egg, milk, and vanilla. Mix in flour mixture. Spread ¼ cup dough very thinly and evenly on greased inverted 9x9x2 pan. Sprinkle with some of combined nuts and ½ cup sugar. Bake 1 pan at a time at 325°F. for 10-12 minutes until golden. While layer is hot, cut into 4½x¾ strips, shape over rolling pin. Repeat, 1 pan at a time, until all dough is used. If strips become too brittle to shape, soften in oven. Note: These are delightfully salty.

Mrs. Bernice Campen, Emerson H. S.
Union City, New Jersey

SWEDISH PIE (Sweden)

Number of Servings — 5

1 egg
¾ c. granulated sugar
1 t. vanilla
Pinch of salt
½ c. flour, sifted
1 t. baking powder
1 c. nuts, chopped finely
½ c. apples, chopped finely

Beat egg until light, add sugar and beat. Add vanilla, salt, flour, and baking powder. Beat well. Fold in nuts and apples. Pour into greased and floured 9" pie plate. Bake in a 350°F. oven until light brown and done. Serve with ice cream or whipped cream.

Mrs. Scott Willock, Albany H. S.
Albany, Ohio

OST KAKA—CHEESE CAKE (Sweden)
Number of Servings — 6-8

3 c. cottage cheese
4 eggs
1 c. sugar
¾ c. flour
½ t. almond extract

Beat eggs well. Add sugar and cottage cheese. Fold in flour, add almond extract. Pour into greased mold. Place in pan of hot water and bake in hot oven until golden brown. May be served with a sweet sauce or jelly.

Mrs. Floyd Fuchs, Evant H. S.
Evant, Texas

SWISS APPLE PIE (Switzerland)
Number of Servings — 5-6

2 eggs, well beaten
¾ c. granulated sugar
½ c. all-purpose flour
1 t. vanilla
1 t. double action baking powder
Pinch of salt
1 heaping c. peeled diced apples
½ c. walnuts

Mix together all the ingredients in a bowl. Pour into a greased pie plate. Bake 30 minutes at 350°F. Note: Do not use a pastry shell for this pie.

Marilyn Harder, Osakis Public School
Osakis, Minnesota

KAFFEBROD (Swedish Tea Ring)
Number of Servings — 16

1 c. milk
¼ c. butter
½ c. sugar
1 t. salt
2 cakes yeast
¼ c. lukewarm water
2 eggs
4½ c. sifted flour
Melted butter
Brown sugar
Cinnamon
Chopped nuts

Scald milk and pour over butter, sugar and salt, crumble yeast into lukewarm water to soften. Cool milk to lukewarm, add yeast. Add well-beaten eggs. Beat in flour to make a soft dough. Turn out on a floured board and knead until smooth. Form into ball and place in a greased bowl. Cover and let rise until double in bulk. When light, shape into 2 rectangular sheets about ¼" thick. Brush with melted butter and sprinkle with brown sugar and cinnamon. Roll in jelly-roll fashion and shape into rings. Place on greased cookie sheets and cut with scissors at 1" intervals almost through ring. Turn slices slightly. Cover and let rise until double in bulk. Bake at 375°F. for 20-30 minutes. While warm, frost with confectioners' frosting and sprinkle with chopped nuts. If desired, sprinkle 1 cup chopped dried fruit on dough before rolling. Makes 2 rings.

Carol Bezold, Kiona-Benton H. S.
Benton City, Washington

SWEDISH COOKIES
Number of Servings — 100

1 lb. oleo or 1 c. butter and 1 c. shortening
2 c. sugar
3 c. plus 2 T. sifted flour
1 t. soda
1 t. baking powder
¼ t. salt (omit if butter is used)
1 t. vanilla
1 c. angel shredded coconut
Candied cherries
Nut halves

Cream shortening. Sift dry ingredients together and add to fat. Then add vanilla and coconut. Chill. Form into very small balls. Place on ungreased cookie sheets. Press down with a glass that has been dipped in flour. Have cookies very thin. Place a nut half or a piece of cherry in center. Bake at 350°F. until slightly brown.

Constance C. Malmsten, Technical H. S.
St. Cloud, Minnesota

SWEDISH NUTS
Number of Servings — 4 Cups

1 lb. nuts — pecans, English walnuts, or almonds can be mixed if desired
1 c. sugar
Dash of salt
2 stiff beaten egg whites
½ c. butter or margarine

Toast nuts in slow oven 325°F. until light brown. Fold sugar and salt into egg whites. Beat until stiff peaks form. Fold nuts into meringue. Melt butter in a 15½x10½x1 jelly pan. Spread nut mixture over butter. Bake in slow oven about 30 minutes 325°F., stirring every 10 minutes, or until nuts are coated with a brown covering and no butter remains in the pan. Cool.

Mrs. JoAnn Braddy, Danville H. S.
Danville, Arkansas

TURKISH PASTE (Turkey)

2 c. sugar
½ c. cold water
¾ c. fresh orange juice
4 T. lemon juice
3 T. gelatin
3 T. grated orange peel
¼ lb. candied cherries
¼ lb. candied pineapple
1 c. pecans

Boil sugar and water to clear syrup. Dissolve 3 tablespoons gelatin in orange juice. Add to syrup. Boil 15 minutes. Add peel and lemon juice. Cook about 5 minutes longer. Cool and add fruits and nuts. Pour in square pan and leave in refrigerator over night. Cut in 1" squares. Roll in confectioners' sugar. Keeps indefinitely.

Mary J. Higgins, Marietta H. S.
Marietta, Georgia

INDEX

RECIPE NOTES

FRP creates successful connections between organizations and individuals through custom books.

 Favorite Recipes® Press

Favorite Recipes Press, an imprint of FRP, Inc., located in Nashville, Tennessee, is one of the nation's best-known and most-respected cookbook companies. Favorite Recipes Press began by publishing cookbooks for its parent company, Southwestern/Great American, in 1961. FRP, Inc., is now a wholly owned subsidiary of the Southwestern/Great American family of companies, and under the Favorite Recipes Press imprint has produced hundreds of custom cookbook titles for nonprofit organizations, companies, and individuals.

Other FRP, Inc., imprints include

CommunityClassics®

Additional titles published by FRP, Inc., are

 *Recipes Worth Sharing*

 *The Hunter's Table*

 *More Recipes Worth Sharing*

 *The Illustrated Encyclopedia of American Cooking*

 *Cooking Up a Classic Christmas*

 *Almost Homemade*

 *The Vintner's Table*

 *Junior Leagues In the Kitchen with Kids: Everyday Recipes & Activities for Healthy Living*

To learn more about custom books, visit our Web site, www.frpbooks.com.